Sociology Windows on Society

An Anthology

Sixth Edition

Robert H. Lauer

Jeanette C. Lauer
U.S. International University

Roxbury Publishing Company
Los Angeles, California

Library of Congress Cataloging-in-Publication Data

Sociology: windows on society / [compiled by] Robert H. Lauer and Jeanette C. Lauer. — 6th ed.
p. cm.
Includes bibliographical references and index
ISBN 1-891487-88-4
1. Sociology. I. Lauer, Robert H. II. Lauer, Jeanette C.
   HM585 .S64 2002
   301—dc21   2001041936
                                                               CIP

Publisher: Claude Teweles
Managing Editor: Dawn VanDercreek
Production Editor: Monica Gomez
Production Assistant: Josh Levine
Typography: Synergistic Data Systems
Cover Design: Marnie Kenney
Cover Photo: Courtesy of www.digitalstock.com

Printed on acid-free paper in the United States of America. This book meets the standards for recycling of the Environmental Protection Agency.

ISBN: 1-891487-88-4

ROXBURY PUBLISHING COMPANY
P.O. Box 491044
Los Angeles, California 90049-9044
Voice: (310) 473-3312 • Fax: (310) 473-4490
E-mail: roxbury@roxbury.net
Website: www.roxbury.net

We wish to dedicate this book to those who have taught us the joy of life: Jon, Kathy, Julie, Jeffrey, Kate, Jeff, Krista, Benjamin, David, and John Robert.

Contents

Unit II: Culture, Socialization, and Social Interaction

* Indicates chapters new to this edition.

---

* Indicates chapters new to this edition.

* Indicates chapters new to this edition.

---

* Indicates chapters new to this edition.

---

* Indicates chapters new to this edition.

* Indicates chapters new to this edition.

Introduction

Any anthology for introductory sociology has two somewhat contradictory obligations: (1) to be interesting, current, and accessible to its readers, and (2) to fairly represent what the discipline is all about. We say that these requirements are contradictory because introductory students are not necessarily interested in, or equipped to fully understand, the many sociological studies that are published. Moreover, sociologists are not always concerned with examining issues that are timely or topical, nor do they write for student readers. In an attempt to strike a balance between these contradictory ideals, we have tried to emphasize sociological substance without sacrificing interest and readability.

To encourage student debate about sociological issues facing society today, this anthology provides a wide variety of articles from both contemporary sources and the classical literature of sociology. Classic selections include readings from the works of Marx, Weber, and Durkheim—all of which are both central to the classic tradition and highly readable.

New to the Sixth Edition

New and expanded coverage is given to major concepts in the unit introductions and to each selection. Contemporary selections in the sixth edition have been updated to include topics of current interest and concern, such as the use of cosmetic surgery to alter appearance; the influence of television on gender roles; sexual betrayal in intimate relationships; gender inequality in medicine; quality of life in nursing homes; Hispanic participation in political life; and the problem of bullying, teasing, and violence in the schools.

Gender continues to be a major focus of this anthology because it is of central concern to people everywhere and is fundamental to many social and political issues in the United States. Moreover, gender has been at the heart of some of the most excit-ing sociological research of recent years. In addition, we emphasize the issues of race/ethnicity and inequality because of their significance in American history and in sociological research.

The selections in this anthology also challenge preconceived notions and conventional wisdom by showing the distinctive power of a sociological viewpoint (for example, Storfer's analysis of the way that parent-child interaction affects I.Q.). As the title suggests, the selections in this anthology can be viewed as "windows" on society. They permit you to see everyday activities in a new light—from the familiar (Bernstein's article on ways that students justify not working) to the more exotic (Harris' study on India's worship of the sacred cow).

A few of the articles in *Sociology: Windows on Society* may prove difficult reading. Nevertheless, we have decided to include these selections for two reasons. First, they are important in accurately presenting what the discipline of sociology is all about. Second, they provide an opportunity to master difficult material—an opportunity that can increase your knowledge and hone your academic skills.

Organization

Windows is now divided into five units. Unit I introduces the enterprise of sociology, illustrating both the perspectives sociologists take and the kinds of methods they use. Unit II features topics related to culture, socialization, and social interaction. Unit III considers various forms of social inequality based on class, race/ethnicity, gender, age, and international stratification, while Unit IV focuses primarily on social institutions. Finally, Unit V addresses two broad social processes: deviance and social change.

Windows can stand alone or be used as a supplement to a standard introductory text. The chart on page xiv cross-references topic areas that commonly appear in introductory sociology texts to related selections in this anthology. Both the primary and secondary emphases of each chapter are listed. This chart will facilitate use of *Windows* as a supplement to any major text.

To enhance understanding, we have highlighted and added discussions of the major concepts in the introductions to the units and the selections. We have also divided the units into parts that clearly identify the major focus of the selections. Review questions and suggested applications follow each selection. The applications can serve as class or small group projects; they offer an opportunity to experience how the process of sociological research is conducted.

The updated *Instructor's Manual/Testing Program* summarizes the conclusions of each article, lists key points, and provides both essay and multiple-choice questions.

We hope these materials will assist instructors in opening the *Windows* on the sociological enterprise to their students.

In Appreciation

The editors and publisher would like to express appreciation to the following individuals whose feedback and revision suggestions helped us prepare the Sixth Edition: E. Doyle McCarthy (Fordham University), Ben Mariante (Stonehill College), Cathy Petrissans (Clarion University of Pennsylvania), Barbara Arrighi (Northern Kentucky University), Kent Sandstrom (University of Northern Iowa), Anne Nurse (The College of Wooster), and Steven Cades (Washington College). We are also grateful to John W. Heeren and Marylee Requa for the insightful work they did on earlier editions. ✦

Use of Selections

S*ociology: Windows on Society* **An Anthology,** Sixth Edition, comfortably stands alone as a single assigned text. However, instructors who use this anthology to supplement another text may find the following chart, which groups the selections, helpful. Primary and secondary emphases are listed separately.

Generic topics for an introductory sociology course:	*Windows* selections in which the topic is a primary emphasis:	*Windows* selections in which the topic is a secondary emphasis:
Introduction	1, 4, 5, 6	2, 3
Research methods	2, 3, 4	6, 9, 18, 19, 36, 41
Culture	7, 8	11, 19, 26, 30, 34, 43, 44
Socialization	9, 10, 11	5, 32, 33, 34
Social interaction	12, 13	5, 6, 21, 22, 25, 32, 33
Social stratification	14, 15, 16, 23	17, 29, 32, 35, 38, 39, 41, 42
Racial/ethnic groups	17, 18, 19, 28, 39	36
Gender	8, 9, 10, 12, 20, 21	13, 16, 22, 24, 27
Sexuality	13	8
Aging	22	35
Family	16, 24, 25, 26	9, 21, 34, 41, 44
Government/politics	27, 28	14, 18, 31, 35, 39
Economy	15, 17, 23, 29, 30, 31	7, 14, 15, 34, 38, 42, 43
Religion	30, 34, 42	3, 7
Education	32, 33	2, 9, 34
Health/medicine	35, 36	6, 8, 22
Deviance	6, 37, 38, 39, 40	3, 8
Collective behavior/social movements	27, 40	36
Demography/urbanization	40, 41	16, 17, 18
Technology/social change	41, 42, 43, 44	7, 8, 10, 23

Contributors

Barbara A. Arrighi teaches sociology at Northern Kentucky University.

Philip Aspden is the executive director of the Center for Research on the Information Society, Pennington, New Jersey.

Joel Best teaches sociology at Southern Illinois University at Carbondale. He is the author of *Threatened Children* (1990) and the editor of *Images of Issues* and *Troubling Children: Studies of Children and Social Problems.*

Darcia Harris Bowman is a staff writer for *Education Week.*

Trudy Bush is an associate editor of *Christian Century.*

Elizabeth Cauffman is assistant professor of psychiatry at the University of Pittsburgh.

Dwight Conquergood teaches in the performance studies department at Northwestern University.

Stephanie Coontz is a member of the faculty at Evergreen State College in Olympia, Washington. Her works include *The Way We Never Were: American Families and the Nostalgia Trip; The Way We Really Are: Coming to Terms With America's Changing Families; The Social Origins of Private Life;* and (with Peta Henderson) *Women's Work, Men's Property.*

Emile Durkheim (1858–1917) is considered one of the principal founders of modern sociology. His major works include *The Division of Labor in Society* (1893), *Rules of Sociological Method* (1895), *Suicide* (1897), and *The Elementary Forms of Religious Life* (1912).

S. Shirley Feldman is senior research scientist, Division of Child Psychiatry, Stanford University.

Kathleen J. Ferraro teaches sociology at Arizona State University.

F. Chris Garcia is professor of political science at the University of New Mexico.

John Garcia is professor of political science at the University of Arizona.

Marvin Harris, a well-known contemporary anthropologist, has published numerous books, including *Cows, Pigs, Wars and Witches; Cannibals and Kings; Our Kind;* and *Culture, People and Nature.*

Rodney Hero is professor of political science at the University of Colorado, Boulder.

Gerald T. Horiuchi teaches sociology at California State University, Fresno.

Donald W. Huffman is professor of sociology at Cedar Crest College, Allentown, Pennsylvania.

Martin Sánchez Jankowski teaches sociology at the University of California, Berkeley, and is chair of the Chicano/Latino Policy Project sponsored by the Institute for the Study of Social Change, also at Berkeley. He is the author of *City Bound: Urban Life and Political Attitudes Among Chicago Youth* and *Islands in the Street: Gangs and American Urban Society.*

John M. Johnson teaches sociology at Arizona State University.

James E. Katz is director of social science research at Bell Communications Research, Morristown, New Jersey.

Jay Klagge teaches management at the University of Phoenix. He specializes in organizational leadership, ethics, and bureaucracy.

Cynthia Loucks is a licensed psychotherapist and a hospice bereavement coordinator.

Karl Marx (1818–1883) is best known for *The Communist Manifesto* (published with Friedrich Engels in 1848) and *Das Kapital* (1867, 1885, 1894). His concern with, and analysis of, social issues makes him important to sociology.

Michael Messner teaches sociology in the Program for the Study of Women and Men in Society at the University of Southern California. His books include *Politics of Masculinities: Men in Movements.*

C. Wright Mills (1916–1962) was a leading critic of modern American civilization. Among his books are *White Collar; The Power Elite; Sociology and Pragmatism; Power, Politics and People;* and, with H. H. Gerth, *From Max Weber: Essays in Sociology.*

Katherine Newman is professor of anthropology at Columbia University. She has written *Declining Fortunes.*

Harry Pachon is president of the Tomas Rivera Policy Institute and Kenan Professor of Political Studies at Pitzer College and Claremont Graduate University.

Barbara J. Risman teaches sociology at North Carolina State University. Her books include *Gender in Intimate Relationships* (with Pepper Schwartz) and *Gender Vertigo: American Families in Transition.*

George Ritzer is a professor of sociology at the University of Maryland, where he has been named Distinguished Scholar-Teacher. His books include *Metatheorizing in Sociology* and *The McDonaldization of Society.*

Lillian B. Rubin is a psychologist and a sociologist. She teaches at CUNY–Queens College. Her books include *Worlds of Pain, Women of a Certain Age, Intimate Strangers, Just Friends,* and *Erotic Wars: What Happened to the Sexual Revolution?*

Kent L. Sandstrom teaches sociology at the University of Northern Iowa. He is the coauthor, with Gary Alan Fine, of *Knowing Children: Participant Observation With Mi-* *nors.* He has also published articles on media conceptions of community planning and parental attitudes toward youth work.

Joshua Sharfstein is a pediatrician who teaches at the Boston University School of Medicine.

JoEllen Shively teaches sociology at the Center for Research on Social Organization at the University of Michigan.

Beth Shulman is a lawyer, author, consultant, and former vice president on an international trade union.

Gregory Squires teaches sociology at the University of Wisconsin–Milwaukee.

Deborah Tannen teaches linguistics at Georgetown University and is the author of *That's Not What I Meant!* An internationally recognized scholar, she has received grants from the National Endowment for the Humanities, the Rockefeller Foundation, and the National Science Foundation.

Max Weber (1864–1920) is another of the founders of modern sociology. His major works include *The Protestant Ethic and the Spirit of Capitalism, Theory of Social and Economic Organization,* and *Methodology of the Social Sciences.*

Susan D. Witt is assistant professor, School of Family and Consumer Sciences, The University of Akron.

Biographical information has been provided where available. Some authors do not appear in this list. ✦

Unit I

The Sociological Enterprise

What is the sociological enterprise? Sociologists study social groups, the interaction within and between groups, and how human behavior is affected. An empirical research study or a theory provides the sociologist with a window view of what is going on in a particular society. The more that sociologists perfect their research techniques and refine their theories, the clearer the view of the inner workings of that society. It is hoped, then, that the "windows" offered in this anthology will give you a sociological perspective not only on society, but also on yourself.

This unit examines various aspects of the sociological enterprise. The first article discusses the "sociological imagination," a distinctive vision of sociology as a discipline. The following two articles demonstrate the diversity of styles in sociological analysis. The next article is an example of critical thinking, an essential part of sociological analysis. The last two articles address the issue of whether sociology can be reduced to biology or psychology—that is, whether human behavior can be explained completely in biological or psychological terms without reference to social factors.

Every discipline uses a distinctive set of concepts to explain the phenomena studied. The "mass" of physicists, the "behavior modification" of psychologists, the "supply and demand" of economists, the "acculturation" of anthropologists, and the "pluralist model of power" of political scientists are among the concepts used by various disciplines. Sociologists also employ specific concepts in an effort to be more precise about explanations. In various unit, part, and selection introductions, therefore, we will briefly explain the important concepts that are introduced. Some of these concepts are words that are commonly used but that have particular (and sometimes different) meanings in sociology and contribute to the distinctive vocabulary of sociological study. You will find these key concepts highlighted in boldface type. ✦

Part One

The Sociological Perspective

Sociology is the scientific study of social life. The founders of sociology wanted to improve the quality of human life and realized that in order to do so they had to understand the workings of society. Their attempt to understand those workings led to the development of the sociological perspective.

The meaning of the sociological perspective is captured in the notion of the **sociological imagination,** a term coined by C. Wright Mills, the author of the first selection. It refers to a way of thinking that enables people to understand the impact of culture, society, and group memberships on their behavior. In contrast to those who try to understand human behavior by studying internal processes in individuals, sociologists explain behavior by examining the social factors that circumscribe the lives of all individuals. ✦

1

The Sociological Imagination

C. Wright Mills

Sociology holds a unique place among the social and behavioral sciences. As a discipline, it studies many of the same phenomena as do the other social sciences but from a distinct vantage point. For example, both sociologists and economists study unemployment. But while economists are more interested in how the rate of unemployment is associated with other economic indicators, sociologists are more likely to be concerned with the broader social context in which joblessness occurs. They ask, is **unemployment** (the number of people out of work and actively looking for jobs) the result of social policies adopted by the government or of decisions made by multinational corporations? More important, sociologists may want to learn the social consequences of unemployment. Does the crime rate rise? Does the incidence of family disruption or domestic violence increase?

Like psychology, sociology is concerned with the individual. Rather than studying the individual in isolation, however, sociologists prefer to examine how each person is socially situated and affected by social factors. How has his or her life been shaped by social class, race and ethnicity, gender, age, and so forth? **Social classes** are groups that are unequal with regard to things valued in a society, such as income, power, and prestige. **Ethnicity** refers to a shared cultural background that leads people to identify with each other; Hispanics, for example, are an ethnic group. **Gender** refers to the social male and female, as distinct from **sex,** the biological male and female. Considerable debate exists about the extent to which the characteristics and behavior of males and females are rooted in social or biological factors.

Sociologists point out that all such social factors come to bear on people's behavior. Humans are social creatures, so that even individual self-expression is related to social circumstances. For instance, a person who is shy by nature is more likely to behave differently when forced to take center stage in a social event, such as a family celebration.

In the following selection, Mills presents his version of the distinctive focus of sociology. In his view, the sociological imagination is reflected by the place of the individual in society and the place of that society in history. Mills looks at social phenomena from the perspective of **conflict theory,** a theory that focuses on contradictory interests, inequalities, and the resulting outcomes. Those outcomes include conflict and social change (alterations in social factors at various levels of social life from the individual to the global). Ironically, in the late 1950s when this piece was written, Mills did not foresee that a greater consciousness of gender would render obsolete the use of the term "men" for both men and women. Nevertheless, his ideas still serve to this day as an excellent guide to the nature of sociology.

Nowadays men often feel that their private lives are a series of traps. They sense that within their everyday worlds, they cannot overcome their troubles, and in this feeling, they are often quite correct: What ordinary men are directly aware of and what they try to do are bounded by the private orbits in which they live; their visions and their powers are limited to the close-up scenes of job, family, neighborhood; in other milieux, they move vicariously and remain spectators. And the more aware they become, however vaguely, of ambitions and of threats which transcend their immediate locales, the more trapped they seem to feel.

Underlying this sense of being trapped are seemingly impersonal changes in the very structure of continent-wide societies. The facts of contemporary history are also facts about the success and the failure of individual men and women. When a society is industrialized, a peasant becomes a worker; a feudal lord is liquidated or becomes a businessman. When classes rise or fall, a man is employed or unemployed; when the rate of investment goes up or down, a man takes new heart or goes broke. When wars happen, an insurance salesman becomes a rocket launcher, a store clerk, a radar man, a wife lives alone, a child grows up without a father. Neither the life of an individual nor the history of a society can be understood without understanding both.

Yet men do not usually define the troubles they endure in terms of historical change and institutional contradiction. The well-being they enjoy, they do not usually impute to the big ups and downs of the societies in which they live. Seldom aware of the intricate connection between the patterns of their own lives and the course of world history, ordinary men do not usually know what this connection means for the kinds of men they are becoming and for the kinds of history-making in which they might take part. They do not possess the quality of mind essential to grasp the interplay of man and society, of biography and history, of self and world. They cannot cope with their personal troubles in such ways as to control the structural transformations that usually lie behind them.

Surely it is no wonder. In what period have so many men been so totally exposed at so fast a pace to such earthquakes of change? That Americans have not known such catastrophic changes as have the men and women of other societies is due to historical facts that are now quickly becoming "merely history." The history that now affects every man is world history. Within this scene and this period, in the course of a single generation, one sixth of mankind is transformed from all that is feudal and backward into all that is modern, advanced, and fearful. Political colonies are freed, new and less visible forms of imperialism installed. Revolutions occur; men feel the intimate grip of new kinds of authority. Totalitarian societies rise, and are smashed to bits—or succeed fabulously. After two centuries of ascendancy, capitalism is shown up as only one way to make society into an industrial apparatus. After two centuries of hope, even formal democracy is restricted to a quite small portion of mankind. Everywhere in the underdeveloped world, ancient ways of life are broken up and vague expectations become urgent demands. Everywhere in the overdeveloped world, the means of authority and of violence become total in scope and bureaucratic in form. Humanity itself now lies before us, the super-nation at either pole concentrating its most coordinated and massive efforts upon the preparation of World War Three.

The very shaping of history now outpaces the ability of men to orient themselves in accordance with cherished values. And which values? Even when they do not panic, men often sense that older ways of feeling and thinking have collapsed and that newer beginnings are ambiguous to the point of moral stasis. Is it any wonder that ordinary men feel they cannot cope with the larger worlds with which they are so suddenly confronted? That they cannot understand the meaning of their epoch for their own lives? That—in defense of selfhood—they become morally insensible, trying to remain altogether private men? Is it any wonder that they come to be possessed by a sense of the trap?

It is not only information that they need—in this Age of Fact, information often dominates their attention and overwhelms their capacities to assimilate it. It is not only the skills of reason that they need—although their struggles to acquire these often exhaust their limited moral energy.

What they need, and what they feel they need, is a quality of mind that will help them to use information and to develop reason; in order to achieve lucid summations of what is going on in the world and of what may be happening within themselves. It is this quality, I am going to contend, that journalists and scholars, artists and publics, scientists and editors are coming to expect of what may be called the sociological imagination.

The sociological imagination enables its possessor to understand the larger historical scene in terms of its meaning for the inner life and the external career of a variety of individuals. It enables him to take into account how individuals, in the welter of their daily experience, often become falsely conscious of their social positions. Within that welter, the framework of modern society is sought, and within that framework the psychologies of a variety of men and women are formulated. By such means the personal uneasiness of individuals is focused upon explicit troubles and the indifference of publics is transformed into involvement with public issues.

The first fruit of this imagination—and the first lesson of the social science that embodies it—is the idea that the individual can understand his own experience and gauge his own fate only by locating himself within his period, that he can know his own chances in life only by becoming aware of those of all individuals in his circumstances. In many ways it is a terrible lesson; in many ways it is a magnificent one. We do not know the limits of man's capacities for supreme effort or willing degradation, for agony or glee, for pleasurable brutality or the sweetness of reason. But in our time we have come to know that the limits of "human nature" are frighteningly broad. We have come to know that every individual lives, from one generation to the next, in some society; that he lives out a biography, and that he lives it out within some historical sequence. By the fact of his living he contributes, however minutely, to the shaping of this society and to the course of its history, even as he is made by society and by its historical push and shove.

The sociological imagination enables us to grasp history and biography and the relations between the two within society. That is its task and its promise. To recognize this task and this promise is the mark of the classic social analyst. It is characteristic of Herbert Spencer—turgid, polysyllabic, comprehensive; of E. A. Ross—graceful, muckraking, upright; of Auguste Comte and Emile Durkheim; of the intricate and subtle Karl Mannheim. It is the quality of all that is intellectually excellent in Karl Marx; it is the clue to Thorstein Veblen's brilliant and ironic insight, to Joseph Schumpeter's many-sided constructions of reality; it is the basis of the psychological sweep of W. E. H. Lecky no less than of the profundity and clarity of Max Weber. And it is the signal of what is best in contemporary studies of man and society.

No social study that does not come back to the problems of biography, of history and of their intersections within a society has completed its intellectual journey. Whatever the specific problems of the classic social analysts, however limited or however broad the features of social reality they have examined, those who have been imaginatively aware of the promise of their work have consistently asked three sorts of questions:

1. What is the structure of this particular society as a whole? What are its essential components, and how are they related to one another? How does it differ from other varieties of social order? Within it, what is the meaning of any particular feature for its continuance and for its change?

2. Where does this society stand in human history? What are the mechanics by which it is changing? What is its place within and its meaning for the development of humanity as a whole? How does any particular feature we are examining affect, and how is it affected by, the historical period in which it moves? And this period—what are its essential features? How does it differ from other periods? What are its characteristic ways of history-making?

3. What varieties of men and women now prevail in this society and in this period? And what varieties are coming to prevail? In what ways are they selected and formed, liberated and repressed, made sensitive and blunted? What kinds of "human nature" are revealed in the conduct and character we observe in this society in this period? And what is the meaning for "human nature" of each and every feature of the society we are examining?

Whether the point of interest is a great power state or a minor literary mood, a family, a prison, a creed—these are the kind of questions the best social analysts have asked. They are the intellectual pivots of classic studies of man in society—and they are the questions inevitably raised by any mind possessing the sociological imagination. For that imagination is the capacity to shift from one perspective to another—from the political to the psychological; from examination of a single family to comparative assessment of the national budgets of the world; from the theological school to the military establishment; from considerations of an oil industry to studies of contemporary poetry. It is the capacity to range from the most impersonal and remote transformations to the most intimate features of the human self—and to see the relations between the two. Back of its use there is always the urge to know the social and historical meaning of the individual in the society and in the period in which he has his quality and his being.

That, in brief, is why it is by means of the sociological imagination that men now hope to grasp what is going on in the world, and to understand what is happening in themselves as minute points of the intersections of biography and history within society. In large part, contemporary man's self-conscious view of himself as at least an outsider, if not a permanent stranger, rests upon an absorbed realization of social relativity and of the transformative power of history. The sociological imagination is the most fruitful form of this self-consciousness. By its use men whose mentalities have swept only a series of limited orbits often come to feel as if suddenly awakened in a house with which they had only supposed themselves to be familiar. Correctly or incorrectly, they often come to feel that they can now provide themselves with adequate summations, cohesive assessments, comprehensive orientations. Older decisions that once appeared sound now seem to them products of a mind unaccountably dense. Their capacity for astonishment is made lively again. They acquire a new way of thinking, they experience a transvaluation of values: in a word, by their reflection and by their sensibility, they realize the cultural meaning of the social sciences.

Perhaps the most fruitful distinction with which the sociological imagination works is between "the personal troubles of milieu" and "the public issues of social structure." This distinction is an essential tool of the so-

ciological imagination and a feature of all classic work in social science.

Troubles occur within the character of the individual and within the range of his immediate relations with others; they have to do with his self and with those limited areas of social life of which he is directly and personally aware. Accordingly, the statement and the resolution of troubles properly lie within the individual as a biographical entity and within the scope of his immediate milieu—the social setting that is directly open to his personal experience and to some extent his willful activity. A trouble is a private matter: values cherished by an individual are felt by him to be threatened.

Issues have to do with matters that transcend these local environments of the individual and the range of his inner life. They have to do with the organization of many such milieux into the institutions of an historical society as a whole, with the ways in which various milieux overlap and interpenetrate to form the larger structure of social and historical life. An issue is a public matter: some value cherished by publics is felt to be threatened. Often there is a debate about what that value really is and about what it is that really threatens it. This debate is often without focus if only because it is the very nature of an issue, unlike even widespread trouble, that it cannot very well be defined in terms of the immediate and everyday environments of ordinary men. An issue, in fact, often involves a crisis in institutional arrangements, and often too it involves what Marxists call "contradictions" or "antagonisms."

In these terms, consider unemployment. When, in a city of 100,000, only one man is unemployed, that is his personal trouble, and for its relief we properly look to the character of the man, his skills, and his immediate opportunities. But when in a nation of 50 million employees, 15 million men are unemployed, that is an issue, and we may not hope to find its solution within the range of opportunities open to any one individual. The very structure of opportunities has collapsed. Both the correct statement of the problem and the range of possible solutions require us to consider the economic and political institutions of the society, and not merely the personal situation and character of a scatter of individuals.

Consider war. The personal problem of war, when it occurs, may be how to survive it or how to die in it with honor; how to make money out of it; how to climb into the higher safety of the military apparatus; or how to contribute to the war's termination. In short, according to one's values, to find a set of milieux and within it to survive the war or make one's death in it meaningful. But the structural issues of war have to do with its causes; with what types of men it throws up into command; with its effects upon economic and political, family and religious institutions; with the unorganized irresponsibility of a world of nation-states.

Consider marriage. Inside a marriage a man and a woman may experience personal troubles, but when the divorce rate during the first four years of marriage is 250 out of every 1,000 attempts, this is an indication of a structural issue having to do with the institutions of marriage and the family and other institutions that bear upon them.

Or consider the metropolis—the horrible, beautiful, ugly, magnificent sprawl of the great city. For many upper-class people, the personal solution to "the problem of the city" is to have an apartment with private garage under it in the heart of the city, and forty miles out, a house by Henry Hill, garden by Garrett Eckbo, on a hundred acres of private land. In these two controlled environments—with a small staff at each end and a private helicopter connection—most people could solve many of the problems of personal milieux caused by the facts of the city. But all this, however splendid, does not solve the public issues that the structural fact of the city poses. What should be done with this wonderful monstrosity? Break it all up into scattered units, combining residence and work? Refurbish it as it stands? Or, after evacuation, dynamite it and build new cities according to new plans in new places? What should those plans be? And who is to decide and to accomplish whatever choice is made? These are structural issues; to confront them and to solve them requires us to consider po-litical and economic issues that affect innumerable milieux.

In so far as an economy is so arranged that slumps occur, the problem of unemployment becomes incapable of personal solution. In so far as war is inherent in the nation-state system and in the uneven industrialization of the world, the ordinary individual in his restricted milieu will be powerless—with or without psychiatric aid—to solve the troubles this system or lack of system imposes upon him. In so far as the family as an institution turns women into darling little slaves and men into their chief providers and unweaned dependents, the problem of a satisfactory marriage remains incapable of purely private solution. In so far as the overdeveloped megalopolis and the overdeveloped automobile are built-in features of the overdeveloped society, the issues of urban living will not be solved by personal ingenuity and private wealth.

What we experience in various and specific milieux, I have noted, is often caused by structural changes. Accordingly, to understand the changes of many personal milieux we are required to look beyond them. And the number and variety of such structural changes increase as the institutions within which we live become more embracing and more intricately connected with one another. To be aware of the idea of social structure and to use it with sensibility is to be capable of tracing such linkages among a great variety of milieux. To be able to do that is to possess the sociological imagination.

Review

1. What does Mills see as the "first fruit" of the sociological imagination?

2. What is the "purpose and task" of the sociological imagination?

3. Why does Mills suggest that the distinction between the "personal troubles of milieu" and the "public issues of social structure" is an essential tool of the sociological imagination?

Application

Select a social problem such as crime, unemployment, homelessness, or discrimination. Over the course of the term, gather at least 15 to 20 articles from newspapers and magazines on the topic. Toward the end of the term, use your sources to write a paper organized around the themes of the "sociological imagination" (i.e., the historical setting, the social structure, and the personal dimensions) and the relationships among them.

Part Two

Studying Social Phenomena

How do sociologists get the information necessary to understand social life? From the first, sociologists have striven to make the discipline a science, to base their findings not on speculation or "common sense" but on theory and data. A **theory,** in simplest terms, is simply a coherent explanation of something. It is a way to understand and explain a social phenomenon. Theory can be used to stimulate a particular line of research. It can also be used to interpret data gathered.

We mentioned conflict theory in the introduction to Mills' article. It is one of three theoretical approaches in sociology. **Structural-functionalism** is a theory focusing on social systems and how their interdependent parts maintain order. **Symbolic interactionist** theory focuses on the interaction between individuals and the resulting construction of social life (see, for example, selections 2 and 36).

Methods are the ways that sociologists gather their data. Just as astronomers use the telescope and physicists use the particle accelerator to gather data, sociologists use their own set of tools: questionnaires, interviews, statistical data provided by the government, experiments, and so on. In this part, we will look at selections that illustrate the two broad categories of methods sociologists use: qualitative (selection 2) and quantitative (selection 3). The fourth selection illustrates the need for critical thinking. ✦

2
Getting It Done

Notes on Student Fritters

Stan Bernstein

Social role *is an important concept in socio-logical analysis. A role is the behavior expected of people who hold a particular position in society (parent, student, worker, citizen, etc.). Roles vary, however, in the extent to which they give individuals flexibility in behaving. As Bernstein suggests in this article, the role of the student in the education system is open-ended. For example, you may be given a class assignment to write a paper. But how long should the paper be and how much research will it require? How should you structure your time to meet the deadline for completion of the assignment? These decisions may be left up to you.*

When students are given the freedom to organize their own efforts, some will not meet the requirements of their instructors. This situation can produce feelings of guilt for the student. Bernstein shows the sources of these feelings and describes the ways in which students fritter away their time. "Fritters," then, are the strategies students use for coping with the open-ended nature of their work.

*Bernstein's article exemplifies the interactionist approach to sociology. Symbolic interactionists emphasize the need for understanding the meaning of things from the actor's point of view. Bernstein illustrates an interactionist approach in three ways. First, he closely analyzes the role of the student in the educative process. Second, Bernstein's method is a version of **participant observation,** in which the researcher takes part in the phenomenon that he or she is observing. Sociologists have used participant observation to study such things as urban gangs, support groups, religious cults, mental hospitals, and various kinds of work settings. Bernstein based his observations on his own experiences*

as a student. He describes various types of fritters based on these observations.

*Third, the discussion of fritters illustrates the internal dialogue people use in adjusting their actions to the actions of others. In this view, the **self** (the capacity to observe, respond to, and direct one's own behavior) consists of two aspects—the "I" and the "me." The "I" is the acting part of the self that operates in the present. ("I'm not going to start that term paper until tomorrow.") The "me" evaluates these actions in terms of the expectations of society. ("It will be difficult for me to do a good term paper if I keep putting it off. My instructor expects me to show more effort.") Out of this internal dialogue, some kind of acceptable justification for delaying work—a fritter—may arise. ("Nobody can expect me to work when it's almost time to eat. I'll start after lunch.")*

Social roles vary in the degree to which their constituent tasks are "closed" or "open" in character. At one extreme are roles such as assembly-line worker, where precise definitions communicate when the task starts, one's progress in it, and when it ends. At the other extreme are roles such as student, when the tasks are highly open or never-ending. The role of student, in particular, involves learning to think and learning the "facts" of various fields. The infinite expandability of these tasks places no practically determined restrictions on the amount of time occupants can dedicate to the role. Like politicians, housewives, and entrepreneurs, students' work is never done. Indeed, students are counseled that people only stop learning when they die. Death is not, students lament, in sight, but learning demands are.

This paper seeks to explore how people cope with roles that are open or never-ending in their demands. In particular, it focuses upon how students justify not working under the ever-present pressure to work. Frequently, when there is work to be done, students fritter away time. An analysis of strategies students adopt in accounting for their time not working will be presented. The objective truth or falsity of the strategies is irrelevant to the purpose of this analysis. What is important is their use in coping with open-ended situations. This analysis treats a student population. The central notion is that of fritter devices or strategies. A fritter is "a justification a student gives to himself for not doing student work in response to felt pressures to work." While the success of a fritter in neutralizing work pressure or guilt is increased by its receiving social support, this consideration is not part of the definition.

The dynamic nature of fritters makes categorizing them difficult. In actual practice, combinations or complex sequences are likely as the student continually reconstitutes his work avoidance as new kinds of justified activity. For ease of presentation, they may be divided into the following four classes: (1) person-based; (2) social relations-based; (3) value-based; and (4) task-based.

Person-Based Fritters

Person-based fritters involve definitions of biological need and personal history.

Biological Necessity

Even a student is human. Being human involves, among other things, the satisfaction of biological needs. These practical necessities are just that—necessities. Therefore, they are foolproof justifications for not working. When, for example, nature calls, what is a person to do?

Similarly, hunger can serve as a justification for work avoidance. Not only can an argument be made for biological necessity, but the student can also argue that hunger impairs studying ability. This argument need not be limited, of course, by actual hunger. The great business done by vending machines in dormitories and the concentration of all-night eating places in areas of high student residence attest to the utility of this justification. Some popular student foods (pizza in particular) are not eaten alone. Time must be spent gathering other people. And once you have them, you can do more with them than eat.

Cleanliness is yet another excellent justification. Anything next to godliness surely takes precedence over work. Washing and showering can serve another function. An entire battery of work-avoidance tactics can be justified by their necessity in keeping the student awake. These activities include preparing and drinking cups of coffee, cold showers, long walks in cold weather, running a half-mile, standing on one's head for a few minutes, listening to Sousa marches, Chopin preludes, or acid rock, and eating rich food. A variety of drugs are now routinely used to fight fatigue. The effects of these are frequently not restricted to fatigue reduction. Subtle and not very subtle alterations of consciousness are common. Attending to these changes can become more interesting than studying. Should these activities fail, or even should they succeed, another way of handling "fatigue" is the I'll-get-up-very-early-tomorrow-morning-when-I'll-be-able-to-work-better fritter. Students have to keep healthy, too. Many regimens, physical and medical, may be required. At some times, it may be crucial that the student get "adequate rest."

Rest on Your Laurels

Focusing on personal history leads to the nostalgia or rest-on-your-laurels fritter. Using this strategy involves employing past accomplishments as justification for present work avoidance. This can take the form of delaying work, since previous history shows (or can be interpreted to suggest) it well within one's capability and therefore not a matter of pressing concern. Or when the present activity proves frustrating to the point of work avoidance, the individual may bolster his esteem by "celebrating" previous successes. A variant on this theme is especially handy for avoiding work when a number of different tasks must be done. Upon completion of one of them, the student may use a you-owe-it-to-yourself justification for work avoidance, the avoidance period being defined as self-payment for a job well done.

Social Relations-Based Fritters

Fritters based upon social relations directly employ other people in the action of avoiding work. The impact of employing other people, however, is not so much in having an audience before which one gives accounts as simply in having an audience. There are three main patterns of social relations fritters.

Group Discussion

The group-discussion fritter is also called the commiseration fritter. Commiserating may be done in a large group or in pairs either in person or over the telephone. It involves "getting together" and consoling one another on the unreasonability or irrationality of the assignment. Complaining about the assigned work is an excellent fritter technique. It justifies work avoidance by directly protesting against the work itself. The more intelligent or discriminating the complaints, the clearer it is that the work task is within the student's later capability. Critical ability may be developed in avoiding studying as well as in doing studying. Sometimes discussions of this sort get around to a comparison of actual work done, leading to the social-comparison fritter.

Social Comparison

Students sometimes compare their progress with one another. When a student discovers he is ahead of others in his work, he can then feel justified in freeing time for work avoidance. This fritter has two aspects. First, there is the time spent gathering comparisons of others. This may involve personal contact or telephoning. Or the comparison others may not be real others working on the same task. Instead, high relative standing earlier in the course may be extrapolated to the present. Because of information from the past, the student may believe he is at present ahead of others. When this is coupled with the perception that relative position is the criterion of final evaluation, it becomes possible, for example, for "curve-breaking" midterm students to free time from final studies and projects. Second, there is the effect of the comparison. The choice of comparison to others is a stra-

tegic choice. For a student to feel justified in his current work avoidance, he must compare his work with someone who is less advanced than he. (Choice of either will vary depending on whether the student wishes to take a break from work or gain incentive to continue it.) The two dangers of this technique for the student are: first, he may choose someone who is, in fact, more advanced in the work; and, second, he may fritter away the time needed for students to catch up and pass him.

Group Work

The decision to study in a group has a number of work-avoidance functions. On the one hand, it immediately makes possible commiseration and social-comparison fritters. Study groups from the same course can, of course, commiserate easily. Students studying together, but for different courses, are able to have even longer commiseration sessions. Each can complain about his course without redundancy and without risk of contradiction or challenge.

Getting a number of people together functions, on the other hand, to increase enormously the range of alternatives to studying. These activities can be justified using any number of the techniques elsewhere mentioned. Work-avoidance maneuvers with group approval are especially difficult to ignore. There is a "risky shift" in the direction of longer fritters, too. This is because, once you have stopped working, it is difficult to know when to suggest to your partners that you should get back to work. It may be hard to stop frittering without being impolite or pressuring. Responsibility for directing attention back to work becomes diffused through the group.

Value-Based Fritters

While the above-mentioned fritter techniques are common and successful, they do not have the guilt-binding power of valuative fritters. One way work can be avoided especially, but not exclusively, in the early college years is using time to discuss values. Political, moral, and aesthetic topics are common in these conversations. Finding out who you are, "getting your shit together," and so on is an important task. Mundane work considerations do not look very important measured against this larger activity. Valuative fritters based on already held values place work and work avoidance within a larger framework of values and choices. It is here that considerations of nonstudent activities enter with greatest effect. Three primary types of valuative fritters may be described and ordered in terms of increasing generality and abstraction.

Higher Good

In the higher-good work-avoidance strategy, the student ranks being a student as less important to him in his scheme of values than other interests and aspects of his identity. Here friendship, love, cultural values (e.g., charity, service), political interests, physical fitness (the sound-mind-in-a-sound-body fritter), and much else can be justified as more worthy of attention for the moment than the study tasks at hand. These other values, of course, vary in strength and, therefore, in their guilt-free binding power in role management. For this reason, the strength of each of the alternative values is enhanced immeasurably if it can be asserted that the opportunity for acting on that value is soon to be gone. Stated another way, *rare events*, or at least infrequent events, have a special ability to bind time from studying, even if the value of the act would otherwise be questionable in relation to the pressure to study. Makes-Jack-a-dull-boy valuative fritters, involving, say, a movie, will be more potent the last day the picture is playing than the first day of an extended run, concerts involving rarely heard performers are able to appease guilt from role violation, and eclipses of the moon draw crowds of guilt-free students as an audience.

Experience Broadens

The experience-broadens fritter is less specific in the sense of presenting a less clear-cut value conflict. It has, nonetheless, the attraction of serving as a ready backup to a post-facto unjustified valuative fritter (say, the movie was lousy, the instruments out of tune, the friend crabby, the eclipse cloud-ridden, or what have you). In such an event, or generally in any event, it can be argued somehow that experience qua experience broadens the person, makes him more complete, or wiser, or what have you. This can bind successfully enormous amounts of time on a scale much larger than the mere work requirements for a specific course. Even career decisions (or decision evasions) can be justified under the experience-broadens rubric. The crucial difference from the higher-good fritter is that any experience will do.

Existential

The most general of valuative fritters is the existential, or the what-the-hell-sort-of-difference-will-it-make, fritter. In this strategy, the decision to work or not work is cast as having no lasting practical or existential effect on the course of one's life. Scholastic failures of prominently successful individuals may be remembered. Einstein's failure of a high school math course can offer solace to the fritterer. If one's activities are ultimately of no consequence anyway, the immediate consequences of work avoidance are not even worthy of consideration. Extreme application of this principle can lead to failure in the student role, in which event one's very studenthood may be justified as an experience-broadens fritter from what one should really be doing.

Task-Based Fritters

Fritters discussed to this point are based upon the student's history, biology, social relations, and values. We come finally to the task itself. Task-based fritters focus upon the direct handling of study time and the allocation of work resources. Specifically, there appear to be four main clusters of task-based fritters: time-related; preparation-related; creativity-related; and task-involved.

Time-Related Fritters

The time symmetry fritter. Many students appear to find it easier to start studying on the hour, half-hour, or, at the very least, quarter-hour than at any other minute. This may be due to the ease these times make for scheduling fritters discussed below. These times are more generally important in plans and schedules between individuals. A common social use of time shapes action. (On a larger scale, weekends, holidays, or Mondays assume special status in the week.) It is, further, "easier" to compute total study time and pages per hour if you start at some such prominent time division. One of the advantages of this technique is that, with a little effort, a large amount of time can be frittered if the activity one chose to do until, say, the quarter-hour starting time, can be extended just a few minutes beyond this starting point. The student is then, by the same logic, justified in waiting until the next prominent time division. Depending on the individual and on the amount of time already spent in time symmetry fritters, the student can choose to wait for the next hour, half-hour, or quarter-hour. As good a fritter technique as this is, there is a problem in its use. Each time it is used in succession, the student feels less justified in invoking the time symmetry fritter. This is sometimes manifested by the setting of the starting time at progressively shorter prominent intervals: e.g., at 7:00, 8:00, 8:30, and then 8:45. In any event, at some point, this technique loses its efficacy. Fortunately, there is a larger-scale, more successful technique which can then be used.

The great divide fritter. At some point, say, in an evening to be devoted to work, it becomes too late to get serious work done (or finish the task, the scheduled amount, or what have you). At this point, the student feels perfectly free to give up for the rest of the night all pretense to studying. It is simply too late to get enough work done to make any work worthwhile. Some other activity is then chosen to occupy the remaining time, but without any need for a higher-good valuative justification. Thus, a particular student might not consider it worthwhile to start studying after 9:00 at night. The time symmetry fritter brought the student up to 8:45, a biological-imperative fritter or a phone-call-for-a-commiseration fritter might be sufficient to add enough time to set up a great divide fritter.

Scheduling fritters. Students justify spending enormous amounts of time making up work schedules. These can be done for the day, evening, week, or whatever the rele-

vant work session to be planned. Plans can be made not just for the coming work, but also for coming work breaks. Fritters of the future become bound into a longer series of work intentions and are in that way neutralized. Of course, scheduling may be resorted to whenever the actual progress of the work falls far enough off schedule to warrant the writing of a new one. Schedule-related fritters, then, become a consideration whenever something goes wrong or could go wrong with the schedule. Indeed, the more detailed the schedule, the greater the chance of derailment.

There are two salient forms of scheduling fritters. First, there are anticipated interruption fritters. If one knows in advance that at a certain point in the work period, studying will be interrupted by some other activity, there is set up a situation in which frittering the time until after the interruption is justified. This can be considered the application of a great divide fritter on a smaller scale. Second, there are disruption-of-sequence fritters. These occur whenever the student, for some reason, performs a task out of order from the planned sequence. If this involves successful completion of the different task, conditions are set up for an owe-it-to-yourself fritter as well as a new scheduling fritter. The disruption of sequence can also justify waiting for a new prominent starting point, like a new day, before actually working.

Deadline change fritters. On occasion a teacher will change the date that some work is due either for the whole class or, by special arrangement, for single students. When this happens, the student feels free to use a postponed-deadline fritter. Since study time is reckoned backward from a deadline date rather than forward to new work opportunities, when the deadline is postponed, time is freed to avoid working. If, for example, a paper due Friday is postponed for one week on Wednesday, the student can wait for the following Wednesday before working again.

Preparation-related fritters

Preparation fritters involve all activities immediately attendant to preparing to study: getting books, paper, pens, cleaning the desk, and what have you. These are easily justified activities, preparatory as they are to work. These immediate preparations are easily escalated. Thus, a student decides that, in the interest of greater efficiency, he should clean his desk top (no matter what the actual nature of his work habits—tidy or abominable). Having done this, a crucial point is reached. He can now actually start to work. Instead, he says while-I'm-at-it and proceeds to clean out the whole desk, or rearrange all his books, or even move on to cleaning the whole room or apartment. This technique is especially interesting, developing as it does from the preparation fritter, in that it quickly ignores the originally work-related starting point. A good job is worth doing well, as long as it isn't the good job you have to do.

Preparation can be difficult (or made difficult), and work can be delayed. In the spread-resources or shuttle fritter the student does not bring, or chooses work for which he cannot bring, all the needed materials to one place for work. Traveling between work sites becomes necessary. What started as the path to work intersects with other paths (perhaps to other places).

Creativity Fritters

Once all the material preparations have been completed there are two other factors left to be prepared—the student and, say, the paper. Let us consider these in reverse order. Preparation of the paper itself will offer many opportunities for work avoidance.

(1) *For the-first-step-is-the-hardest.* This can mean working for a long time on an outline, or, commonly, working hard at getting exactly the proper first sentence or first paragraph. The opening of a paper is felt in an important way to constrain the range of alternatives, stylistic and organizational, for the rest of the work. It becomes, therefore, of utmost importance that the opening be precisely correct—no matter how much time it takes.

(2) *In addition, the student must be ready to work.* Every creative endeavor, however, has an incubation period and every endeavor, creative or not, requires motiva-

tion. Both needs can require time, justified time. It is best to wait until you are bursting with ideas or are sufficiently motivated, even if the motivation is guilt due to unsuccessful previous application of fritter techniques. This is therefore the let-it-brew-for-a-while fritter (closely related to this is the I'll-lie-down-and-think-about-it fritter; the possible danger in this tactic is, of course, very clear; listing all things people are designed to do horizontally, studying is one of the lowest on the list).

(3) *Related to these is the I'm-sure-there-is-something-else fritter.* No matter how much advanced preparation there has already been, the conscientious student is justified in allowing some free time to think of something else which should be included (say, in a paper, or when considering how to psych out the teacher's exam questions). This is especially useful when, for example, a paper is on a topic requiring an interdisciplinary approach or a number of different viewpoints for elucidation. The "something else" can then be in an area only vaguely related to the original topic. This justification can thus successfully be used to allow additional time for readings and thinking more and more peripheral to the original topic—i.e., to the work itself. When the task is taking a test, students can spend a great deal of time trying to psych out the teacher. Information on prior exams and teacher's specialization or personal quirks may be important in deciding what significant knowledge is.

Task-Involved Fritters

Finally, the student, to remain in concept and in fact a student, must occasionally actually work. Once work is started, however, there are still some devices which can be used to slow it or end it quickly without endangering one's view of self as student.

(1) One important consideration, especially to someone who has been using scheduling fritters, is a reliable measure of how quickly the work is going. Time

is thus justifiably spent computing pages, hours, words per minute, or what have you. This is the what's-my-rate fritter.

(2) Every work goal can be divided into subgoals whose individual accomplishments are significant since each contributes to the final completion. This is the principle behind the logical-stopping-point fritter. Small owe-it-to-yourself fritters are justified by the completion of the subgoals. As the time symmetry fritter has prominent dividing points for the time continuum, so the logical-stopping-point fritter divides up the work task itself. Thus, for example, one may set up subgoals such that one is justified in taking a break after completing only a single chapter in an assigned book. This technique, however, like the time symmetry fritter, is conducive to fractionalization. The subgoal can shift from finish the chapter to finish the topic of discussion or, more extremely, the page or the paragraph.

(3) Sometimes the student has more than one project to work on at once. The jack-of-all-trades fritter is a way of avoiding working too hard on any one subject by shifting from task to task before the work gets too taxing in any one of them.

Recovery Fritters

Sometimes the student does not complete the task when it is due. If he can get an open-ended extension, he is free to postpone additional work for a long time. This is the effect of the you-can't-pick-up-spilled-milk fritter.

Concluding Remarks

There are features of the student role which facilitate the use of these strategies. Students are granted great liberty in the planning of their use of time. Student time is more often "individual time" than "social time." Time demands are stricter in high schools than in colleges. Required class time and daily evaluated assignments are less characteristic of the college years. The schools frequently cite the increased maturity of the students as the reason for the greater liberty permitted. However, time use in statuses occupied by even more mature adults are frequently more regulated by institutions. Perhaps most important, the student is in a transitional role. The schools and the population as a whole are not favorably disposed to lifetime students. It is an early stage in commitment to professional careers and a late stage in formal education for yet other careers. Widespread use of fritter techniques can ease the difficulties of early commitment for the former and aid the termination of formal education for the latter.

Review

1. How does Bernstein define fritters?

2. Name and describe each of the four classes of fritters.

3. What are the main differences among the four classes of fritters?

4. What can account for greater use of fritters by college students than high school students or adults not in college?

Applications

1. For a one-week period, record the number of times you use various fritters, on which days, at what times, and related to what areas of study. Give examples of each. Use the specific types and subtypes discussed by Bernstein. Discuss your use of fritters compared to their use by students in general as brought out by Bernstein.

2. For a one-week period pay close attention to what other students say to you directly or what you overhear being said regarding their use of fritters. Record the numbers and types. Compare your findings to those of Bernstein.

Reprinted from: Stan Bernstein, "Getting It Done: Notes on Student Fritters." In *Urban Life and Culture*, Vol. I, No. 3, October 1972. Copyright © 1972 by Sage Publications. Reprinted by permission. ✦

3
Egoistic Suicide

Emile Durkheim

Sociologists often make use of existing sources (e.g., census data or crime rates) for research purposes. Organizing these data into an appropriate statistical format is just the beginning of the sociologist's work. Since the facts never speak for themselves, the sociologist must determine how the statistics express underlying social processes. Facts without such interpretation are meaningless to the scientific enterprise.

The best sociological interpretation is that which is applicable to society at large. In this sense, Durkheim's book on suicide has become the standard model for statistical and quantitative sociology. In the selection that follows, Durkheim takes the observed differences between Catholic and Protestant suicide rates as indicating differing degrees of social integration in these two faiths. In turn, this interpretation affirms a more general theory about the processes of integration in all social groups.

Beyond serving as an exemplar for later quantitative research, Durkheim's study can be seen as a critique of common-sense notions about suicide. Self-destruction is most often seen in egoistic terms—an individual acting out of psychological causes such as depression or unhappiness. The premise that the causes of suicide are psychological is actually an expression of individualist beliefs dominant in present-day society. This premise has not always existed. And, as Durkheim shows, the belief in individualism itself has social causes. There is, then, irony in his reference to this social cause of suicide as "egoistic."

If one casts a glance at the map of European suicide, it is at once clear that in purely Catholic countries like Spain, Portugal, Italy, suicide is very little developed, while it is at its maximum in Protestant countries, in Prussia, Saxony, Denmark. The following averages compiled by Morselli confirm this first conclusion:

Average of Suicides per Million Inhabitants

Protestant states (Protestant and Catholic)	96
Catholic states	58
Greek Catholic states	40

The low proportion of the Greek Catholics cannot be surely attributed to religion, for as their civilization is very different from that of the other European nations, this difference of culture may be the cause of their lesser aptitude. But this is not the case with most Catholic or Protestant societies. To be sure, they are not all on the same intellectual and moral level; yet the resemblances are sufficiently essential to make it possible to ascribe to confessional differences the marked contrast they offer in respect to suicide.

The only essential difference between Catholicism and Protestantism is that the second permits free inquiry to a far greater degree than the first. Of course, Catholicism by the very fact that it is an idealistic religion concedes a far greater place to thought and reflection than Greco-Latin polytheism or Hebrew monotheism. It is not restricted to mechanical ceremonies but seeks the control of the conscience.

So it appeals to conscience, and even when demanding blind submission of reason, does so by employing the language of reason. None the less, the Catholic accepts his faith ready made, without scrutiny. He may not even submit it to historical examination since the original texts that serve as its basis are proscribed. A whole hierarchical system of authority is devised, with marvelous ingenuity, to render tradition invariable. All variation is abhorrent to Catholic thought. The Protestant is far more the author of his faith. The Bible is put in his hands and no interpretation is imposed upon him. The very structure of the reformed cult stresses this state of religious individualism. Nowhere but in England is the Protestant clergy a hierarchy; like the worshipers, the priest has no other source but himself and his conscience. He is a more instructed guide than the run of worshipers but with no special authority for fixing dogma. But what best proves that this freedom of inquiry proclaimed by the founders of the Reformation has not remained a Platonic affirmation is the increasing multiplicity of all sorts of sects so strikingly in contrast with the indivisible unity of the Catholic Church.

We thus reach our first conclusion, that the proclivity of Protestantism for suicide must relate to the spirit of free inquiry that animates this religion. Let us understand this relationship correctly. Free inquiry itself is only the effect of another cause. When it appears, when men, after having long received their ready-made faith from tradition, claim the right to shape it for themselves, this is not because of the intrinsic desirability of free inquiry, for the latter involves as much sorrow as happiness. But it is because men henceforth need this liberty. This very need can have only one cause: the overthrow of traditional beliefs. If they still asserted themselves with equal energy, it would never occur to men to criticize them. If they still had the same authority, men would not demand the right to verify the source of this authority. Reflection develops only if its development becomes imperative, that is, if certain ideas and instinctive sentiments which have hitherto adequately guided conduct are found to have lost their efficacy. Then reflection intervenes to fill the gap that has appeared, but which it has not created. Just as reflection disappears to the extent that thought and action take the form of automatic habits, it awakes only when accepted habits become disorganized. It asserts its rights against public opinion only when the latter loses strength, that is, when it is no longer prevalent to the same extent. If these assertions occur not merely occasionally and as passing crises, but become chronic, if individual consciences keep reaffirming their autonomy, it is because they are constantly subject to conflicting impulses, because a new opinion has not been formed to replace the one no longer existing. If a new system of beliefs were constituted

which seemed as indisputable to everyone as the old, no one would think of discussing it any longer. Its discussion would no longer even be permitted, for ideas shared by an entire society draw from this consensus an authority that makes them sacrosanct and raises them above dispute. For them to have become more tolerant, they must first already have become the object of less general and complete assent and been weakened by preliminary controversy.

Thus, if it is correct to say that free inquiry once proclaimed multiplies schisms, it must be added that it presupposes them and derives from them, for it is claimed and instituted as a principle only in order to permit latent or half-declared schisms to develop more freely. So if Protestantism concedes a greater freedom to individual thought than Catholicism, it is because it has fewer common beliefs and practices. Now, a religious society cannot exist without a collective *credo* and the more extensive the *credo* the more unified and strong is the society. For it does not unite men by an exchange and reciprocity of services, a temporal bond of union which permits and even presupposes differences, but which a religious society cannot form. It socializes men only by attaching them completely to an identical body of doctrine and socializes them in proportion as this body of doctrine is extensive and firm. The more numerous the manners of action and thought of a religious character are, which are accordingly removed from free inquiry, the more the idea of God presents itself in all details of existence, and makes individual wills converge to one identical goal. Inversely, the greater concessions a confessional group makes to individual judgment, the less it dominates lives, the less its cohesion and vitality. We thus reach the conclusion that the superiority of Protestantism with respect to suicide results from its being a less strongly integrated church than the Catholic Church.

The beneficent influence of religion is not due to the special nature of religious conceptions. If religion protects man against the desire for self-destruction, it is not that it preaches the respect for his own person to him with arguments *sui generis*, but because it is society. What constitutes this society is the existence of a certain number of beliefs and practices common to all the faithful, traditional and thus obligatory. The more numerous and strong these collective states of mind are, the stronger the integration of the religious community and also the greater its preservative value. The details of dogmas and rites are secondary. The essential thing is that they be capable of supporting a sufficiently intense collective life. And because the Protestant church has less consistency than the others it has less moderating effect upon suicide.

So we reach the general conclusion: suicide varies inversely with the degree of integration of the social groups of which the individual forms a part.

But society cannot disintegrate without the individual simultaneously detaching himself from social life, without his own goals becoming preponderant over those of the community, in a word without his personality tending to surmount the collective personality. The more weakened the groups to which he belongs, the less he depends on them, the more he consequently depends only on himself and recognizes no other rules of conduct than what are founded on his private interests. If we agree to call this state egoism, in which the individual ego asserts itself to excess in the face of the social ego and at its expense, we may call egoistic the special type of suicide springing from excessive individualism.

But how can suicide have such an origin?

First of all, it can be said that, as collective force is one of the obstacles best calculated to restrain suicide, its weakening involves a development of suicide. When society is strongly integrated, it holds individuals under its control, considers them at its service and thus forbids them to dispose willfully of themselves. Accordingly it opposes their evading their duties to it through death. But how could society impose its supremacy upon them when they refuse to accept this subordination as legitimate? It no longer then possesses the requisite authority to retain them in their duty if they wish to desert; and conscious of its own weakness, it even recognizes their right to do freely what it can

no longer prevent. So far as they are the admitted masters of their destinies, it is their privilege to end their lives. They, on their part, have no reason to endure life's sufferings patiently. For they cling to life more resolutely when belonging to a group they love, so as not to betray interests they put before their own. The bond that unites them with the common cause attaches them to life and the lofty goal they envisage prevents their feeling personal troubles so deeply. There is, in short, in a cohesive and animated society a constant interchange of ideas and feelings from all to each and each to all, something like a mutual moral support, which instead of throwing the individual on his own resources, leads him to share in the collective energy and supports his own when exhausted.

But these reasons are purely secondary. Excessive individualism not only results in favoring the action of suicidogenic causes, but it is itself such a cause. It not only frees man's inclination to do away with himself from a protective obstacle, but creates this inclination out of whole cloth and thus gives birth to a special suicide which bears its mark. This must be clearly understood for this is what constitutes the special character of the type of suicide just distinguished and justifies the name we have given it. What is there then in individualism that explains this result?

***

A whole range of functions concern only the individual; these are the ones indispensable for physical life. Since they are made for this purpose only, they are perfected by its attainment. In everything concerning them, therefore, man can act reasonably without thought of transcendental purposes. These functions serve by merely serving him. In so far as he has no other needs, he is therefore self-sufficient and can live happily with no other objective than living. This is not the case, however, with the civilized adult. He has many ideas, feelings and practices unrelated to organic needs. The roles of art, morality, religion, political faith, science itself are not to repair organic exhaustion nor to provide sound functioning of the organs. All this supra-physical life is built and expanded not because of the demands of the cosmic environment but because of the demands of the social environment. The influence of society is what has aroused in us the sentiments of sympathy and solidarity drawing us toward others; it is society which, fashioning us in its image, fills us with religious, political and moral beliefs that control our actions. To play our social role we have striven to extend our intelligence and it is still society that has supplied us with tools for this development by transmitting to us its trust fund of knowledge.

Through the very fact that these superior forms of human activity have a collective origin, they have a collective purpose. As they derive from society they have reference to it; rather they are society itself incarnated and individualized in each one of us. But for them to have a *raison d'etre* in our eyes, the purpose they envisage must be one not indifferent to us. We can cling to these forms of human activity only to the degree that we cling to society itself. Contrariwise, in the same measure as we feel detached from society we become detached from that life whose source and aim is society. For what purpose do these rules of morality, these precepts of law binding us to all sorts of sacrifices, these restrictive dogmas exist, if there is no being outside us whom they serve and in whom we participate? What is the purpose of science itself? If its only use is to increase our chances for survival, it does not deserve the trouble it entails. Instinct acquits itself better of this role; animals prove this. Why substitute for it a more hesitant and uncertain reflection? What is the end of suffering, above all? If the value of things can only be estimated by their relation to this positive evil for the individual, it is without reward and incomprehensible. This problem does not exist for the believer firm in his faith or the man strongly bound by ties of domestic or political society. Instinctively and unreflectively they ascribe all that they are and do, the one to his Church or his God, the living symbol of the Church, the other to his family, the third to his country or party. Even in their sufferings they see only a means of glorifying the group to which they belong and thus do homage to it. So, the Christian ultimately desires and seeks suffering to testify more fully to his contempt for the flesh and more fully resemble his divine model. But the more the believer doubts, that is, the less he feels himself a real participant in the religious faith to which he belongs, and from which he is freeing himself; the more the family and community become foreign to the individual, so much the more does he become a mystery to himself, unable to escape the exasperating and agonizing question: to what purpose?

If, in other words, as has often been said, man is double, that is because social man superimposes himself upon physical man. Social man necessarily presupposes a society which he expresses and serves. If this dissolves, if we no longer feel it in existence and action about and above us, whatever is social in us is deprived of all objective foundation. All that remains is an artificial combination of illusory images, a phantasmagoria vanishing at the least reflection; that is, nothing which can be a goal for our action. Yet this social man is the essence of civilized man; he is the masterpiece of existence. Thus we are bereft of reasons for existence; for the only life to which we could cling no longer corresponds to anything actual; the only existence still based upon reality no longer meets our needs. Because we have been initiated into a higher existence, the one which satisfies an animal or a child can satisfy us no more and the other itself fades and leaves us helpless. So there is nothing more for our efforts to lay hold of, and we feel them lose themselves in emptiness.

In this sense it is true to say that our activity needs an object transcending it. We do not need it to maintain ourselves in the illusion of an impossible immortality; it is implicit in our moral constitution and cannot be even partially lost without this losing its *raison d'etre* in the same degree. No proof is needed that in such a state of confusion the least cause of discouragement may easily give birth to desperate resolutions. If life is not worth the trouble of being lived, everything becomes a pretext to rid ourselves of it.

But this is not all. This detachment occurs not only in single individuals. One of the constitutive elements of every national temperament consists of a certain way of estimating the value of existence. There is a collective as well as an individual humor inclining peoples to sadness or cheerfulness, making them see things in bright or sombre lights. In fact, only society can pass a collective opinion on the value of human life; for this the individual is incompetent. The latter knows nothing but himself and his own little horizon; thus his experience is too limited to serve as a basis for a general appraisal. He may indeed consider his own life to be aimless; he can say nothing applicable to others. On the contrary, without sophistry, society may generalize its own feeling as to itself, its state of health or lack of health. For individuals share too deeply in the life of society for it to be diseased without their suffering infection. What it suffers they necessarily suffer. Because it is the whole, its ills are communicated to its parts. Hence it cannot disintegrate without awareness that the regular conditions of general existence are equally disturbed. Because society is the end on which our better selves depend, it cannot feel us escaping it without a simultaneous realization that our activity is purposeless. Since we are its handiwork, society cannot be conscious of its own decadence without the feeling that henceforth this work is of no value. Thence are formed currents of depression and disillusionment emanating from no particular individual but expressing society's state of disintegration. They reflect the relaxation of social bonds, a sort of collective asthenia, or social malaise, just as individual sadness, when chronic, in its way reflects the poor organic state of the individual. Then metaphysical and religious systems spring up which, by reducing these obscure sentiments to formulae, attempt to prove to men the senselessness of life and that it is self-deception to believe that it has purpose. Then new moralities originate which, by elevating facts to ethics, commend suicide or at least tend in that direction by suggesting a minimal existence. On their appearance they seem to have been created out of whole cloth by their makers who are sometimes blamed for the pessimism of their doctrines. In reality they are an effect rather than a cause; they merely symbolize in abstract language and systematic form the physiological distress of the body social. As these currents are collective, they have, by virtue of their origin, an authority which they impose upon the individual and they drive him more vigorously on the way to which he is already inclined by the state of moral distress directly aroused in him by the disintegration of society. Thus, at the very moment that, with excessive zeal, he frees himself from the social environment, he still submits to its influence. However individualized a man may be, there is always something collective remaining—the very depression and melancholy resulting from this same exaggerated individualism. He effects communion through sadness when he no longer has anything else with which to achieve it.

Hence this type of suicide well deserves the name we have given it. Egoism is not merely a contributing factor in it; it is its generating cause. In this case the bond attaching man to life relaxes because that attaching him to society is itself slack. The incidents of private life which seem the direct inspiration of suicide and are considered its determining causes are in reality only incidental causes. The individual yields to the slightest shock of circumstance because the state of society has made him a ready prey to suicide.

Review

1. What types of countries, according to Durkheim, are likely to have high suicide rates? Explain why.

2. How does Durkheim define the egoistic type of suicide?

3. What are the origins of egoistic suicide?

4. How does Durkheim differentiate between social man and physical man?

Applications

1. Compare suicide rates of the different countries mentioned by Durkheim, as well as other countries. Are there differences in the rate according to whether

the society is predominantly Catholic, Protestant, Jewish, Hindu, or nonreligious? Are Durkheim's conclusions relevant today?

2. Interview four people—a Catholic, a Protestant, a Jew, and an atheist. Develop an interview format that addresses

a. attitudes toward suicide

b. the group's position on suicide

c. perceptions of causes and reasons for suicide

d. perceptions about the importance of religion in causing or preventing suicide

e. perceptions about societal influences on suicide—both causes and prevention

Summarize your findings, contrasting them with Durkheim's.

Reprinted from: Emile Durkheim, "Egoistic Suicide." In *Suicide: A Study in Sociology*, by Emile Durkheim, translated by John A. Spaulding and George Simpson. Edited by George Simpson. Adapted with permission of the Free Press, a division of Simon and Schuster, Copyright © 1951; © renewed 1979 by the Free Press. ✦

4

'It's Awful! It's Terrible! It's . . . Never Mind'

Steven A. Holmes

How do people know what they know? It's a question posed and extensively discussed by philosophers. It's also a question raised by sociologists, who frequently challenge both the conventional wisdom and the opinions of experts.

Much of what people know comes from the media. You read in a magazine article, for example, that half of all marriages fail. You tell this to friends, who pass it on to others. Soon, it is a part of the conventional wisdom—everyone knows that half of all marriages fail. The problem is, it isn't true that half of all marriages fail. Half of all marriages have never failed. Among some younger age groups, half of all marriages would ultimately fail if the divorce rate had remained as high as it was in the late 1970s. But the rate has fallen somewhat, so the proportion of marriages that ultimately fail is uncertain.

In this selection, Holmes provides some additional examples of information reported in the media that was either wrong or misleading. Why does it matter? Well, if you go into marriage believing that you have a 50-50 chance of divorcing, you may not be as committed or as willing to work through problems as you would be if you thought that most marriages succeed. If you read that high-tension electrical wires cause cancer, you may avoid living somewhere that would have been an ideal home for you. If you agree that people are poor because they are unwilling to work, you may oppose government programs to help the poor.

Information, in other words, affects what people do as well as what they believe. It is im-portant, therefore, to engage in critical thinking when you sort through the information that comes to you. And as Holmes notes, critical thinking is needed whether the information comes from a popular or a professional source. Experts are not infallible.

Critical thinking does not mean cynicism—as though you can't believe anyone or anything. It means exercising caution in the face of massive amounts of information, not dismissing all information as tainted or purely a matter of opinion.

Critical thinking means the willingness to raise such questions as these: Is this information consistent with my experience (keeping in mind that it may be true even if it isn't consistent)? Is it consistent with other things I know? Is it reasonable? What is the basis for the facts presented? Are the conclusions the only ones that can be drawn from the facts? Is the source a generally reliable one? And so on. Critical thinking, in sum, is the rational road between the extremes of gullibility and cynicism.

The reports were shocking, even enraging, the type that can make one wonder where American society is headed. In 1995, several research organizations reported that a hefty percentage—in one study, 65 percent—of teen-age mothers had babies by adult men. The image of lecherous men seducing troubled young girls barely past menarche prompted several states to step up enforcement of statutory rape laws, both to protect the girls and to reduce out-of-wedlock births.

There was one problem, though. The image was largely wrong. What many news reports on the studies neglected to mention was that 62 percent of the teen-age mothers were 18 or 19 years old and, therefore, like the fathers of their babies, adults. Also ignored was the fact that the researchers did not differentiate between married and single teenagers. Subsequent studies have determined that of all those age 15 to 17 who gave birth, only 8 percent were unmarried girls made pregnant by men at least five years older.

"It's a sizable minority," said John Hutchins, a spokesman for the National Campaign to Prevent Teen Pregnancy, "a percentage that we should definitely be concerned about. But it is still a small percentage. If all of our attention is placed on that, we're not understanding the full problem."

The tale of the predatory males is just one example of what has become a disquieting trend. Call it the "whoops factor," a phenomenon that starts with shoddy research or the misinterpretation of solid research, moves on quickly to public outcry, segues swiftly into the enactment of new laws or regulations and often ends with news organizations and some public policy mavens sounding like the late Gilda Radner's character, Emily Litella, as they sheepishly chirp, "Never mind!"

Arson, Rape, Poison

The public has been buffeted by reports suggesting a campaign to torch black churches, a surge in juvenile crime, rampant child abuse in day-care centers, a rape crisis on college campuses and the continued poisoning of the country by cancer-causing chemicals like alar, saccharin or cyclamates or by electromagnetic forces emanating from high-voltage power wires.

Last week a panel of scientists from the National Cancer Institute and some leading hospitals reported after an exhaustive study that there is no evidence that living near power lines causes elevated rates of childhood leukemia. The link had been suggested by a poorly designed 1979 study by researchers at the University of Colorado. After that study was reported, parents of children with cancer sued power companies, and property values near power lines plummeted.

While there tends to be enough truth in many of these claims to warrant serious investigation and remedial action, some of the initial reports are so overblown as to produce panic and then cynicism. "It's what I call the Weather Channel phenomenon," said Robert Thompson, a professor of radio and television at Syracuse University. "Five minutes into watching it, you're convinced that you have to be really concerned about that front moving in. The next thing you

know you've turned off the TV in a state of panic, feeling that you should be sand-bagging your house."

When the brewing problem is exposed as a kind of Comet Kohoutek of social pathology, there is a sense of betrayal, complacency and, finally, attention is drawn away from the true extent of the problem to the methodology that was used to unearth it.

"A brilliant sleight-of-hand gets achieved," Mr. Thompson said. "These are problems that are difficult to solve. And if we divert attention to a debate on how they are covered or how they are measured, then we don't have to make the tough choices on how to actually address them."

Underneath the embarrassing retreats from what in hindsight seems shabby research, superficial journalism or a triumph of politically motivated public relations lies a much deeper problem: Americans' willingness, almost eagerness, to accept a Hobbesian view of man as a brutish thug who if left unchecked would sow chaos and destruction. In this atmosphere, even reports like the one claiming that one quarter of all female college students are raped each year are readily believed.

Moreover, "people are always looking for one single-bullet answer," said Kristin Moore, president of Child Trends Inc., a Washington-based research organization specializing in adolescent sexual issues. "But things are more complicated than people want them to be."

And they are more complicated than many reporters and editors want them to be. Cramped by space and time, and usually not having much knowledge of statistics, journalists are often bamboozled by "experts" bearing impressive numbers or they fail to put the numbers in historical or demographic perspective.

"The media do not have the time, inclination or skill to really dig deeply into reports of research or claims made by political leaders," said Alfred Blumstein, a professor of criminology at Carnegie Mellon University in Pittsburgh. "It merely transmits them, and transmits them in a way to make headlines or sound bites on TV."

Thus, when the Department of Health and Human Services estimated in 1983 that 1.5

million children are reported missing each year, few people questioned the information. With the imprimatur of the Federal Government, a national campaign sprang up that included pictures of missing children on milk cartons and campaigns instructing children how to avoid being kidnapped.

Later, more rigorous studies would find that 3,200 to 4,600 children a year are abducted by strangers. To be sure, that is a large number. But it is dwarfed by the more than 350,000 children who, the Justice Department estimated later, are snatched by a parent in custody disputes, and it is nowhere near 1.5 million.

The definition of a particular group as victims—often with solid historical and contemporary evidence—also helps color the public's receptivity to studies or claims about them.

For example, last year, a spate of fires at African-American churches conjured images of white nightriders running amok or a reprise of the 1963 Birmingham church bombing. President Clinton appointed a task force to look into the problem. Last month, the task force reported that there was no national conspiracy of hate groups; the fires stemmed in part from racism but also from financial profit, burglary and personal revenge. Indeed, about one-third of the 76 people arrested in the church cases between Jan. 1, 1995, and May 27, 1997, were black.

Often, the unwillingness of reporters to ask hard questions or of policy makers to provide a context for data can lead regulators and lawmakers into broad-brush policies that waste resources and political capital.

In May, the House of Representatives, in response to reports of surging juvenile crime and an increase in the number of young killers, voted to offer states $1.5 billion in financial incentives to require that juveniles accused of violent crimes be tried as adults. Even as the House acted, the Bureau of Criminal Justice Statistics reported that while juvenile homicides had risen, they were highly concentrated. The bureau determined that in 1995, one-third took place in just 10 of the counties in the country. It added that 84 percent of the nation's counties had no juvenile homicides at all.

Review

1. What does Holmes mean by the "whoops" factor?

2. Why do the media sometimes report false or misleading information?

3. What are the consequences of false or misleading information?

Applications

1. Use the *Readers' Guide to Periodical Literature* to look up articles that pertain to two or more of the cases cited by Holmes. Do any of the articles acknowledge the possibility that the information might be erroneous or incomplete? Practice your critical-thinking skills by making a list of questions that could be raised about the claims in the article, questions that might lead you to look for additional evidence.

   Now look through a recent magazine or newspaper. Find an article that makes a claim about some social or natural phenomenon. Make a list of questions that you would like to have answered before accepting the conclusions of the article.

2. Even though claims are made and later retracted, some people read or hear about the original claim but not the retraction. How many people do you think still accept some of the erroneous claims made in this article? Interview a dozen people. Take each of the claims that Holmes describes, and put them into this kind of format: "A report appeared that 65 percent of teen-age mothers have children by adult men. Have you heard of the report? Do you think it is true? Why or why not?"

   How many people recall the reports? How many believed then whether or not they had heard of them? How many knew both of the original reports and the retractions?

Part Three

Biology, Psychology, or Sociology?

In recent decades, the field of **sociobiology** has tried to reduce the explanation of human behavior to biological factors. Everything from criminal behavior to acts of altruism has been explained as being genetically based and/or in harmony with evolutionary advantage (i.e., with survival of the species). Some psychologists, on the other hand, have tried to understand all human behavior solely in terms of qualities of the individual.

Sociologists do not deny the import of either biological or psychological factors. They know that individual needs and drives vary because of genetic makeup. They recognize that some aspects of the individual's makeup—such as personality factors—help explain that individual's behavior. At the same time, sociologists stress the importance of studying the social factors that also are essential for an understanding of human life and human behavior. The two selections in this part illustrate the significance of social factors, showing that even such things as IQ and drinking patterns reflect social as well as genetic and psychological factors. ✦

5
Intelligence and Giftedness

Miles D. Storfer

The power of a social explanation for human behavior is most apparent when it is contrasted with a widely accepted biological explanation. Consider the matter of intelligence, for example. What determines your IQ? Most people think of IQ as biological, as part of their genetic inheritance.

If IQ scores are genetically based, however, we would expect that children in the same family would have similar scores. And we would expect that, say, a third child in the family would have as good a chance as a first or second child of having a slightly higher score than his or her siblings. In point of fact, however, first children tend to score higher than subsequent children in the family. How can we explain this? This article reviews research that looks at the issue of higher scores of firstborns and identifies some of the social factors that help explain the phenomenon.

The issue is important from both a societal and a family perspective. From the societal point of view, if IQ scores are genetically fixed, there is little point in wasting money on remedial programs in education. Moreover, slogans like "you can be anything you want" are not only wrong but harmful, because they encourage expectations that are genetically doomed to failure. In contrast, if it is possible to intervene in children's lives and increase IQ scores beyond what they would have been without the intervention, one could argue that there is a societal responsibility to make the effort.

From a family perspective, the issue is important because parents want the best for their children. Can a parent do something to increase a child's IQ? The answer is yes. And the article identifies the kind of parent-child interaction that is necessary.

Introduction

This chapter explores possible relationships between parental interaction with infants and toddlers and their later cognitive development. It begins with an analysis of studies that have examined the differences in parents' behavior toward first-born and later born children, on the basis that these differences are likely to be a significant source of the first-born IQ advantage. . . .

First-born—Later born Differences in the Early Home Environment

Are there any systematic differences in the way mothers attend to their oldest child during infancy and toddlerhood, compared with their behavior toward later borns?

A review of the literature strongly suggests that there are considerable differences in the nature and quality—but not necessarily in the overall quantity—of stimulation received by first-borns and later borns during infancy and early childhood.

One such study (Jacobs and Moss, 1976) compared the behavior of mothers toward their first-born child at three months of age with the behavior of these same mothers toward their second-born child at a similar age and found several important differences: (1) virtually no mother spoke to her second-born child as frequently as the average mother in this study spoke to her first-born child; (2) virtually no mother imitated the vocalization of her second-born child as often as she did her first-born's; and (3) in each of the other measures of maternal interaction . . . , at least two-thirds of the second-born infants received less maternal attention than did the average first-born. In response to the higher frequency of maternal attention, these first-born infants smiled more often than did their younger siblings and vocalized more frequently. . . .

Lewis and Kreitzberg (1979) found the following substantial differences in maternal behavior toward first-borns and later borns at three months of age in a rather large study (193 families):

- The mothers of first-borns vocalized more frequently to their infants (58 percent) than did the mothers of later borns (with second-borns receiving slightly more frequent maternal vocalizations than did third or later borns).

- The mothers of first-borns looked at their infants 42 percent more frequently and smiled at and laughed with them 40 percent more often than did the mothers of later borns.

- Although there was little difference in the proportion of time that the mothers of first-borns and later borns spent holding their children, the mothers of first-borns spent almost twice as much time rocking their children.

- These first-borns were also played with more frequently (70 percent) than the later borns and were given toys and pacifiers nearly twice as often.

In response, these first-borns spent 24 percent more time looking at their mothers, 33 percent more time smiling at and laughing with them, and 36 percent more time playing with objects. Although infant vocalizations to the mother showed only a slight diminution when first and second-borns were compared, they showed a much more substantial (25 percent) reduction when first-borns were compared to third-borns or fourth-borns. . . .

In toddlerhood, first-borns appear to receive a greater variety of stimulation than do later borns, and these differences are associated with IQ performance at a later age (Gottfried and Gottfried, 1984). . . . In another (unfortunately smaller) study, which contrasted maternal interactions with first-born and later born toddlers (White, Kahan, and Attanucci, 1979), major differences were found in response to the following questions:

- What percentage of the time do mothers respond immediately to their children's overtures? (first-borns, 90.3 percent; later borns, 76.7 percent).

- When responding to their toddlers' questions, what percentage of the time do mothers provide related ideas?

(first-borns, 68.8 percent; later borns, 31.1 percent).

- What percentage of the observation time is spent in adult-initiated mother/toddler interactions? (firstborns, 24.0 percent; later borns, 6.6 percent).

- What is the average duration of adult-mediated interactions? (first-borns, 7.1 seconds; later borns, 4.3 seconds).

- What degree of language complexity do mothers use in responding to their toddlers? (1) complex sentences: first-borns, 22.2 percent; later borns, 5.5 percent; (2) one-word answers: first-borns, 4.3 percent; later borns, 17.5 percent; (3) phrases: first-borns, 59.1 percent; later borns, 64.6 percent; (4) no response: first-borns, 5.6 percent; later borns, 12.4 percent.

These researchers also evaluated the frequency with which a mother responded verbally to her child's initiatives at what they thought to be an appropriate level and concluded that first-borns received appropriate responses 83 percent of the time, compared with only 35 percent for later borns. . . .

Two recent studies by Bornstein and Tamis-LeMonda (1989) lend additional support to the proposition that maternal responsiveness has a strong influence on cognitive development. One, of fifty-two first-born five-month-old infants, found that mothers' prompt, contingent, and appropriate responsiveness to their infants' nondistress activities bore statistically significant correlations with these infants' habituation speed and with their "novelty preference" scores, even after the effects of these mothers' noncontingent stimulation were partialled out. The other study, of twenty first-born four-month-olds, reported a correlation of +.60 between maternal responsiveness to infants' nondistressful vocalizations, facial expressions, body movements, and the like and four-year IQ scores. . . .

Mother/Infant Interactive Behavior and IQ Development: Overview

The preceding analysis of differences in maternal behavior toward first-borns and later borns during infancy suggests that (1) the total amount of environmental stimulation seems to be of far less importance in determining a child's cognitive development than the amount of stimulation specifically directed toward the child; (2) effective maternal gaze behavior patterns, as evidenced by eye contact and the pleasure derived therefrom, promote cognitive development; and (3) imitating an infant's vocalization is of special importance in early cognitive development.

Other aspects of early parental behavior that appear to contribute to children's emerging intellectual development include (1) encouraging the child to attend to objects and events in the environment; (2) naming specific objects (especially the parts of an infant's body during activities such as bathing); (3) choosing appropriate mechanisms for attaining and maintaining a state of "quiet alertness" in early infancy and using this state to provide appropriate visual and auditory stimulation; and (4) providing opportunities for so-called contingent responsivity—by creating situations that enable infants to learn that, through their actions, they can affect their surroundings in particular ways.

Encouragement of Attention

Several studies indicate that the extent to which mothers encourage their infants and toddlers to attend to objects and events in the environment has a strong relationship with subsequent IQ performance, particularly in verbal areas.

In one of these studies, where the level of parental education averaged a college degree (Ruddy and Bornstein, 1982; Bornstein, 1985), a strong association was found between (1) maternal encouragement assessed at four months and thirteen months of age and (2) later intellectual performance. The correlation between "encouragement of attention" assessed at four months and Wechsler IQ scores at four years was quite strong: +.51. At this early age, the encouragement-assessment factor included handing the baby a toy, pointing to a picture, or naming an object. At thirteen months of age, bringing a new property, object, or event in the environment to a toddler's attention (as opposed to elaborating on something that was already under the child's purview) was highly correlated with an early development of verbal comprehension. . . .

In a study of 168 essentially middle-class families, Olson, Bates, and Bayles (1984) again found "encouragement of attention" at six and thirteen months to be predictive of cognitive competence. Two of these researchers' six-month variables, "verbal stimulation" and "mother object stimulation" ("offer toy to infant, offer and demonstrate toy, and return object to infant"), were modestly but persuasively predictive of "academic competence" at age six (Olson, Bayles, and Bates, 1986). At thirteen months, the researchers' "maternal teaching" measure (which included drawing a toddler's attention to an object, offering the object, offering and demonstrating an object, questioning, naming, and accepting the toddler's actions) was strongly correlated (+.49) with these authors' measures of cognitive competence at twenty-four months. . . .

Gaze Behavior and Vocal Imitation

It seems to be part of instinctive behavior for mothers to imitate their infants' facial expressions and vocalizations. At the same time, newborn infants themselves have a clearly demonstrated capacity to imitate facial expressions (Meltzoff and Moore, 1983) and also appear to possess an indigenous readiness to match vocal imitations (Papousek, Papousek, and Bornstein, 1985).

The extraordinary importance of imitating an infant's vocalizations to normal cognitive development has been aptly demonstrated. Further, several studies suggest that there are longitudinal linkages between effective gaze behavior in infancy and childhood IQ. Let us then turn at once to a discussion of these behaviors.

The Tehran Study (Hunt, Mohandessi, Ghodssi, and Akiyama, 1976)

In an orphanage in Tehran, where only routine custodial care was provided, virtually all the children reared there from infancy suffered a progressive decline in IQ until it tended to stabilize (most frequently at slightly above 60 points). When a regimen designed to foster imitative skills was introduced (Hunt, 1981), however, the effects were quite dramatic. Where previously the infants would have had little or no expressive speech at three years of age, all the children receiving this regimen had acquired vocabularies of fifty words or more by seventeen to twenty-two months of age. The strategy employed was as follows:

Caretakers were instructed to initiate vocal games with their charges, either by imitating the spontaneous vocalizations of the infants in their care or by vocalizing sounds that they had heard an infant make repeatedly. The program began once an infant had been heard to repeatedly vocalize several different sounds. The caretaker began by uttering one of the sounds in the infant's repertoire and, when the infant repeated it, uttered it again. After several repetitions, the caretaker shifted to another of the sounds from the infant's repertoire to get a new vocal interchange going. After three different sounds were routinely repeated, the caretaker gradually reduced the number of times that each sound was repeated before shifting sounds, with the aim of getting the infant to immediately follow from one pattern to another, in effect playing a game of "follow the leader."

This vocal game was part of the caretaker-infant interaction during each stint of bathing, dressing, feeding, toileting, and so on. After the infant had acquired facility in this game, the caretaker introduced new vocal patterns from the native (Persian) language: new in the sense that the caretaker had never heard the infant make them. The caretaker uttered these unfamiliar sounds repeatedly as the infant, through successive approximations, came closer to repeating the sounds modeled for him.

Once the infant acquired the ability to copy novel sounds, the caretaker fostered the beginning of naming (or semantic mastery) by mentioning the names of the parts of the infant's body as they were touched by the washcloth during bathing (beginning with those body parts visible to the infant).

In summary, caretakers (1) imitated the cooings and babblings of infants in their charge to get vocal games going; (2) expanded this game into a vocal "follow the leader" by using familiar vocal patterns; (3) modeled unfamiliar vocal patterns; and (4) sharpened the "game" conditions by teaching the infants to associate parts of their bodies with the sounds of the names of these parts as a means of teaching that sounds have meaning.

Smiling, Cooing, and Imitation: Timetables and Potential Importance

Several studies suggest that the best way to sustain communication with an infant is to closely attend to and imitate the infant's behavior. Maternal overactivity born of attempts to gain attention, however, appears to be adversive and causes the infant to gaze away. For example, in one study (Field, 1977) an inverse relationship between maternal activity and infant gaze was found in each of three interactive situations: "attention-getting," "spontaneous," and "imitative" situations. . . . Thus, infant gaze can be thought of as a signal indicating the readiness of the infant to engage in interaction, while gaze aversion appears to indicate a wish to terminate or temporarily suspend an interaction.

A mother's imitation of her infant's expressions and vocalizations appears to occur quite naturally, as evidenced by studies of mother-infant interactions when hospitals allow mothers to spend most of their time with their newborns (Hunt, Mohandessi, Ghodssi, and Akiyama, 1976).

Mothers and infants also enjoy cooing at each other. A pattern of alternate cooing and waiting has been observed in infant-mother interactions both at four and at eight weeks of age. Infants appear to seek opportunities for such vocal dialogues and take great pleasure in these interactions.

Vigorous smiling and cooing in response to the human face can be readily elicited in young infants. Increasing rapidly during the second and third months of life, these responses reach a peak at approximately fourteen weeks and appear to be dependent on a proper alignment of the mother's face to the face of the infant (Watson, 1972). During the third and fourth months of life, "a face stimulus" can elicit vigorous smiling but only if it is aligned with the infant's face in a zero-degree orientation. Only half as much smiling will be elicited in response to either a 90-degree or a 180-degree facial orientation.

A series of experiments has demonstrated that this phenomenon of vigorous smiling and cooing also occurs in response to an inanimate object (for instance, a mobile) if the infant has learned that the object will behave in a manner contingent upon its behavior (Badger, 1977). For example, after three to five days of ten-minute-a-day exposure to a contingently responsive mobile, almost all infants are reported to respond with vigorous smiling and cooing, as follows:

- If the mobile's performance is clearly contingent on the infant's doing something (such as touching its head to a pillow or moving its leg), the infant will do considerably more of that activity.

- If the mobile moves, but its movement is not contingent on the infant's activity, the infant will alter its activity level back to baseline after several attempts to get the mobile to move.

- If, however, an ambiguous response occurs (the mobile sometimes moves contingently and sometimes doesn't) the infant's movements will fall well below baseline, as it tries to avoid the situation.

Badger suggests that these findings may explain an infant's vigorous response to the zero-degree facial orientation. Because most caretaking activities (such as feeding and diaper changing) are more commonly associated with a ninety-degree facial alignment, this response is clearly not related to primary rewards. Indeed, it is usually only when a mother begins playing with her baby that she aligns herself at zero degrees and that her facial and verbal behavior begins to respond to its actions and reactions. Therefore, one might conclude that infants greatly enjoy the process of assimilating response-contingent stimulation and are vigorously

expressive of their pleasure in achieving control of their environment. . . .

Mothers who are initially frustrated by the early unresponsiveness of their infants and are then shown how to engage them in vocal games (which are begun by repeating their infants' spontaneous vocalizations) have generally been able to elicit smiles, laughter, and joy as a result of these efforts (Uzgiris, 1972).

In middle-class and upper-middle-class homes, so-called pseudoimitation (an infant's responding in kind to familiar vocalizations modeled by another person) is achieved at about eight weeks of age (Hunt, 1981; Uzgiris, 1972). "True" imitation (that is, imitation of vocal sounds generally unfamiliar to an infant) appears to occur at about eight to ten months of age. Once this latter capacity emerges, it seems to provide a basis for the acquisition of the names of objects.

Reciprocal vocal imitation provides the earliest opportunity for infants to compare both imitative and imitating products and discover similarities between them. Several prominent researchers (for example, Papousek, Papousek, and Bornstein, 1985) suggest that it might be highly productive for adults to imitate infants' first quiet vocalizations and to elaborate on them by repeating them several times and then varying the vocalization (such as the pitch) in some small measure. Mothers quite naturally use pitch contour to obtain and sustain their babies' attention and to encourage eye contact and smiling, and they also use exaggerated intonational contouring of utterances in face-to-face play (Stern, Spieker, and MacKain, 1982). Three- to six-month-old infants seem to very much enjoy opportunities to imitate pitch (tones) and, with sufficient practice, become reasonably good at it (Kessen, Levine, and Wendrich, 1979). . . .

Verbal Stimulation, 'Informative Talk,' and Affective Tone

The evidence that certain kinds of vocal stimulation (for instance, encouraging attention, providing related ideas [after saying "ball," adding "big ball"], and using vocal imitation) are beneficial to cognitive development would seem to imply that the greater the overall amount of child-directed vocal stimulation, the greater the likelihood of IQ enhancement.

Such a conclusion, however, is not necessarily warranted. Rather, there is evidence that—beyond a given amount of verbal stimulation—it is the quality of the verbally interactive relationship between child and caretaker and not the quantity of verbal stimulation that matters. . . .

If we are willing to accept the scores on the early infant IQ predictors . . . as mechanisms for detecting and exploring potential causal links between maternal interactive behavior and later cognitive development, several conclusions might be drawn. One . . . is the high correspondence found between maternal encouragement of attention and scores on habituation paradigms. Another, if we accept the premise that a three-month-old's "mother-stranger vocal discrimination" behavior is often a precursor of verbal IQ during childhood, is that we can use these three-month Differential Vocal Response (DVR) scores as a surrogate for childhood IQ by comparing the behavior patterns of mothers whose children have relatively high and relatively low DVR scores. This type of analysis yields two important conclusions: First, a moderate amount of maternal vocalization to a three-month-old is associated with higher DVR scores than either a high or low amount, and, second, the degree to which a child is valued and desired by its caretakers seems to have an appreciable effect on DVR scores at this age.

This first conclusion has been replicated in a number of diverse populations by Roe and her colleagues. In one of these studies— of first-born American children, subdivided into low-maternal-education and high-maternal-education subsamples (Roe and Bronstein, forthcoming)—infants in the "high-ed" group vocalized twice as much to their mothers as they did to the strangers, but the "low-ed" group responded equally to the mothers' and strangers' overtures. Nevertheless, over the course of the two observation periods, the total amount of infant vocal response was equal between the two groups. The primary difference was that the "high-

ed" group responded more to their mothers and less to the strangers, but the infants from "low-ed" families responded equally to both. Within each of these educational strata, however, the highest DVR scores were associated with a mid-level amount of maternal vocal stimulation (recorded in a naturalistic setting), and the lowest scores were associated with high and low levels of such stimulation. The mother's affective tone also appears to have a substantial impact on DVR scores, as suggested by the following findings:

- In Greece, where (1) male children tend to be "more valued and desired by parents than female children" and (2) where males, both as children and adults, score "significantly higher than females on most cognitive tests, including verbal cognitive tests" (Roe, 1987, p. 2), the vocal response rates of the males to their mothers were two and a half times higher than to strangers. Among the females, however, the rates were nearly equal (Roe and others, 1985). In an additional study of twenty-five institutionally reared Greek children (Roe, 1987), DVR scores were negative for the males (they vocalized more to strangers than to caretakers) and neutral for the females. By contrast, in the American populations studied, no sex difference was observed.

- Whether or not a baby was "planned" has been shown to be related to DVR scores (Roe and Bronstein, forthcoming); even though this relationship is compounded by its interaction with educational level, it may in fact signify an important cause of SES differences.

Contingent Responsivity

The term contingent responsivity refers to creating or using opportunities for the environment to respond quickly and predictably to an infant's actions (his or her movements or vocalizations). Teaching an infant that he or she can exercise control over the environment and exposure to early contingent action-outcome pairings lay the groundwork for subsequent learning and promote feelings of competence and a greater readiness to explore and master the environment (Brinker and Lewis, 1982).

Several studies suggest that providing infants with opportunities to control their environment can have a substantial impact on their intellectual development. For example, in a longitudinal study in which IQ scores at five years of age were compared with interactions between mothers and children during home visits at eight, twenty-one, and twenty-four months (Beckwith and Cohen, 1984), those toddlers who were evaluated as receiving consistently responsive care from their mothers during each of the three home visits had markedly higher Stanford-Binet IQ scores at age five, as follows:

- In the higher SES subsample, the scores of the children who received "consistently responsive" behavior averaged 114.5, compared with 104.0 for those where maternal behavior was not consistently responsive.

- In the lower SES subsample, the scores of the children who received "consistently responsive" behavior averaged 117.7, compared with where maternal behavior was not consistently responsive.

This study also found that, after factoring out SES, there were still significant relationships between IQ and (1) contingent maternal vocalization at one month of age and (2) maternal responsivity to distress at eight months of age.

In a follow-up evaluation at age twelve (Beckwith and Cohen, 1989), the offspring of those mothers who were adjudged at eight and twenty-four months to be more "verbally responsive" to the vocalizations of their children than the median scored 14 points higher (on the WISC-R) than did the children who "had been treated unresponsively" at both of these ages. . . .

Another study, which sought to discern links between children's IQ scores at six years of age and maternal interactive behavior at three months of age (Coates and Lewis, 1984), found strong associations between (1) Wechsler vocabulary subtest scores and the combination of the mother's vocal responsivity and her response to her infant's distress by holding, touching, and other "proximal" behavior (these two factors explained a fourth of the verbal IQ variance); and (2) Wechsler blockdesign subtest scores and vocal responsivity (this also explained a fourth of the variance).

Conclusions

The studies presented in this chapter strongly suggest that specific interactive behaviors between mothers and infants can have a considerable and seemingly lasting influence on childhood IQ scores. Behaviors of particular importance appear to include ample rocking, imitating infants' vocalizations, using gaze behavior effectively, encouraging attention to objects and events in the environment, seeking opportunities to use contingent responsivity as a teaching tool, responding immediately to an infant's or toddler's overtures and providing related ideas as part of verbal responses, and using an appropriate level of sentence complexity. . . .

References

Badger, E. (1977). The Infant Stimulation/ Mother Training Program. In B. M. Caldwell and D. J. Stedman (Eds.), *Infant Education: A Guide for Helping Handicapped Children in the First Three Years*. New York: Walker.

Beckwith, L., and Cohen, S. E. (1984). Home Environment and Cognitive Competence in Preterm Children During the First 5 Years. In A. W. Gottfried (Ed.), *Home Environment and Early Cognitive Development*. Orlando, Fla.: Academic Press.

Beckwith, L., and Cohen, S. E. (1989). Maternal Responsiveness with Preterm Infants and Later Competency. In M. H. Bornstein (Ed.), *Maternal Responsiveness: Characteristics and Consequences. New Directions for Child Development*, no. 43. San Francisco: Jossey-Bass.

Bornstein, M. H. (1985). How Infant and Mother Jointly Contribute to Developing Cognitive Competence in the Child. *Proceedings of the National Academy of Sciences*, 82, pp. 7470–7473.

Bornstein, M. H., and Tamis-LeMonda, C. S. (1989). Maternal Responsiveness and Cognitive Development in Children. In M. H. Bornstein (Ed.), *Maternal Responsiveness:*

Characteristics and Consequences. New Directions for Child Development, no. 43. San Francisco: Jossey-Bass.

Brinker, R. P., and Lewis, M. (1982). Contingency Intervention in Infancy. In J. Anderson and J. Cox (Eds.), *Curriculum Materials for High Risk and Handicapped Infants*. Chapel Hill, N.C.: Technical Assistance and Development System.

Coates, D. L., and Lewis, M. (1984). Early Mother-Infant Interaction and Infant Cognitive Status as Predictors of School Performance and Cognitive Behavior in Six-Year-Olds. *Child Development*, 55, pp. 1219–1230.

Field, T. M. (1977). The Effects of Early Separation, Interactive Deficits, and Experimental Manipulations on Infant-Mother Face-to-Face Interaction. *Child Development*, 48, pp. 763–771.

Gottfried, A. W., and Gottfried, A. E. (1984). Home Environment and Cognitive Development in Young Children of Middle-Socioeconomic-Status Families. In A. W. Gottfried (Ed.), *Home environment and Early Cognitive Development.*, Orlando, Florida: Academic Press.

Hunt, J. McV. (1981). Experiential Roots of Intention, Initiative, and Trust. In H. I. Day (Ed.), *Advances in Intrinsic Motivation and Esthetics*. New York: Plenum.

Hunt, J. McV., Mohandessi, K., Ghodssi, M., and Akiyama, M. (1976). The Psychological Development of Orphanage-Reared Infants: Interventions with Outcomes (Tehran). *Genetic Psychology Monographs*, 94, pp. 177–226.

Jacobs, B. S., and Moss, H. A. (1976). Birth Order and Sex of Sibling as Determinants of Mother and Infant Interaction. *Child Development*, 47, pp. 315–322.

Kessen, W., Levine, J., and Wendrich, A. (1979). The Imitation of Pitch in Infancy. *Infant Behavior and Development*, 2, pp. 93–99.

Lewis, M., and Kreitzberg, V. S. (1979). Effects of Birth Order and Spacing on Mother-Infant Interactions. *Developmental Psychology*, 15, pp. 617–625.

Meltzoff, A. N., and Moore, M. J. (1983). Newborn Infants Imitate Adult Facial Gestures. *Child Development*, 54, pp. 702–709.

Olson, S. L., Bates, J. E., and Bayles, K. (1984). Mother-Infant Interaction and the Development of Individual Differences in Children's Cognitive Competence. *Developmental Psychology*, 20, pp. 166–179.

Olson, S. L., Bayles, K., and Bates, J. E. (1986). *Predicting Social and Cognitive Competence at Age Six from Early Mother-Child Interactions*.

Paper presented at the International Conference on Infant Studies, Los Angeles.

Papousek, M., Papousek, H., and Bornstein, M. H. (1985). The Naturalistic Vocal Environment of Young Infants: On the Significance of Homogeneity and Variability in Parental Speech. In T. M. Field and N. A. Fox (Eds.), *Social Perception in Infants*. Norwood, N.J.: Ablex.

Roe, K. V. (1987). *Planned vs. Unplanned Status of Infant and Vocal Interaction with Mother and Stranger*. Paper presented at biennial meeting of the Society for Research in Child Development, Baltimore, Md., Apr.

——. (forthcoming). Vocal Stimulation and Cognitive Processing. *Infant Behavior and Development*.

Roe, K. V., and Bornstein, R. (forthcoming). Maternal Education and Infant Cognitive Processing. *International Journal of Behavioral Development*.

Roe, K. V, McClure, A., and Roe, A. (1982). Vocal Interaction at Three Months and Cognitive Skills at Age 12 Years. *Developmental Psychology*, 18, pp. 15–16. Vocal Interaction at Three Months and Cognitive Skills at Age 12 Years. *Developmental Psychology*, 21, pp. 372–384.

Ruddy, M. G., and Bornstein, M. H. (1982). Cognitive Correlates of Infant Attention and Maternal Stimulation over the First Year of Life. *Child Development*, 53, pp. 183–188.

Stern, D. N., Spieker, S., and MacKain, K. (1982). Intonation Contours as Symbols in Maternal Speech to Prelinguistic Infants. *Developmental Psychology*, 18, pp. 727–735.

Uzgiris, I. C. (1972). Patterns of Vocal and Gestural Imitation in Infants. In F. J. Monks and others (Eds.), *Determinants of Behavior Development*. Orlando, Fla.: Academic Press.

Watson, J. S. (1972). Smiling, Cooing, and the Game. *Merrill-Palmer Quarterly*, 18, pp. 324–339.

White, B. L., Kahan, B. T., and Attanucci, J. (1979). *The Origins of Human Competence*. Lexington, Mass.: Lexington Books.

Review

1. How do mothers relate differently to their first-born children than to their other children?

2. What are the consequences of the differing patterns of interaction?

3. How did Tehran caretakers increase the IQ of children?

4. What is meant by contingent responsivity and why is it important?

Applications

1. Assuming that fathers as well as mothers can enhance their children's IQs, make a list of the behaviors noted in this selection that are important. If you are married, discuss with your spouse what each of you can do to maximize your children's IQ. If you are not married, save your list for future reference and share it with your spouse when you have children. You can also share the list with friends and family.

2. One reason parents relate differently to first-born and later children is a practical one—the lack of time and energy. Interview a number of parents who have two or more children. Ask them to describe how the demands of time and energy affected the way they related to or dealt with their children as their families grew in size.

Reprinted from: Miles D. Storfer, "Intelligence and Giftedness: The Contributions of Heredity and Early Environment." In *Intelligence and Giftedness: The Contributions of Heredity and Early Environment*, pp. 157–175. Reprinted with permission from Miles D. Storfer. San Francisco: Jossey-Bass, 1990. Copyright © 1990 Jossey-Bass Inc., Publishers. Reprinted by permission. All rights reserved. ✦

6
Drinking During Adolescence

Laurie Chassin
Christian DeLucia

What is America's most serious drug problem? You're right if you said alcohol. More than 20 million Americans are either alcoholics or problem drinkers. **Alcohol abuse,** which we define as drinking to the point of detrimental consequences to the user and to others, is not only widespread but is also becoming a problem at increasingly younger ages.

Why do so many Americans, including so many adolescents, drink excessively? A popular perception is that an alcoholic is "sick" and that alcoholism is a "disease." Presumably, then, adolescents who are heavy drinkers do so because they are in the initial stages of the disease.

The disease theory is a biological explanation: Some people are genetically disposed to alcoholism and can only get rid of the disease by avoiding alcohol altogether. Others use a psychological explanation: Alcoholism reflects a psychological disorder. But if alcoholism results merely from a genetically based vulnerability to alcohol or from a personality disorder, how can we explain people who are heavy drinkers but who never become alcoholics? How can we explain adolescents who drink excessively while in college but only drink moderately thereafter? And why do adolescents begin drinking in the first place?

In this article, Chassin and DeLucia identify the varied social factors associated with adolescent drinking. Among the important factors are **norms,** one of the more interesting elements of culture. Norms are the rules, such as standards and laws, that define the behavior required or expected in society. The extent to which the rules are enforced varies. **Folkways** are norms that are preferred or appropri-

ate ways of behaving but not essential to the well-being of society. **Mores,** in contrast, are norms that are essential to social well-being. They are therefore enforced far more rigorously than folkways. Some norms are incorporated into the laws of a society. But even those that are not laws are powerful influences on behavior.

Both family and peer norms affect adolescent drinking. Also important is the extent to which social norms are incorporated into the law. In any society, the more important the norm is considered to be, the more likely it is to become a law and the less likely people are to deviate. Thus, laws that reinforce the norm against adolescent drinking by regulating the availability of alcohol decrease adolescent use and abuse of the drug.

Researchers typically consider adolescence to be the developmental period during which youth are most at risk for initiating alcohol use. Many developmental theorists view adolescence as occurring from approximately age 10 (i.e., the beginning of pubertal development) through age 25 (i.e., when adult roles are established) (Feldman and Elliott 1990). This article, however, applies a more restrictive definition and primarily considers alcohol consumption from early adolescence through the high school years (i.e., approximately ages 10 to 18).

Prevalence data suggest that most adolescents report some exposure to alcohol use and that use increases with age (Johnston et al. 1995). In terms of current consumption, recent national student survey data show that 25 percent of 8th graders and 50 percent of 12th graders report consuming alcohol within the past month (Johnston et al. 1995). Moreover, a substantial proportion of those drinkers consume heavily[1]: 15 percent of the 8th graders and 28 percent of the 12th graders report having five or more drinks in a row in the past 2 weeks, and just under 3 percent of the 12th graders report daily use. National surveys have found some gradual declines in adolescent drinking since the peaks of the early 1980's, but the most recent trends, which show some small (i.e., not statistically significant) increases (Johnston et al. 1995), are less clear.

The prevalence of adolescent drinking also varies demographically. Boys report more heavy drinking than do girls, and among high school seniors, white adolescents report more heavy drinking than do Hispanic or African-American adolescents. For example, 1994 national data for 12th graders found that 32 percent of non-Hispanic Caucasians, 24 percent of Hispanics, and 14 percent of African-Americans reported consuming five or more drinks in a row in the past 2 weeks (Johnston et al. 1995). However, because these ethnic differences are less apparent at earlier grades, they could be caused partially by ethnic differences in school dropout rates (Johnston et al. 1995). (School-based surveys collect data on current students only; thus, these surveys cannot determine the alcohol consumption patterns of same-age school dropouts. To the degree that dropout rates vary by ethnicity, the survey results will be skewed.) Inconsistent definitions, as well as inter- and intracultural diversity, complicate comparisons among ethnic groups. In general, however, compared with other ethnic groups, Native American adolescents typically report the highest consumption rates, and Asian-American youth report the lowest (Johnstone 1994).

Diagnosis of Alcohol Abuse and Dependence Among Adolescents

As with adult alcohol use, an examination of adolescent drinking patterns and problems requires consideration of (1) the quantity and frequency of consumption, (2) alcohol-related negative life consequences, and (3) alcohol-dependence symptoms (Bailey and Rachal 1993). Beyond the examination of simple consumption patterns, however, a striking lack of empirical work exists on the prevalence of clinical alcohol abuse or dependence[2] among adolescents of high school age or younger.

This void likely is attributable to the low prevalence of alcohol abuse and dependence diagnoses in early and middle adolescence compared with the dramatic increase in alcohol problems after the high school years. For example, Cohen and colleagues (1993) found prevalence rates[3] of 4 percent or less among adolescents younger than age 16. In contrast, prevalence rates of 8.9 percent and 20.3 percent, respectively, were found for females and males ages 17 to 20 (Cohen et al. 1993).

Simply applying adult diagnostic criteria, however, may not be the best way to describe the drinking patterns and problems that occur during early and middle adolescence. Using other measures, the discrepancy between prevalence rates for younger and older adolescents could diminish. For example, Martin and colleagues (1995) found that common adult symptoms of alcohol abuse and dependence, such as medical problems and alcohol withdrawal symptoms, rarely occurred in adolescents. In addition, many adolescents who did not have an alcohol-dependence diagnosis reported a marked increase in the amount of alcohol needed to attain a desired effect (i.e., tolerance). In fact, Martin and colleagues (1995) suggest that a marked increase in consumption may be a normative feature of adolescent drinking rather than a phenomenon linked specifically to alcohol dependence. Research is now under way to refine methods for diagnosing clinical alcohol abuse and dependence in adolescents (Martin et al. 1995).

Consequences of Adolescent Drinking

Adolescent alcohol use (particularly heavy use) is associated with many negative outcomes (see Table 6.1). Although medical consequences of alcohol abuse in adolescents are rarely studied, a few studies have produced evidence that describes such effects. For example, adolescent alcohol abusers show elevations in liver enzymes (Arria et al. 1995), an early indicator of liver damage. These adolescents also demonstrate higher rates of multiple drug use (Arria et al. 1995) and poorer language function than do adolescents without alcohol abuse or dependence diagnoses (Moss et al. 1994). However, they do not show signs of brain damage on neuropsychological tests (Moss et al. 1994).

Table 6.1
Negative Outcomes Associated With Adolescent Alcohol Use (Especially Heavy Use)

Health-Related Outcomes
  Elevations in liver enzymes
  Use of other drugs
  Fatal motor vehicle crashes
  Unintentional injuries
  Homicide
  Suicide
  Early sexual activity
  More frequent sexual activity
  Less frequent condom use

Psychosocial Outcomes
  Poorer language function
  Interference with development of adolescent competencies
  Interference with development of social and coping skills

Perhaps of even greater public health significance is the fact that adolescent alcohol consumption is correlated with the three leading causes of death in this age group: unintentional injuries, homicide, and suicide (U.S. Department of Health and Human Services [USDHHS] 1991). More than one-half of all fatal motor vehicle crashes among 15- to 24-year-olds involve alcohol, and approximately one-half of all homicides in this age group are associated with alcohol use (USDHHS 1991). Moreover, the percentage of intoxicated drivers involved in fatal crashes is higher at younger ages, reaching a peak among young adults (i.e., 34 percent for drivers ages 21 to 24 in 1991), then declining among older adults (i.e., 16 percent for drivers ages 45 to 64 in 1991) (National Center for Statistics and Analysis 1992). National data also suggest that alcohol use was associated with suicidal thoughts and suicide attempts among the 8th and 10th graders who were surveyed (Windle et al. 1992).

The association between adolescent alcohol consumption and risky sexual behavior also is of public health importance. Adolescent alcohol use is associated with earlier initiation of sexual activity, more frequent sexual activity, and less frequent condom use (Cooper et al. 1994), all of which raise the risk for HIV infection and other sexually transmitted diseases. In addition, adolescents (particularly white adolescents) report riskier sexual behavior on occasions when they have used alcohol or other drugs (AOD's) than on occasions when they have not (Cooper et al. 1994).

However, the association between adolescent drinking and these serious negative health risks does not imply a causal relationship. As other researchers have indicated (Donovan 1993; Leigh and Stall 1993), adolescent alcohol use is associated with personality characteristics such as impulsiveness and sensation seeking. Thus, it may be these underlying personality characteristics, rather than simply alcohol use, that increase the risk for traffic crashes, risky sexual behavior, violence, and suicide.

A similar argument has been made concerning the relationship between alcohol use and other drug use. Alcohol is used at earlier ages than are other drugs, and alcohol use increases the risk for later use of illegal drugs (Yamaguchi and Kandel 1984). Early onset of alcohol use (i.e., before age 15) is associated with greater risk for other substance use and the development of later alcohol-related problems (Robins and Pryzbeck 1985). However, although alcohol, like cigarettes, may lead to other forms of substance use, this pattern does not imply that alcohol use "causes" such substance use.

In terms of psychosocial development, Baumrind and Moselle (1987) speculate that heavy AOD use in adolescence interferes with the development of emerging adolescent competencies, including social and coping skills. Because most adolescents report some alcohol use, however, these deficits may be limited to those adolescents who drink particularly heavily or frequently. In fact, in the general population, drinking in adolescence has been associated with enhanced social functioning, less loneliness, and more positive emotional states (i.e., positive affect) in early adulthood (Newcomb and Bentler 1988).

Risk Factors for Adolescent Drinking

Risk factors for adolescent drinking can be organized into categories that include sociocultural, family, peer, and intrapersonal factors as well as factors related to adolescents' beliefs about alcohol.

Sociocultural Factors

One sociocultural factor affecting adolescents is their degree of access to alcohol. Although few studies have focused specifically on adolescents (Holder 1994), the existing research suggests that greater alcohol availability is associated with higher rates of drinking. In contrast, greater regulation of alcohol availability is associated with older ages of initiation, decreased consumption, and fewer alcohol-related problems (Single 1994). In particular, computer simulations indicate that policies raising the legal drinking age or increasing prices with alcohol taxes are associated with lower rates of adolescent alcohol consumption and reduced mortality from traffic crashes among youth ages 18 to 20 (Grossman et al. 1994). Research on other sociocultural factors, such as the impact of alcohol advertising and alcohol warning labels, is equivocal and has produced limited data on adolescents (Mackinnon 1995; Single 1994).

Family Factors

Many theories (e.g., social control theory, social learning theory, and problem behavior theory) include a focus on family factors that influence adolescent alcohol use (Jacob and Leonard 1994). Empirical studies have produced fairly consistent support for these theories. Families in which parents use alcohol to excess, show high levels of antisocial behavior (including antisocial personality disorder),[4] or both are said to model alcohol-abusing behavior, a factor termed "family modeling." These families are more likely to have adolescent children who use alcohol. . . . Families in which parents provide low levels of social support, show little monitoring of their children's behavior, use inconsistent discipline practices, and exhibit high levels of conflict and low levels of closeness—traits known as family socialization factors—also are more likely to have adolescent children who use alcohol (Barnes et al. 1986). Most empirical studies have been conducted with biological families, however, which may lead to overestimating the magnitude of such family influences, because the behavior of offspring reflects shared genes as well as shared environment (McGue et al. 1996). (In contrast, studies of adoptees can help isolate environmental factors from genetic ones.)

Potentially important components of family influence on adolescent drinking are the drinking behavior and social influence of siblings (Jacob and Leonard 1994). Siblings' levels of alcohol consumption are correlated for both biological and adoptive siblings. These correlations are stronger for siblings who are close in age and of the same sex (McGue et al. 1996). Siblings may provide direct modeling influences as well as more indirect influences through exposure to a particular high-risk peer group (Rowe and Gulley 1992).

Peer Factors

Peer drinking and peer acceptance of drinking (i.e., positive attitudinal tolerance of drinking) have been consistently associated with adolescent drinking, and adolescent drinking typically occurs in peer social contexts (Hughes et al. 1992; Margulies et al. 1977). Adolescents whose friends frequently drink are more likely to increase their own drinking over time, and adolescents who frequently drink are more likely to increase their affiliations with alcohol-using peers (Curran et al. in press). Thus, adolescents who drink are more likely to select friends who drink, and those friends in turn influence adolescents' drinking.

In understanding adolescents' risk for drinking, one must consider what leads adolescents to affiliate with alcohol-using peers. Some research suggests that poor parenting practices create early childhood deficits in social skills and self-regulation, particularly with regard to aggressive behavior, which result in rejection from mainstream peer groups (Brown et al. 1993; Patterson et al. 1989). Children who are rejected from these mainstream peer groups then affiliate with deviant peers; in turn, participation in deviant peer networks increases the risk for drinking and other forms of substance use (Kaplan 1980). This research demonstrates a link between the parenting factors and the peer factors that lead to adolescent drinking.

Intrapersonal Factors

Adolescents who report high levels of alcohol consumption are characterized by a constellation of personality traits indicating low levels of self-regulation (see Table 6.2). These adolescents are more likely to be aggressive and to have high attitudinal tolerance for deviant behavior, low value and expectations for academic success, and high levels of sensation seeking and impulsivity (Brook et al. 1992; Jessor and Jessor 1977). These characteristics also describe adolescents with clinical levels of alcohol abuse or dependence (Moss and Kuruscu 1995).

Table 6.2
Personality Characteristics Associated With Adolescent Alcohol Use

Characteristics
  Low self-regulation
  Aggressiveness
  Highly tolerant attitudes toward deviant behavior
  Low value of and expectation for academic success
  Sensation seeking
  Impulsivity
  Low self-esteem

Possible Other Characteristics
  Negative emotional states (e.g. depression)
  High emotional intensity
  Low threshold for emotional response

The role of other intrapersonal factors is more controversial. For example, it is unknown whether intense emotional responses and a tendency to overreact (i.e., emotional reactivity) or negative emotional states, such as depression and anxiety, are linked to adolescent alcohol use. Some data link negative emotional states, particularly depression, to adolescent alcohol use (Colder and Chassin 1993; Hussong and Chassin 1994). However, studies over time that attempt to predict later alcohol use based on previously measured levels of negative emotional states do not always confirm this relationship (Chassin et al. 1996). Thus, it is unclear whether negative emotional states are a cause or a result of adolescent alcohol use, although depressive disorders (Deykin et al.

1992) and anxiety disorders (Clark et al. 1994) have been associated with clinical alcoholism in adolescence.

Moreover, the combination of low self-regulation and high levels of negative emotional states (i.e., negative affect) may be associated particularly with adolescent alcohol use (Pandina et al. 1992).

The onset of adolescent alcohol use among middle school students also has been linked to low levels of self-esteem (Kaplan 1980). According to Kaplan's self-derogation theory, adolescents who receive failure feedback from mainstream sources (e.g., peer rejection or poor school achievement) seek out deviant peer affiliations in order to increase their sense of self-worth. Although these deviant peer affiliations do raise self-esteem, they also raise risk for AOD use.

Beliefs About Alcohol

Adolescents form beliefs about alcohol's effects before actually engaging in alcohol consumption, and these expectations (i.e., alcohol expectancies) are related to their drinking behavior. For example, Christiansen and colleagues (1989) found that positive expectancies of alcohol predicted adolescents' drinking behavior (and problem drinking) 12 months later. Moreover, among 12- to 14-year-old abstainers, adolescents who expected to gain greater social acceptance (i.e., social facilitation) as a result of drinking were more likely to begin to drink, and they increased their alcohol consumption at faster rates than did their same-age peers who did not show these expectancies (Smith et al. 1995). Alcohol expectancies are a potentially important risk factor for adolescents, because they may integrate adolescents' knowledge about alcohol from sources such as media, peer, and family models as well as from their own experiences. Thus, many different influences can shape adolescents' beliefs about alcohol, and these beliefs in turn influence adolescents' drinking behavior.

Summary and Conclusions

Understanding alcohol use in adolescence is critical, because during these years, many people initiate drinking, and early drinking problems can appear. Although some experimentation with drinking is virtually universal and normative in adolescence, alcohol use during this period also is linked to negative adolescent health outcomes, including unintentional injuries, homicide, suicide, and unsafe sexual practices. At a broad social level, adolescent drinking is related to alcohol availability as well as to laws, social norms, and prices regulating such availability. In addition, adolescents who drink alcohol are more likely to come from families in which parental drinking, sibling drinking, and lower levels of parental control and support occur. Youth who drink also are more likely to have friends who model and tolerate alcohol use, show lower levels of self-regulation, and have more positive expectancies about alcohol's effects. Much of the research to date, however, has related these risk factors to the frequency or quantity of drinking rather than to alcohol abuse or dependence among adolescents. Thus, it has been difficult to distinguish predictive factors specific to adolescent problem drinking or clinical alcohol abuse or dependence from predictors of alcohol consumption in general. An understanding of the factors that determine which adolescents are particularly vulnerable to the negative effects of alcohol consumption is an important step for preventing alcohol-related problems among adolescents.

Endnotes

1. The term "heavy alcohol consumption" is not used consistently in the alcohol research literature, and the studies referred to in this article likewise define the concept in different ways. Unless otherwise specified, this article defines heavy consumption as having five or more drinks in a row within the past two weeks.

2. Definition of the terms "alcohol abuse" and "alcohol dependence" can vary in the alcoholism literature. Generally, however, a person clinically diagnosed with alcohol abuse or alcohol dependence must meet specific criteria (e.g., as defined in the American Psychiatric Association's Diagnostic and Statistical Manual of Mental Disorders, Fourth Edition). These criteria include the experience of with-

drawal symptoms and increased tolerance to the effects of alcohol as well as impaired control over drinking.

3. Using criteria from the American Psychiatric Association's Diagnostic and Statistical Manual of Mental Disorders, Third Edition, Revised.

4. Antisocial personality disorder is a pattern of irresponsible and antisocial behavior beginning early in life and continuing through adulthood.

References

Arria, A.M.; Dohey, M.A.; Mezzich, A.C.; Bukstein, O.G.; and Van Thiel, D.H. "Self-reported health problems and physical symptomatology in adolescent alcohol abusers." *Journal of Adolescent Health* 16(3):226–231, 1995.

Bailey, S.C., and Rachal, J.V. "Dimensions of adolescent problem drinking." *Journal of Studies on Alcohol* 54(5):555–565, 1993.

Barnes, G.M.; Farrel, M.P.; and Cairns, A. "Parental socialization factors and adolescent drinking behaviors." *Journal of Marriage and the Family* 48(1):27–36, 1986.

Baumrind, D., and Moselle, K.A. "A developmental perspective on adolescent drug abuse." *Advances in Alcohol and Substance Abuse* 4(3–4):41–67, 1987.

Brook, J.S.; Cohen, P.; Whiteman, M.; and Gordon, A.S. "Psychosocial risk factors in the transition from moderate to heavy use or abuse of drugs." In: Glantz, M., and Pickens, R., eds. *Vulnerability to Drug Abuse*. Washington, DC: American Psychological Association, 1992. pp. 359–388.

Brown, B.B.; Mounts, N.; Lamborn, S.D.; and Steinberg, L. "Parenting practices and peer group affiliation in adolescence." *Child Development* 64(2):467–482, 1993.

Chassin, L.; Curran, P.J.; Hussong, A.M.; and Colder, C.R. "The relation of parent alcoholism to adolescent substance use: A longitudinal follow-up study." *Journal of Abnormal Psychology* 105(1):70–80, 1996.

Christiansen, B.A.; Smith, G.T.; Roehling, P.V.; and Goldman, M.S. "Using alcohol expectancies to predict adolescent drinking behavior after one year." *Journal of Consulting and Clinical Psychology* 57(1):93–99, 1989.

Clark, D.B.; Jacob, R.G.; and Mezzich, A. "Anxiety and conduct disorders in early onset alcoholism." *Annals of the New York Academy of Sciences* 708:181–186, 1994.

Cohen, P.; Cohen, J.; Kaseb, S.; Velez, C.N.; Hartmark, C.; Johnson, J.; Rojas, M.; Brook, J.; and Streuning, E.L. "An epidemiological study of disorders in late childhood and adolescence—I. Age- and gender-specific prevalence." *Journal of Child Psychology and Psychiatry and Allied Disciplines* 34(6):851–867, 1993.

Colder, C.R., and Chassin, L. "The stress and negative affect model of adolescent alcohol use and the moderating effects of behavioral under-control." *Journal of Studies on Alcohol* 54(3):326–333, 1993.

Cooper, M.L.; Peirce, R.S.; and Huselid, R.F. "Substance use and sexual risk taking among black adolescents and white adolescents." *Health Psychology* 13(3):251–262, 1994.

Curran, P.J.; Stice, E.; and Chassin, L. "The relation between adolescent alcohol use and peer alcohol use: A longitudinal random coefficients model." *Developmental Psychology*, in press.

Deykin, E.Y.; Buka, S.L.; and Zeena, T.H. "Depressive illness among chemically dependent adolescents." *American Journal of Psychiatry* 149(10):1341–1347, 1992.

Donovan, J.E. "Young adult drinking-driving: Behavioral and psycho-social correlates." *Journal of Studies on Alcohol* 54(5):600–613, 1993.

Feldman, S.S., and Elliott, G.R. "Capturing the adolescent experience." In: Feldman, S.S., and Elliott, G.R., eds. *At the Threshold: The Developing Adolescent*. Cambridge: Harvard University Press, 1990. pp. 1–14.

Grossman, M.; Chaloupka, F.J.; Saffer, H.; and Laixuthai, A. "Effects of alcohol price policy on youth: A summary of economic research." *Journal of Research on Adolescence* 4(2):347–364, 1994.

Holder, H.D. Commentary: "Alcohol availability and accessibility as part of the puzzle: Thoughts on alcohol problems and young people." In: Zucker, R.; Boyd, G.; and Howard, J., eds. *The Development of Alcohol Problems: Exploring the Biopsychosocial Matrix of Risk*. National Institute on Alcohol Abuse and Alcoholism Research Monograph No. 26. NIH Pub. No. 94–3495. Bethesda, MD: The Institute, 1994, pp. 249–254.

Hughes, S.O.; Power, T.G.; and Francis, D.J. "Defining patterns of drinking in adolescence: A cluster analytic approach." *Journal of Studies on Alcohol* 53(1):40–47, 1992.

Hussong, A.M., and Chassin, L. "The stress-negative affect model of adolescent alcohol use: Disaggregating negative affect." *Journal of Studies on Alcohol* 55(6):707–718, 1994.

Jacob, T., and Leonard, K. "Family and peer influences in the development of adolescent alcohol abuse." In: Zucker, R.; Boyd, G.; and Howard, J., eds. *The Development of Alcohol Problems: Exploring the Biopsychosocial Matrix of Risk*. National Institute on Alcohol Abuse and Alcoholism Research Monograph No. 26. NIH Pub. No. 94–3495. Bethesda, MD: The Institute, 1994. pp. 123–155.

Jessor, R., and Jessor, S.L. "Personality and problem behavior." *Problem Behavior and Psychosocial Development: A Longitudinal Study of Youth*. New York: Academic Press, 1977. pp. 95–111.

Johnston, L.D.; O'Malley, P.M.; and Bachman, J.G. "Prevalence of drug use among eighth, tenth, and twelfth grade students." *National Survey Results on Drug Use From the Monitoring the Future Study, 1975–1994: Volume 1. Secondary School Students*. NIH Pub. No. 95–4026. Rockville, MD: National Institute on Drug Abuse, 1995. pp. 39–76.

Johnstone, B.M. "Sociodemographic, environmental, and cultural influences on adolescent drinking behavior." In: Zucker, R.; Boyd, G.; and Howard, J., eds. *The Development of Alcohol Problems: Exploring the Biopsychosocial Matrix of Risk*. National Institute on Alcohol Abuse and Alcoholism Research Monograph No. 26. NIH Pub. No. 94–3495. Bethesda, MD: The Institute, 1994. pp. 169–203.

Kaplan, H.B. "Antecedents of self-derogation." *Deviant Behavior in Defense of Self*. New York: Academic Press, 1980. pp. 79–110.

Leigh, B.C., and Stall, R. "Substance use and risky sexual behavior for exposure to HIV: Issues in methodology, interpretation, and prevention." *American Psychologist* 48(10):1035–1045, 1993.

Mackinnon, D.P. "Review of the Effects of the Alcohol Warning Label." In: Watson, R.R., ed. *Alcohol, Cocaine, and Accidents: Drug and Alcohol Abuse Reviews* 7. Totowa, NJ: Humana Press, 1995. pp. 131–161.

Margulies, R.Z.; Kessler, R.C.; and Kandel, D.B. "A longitudinal study of onset of drinking among high school students." *Journal of Studies on Alcohol* 38(5):897–912, 1977.

Martin, C.S.; Kaczynski, N.A.; Maisto, S.A.; Burkstein, O.M.; and Moss, H.B. "Patterns of DSM-IV alcohol abuse and dependence symptoms in adolescent drinkers." *Journal of Studies on Alcohol* 56(6):672–680, 1995.

McGue, M.; Sharma, A.; and Benson, P. "Parent and sibling influences on adolescent alcohol use and misuse: Evidence from a U.S. adoption cohort." *Journal of Studies on Alcohol* 57(i):8–18, 1996.

Moss, H.B., and Kuruscu, L. "Aggressivity in adolescent alcohol abusers: Relationship with conduct disorder." *Alcoholism: Clinical and Experimental Research* 19(3):642–646, 1995.

Moss, H.B.; Kuruscu, L.; Gordon, H.W.; and Tarter, R.E. "A neuropsychologic profile of adolescent alcoholics." *Alcoholism: Clinical and Experimental Research* 18(1): 159–163, 1994.

National Center for Statistics and Analysis. *1991 Alcohol Fatal Crash Facts*. Washington, DC: National Highway Traffic Safety Administration, 1992.

Newcomb, M.D., and Bentler, P.M. *Consequences of Adolescent Drug Use: Impact on the Lives of Young Adults*. Newbury Park, CA: Sage Publications, 1988.

Pandina, R.J.; Johnson, V.; and Labouvie, E.W. "Affectivity: A Central Mechanism in the Development of Drug Dependence." In: Glantz, M., and Pickens, R., eds. *Vulnerability to Drug Abuse*. Washington, DC: American Psychological Association, 1992. pp. 179–210.

Patterson, G.R.; Debarsyshe, B.D.; and Ramsey, E. "A developmental perspective on antisocial behavior." *American Psychologist* 44(2):329–335, 1989.

Robins, L.N., and Pryzbeck, T.R. "Age of onset of drug use as a factor in drug and other disorders." In: Jones, C.L., and Battjes, R.J., eds. *Etiology of Drug Abuse: Implications for Prevention*. National Institute on Drug Abuse Research Monograph No. 56. DHHS Pub. No. (ADM)85–1335. Rockville, MD: National Institute on Drug Abuse, 1985. pp. 178–192.

Rowe, D.C., and Gulley, B.L. "Sibling effects on substance use and delinquency." *Criminology* 30(2):217–233, 1992.

Single, E. "The impact of social and regulatory policy on drinking behavior." In: Zucker, R.; Boyd, G.; and Howard, J., eds. *The Development of Alcohol Problems: Exploring the Biopsychosocial Matrix of Risk*. National Institute on Alcohol Abuse and Alcoholism Research Monograph No. 26. NIH Pub. No. 94–3495. Bethesda, MD: The Institute, 1994. pp. 209–248.

Smith, G.T.; Goldman, M.S.; Greenbaum, P.E.; and Christiansen, B.A. "Expectancy for social facilitation from drinking: The divergent paths of high-expectancy and low-expectancy adolescents." *Journal of Abnormal Psychology* 104(1):32–40, 1995.

U.S. Department of Health and Human Services. *Healthy people 2000: National health promotion and disease prevention objectives*. NIH Pub. No. (PHS)91–50212. Washington, DC: U.S. Govt. Print. Off., 1991.

Windle, M.; Miller-Tutzauer, C.; and Domenico, D. "Alcohol use, suicidal behavior, and risky activities among adolescents." *Journal of Research on Adolescence* 2(4):317–330, 1992.

Yamaguchi, K., and Kandel, D.B. "Patterns of drug use from adolescence to young adulthood: III. Predictors of progression." *American Journal of Public Health* 74(7):673–681, 1984.

Review

1. How does alcohol use by adolescents vary among racial and ethnic groups?

2. What are the consequences of alcohol use by adolescents?

3. What factors put adolescents at risk for drinking?

Application

Develop a questionnaire to use for interviewing students about their understanding of excessive drinking. Ask the students how they would define excessive drinking (in terms of number of consecutive drinks within a given time period). Get their perception of how much excessive drinking occurs on campus, and what groups (by sex, race/ethnicity, year in college, and major) are more likely to engage in such drinking. Finally, ask them why they think people drink excessively, and why the groups they identified drink more heavily than others.

Note each respondent's sex and race/ethnicity. Summarize your findings. How do the definitions of excess compare with that used by Chassin and DeLucia. To which group(s) do your respondents attribute the most drinking? Why? Do the answers given vary by the respondents' age or race/ethnicity? How?

Reprinted from: Laurie Chassin and Christian DeLucia. "Drinking During Adolescence." In *Alcohol Health & Research World* 20 (1996):175–80. Reprinted by permission. ✦

Unit II

Culture, Socialization, and Social Interaction

This unit introduces more of the fundamental concepts in contemporary sociology. These concepts are essential to understanding the sociological perspective.

Take the concept of **culture,** for instance. In contrast to the popular use of the term as a synonym for refinement, sociologists and anthropologists define culture as everything that people create, ranging from technology to art to moral codes to customs. Thus, you can think of culture in contrast to nature. It is generally accepted that animals and insects adapt to their environment by instinctive means set by nature. On the other hand, the great variety of human adaptations to the environment depend on culture for their explanation. Since culture is learned rather than genetically transmitted, it is more readily changeable than nature's arrangements.

The first two articles in this unit, selections 7 and 8, show the impact of norms. Like roles, norms are crucial for maintaining social order. They let you generally know what to expect from people even though you don't know them or know much about them. Norms can lead people in one society to behave in ways that appear odd or irrational to those in other societies. But all societies have norms, and those norms help maintain social order.

Order is also maintained through **socialization,** the fundamental process by which individuals learn about and adjust to their surrounding social world. All human beings are born into a particular social context in which they must learn to function. If the socialization is effective, the individual will internalize the culture, believing that this is the right way of life. Thus, the individual will fit in with the culture, follow its ways, and perpetuate them.

Socialization is one way in which children learn what it means to be male and female. As with intelligence, gender is not a purely biological phenomenon. Selections 9, 10, and 11 illustrate the socialization process by examining three aspects of learning gender roles: the outcome when children are subjected to contradictory socializing forces, the influence of television, and the impact of sports on male identity.

Another concept addressed in this section is **interaction.** While we often speak about the commanding imperatives of culture and society ("Society says you must . . . "), these mandates take on significance only in the context of communication between individuals. Selections 12 and 13 approach these social-psychological concerns in different ways. Selection 12 looks at the differing conversational styles of men and women. Selection 13 looks at an aspect of sexual interaction—the motives for, and consequences of, sexual betrayal in an intimate relationship. ✦

Part One

Culture

Culture includes everything created by people: their technology, their system of knowledge and beliefs, their art, their morals and laws, their customs, and all other products of human thought and action. By asserting that culture is the creation of human thought and action, sociologists stress that social life is the result of human interaction and human decisions rather than of instincts.

In a sense, then, all the selections in this book deal with culture in one way or another. In this part, however, we focus on norms and the way in which particular norms in two different societies—India and the United States—lead to behavior not found in many other societies. ✦

7
India's Sacred Cow

Marvin Harris

Structural-functional reasoning in sociology looks at cultural items such as norms, beliefs, institutions, and behavior patterns in terms of their consequences for social groups. When all the consequences are thoroughly assessed, a seemingly irrational belief or practice may appear more reasonable because of the functions it serves for the group. For example, a primitive tribe doing a rain dance to end a drought may seem irrational to an observer. But the collective ritual of the dance may keep tribal morale high until rain does come and thereby help preserve the group in the face of a crisis.

*A cultural practice that strikes many observers as highly irrational is the strong reverence for cattle in India. Westerners (and even some Indians themselves) have long considered cattle worship to be a key element in India's continual flirtation with famine. Indian people go hungry while sacred cows are fed by the government. What could be more irrational? In his analysis of the Indian **ecosystem** (the system of living things, their environment, and their interrelationships), Harris finds these critics to be shortsighted. As an ecologist, he is concerned with how a population adapts to its environment, given the technology and resources available. He is also interested in the prominent place cattle occupy in India's system of agricultural production. Most Indian farmers have small plots of land, so cattle are useful for fertilizer and for hauling. They also supply the farm family with milk, and their waste products serve as fuel and floor covering material. And cattle supply meat and leather for the larger economy. Most important, since cattle primarily eat what is inedible to humans, the two species are not in competition with each other for food. Devotion to cattle ensures that even when famine threatens, Indians will not slaughter their cattle to prevent starvation. To do so would cause even more severe problems in the long run.*

. . . Hindus venerate cows because cows are the symbol of everything that is alive. As Mary is to Christians the mother of God, the cow to Hindus is the mother of life. So there is no greater sacrilege for a Hindu than killing a cow. Even the taking of human life lacks the symbolic meaning, the unutterable defilement, that is evoked by cow slaughter.

According to many experts, cow worship is the number one cause of India's hunger and poverty. Some Western-trained agronomists say that the taboo against cow slaughter is keeping one hundred million "useless" animals alive. They claim that cow worship lowers the efficiency of agriculture because the useless animals contribute neither milk nor meat while competing for croplands and foodstuff with useful animals and hungry human beings. A study sponsored by the Ford Foundation in 1959 concluded that possibly half of India's cattle could be regarded as surplus in relation to food supply. And an economist from the University of Pennsylvania stated in 1971 that India has thirty million unproductive cows.

It does seem that there are enormous numbers of surplus, useless, and uneconomic animals, and that this situation is a direct result of irrational Hindu doctrines. . . .

Love of cow affects life in many ways. Government agencies maintain old age homes for cows at which owners may board their dry and decrepit animals free of charge. In Madras, the police round up stray cattle that have fallen ill and nurse them back to health by letting them graze on small fields adjacent to the station house. Farmers regard their cows as members of the family, adorn them with garlands and tassels, pray for them when they get sick, and call in their neighbors and a priest to celebrate the birth of a new calf. Throughout India, Hindus hang on their walls calendars that portray beautiful, bejeweled young women who have the bodies of big fat white cows. Milk is shown jetting out of each teat of these half-woman, half-zebu goddesses.

Starting with their beautiful human faces, cow pinups bear little resemblance to the typical cow one sees in the flesh. For most of the year their bones are their most prominent feature. Far from having milk gushing from every teat, the gaunt beasts barely manage to nurse a single calf to maturity. The average yield of whole milk from the typical hump-backed breed of zebu cow in India amounts to less than 500 pounds a year. Ordinary American dairy cattle produce over 5,000 pounds, while for champion milkers, 20,000 pounds is not unusual.But this comparison doesn't tell the whole story. In any given year about half of India's zebu cows give no milk at all—not a drop. . . .

Mohandas K. Gandhi was an ardent advocate of cow love and wanted a total ban on cow slaughter. When the Indian constitution was drawn up, it included a bill of rights for cows which stopped just short of outlawing every form of cow killing. Some states have since banned cow slaughter altogether, but others still permit exceptions. The cow question remains a major cause of rioting and disorders, not only between Hindus and the remnants of the Moslem community, but between the ruling Congress Party and extremist Hindu factions of cow lovers. . . .

To Western observers familiar with modern industrial techniques of agriculture and stock raising, cow love seems senseless, even suicidal. The efficiency expert yearns to get his hands on all those useless animals and ship them off to a proper fate. And yet one finds certain inconsistencies in the condemnation of cow love. When I began to wonder if there might be a practical explanation for the sacred cow, I came across an intriguing government report. It said that India had too many cows but too few oxen. With so many cows around, how could there be a shortage of oxen? Oxen and male water buffalo are the principal source of traction for plowing India's fields. For each farm of ten acres or less, one pair of oxen or water buffalo is considered adequate. A little arithmetic shows that as far as plowing is concerned, there is indeed a shortage rather than a surplus of animals. India has 60 million farms, but only 80 million traction animals. If each farm had its quota of two oxen or two water buffalo, there ought to be 120 million traction animals— that is, 40 million more than are actually available. . . .

The shortage of draft animals is a terrible threat that hangs over most of India's peasant families. When an ox falls sick a poor farmer is in danger of losing his farm. . . . The Indian farmer who can't replace his sick or deceased ox is in much the same situation as an American farmer who can neither replace nor repair his broken tractor. But there is an important difference: tractors are made by factories, but oxen are made by cows. A farmer who owns a cow owns a factory for making oxen. With or without cow love, this is a good reason for him not to be too anxious to sell his cow to the slaughterhouse. One also begins to see why Indian farmers might be willing to tolerate cows that give only 500 pounds of milk per year. If the main economic function of the zebu cow is to breed male traction animals, then there's no point in comparing her with specialized American dairy animals, whose main function is to produce milk. Still, the milk produced by zebu cows plays an important role in meeting the nutritional needs of many poor families. Even small amounts of milk products can improve the health of people who are forced to subsist on the edge of starvation. . . .

Agriculture is part of a vast system of human and natural relationships. To judge isolated portions of this "ecosystem" in terms that are relevant to the conduct of American agribusiness leads to some very strange impressions. Cattle figure in the Indian ecosystem in ways that are easily overlooked or demeaned by observers from industrialized, high-energy societies. In the United States, chemicals have almost completely replaced animal manure as the principal source of farm fertilizer. American farmers stopped using manure when they began to plow with tractors rather than mules or horses. Since tractors excrete poisons rather than fertilizers, a commitment to large-scale machine farming is almost of necessity a commitment to the use of chemical fertilizers. And around the world today there has in fact grown up a vast integrated petrochemical-tractor-truck industrial complex that produces farm machinery, motorized transport, oil and gasoline, and chemical fertilizers and pesticides upon which new high-yield production techniques depend.

For better or worse, most of India's farmers cannot participate in this complex, not because they worship their cows, but because they can't afford to buy tractors. Like other underdeveloped nations, India can't build factories that are competitive with the facilities of the industrialized nations nor pay for large quantities of imported industrial products. To convert from animals and manure to tractors and petrochemicals would require the investment of incredible amounts of capital. Moreover, the inevitable effect of substituting costly machines for cheap animals is to reduce the number of people who can earn their living from agriculture and to force a corresponding increase in the size of the average farm. We know that the development of large-scale agribusiness in the United States has meant the virtual destruction of the small family farm. Less than 5 percent of U.S. families now live on farms, as compared with 60 percent about a hundred years ago. If agribusiness were to develop along similar lines in India, jobs and housing would soon have to be found for a quarter of a billion displaced peasants.

Since the suffering caused by unemployment and homelessness in India's cities is already intolerable, an additional massive build-up of the urban population can only lead to unprecedented upheavals and catastrophes.

With this new alternative in view, it becomes easier to understand low-energy, small-scale, animal-based systems. As I have already pointed out, cows and oxen provide low-energy substitutes for tractors and tractor factories. They also should be credited with carrying out the functions of a petrochemical industry. India's cattle annually excrete about 700 million tons of recoverable manure. Approximately half of this total is used as fertilizer, while most of the remainder is burned to provide heat for cooking. The annual quantity of heat liberated by this dung, the Indian housewife's main cooking fuel, is the thermal equivalent of 27 million tons of kerosene, 35 million tons of coal, or 68 million tons of wood. Since India has only small reserves of oil and coal and is already the victim of extensive deforestation, none of these fuels can be considered practical substitutes for cow dung. The thought of dung in the kitchen may not appeal to the average American, but Indian women regard it as a superior cooking fuel because it is finely adjusted to their domestic routines. Most Indian dishes are prepared with clarified butter known as *ghee*, for which cow dung is the preferred source of heat since it burns with a clean, slow, long-lasting flame that doesn't scorch the food. This enables the Indian housewife to start cooking her meals and to leave them unattended for several hours while she takes care of the children, helps out in the fields, or performs other chores. American housewives achieve a similar effect through a complex set of electronic controls that come as expensive options on late-model stoves.

Cow dung has at least one other major function. Mixed with water and made into a paste, it is used as a household flooring material. Smeared over a dirt floor and left to harden into a smooth surface, it keeps the dust down and can be swept clean with a broom.

Because cattle droppings have so many useful properties, every bit of dung is carefully collected. Village small fry are given the task of following the family cow around and of bringing home its daily petrochemical output. In the cities, sweeper castes enjoy a monopoly on the dung deposited by strays and earn their living by selling it to housewives.

From an agribusiness point of view, a dry and barren cow is an economic abomination. But from the viewpoint of the peasant farmer, the same dry and barren cow may be a last desperate defense against the moneylenders. There is always the chance that a favorable monsoon may restore the vigor of even the most decrepit specimen and that she will fatten up, calve, and start giving milk again. This is what the farmer prays for; sometimes his prayers are answered. In the meantime, dung-making goes on. And so one gradually begins to understand why a skinny old hag of a cow still looks beautiful in the eyes of her owner.

Zebu cattle have small bodies, energy-storing humps on their back, and great powers of recuperation. These features are adapted to the specific conditions of Indian agriculture. The native breeds are capable of surviving for long periods with little food or water and are highly resistant to diseases that afflict other breeds in tropical climates. Zebu oxen are worked as long as they continue to breathe. . . .

But sooner or later there must come a time when all hope of an animal's recovery is lost and even dungmaking ceases. . . . By slaughtering or selling his aged and decrepit animals, a farmer might earn a few more rupees or temporarily improve his family's diet. But in the long run, his refusal to sell to the slaughterhouse or kill for his own table may have beneficial consequences. An established principle of ecological analysis states that communities of organisms are adapted not to average but to extreme conditions. The relevant situation in India is the recurrent failure of the monsoon rains. To evaluate the economic significance of the antislaughter and anti-beef-eating taboos, we have to consider what these taboos mean in the context of periodic droughts and famine.

The taboo on slaughter and beef eating may be as much a product of natural selection as the small bodies and fantastic recuperative powers of the zebu breeds. During droughts and famines, farmers are severely tempted to kill or sell their livestock. Those who succumb to this temptation seal their doom, even if they survive the drought, for when the rains come, they will be unable to plow their fields. I want to be even more emphatic. . . . Cow love with its sacred symbols and holy doctrines protects the farmer against calculations that are "rational" only in the short term. To Western experts it looks as if "the Indian farmer would rather starve to death than eat his cow." The same kinds of experts like to talk about the "inscrutable Oriental mind" and think that "life is not so dear to the Asian masses." They don't realize that the farmer would rather eat his cow than starve, but that he will starve if he does eat it. . . .

From a Western agribusiness viewpoint, it seems irrational for India not to have a meat-packing industry. But the actual potential for such an industry in a country like India is very limited. A substantial rise in beef production would strain the entire ecosystem, not because of cow love but because of the laws of thermodynamics. In any food chain, the interposition of additional animal links results in a sharp decrease in the efficiency of food production. The caloric value of what an animal has eaten is always much greater than the caloric value of its body. This means that more calories are available per capita when plant food is eaten directly by a human population than when it is used to feed domesticated animals.

Because of the high level of beef consumption in the United States, three-quarters of all our croplands are used for feeding cattle rather than people. Since the per capita calorie intake in India is already below minimum daily requirements, switching croplands to meat production could only result in higher food prices and a further deterioration in the living standards for poor families. I doubt if more than 10 percent of the Indian people will ever be able to make beef an important part of their diet, regardless of whether they believe in cow love or not.

I also doubt that sending more aged and decrepit animals to existing slaughterhouses would result in nutritional gains for the people who need it most. Most of these animals get eaten anyway, even if they aren't sent to the slaughterhouse, because throughout India there are low-ranking castes whose members have the right to dispose of the bodies of dead cattle. In one way or another, twenty million cattle die every year, and a large portion of their meat is eaten by these carrion-eating "untouchables". . . .

Like everything else I have been discussing, meat eating by untouchables is finely adjusted to practical conditions. The meat-eating castes also tend to be the leather-working castes, since they have the right to dispose of the skin of the fallen cattle. So despite cow love, India manages to have a huge leathercraft industry. Even in death, apparently useless animals continue to be exploited for human purposes.

I could be right about cattle being useful for traction, fuel, fertilizer, milk, floor covering, meat, and leather, and still misjudge the ecological and economic significance of the whole complex. Everything depends on how much all of this costs in natural resources and human labor relative to alternative modes of satisfying the needs of India's huge population. These costs are determined largely by what the cattle eat. Many experts assume that man and cow are locked in a deadly competition for land and food crops. This might be true if India's farmers followed the American agribusiness model and fed their animals on food crops. But the shameless truth about the sacred cow is that she is an indefatigable scavenger. Only an insignificant portion of the food consumed by the average cow comes from pastures and food crops set aside for their use. . . .

The major constituent in the cattle's diet is inedible by-products of human food crops, principally rice straw, wheat bran, and rice husks. . . . Probably less than 20 percent of what the cattle eat consists of humanly edible substances; most of this is fed to working oxen and water buffalo rather than to dry and barren cows. Odend'hal found that in his study area there was no competition between cattle and humans for land or the food supply: "Basically, the cattle convert items of little direct human value into products of immediate utility."

One reason why cow love is so often misunderstood is that it has different implications for the rich and the poor. Poor farmers use it as a license to scavenge while the wealthy farmers resist it as a rip-off. To the poor farmer, the cow is a holy beggar; to the rich farmer, it's a thief. Occasionally the cows invade someone's pastures or planted fields. The landlords complain, but the poor peasants plead ignorance and depend on cow love to get their animals back. If there is competition, it is between man and man or caste and caste, not between man and beast. . . .

Cow-slaughter enthusiasts base their recommendation on an understandable error. They reason that since the farmers refuse to kill their animals, and since there is a religious taboo against doing so, therefore it is the taboo that is mainly responsible for the high ratio of cows to oxen. Their error is hidden in the observed ratio itself: 70 cows to 100 oxen. If cow love prevents farmers from killing cows that are economically useless, how is it there are 30 percent fewer cows than oxen? Since approximately as many female as male animals are born, something must be causing the death of more females than males. The solution to this puzzle is that while no Hindu farmer deliberately slaughters a female calf or decrepit cow with a club or a knife, he can and does get rid of them when they become truly useless from his point of view. Various methods short of direct slaughter are employed. To "kill" unwanted calves, for example, a triangular wooden yoke is placed about their necks so that when they try to nurse they jab the cow's udder and get kicked to death. Older animals are simply tethered on short ropes and allowed to starve—a process that does not take too long if the animal is already weak and diseased. Finally, unknown numbers of decrepit cows are surreptitiously sold through a chain of Moslem and Christian middlemen and end up in the urban slaughterhouses.

If we want to account for the observed proportions of cows to oxen, we must study rain, wind, water, and land-tenure patterns, not cow love. The proof of this is that the proportion of cows to oxen varies with the relative importance of different components of the agricultural system in different regions of India. The most important variable is the amount of irrigation water available for the cultivation of rice. Wherever there are extensive wet rice paddies, the water buffalo tends to be the preferred traction animal, and the female water buffalo is then substituted for the zebu cow as a source of milk. That is why in the vast plains of northern India, where the melting Himalayan snows and monsoons create the Holy River Ganges, the proportion of cows to oxen drops down to 47 to 100. As the distinguished Indian economist K.N. Raj has pointed out, districts in the Ganges Valley where continuous year-round rice-paddy cultivation is practiced have cow-to-oxen ratios that approach the theoretical optimum. This is all the more remarkable since the region in question—the Gangetic plain—is the heartland of the Hindu religion and contains its most holy shrines. . . .

Do I mean to say that cow love has no effect whatsoever on the cattle sex ratio or on other aspects of the agricultural system? No. What I am saying is that cow love is an active element in a complex, finely articulated material and cultural order. . . .

Since the effective mobilization of all human action depends upon the acceptance of psychologically compelling creeds and doctrines, we have to expect that economic systems will always oscillate under and over their points of optimum efficiency. But the assumption that the whole system can be made to work better simply by attacking its consciousness is naive and dangerous. Major improvements in the present system can be achieved by stabilizing India's human population, and by making more land, water, oxen, and water buffalo available to more people on a more equitable basis. The alternative is to destroy the present system and replace it with a completely new set of demographic, technological, politico-economic, and ideological relationships—a whole new ecosystem. Hinduism is undoubtedly a conservative force, one that makes it more difficult for the "development" experts and "modernizing" agents to destroy the old system and to replace it with a high-energy industrial and agribusiness complex. But if you think that a high-energy industrial and agribusiness complex will necessarily be more "rational" or "efficient" than the system that now exists, forget it.

Contrary to expectations, studies of energy costs and energy yields show that India makes more efficient use of its cattle than the United States does. In Singur district in West Bengal, Dr. Odend'hal discovered that the cattle's gross energetic efficiency, defined as the total of useful calories produced per year divided by the total calories consumed during the same period, was 17 percent. This compares with a gross energetic efficiency of less than 4 percent for American beef cattle raised on Western range land. As Odend'hal says, the relatively high efficiency of the Indian cattle complex comes about not because the animals are particularly productive, but because of scrupulous product

utilization by humans: "The villagers are extremely utilitarian and nothing is wasted."

Wastefulness is more a characteristic of modern agribusiness than of traditional peasant economies. Under the new system of automated feed-lot beef production in the United States, for example, cattle manure not only goes unused, but it is allowed to contaminate ground water over wide areas and contributes to the pollution of nearby lakes and streams.

The higher standard of living enjoyed by the industrial nations is not the result of greater productive efficiency, but of an enormously expanded increase in the amount of energy available per person. In 1970 the United States used up the energy equivalent of twelve tons of coal per inhabitant, while the corresponding figure for India was one-fifth ton per inhabitant. The way this energy was expended involved far more energy being wasted per person in the United States than in India. Automobiles and airplanes are faster than oxcarts, but they do not use energy more efficiently. In fact, more calories go up in useless heat and smoke during a single day of traffic jams in the United States than is wasted by all the cows of India during an entire year. The comparison is even less favorable when we consider the fact that the stalled vehicles are burning up irreplaceable reserves of petroleum that it took the earth tens of millions of years to accumulate. If you want to see a real sacred cow, go out and look at the family car.

Review

1. What effects does India's love of cows have on life in that country?

2. What are the negative aspects of India's cow love, according to its critics?

3. What actual functions does cow love serve for the Indian people?

Applications

1. Many Westerners maintain that cow love as practiced in India is irrational, especially considering India's need for more food for the people in times of

famine. Some sociologists might consider such a belief to be ethnocentric, i.e., viewing Western ways as superior and India as inferior. But people in other societies might consider our refusal to eat dog meat as irrational when there are people starving in the United States. Peruse the popular media looking for common practices, beliefs, and values that are part of American culture but that you think could be considered irrational by others (e.g., our not eating dogs). Report your findings.

2. Develop and use an interview questionnaire on the ideas brought out in this article pertaining to cow love. Interview several people, including one or more of Indian ancestry if possible. Summarize your findings.

3. Describe ethnocentric responses you have had while traveling in another country or a different part of the United States. What bothered you and why?

8
Cosmetic Surgery
Beauty as Commodity

Debra Gimlin

Every society has norms that deal with physical appearance—how a person should look in order to be attractive. In preindustrial societies, these norms involve such things as decorating or altering the body (including scarring, elongation of the neck, shaping the head from infancy, etc.). In our society, some of the norms about appearance vary between groups. Among youth, for example, body piercing is considered attractive, while many older adults find the practice repugnant. Other norms are more pervasive—such as standards for the kind of body an attractive person should have. For a woman, that ideal includes being slender, in contrast to a hundred years ago, when the "full-figured" woman was considered the most attractive.

In an effort to attain the requisite slimness, some women succumb to eating disorders. Others, including teenage girls, use various surgical procedures to enhance their beauty, including breast augmentation, eyelid surgery, liposuction (to remove fat), reshaping of the nose, and the "tummy tuck" to tighten the abdomen.

In this article, Gimlin describes how women succumb to the norm of attractiveness by resorting to cosmetic surgery. Ironically, in so doing, they break another norm—that attractiveness should be "natural" or attained by more natural means, such as diet and exercise. Gimlin also notes how women justify breaking one norm in order to satisfy the other one.

After several unsuccessful attempts to schedule an appointment with her, I finally managed to meet with Jennifer, a 29-year-old grade school teacher who volunteered to talk with me about the cosmetic surgery that she had undergone. On a typically cold November afternoon, I spoke with Jennifer in her apartment on the south shore of Long Island. Jennifer, who is 5' 6" tall and has long, straight blond hair and expressive light blue eyes, was dressed in an oversized gray pullover and black sweat pants. While we talked, she peeled and sliced the crudités that would be her contribution to the "pot luck" engagement party that she would be attending later that evening.

Sitting at her kitchen table for nearly two hours, Jennifer and I discussed her decision to have cosmetic surgery. During our conversation, I noticed that by far the most prominent—and largest—feature in her small studio apartment was the enormous black and chrome stair-climbing machine set slightly off from the center of the living-room/bedroom. I learned that Jennifer spends 40 minutes each day on this machine and works out with weights at a nearby gym three to four times per week. She eats no meat, very little oil or fat, no sweets and drinks very little alcohol. Despite her rigorous body work routine, Jennifer's legs have remained a disappointment to her. Rather than appearing lean and muscular, they look, by her account, thick and shapeless—particularly around her lower thighs and knees. Jennifer says that her decision to have liposuction performed was motivated primarily by her inability to reshape her legs through diet and exercise. During the procedure, the fatty deposits were removed from the insides of Jennifer's knees, making her legs appear slimmer and more toned.

During the time I spent with Jennifer, she discussed her reasons for having liposuction, including her own significant ambivalence about taking surgical steps to alter her body. Jennifer argued that, if possible, she would have preferred to shape her body through aerobics, weight training and dieting, and that liposuction was, for her, a last, desperate option. By her account, plastic surgery was an attempt to alter physical attributes that Jennifer referred to as "genetic flaws," attributes that she could change through no other available means. Expressing some shame, as she says, "for taking the easy way out," Jennifer's feelings of guilt are not so great that she regrets having surgery. Indeed, quite the opposite is true; Jennifer plans to have a second liposuction in the near future, this time to remove the fatty tissue from her upper and inner thighs.

Cosmetic surgery stands, for many theorists and social critics, as the ultimate symbol of invasion of the human body for the sake of physical beauty. It has epitomized for many—including myself—the astounding lengths to which contemporary women will go in order to obtain bodies that meet current ideals of attractiveness. Moreover, plastic surgery is perceived by its critics as an activity that is somehow *qualitatively* different from other efforts at altering the body (including aerobics, hairstyling, or even dieting) in that it is an activity so extreme, so invasive, that it leaves no space for interpretation as anything but subjugation. Even more than women who may participate in other types of body-shaping activities, those who undergo cosmetic surgery appear to many observers—both casual and academic—to be so obsessed with physical appearance that they are willing to risk their very existence in order to become more attractive.

While cosmetic surgery has been dealt powerful (and some would say well-deserved) blows from the score of feminist writers who criticize body work generally (Dally 1991; Kaw 1994), the cosmetic surgery industry is nonetheless rapidly expanding (Wolf 1991). Three hundred million dollars are spent every year on cosmetic surgery and the amount is increasing annually by 10 percent (Davis 1995, p. 21). In 1988, more than two million Americans underwent some form of cosmetic surgery. Between 1984 and 1986 alone, the number of cosmetic operations in the U.S. tripled (Wolf 1991, p. 251). Ninety percent of these operations are performed on women: virtually all breast augmentations and reductions, 90 percent of face-lifts, 86 percent of eyelid reconstructions, and 61 percent of rhinoplasties (better known as "nose jobs"). In 1987, American women had 94,000 breast reconstructions, 85,000 eyelid surgeries, 82,000 nose jobs, 73,230 liposuctions, and 67,000 face-lifts (American Society for Plastic and Reconstructive Surgeons 1988). At the end of World War II, there were only about one hundred plastic surgeons in the United States; today there are approximately four thousand along with an unknown number of additional specialists, mostly dermatologists, also performing face-lifts, eyelid surgeries and other "minor" procedures (Davis 1995, p. 21).

Criticisms of surgical alteration of the female body multiply nearly as rapidly as the procedures themselves. One of the main critiques of cosmetic surgery derives from the dangers involved in many of the procedures. Cosmetic surgery is undeniably painful and risky and each operation involves its own potential complications. For instance, pain, numbness, bruising, discoloration and depigmentation frequently follow a liposuction, often lingering up to six months after the operation. Similarly, face-lifts can damage nerves, leaving the patient's face permanently numb. More serious disabilities include fat embolisms, blood clots, fluid depletion, and in some cases, death. Indeed, health experts estimate that the chance of serious side effects from breast augmentation are between 30 percent and 50 percent. The least dramatic and most common of these include decreased sensitivity in the nipples, painful swelling or congestion of the breasts, and hardening of the breasts that makes it difficult to lie down comfortably or to raise the arms without the implants shifting (Goldwyn 1980). More serious is the problem of encapsulation, where the body reacts to foreign materials by forming a capsule of fibrous tissue around the implants. This covering can sometimes be broken down manually by the surgeon, but even when successful, this procedure is extremely painful. When it is unsuccessful, the implants must be removed; in some cases, the surgeon is actually forced to chisel the hardened substance from the patient's chest wall.

Clearly, the recipient of cosmetic surgery may very well emerge from the operation in worse shape than when she went in. Unsuccessful breast augmentations are often disfiguring, leaving the recipient with unsightly scars and deformation. An overly tight face-lift produces a "zombie" look, in which the countenance seems devoid of expression. Following a liposuction, the skin can develop a corrugated, uneven texture so that the recipient looks worse than she did before the surgery.

Finally, some criticisms of cosmetic surgery focus on the implications of such procedures for contemporary conceptualizations of the body and identity. In particular, cosmetic surgery has expanded in conjunction with such developments in medical equipment as magnifying lenses, air drills for severing bone and leveling skin, and perfected suturing materials, all enabling surgical interventions to be performed with better results and less trauma for the patient (Meredith 1988). According to some critics, these developments, and the increasing flexibility in body altering that they permit, are inextricably linked to cultural discourses likening the body to what Susan Bordo (1990) has called "cultural plastic." The body is now understood as having a potential for limitless change, "undetermined by history, social location or even individual biography" (p. 657). Not only has the body come to stand as a primary symbol of identity, but it is a symbol whose capacity for alteration and modification is understood to be unlimited. The body, instead of a dysfunctional object requiring medical intervention, becomes a commodity, not unlike "a car, a refrigerator, a house, which can be continuously upgraded and modified in accordance with new interests and greater resources" (Finkelstein 1991, p. 87). The body is a symbol of selfhood, but its relation to its inhabitant is shaped primarily by the individual's capacity for material consumption. . . .

Research and Methods

The research for this chapter involves field work in a Long Island plastic surgery clinic and interviews with the clinic's surgeon [Dr. John Norris] and 20 of his female patients. . . . The women I interviewed ranged in age from 24 to 50. The procedures they underwent include breast augmentations, nose jobs, face-lifts, eye reshaping, tummy tucks, and liposuctions. The women are Asian American or European American;

among the latter, the group members' geographical heritage varies in terms of Eastern and Western, Northern and Southern Europe. Three of the women are of Semitic ancestry. All but one (a full-time mother) held salaried jobs or were students at the time of the interviews. They were employed as opticians, medical technicians, receptionists, insurance agents, teachers, office administrators, hairstylists, and secretaries.

Stories of a Face-Lift: Ann Marie

Ann Marie, a slender, soft-spoken 50-year-old medical technician with upswept blonde hair, was one of the first surgery patients I interviewed for this research. Married for nearly 30 years, Ann Marie carried herself with a careful gentility. The type of woman my mother would refer to as a "lady," Ann Marie's daintiness and obvious concern for her appearance made me self-conscious of the bulky sweater and combat boots I was wearing. Dressed in snug-fitting woolen pants, low-heeled brown pumps, and a fuzzy light mauve sweater, Ann Marie invited me into her small, tidy home and asked demurely if I would like coffee. Anxious to begin my first interview with someone who had had a face-lift, I refused her offer. Ann Marie brought her own drink back from the kitchen in a tiny, flower-painted china cup and saucer and began telling me about her experiences with plastic surgery.

Somewhat to my surprise, Ann Marie was not at all shy about discussing her face-lift. In fact, she actually seemed eager to tell me the reasons for her decision. By her account—and, as anyone with even the most limited understanding of physiology would expect—Anne Marie's appearance began to change in her late thirties and forties. She developed "puffiness underneath the eyes," and "drooping upper eyelids." Most unattractive by Ann Marie's account, "the skin of my throat started getting creepy." In her words, "You get to an age" when "you look in the mirror and see lines that were not there before." Because her physical appearance had begun to reflect the aging process, she explained, "All of a sudden the need [for cosmetic surgery] was there."

While Ann Marie described her need for a face-lift as "sudden," she actually planned to have the procedure long before she believed that she needed it. Ann Marie recalled that "about ten years ago," she spoke with several close friends about having a face-lift at some point in the distant future. She explained,

> We talked about it a long time ago. I guess I have never accepted the axiom of growing old gracefully. I have always sworn I would never picture myself as a chubby old lady.

Ann Marie and her friends "talked and decided that when the time was just right, we would definitely do it." Even so, Ann Marie was the only member of the group who actually went through with the surgery.

Despite her seemingly firm decision, Ann Marie did not enter into cosmetic surgery lightly. Instead, she considered having the procedure over several years, during which she "thought about it from time to time. There was a lot to be considered." In her estimation, "Having plastic surgery is not something to undertake lightly." Among the issues she contemplated were the physical dangers involved in the operation, the potential for looking worse after the surgery than before and the importance of choosing a well-qualified doctor with an excellent reputation. She explained,

> You are putting your face in the hands of a surgeon; there is the possibility of absolute disaster, very possibly permanently. You have to choose the surgeon very carefully.

Ann Marie chose John to perform the face-lift. Largely because he had performed an emergency procedure for her just over one year earlier, Ann Marie claimed that she felt completely comfortable with her selection of a surgeon. She explained,

> John was recommended to me by my dermatologist. I had an infection on my face; it was quite serious. The dermatologist told me I had to go to a plastic surgeon and John was the only one he would recommend.

Because of the dermatologist's recommendation and her satisfaction with John's ear-lier work, Ann Marie returned to him when she decided to have the face-lift. She visited his office in Long Island for a consultation and, not long after her appointment, decided to have the procedure.

During their first meeting, Ann Marie learned what she refers to as two "surprises." She learned the price of the operation and that she would have to stop smoking, due to the health risks associated with nicotine intake. According to Ann Marie, John explained that she must stop smoking because "you will not heal as well if you continue to smoke. Because it impedes circulation, smoking decreases your ability to heal properly." She said, "The most difficult part was to stop smoking. I was puffing away a pack and a half a day for over 20 years." John told Ann Marie that she would not be able to smoke for three months in advance of the surgery. She said, "I thought, 'What? I will never be able to do this.' But I did, I stopped cold. That was the real sacrifice for me."

While giving up cigarettes may have been the greatest sacrifice for Ann Marie, there were clearly many others. For a full year, Ann Marie had to work "one day job, one night job, occasionally a third job" in order to afford the surgery. She had to "bank" four weeks of overtime at her primary job so that she could take time off to recover from the procedure. She also postponed repairs on her home because she could not afford to pay for both the repairs and the operation. She explained, "There were things my house needed but my feeling was, I needed a face-lift more than my house did." Like many of John's patients, having cosmetic surgery was a priority for Ann Marie.

Ann Marie spent most of our interview explaining her reasons for having the face-lift. By providing me with a long and detailed account of her need for the procedure, she hints at an awareness that her behavior is somehow subject to criticism, that it might, for example, be construed by others as superficial or shallow. With a hint of defensiveness in her tone, Anne Marie explained that she "needed" the face-lift—despite its financial costs and physical risks—not merely because she is concerned with her appearance, but instead, because of pressures in "the work field." She says,

> Despite the fact we have laws against age discrimination, employers do find ways of getting around it. I know women my age who do not get jobs or are relieved of jobs because of age. This [the face-lift] will ensure my work ability.

Ann Marie, by her account, decided to have a face-lift not out of narcissism but out of concerns for her professional well-being. Justifying her behavior as a career decision, she implies that she is sensitive to the social disapproval of plastic surgery, that she knows that the behavior requires some justification.

And yet, even though Ann Marie believes that looking younger would help her professionally, she also admitted that she had "not seen anything that has really changed in that area [her career]." Instead, the procedure had affected her primarily "on a personal basis, a social basis." Explaining these effects in more detail, she said,

> I meet people I haven't seen for two or three years who will say, "There is something different about you, but I don't know what it is." I met a sister of a very good friend of mine in June, which is five months after my surgery. She looked at me and said, "I don't know you." I said, "Of course you do. I've known you nearly all of my life." She realized who I was and was astounded at my appearance.

Plastic surgery, then, in Ann Marie's telling, provides an account of herself as a younger woman that has, in turn, improved her self-image. By attributing a series of positive experiences—and the resulting improvement in her self-perception—to her face-lift, Ann Marie justifies her decision to have cosmetic surgery. . . .

"A Deep Dark Secret": Having Liposuction

John arranged for me to speak with a woman named Bonnie, who was planning, but had not yet had, cosmetic surgery. In sharp contrast to the other women John suggested I interview, Bonnie was hesitant to speak with me about the procedure, because, as she later acknowledged, she considered it to be "a deep dark secret" which she had discussed with no one but her husband of five months. Bonnie worked out at the same gym that both John and I frequented. Because she and I were previously acquainted, John suggested that Bonnie speak with me about the procedure she was considering and she agreed. Over the next six months, Bonnie and I met several times to discuss cosmetic surgery; during that period, she decided to have liposuction, underwent the procedure, and recovered from it.

Having recently completed a masters degree in a New England university, Bonnie moved to the east end of Long Island to take a position as a chemist in a large biomedical research firm. She explained to me that she had, over the years, spoken casually to various women about cosmetic surgery, and had "fantasized about" having liposuction herself, though she had never considered it seriously. Prior to having the operation, Bonnie told me why she had been reluctant, even though the procedure had always been, as she described, a "fantasy" of hers. She explained her hesitation as follows:

> It's always seemed to me to be one step too far. I have dieted and exercised my whole life, find sometimes I've gone over the edge and done some things that probably weren't very healthy, but I could always stop myself before I became totally obsessed. I guess I have always thought that I would never get so obsessed that I would allow my body to be cut into just so I could look better. At least that's what I had always hoped. I couldn't imagine myself as one of 'them,' as one of those weak women who would go that far.

Despite her stated objections to cosmetic surgery and her characterization of its patients as "weak," Bonnie considered, and, after extensive deliberation, underwent, liposuction on the outside of her upper thighs. Bonnie described this area of her body as

> . . . flabby, no matter what I do. I've always had these lumps that I couldn't get rid of. My friends used to tease me because whenever I'd look at myself in the mirror, I'd always push that part of my leg in, so

you couldn't see the lumps. I wanted to imagine how I'd look without them. I exercise five or six times a week; I cycle with my husband. I do all the weightlifting that is supposed to tone up the muscles in those areas. Nothing works!

Despite her frustrations, Bonnie had never seriously investigated the procedure until, at age 26, she finished graduate school and began full-time employment. She explained, "This is the first time I've ever made enough money to think about doing something like this. The liposuction will cost $2,000, which is less than it usually costs because I won't have to have general anesthesia, but it's still a lot of money." Bonnie noted that she would never have seriously considered having cosmetic surgery while she was living near her family and friends.

> The other thing is that I wouldn't want any of my friends or family to know about it, only my husband. My family would all be like, "You don't need to have that done. You're crazy. You are thin enough already." That doesn't keep me from thinking these lumps on my thighs are really ugly. They are the only thing I see when I look in the mirror.

Bonnie continued, explaining that her hesitance to discuss her desire to have liposuction with her friends stems from their perception of cosmetic surgery as part of a process of "giving in to pressure, giving in to these ideals about how women should look, when none of us real women are ever going to look like that." Bonnie believed that her friends would react to her interest in plastic surgery by making her 'feel so ashamed, like I am not strong enough to accept myself like I am, like I hate my female body.'

Bonnie was one of the few women I interviewed who articulated her ambivalence about plastic surgery in what could be construed as political, rather than exclusively personal, terms. Her description of her friends' imagined protests to liposuction was one of many examples of her concern with the political meaning of her actions. Bonnie also explained that her own interpretation of cosmetic surgery was the main source of her dilemma over having the procedure. She said,

I am not worried about problems with the operation itself. I know that Dr. Norris has a great reputation. I've talked to other people at the gym who have used him and they were all really happy. He does so much of this stuff, I'm sure he's really good at it.

Bonnie's concerns focused instead on the social and cultural significance of her action. She said, "If I am proud to be a woman, then I should be proud to look like a woman, with a woman's butt and a woman's thighs." Reacting to her own accusations, she said, "I am proud to be a woman, but I really hate it when I get a glimpse of my backside and I just look *big*. I feel terrible knowing that it is those areas of my body which are understood to be most 'female' that I dislike the most." Expressing her interest in cosmetic surgery as her only viable option for reducing dissatisfaction with her appearance, she added,

> I don't really know how to get around it, though, because I really do not like those parts of my figure. Plastic surgery seems like a pretty good way, and really, a pretty easy way, to deal with that dissatisfaction, to put those negative feelings behind me . . . to move on with the rest of my life. . . . Like, I'd really like to put on a pair of biking shorts and not even have it cross my mind that my butt is going to look big in them. I'd love to get dressed for work in the morning, and have only the work in front of me, rather than, you know, what's literally behind me, be the thing that concerns me the most.

Bonnie is explicitly aware that the body and the self are understood culturally to be equivalent. When she says that she dislikes the "female" parts of her figure, one can easily imagine replacing the term "figure" with the term "self." Indeed, it is Bonnie's ambivalence about her female identity that is most troubling to her; by eradicating the physical signs of femininity—and the imperfection which is necessarily a component of those attributes—she believes she will be able to construct a self that will be less imperfect and more culturally acceptable, and which will, as she puts it, allow her to "move on with the rest of" her life. Bonnie contends that having plastic surgery will allow her to focus more attention on other activities and concerns, including her career, the sports she enjoys, and her new marriage. At the same time, her decision to undergo liposuction comes at a considerable cost for Bonnie, who says explicitly that, if possible, she would prefer to change her perceptions rather than her body. The "pressure" she feels, however, limits Bonnie's ability to actively rework her self-image, leaving her to choose between two options—plastic surgery or a negative self-concept—neither of which is satisfactory. Bonnie's decision to undergo liposuction suggests that, in the end, the costs associated with having plastic surgery were somehow less significant than were those attached to accepting her appearance flaws.

Ann Marie and Bonnie present two quite disparate images of the concerns women face as they consider having cosmetic surgery. While Anne Marie struggled to work out the financial and physical requirements of her face-lift, Bonnie agonized over the political dimension of her decision to have liposuction. So distinct are these preoccupations, in fact, that they can be conceptualized as opposite ends of a continuum, along which the perspectives of the other 18 women I interviewed can be placed. For most of these women, the political implications of cosmetic surgery, though not entirely ignored, were far less significant than they were for Bonnie. Compared to her, the other women I interviewed were more often concerned with the health risks and financial costs involved in cosmetic surgery and, even more significantly, with how they would look after their procedures.

While the character of Anne Marie's and Bonnie's pre-operative anxieties took different forms, both constructed elaborate accounts regarding their entitlement to plastic surgery. Like Anne Marie and the other women whose voices I will recount later in this article, Bonnie justifies her decision to have plastic surgery by explaining that she has done all that is humanly possible to alter a failed body and argues that no act short of plastic surgery will allow her to live peacefully with herself. Significantly, the women I talked to provided accounts in which they attempted to dissociate themselves from responsibility for perceived bodily flaws. Each woman's body was imperfect not because she had erred in her body work but because of aging, genetics, or some other physical condition that the woman could not control. In effect, they argued that their flawed bodies were incorrect indicators of character, and, as such, effectively lie about who the women really are. Accounts like these not only justify cosmetic surgery but attempt to convert it into an expression of a putatively true identity. Plastic surgery becomes for them not an act of deception, but an effort to align body with self.

"The Body I Was Meant to Have": Why Women Have Cosmetic Surgery

While some writers have dealt with cosmetic surgery as if it were an attempt to accomplish idealized female beauty in order to gain the approval of men (Wolfe 1991), the women I spoke with claimed that the goal of plastic surgery is neither to become beautiful, nor to be beautiful for husbands, boyfriends, or other significant individuals. Indeed, these women adamantly insisted that they altered their bodies for their own satisfaction, in effect utilizing such procedures to create what they conceptualize as a normal appearance—an appearance that reflects a normal self. While I do not accept their accounts without some skepticism, I believe that women who have plastic surgery are not necessarily doing so in order to become beautiful nor to please particular individuals. Instead, when women have plastic surgery, they are responding to highly restrictive notions of normality and the "normal" self, notions which neither apply to the population at large (in fact, quite the reverse) nor leave space for ethnic variation. In effect, plastic surgery, as I have argued earlier, "works" for women who have these procedures, but it works only within the context of a culture of appearance that is highly restrictive and which is less a culture of beauty than it is a system of control based on the physical representations of gender, age, and ethnicity.

Throughout the interviews, my respondents claimed that prior to having surgery, some particular physical feature stood in the way of their looking "normal." This feature distinguished them from others and prohibited them from experiencing, as Marcy, a 25-year-old student, explained, "a happy, regular life." Marcy decided at age 16 to have the bony arch in the middle of her nose removed and its tip shortened. Prior to having the procedure, Marcy had never been involved in a romantic relationship, a fact that she attributed to her "hook" nose and unattractive appearance. Marcy said,

> I have always felt terrible about how pronounced it was. No matter how I wore my hair, it was in the middle of my face and everybody noticed it. It's not like I could just wear my bangs long.

Marcy decided to have rhinoplasty near a date that was particularly symbolic for her. She explained, "I was having my nose done just before Valentine's Day. I thought to myself, maybe if I have my nose done for Valentine's Day, by next Valentine's Day, I'll have a valentine!" Although she did not find a valentine for the following year—she explained that "[dating] didn't happen until a few years later"—Marcy claimed that over time, she was able to experience pleasure that she would have missed without having her nose surgically altered.

Because Marcy uses cosmetic surgery to make herself more appealing to others, her experience seemingly supports the criticisms of authors like Wolf (1991). However, a central feature of Marcy's account is that she does not expect plastic surgery to make her beautiful. Neither does she believe that winning male affection requires her to be beautiful. Quite the contrary, Marcy clearly imagines that a merely normal appearance is sufficient to garner the male attention that she desires.

The women I interviewed frequently described the ways in which their physical features had kept them from living ordinary lives. For example, Barbara, a 29-year-old bookkeeper, told me that her breasts—which were, by her account, too small to fill out attractive clothing—made her appear "dumpy" and ill-proportioned. Her "flaw" had, in turn, contributed to the negative self-image Barbara described having in her teens and early twenties, and this negative self-image served to limit the education and career goals Barbara set for herself, the friendships she attempted to foster, and the romantic and sexual relationships she pursued. Barbara decided to have her breasts augmented (from a 36A to a 36D) to make herself, as she said, "more attractive to myself and others." While her larger breasts have in fact made Barbara feel more attractive, like other patients I interviewed, she nevertheless laments her (and all women's) inability to be self-confident despite self-perceived physical shortcomings. She said,

> For women, the appearance is the important thing. That's too bad that we can't worry about not being judged. [Small breasts] made a big difference in how I felt myself being perceived and how I felt about myself as a person.

Prior to having cosmetic surgery, Barbara was both abnormal (because her small breasts made her appear and feel awkward and self-conscious) and, at the same time, normal for her gender (in that all women are abnormal because they all fail to meet standards for female beauty).

Because physical attractiveness shapes the way women are "judged," appearance must be guarded as women age. Like Ann Marie, several of the patients I interviewed underwent cosmetic procedures aimed at reducing the natural signs of aging. These women claimed that aging had changed an acceptable appearance into an unacceptable one, with the resulting appearance reflecting negatively on identity. For instance, Sue, a 44-year-old optician, decided to have the loose skin around her eyes tightened. She explained why she had the operation:

> My eyes had always been alright, nice eyes. I guess I had always liked my face pretty well, but with age, the skin around them started getting puffy. They just didn't look nice anymore. I looked tired, tired and old. That's why I had them fixed.

While Sue had, according to her own account, once been satisfied with her appearance—even thinking her eyes were "nice"—she grew to dislike her face as the signs of aging became apparent. Basically, Sue had lost an acceptable appearance over time and so used cosmetic surgery to regain the face she liked "pretty well."

The women who had cosmetic surgery told me that they had chosen to have these procedures not to make themselves beautiful or outstanding in any particular way, but instead simply to regain normal physical characteristics that they once had but had lost through the aging process (see Davis 1995 for similar findings). . . . Youth—or at least a youthful appearance—is not the only characteristic women attempt to construct or regain through aesthetic procedures. Indeed, three of the patients I interviewed—all of whom were under the age of 30—had cosmetic surgery in order to reduce the physical markers of ethnicity. These women underwent procedures intended to make their physical features more closely approximate those associated with Anglo-Saxon nationalities. Marcy, a Jewish woman who—as described earlier—had rhinoplasty to diminish the "hook" in her nose, noted that the procedure also removed physical features "more frequently associated with Jewish people." Jodie, a 28-year-old student who also had her nose reshaped, said, "I had this Italian bump on my nose. It required a little shaving. Now, it looks better." By a "better" nose, Jodie implies a more Anglo-Saxon, less Italian, and, therefore, less ethnic nose. And Kim, a 22-year-old Taiwanese-American student, underwent a procedure to make her eyes appear more oval in shape. She said, "We [Taiwanese people] regard girls with wide, bright eyes as beautiful. My eyes used to look a little bit as if I was staring at somebody. The look is not soft; it is a very stiff look." While none of these women are consciously attempting to detach themselves from ethnicity per se, they nevertheless chose to ignore the fact that their efforts to appear more "normal" are, by definition, explicitly intended to diminish the physical markers of that ethnicity. Clearly indifferent to the loss of ethnic identity that their actions imply, these women simply accept the notion that normalized (i.e., Anglo-Saxon) features are more attractive than ethnic ones.

As I listened to these women's accounts of their cosmetic surgery, I was struck by the fact that all of them claimed—quite adamantly, in fact—to have benefited from their participation in an activity that has garnered widespread and hostile criticism from feminists and nonfeminists alike. These women contended that plastic surgery was, for them, a logical, carefully thought-out response to distressing circumstances that could not otherwise be remedied. Moreover, as a result of their procedures, the women perceive themselves to be more socially acceptable, more normal, and, in several cases, more outgoing. As Bonnie, the woman whose political concerns made her initially reluctant to undergo liposuction, explained, "I got exactly what I wanted from this. My body isn't extraordinarily different, but now I feel like, well, I have a cute bottom. I have a cuter figure. I don't feel like the-one-with-the-big-butt anymore. And for me, that lets me put my body issues away pretty much."

At the same time, implying that some remnants of her original ambivalence about having cosmetic surgery still remained, Bonnie explained that she wishes she could have said, "To hell with it, I am going to love my body the way it is . . . but I had tried to do that for 15 years and it didn't work." She adds, "Now, I know I'll never look like Cindy Crawford, but I can walk around and feel like everything is good enough."

During my interviews with these patients, I was also struck by the fact that plastic surgery provides for the pleasure not only of the observers/lovers/partners of the women who undergo these procedures, but also of the women themselves. For instance, some of these women say that they are able to wear clothes that they did not feel attractive in prior to their operations; others, as I mentioned earlier, claim to have greater self-confidence or to be more extroverted. In one such example, Jennifer, the 29-year-old teacher who had liposuction to remove fatty tissue from the inside of her knees, explained,

When I walk out that door in the morning, my head might be a little bit higher when I'm wearing a certain outfit. Like before I had [liposuction] done, it used to be, I feel good, but I hope no one will notice that my legs aren't too nice.

The clothing these women are now able to wear includes items such as bathing suits, dresses with low-cut necklines, and lingerie—all of which are likely to be feminine and revealing. Wearing these clothes, and perceiving themselves as attractive in them, shapes the women's perceptions of themselves and increases their self-confidence. For example, Tara, a 27-year-old student, told me that before she had breast augmentation surgery, she avoided wearing bathing suits in public and had refused to shop for bras. She said,

> [Breast augmentation] has given me more self-confidence than I ever had. I fit in when I'm with my girlfriends now. Before, I never went to the beach with anybody around. After I had [plastic surgery], I couldn't wait to buy a bra. I could never buy one before because I was so pathetically small.

By her account, prior to having breast augmentation, Tara had been too "pathetically small" to enjoy going to the beach or shopping with friends. Having plastic surgery, however, served to make Tara appear more normal. Being able to "fit in," Tara now participates in activities from which she previously felt excluded.

Barbara, who also had breast augmentation surgery, recounted a similar experience. She said,

> I used to wear super-padded bras when I dressed up but they just never did it for me. I didn't look like the other women. But now, like tonight, I am going to a party and I know I'll be able to fill out the dress.

Barbara added, "[Breast augmentation] has made me feel very confident. I think that's the difference."

Sandra, a 43-year-old office manager who had liposuction to reduce her "thick thighs" and "saddlebag" hips, explained that she underwent the procedure not only to appear youthful or to wear feminine clothing, but also to approximate a cultural ideal involving social class. She said,

> I used to put on nice clothes and still look like a bag lady, you know, unsophisticated. Now I feel like I can wear good clothes and look like they are appropriate for me. Now my *body fits the clothes*.

Here, Sandra likens appearance to a tableau of social class, both in the context of the clothing one chooses and the extent to which one's body appears to be "appropriate" for that clothing (and the social standing that it implies). Simply put, before Sandra's surgery, her "flabby" body suggested a lower social status than did her clothing. Despite her efforts to wear "nice clothes"—i.e., clothes that would not be considered appropriate for a "bag lady"—her body undermined her efforts to use appearance to stake out a particular social location. In effect, Sandra's body not only makes her clothing an ineffective class identifier, but also invalidates Sandra's claims to a particular status. Plastic surgery, however, allows Sandra to more effectively display social class through clothing. Bringing her body into line with her self-appointed social class—particularly as its enactment relies upon clothing—cosmetic surgery serves as a tool for legitimizing Sandra's claims to social status. . . .

Plastic Surgery and Inauthenticity: The High Price of Body Work

In its own terms, the process of making an abnormal body into a normal one, plastic surgery succeeds. The women who have undergone plastic surgery believe themselves to possess, as they had not before, the bodily expression of a normative self. However, at the same time, plastic surgery fails. If women are attempting to use plastic surgery to recreate themselves—to make claims through the body about who and what they are—they must also deal with charges of shallowness. In high irony, the very same women who are attracted to plastic surgery because of a belief that the body is an indicator of the self must now deal with charges that the surgically altered body is a deception, that it is an inauthentic representation of the self. Some of the costs of cosmetic surgery—including the danger of physical damage and the high financial price—are obvious to those who have undergone these procedures and, perhaps, even to those who have not. Most of the women I talked to had plastic surgery only after serious consideration (often accompanied by research into the medical technology involved in the operations). Likewise, few could easily afford the surgery they underwent; nearly all of them had to sacrifice some other large purchase or to weather some financial hardship in order to have the surgery. Some have accrued considerable debt while others have had to request financial help from relatives. Only a very few of the women I interviewed were able to waylay some of the costs through insurance.

It is, however, the other costs associated with cosmetic surgery that I wish to focus on here. In particular, I want to explore the taint of inauthenticity that women must deal with after surgery. Despite their efforts to tell a story in which they have earned the right to plastic surgery, the women who have undergone that surgery are still alert to charges that they have merely bought a new appearance. At the same time that their bodies approximate normality, the method that they use invites charges that their character is suspect. Not the results of plastic surgery, but the very fact of having had plastic surgery, becomes the primary indicator of identity. Although the women I interviewed do not formulate the complexities and contradictions involved in their activities in the way I have here, the accounts they construct show that they struggle to deal with a self-concept that continues to be deviant despite the women's normal appearances. Indeed, the accounts themselves—which attempt to deny inauthenticity by positioning cosmetic surgery as somehow owed to the women who partake of it—show that plastic surgery fails to align body and self.

While the women's accounts take a variety of forms, they suggest a singular conclusion with regards to the success of plastic surgery for establishing a normative identity. More specifically, women like Anne Marie and Bonnie invoke their rigorous body work regimens as evidence of moral value and as the basis for their entitlement to cosmetic surgery. At the same time, they remain unsatisfied with the results, physical and moral, of this body work. Unlike the women I studied in an aerobics class—who, by virtue of their hard work, successfully undermined the body's power to reflect character—the women who had plastic surgery seemed unable to escape the social and moral meanings they attributed to their own bodies. Had they accepted the hard work they put into exercise and dieting as an adequate indicator of identity, they would not have needed to turn to plastic surgery to correct what they saw as their bodies' failings. Needing to establish the act of plastic surgery (as distinct from its results) as irrelevant for selfhood and needing to position the surgically altered body as the putatively true indicator of selfhood, women who have had plastic surgery revert to accounts that have already proved unsuccessful. The critical implications for self inherent in cosmetic surgery itself require women to resort to accounts that they know—either consciously or unconsciously—will fail to support the identity claims of youth or ethnicity that they want to make. Indeed, in the very act of making these claims, women who have undergone plastic surgery attest to the failure of that surgery to position the transformed body as a convincing representation of the self.

Conclusion

My research points to three general conclusions. The first bears on the reasons women have plastic surgery and suggests a modification of the criticisms of such procedures. The second bears on the ways in which women create accounts of plastic surgery, an omission from the criticisms of plastic surgery. The third returns more sympathetically to those criticisms.

First, none of the women I spoke to embarked casually on plastic surgery. The costs of these procedures—measured in dollars and in the risk of physical damage—are well known to those who have undergone cosmetic surgery. Most of these women had plastic surgery only after serious consideration, often accompanied by research into the medical technology involved in the operations. Nearly all either had to sacrifice another large purchase or to weather some sort of financial hardship to pay for the surgery. More importantly, although physicians may serve as gatekeepers, preventing some women from receiving surgery, physicians do not, in any direct sense, recruit patients. Neither did the women I spoke to report that they underwent surgery at the urging of a specific other—husband, parent, lover, or friend. Rather, the decision to seek surgery seems to have been driven by the desires of women themselves, at least in the immediate circumstances. To be sure, the women's decisions to undergo surgery were shaped by broader cultural considerations—by notions of what constitutes beauty, by distinctively ethnic notions of beauty, and, most importantly, by the assumption that a woman's worth is measured by her appearance. Yet to portray the women I talked to as some sort of "cultural dopes," tossed and battered by cultural forces beyond their understanding, as passively submitting to the demands of beauty, is to badly misrepresent them. A more appropriate image, I would suggest, is to present them as savvy cultural negotiators, attempting to "make out" as best they can within a culture that limits their options. Those who undergo plastic surgery may (ultimately) be wrong, but they are not foolish. They know what they are doing. Their goals are realistic and they, in fact, achieve most of what they set out to accomplish with plastic surgery. Although their actions surely do, in the long run, contribute to the reproduction of a beauty culture that carries heavy costs for them and for all women, in the short run they have succeeded in their own more limited purposes.

Second, plastic surgery demands accounts . . . those who undertook plastic surgery are working hard to justify themselves . . . they do this in two steps. First, they must convince themselves that they deserve the surgery, whether by the hard work they put in at the gym or the effort they invest in saving the money that surgical procedures require. In so doing, they make the surgery, psychologically and ideologically, their own. Second, they must convince themselves that the revised appearances they *have been given*, however well earned, are somehow connected to the self—i.e., that they are innocent of the charges of inauthenticity. To do this, they invoke essentialist notions of the self and corresponding notions of the body as accidental, somehow inessential, or a degeneration from a younger body that better represented who they truly are. . . .

Finally, I return more sympathetically to the criticisms of plastic surgery. . . . In the other settings I studied, the local production of an alternative culture is very much in evidence. Among the women who chose to have plastic surgery, there are the aesthetic judgments of their plastic surgeon and the ignored expressed opposition of friends and family, but no local culture of their own. Elsewhere women are challenging, however haltingly, however partially, a beauty culture. In contrast, the women who undergo plastic surgery are simply making do, perhaps as best they can, within a culture that they believe rewards them for their looks.

References

Bordo, S. (1990). "Material girl": The effacements of postmodern culture. *Michigan Quarterly Review*, 29, 653–677.

Dally, A. (1991). *Women Under the Knife: A History of Surgery*. London: Hutchinson Radius.

Davis, K. (1995). *Reshaping the Female Body: The Dilemma of Cosmetic Surgery*. New York: Routledge.

Finkelstein, J. (1991). *The Fashioned Self*. Philadelphia, PA: Temple University Press.

Gimlin, D. (Forthcoming). *Bodywork: The Business of Beauty in Women's Lives*. Berkeley: University of California Press.

Goldwyn, R. M. (Ed.) (1980). *Long-Term Results in Plastic and Reconstructive Surgery*. 2nd edition. Boston: Little, Brown and Company.

Kaw, E. (1994). Opening faces: The politics of cosmetic surgery and Asian American women. In N. Sault (Ed.), *Many Mirrors: Body Image and Social Relations* (pp. 241–265). New Brunswick, NJ: Rutgers University Press.

Meredith, B. (1988). *A Change for the Better*. London: Grafton Books.

Wolf, N. (1991). *The Beauty Myth: How Images of Beauty Are Used Against Women.* New York: William Morrow.

Review

1. What are the cultural forces behind the use of cosmetic surgery?

2. What kinds of reasons do women give for justifying their cosmetic surgery?

3. How do women feel about themselves after having cosmetic surgery?

Applications

1. Look at clothing ads in a newspaper or magazine. If you were an alien whose only information about humans was the models in these ads, how would you describe the way humans look? What proportion of people do you think actually look that way?

2. Although this article focuses on women, men undergo a certain amount of cosmetic surgery because they are dissatisfied with their physical appearance. Make an informal survey of friends and acquaintances—try to get an equal number of males and females. Tell them a little about this article then ask them how they feel about their own bodies. Are they basically satisfied or somewhat dissatisfied with the way they look? If they could change something about their appearance, what would it be? Are there differences between the responses of the males and females? How do your findings square with what Gimlin found in her research?

Part Two

Becoming a Social Creature

Socialization occurs throughout life, but some of the most important socialization takes place during childhood. Foremost among the socializing agents is the family. From birth, the family influences a child's development by such behaviors as the way the parents hold the baby, look at it, talk to it, and respond to its needs. As the child grows, the parents teach values and norms.

Family socialization is reinforced or modified by experiences at school and with peers, by the mass media, and by interaction with others.

In this part, we look at three of the agents of socialization: family, television, and organized sports. In each selection, the question addressed is how the particular agent affects the development of gender roles. ✦

9
As the Twig Is Bent

Children Reared in Feminist Households

Barbara J. Risman
Kristen Myers

In a perfectly integrated society, all elements would work together harmoniously and flawlessly. All the various agents of socialization would be consistent with each other. But no society is perfectly integrated. As a result, the agents of socialization are not always consistent, and sometimes may even contradict one another. For example, parents and teachers may admonish teens to avoid drugs, while peers may pressure them to experiment with drugs.

Contradictory messages and pressures from socializing agents occur throughout people's lives. For instance, a man who was urged by his parents and encouraged by his new employer to work more than the required minimum found himself facing hostile colleagues when he tried to forego the morning coffee break and remain at his desk.

How do people deal with such contradictions? Obviously, they have many options. In this selection, the researchers look at how children reared in feminist households handle the conflict between parental teachings of nonsexist attitudes and behavior and the attitudes and behavior of the less-than-egalitarian world in which they must function. The authors gathered their material by finding fifteen "fair" families (those in which husband and wife agreed that they had an egalitarian relationship) and interviewing the twelve boys and nine girls from those families. They also had some of the children write poetry and free play.

The article illustrates an important sociological principle: How an individual behaves is a function not only of his or her personal attitudes and inclinations but also of the social forces that come to bear on him or her in particular social contexts. Those who adapt to the social context may pay a price in the sense of compromising their standards or preferences. Those who do not adapt may pay the even heavier price of ostracism. Most people adapt at least enough to be an acceptable part of some group.

In recent years, sociologists have come to define gender as a social construct to be negotiated rather than as a fixed entity (West and Zimmerman 1987; Connell 1987; Risman and Schwartz 1989; Howard et al. 1996). In this view, gender is neither simply an attribute of individuals nor a constraint of the social structure. Instead, when people interact in their daily lives, they "do gender" which helps to reproduce the larger, gendered social structure. West and Zimmerman (1987) argue that individuals are actors working within structural constraints rather than passive pawns. The conceptualization of gender as behavior that may or may not be enacted allows those concerned with inequality to hope for change: What would happen if we decided not to do gender, or to do it differently? Would we radically alter the social structure as we know it, or are larger social pressures strong enough to override individual insurgency?. . .

Learning How to Behave: Acting Versus Reacting

Sociologists have only rarely—and quite recently—studied children's gender. Therefore, much of the literature to be reviewed originates in other disciplines. When children are studied, in both sociology and psychology, the predominant questions center around the ways in which children learn to be boys or girls. We organize this literature analytically, for purposes of discussion, based on the presumptions about children's role in their own socialization. We divide this scholarship into three categories: that which sees children as the primary actors in the gendering process, or cognitive theories; that which sees children's gender as something that is imposed by the larger culture, and that is reinforced through structural constraints, or socialization theories; and that which argues that children are constrained by long-standing gender norms, but which sees children as participating in and negotiating the enactment of gender or social constructionist theories.

We briefly summarize these analytic categories. First, theories where children are the primary actors [including Piaget (1932); Kohlberg (1966); Maccoby (1992); and Martin (1993)] are theories of cognitive development which argue that children play an active role in gender acquisition, rather than passively absorbing appropriate information from their parents and peers. Instead, children seek relevant information, and they organize it into predictable patterns. They begin to do this at a young age in order to make sense out of their worlds. This perspective puts undue emphasis on the child as rational actor freely picking and choosing among the available options, and selecting gender as the most salient organizing force in society (Bem 1993).

The second category—which conceptualizes gender as structurally imposed upon children—includes Parsons and Bales (1955); Inkeles (1968); Bandura (1962, 1971); Cahill (1987); Deaux (1984); Fagot et al. (1992); Hutson (1983); Stern and Karraker (1989); and Eisenberg et al. (1985). This perspective sees the socialization process as a one-way conduit of information from adult to child. Beginning at birth, people in society (parents, teachers, and peers) reward children for learning the behavior of the same sex. Because they receive positive feedback for "correct" behavior, children imitate same-sex behavior, and "encode" it into their behavioral repertoires. Once encoded, the child's gender is set. This socialization perspective offers a static picture of gender with the child as a relatively acquiescent recipient of appropriate models of behavior, which in turn offer little room for improvisation and change. This is typical of role theo-

rists in general (Kreps et al. 1994). It also does not allow for the enactment of multiple masculinities and femininities (Connell 1992), thereby reifying and valorizing a gender dichotomy.

The last category is more consistent with a social constructionist perspective. In recent years, sociologists have taken a more critical look at the gender socialization of children, arguing that socialization is not a one-way conduit of information, with adults providing role models and sanctions, and with the children hitting, missing and eventually getting it "right" [for more, see Corsaro (1985), Alanen (1988), and Giddens (1979)]. Instead, the children participate in the process as social actors. Research in this tradition is quite new. For example, Borman and O' Reilly (1987) find that kindergarten children in same-sex play groups initiate play in similar manners, but that the topics for play vary by gender. That is, boys and girls play different types of games, thereby creating different conversational and negotiation demands. Thorne (1993) examines groups of children in classrooms and school yards, illustrating how "kids" actively create and police gender boundaries, forming various strata among themselves. She asserts that gender relations are not invariant, but instead can change according to the context and the actors involved. Thorne criticizes most socialization and development frameworks for presupposing a certain outcome: that boys will learn appropriate masculinities, girls will learn appropriate femininities; and if they fail to do so, they will either be punished or labeled deviant. She argues that this future-oriented perspective distorts the children's every day realities, which are crucial to their on-going gendered negotiations. As she says, "children's interactions are not preparation for life, they are life itself" (p. 3).

Bem (1993) improves upon both cognitive and socialization theories by linking them. Bem argues that children try to make sense of the world by forming categories, or "schema," but these categories are shaped by the ubiquitous presence of existing gender categories in society. She argues that learning gender is subtle, transmitted to children by adults both consciously and unconsciously, so that the dominant way of understanding the social world is seen as the only way to understand it. Existing gender divisions are hegemonic and therefore usually unquestioned by both children and adults. Therefore, calling into question the taken-for-granted gendered organization of society is difficult and unlikely, though not impossible.

It seems quite reasonable that all three processes occur. Children who live in gendered societies do, no doubt, develop gender schema and code themselves as well as the world around them in gendered terms. But this seems much more likely to be the result of their lived experiences in patriarchal societies and not the consequence of some innate drive for cognitive development. While children do indeed develop cognitive gender schema, adults and older children also treat boys and girls quite differently. Gender socialization is apparent in any observation of children's lives. And, while children are being socialized, they react, negotiate, and even reject some of the societal pressures as they interact with each other, and adults. Children are actors in the gendering process, but that does not mean that we must ignore the impact of differential reinforcement of gender-appropriate behavior on them. The cognitive effects of living in a gendered (and sexist) society, the reality of gender socialization, and the active efforts of boys and girls to negotiate their own worlds interact to affect their future options and constraints.

Unequal Outcomes: Reproducing Gender Inequalities

Even when we recognize that children both act and react throughout the gendering process, we cannot overlook the strong empirical data which suggests that boys and girls are differentially prepared for their adult roles. Boys are still routinely socialized to learn to work in teams and to compete; girls are still routinely socialized to value nurturing (just notice the relative numbers of boys and girls in team sports versus those dedicated readers to the very popular book series, *The Babysitters Club*). Thorne (1993)

has shown very convincingly that there is much more cross-over gender play than dichotomous thinking presumes; and yet other research continues to indicate the consequences of gender socialization on children (Lever 1978; Luttrell 1993; Hawkins 1985; Wilder et al. 1985; Signorelli 1990; Maccoby 1992; Hutson 1993). There is also much evidence that gender socialization differs by social class, ethnicity and religion (Peterson and Rollins 1987; Collins 1990).

Lever's (1978) classic study of boys' and girls' play offers insight into the ways in which boys and girls are differentially prepared for their futures: men are presumed to belong in the public, competitive sphere and women in the private, nurturing sphere. Boys' games were more likely to be outside, involve teams and be age-integrated. Girls were more likely to play make believe games with one or two others, and to break up a game rather than work through conflict. After interviewing two groups of working class women about their gendered experiences in school, Luttrell (1993) suggests that school is politically embattled, and femininity is used to undermine working class girls' academic confidence and success in school. Hawkins (1985) argues that girls often do not receive sufficient support with regard to learning computer skills; they are thereby somewhat handicapped in an increasingly computer-reliant world. Wilder et al. (1985) echo this argument, examining the ideology that technology is a male domain. In surveys of 1,600 children in kindergarten through twelfth grade, they find that girls like computers less than boys and therefore use them less. In a survey of first year college students, they find that women students feel less competent with computer technology, regardless of their skill or experience.

Gender specific experiences aren't limited to play and school. Because human beings are helpless at birth and, in our society, adulthood may not arrive for more [than] two decades, children are dependent upon families for a very long time. Therefore, parents and the immediate family are one source of existing gendered expectations (Maccoby 1992). The research we have discussed above points to the negative impact of gender-typing on their psyches, their acquisition of competitive market skills, necessary nurturing skills, and their interaction with each other. Research indicates that parents participate in gender-typing by often rewarding gender-typical play and punishing gender-atypical play (Hutson 1983). In order to help combat gender inequality, we must carefully attend to both gendering processes and the negotiation of gender among children. While several scholars have documented that some families in our society are moving in the direction of shared parenting, we have as yet little information about how effective such changes in parenting style might be in a society in which gendering processes continue to occur in other social realms (Coltrane 1996; Marsiglio 1995; Schwartz 1994; Segal 1990).

In this paper, we examine children whose parents have attempted to break the chain of gender inequality that begins at birth. We focus particularly on the ways in which children grapple with and enact gender. The children in this study are living in a different context than children in more mainstream families: these are children whose parents . . . have an ideological and practical commitment to organizing their homes and families in an egalitarian manner. Whereas mainstream parents may react with delight when their daughter wants to be Barbie for Halloween and their son wants toy guns for his birthday, the parents in this study are likely to be dismayed. Rather than receiving reinforcement from their parents when they enact hegemonic behavior, these children are likely to encounter disappointment or concern. So, how do these children negotiate gender given their atypical parents? . . .

The Complicated Worlds of Fair Children

In examining the stories, poems, and conversations of the children, we have drawn two main findings. The inconsistencies between the children's egalitarian beliefs and their experiences with peers are the major and consistent finding in these data. The second finding, also consistent, is that identities seem to be forged more from lived experiences than from ideology. The disjunction between ideology, experience, and identity seems to be a common thread woven through all these children's stories. In discussing the findings and providing the words of the children themselves, we refer to the gender of the child. We recognize that, in focusing repeatedly on gender, we may be reinforcing the notion of gender differences rather than similarities; that is not our intention. It is simply a necessary means of distinguishing subjects and the differential experiences.

We divide our findings into three major categories: ideology, experiences and identities of the children. In analyzing the data, we realized that gender operates on several levels for these children. They all espouse a certain rhetoric of gender which they have learned in part from living in "fair" families. We find that this rhetoric is not always in sync with the children's gendered experiences and behaviors, so we address them separately. And, last, we find that the children have internalized notions of gender which affect their identities as girls and boys.

Ideology

Approximately 80 percent of the children (16 of 21) entirely adopted their parents' egalitarian or feminist views on gender. Two of the children without such views were four year olds whose answers were better described as inconsistent than traditional. These children knew that occupations were currently sex-segregated but believed they shouldn't be. They didn't see any jobs in families that ought to be either for men or women. One 10 year old boy actually became annoyed as we questioned him about what men and women should do. He retorted in an irritated voice and rolled his eyes: "I told you I think anybody can do these jobs. . . . I think that saying just men or just women could do these jobs isn't being equal." The children over six years of age didn't have any problem differentiating what was true from what should be so.

Most of both boys and girls not only believed that men and women should be free to work in any occupation and share the family labor, they also understood that male privilege existed in contemporary society. This nine year old girl told us that she believed very much in feminism because "I don't think that it is the least bit fair that in most places males have the main power. I think that women play an important part and should be free to do what they want to do." Similarly, a 15 year old told us, in response to a question about what he liked about being a boy, "It's probably easier being a guy at least it is now because of stereotypes and prejudices and everything." Overall, most of these children were sophisticated, true believers in gender equality and the capabilities of men and women to be in the same jobs and family roles. The influence of their parents as ideological conduits and role models was evident in these children's attitudes.

Experiences

These children may have had "politically correct" attitudes about gender equality for men and women, but when that ideology contradicted their experiences as boys and girls, the experiential data won hands-down. Despite their answers to what should be for grown-ups, these children gave remarkably typical answers about the differences between boys and girls. In order to find out their "gut" beliefs about boys and girls, we probed their experiences with a variety of techniques. We asked them how their lives would be different if a magician turned them into a girl/boy. We provided them short scenarios using stereotypically male and female adjectives (e.g. weak, strong, fearful, adventuresome) and asked them to circle a male or female diagram, and then asked why. We asked what they liked and disliked about being a girl or boy. We asked them to write poems which began with the line "If I were a boy/girl" using the opposite sex category. We showed them different pictures of a boy and a girl (similar in the fact that both sat on the same sofa), and we asked them to tell us a story about each child. We followed up every comment which would help us assess their experiences.

None of the four, five or six year olds had yet begun to believe that boys and girls were different. These egalitarian parents managed to exert some insulation for their preschoolers from typical American norms—perhaps by choice of paid care giving arrangements and selection of friends. This finding differs from theories based on developmental psychological research [e.g. Kohlberg (1966), Kohlberg and Ullian (1974)], which suggests that children necessarily begin sex-stereotyping as early as four years old.

Once children hit seven years of age, however, their non-familial experiences have broadened considerably, as have their ideas about differences between the sexes. We found the descriptions of school age children remarkably consistent—and stereotypical—across sex and age categories. Girls were sweet and neat; boys were athletic and disruptive. . . . These children offered unequivocal support for the belief in major sex differences between boys and girls within minutes of having parroted their parents' [feminist] views about the equality and similarity of men and women.

Three of these children qualified these stereotypical answers. An 8 year old boy made a point of telling us that he knew girls could be into sports or computers, he just didn't personally know any who were. A 7 year old girl was sure that girls were better behaved and boys were mean, but she also sometimes wanted to be a boy because they seemed to have more playful and active games. A 10 year old boy knew that some girls were "like boys," and he even let such a girl try out for his spy club. And one 6 year old boy made the very acute observation that girls played different games on the playground but the same games as boys in the neighborhood [Thorne (1993) finds the same thing]. This little boy had a close neighborhood girl friend, but we observed that when the other boys came around, he left her alone. Crossing gender for play was fine with him, but not at the expense of ridicule from the other boys. Our observation was reinforced by his parents' independently mentioning this pattern.

When family experiences collided head on with experiences with peers, the family influences were dwarfed. For example, one six year old boy told us that if a magician were to turn him into a girl, he'd be different because he'd have long hair. This boy's father had a long straight black ponytail which went to the middle of his back, and his mother's hair hardly reached below her ears. A four year old boy told us that if a magician were to turn him into a girl, he'd have to do housework—despite his father's flexible work schedule, which allowed him to spend more time in domestic pursuits than his wife. Children knew that women and men were equal; it was boys and girls who were totally different. It almost seemed as if these children believed that boys and girls were opposites, but men and women were magically transformed into equal and comparable people.

Seven of these children spoke explicitly about male privilege among peers or at school. A 9 year old girl told us that sometimes she wished to be a boy because when

> teachers need help like to carry a box to their classroom, they always come in and say, like, can I borrow a couple of your boys, and never say, "can I borrow a couple of your students?" And so the girls never get to do any of the stuff and leave the classroom . . . it's always the boys that get to leave. And like, little trips and stuff, when we used to go on field trips, the boys would always have to carry a basket of lunches, and go ahead, and like, when they had stuff to bring from the car, it'd always be boys that'd get to go to the car and eat and the girls, like, had to stay on the bus and just sit there and wait while some boys got to go there and the girls never got to do it, do that stuff . . . you get left out because you're a girl. . . . But I'm not wimpy.

The 7 year old girl told us that she was "more hyper" than most girls and many of her friends were boys because they were more active and playful. A 10 year old boy mentioned "racism against women" in sports. One 9 year old girl was an avowed feminist who also espoused implicitly essentialist notions about girls' innate cooperativeness versus boys' innate combativeness. She thought girls ought to have more power in the world because they were better people. The following paragraph written by an 8 year old boy was an articulate statement about male privilege, but such an un-

derstanding of such privilege was widely shared by all of the children, though not usually so well articulated.

> If I were a girl I'd have to attract a guy—wear makeup; sometimes, wear the latest style of clothes and try to be likeable. I probably wouldn't play any physical sports like football or soccer. I don't think I would enjoy myself around men in fear of rejection or under the pressure of attracting them.

Therefore, while boys and girls shared the perception that boys were troublemakers, sarcastic, and athletic, they also sensed that boys had advantages. Only a few of the boys were, in fact, conscious that they belonged to a group for which they had internalized negative characteristics. One aware boy answered our question about how he was different from other guys this way[:] "I think I'm taller. I don't like bullying people around that much. When one of my friends starts fighting somebody or arguing with somebody, I don't join in. I steer clear of them. I try to get in as few fights as possible." This boy built his identity in sports (his room was a baseball shrine and his activities were sports, sports, and more sports), but tried to distance himself from the violent aspects of peer group masculinity. Another boy told us that if he were magically transformed into a girl, he would be nicer to his friends. These boys had internalized very negative attitudes toward their own group—and at some level, themselves. In no case did any girl tell us how bad girls as a group were. When girls talked about how they were similar and different from other girls, their answers were idiosyncratic. These children "knew" that boys and girls were very different; they "knew" that boys had advantages; but they also "knew" that girls were nicer people.

Identity

These boys and girls were consistent when they explained how boys and girls were different. The unanimity dissolved when we began to look at how they forged their own identities. Only six of these children seemed to have fashioned selves which unambiguously fit into their own stereotyped notions of childhood gender. The interview and observational data collected in these families identified six children (the 11 year old Germane girl, the 12 year old Potadman boy, the 8 year old Pretzman boy, the 10 year old Stokes girl, the 6 year old Green girl, and the 9 year old Sykes girl) who described themselves in consistently gendered fashion, and who were so identified in observational data. The first obvious finding was that these children's attitudes and identities were not consistent. The Pretzman boy, Stokes girl, Green girl, and Sykes girl are very self-consciously egalitarian, even feminist. The Germane girl and the Potadman boy, however, were two of the children with more traditional beliefs about gender. The Pretzman and Potadman children were "all-boy;" the Sykes, Stokes, Green and Germane children "all-girl."

What does "all-boy" or "all-girl" mean? In this instance, we refer back to the list created by the children themselves. The children suggested boys were active, into sports, mean, bad, freer than girls, sarcastic, cool, aggressive, athletic, tough, stronger than girls, into fights, troublemakers, competitive, bullies, and into computers. These six children could indeed be described exclusively by characteristics in this list, with no reference to those traits which were used to describe girls. Now, this doesn't mean that every characteristic was applicable, only that no characteristics from the opposite sex list fit at all. For example, there was no indication that the Pretzman boy was mean or a troublemaker, just the opposite. He was an academically gifted child who took school very seriously, and followed directions impeccably, yet all his interests were masculine—sports, [L]eggos, [S]tar-trek, computers. He described himself as "strong" and used that criterion to differentiate boys and girls. He didn't play much with girls, and there was simply no indication of cross-gender behavior or traits either in the interview or as we watched him at home. The Potadman boy was similar. His main interest and identity seemed to be attached to sports. He was interpersonally instrumental, answering us with short, not-too-reflective comments. In traditionally masculine fash-

ion, his friendships were described almost entirely in terms of sharing activities.

The four girls who were "all-girl" could be described by using the characteristics the children provided for us about girls: nice, behave well, quiet, cooperative, good, sweet, not into sports, not sneaky, nice to friends, less free. While none of these girls embodied every one of these traits, it is unlikely that these girls would be described by any of the traits in the "boy" list. One shared characteristic was their distaste for competitive sports. The Germane girl provided an easy comparison to the Potadman boy discussed above. Her very favorite games were make-believe fantasies, and her favorite activity was dance. Her favorite possessions: dolls and stuffed animals. The Stokes 10 year old was similarly gendered. Her very favorite activities were reading, writing poems and art. She was adamant about disliking sports, and she knew why: she didn't like any activity where you had to be pushy or aggressive. The Green daughter had three doll houses, and not a "boy" toy in the house. Because we interviewed the entire family, we knew that this child preferred girl toys in spite of her parents' teaching. Her parents were very conscious of encouraging her to make her own choices and develop her own potential; the mother told us she "was working on" trying to get her daughter to be willing to play some sports, at least at school during recess.

These six children, raised by egalitarian parents and often holding feminist attitudes themselves, nevertheless fashioned selves which are unambiguously gendered. The following poem sums up what these children thought when they imagined being the opposite sex. The essay was written by the Sykes girl in response to our request to write a verse which began with the phrase, "If I were a boy." She wrote,

> If I were a boy, I'd know my parents had made a mistake, and that I should have been a girl. I'd always feel that I didn't belong because the girls were who I wanted to play with; but they wouldn't let me, and I didn't want to be with the boys.

This 9 year old girl provided an interesting and stark example of the disjunction between identity and ideology. She lived in one of our most self-consciously feminist and progressive families. They saw themselves as living outside the mainstream, with no television so their daughter avoided excess materialism. All three Sykes were avowed feminists. And yet, the daughter was one of the most feminine in the sample—her long wavy hair flowed below her waist. She loved and collected china tea cups, hated competitive sports, and loved nature and hiking. She saved a bug from destruction during a home observation, and she carried it tenderly outside. In honor of the interview, she put on her favorite bedclothes, a long nightgown with a pink bow. This child was very smart, and knew it. She intended to succeed professionally, maybe in a scientific career. So perhaps she too, despite her feminine self-presentation and dislike for most things male, was actually more actively crossing over gender boundaries than we could determine in our limited access to her life.

The other 15 children had also fashioned gendered selves. The boys were much more likely to enjoy sports, the girls to enjoy dance. Despite their parents' role-modeling, despite their own ideologies, all of these girls were more feminine than masculine. All of these boys were more masculine [than] feminine. But all of the rest of these children, to varying degrees, crossed over gender lines in interests and interpersonal style. All but one of the girls was either involved in at least one competitive sport or expected to be when she got older. All of the boys stood out some way as exceptions to hegemonic masculinity. An interesting sex difference existed, however. All the girls told us in quite explicit terms just how they were different from other girls, but the boys often denied any differences from other boys, differences that our interview and observational team noted. For example, one girl knew she was different from other girls because she loved team sports and would like to be a boy, except that she knew "they aren't always very nice." A 4 year old liked to climb trees, as well as play fantasy games about babies. She knew she was "nice, like other girls" but wanted to be "cool" like boys. She told us her future goal was to "be a mommy so I can work hard and like my job."

In seeing this child in public settings in the last few years, we know that she has become an enthusiastic baseball player with a square and chunky frame. She looks tough on the field. Another child believed she was more active [than] other girls, but she was also "real sweet," liked horses, and was nice to her friends (all characteristics she sees as different from boys). Yet another child told us she was "not like other girls particularly." She had friends who were boys, although her best friend was another girl. But she liked being a girl because she could do whatever she wanted.

The boys whom we coded as portraying some cross-over behaviors and interpersonal style were much less likely to notice it themselves. While some of the data reported here came directly from the interviews, much of it also relied on subtle inconsistencies in their own words, body language, and, to some extent, the "gut" feelings of the interview and observational team as recorded in field notes. Both of the older Potadman boys (15 and 17 years of age) told us some hopes and dreams which seemed to cross-over gender stereotypes. The 15 year old babysat and loved domestic work, to vacuum and cook. He would like to stay home with his children if his wife could earn a high enough income. His very tall older brother, whose long pony tail reaching below his waist was his most distinctive visual characteristic, hated to work out, and found it unfair that women can be considered sexy without being muscular but that men can't. He wrote poetry and never has been into sports, although he did like volleyball. He described himself as an intellectual outsider, and seemed comfortable—if somewhat vulnerable—with the status.

Four little boys—all aged 4 or 5—also told us their androgynous preferences. One liked lots of boys' games, particularly baseball. But he also wanted to be like his sister, played housekeeping at day care, and enjoyed playing "dress-up" in his sister's clothes. Another boy's favorite movie characters were Aladdin and the Little Mermaid, and he had shoes adorned with the likenesses of both. A 4 year old boy thought being "silly" was the best part of being a boy.

While he liked guns and had mostly boys as friends, his answers to most questions seemed gender-neutral. Similarly, one 5 year old boy liked boys' toys and baseball, but many of his favorite activities seemed gender-neutral: board games, and playing out of doors with both boys and girls. His body language and self-presentation, his greater enthusiasm for non-gendered subjects, brought to mind the characteristic "gentle." One 6 year old boy preferred stereotypically boy toys, and he took Tae Kwon Do, but like the 15 year old above, he too would like to not work at all, to "spend more time with his children." Even when these boys talked about their stereotypical behaviors, they never seemed rough or tough; they seemed warm and caring.

There were two boys whose words contradicted their behavior (as reported by parents) and our observations. One 10 year old boy seemed to try too hard at his self-presentation. He wanted us to think he was tough, mean, and sneaky—a real boy. But the boy we met was warm, kind, and soft-spoken, even as he told us about his war games. This son of two nonfiction writers wanted a blue-collar job where he could wear "lots of armor" and be tough. But all of these words did not square with what we found—a 10 year old who played gently with his sister. He came back from the bathroom, interrupted our interview and his 4 year old sister's interview, to bring her to look out the bathroom window. He wanted to make sure she didn't miss the full moon. He talked to her quietly, handled her gently. When we noticed some Barbie-dolls in his closet and asked what kind of games he played with them, he answered, "Oh, I mostly kill them. They're my sister's." His mother told us otherwise, that both children played fantasy games with the dolls. He alluded to this himself later on: "I like the Ken doll because he is a basketball star." This boy twitched, visibly, when he spoke about gender preferences. The interview was poignant: he knew that boys were "supposed" to be mean and sneaky, and he wanted very much to fulfill those expectations, or at least to make us believe that he did. But we could not believe it; he gave too many contradictory signals.

We had a similar experience with the 10 year old Woods boy. He was a baseball fanatic and his room was entirely in Carolina Blue, rug and all. He talked about liking to compete. Both of these characteristics are hegemonically masculine, and they were clearly central to his identity. And yet, he described his baby brother in loving terms, and in three straight losses in an UNO card game with his interviewer, he never once showed any competitive spirit nor disappointment in losing. He emanated warmth, as did his father. He also differentiated himself from other boys because he wasn't a bully and didn't like to fight. These children's behavior challenged the boundaries of a rigid gender dichotomy, redefining athletics and competition as less hegemonically masculine.

Summary

The children in fair families have adopted their parents' egalitarian views. They believe men and women are equal, and that no jobs—inside or outside the family—ought to be sex-linked. But beyond these abstract statements concerning beliefs, these children depend on their own lived experiences for understanding gender in their childhood worlds. And they "know" that boys and girls are different—very different. The children—including the boys themselves—describe boys as a group as not only athletic, but also mean and troublesome. Girls are described as sweet, quiet, and well-behaved. Six of these children met their own criteria for being "all-boy" or "all-girl," while the rest portrayed some examples of cross-gender behavior. The girls knew and reported how they were different from other girls, the boys didn't.

One way to interpret the inconsistencies that we observed between children's ideology and their behavior and identities is that gender socialization has many sources, which are sometimes contradictory. Parents may be the primary socializing agents, but children are influenced by myriad social pressures outside of the family to conform to existing gendered norms. We think this is part of the story. While these parents have struggled to raise their children without oppressive gendered categories, the parents are unable to completely cloister their children. They go to school, synagogue or church, and to their friends' homes—places where gender is done differently.

The closest we came to finding a case where the parents had completely controlled their children's gendered environment was with a family whose two children were under four years old. The children were too young to be interviewed, but one interviewer played with them and observed them for three hours while other team members interviewed their parents. What we saw was remarkable. The parents and their private child care worker had carefully eliminated gender distinctions from their children's lives: they changed pronouns in books to be gender neutral; they never referred to their children as "girls" but as people; and they concentrated instead on teaching love for all people, flora, and fauna. In talking with the older child (who was three years old—her sister was an infant), the interviewer asked her if she was a boy or a girl. The child proudly responded that she was a person. She did not yet differentiate along gendered lines. We wondered what life would be like for this child when her parents could no longer shelter her and her sister from the hegemonically gendered organization of larger society. Nevertheless, she was the only child we observed who lived this seemingly non-gendered life.

Another way to look at these inconsistencies is to see them as a gradual process of gender revolution. These children may be challenging the rigid proscriptions of a gender dichotomy. Sociologists have begun to recognize (see especially Connell 1987 and 1995) that there are multiple masculinities and femininities, but most of society still wholly adopt[s] and enforce[s] a simple dichotomy. These children's actions challenge the existing gender structure of society in that they reject the dichotomy. Being competitive and into sports does not impede a boy's ability to be tender and loving. Girls can wear hair bows and pink dresses and still be feminists. One set of characteristics does not preclude the co-existence of the other. They straddle the boundaries. The strad-

dling makes some children nervous—like the 10 year boy who twitched—because they know they're unusual. But many consider their duality to be normal. These children are not post-gendered in that they obliterate the differences between boys and girls; on the contrary, they embrace and occasionally celebrate them. They are post-gendered because they do not use these differences as dichotomies nor as a basis for ranking each other. What all of these children have in common is a focus on kindness and gentleness. They can be masculine or feminine or both, but they are all humanitarian. . . .

References

Alanen, L. (1988). Rethinking childhood. *Acta Sociologica*, 31, 53–67.

Bandura, A. (1962). Social Learning Through Imitation. In M. Jones (Ed.), *Nebraska Symposium on Motivation*, volume 10, (pp. 211–274). Lincoln: University of Nebraska Press.

—— (1971). *Psychological modeling: Conflicting theories*. Chicago: Aldine-Atherton.

Bem, S. L. (1993). *The Lenses of Gender*. New Haven: Yale University Press.

Borman, K. M., and P. O'Reilly. (1987). Learning Gender Roles in Three Urban U.S. Kindergarten Classrooms. *Child and Youth Services*, 8, 43–66.

Cahill, S. E. (1987). Language Practices and Self-Definition: The Case of Gender Identity Acquisition. *Sociological Quarterly*, 27, 295–311.

Collins, P. Hill (1990). *Black Feminist Thought*. Boston: Unwin Hyman.

Coltrane, S. (1996). *Family Man: Fatherhood, Housework and Gender Equity*. Oxford: Oxford University Press.

Connell, R. W. (1987). *Gender and Power*. Stanford: Stanford University Press.

—— (1992). A Very Straight Gay: Masculinity, Homosexual Experience, and the Dynamics of Gender. *American Sociological Review*, 57, 735–751.

—— (1995). *Masculinities*. Berkeley: University of California Press.

Corsaro, W. A. (1985). *Friendship and Peer Culture in the Early Years*. Norwood: Ablex Publishing.

Deaux, K. (1984). From Individual Differences to Social Categories: Analysis of a Decade's Research on Gender. *American Psychologist*, 39, 105–116.

Eisenberg, N., S. A. Wolchik, R. Hernandez, and J. F. Pasternack. (1985). Parental Socialization of Young Children's Play: A Short-term Longitudinal Study. *Child Development*, 56, 1506–1513.

Fagot, B. I., M. D. Leinbach, and C. O'Boyle. (1992). Gender Labeling, Gender Stereotyping, and Parenting Behaviors. *Developmental Psychology*, 28, 225–230.

Giddens, A. (1979). *Central Problems in Social Theory*. Berkeley: University of California Press.

—— (1984). *The Constitution of Society*. Berkeley: University of California Press.

Hawkins, J. (1985). Computers and Girls: Rethinking the Issues. *Sex Roles*, 13, 165–180.

Howard, J., B. Risman, M. Romero, and J. Sprague. (1996). *The Gender Lens Book Series*. Thousand Oaks, CA: Forge and Sage Publishers.

Hutson, A. H. (1993). Sex-Typing. In E. M. Hetherington and P. H. Mussen (Eds.) *Handbook of Child Psychology*, volume 4. New York: Wiley.

Inkeles, A. (1968). Society, Social Structure and Child Socialization. In J. Clausen (Ed.) *Socialization and Society*. Boston: Little, Brown.

Kohlberg, L. (1966). A Cognitive-developmental Analysis of Children's Sex-role Concepts and Attitudes. In E. E. Maccoby (Ed.) *The Development of Sex Differences*. Stanford: Stanford University Press.

Kohlberg, L., and D. Z. Ullian. (1974). Stages in the Development of Psychosocial Concepts and Attitudes. In R. C. Friedman, R. N. Richart, and R. L. Vande Wiele (Eds.) *Sex Differences in Behavior*. New York: Wiley.

Kreps, G. A., and S. L. Bosworth; with J. A. Mooney, S. T. Russell, and K. A. Myers. (1994). *Organizing, Role Enactment, and Disaster: A Structural Theory*. Newark: University of Delaware Press.

Lever, J. (1978). Sex Differences in the Complexity of Children's Play and Games. *American Sociological Review*, 43, 471–483.

Luttrell, W. (1993). The Teachers, They All Had Their Pets: Concepts of Gender, Knowledge and Power. *Signs*, 18, 505–546.

Maccoby, E. E. (1992). The Role of Parents in the Socialization of Children: An Historical Overview. *Developmental Psychology*, 28, 1006–1017.

Marsiglio, W. (1995). *Fatherhood: Contemporary Theory, Research, and Social Policy*. Thousand Oaks, CA: Sage.

Martin, C. L. (1993). New Directions for Investigating Children's Gender Knowledge. *Developmental Review*, 13, 184–204.

Parsons, T., and R. Bales. (1955). *Family Socialization and Interaction Process*. Glencoe: Free Press.

Peterson, G. W., and B. C. Rollins. (1987). Parent-child Socialization. In M. Sussman and S. Steinmetz (Eds.) *Handbook of Marriage and the Family*. New York: Plenum.

Piaget, J. (1932). *The Moral Judgement of the Child*. London: Kegan Paul.

Risman, B. (Forthcoming). *Gender Vertigo: American Families in Transition*. New Haven: Yale University Press.

Risman, B., and P. Schwartz. (1989). *Gender in Intimate Relationships: A Microstructural Approach*. Belmont, CA: Wadsworth.

Rosenthal, R., and L. Jacobsen. (1968). *Pygmalion in the Classroom: Teacher Expectations and Pupil's Intellectual Development*. New York: Holt.

Schwartz, P. (1994). *Peer Marriage: How Love Between Equals Really Works*. New York: Free Press.

Segal, L. (1990). *Slow Motion: Changing Masculinities, Changing Men*. New Brunswick: Rutgers University Press.

Signorelli, N. (1990). Children, Television, and Gender Roles. *Journal of Adolescent Health Care*, 11, 50–58.

Stern, M., and K. H. Karraker. (1989). Sex Stereotyping of Infants: A Review of Gender Labeling Studies. *Sex Roles*, 20, 501–522.

Thorne, B. (1993). *Gender Play*. New Brunswick: Rutgers University Press.

West, C., and D. Zimmerman. (1987). Doing Gender. *Gender and Society*, 1, 125–151.

Wilder, G., D. Mackie, and J. Cooper. (1985). Gender and Computers: Two Surveys of Gender-related Attitudes. *Sex Roles*, 13, 215–228.

Review

1. Explain the three major theories by which social scientists explain how children learn to be boys and girls.

2. Describe the ideology of children reared in feminist homes.

3. How do children reared in feminist homes handle the contradiction between their ideology and their experiences?

4. What happens to the identities of children reared in feminist homes?

Applications

1. Think about the messages you got while growing up about the meaning of being male and female. Those messages came to you through both what people said and what they did. Compare the messages you got from various sources: parents, friends, teachers, religion, and mass media. Describe any inconsistencies. How do your current beliefs square with these varied messages? Do you, like the children in the above study, find yourself acting in ways that compromise your ideals? Why or why not?

2. One of the issues explored in Risman and Myers' research is the extent to which certain occupations are more appropriate for one sex than the other. Get a list of occupations from the *Statistical Abstract of the United States* or from books about careers. Do you believe that some occupations are more appropriate for one sex than the other? If so, which ones and why? If not, why? Ask the same questions of your friends. Summarize the reasons offered by both those who believe either sex can manage any occupation and those who believe some occupations are more appropriate for one sex over the other.

10

How Television Shapes Children's Gender Roles

Susan D. Witt

"The child is the father of the man" (or, perhaps, "mother of the woman"). This adage underscores the importance of early socialization, which includes learning **gender roles,** the behavior associated with being either male or female in a particular society.*

Sociologists do not deny the importance of biological factors, but they concentrate on the social factors that shape gender behavior. They stress the fact that males and females do not act in particular ways simply because they are biologically different. Rather, every society has norms about what it means to be male or female.

The fact that gender roles are not completely rooted in the imperatives of biological makeup is supported by variations between societies. Support is also found in gender role norms that have no biological explanation. For example, American women were long barred from many occupations (such as surgeon, police officer, and carpenter) on the grounds that they were emotionally or physically incapable or that the work was simply inappropriate for a woman. Such grounds cannot be defended biologically.

How do people learn and accept norms? The agents of socialization include the family, school, religious institutions, and the mass media. In this selection, Susan Witt discusses one of the important tools of gender role socialization among the mass media: television. She points out how television portrayals of males and females perpetuate gender bias. The more children watch and accept the portrayals, the more they are likely to believe that men

are decisive leaders and women are dependent followers.

Children often internalize gender role stereotypes from books, songs, television, and the movies (Thorne 1993). Television, however, is perhaps the most influential form of media (Lauer & Lauer 1994). Research on television viewing and children's socialization indicates that television has a great impact on children's lives.

Studies show preschoolers spend an average of nearly 30 hours a week watching television; some spend more time watching television than doing anything else except sleeping (Anderson, Lorch, Field, Collins, & Nathan 1986; Aulette 1994; Kaplan 1991). Nielsen Media Research has found that by the time children are 16 years old, they have spent more time watching television than going to school (as cited in Basow 1992). As a result, children are exposed to about 20,000 advertisements a year (Stoneman & Brody 1981). By the time a child graduates from high school, he will have witnessed 13,000 violent deaths on television (Gerbner & Gross 1976).

Television influences both children's prosocial and antisocial behaviors (Ahammer & Murray 1979; Bandura 1986; Comstock & Paik 1991; Strasburger 1995), as well as their attitudes about race and gender (Liebert & Sprafkin 1988).

Development of Children

As children grow and develop, they take in information and acquire knowledge at a rapid pace. As they develop their cognitive abilities, they assimilate new information and accommodate it to what they already know (Piaget 1954). Children's ideas about how the world works come from their experiences and from the attitudes and behaviors they see around them. The young child who believes that only women are nurses and only men are doctors may have developed this understanding because the first doctor he or she saw was a man, who was assisted by a female nurse. This "man as doctor, woman as nurse" idea may have been reinforced further by parents, books, conversations with friends, and television. If the child frequently meets such gender biases and gender stereotypes, this knowledge will be incorporated into future perceptions. Keeping in mind that young children with developing minds watch many hours of television, and recalling how television reinforces gender stereotypes, it is not surprising when children develop stereotyped beliefs.

Of the various factors that help shape gender-typed behaviors, role models and imitation are extremely influential (Bandura 1977; Basow 1992; Beal 1994; Hargreaves & Colley 1986). Research suggests that children who view violent programming on television will behave more aggressively with peers (Bandura 1977; Strasburger 1995). It is also true that children who view prosocial behaviors on television are more likely to exhibit those types of behaviors themselves. Young children will imitate and repeat behaviors they see on television. Consequently, children may exhibit these gender-biased behaviors and develop the gender-biased attitudes that they see modeled on television.

Developing autonomy, initiative, and a sense of industriousness [is] critical to young children's positive development (Erikson 1964). Children who witness female characters on television programs who are passive, indecisive, and subordinate to men, and who see this reinforced by their environment, will likely believe that this is the appropriate way for females to behave. Female children are less likely to develop autonomy, initiative, and industriousness if they rarely see those traits modeled. Similarly, because male characters on television programs are more likely to be shown in leadership roles and exhibiting assertive, decisive behavior, children learn this is the appropriate way for males to behave (Cantor 1977; Carter 1991; Seidman 1999).

Gender Bias in Television

The National Institute of Mental Health has determined:

- Men are usually more dominant in male-female interactions.

- Men on television are often portrayed as rational, ambitious, smart, competitive, powerful, stable, violent, and tolerant, while women are sensitive, romantic, attractive, happy, warm, sociable, peaceful, fair, submissive, and timid.

- Television programming emphasizes male characters' strength, performance, and skill; for women, it focuses on attractiveness and desirability.

- Marriage and family are not important to television's men. One study found that for nearly half the men, it wasn't possible to tell if they were married, a fact that was true for only 11 percent of the women (National Institute of Mental Health, as cited in Lauer & Lauer 1994, p. 73).

About two-thirds of characters in television programs are male, a figure that has remained constant since the 1950s (Condry 1989; Huston et al. 1992; Seidman 1999). In interactions between men and women, women frequently are defined by their relationships with men (Beal 1994).

Furthermore, television often does not reflect the reality of the work force. For example, 75 percent of the women on TV are depicted as being in the labor force, compared with the truer figure of about 56 percent (Basow 1992; Lauer & Lauer 1994). Most women on television are shown working in a profession. Most women in real life, however, are in low-paying, low-status jobs (Basow 1992). Less than 10 percent of women in the United States make more than $50,000 a year (Beal 1994).

Most females on prime time television are young, attractive, thin, and have an ornamental quality (Davis 1990). Most of these characters are either under 35 or over 50—middle-age women are rare (Beal 1994). Females consistently are placed in situations where looks count more than brains, and helpless and incompetent behaviors are expected of them (Boyer 1986). Men are twice as likely as women to be shown as competent and able to solve problems (Boyer 1986). Gender stereotypes abound on television, with women being depicted as sex objects more frequently than men, and men portrayed as inept when handling children's needs (Horovitz, as cited in Basow 1992; Seidman 1999).

On music television, a popular program choice among young viewers, females often are shown in degrading positions. Music videos frequently show women as sex objects, and as trying to gain the attention of a male who ignores them (Sherman & Dominick 1986). Rap music videos, for example, frequently portray women as objects of lust (Basow 1992; Seidman 1999). Women are four times more likely than men to be provocatively dressed in these videos (Atkin, Moorman, & Lin 1991), while men are almost always fully clothed (Tavris & Wade 1984).

While early television commercials were criticized for being overwhelmingly biased in favor of males, a study of commercials broadcast between 1971 and 1985 indicated a better balance of male and female characters (Bretl & Cantor 1988). Even so, women are most often shown in the role of wife and mother, or demonstrating products for the home (Osborn, as cited in Basow 1992). Another aspect of television advertising that is overwhelmingly a masculine province is voiceovers and narration, in which 83–90 percent of the voices are male (Basow 1992).

What Children Are Watching

While some children's programming has come under attack for being violent, irrelevant, or sexist (Carter 1991; Streicher 1974), other programs for children, such as "Sesame Street," are regularly lauded for attempting to meet children's developmental needs. Sexism, however, can be found even among the Muppets, most of whom all have male names or male voices (Cobb, Stevens-Long, & Goldstein 1982). Even Miss Piggy, a female character, is voiced by a male.

A study of Saturday morning cartoons revealed that females were pictured less often than males, were less active than males, played fewer roles than males, played fewer lead roles than males, and worked primarily in the home (Streicher 1974). Although these findings were obtained more than 25 years ago, no significant improvement is evident.

Recent studies of children's Saturday morning programs feature males in dominant roles, while showing females in peripheral roles (Carter 1991; Thompson & Zerbinos 1995). Children's programs on the Public Broadcasting System consistently show fewer females than males. Furthermore, television programs evidence a greater range of occupations for males than females (Cantor 1977; Thompson & Zerbinos 1995). This discrepancy in occupations between males and females also appears in music videos, where more than nine out of 10 occupational roles that were classified as stereotypically male (e.g., physician, mechanic, firefighter) were played by male actors (Seidman 1999). It has been suggested the preferences of boys are given precedence over those of girls because boys represent 53 percent of the Saturday viewing audience (Watson, as cited in Basow 1992).

Gender stereotypes are common on daytime soap operas as well; women often are shown as hopeless individuals, unable to solve problems without assistance (Basow 1992). Children frequently watch these programs after school, reinforcing notions of women as subordinate, passive, and indecisive.

In commercials for children's programs, boys are shown more frequently and in more active roles; girls' behavior is much more likely to be passive (O'Connor 1989). Advertisers indicate that using male models generates more product sales to children of both sexes than using female models (Schneider 1987). It also has been suggested that girls watch male-dominated programs and commercials simply because that is what is available. Given the option, however, girls will become loyal to programming that is more gender-neutral (Schneider 1987).

Children without television have been shown to be less stereotyped in their gender role attitudes (Kimball 1986). Furthermore, children who view programs with non-traditional gender roles tend to have non-traditional gender role perceptions (Rosenwasser, Lingenfelter, & Harrington 1989). Because children model the behavior they see on television, they are likely to perpetuate gender stereotypes they view (Basow 1992; Strasburger 1995).

Summary

Research indicates that television has a socializing influence on children regarding their attitudes toward gender roles. Gender role stereotypes seen on television are, in turn, reinforced by parents, friends, and school, contributing to the child's sense of what it means to be male or female in society. Television sends forceful and compelling messages about societally approved gender roles, which are often stereotyped, biased, and outdated. As children continue to develop and grow, they are exposed to more and more examples of such gender biases and stereotypes.

Traditional gender roles, wherein men are encouraged to be decisive and to show leadership qualities while women are encouraged to be deferential and dependent, do not benefit anyone, particularly women. Traditional gender roles discourage the full range of expression and accomplishment. Children should be allowed to develop a sense of self in a gender-fair environment that encourages everyone to fully feel a part of society.

References

Ahammer, I. M., & Murray, J. P. (1979). Kindness in the kindergarten: The relative influence of role playing and prosocial television in facilitating altruism. *International Journal of Behavioral Development*, 2, 133–157.

Anderson, D. R., Lorch, E. P., Field, D. E., Collins, P., & Nathan, J. G. (1986). Television viewing at home: Age trends in visual attention and time with TV. *Child Development*, 57, 1024–1033.

Atkin, D. J., Moorman, J., & Lin, C. A. (1991). Ready for prime time: Network series devoted to working women in the 1980s. *Sex Roles*, 25, 677–685.

Aulette, J. R. (1994). *Changing Families*. Belmont, CA: Wadsworth Publishing Company.

Bandura, A. (1977). *Social Learning Theory*. Englewood Cliffs, NJ: Prentice-Hall.

Bandura, A. (1986). *Social Foundations of Thought and Action: A Social Cognitive Theory*. Englewood Cliffs, NJ: Prentice-Hall.

Basow, S. A. (1992). *Gender Stereotypes and Roles* (3rd ed.). Pacific Grove, CA: Brooks/Cole Publishing.

Beal, C. (1994). *Boys and Girls: The Development of Gender Roles*. New York: McGraw-Hill.

Boyer, P. J. (1986). TV turns to the hard boiled male. *New York Times*, February 16, pp. H1, H29.

Bretl, D. J., & Cantor, J. (1988). The portrayal of men and women in U.S. television commercials: A recent content analysis and trends over 15 years. *Sex Roles*, 18, 595–609.

Cantor, M. (1977). Women and public broadcasting. *Journal of Communication*, 27, 14–19.

Carter, B. (1991). Children's TV, where boys are king. *New York Times*, May 1, pp. A1, C18.

Cobb, N. J., Stevens-Long, J., & Goldstein, S. (1982). The influence of televised models on toy preference in children. *Sex Roles*, 8, 1075–1080.

Comstock, G., & Paik, H. (1991). *Television and the American Child*. San Diego, CA: Academic Press.

Condry, J. (1989). *The Psychology of Television*. Hillsdale, NJ: Erlbaum.

Davis, D. M. (1990). Portrayals of women in prime time network television: Some demographic characteristics. *Sex Roles*, 23, 325–332.

Erikson, E. (1964). *Childhood and Society* (2nd ed.). New York: Norton.

Gerbner, G., & Gross, L. (1976). The scary world of TV's heavy viewer. *Psychology Today*, April, 41–45.

Hargreaves, D., & Colley, A. (1986). *The Psychology of Sex Roles*. London: Harper & Row, Publishers.

Huston, A. C., Donnerstein, E., Fairchild, H., Feshbach, N. D., Katz, P., Murray, J. P., Rubenstein, E. A., Wilcox, B. L., & Zuckerman, D. (1992). *Big World, Small Screen: The Role of Television in American Society*. Lincoln, NE: University of Nebraska Press.

Kaplan, P. (1991). *A Child's Odyssey*. St. Paul, MN: West Publishing.

Kimball, M. M. (1986). Television and sex role attitudes. In T. M. Williams (Ed.), *The Impact of Television: A Natural Experiment in Three Communities* (pp. 265–301). Orlando, FL: Academic Press.

Lauer, R. H., & Lauer, J. C. (1994). *Marriage and Family: The Quest for Intimacy*. Madison, WI: Brown & Benchmark.

Liebert, R. M., & Sprafkin, J. (1988). *The Early Window: Effects of Television on Children and Youth* (3rd ed.). New York: Pergamon Press.

Lott, B. (1989). Sexist discrimination as distancing behavior: II. Prime time television. *Psychology of Women Quarterly, 13*, 341–355.

O'Connor, J. J. (1989). What are commercials selling to children? *New York Times,* June 6, p. A28.

Piaget, J. (1954). *The Construction of Reality in the Child.* New York: Basic Books.

Rosenwasser, S. M., Lingenfelter, M., & Harrington, A. F. (1989). Nontraditional gender role portrayals on television and children's gender role perceptions. *Journal of Applied Developmental Psychology, 10,* 97–105.

Schneider, C. (1987). Children's television: The art, the business, and how it works. Lincolnwood, NJ: NTC Business Books.

Seidman, S. A. (1999). Revisiting sex role stereotyping in MTV videos. *International Journal of Instructional Media, 26,* 11–22.

Sherman, B. L., & Dominick, J. R. (1986). Violence and sex in music videos, TV, and rock-n-roll. *Journal of Communication, 36,* 79–93.

Stoneman, Z., & Brody, G. H. (1981). Peers as mediators of television food advertisements aimed at children. *Developmental Psychology, 17,* 853–858.

Strasburger, V. C. (1995). *Adolescents and the Media.* Newbury Park, CA: Sage.

Streicher, H. (1974). The girls in the cartoons. *Journal of Communication, 24,* 125–129.

Tavris, C., & Wade, C. (1984). *The Longest War: Sex Differences in Perspective* (2nd ed.). San Diego, CA: Harcourt, Brace, Jovanovich.

Thompson, T. L., & Zerbinos, E. (1995). Gender roles in animated cartoons: Has the picture changed in 20 years? *Sex Roles: A Journal of Research, 32*(9–10), 651–673.

Thorne, B. (1993). *Gender Play: Girls and Boys in School.* New Brunswick, NJ: Rutgers University Press.

Review

1. How does television influence children's development, including their attitudes and beliefs?

2. How are males and females portrayed on television?

3. What images of males and females emerge from children's cartoons?

4. How would you summarize the net impact of television on children's images of males and females?

Applications

1. Recall the television programs you watched most when you were a child. What do you remember about the ways males and females were portrayed? Did those programs reflect some of the same biases described by Witt? How do your beliefs about appropriate gender roles square with the programs you watched? What other factors have influenced your beliefs?

2. Watch a number of prime-time television programs. Use the various forms of bias Witt identifies as a checklist for each of the programs and for the commercials as well. How would you rate the programs? Are some more biased than others? How do the commercials compare with the programs? If the programs you watched are typical of all programming, what conclusions would you draw about the extent of gender bias today?

11

The Meaning of Success

The Athletic Experience and the Development of Male Identity

Michael Messner

Many selections in this anthology discuss
women's roles and how they compare with
those of men. This reading focuses exclusively
on males and their participation in organized
athletics while growing up. It has been widely
accepted that such participation develops
highly valued personal qualities such as discipline and competitiveness that will translate
into success later in life. In recent years, however, this belief has been questioned by social
scientists who point out that fewer than 1 percent of high school and college athletes actually achieve professional success in sports.
Many of these athletes see themselves as failures regardless of how outstanding their performance.

Messner's study goes beyond conventional
formulas about whether participation in
sports breeds success or failure. He explores
the lives of 30 former male athletes to discover
how their participation in sports and notions
of success in sports affected the development
of their male identity as well as their relationships to work and with other people.

What is the relationship between participation in organized sports and a young
male's developing sense of himself as a success or failure? And what is the consequent
impact on his self-image and his ability to
engage in intimate relationships with others? Through the late 1960s, it was almost

universally accepted that "sports builds
character" and that "a winner in sports will
be a winner in life." Consequently, some liberal feminists argued that since participation in organized competitive sports has
served as a major source of socialization for
males' successful participation in the public
world, girls and young women should have
equal access to sports. Lever, for instance,
concluded that if women were ever going to
be able to develop the proper competitive
values and orientations toward work and
success, it was incumbent on them to participate in sports.[1]

In the 1970s and 1980s, these uncritical
orientations toward sports have been questioned, and the "sports builds character" formula has been found wanting. Sabo points
out that the vast majority of research does
not support the contention that success in
sports translates into "work success" or
"happiness" in one's personal life.[2] In fact, a
great deal of evidence suggests that the contrary is true. Recent critical analyses of success and failure in sports have usually
started from assumptions similar to those of
Sennett and Cobb and of Rubin[3]: the disjuncture between the *ideology* of success (the
Lombardian Ethic) and the socially structured *reality* that most do not "succeed"
brings about widespread feelings of failure,
lowered self-images, and problems with interpersonal relationships.[4] The most common argument seems to be that the highly
competitive world of sports is an exaggerated reflection of advanced industrial capitalism. Within any hierarchy, one can actually work very hard and achieve a lot, yet still
be defined (and perceive oneself) as less than
successful. Very few people ever reach the
mythical "top," but those who do are made
ultravisible through the media.[5] It is tempting to view this system as a "structure of failure" because, given the definition of *success*,
the system is virtually rigged to bring about
the failure of the vast majority of participants. Furthermore, given the dominant values, the participants are apt to blame themselves for their "failure." Schafer argues that
the result of this discontinuity between
sports values–ideology and reality is a "widespread conditional self-worth" for young

athletes.[6] And as Edwards has pointed out, this problem can be even more acute for black athletes, who are disproportionately channeled into sports, yet have no "social safety net" to fall back on after "failure" in sports.

Both the traditional "sports builds character" and the more recent "sports breeds failures" formulas have a common pitfall: Each employs socialization theory in an often simplistic and mechanistic way. Boys are viewed largely as "blank slates" onto which the sports experience imprints values, appropriate "sex-role scripts," and orientations toward self and world. What is usually not taken into account is the fact that boys (and girls) come to the sports experience with an *already gendered* identity that colors their early motivations and perceptions of the meaning of games and sports. As Gilligan points out, observations of young children's game-playing show that girls bring to the activity a more pragmatic and flexible orientation toward the rules—they are more prone to make exceptions and innovations in the middle of the game in order to make the game more "fair" and maintain relationships with others.[7] Boys tend to have a more firm, even inflexible orientation to the rules of the game—they are less willing to change or alter rules in the middle of the game: to them, the rules are what protects any "fairness." This observation has profound implications for sociological research on sports and gender: The question should not be *simply* "how does sports participation affect boys [or girls]?" but should add "what is it about a developing sense of male identity that attracts males to sports in the first place? And how does this socially-constructed male identity develop and change as it interacts with the structure and values of the sports world?" In addition to being a social-psychological question, this is also a *historical* question: Since men have not at all times and places related to sports the way they at present do, it is important to explore just what kinds of men exist today. What are their needs, problems, and dreams? How do these men relate to the society they live in? And how do organized sports fit into this picture?

The 'Problem of Masculinity' and Organized Sports

In the first two decades of this century, men feared that the closing of the frontier, along with changes in the workplace, the family, and the schools was having a "feminizing" influence on society.[8] One result of the anxiety men felt was the creation of the Boy Scouts of America as a separate sphere of social life where "true manliness" could be instilled in boys *by men*.[9] The rapid rise of organized sports in roughly the same era can be attributed largely to the same phenomenon. As socioeconomic and familial changes continued to erode the traditional bases of male identity and privilege, sports became an increasingly important cultural expression of traditional male values—organized sports became a "primary masculinity-validating experience."[10]

In the post–World War II era, the bureaucratization and rationalization of work, along with the decline of the family wage and women's gradual movement into the labor force, have further undermined the "breadwinner role" as a basis for male identity, thus resulting in a "problem of masculinity" and a "defensive insecurity" among men.[11] As Mills put it, the ethic of success in postwar America "has become less widespread as fact, more confused as image, often dubious as motive, and soured as a way of life [yet] there are still compulsions to struggle, to 'amount to something.'"[12]

How have men expressed this need to "amount to something" within a social context that seems to deny them the opportunities to do so? Again, organized sports play an important role. Both on a personal-existential level for athletes and on a symbolic-ideological level for spectators and fans, sports have become one of the "last bastions" of traditional male ideas of success, of male power and superiority over—and separation from—the perceived "feminization" of society. It is likely that the rise of football as "America's number-one game" is largely the result of the comforting *clarity* it provides between the polarities of traditional male power, strength, and violence and the contemporary fears of social feminization.

Daniel Levinson's concept of the "individual life structure" is a useful place to begin to construct a gestalt of the life of the athlete.[13] Levinson demonstrates that as males develop and interact with their world, they continue to change throughout their lives. A common theme during developmental periods is the process of individuation, the struggle to separate, to "decide where he stops and where the world begins."

> In successive periods of development, as this process goes on, the person forms a clearer boundary between self and world. . . . Greater individuation allows him to be more separate from the world, to be more independent and self-generating. But it also gives him the confidence and understanding to have more intense attachments in the world and to feel more fully a part of it.[14]

This dynamic of separation and attachment provides a valuable social-psychological framework for examining the experiences and problems faced by the athlete as he gropes for and redefines success throughout his life course. In what follows, Levinson's framework is utilized to analyze the lives of 30 former athletes interviewed between 1983 and 1984. Their *interactions* with sports are examined in terms of their initial boyhood attraction to sports: how notions of success in sports connect with a developing sense of male identity; and how self-images, relationships to work and other people, change and develop after the sports career ends.

Boyhood: The Promise of Sports

Given how very few athletes actually "make it" through sports, how can the intensity with which millions of boys and young men throw themselves into athletics be explained? Are they simply pushed, socialized, or even *duped* into putting so much emphasis on athletic success? It is important here to examine just what it is that young males hope to get out of the athletic experience. And in terms of *identity*, it is crucial to examine the ways in which the structure and experience of sports activity meets the developmental needs of young males. The story of

Willy Rios sheds light on what these needs are. Rios was born in Mexico and moved to the United States at a fairly young age. He never knew his father, and his mother died when he was only nine years old. Suddenly he felt rootless, and at this time he threw himself into sports, but his motivations do not appear to be based upon a need to compete and win.

> Actually, what I think sports did for me is it brought me into kind of an instant family. By being on a Little League team, or even just playing with all kinds of different kids in the neighborhood, it brought what I really wanted, which was some kind of closeness.

Similar statements from other men suggest that a fundamental motivational factor behind many young males' sports strivings is a need for connection, "closeness" with others. But why do so many boys see *sports* as an attractive means of establishing connections with others? Chodorow argues that the process of developing a gender identity yields insecurity and ambivalence in males.[15] Males develop "rigid ego boundaries" that ensure separation from others, yet they retain a basic human need for closeness and intimacy with others. The young male, who both seeks and fears attachment with others, thus finds the rulebound structure of games and sports to be a psychologically "safe" place in which he can get (nonintimate) connection with others within a context that maintains clear boundaries, distance, and separation from others. At least for the boy who has some early successes in sports, some of these ambivalent needs can be met, for a time. But there is a catch: For Willy Rios, it was only after he learned that he would get attention (a certain kind of connection from other people for being a good athlete—indeed, that this attention was *contingent on his being good)*that narrow definitions of success, based on performance and winning, became important to him. It was years before he realized that no matter how well he performed, how successful he became, he would not get the closeness that he craved through sports.

> It got to be a product in high school. Before, it was just fun, and having accep-

tance, you know. Yet I had to work for my acceptance in high school that way, just being a jock. So it wasn't fun any more. But it was my self-identity, being a good ballplayer. I was realizing that whatever you excel in, you put out in front of you. Bring it out. Show it. And that's what I did. That was my protection. . . . It was rotten in high school, really.

This conscious striving for successful achievement becomes the primary means through which the young athlete seeks connections with other people. But the irony of the situation, for so many boys and young men like Willy Rios, is that the athletes are seeking to get something from their success in sports that sports usually cannot deliver—and the *pressure* that they end up putting on themselves to achieve that success ends up stripping them of the ability to receive the one major thing that sports really *does* have to offer: fun.

Adolescence: You're Only as Good as Your Last Game

Adolescence is probably the period of greatest insecurity in the life course, the time when the young male becomes most vulnerable to peer expectations, pressures, and judgments. None of the men interviewed for this study, regardless of their social class or ethnicity, seemed fully able to "turn a deaf ear to the crowd" during their athletic careers. The crowd, which may include immediate family, friends, peers, teammates, as well as the more anonymous fans and media, appears to be a crucially important part of the process of establishing and maintaining the self-images of young athletes. By the time they were in high school, most of the men interviewed for this study had found sports to be a primary means through which to establish a sense of manhood in the world. Especially if they were good athletes, the expectations of the crowd became very powerful and were internalized (and often *magnified*) within the young man's own expectations. As one stated, by the time he was in high school, "it was *expected* of me to do well in all of my contests—I mean by my coach and my peers, and my family. So I in turn expected to do well, and if I didn't do well, then I'd be very disappointed."

When so much is tied to your performance, the dictum that "you are only as good as your last game" is a powerful judgment. It means that the young man must continually prove, achieve, and then *re*prove, and *re*achieve his status. As a result, many young athletes learn to seek and *need* the appreciation of the crowd to feel that they are worthy human beings. But the internalized values of masculinity along with the insecure nature of the sports world mean that the young man does *not* need the crowd to feel *bad* about himself. In fact, if one is insecure enough, even "success" and the compliments and attention of other people can come to feel hollow and meaningless. For instance, 48-year-old Russ Ellis in his youth shared the basic sense of insecurity common to all young males, and in his case it was probably compounded by his status as a poor black male and an insecure family life. Athletics emerged early in life as the primary arena in which he and his male peers competed to establish a sense of self in the world. For Ellis, his small physical stature made it difficult to compete successfully in most sports, thus feeding his insecurity—he just never felt as though he belonged with "the big boys." Eventually, though, he became a top middle-distance runner. In high school, however:

Something began to happen there that later plagued me quite a bit. I started doing very well and winning lots of races and by the time the year was over, it was no longer a question for me of *placing*, but *winning*. That attitude really destroyed me ultimately. I would get into the blocks with worries that I wouldn't do well—the regular stomach problems—so I'd often run much less well than my abilities—that is, say, I'd take second or third.

Interestingly, his nervousness, fears, and anxieties did not seem to be visible to "the crowd":

I know in high school, certainly, they saw me as confident and ready to run. No one assumed I could be beaten, which fascinated me, because I had never been good at understanding how I was taken in other people's minds—maybe because I spent so much time inventing myself in their regard in my own mind. I was projecting my fear fantasies on them and taking them for reality.

In 1956 Ellis surprised everyone by taking second place in a world-class field of quarter-milers. But the fact that they ran the fastest time in the world, 46.5, seemed only to "up the ante," to increase the pressures on Ellis, then in college at UCLA.

Up to that point I had been a nice zippy kid who did good, got into the *Daily Bruin* a lot, and was well-known on campus. But now an event would come up and the papers would say, 'Ellis to face so-and-so.' So rather than my being *in* the race, I *was* the race, as far as the press was concerned. And that put a lot of pressure on me that I never learned to handle. What I did was to internalize it, and then I'd sit there and fret and lose sleep, and focus more on not winning than on how I was doing. And in general, I didn't do badly—like one year in the NCAA's I took fourth—you know, in the *national finals*. But I was focused on winning. You know, later on, people would say, 'Oh wow, you took fourth in the NCAA?—you were *that good*?' Whereas I thought of these things as *failures*, you know?

Finally, Ellis's years of training, hopes, and fears came to a head at the 1956 Olympic trials, where he failed to qualify, finishing fifth. A rival whom he used to defeat routinely won the event in the Melbourne Olympics as Ellis watched on television.

That killed me. Destroyed me. . . . I had the experience many times after that of digging down and finding that there was infinitely more down there than I ever got—I mean, I know that more than I know anything else. Sometimes I would really feel like an eagle, running. Sometimes in practice at UCLA running was just exactly like flying—and if I could have carried that attitude into events, I would have done much better. But instead, I'd worry. Yeah, I'd worry myself sick.

As suggested earlier, young males like Russ Ellis are "set up" for disappointment, or worse, by the disjuncture between the narrow Lombardian definition of success in the sports world and the reality that very few ever actually reach the top. The athlete's sense of identity established through sports is therefore insecure and problematic, *not simply* because of the high probability of "failure," but also because *success* in the sports world involves the development of a personality that *amplifies* many of the most ambivalent and destructive traits of traditional masculinity. Within the hierarchical world of sports, which in many ways mirrors the capitalist economy, one learns that if he is to survive and avoid being pushed off the ever-narrowing pyramid of success, he must develop certain kinds of relationships—to himself, to his body, to other people, and to the sport itself. In short, the successful athlete must develop a highly goal-oriented personality that encourages him to view his body as a tool, a machine, or even a weapon utilized to defeat an objectified opponent. He is likely to have difficulty establishing intimate and lasting friendships with other males because of low self-disclosure, homophobia, and cut-throat competition. And he is likely to view his public image as a "success" as far more basic and fundamental than any of his interpersonal relationships.

For most of the men interviewed, the quest for success was not the grim task it was for Russ Ellis. Most men did seem to get, at least for a time, a sense of identity (and even some happiness) out of their athletic accomplishments. The attention of the crowd, for many, affirmed their existence as males and was thus a clear motivating force. Gary Affonso, now 42 years old and a high school coach, explained that when he was in high school, he had an "intense desire to practice and compete."

I used to practice the high jump by myself for hours at a time—only got up to 5'3"—scissor! [*Laughs*] But I think part of it was, the track itself was in view of some of the classrooms, and so as I think back now, maybe I did it for the attention, to be seen. In my freshman year, I chipped my two front teeth in a football game, and after that I always had a gold tooth, and I was always self-conscious about that. Plus I had my glasses, you know. I felt a little conspicuous.

This simultaneous shyness, self-consciousness, and conspicuousness *along with* the strongly felt need for attention and external validation (attachment) so often characterize athletes' descriptions of themselves in boyhood and adolescence. The crowd, in this context, can act as a distant, and thus nonthreatening, source of attention and validation of self for the insecure male. Russ Ellis's story typifies that what sports seem to *promise* the young male—affirmation of self and connection with others—is likely to be *undermined* by the youth's actual experience in the sports world. The athletic experience also "sets men up" for another serious problem: the end of a career at a very young age.

Disengagement Trauma: A Crisis of Male Identity

For some, the end of the athletic career approaches gradually like the unwanted houseguest whose eventual arrival is at least *known* and can be planned for, thus limiting the inevitable inconvenience. For others, the athletic career ends with the shocking suddenness of a violent thunderclap that rudely awakens one from a pleasant dream. But whether it comes gradually or suddenly, the end of the playing career represents the termination of what has often become the *central aspect* of a young male's individual life structure, thus initiating change and transition in the life course.

Previous research on the disengagement crises faced by many retiring athletes has focused on the health, occupational, and financial problems frequently faced by retiring professionals.[16] These problems are especially severe for retiring black athletes, who often have inadequate educational backgrounds and few opportunities within the sports world for media or coaching jobs.[17] But even for those retiring athletes who avoid the pitfalls of financial and occupational crises, substance abuse, obesity, and ill health, the end of the playing career usually involves a crisis of identity. This identity crisis is probably most acute for retiring *professional* athletes, whose careers are coming to an end right at an age when most men's careers are beginning to take off.

As retired professional football player Marvin Upshaw stated,

> You find yourself just scrambled. You don't know which way to go. Your light, as far as you're concerned, has been turned out. You miss the roar of the crowd. Once you've heard it, you can't get away from it. There's an empty feeling— you feel everything you wanted is gone. All of a sudden you wake up and you find yourself 29, 35 years old, you know, and the one thing that has been the major part of your life is gone. It's gone.

The interaction between self and other through which the athlete attempts to solidify his identity is akin to what Cooley called "the looking-glass self." If the athletic activity and the crowd can be viewed as a *mirror* into which the athlete gazes and, in Russ Ellis's words, "invents himself," we can begin to appreciate how devastating it can be when that looking-glass is suddenly and permanently *shattered*, leaving the young man alone, isolated, and disconnected. And since young men often feel comfortable exploring close friendships and intimate relationships only *after* they have established their separate work-related (or sports-related) positional identity, relationships with other people are likely to become more problematic than ever during disengagement.

Work, Love, and Male Identity After Disengagement

Eventually, the former athlete must face reality: At a relatively young age, he has to start over. In the words of retired major league baseball player Ray Fosse, "Now I gotta get on with the rest of it." How is "the rest of it" likely to take shape for the athlete after his career as a player is over? How do men who are "out of the limelight" for a few years come to define themselves as men? How do they define and redefine success? How do the values and attitudes they learned through sports affect their lives? How do their relationships with friends and family change over time?

Many retired athletes retain a powerful drive to reestablish the important relationship with the crowd that served as the primary basis for their identity for so long. Many men throw themselves wholeheartedly into a new vocation—or a confusing *series* of vocations—in a sometimes pathetic attempt to recapture the "high" of athletic competition as well as the status of the successful athlete in the community. For instance, 35-year-old Jackie Ridgle is experiencing what Daniel Levinson calls a "surge of masculine strivings"[18] common to men in their mid 30s. Once a professional basketball player, Ridgle seems motivated now by a powerful drive to be seen once again as "somebody" in the eyes of the public. When interviewed, he had recently been hired as an assistant college basketball coach, which made him feel like he again had a chance to "be somebody."

> When I say 'successful,' that means somebody that the public looks up to just as a basketball player. Yet you don't have to be playing basketball. You can be anybody: You can be a senator or a mayor, or any number of things. That's what I call successful. Success is recognition. Sure, I'm always proud of myself. But there's that little goal there that until people respect you, then—[*Snaps fingers*]. Anybody can say, 'Oh, I know I'm the greatest thing in the world,' but *people* run the world, and when *they* say you're successful, then you *know* you're successful.

Indeed, men, especially men in early adulthood, usually define themselves primarily in terms of their position in the public world of work. Feminist literature often criticizes this establishment of male identity in terms of work—success as an expression of male privilege and ego satisfaction that comes at the expense of women and children. There is a great deal of truth to the feminist critique: A man's socially defined need to establish himself as "somebody" in the (mostly) male world of work is often accompanied by his frequent physical absence from home and his emotional distance from the family. Thus, while the man is "out there" establishing his "name" in public, the woman is usually home caring for the day-to-day and moment-to-moment needs of her family (regardless of whether or not she also has a job in the paid labor force). Tragically,

only in midlife, when the children have already "left the nest" and the woman is often ready to go out into the public world, do some men discover the importance of connection and intimacy.

Yet the interviews indicate that there is not always such a clean and clear "before-after" polarity in the lives of men between work–success and care–intimacy. The "breadwinner ethic" as a male role *has* most definitely contributed to the perpetuation of male privilege and the subordination and economic dependence of women as mothers and housekeepers. But given the reality of the labor market, where women still make only 62 cents to the male dollar, many men feel very responsible for providing the majority of the income and financial security for their families. For instance, 36-year-old Ray Fosse, whose father left his family when he was quite young, has a very strong sense of commitment and responsibility as a provider of income and stability in his own family.

> I'm working an awful lot these days and trying not to take time away from my family. A lot of times I'm putting the family to sleep, and working late hours and going to bed and getting up early and so forth. I've tried to tell my family this a lot of times: The work that I'm doing now is gonna make it easier in a few years. That's the reason I'm working now, to get that financial security, and I feel like it's coming very soon . . . but, uh, you know, you go a long day and you come home, and it's just not the quality time you'd like to have. And I think when that financial security comes in, then I'm gonna be able to forget about everything.

Jackie Ridgle's words mirror Fosse's. His two jobs and strivings to be successful in the public world mean that he has little time to spend with his wife and three children.

> I plan to someday. Very seldom do you have enough time to spend with your kids, especially nowadays, so I don't get hung up on that. The wife do sometimes, but as long as I keep a roof over their heads and let 'em know who's who, well, one day they'll respect me. But I can't just get bogged down and take any old job, you know, a filling station job or some-

thing. Ah, hell, they'll get more respect, my kids for me, right now, than they would if I was somewhere just a regular worker.

Especially for men who have been highly successful athletes (and never have had to learn to "lose gracefully"), the move from sports to work-career as a means of establishing connection and identity in the world is a "natural" transition. Breadwinning becomes a man's socially learned means of seeking attachment, both with his family and, more abstractly, with "society." What is salient (and sometimes tragic) is that the care that a woman gives her family usually puts her into direct daily contact with her family's physical, psychological, and emotional needs. A man's care is usually expressed more abstractly, often in his absence, as his work removes him from day-to-day, moment-to-moment contact with his family.

A man may want, even crave, more direct connection with his family, but that connection, and the *time* it takes to establish and maintain it, may cause him to lose the competitive edge he needs to win in the world of work—and that is the arena in which he feels he will ultimately be judged in terms of his success or failure as a man. But it is not simply a matter of *time* spent away from the family which is at issue here. As Dizard's research shows clearly, the more "success oriented" a man is, the more "instrumental" his personality will tend to be, thus increasing the psychological and emotional distance between himself and his family.[19]

If the analysis presented here is correct, the developing psychology of young boys is predisposed to be attracted to the present structure and values of the sports world, so any attempt *simply* to infuse cooperative and egalitarian values into sports is likely to be an exercise in futility. The need for equality between men and women, in the public realm as well as in the home, is a fundamental prerequisite for the humanization of men, sports, and society. One of the most important changes that men could make would be to become more equally involved in parenting. The development of early bonding between fathers and infants (in addition to that between mothers and infants), along with nonsexist childrearing in the family, schools, and sports would have far-reaching effects on society: Boys and men could grow up more psychologically secure, more able to develop balance between separation and attachment, more able at an earlier age to appreciate intimate relationships with other men without destructive and crippling competition and homophobia. A young male with a more secure and balanced personality might also be able to *enjoy* athletic activities for what they really have to offer: the opportunity to engage in healthy exercise, to push oneself toward excellence, and to bond together with others in a challenging and fun activity.

Endnotes

1. Lever, J., "Sex Differences in the Games Children Play," *Social Problems* 23, 1976.

2. Sabo, D., "Sport Patriarchy and Male Identity: New Questions about Men and Sport," *Arena Review*, 9, no. 2, 1985.

3. Sennett, R. and J. Cobb, *The Hidden Injuries of Class* (New York: Random House, 1973); and L.B. Rubin, *Worlds of Pain: Life in the Working Class Family* (New York: Basic Books, 1976).

4. Ball, D.W., "Failure in Sport," *American Sociological Review* 41, 1976; J.J. Coakley, *Sports in Society* (St. Louis: Mosby, 1978); D.S. Harris and D.S. Eitzen, "The Consequences of Failure in Sport," *Urban Life*, July 1978, 2; G.B. Leonard, "Winning Isn't Everything: It's Nothing," in *Jock: Sports and Male Identity*, ed. D. Sabo and R. Runfola (Englewood Cliffs, N.J.: Prentice-Hall, 1980); W.E. Schafer, "Sports and Male Sex Role Socialization," *Sport Sociology Bulletin* 4, Fall 1975; R.C. Townsend, "The Competitive Male as Loser," in *Jock*, eds. Sabo and Runfola, and T. Tutko and W. Bruns, *Winning Is Everything and Other American Myths* (New York: Macmillan, 1976).

5. In contrast with the importance put on sports success by millions of boys, the number who "make it" is incredibly small. There are approximately 500 players in major-league baseball, with an average career span of 7 years. Approximately 6–7 percent of all high school football players ever play in college. Roughly 8 percent of all draft-eligible college football and basketball athletes are drafted by the pros, and only 2 percent sign a profes-

sional contract. The average career for NFL athletes is now 4 years, and for the NBA it is only 3.4 years. Thus the odds of getting anywhere *near* the top are very thin—and if one is talented and lucky enough to get there his stay will be brief. See H. Edwards, "The Collegiate Athletic Arms Race: Origins and Implications of the 'Rule 48' Controversy," *Journal of Sport and Social Issues* 8, 1, Winter-Spring 1984; Harris and Eitzen, "Consequences of Failure;" and P. Hill and B. Lowe, "The Inevitable Metathesis of the Retiring Athlete," *International Review of Sports Sociology* 9, nos. 3–4, 1978.

6. Schafer, "Sport and Male Sex Role," p. 50.

7. Gilligan, C., *In a Different Voice: Psychological Theory and Women's Development* (Cambridge: Harvard University Press, 1982); J. Piaget, *The Moral Judgment of the Child* (New York: Free Press, 1965); and Lever, "Games Children Play."

8. Filene, P. G., *Him/Her/Self: Sex Roles in Modern America* (New York: Harcourt Brace Jovanovich, 1975).

9. Hantover, J., "The Boy Scouts and the Validation of Masculinity," *Journal of Social Issues* 34, 1978, 1.

10. Dubbert, J.L., *A Man's Place: Masculinity in Transition* (Englewood Cliffs, NJ: Prentice-Hall, 1979).

11. Tolson, A., *The Limits of Masculinity* (New York: Harper & Row, 1977).

12. Mills, C.W., *White Collar.* (London: Oxford University Press, 1951).

13. Levinson, D.J., *The Seasons of a Man's Life* (New York: Baltimore, 1978).

14. *Ibid.*, p. 195.

15. Chodorow, N., *The Reproduction of Mothering* (Berkeley: University of California Press, 1978).

16. Hill and Lowe, "Metathesis of Retiring Athlete," pp. 3–4; and B.D. McPherson, "Former Professional Athletes' Adjustment to Retirement," *Physician and Sports Medicine*, August 1978.

17. Edwards, "Collegiate Athletic Arms Race."

18. Levinson, *Seasons of a Man's Life*.

19. Dizard, J.E., "The Price of Success," in *Social Change in the Family*, ed. J.E. Dizard (Chicago: Community and Family Study Center, University of Chicago, 1968).

Review

1. What appear to be the differences between young girls' and young boys' orientations to game-playing activities?

2. Briefly discuss and contrast the traditional "sports build character" position with the opposing "sports build failure" position.

3. What do young males appear to be seeking in their strivings for successful athletic achievement?

4. What does the end of the athletic playing career actually represent to an athlete?

5. According to a feminist critique, what does a male's need to establish his identity in the world of work do to his home and family life?

Applications

1. *Survey:* Develop a questionnaire to be administered to male and female high school or college students. Include questions that pertain to attitudes toward beliefs about

    a. equal access of males and females to sports participation

    b. the value of sports participation to character development, career preparation, interpersonal relationships, self-image and self-esteem, and the view of one's body

    c. the ideal age range for sports participation

    d. the negative consequences of sports participation

    e. the motivation for participating in sports

    f.   the importance of others' expectations

    g. the adage "sports build character" versus "sports build failure"

    h. differences in males' and females' orientations toward sports participation

    i. effects on the athlete when playing career activities end

2. *Interview:* Conduct one or two in-depth interviews with a male high school or college athlete and an adult male who has ended his sports playing career. Ask open-ended questions that cover the same points as your questionnaire.

Part Three

Social Interaction

Interaction with others has two crucial functions in human life. First, it maintains people's values and beliefs. No human can hold to purely idiosyncratic ways and retain his or her sanity. People believe in what they do, value what they do, and act as they do because we share those things with a certain number of others.

Second, interaction shapes people's development. You are the kind of person you are because of your interaction experiences. You learn through interaction, for example, what it means to engage in social roles. Interac-

tion helps you to understand a particular role both by explicit teaching ("good girls don't act that way") and by example (observing others who hold that role).

Your roles, then, guide the way you behave. In this part, we see how gender roles affect conversations between men and women (selection 12). Because roles are a central part of social order, violations incur negative reactions. Thus, selection 13 examines why a violation (sexual betrayal by a lover) might occur and the way in which the violation affects the partners. ✦

12

'You Just Don't Understand'

The Role of Gender in Conversational Interruptions

Deborah Tannen

*The positions of men and women in society can be studied in various ways. For example, the ratio of men to women in elective office or the pay differential between genders in similar job positions can be investigated and compared. The subtle differences in the styles of interaction between men and women underlie many major facets of the role of gender. The paired concepts of "message" and "metamessage" provide some initial insight into these differences. **Message** refers to the apparent content of a communication, while **metamessage** refers to its structure and its interpretation within a relationship. Men, for instance, often feel that asking for help or directions contains the metamessage that they are less competent than the person being asked.*

In general, Tannen feels that women tend to be more attuned to metamessages than men. In this selection, she focuses primarily on the nature of conversational interruption and the part that gender plays in its occurrence. She admits a certain complexity to this interaction because many instances of assumed interruptions can be more accurately defined as "cooperative overlapping." That is, one person begins speaking over the words of another in an effort to show support for the point the first speaker is making. Women are more likely to do this when they engage in "rapport talk"—conversation that establishes connections and matches experiences. The metamessage of rapport talk, therefore, is one of empathy for conversational partners. Men, on the other hand, are more likely to engage in "report talk" by which they try to hold center stage through

storytelling, displaying knowledge or skills, and so on. The metamessage here is that the speaker is preserving or improving his status in relation to others.

Here is a joke that my father likes to tell.

A woman sues her husband for divorce. When the judge asks her why she wants a divorce, she explains that her husband has not spoken to her in two years. The judge asks the husband, "Why haven't you spoken to your wife in two years?" He replies, "I didn't want to interrupt her."

This joke reflects the commonly held stereotype that women talk too much and interrupt men.

In direct contradiction of this stereotype, one of the most widely cited findings to emerge from research on gender and language is that men interrupt women. I have never seen a popular article on the subject that does not cite this finding. It is deeply satisfying because it refutes the misogynistic stereotype that accuses women of talking too much, and it accounts for the experience reported by most women, who feel they are often cut off by men.[1]

Both claims—that men interrupt women and that women interrupt men—reflect and bolster the assumption that an interruption is a hostile act, a kind of conversational bullying. The interrupter is seen as a malevolent aggressor, the interrupted an innocent victim. These assumptions are founded on the premise that interruption is an intrusion, a trampling on someone else's right to the floor, an attempt to dominate.

The accusation of interruption is particularly painful in close relationships, where interrupting carries a load of metamessages—that a partner doesn't care enough, doesn't listen, isn't interested. These complaints strike at the core of such a relationship, since that is where most of us seek, above all, to be valued and to be heard. But your feeling interrupted doesn't always mean that someone set out to interrupt you. And being accused of interrupting when you know you didn't intend to is as frustrating as being cut off before you've made your point.

Because the complaint "You interrupt me" is so common in intimate relationships, and because it raises issues of dominance and control that are fundamental to the politics of gender, the relationship between interruption and dominance bears closer inspection. For this, it will be necessary to look more closely at what creates and constitutes interruption in conversation.

Do Men Interrupt Women?

Researchers who report that men interrupt women come to their conclusion by recording conversation and counting instances of interruption. In identifying interruptions, they do not take into account the substance of the conversations they studied: what was being talked about, speakers' intentions, their reactions to each other, and what effect the "interruption" had on the conversation. Instead, mechanical criteria are used to identify interruptions. Experimental researchers who count things need operational criteria for identifying things to count. But ethnographic researchers—those who go out and observe people doing naturally whatever it is the researchers want to understand—are as wary of operational criteria as experimenters are wedded to them. Identifying interruptions by mechanical criteria is a paradigm case of these differences in points of view.

Linguist Adrian Bennett explains that "overlap" is mechanical: Anyone could listen to a conversation, or a tape recording of one, and determine whether or not two voices were going at once. But interruption is inescapably a matter of interpretation regarding individuals' rights and obligations. To determine whether a speaker is violating another speaker's rights, you have to know a lot about both speakers and the situation. For example, what are the speakers saying? How long has each one been talking? What has their past relationship been? How do they feel about being cut off? And, most important, what is the content of the second speaker's comment, relative to the first: Is it a reinforcement, a contradiction, or a change in topic? In other words, what is the second speaker trying to do? Apparent support can subtly undercut, and an apparent change of topic can be an indirect means of support—as, for example, when an adolescent boy passes up the opportunity to sympathize with his friend so as not to reinforce the friend's one-down position.

All these and other factors influence whether or not anyone's speaking rights have been violated and, if they have been, how significant the violation is. Sometimes you feel interrupted but you don't mind. At other times, you mind very much. Finally, different speakers have different conversational styles, so a speaker might feel interrupted even if the other did not intend to interrupt.[2]

Here is an example that was given by Candace West and Don Zimmerman to show a man interrupting a woman. In this case I think the interruption is justified in terms of interactional rights. (The vertical lines show overlap.)

> FEMALE: So uh you really can't bitch when you've got all those on the same day but I uh asked my physics professor if I couldn't change | that
>
> MALE: | Don't touch that.
>
> FEMALE: What? (pause)
>
> MALE: I've got everything jus' how I want it in that notebook, you'll screw it up leafin' through it like that.[3]

West and Zimmerman consider this an interruption because the second speaker began while the first speaker was in the middle of a word (*change*). But considering what was being said, the first speaker's rights may not have been violated. Although there are other aspects of this man's talk that make him seem like a conversational bully, interrupting to ask the woman to stop leafing through his notebook does not in itself violate her right to talk. Many people, seeing someone handling their property in a way that was destroying their painstaking organization of it, would feel justified in asking that person to stop immediately, without allowing further damage to be done while waiting for the appropriate syntactic and rhetorical moment to take the floor.

Sociologist Stephen Murray gives an example of what he regards as a prototypical case of interruption where someone cuts in to talk about a different topic when the first speaker has not even made a single point. Here is his example:

H: I think｜that

W: ｜Do you want some more salad?

This simple exchange shows how complex conversation can be. Many people feel that a host has the right, if not the obligation, to offer food to guests, whether or not anyone is talking. Offering food, like asking to have salt or other condiments passed, takes priority, because if the host waited until no one was talking to offer food, and guests waited until no one was talking to ask for platters beyond their reach, then the better the conversation, the more likely that many guests would go home hungry.

This is not to say that any time is the right time to interrupt to offer food. If a host *habitually* interrupts to offer food *whenever* a partner begins to say something, or interrupts to offer food just when a speaker reaches the climax of a story or the punchline of a joke, it might seem like a violation of rights or the expression of mischievous motives. But the accusation of interrupting cannot be justified on the basis of a single instance like this one. Conversational style differences muddy the waters. It may be that one person grew up in a home where conversation was constant and all offers of food overlapped ongoing talk, while another grew up in a home where talk was sparse and food was offered only when there was a lull in the conversation. If two such people live together, it is likely that one will overlap to offer food, expecting the other to go on speaking, but the overlap-aversant partner will feel interrupted and maybe even refuse to resume talking. Both would be right, because interruption is not a mechanical category. It is a matter of individual perceptions of rights and obligations, as they grow out of individual habits and expectations.

In these examples, an overlap—two voices talking at once—is not necessarily an interruption, that is, a violation of someone's speaking rights. There are also instances where speakers do feel that their rights have been infringed on, and may even feel interrupted, when there is no overlap. An example of such an instance appears in Alice Greenwood's analysis of dinner table conversations among her three children (twins Denise and Dennis, twelve, and Stacy, eleven) and their friends. In the following example, Denise and Stacy have performed a verbal routine for the benefit of their brother's dinner guest, Mark, fourteen. This dialogue, which Greenwood calls the Betty routine, is one the sisters often perform together. Before they start, they get Mark's attention: Denise says, "Listen to this. Mark, listen to this." Then Denise and Dennis announce, "It's so funny." But Mark doesn't agree:

DENISE: [In Betty voice] Excuse me, are you Betty?. . .

STACY: Oh, yes.

DENISE: [In Betty voice] Betty who?

STACY: [In Betty voice] Bettybitabitabittabuttabut— [Dennis, Denise, and Stacy laugh.]

MARK: Whaaaat? [Dennis, Denise, and Stacy laugh hysterically.][4]

Although this routine sparks delighted laughter from the three siblings, and on other occasions also sparked laughter among friends, Mark did not laugh and claimed not to get the joke. Denise and Stacy tried to explain it to him:

DENISE: I said, 'Betty who?' like you say 'Betty Jones.' Then she says, 'Bettybitabita—'

➜ DENNIS: Did anyone eat from this yet?

MARK: No. Actually, what I was going to say was can I try that soup? It looks quite good.

➜ DENISE: Listen, listen, listen, listen.

MARK: Say it in slow motion, okay?

STACY: Betty bought a bit of bitter butter and she said, 'This butter's bitter. If I put it in my batter, it will make my batter bitter.' So Betty bought a bit of better butter to—

DENISE: You never heard that before?

MARK: No. Never.

DENISE: Mark, seriously?

MARK: Seriously.

DENISE: It's like the
  famous to—|

→ STACY: |tongue twister.

MARK: No. The famous tongue twister is
Peterpiperpicked—|

→ DENISE: |Same thing. It's like
that. It's like that one.

MARK: You keep interrupting me.

In this excerpt, Denise and Stacy repeatedly cut each other off, as shown by the arrows and vertical lines, but there is no indication that either resents it. They do seem to mind their brother Dennis's overlapping to ask about the food ("Did anyone eat from this yet?") because he's interrupting their explanation (Denise protests, "Listen, listen, listen, listen"). The girls are supporting each other, talking on the same team.

Most striking is Mark's complaint, "You keep interrupting me." This is intriguing because what Mark was saying when he got interrupted ("No. The famous tongue twister is Peterpiperpicked—") was actually an interruption of the girls' explanation, even though his voice did not overlap theirs. The same is true for the previous time they "interrupted" him: Just as Denise said, "All right. Watch this," Mark began to ask, "Is it as funny as a—" but he didn't get to finish because Dennis laughed and Denise launched the routine, as announced. So Mark's protest seems like a real-life instance of the humorous line "Don't talk while I'm interrupting you."

Mark also took an oppositional stance, even though he was really supporting rather than disagreeing. The girls just said that their tongue twister was "like the famous tongue twister." If Mark had simply offered "the famous tongue twister" (Peter Piper picked a peck of pickled peppers), then his interruption would have been supportive, furnishing the end of Denise's explanation. Instead, he began by saying "No," as if they had been claiming that theirs was *the* famous tongue twister.

In this conversation, the girls were trying to include Mark in their friendly banter. Greenwood found, in studying her children's conversations with their friends, that the more interruptions a conversation contained, the more comfortable the children felt in it and the more they enjoyed it. But Mark refused to be part of their fun by insisting on his right to hold the floor without interruption. Perhaps his being a few years older was a factor. Perhaps he did not like being cast in the role of audience. Perhaps he felt he was being put down when Denise asked, "You never heard that before? . . . Mark, seriously?" Whatever the reason, Denise, Stacy, and Dennis were doing rapport-talk, and Mark wanted to do something more like report-talk. It is not surprising that Denise later told her mother that she didn't like Mark.

Although Denise did "interrupt" Mark to tell him he had the idea ("Same thing. It's like that"), there is no evidence that she was trying to dominate him. Furthermore, though Denise and Stacy interrupted each other, there is no evidence that they were trying to dominate each other. There is, however, some evidence that Mark might have been trying to dominate Stacy and Denise, for example by refusing to laugh at their jokes and rejecting their explanation of their verbal routine, even though he did not overlap their speech. So it is not the interruption that constitutes dominance but what speakers are trying to do when they talk to each other.

Claiming that an interruption is a sign of dominance assumes that conversation is an activity in which one speaker speaks at a time, but this reflects ideology more than practice. Most Americans *believe* one speaker *ought* to speak at a time, regardless of what they actually do. I have recorded conversations in which many voices were heard at once and it was clear that everyone was having a good time. When I asked people afterward their impressions of the conversation, they told me that they had enjoyed themselves. But when I played the tape back for them, and they heard that people had been talking all together, they were embarrassed and made comments like "Oh, God, do we really do that?" as if they had been caught with their verbal pants down.

In a book entitled *Conversational Style*, I analyzed two and a half hours of dinner table conversation among six friends. Looking back on the conversation, some of the friends told me they had felt that others had "dominated" the conversation—and when I first listened to the tape, I too thought that it looked that way. But the accused pleaded innocent: They claimed they had not intended to dominate; in fact, they wondered why the others had been so reticent. Only by comparing different parts of the conversation to each other was I able to solve the puzzle.

The inadvertent interruptions—and the impression of domination—came about because the friends had different conversational styles. I call these styles "high considerateness" and "high involvement," because the former gave priority to being considerate of others by not imposing, and the latter gave priority to showing enthusiastic involvement. Some apparent interruptions occurred because high-considerateness speakers expected longer pauses between speaking turns. While they were waiting for the proper pause, the high-involvement speakers got the impression they had nothing to say and filled in to avoid an uncomfortable silence. Other unintended interruptions resulted when high-involvement speakers chimed in to show support and participation: High-considerateness speakers misinterpreted the choral support as attempts to yank the floor away from them, and they stopped, to avoid what to them would have been a cacophony of two voices at once. Ironically, these interruptions were not only the interpretations of the apparent victims—they were their creations. When high-involvement speakers used exactly the same techniques with each other, the effect was positive rather than negative: Chiming in with speakers didn't stop anybody from talking. It greased the conversational wheels and enlivened spirits. . . .

Cultural Differences

In my study of dinner table conversation, the three high-involvement speakers were New York City natives of Jewish background. Of the three high-considerateness speakers, two were Catholics from southern California and one was from London, England. Although a sample of three does not prove anything, nearly everyone agrees that many (obviously not all) Jewish New Yorkers, many New Yorkers who are not Jewish, and many Jews who are not from New York have high-involvement styles and are often perceived as interrupting in conversations with speakers from different backgrounds, such as the Californians in my study. But many Californians expect shorter pauses than many Midwesterners or New Englanders, so in conversations between them, the Californians end up interrupting. Just as I was considered extremely polite when I lived in New York but was sometimes perceived as rude in California, a polite Californian I know was shocked and hurt to find herself accused of rudeness when she moved to Vermont.

The cycle is endless. Linguists Ron and Suzanne Scollon show that Midwestern Americans, who may find themselves interrupted in conversations with easterners, become aggressive interrupters when they talk to Athabaskan Indians, who expect much longer pauses. Many Americans find themselves interrupting when they talk to Scandinavians, but Swedes and Norwegians are perceived as interrupting by the longer-pausing Finns, who are themselves divided by regional differences with regard to length of pauses and rate of speaking. As a result, Finns from certain parts of the country are stereotyped as fast talking and pushy, and those from other parts of the country are stereotyped as slow talking and stupid, according to Finnish linguists Jaakko Lehtonen and Kari Sajavaara.

Anthropologists have written about many cultures in the world where talking together is valued in casual conversation. This seems to be the norm in more parts of the world than the northern European norm of one-speaker-speaks-at-a-time. Karl Reisman coined the term *contrapuntal conversations* to describe the overlapping style he observed in Antigua. Karen Watson borrowed his term to describe Hawaiian children's verbal routines in which they jointly joke and engage in "talk story." Watson explains that for these children, taking a turn is not a matter of individual performance but "partnership in performance." Michael Moerman makes similar observations about Thai conversation. Reiko Hayashi finds far more simultaneous speech among Japanese speakers in casual conversation than among Americans. Jeffrey Shultz, Susan Florio, and Frederick Erickson found that an Italian-American boy who was considered a serious behavior problem at school was simply chiming in as was appropriate and normal in his home. All of these researchers document overlapping speech that is not destructive, not intended to exercise dominance and violate others' rights. Instead, it is cooperative, a means of showing involvement, participation, connection. In short, simultaneous talk can be rapport-talk.

Women as Cooperative Overlappers

Paradoxically (in light of the men-interrupt-women research), and most important for our discussion here, another group that has been found to favor conversations in which more than one person speaks at a time is women. Folklorist Susan Kalcik was one of the first to observe women's use of overlapping talk by taping a women's group. In reviewing studies that compared all-male and all-female interaction, linguists Deborah James and Janice Drakich found that, of those reporting differences, the great majority observed more interruptive talk among the females.

Linguist Carole Edelsky inadvertently uncovered women's preference for overlapping talk when she set out to determine who talked more at a series of faculty committee meetings. She found that men talked more than women if one person was speaking while the others listened silently, but women talked as much as men during periods when more than one voice was heard at the same time. In other words, women were less likely

to participate when the situation felt more like report-talk, more likely to do so when it felt like rapport-talk. Cooperative overlapping framed parts of the meeting as rapport-talk.

Following is an example of women in casual conversation overlapping in a highly cooperative and collaborative way. It comes from a conversation recorded at a kitchen table by linguist Janice Hornyak, who was a party to the conversation. Jan and her mother, Peg, who are from a southern state, were visiting relatives in the North, where Jan got to see snow for the first time. Peg and Marge, who are sisters-in-law, reminisce, for Jan's benefit, about the trials of raising small children in a part of the country where it snows. (Jan's mother raised her older children in the North but moved to the South before Jan was born.)

PEG: The part I didn't like was putting everybody's snow pants and boots and |

→ MARGE: |Oh yeah, that | was the worst part

PEG: | and scarves

→ MARGE: and get them all bundled up in boots and everything and they're out for half an hour and then they come in and they're all covered with this snow and they get that *shluck* all over |

→ PEG: |All that wet stuff and

→ JAN: That's why adults don't like snow, huh?

MARGE: That's right.

PEG: Throw all the stuff in the dryer and then they'd come in and sit for half | an hour

MARGE: | and in a little while they'd want to go back out again.

PEG: Then they want to go back out again.[5]

All three speakers in this example initiate turns that either latch onto or intrude into other speakers' turns. Peg and Marge play a conversational duet: They jointly hold one conversational role, overlapping each other without exhibiting (or reporting) resentment at being interrupted.

Hornyak points out the even more intriguing fact that these speakers often end a comment with the conjunction *and*, creating the appearance of interruption when there is none, as when Peg says, "All that wet stuff and." Hornyak claims that this strategy is used by many speakers in her family, and is satisfying and effective when used with each other. She is criticized, however, for using this same strategy among others, who protest that it confuses them. They may even get the impression that someone who ends a sentence with *and* doesn't know whether or not she is finished.

Why would anyone want to create the impression of interruption when there is none? One reason that speakers from some cultural groups leave little or no pause between turns is that they see silence in friendly conversation as a sign of lack of rapport. Overlapping is a way to keep conversation going without risking silence. I should note, though, that Hornyak and the family members she taped do not speak loudly or quickly or all at once. Their overlaps, though frequent, are brief, ending sentences with *and* is a way to achieve the appearance of interruption when there is minimal overlap.

Though Hornyak feels the strategy of creating the appearance of overlap by ending a sentence with *and* is peculiar to her family, others have commented that they know people who do this. At least one man I spoke to said that his mother (to his father's chagrin) regularly ends her comments with *and uh*, and that her mother and all her sisters do it too—but her father and brother don't. This man also considered this a family style. Although it clearly does run in families, the style seems to result from a combination of gender and culture.

Gender and culture also dovetail in another example of the false appearance of interruption. William Labov and David Fanshel, in a study of a psychotherapy session between a nineteen-year-old patient called Rhoda and a social worker, show that Rhoda never ended a speaking turn by falling silent. Instead, when she had said all she wanted to say, she began to repeat herself. Her repetitions were an invitation to the therapist to begin speaking by interrupting her. Both client and therapist were New Yorkers, Jewish, and women.

Cultural Explanations: A Mixed Blessing

The realization that people with similar cultural backgrounds have similar ways of talking often comes as a revelation and a relief to people who thought they had personal quirks or even psychological problems. For example, a Greek-American man I interviewed for a study of indirectness in conversation had been told by friends and lovers throughout his life that there was something wrong with him, because he always beat around the bush instead of coming out and saying what was on his mind. He told me that his parents spoke that way, and I told him that I had found that Greeks often tended to be more indirect than Americans, and Greek-Americans were somewhere in the middle. This man was enormously relieved, saying that my explanation rang a bell. He went on to say:

> I see it as either something heroically different or a real impediment. . . . Most of the time I think of it as a problem. And I can't really sort it out from my family and background. . . I don't know if it's Greek. I just know that it's me. And it feels a little better to know that it's Greek.

Viewing his "family" style as an ethnic style relieved this man of the burden of individual pathology otherwise implied by being different from most of the people he communicated with.[6]

But the tendency of people from similar cultural backgrounds to have habitual ways of speaking that are similar to each other's and different from those of people from other cultural backgrounds has had unfortunate, even tragic consequences. When people who are identified as culturally different have different conversational styles, their ways of speaking become the basis for negative stereotyping. As I mentioned earlier, anti-Semitism classically attributes loudness, aggressiveness, and "pushiness" to

Jewish people—making a leap from ways of speaking to character. For example, in a letter to Henry Miller, Lawrence Durrell described a Jewish fellow writer: "He is undependable, erratic, has bad judgment, loud-mouthed, pushing, vulgar, thoroughly Jewish. . . ."[7]

The perception that Jews (or New Yorkers—the categories are often fused in many people's minds) are loud and pushy simply blames the minority group for the effect of their style *in interaction with others who use a different style*. Anthropologist Thomas Kochman shows that a parallel style difference underlies the stereotyping of "community" blacks as inconsiderate, overbearing, and loud. When members of one group have the power to persecute members of the other, the results of such misjudgments are truly tragic.

If cultural differences are likely to cause misjudgment in personal settings, they are certain to do so in international ones. I would wager that the much-publicized antipathy between Nancy Reagan and Raisa Gorbachev resulted from cultural differences in conversational style. According to Nancy Reagan, "From the moment we met, she talked and *talked*—so much that I could barely get a word in, edgewise or otherwise." I suspect that, if anyone asked Raisa Gorbachev, she would say she'd been wondering why her American counterpart never said anything and made her do all the conversational work.[8]

Of course not all Russians or Jews or New Yorkers or blacks are high-involvement speakers. Many use the style in some situations but not others. Some have erased, modified, or never used such styles at all. No group is homogeneous; for example, the high-involvement style I describe is more common among East European than German Jewish speakers. But many Jewish speakers do use some variety of high-involvement style in some situations, as do many Italian, Greek, Spanish, South American, Slavic, Armenian, Arab, African, and Cape Verdean speakers—and members of many other groups I have not mentioned.

A Word of Caution

The juxtaposition of these two lines of inquiry—gender and interruption on the one hand, and ethnicity as conversational style on the other—poses a crucial and troubling dilemma. If it is theoretically wrong-headed, empirically indefensible, and morally insidious to claim that speakers of particular ethnic groups are pushy, dominating, or inconsiderate because they appear to interrupt in conversations with speakers of different, more "mainstream" ethnic backgrounds, can it be valid to embrace research that "proves" that men dominate women because they appear to interrupt them in conversation? If the researchers who have found men interrupting women in conversation were to "analyze" my audiotapes of conversations among New York Jewish and California Christian speakers, they would no doubt conclude that the New Yorkers "interrupted" and "dominated"—the impression of the Californians present. This was not, however, the intention of the New Yorkers, and—crucially—not the result of their behavior alone. Rather, the pattern of apparent interruption resulted from the *difference* in styles. In short, such "research" would do little more than apply the ethnocentric standards of the majority group to the culturally different behavior of the minority group.

In a parallel way, claims that men dominate women because they interrupt them in conversation accept the assumption that conversation is an enterprise in which only one voice should be heard at a time. This erroneous assumption has significant negative consequences for women. Many women, when they talk among themselves in situations that are casual, friendly, and focused on rapport, use cooperative overlapping: Listeners talk along with speakers to show participation and support. It is this practice, when overheard, that has led men to stereotype women as noisily clucking hens. And women who enjoy such conversations when they have them may later feel embarrassed and guilty, because they accept the one-speaker-at-a-time ethic that is more appropriate to men's "public speaking" conversational style, or report-talk, than it is to women's "private speaking" style, which emphasizes rapport-talk.

Juxtaposing research claiming that men interrupt women with my study of dinner table conversation provides a linguistic parallel but a political contrast. Jews are a minority in the United States, as are blacks and members of the other groups that I mentioned as having high-involvement style. Minorities are at a disadvantage. But in the male-female constellation, it is women who are at a social and cultural disadvantage. This transforms the political consequences of blaming one group for dominating the other.

Most people would agree that women as a class are dominated by men as a class in our culture, as in most if not all cultures of the world. Therefore, many would claim that viewing gender differences as cross-cultural communication is copping out, covering up real domination with a cloth of cultural difference. Though I am sympathetic to this view, my conscience tells me that we cannot have it both ways. If we accept the research in one paradigm—the men-interrupt-women one—then we are forced into a position that claims that high-involvement speakers, such as blacks and Jews and, in many circumstances, women, are pushy, aggressive, or inconsiderately or foolishly noisy.[9]

The consequences of such a position are particularly dangerous for American women of ethnic or regional backgrounds that favor high-involvement conversational styles. The United States witnessed a dramatic example of just such consequences when Geraldine Ferraro, a New Yorker of Italian extraction, ran for vice president and was labeled a bitch by Barbara Bush, a woman of more "mainstream" background. The view of high-involvement style as dominance, taken from the men-interrupt-women paradigm, yields the repugnant conclusion that many women (including many of us of African, Caribbean, Mediterranean, South American, Levantine, Arab, and East European backgrounds) are dominating, aggressive, and pushy—qualities that are perceived as far more negative in women than in men.

As a woman who has personally experienced the difficulty many women report in making themselves heard in some interactions with men (especially "public" situations), I am tempted to embrace the studies that men interrupt women: It would allow me to explain my experience in a way that blames others. As a high-involvement-style speaker, however, I am offended by the labeling of a feature of my conversational style as loathsome, based on the standards of those who do not share or understand it. As a Jewish woman raised in New York who is not only offended but frightened by the negative stereotyping of New Yorkers and women and Jews, I recoil when scholarly research serves to support the stereotyping of a group of speakers as possessing negative intentions and character. As a linguist and researcher, I know that the workings of conversation are more complex than that. As a human being, I want to understand what is going on.

Who's Interrupting?

The key to understanding what is going on, at least in part, is the distinction between rapport-talk and report-talk—the characteristic ways that most women use language to create a community and many men use it to manage a contest. As a result, though both women and men complain of being interrupted by each other, the behaviors they are complaining about are different.

In many of the comments I heard from people I interviewed, men felt interrupted by women who overlapped with words of agreement and support and anticipation of how their sentences and thoughts would end. If a woman supported a man's story by elaborating on a point different from the one he had intended, he felt his right to tell his own story was being violated. He interpreted the intrusion as a struggle for control of the conversation.

For example, a man was telling about some volunteer work he had done as a cashier at a charity flea market. At the end of the day, there had been a shortfall in his cash register, which he had to make up from his own pocket. A woman listening to him kept overlapping his story with comments and expressions of sympathy, elaborating on how unfair it was for him to have to pay when he had been volunteering his time. As a matter of fact, the man had not been telling his experience in order to emphasize the injustice of it, and he felt interrupted and "manipulated" by the woman, whom he saw as trying to take over his story. Her offense was an excess (in his view) of rapport-talk.

This brings me back to my father, and why he might take particular relish in telling the joke about the man who didn't talk to his wife because he didn't want to interrupt her. My father believes that only one person should speak at a time. As a result, he often has a hard time getting the floor in conversations involving my mother, my two sisters, and me, since we overlap and do not leave pauses between our comments. He also feels that once he begins to talk, he should be permitted to continue until he is satisfied that he has explained his ideas completely. My mother and sisters and I feel that in a casual conversation among friends or family, it is acceptable to chime in when you think you know what others are getting at; if you're wrong, they are free to correct you, but if you're right, everyone prefers the show of connection and rapport that comes from being understood without having to spell everything out.

My father's view of this situation surfaced some years ago when he was talking and my mother chimed in. He wistfully sighed and said to my mother, "You have an advantage, dear. If I want to say something, I have to wait until no one else is talking. But you can say what you want whenever you think of it." For her part, my mother can't understand why my father needs special privileges to say something—why doesn't he just jump in like the rest of us? And I can recall feeling as a teenager that listening to my father, who is an attorney, explain something to me was like hearing a summation to the jury.

So both the man and the women in my family feel oppressed, at times, by others' ways of talking—he because he is interrupted and doesn't find the pauses he needs to enter the conversation, and we because he forbids and eschews overlaps and won't just take part like everyone else. The women in

the family value overlaps and interruptions as shows of involvement in rapport-talk, and the man in the family values not being imposed on in report-talk. And he approaches casual conversations at home more like report-talk than the women do.

Then what is the source of women's complaints that they are interrupted by men? Just as my sisters, my mother, and I expect my father to toss out brief comments like the rest of us, men who approach conversation as a contest in which everyone competes for the floor might be treating women as equals, expecting them to compete for the floor like everyone else. But women are far less likely to do so, since they do not regard conversations as contests and have little experience in fighting for the right to be heard. Quite the opposite, Elizabeth Aries found that women who talked a lot in discussion groups often invited quieter group members to speak.

Uncooperative Overlapping

Whereas women's cooperative overlaps frequently annoy men by seeming to co-opt their topic, men frequently annoy women by usurping or switching the topic. An example of this kind of interruption is portrayed in "You're Ugly, Too," a short story by Lorrie Moore. The heroine of this story, a history professor named Zöe, has had an ultrasound scan to identify a growth in her abdomen. Driving home after the test, she looks at herself in the rear-view mirror and recalls a joke:[10]

> She thought of the joke about the guy who visits his doctor and the doctor says, "Well, I'm sorry to say, you've got six weeks to live."
>
> "I want a second opinion," says the guy. . . .
>
> "You want a second opinion? O.K.," says the doctor. "You're ugly, too." She liked that joke. She thought it was terribly, terribly funny.

Later in the story, at a Halloween party, Zöe is talking to a recently divorced man named Earl whom her sister has fixed her up with. Earl asks, "What's your favorite joke?" This is what happens next:

"Uh, my favorite joke is probably—O.K., all right. This guy goes into a doctor's office, and—"

"I think I know this one," interrupted Earl, eagerly. He wanted to tell it himself. "A guy goes into a doctor's office, and the doctor tells him he's got some good news and some bad news—that one, right?"

"I'm not sure," said Zöe. "This might be a different version."

"So," the guy says, "Give me the bad news first," and the doctor says, "O.K.—You've got three weeks to live." And the guy cries, "Three weeks to live! Doctor, what is the good news?" And the doctor says, "Did you see that secretary out front? I finally fucked her."

Zöe frowned.

"That's not the one you were thinking of?"

"No." There was accusation in her voice. "Mine was different."

"Oh," said Earl. He looked away and then back again. "What kind of history do you teach?"

When Earl interrupts Zöe, it is not to support her joke but to tell her joke for her. To make matters worse, the joke he tells isn't just different; it's offensive. When he finds out that his joke was not the same as hers, he doesn't ask what hers was. Instead, he raises another topic entirely ("What kind of history do you teach?").

Most people would agree that Earl's interruption violated Zöe's speaking rights, because it came as Zöe was about to tell a joke and usurped the role of joke teller. But Zöe yielded quickly to Earl's bid to tell her joke. As soon as he said "some good news and some bad news," it was obvious that he had a different joke in mind. But instead of answering "No" to his question ". . . that one, right?" Zöe said, "I'm not sure. This might be a different version," supporting his bid and allowing for agreement where there really was disagreement. Someone who viewed conversation as a contest could have taken back the floor at this point, if not before. But Zöe seemed to view conversation as a game requiring each speaker to support the other's words. If they had known each other well

enough to argue about this later, Earl might have challenged, "Why didn't you stop me when you saw I was going to tell a different joke, instead of letting me go on and then getting mad?"

Another part of the same story shows that it is not overlap that creates interruption but conversational moves that wrench a topic away from another speaker's course. Zöe feels a pain in her stomach, excuses herself, and disappears into the bathroom. When she returns, Earl asks if she's all right, and she tells him that she has been having medical tests. Rather than asking about her health, Earl gives her some food that was passed around while she was in the bathroom. Chewing, she says, "With my luck it'll be a gall bladder operation." Earl changes the subject: "So your sister's getting married? Tell me, really, what you think about love." Zöe begins to answer:

"All right. I'll tell you what I think about love. Here is a love story. This friend of mine—"

"You've got something on your chin," said Earl, and he reached over to touch it.

Like offering food, taking something off someone's face may take priority over talk, but doing so just as Zöe starts to tell a story seems like a sign of lack of interest in her story, and lack of respect for her right to continue it. Furthermore, this is not an isolated incident, but one in a series. Earl did not follow up Zöe's revelation about her health with questions or support, didn't offer advice, and didn't match her revelation with a mutual one about himself. Instead, he shifted the conversation to another topic—love—which he might have felt was more appropriate than a gallbladder operation for initiating a romantic involvement. For the same reason, taking something off her chin may have been too good an opportunity for touching her face to pass up. Indeed, many of his moves seem to be attempts to steer the conversation in the direction of flirting.

Who's Driving?

Interruption, then, has little to do with beginning to make verbal sounds while someone else is speaking, though it does have to do with issues of dominance, control, and showing interest and caring. Women and men feel interrupted by each other because of the differences in what they are trying to accomplish with talk. Men who approach conversation as a contest are likely to expend effort not to support the other's talk but to lead the conversation in another direction, perhaps one in which they can take center stage by telling a story or joke or displaying knowledge. But in doing so, they expect their conversational partners to mount resistance. Women who yield to these efforts do so not because they are weak or insecure or deferential but because they have little experience in deflecting attempts to grab the conversational wheel. They see steering the conversation in a different direction not as a move in a game, but as a violation of the rules of the game.

Being blamed for interrupting when you know you didn't mean to is as frustrating as feeling interrupted. Nothing is more disappointing in a close relationship than being accused of bad intentions when you know your intentions were good, especially by someone you love who should understand you, if anyone does. Women's effusion of support can be irritating to men who would rather meet with verbal sparring. And a left jab meant in the spirit of sparring can become a knockout if your opponent's fists are not raised to fight. . . .

Endnotes

1. The researchers most often cited for the finding that men interrupt women are Candace West and Don Zimmerman (for example, West and Zimmerman, 1983, 1985; Zimmerman and West, 1975). However, many others have come to similar conclusions (for example, Eakins and Eakins, Greif). Deborah James and Janice Drakich are currently reviewing the literature on interruption.

2. The point that violation of speaking rights is a matter of degree is made by Stephen Murray.

3. The example comes from West and Zimmerman, 1983, p. 105. The numbers in parentheses show seconds of pause. Vertical lines show overlap: two voices speaking at once.

4. Transcription is based on Greenwood's, with minor adjustments for readability and changes of names. Vertical lines show latching: The second speaker began with no overlap but no perceptible pause either.

5. Janice Hornyak recorded, transcribed, and analyzed this excerpt in conjunction with my course in discourse analysis at Georgetown University, spring 1989.

6. My study of indirectness in Greek and American conversational style is reported in Tannen (1982).

7. The excerpt from Durrell's letter to Miller is taken from Vivian Gornick, "Masters of Self-congratulation," a review of *The Durrell-Miller Letters*, ed. by Ian S. MacNiven, in *The New York Times Book Review*, November 20, 1988, p. 47.

8. The quote from Nancy Reagan is from her book, *My Turn*, as excerpted in *Newsweek*, October 23, 1989, p. 66.

9. The argument that Maltz and Borker and I are covering up real male domination with the cross-cultural hypothesis is cogently argued in a paper by Nancy Henley and Cheris Kramarae.

10. Lorrie Moore, "You're Ugly, Too," *The New Yorker*, July 3, 1989, pp. 34, 38, 40.

References

Eakins, Barbara Westbrook, and R. Gene Eakins. 1978. *Sex Differences in Communication*. Boston: Houghton Mifflin.

Greenwood, Alice. 1989. *Discourse Variation and Social Comfort: A Study of Topic Initiation and Interruption Patterns in the Dinner Conversation of Preadolescent Children*. Ph.D. dissertation, City University of New York.

Greif, Esther Blank. 1980. "Sex Differences in Parent-Child Conversations." *Women's Studies International Quarterly* 3:2/3, 253–258.

Henley, Nancy, and Cheris Kramarae. Forthcoming. "Miscommunication, Gender, and Power." *Handbook of Miscommunication and Problematic Talk*, ed. by Nikolas Coupland, John Wiemann, and Howard Giles. Bristol: Multilingual Matters.

James, Deborah, and Janice Drakich. 1989. "Understanding Gender Differences in Amount of Talk." Ms., Linguistics Department, University of Toronto, Scarborough Campus.

Maltz, Daniel N., and Ruth A. Borker. 1982. "A Cultural Approach to Male-Female Miscommunication." *Language and Social*

Identity, ed. by John J. Gumperz, 196–216. Cambridge: Cambridge University Press.

Murray, Stephen O. 1985. "Toward a Model of Members' Methods for Recognizing Interruptions." *Language in Society* 13, 31–41

Tannen, Deborah. 1982. "Ethnic Style in Male-Female Conversation." *Language and Social Identity*, ed. by John J. Gumperz, 217–231. Cambridge: Cambridge University Press.

West, Candace, and Don H. Zimmerman. 1983. "Small Insults: A Study of Interruptions in Cross-Sex Conversations Between Unacquainted Persons." *Language, Gender, and Society*, ed. by Barrie Thorne, Cheris Kramarae, and Nancy Henley, 103–117. Rowley, MA: Newbury House.

West, Candace, and Don H. Zimmerman. 1985. "Gender, Language, and Discourse." *Handbook of Discourse Analysis*, vol. 4: *Discourse Analysis in Society*, ed. by Tuen A. van Dijk, 103–124. London: Academic Press.

Zimmerman, Don H., and Candace West. 1975. "Sex Roles, Interruptions, and Silences in Conversations." *Language and Sex: Difference and Dominance*, ed. by Barrie Thorne and Nancy Henley, 105–129. Rowley, MA: Newbury House.

Review

1. Why do men feel that women are trying to control conversations? What conversational style do women use?

2. What are the differences between women and men in what they are attempting to accomplish with talk?

3. How do one's family and upbringing influence one's conversational style later in life?

4. What are the differences between "high-involvement" and "high-considerateness" conversational styles?

Application

Tape-record dinner conversations among your family or friends for three nights. Attempt to identify interruptions, overlapping, and conversational styles. Discuss your findings as they coincide or conflict with Tannen's article.

13
Sexual Betrayal

Perspectives of Betrayers and the Betrayed

S. Shirley Feldman
Elizabeth Cauffman

One of the most intense and intimate forms of human interaction is sex. While sex is a basic drive, it is also a behavior shaped by social factors. People learn how to be sexual creatures. Individuals learn how to express sexual needs in socially acceptable ways. For example, a particular sexual behavior may be highly valued in some societies and disapproved of or hardly practiced in others. Thus, mouth-to-mouth kissing is a desired sexual behavior in most societies, but in some it is regarded as repulsive and is avoided.

One norm found in most societies is that a committed intimate relationship (dating or marriage) implies no sexual relationships with someone outside the relationship. A significant amount of literature exists about the consequences of infidelity for marriage, but very little has been written about infidelity among those who are in a committed but unmarried relationship.

In this selection, Feldman and Cauffman report on their research to address this gap in our knowledge. Using a sample of adolescents and young adults, they explore the experience of sexual betrayal from the point of view of both those who betray and those who were betrayed.

Introduction

Although romantic relationships are common during the adolescent years, their dynamics are poorly understood. In particular, the causes and consequences of sexual infidelity during adolescence and young adulthood remain virtually unexplored, despite the fact that such betrayals may have significant emotional and interpersonal consequences.

Previous research has found that adolescents consider "betrayal" to include activities such as dating, spending time, becoming emotionally involved, or having sexual relations with someone other than one's romantic partner (Roscoe et al., 1988). Sexual betrayal, in contrast to general betrayal, is limited to sexual activities (including petting and sexual intercourse) outside a supposedly exclusive relationship. Sexual betrayal, in the context of the present discussion, refers to the unilateral breaking of a commitment to be sexually monogamous, without the awareness or sanction of one's romantic partner (Lieberman, 1988).

Although young people have become more permissive over the past few decades, and although they engage in sexual intercourse at younger ages and have experience with a variety of different partners over time (Katchadourian, 1990), adolescents do not endorse sexual promiscuity. In fact, sexual activity among most teens occurs in the context of a relationship of some importance to them (Moore and Rosenthal, 1993). Furthermore, youths typically pursue only one relationship at a time in a practice known as serial monogamy. Sexual infidelity, in dating as well as in marriage, is seen as a major rule violation that is strongly disapproved of by people of all ages (Greely, 1991; Hansen, 1987; Lieberman, 1988; Sheppard et al., 1995; Thompson, 1984; Weis and Slosnerick, 1981).

Yet, despite strong societal sanction against betrayal or sexual infidelity, such occurrences are relatively common. Available data, though quite sparse and of questionable generalizability, suggest that approximately 50 percent of adult men and 40 percent of adult women engage in extramarital relations (Lawson and Samson, 1988; Thompson, 1984). Among adolescents, the data are even less substantial, but current estimates of betrayal range from 20 percent to 64 percent, depending on the definition of betrayal (Hansen, 1987; Roscoe et al., 1988; Sheppard et al., 1995). Although the incidence of betrayal is generally higher among males than among females (Hansen, 1987; Townsend and Levy, 1990), there is some evidence that this gap may be narrowing (Thompson, 1984) or even disappearing (Roscoe et al., 1988; Seal et al., 1994; Sheppard et al., 1995).

Betrayal during the adolescent years may occur as a consequence of the need to balance developmental tasks with competing demands. Sexual activity, for example, is often part of age-typical explorations of intimacy. During the teenage years, adolescents move from a focus on same-sex friendships to a focus that includes opposite-sex friendships and romances. According to previous research, the defining features of friendship during the adolescent years are trust and loyalty (Berndt and Perry, 1990). As adolescents grow to expect these characteristics in their friendships, they are also likely to expect these same qualities in their romantic relationships. According to Sullivan (1953), for adolescents to achieve satisfactory relations with members of the opposite sex, they must integrate their "lust dynamism" with their need for both security and intimacy.

The establishment of a clear sense of identity is another important developmental task of adolescence, a task that in recent decades has extended into young adulthood. The study of identity development is dominated by Erikson's (1968) proposition that the period of adolescence (and young adulthood) is a time of "identity crisis" during which, experimentation and exploration of the self lead to a coherent sense of identity. Forging an autonomous sense of self, however, is not a process that can be carried out in isolation. Interactions with others are necessary to provide a context in which an individual's identity can be defined. Accordingly, participation in intimate relationships is an important aspect of establishing one's own sense of identity. At the same time, however, it can be argued that, because a truly intimate relationship involves sharing one's deepest thoughts and feelings, one must have a self before one can share it with another. Thus, it seems plausible that intimacy and identity

develop in tandem, with gradual advances in identity leading to the possibility of increasing levels of intimacy, which in turn foster further progress in establishing an identity (Dyk and Adams, 1987).

The developmental need to establish intimate relationships as well as to develop a coherent sense of self may place conflicting demands on the adolescent. These demands may place adolescents in the difficult position of choosing between the exploration of self and developing an intimate connection with others. Acts of betrayal may have serious consequences for the development of intimacy, yet adolescents also may need to experiment with different romantic partners in order to develop a clear sense of identity. This paradox may explain why incidents of betrayal are common, despite being viewed as morally wrong. Indeed, one would expect acts of betrayal to result in high levels of cognitive dissonance, as the betrayer attempts to integrate behaviors and beliefs that are inconsistent.

The Experience of Sexual Betrayal

We know relatively little about the effects of sexual betrayal on unmarried adolescents and young adults, because little research is available on the subject. The extant research typically focuses on hypothetical betrayal. Subjects are asked about possible reasons for betrayal and what they might do if they learned their partner was unfaithful (Roscoe et al., 1988), or they are asked to respond to vignettes (Mongeau et al., 1994) or to complete stories involving sexual betrayal (Kitzinger and Powell, 1995).

The picture that emerges from such research is fragmentary. The most common motives generated by college students for betrayal [include] dissatisfaction or boredom with the relationship, seeking revenge on the partner, uncertainty about the relationship, and need for variety or experimentation. Emotions experienced in response to marital infidelity (measured using a story completion test) depend in part on the age and gender of the subject and the gender of the aggrieved, but generally include anger, emotional pain, indifference, and desire for revenge. Anticipated consequences of the betrayal to the relationship, as described by "victims" of imagined betrayal, include terminating the relationship, seeking the reason for the betrayal, discussing the issue with the partner, and doing nothing. Whether these responses to hypothetical betrayal reflect the likelihood of responses to actual incidents is, as yet, unknown.

In light of the paucity of research on extradyadic betrayal in adolescents and young adults, we also examined the results of research on marital infidelity, as a way of informing our thinking, despite the fact that marital infidelity is judged as a more serious moral violation than dating infidelity (Lieberman, 1992; Sheppard et al., 1995). Motives for marital infidelity, as reported by perpetrators, include marital dissatisfaction, sexual dissatisfaction, desire for excitement or enhancement of self-esteem, and falling in love with a new partner (DeBurgher, 1972; Erlbaum, 1982; Glass and Wright, 1992; Wiggins and Lederer, 1984). Responses of the aggrieved to the discovery of marital infidelity by their spouse include termination of the relationship, ignoring the partner, reappraising the situation, and discussing the incident with the erring partner (Buunk, 1980). The viewpoint of the perpetrator is, in general, underrepresented in the available research.

Overall, our knowledge of the experience of betrayal is quite limited. The goal of our study is to obtain a detailed picture of betrayal experiences among adolescents and young adults, and to examine the viewpoint of the perpetrator as well as the aggrieved.

Gender Differences in Sexual Betrayal

Gender differences are pervasive in the areas of sexuality and sex roles. One thus would expect that gender differences may be salient in the area of betrayal as well. Indeed, gender differences in attitudes toward and incidence of betrayal have been found, with more males than females reporting extramarital infidelity, although this gender gap has been declining (Sponaugle, 1989). Among adolescents and unmarried young adults, gender differences in sexual betrayal are either modest in magnitude (with males

engaging in somewhat more betrayal than females) or absent (Roscoe et al., 1988; Sheppard et al., 1995). Gender differences in motives for betrayal are similar for adults engaged in marital infidelity and youths responding to hypothetical extradyadic infidelity. In general, women tend to approve more of love justifications for extramarital involvement and dissatisfaction with the existing relationship, whereas men approve more of such justifications as sexual attraction or unavailability of the spouse (Glass and Wright, 1992; Roscoe et al., 1988). Similarly, Wiederman and Allgeier (1993) find that women are more upset by situations implying emotional infidelity, whereas men are more upset by implications of sexual infidelity. Other research suggests that women equate sex with love, whereas men hold these two concepts as separate (Glass and Wright, 1992). . . .

Although gender differences have received significant research attention, the behaviors, reactions, and experiences of perpetrators and victims of sexual betrayal have not been explored in detail. In the present study, we examine incidents of betrayal from both points of view. More specifically, we examine the partners with whom the perpetrator betrays, the motives for the betrayal, the affective response, and the effect on the relationship.

Goals of the Present Study

Extant research and theory suggest that betrayal may be a frequently occurring experience as youths struggle to forge an identity (which involves experimentation), develop intimacy (which carries with it an expectation of monogamy), and incorporate sexuality into both of these aspects of their personality. Betrayal, studied mostly in marriages, generates emotional upheaval and fosters a reconsideration of the value of the romantic relationship. Here our goal is to describe more fully the occurrence and experience of sexual betrayal in adolescents and young adults. To this end, we explore four specific issues:

1. the incidence of sexual betrayal in youths who have been in a romantic re-

lationship, as reported by the perpetrator as well as the aggrieved;

2. the subjective experience surrounding betrayal of both the aggrieved and the perpetrator, including such descriptive information as

   • who is the betrayal partner,
   • how did the aggrieved learn about the betrayal,
   • what were the motives for the betrayal,
   • what was the emotional response to the betrayal, and
   • what was the resultant effect on the relationship;

3. differences in the experience of betrayal as described from the viewpoint of the aggrieved and the viewpoint of the perpetrator;

4. gender differences in both incidence and experience of betrayal.

Method

In a cross-sectional study of several hundred youth, we administered questionnaires to assess betrayal behaviors as well as reactions to betrayal. We assessed the reactions of youths to their own acts of betrayal as well as to betrayal by others. The [final] sample of 216 subjects was approximately equally divided between females (52 percent) and males (48 percent). Subjects were between 18 and 24 years old, with a mean age of 20.6 years. A majority (81 percent) were born in the United States. Fifty-nine percent came from nondivorced families; 41 percent had divorced parents. The ethnicity of the sample was as follows: non-Hispanic White (hereafter referred to as White) 55 percent, Latino 10 percent, African American 7 percent, Asian American 15 percent, Other 13 percent.

Results

Incidence of Betrayal

Youths 18 to 24 years old report significant experience with betrayal in romantic relationships . . . 40 percent reported having been the perpetrator and more than half reported having been the aggrieved. More than 25 percent report having experienced both sides of betrayal (i.e., as both perpetrator and aggrieved), and two-thirds had been in a relationship that involved betrayal (where they were either the perpetrator or the aggrieved). Thus, experience with sexual betrayal in some form was normative for this sample. Among those subjects who betrayed their partner, 62 percent reported that the betrayal involved sexual intercourse, whereas the remainder engaged in petting only. Among aggrieved subjects, 71 percent reported that their partner engaged in sex with another person, whereas, the remainder reported that their partner engaged in petting without intercourse.

Betrayal: Viewpoint of the Perpetrator

In this section, analyses are confined to the 40 percent of the sample (n = 86) who reported that they had betrayed one or more partners. . . . For the majority of perpetrators (65 percent), the new partner was well known to them prior to the betrayal. The most common betrayal partners included acquaintances, casual friends, and ex-lovers. Relatively fewer youths betrayed their partner with a stranger.

Perpetrators reported a variety of motives for betrayal, with magnetic attraction toward the new partner the most frequent category and vindictiveness (e.g., trying to hurt partner or make partner jealous) the least frequent. Motives falling into three other clusters were each mentioned by about half of the perpetrators. These clusters include bad relations with the regular partner, confidence that they could avoid detection, and being unsure of the existing relationship. . . . The most frequently mentioned motives (noted by 40 percent or more of the sample) were sexual attraction to the new partner, inability to resist temptation, (regular) partner out of town or otherwise unavailable, and being under the influence of alcohol or drugs at the time of the betrayal.

Perpetrators experienced a wide range of emotional responses to their own acts of betrayal. Almost as many subjects reported one or more positive emotions (43 percent) as reported negative emotions (50 percent). However, cognitive-affective emotions were the most commonly reported, with almost three-quarters of the perpetrators reporting at least one such emotion as being mostly or very much how they felt. An examination of the incidence of the specific emotions reveals that guilt was the most prevalent emotion (endorsed by 63 percent). Feeling ashamed, confused, and immoral were each characteristic of more than a third of the sample.

According to the perpetrators, their acts of betrayal typically were revealed to the aggrieved partner. Forty-two percent of their partners never found out (and an additional two percent did not find out until after the relationship had been terminated). In cases in which the partner did find out (n = 36), 83 percent of the perpetrators claim to have confessed, 8 percent reported that the existing partner just "figured it out" and another 8 percent reported that the partner learned about the betrayal from a third party.

The reactions of aggrieved partners to the news of the betrayal (as described by the perpetrator) were quite variable. A small minority of the aggrieved partners refused to talk about the betrayal, and a similar small percentage became violent, either smashing an object, threatening, or actually hitting the perpetrator. Other aggrieved partners purportedly discussed the issue calmly. The majority (64 percent), however, expressed considerable upset, either sulking or withdrawing, insulting or yelling at the perpetrator (getting mad), or being upset in unspecified ways. Clearly, the perpetrators paint a picture of a strong and negative reaction by the aggrieved partner.

After the aggrieved found out about the betrayal (as was the case for 56 percent of the perpetrator sample), the relationship generally underwent some changes. According to the perpetrator, the relationship was terminated in 60 percent of the cases, somewhat more often by the perpetrator than by the aggrieved. The relationship continued for the remaining 40 percent, with more than half of these couples agreeing to be monogamous and the remainder agreeing to date others or

to define more clearly permissible behaviors with others.

In summary, the perpetrators' accounts reveal betrayal to be a common but nonetheless emotionally charged event in the lives of adolescents and young adults. Close to half of those in a long-term relationship reported that they had betrayed at least one of their partners, usually with a person already known to them, and motivated by magnetic attraction to a new partner. The perpetrators seemed aware that they had violated moral standards, as indicated by the high prevalence of guilt. Although a significant minority reported "getting away" with their infidelity, those whose partners found out claimed they confessed. In a majority of cases, the betrayal led to the dissolution of the relationship. Notably, however, there was considerable variation in responses to all the questions.

Betrayal: Viewpoint of the Aggrieved

The aggrieved reported discovering their partner's betrayal in a number of different ways. The information was obtained from the erring partner in 50 percent of the cases, from a third party in 30 percent of the cases, and by "just figuring it out" for themselves in 20 percent of the cases. It is noteworthy that their descriptions, although matching the pattern of responses provided by the perpetrators, differ in important details. The aggrieved were less likely to state that the perpetrator confessed, and more likely to claim that the aggrieved had figured it out or that a third party had relayed the information.

Although, betrayal by a romantic partner was normative in this sample of late adolescents and young adults, it was nevertheless an emotionally laden event for the aggrieved. A majority of the aggrieved expressed negative emotions as being mostly or very characteristic of their reactions, with anger, sadness/depression, and frustration reported by 50 percent or more of the sample. Cognitive-affective emotions such as disappointment and mistrust also were reported by more than half the sample of the aggrieved.

The immediate reactions by the aggrieved to news of the betrayal ranged from ignoring the issue (10 percent), to calm discussion (19 percent), to being clearly upset (55 percent including such behaviors as being upset/crying, withdrawing/sulking, yelling/insulting, and violence). . . .

Upon discovery of the betrayal, the majority of the aggrieved reported that the relationship was terminated—usually by the aggrieved, but in approximately one-third of the cases by the perpetrator. About a quarter of the aggrieved report that the relationship was renegotiated, either to affirm monogamy or to permit dating with others and more clearly define acceptable behavior with others. When we compared the accounts of the aggrieved and the perpetrators of the effects of betrayal on the relationship, similarities and differences are observed. The perpetrator and the aggrieved agreed that a majority of the relationships were terminated. However, the aggrieved were less likely than the perpetrators to claim that the perpetrators broke up the relationship (18 percent vs. 34 percent, respectively) and they were more likely to claim that the aggrieved broke off the relationship (54 percent vs. 26 percent, respectively). Thus, there appears to be a self-serving action bias on the part of the informant, indicating that the informant exercised some control over events following the betrayal.

In summary, the aggrieved typically discovered their partner's betrayal because the partner confessed. The predominant emotional reactions included anger, sadness, disappointment, and mistrust. In dealing with their partners, the aggrieved exhibited marked distress and often terminated the relationship. Overall, there was general correspondence between reports by the aggrieved and by the perpetrators regarding how the aggrieved learned about and dealt with the betrayal, as well as what happened to the relationship. However, the aggrieved and the perpetrators alike tended to attribute responsibility for events in the aftermath of the betrayal to themselves more often than to the other party.

Gender Differences

Gender differences in the incidence of betrayal were not observed. Males and females were equally likely to be perpetrators and equally likely to be the aggrieved as well. Gender differences were generally absent in the perpetrators' reports of betrayal. Males and females were alike in whom they chose as a new partner, the motives they gave for betrayal, whether and how their partners discovered the betrayal, the emotions the perpetrators experienced, and what happened when their partners confronted them about the betrayal. Male and female perpetrators differed in their descriptions of the effect of betrayal on the relationship with more males describing termination by the aggrieved and more females describing termination by the perpetrator.

Gender differences also were generally absent in reports by the aggrieved. Males and females were alike in their reports of how betrayal was discovered, the emotions experienced, and the effect on the relationship. There were, however, some gender differences in descriptions of the aggrieved's confrontation with the partner. Aggrieved females were more likely than aggrieved males to make up after crying and being upset, and were less likely to either withdraw/sulk or be violent.

Discussion

This study is the first investigation of the subjective experiences and emotional reactions of adolescents and young adults to sexual betrayal in their own relationships. In contrast to other studies, our study examines sexual betrayal rather than general betrayal (which includes emotional betrayal in the absence of any physical intimacy), and focuses, in particular, on youth who, despite an agreement to be monogamous, actually experienced betrayal. In addition, our study investigates the viewpoint of the perpetrator as well as the aggrieved in the betrayal relationship, and includes a diverse sample of youth, including youth from two-year community and city colleges as well as four-year colleges. Our findings indicate that most youth in supposedly monogamous relationships are familiar with betrayal and find it both emotionally charged and painful. . . .

Incidence of Betrayal

Approximately two-thirds of the sample had experienced betrayal, either as the perpetrator or as the aggrieved. Although this prevalence of acts of betrayal is high, involving a majority of youth who had ever been in a romantic relationship, this figure is probably a significant underestimate of the actual incidence of betrayal because not all aggrieved discovered the betrayal of their partner. In fact, perpetrators in our study claim that more than 40 percent of their partners never learned of the betrayal.

The incidence of betrayal among our subjects can be compared to other reports of betrayal. Despite significant variability across studies in measures, definitions of betrayal, and samples, all studies concur that betrayal is a frequent event in the relationships of youth. In our data, 40 percent of the sample described themselves as perpetrators of sexual betrayal in at least one relationship, a figure that falls between the 38 percent incidence of general betrayal in the most important relationship reported by Sheppard et al. (1995) and the 51 percent reported by Roscoe et al. (1988). Similarly, 66 percent of our sample reported having been either the perpetrator or aggrieved in sexual betrayal, similar to the 63 percent reported by Hansen (1987).

There are several possible explanations for the fact that acts of betrayal appear so commonplace among teens and young adults. First, adolescents may experience significant difficulty communicating clearly with their partners about sexuality, commitments, and expectations for limiting sexual activities with others, a problem also found in adults (Blumstein and Schwartz, 1983; Sprecher and McKinney, 1993). Accordingly, misunderstandings are likely to occur. Second, betrayal in this age group may result from the complexities of balancing growing levels of intimacy (with its need for commitment and fidelity) with the establishment of a strong sense of identity (with its need for experimentation and exploration of alternatives). The emotions experienced by youth subsequent to betrayal give some support to this interpretation. For example, whereas 63 percent of perpetrators felt guilty, 43 percent

reported feeling happy, proud, or excited. The fact that betraying one's partner can elicit positive emotions as well as negative ones suggests that the underlying motives of this act may be deeply rooted. Because adolescents are still exploring their own identities, experiences such as betrayal can elicit positive reactions in addition to feelings of guilt.

Motives for Betrayal

A significant strength of our study is its focus on actual incidents of betrayal, rather than responses to hypothetical situations. Data from the present study suggest that asking people to provide motives for hypothetical betrayal or using projective tests of motives for betrayal may not provide an accurate view of the motives involved in actual acts of betrayal. . . . Compared to our subjects, youth explaining the motives in a hypothetical case of betrayal underestimated both sexual attraction toward a new partner (12 percent in Roscoe's study vs. 53 percent in our study) and the influence of sexual dissatisfaction with the ongoing relationship (10 percent vs. 30 percent). Youth who generated motives to explain hypothetical betrayal also underestimated, relative to our sample, the importance of situational considerations such as temporary absence of the partner (8 percent vs. 40 percent) and the effects of drugs and alcohol (0 percent in Roscoe's study vs. 40 percent in our study). Given such differences, we conclude that if the motives for betrayal are to be understood, we must not rely on hypothetical measures; instead, we must explore the dynamics of actual events.

The data provided by perpetrators regarding their motives yield useful insight into the conscious factors responsible for betrayal. The most commonly reported motives can be classified either as "pushes" or as "pulls," using the terminology of Buunk (1987). Pushes include high costs and low rewards associated with the ongoing relationship (e.g., bad relations, being unsure of relations), whereas pulls include high rewards and low costs of betrayal (e.g., magnetic attraction, certainty of avoiding detection). Several other, less common classes of motives that were neither "pushes" nor "pulls" (e.g., vindictiveness, drugs/alcohol) also were reported. In general, though, pulls (especially sexual attraction, partner being away) were the strongest motives reported by this age group. Such motives may be conceptualized in terms of serving the search for identity, such as the need for exploration and experimentation, although this explanation was not tested explicitly in the present study.

The prevalence of situational contributors to betrayal is notable. The absence of a partner and being under the influence of either drugs or alcohol were each given as motives by more than 40 percent of those who had betrayed a partner. Furthermore, these environmental situations are extremely common among youth. For example, separation of romantic partners may result from such common situations as partners attending different colleges or attending the same college but returning home to different parts of the country for vacations. Separations also result from work demands and opportunities, and recreational plans with same-sex friends. Similarly, alcohol and drug use by youth is normative. It is estimated that, in 1992, 41 percent of youth in a large-scale study consumed five or more alcoholic drinks in a row on at least one occasion in the two weeks prior to the study (Johnston et al., 1993). Thus, the environmental contexts of many youths put them at significant risk of betrayal. What we do not know, however, is whether alcohol and drugs impair judgment so that youth engage in behaviors they would not otherwise undertake, or whether youth take alcohol/drugs to reduce their inhibitions and help to set aside ethical or other concerns to make betrayal easier.

In our interviews, youth often gave elaborate answers to explain how they came to betray their partners, often alluding to more than one motive. For example, a 21-year-old female who went away to summer school while in an ongoing monogamous relationship explains:

I was starting to have pretty severe doubts. I'd never dated anybody else and I was starting to wonder, Why am I tied down? I went into my [friend's] room one day and said, That's it. I'm not in love with my boyfriend anymore. . . . When I go home, I am going to break up with him and within a couple of days I hooked up with someone to whom I was really attracted . . . and we had sex a short while later. . . . Technically, I cheated on him [my old boyfriend].

Similarly, a 23-year-old male, who had betrayed his partner only once, described how his girlfriend's absence was the primary motive:

The girl I was dating left to study in Mexico for a while and before she left we agreed, even though our relationship was not on the best of terms, that we would still be expecting to keep seeing each other when she got back. I don't know if I believed that or . . . I didn't want her to be unhappy there. . . . When she was gone I started messing around with another girl and it turned into a big mess. . . .

A surprising but significant result of our questionnaire study was the general lack of gender differences in the prevalence of and motives for betrayal. The lack of gender differences is consistent with the view that betrayal emerges as a consequence of dealing with developmental tasks that are common for both males and females during late adolescence. . . .

Comparing the Viewpoints of the Aggrieved and the Perpetrator

The present study examines the perspective of the perpetrator as well as the aggrieved. There were few surprises regarding the aggrieved's emotions. We expected and found that the aggrieved experience high rates of negative emotions (anger, frustration, and sadness) and high rates of cognitive-affective emotions (disappointment, mistrust, confusion, and insecurity). These findings agree with those reported by others studying adolescents (Kitzinger and Powell, 1995) and adults (Buunk, 1995). Of greater interest are some relatively low-incidence responses indicating that some youth assume responsibility for bad things that happen to them. A small percentage of aggrieved youth felt inadequate (18 percent) and guilty (7 percent) in response to their partner's betrayal.

Perpetrators' emotions were significantly more variable than those of the aggrieved. Only one response—guilt—was experienced by more than half of the sample (63 percent), whereas three emotions—feeling ashamed, immoral, or confused—were reported by approximately one-third of the sample. Thus, the most frequently experienced emotions had a strongly self-evaluative component, giving evidence that youth were aware that they were breaking community or personal standards. A 19-year-old female who betrayed her partner describes her reaction:

> I broke out, um, I broke out in spots. It ... was from stress. . . . That's what the doctor told me. I had so much inside of me that I needed to let out, and I just broke out in spots all over my body. I felt so incredibly guilty and I knew if I told [my partner] that I might not be able to have the same relationship, and I didn't want to jeopardize it, 'cause once [the betrayal] happened . . . it really made me realize how special he was to me, and, um, I just felt incredibly guilty and I wanted to tell him, but I couldn't, I guess.

More surprising than the reports of guilt and other cognitive-affective responses was that 40 percent of the perpetrators reported one or more positive emotions. One of our interview respondents, a male 22 years old, illustrates this as he describes the first time he betrayed a partner:

> At the time, it was a new experience for me, and I was just kind of experimenting . . . and I didn't really feel bad about doing that for some reason. . . . I thought this is kind of neat, people do this all the time, I'm just seeing what it's like.

We suggest that the positive emotional responses reported by many youth indicate not that they are happy that they betrayed a partner, but that they were celebrating their ability to attract a new partner and the success of their experimentation. Thus, through betrayal, they proved to themselves that they were attractive to others and that they had options.

In describing the betrayal experience, the perpetrators and the aggrieved generally agree on some key dimensions. For example,

they agree that confession by the perpetrator is the most common way in which the aggrieved discover betrayal, that upset is the most common reaction by the aggrieved, and that the relationship is terminated in a majority of cases. Clearly, as evidenced by the emotional reactions reported, and by the number of couples who chose to terminate the relationship, infidelity is a major distressing event in the lives of youth. This finding stands in contrast to that reported by Roscoe et al. (1988), who asked youth about responses to hypothetical betrayal. He found a more rational approach. More youth in his sample expected that they would be calm and reasonable in discussing betrayal, with a focus on finding out the reason for the betrayal, working toward improving the relationship, and forgiveness. In contrast, in our study, the reports of both the perpetrators and the aggrieved describe considerably more pain and emotion than rationality and calmness in confronting an actual betrayal.

Despite some general agreement, the aggrieved and the perpetrators differed significantly in their reports of the details surrounding the discovery of betrayal. For example, both the perpetrators and the aggrieved were likely to see themselves as more instrumental than their partner in shaping events in the aftermath of the betrayal. Thus, there appears to be a self-protective and self-enhancing "action bias" on the part of informants, with each member of the dyad likely to overestimate his or her own role in dealing with the betrayal. This may give a sense of control, if not of the original situation, then at least of its aftermath.

The development of intimacy and trust during adolescence is a challenging task. Balancing these tasks with the exploration of one's identity places further strains on adolescents. The data presented here paint a picture in which males and females alike often betray their romantic partners, leading to guilt because they do not condone such behavior, but also, for many, leading to feelings of happiness and excitement as their interpersonal horizons and their insight regarding their own identity expand. Meanwhile, many youth experience betrayal by a partner and suffer negative emotions, which forces them to reevaluate the relationship.

References

Berndt, T., and Perry, T. (1990). Distinctive features and effects of early adolescent friendships. In Montemayor, R., Adams, G., and Gullota, T. (eds.), *Advances in Adolescence Research* (Vol. 2). Sage, Beverly Hills, CA, pp. 269–287.

Blumstein, P., and Schwartz, P. (1983). *American Couples*. Morrow, New York.

Buss, D. (1995). Psychological sex differences: Origins through sexual selection. *Am. Psychol.* 50: 164–168.

Buunk, B. (1980). Extramarital sex in the Netherlands: Motivation in social and marital context. *Altern. Lifestyles* 111–39.

——. (1987). Conditions that promote breakups as a consequence of extra dyadic involvements. *J. Soc. Clin. Psychol.* 5: 271–285.

——. (1995). Sex, self-esteem, dependency, and extradyadic sexual experience as related to jealousy response. *J. Soc. Pers. Relat.* 12: 147–153.

DeBurgher, J. E. (1972). Sex in troubled marriages. *Sex. Behav.* 2: 23–62.

Dyk, P., and Adams, G. (1987). The association between identity development and intimacy during adolescence: A theoretical treatise. *J. Adolesc. Res.* 2: 223–235.

Erikson, E. (1968). *Childhood and Society* (2nd Ed.). Norton, New York.

Erlbaum, P. L. (1982). The dynamics, implications, and treatment of extramarital sexual relationships for the family therapist. *J. Marit. Fam. Therapy* 7: 489–495.

Feldman, S. S., and Cauffman, E. (1999, in press). Your cheatin' heart: Sexual betrayal attitudes and behaviors and their correlates. *J. Res. Adolesc.* 9.

Glass, S. P., and Wright, T. L. (1992). Justifications for extramarital relationships: The association between attitudes, behaviors, and gender. *J. Sex Res.* 29: 361–387.

Greely, A. M. (1991). *Faithful Attraction: Discovering Intimacy, Love and Fidelity in American Marriage*. New York, Doherty.

Hansen, G. L. (1987). Extra dyadic reactions during courtship. *J. Sex Res.* 23: 382–390.

Johnston, L. D., O'Malley, P. M., and Bachman, J. G. (1993). National Survey Results on Drug Use from Monitoring the Future Study, 1975–1992. Volume 1. Secondary School Students. U.S. Department of Health and Human Services (National Institute on Drug Abuse Publ. No. 93-3597). U.S. Government Printing Office, Washington, DC.

Katchadourian, H. (1990). Sexuality. In Feldman, S. S., and Elliot, G. R. (eds.), *At the Threshold: The Developing Adolescent*. Harvard University Press, Cambridge, MA, pp. 330–351.

Kitzinger, C., and Powell, D. (1995). Engendering infidelity: Existentialist and social constructionist readings of a story completion task. *Fem. Psychol.* 5: 345–372.

Lawson, A., and Samson, C. (1988). Age, gender and adultery. *Br. J. Sociol.* 39: 409–440.

Lieberman, B. (1992). Extrapremarital intercourse: Attitudes toward neglected sexual behavior. *J. Sex Res.* 24: 296–298.

Mongeau, P., Hale, J., and Alles, M. (1994). An experimental investigation of accounts and attributions following sexual infidelity. *Commun. Monogr.* 61: 326–344.

Moore, S., and Rosenthal, D. A. (1993). *Sexuality in Adolescence*. New York, Routledge.

Roscoe, B., Cavanaugh, L., and Kennedy, D. (1988). Dating infidelity: Behaviors, reasons, and consequences. *Adolescence* 23: 35–43.

Seal, D. W., Agostinelli, G., and Hanneft, C. (1994). Extradyadic romantic involvement: Moderating of sociosexuality and gender. *Sex Roles* 31: 1–22.

Sheppard, V., Nelson, E., and Andreoli-Mathie, V. (1995). Dating relationships and infidelity: Attitudes and behavior. *J. Sex Marit. Therapy* 21: 202–212.

Sponaugle, G. C. (1989). Attitudes towards extramarital relations. In McKenney, K., and Sprecher, S. (eds.), *Human Sexuality: The Societal and Interpersonal Context*, 187–209. Norwood, NJ, Ablex.

Sprecher, S., and McKinney, K. (1993). *Sexuality*. Sage, Newbury Park, CA.

Sullivan, H. S. (1953). *Conceptions of Modern Psychiatry*. Norton, New York.

Thompson, A. P. (1983). Extramarital sex: A review of research literature. *J. Sex Res.* 19: 1–22.

Thompson, A. P. (1984). Emotional and sexual components of extramarital relations. *I Marr. Fam.* 46: 35–42.

Townsend, J. M., and Levy, G. D. (1990). Effect of potential partner's costume and physical attractiveness on sexuality and partner selection. *J. Psychol.* 127: 371–389.

Weis, D. L., and Slosnerick, M. (1981). Attitudes toward sexual and nonsexual extramarital involvement among a sample of college students. *J. Marr. Fam.* 43: 349–358.

Wiederman, M. W., and Allgeier, E. R. (1993). Gender differences in sexual jealousy: Adaptionist as social learning explanation. *Ethnol. Sociobiol.* 14: 115–140.

Wiggins, J. D., and Lederer, D. A. (1984). Differential antecedents of infidelity in marriage. *Am. Ment. Health Couns. Assoc.* 16: 152–161.

Review

1. How common is betrayal among unmarried couples, and what are some possible explanations for betrayal?

2. Describe the various motives that young people give for sexual betrayal.

3. Discuss the similarities and the differences the authors report between the aggrieved and the perpetrators.

Applications

1. If you have been sexually betrayed or have sexually betrayed someone, compare your experience with the results of this research. How do your feelings and motivations compare with those the authors report? Were there aspects of the betrayal experience that were important but not covered in this article?

2. Search the term "sexual betrayal" on the internet. Are there materials on betrayal among the unmarried, or are they mainly or exclusively on betrayal in marriage? Find a personal account or some research data on marital betrayal. Compare the materials with the authors' findings. What are the similarities and differences in the experiences of those betrayed by a spouse and the unmarried studied by the authors?

Reprinted from: S. Shirley Feldman and Elizabeth Cauffman, "Sexual Betrayal Among Late Adolescents: Perspectives of the Perpetrator and the Aggrieved," *Journal of Youth and Adolescence* 28 (April, 1999):235–47. Used by permission of Plenum Publishers. ✦

Unit III

Inequality

Inequality is a central concept in sociological analysis. Inequality exists in all societies, because every society has a **stratification** system—an arrangement of the society into groups that are unequal with regard to things valued in that society. In the United States and other modern societies, the groups are called **social classes,** and the "things valued" include wealth and possessions, power, and prestige. In general, those at the top of the stratification system have the highest incomes, the best occupations (which bring them prestige as well as income), and the most power.

Equality is one of humanity's most profound ideals. Whether embodied in the Founding Fathers' notion that "all men are created equal," Marx's vision of a communist society of equal rewards, or the feminist goal of an Equal Rights Amendment, the desire for equality has stirred the passions of the masses throughout history.

Nevertheless, no society with complete equality has ever existed. And, while the ideal itself is still important to many people, others deny its value or at least its practicality. For instance, the prominent sociological theory of structural functionalism asserts that unequal rewards must necessarily be attached to various positions in a society in order to motivate people to hold those positions. In this view, the complete equality of rewards would be a "sociological monstrosity." How could people be motivated to take up important but arduous jobs without concomitant higher rewards? Such a society, according to these theorists, could not work.

Another way to look at the issue is more pragmatic. We accept the fact that inequality always has and always will exist. The issue then is, how much inequality is acceptable? It is unlikely that consensus can be obtained on this issue. Therefore, society will experience ongoing conflict as various groups strive to obtain what they view as their fair share of valued things.

The selections in this unit (selections 14–23) illustrate this last point. They each involve some kind of conflict between groups over the fairness of the distribution of valued things. Many people not only have less but also feel they have been deprived by those above them in the stratification system. For them inequality means not just that they have fewer things that are valued than others, but that they have less than their rightful share. The deprived groups include the lower social classes, people in lower-level occupations, the homeless, some racial/ethnic groups, women, the aged, and those in poorer nations. ✦

Part One

The Nature of Inequality

While structural functionalism can be used to justify a certain amount of inequality, conflict theory is generally used to attack inequalities. There are, in other words, different perspectives on the causes and consequences of inequality in a society.

One point, however, is indisputable: Everyone in the world lives in a system of inequality. There are no societies where perfect equality exists. The kind of inequality any particular individual faces, however, may vary from one society to another. The selections in this part illustrate the diverse nature of inequality. Selection 14 offers Marx's classic statement about social classes. Selection 15 dramatizes the extent of inequality between chief executive officers and workers in low-wage jobs in the United States. Selection 16 examines the plight of those at the bottom of America's stratification system. ✦

14
The Communist Manifesto

Karl Marx
Friedrich Engels

The work of Marx must be regarded as the starting point for the sociological analysis of stratification in societies. His fundamental insight is that societies are divided into potentially conflicting groups on the basis of the ownership or control of productive property (land, natural resources, commercial and industrial enterprises, etc.). In Marx's view, the primary division in industrial society is between the capitalists (or bourgeoisie) and the workers (or proletariat). While he recognized the existence of other classes in industrial society, they were of secondary importance. After all, it is the class conflict between the bourgeoisie and the proletariat that will propel society on to its next historical stage, socialism.

While Marx was incorrect in a number of his predictions about the future of capitalism, many of his ideas have stood the test of time and continue to illuminate current events. For instance, Marx observed that although the ruling class in a society is dominant by virtue of its superior material or economic position, this dominance is also reflected in the legal and political system and in the whole range of beliefs and ideology. Ideas, then, simply mirror material reality. Therefore, revolutionary ideas are impotent without a basis in material reality, such as a proletarian class experiencing privation and misery.

Marx overestimated the extent to which capitalism would inflict miserable working and living conditions on the proletariat. He never anticipated the welfare state or government intervention on behalf of workers. Yet his insight into the inherent conflict of interest between the owners and the workers is still valid. As the history of the labor movement dramatizes, any gains made by those in the lower levels of the stratification system come through struggle, threat, and coercive action rather than through the generosity and sense of fair play of those in positions of power.

I. Bourgeois and Proletarians

The history of all hitherto existing society is the history of class struggles.

Freeman and slave, patrician and plebeian, lord and serf, guild-master and journeyman, in a word, oppressor and oppressed, stood in constant opposition to one another, carried on an uninterrupted, now hidden, now open fight, a fight that each time ended either in a revolutionary reconstitution of society at large, or in the common ruin of the contending classes.

In the earlier epochs of history, we find almost everywhere a complicated arrangement of society into various orders, a manifold gradation of social rank. In ancient Rome we have patricians, knights, plebeians, slaves; in the Middle Ages, feudal lords, vassals, guild-masters, journeymen, apprentices, serfs; in almost all of these classes, again, subordinate gradations.

The modern bourgeois society that has sprouted from the ruins of feudal society has not done away with class antagonisms. It has but established new classes, new conditions of oppression, new forms of struggle in place of the old ones.

Our epoch, the epoch of the bourgeoisie, possesses, however, this distinctive feature: it has simplified the class antagonisms. Society as a whole is more and more splitting up into two great hostile camps, into two great classes directly facing each other: Bourgeoisie and Proletariat.

From the serfs of the Middle Ages sprang the chartered burghers of the earliest towns. From these burgesses the first elements of the bourgeoisie were developed.

The discovery of America, the rounding of the Cape, opened up fresh ground for the rising bourgeoisie. The East-Indian and Chinese markets, the colonization of America, trade with the colonies, the increase in the means of exchange and in commodities generally, gave to commerce, to navigation, to industry, an impulse never before known, and thereby, to the revolutionary element in the tottering feudal society, a rapid development.

The feudal system of industry, in which industrial production was monopolized by closed guilds, now no longer sufficed for the growing wants of the new markets. The manufacturing system took its place. The guild-masters were pushed on one side by the manufacturing middle-class; division of labor between the different corporate guilds vanished in the face of division of labor in each single workshop. Meantime the markets kept ever growing, the demand, ever rising. Even manufacture no longer sufficed. Thereupon steam and machinery revolutionized industrial production. The place of manufacture was now taken by the giant, modern industry, the place of the industrial middle-class, by industrial millionaires, the leaders of whole industrial armies, the modern bourgeoisie.

Modern industry has established the world market, for which the discovery of America paved the way. This market has given an immense development to commerce, to navigation, to communication by land. This development has, in its turn, reacted on the extension of industry; and in proportion as industry, commerce, navigation, railways extended, in the same proportion the bourgeoisie developed, increased its capital, and pushed into the background every class handed down from the Middle Ages. We see, therefore, how the modern bourgeoisie is itself the product of a long course of development, of a series of revolutions in the modes of production and of exchange. . . .

The bourgeoisie has played a most revolutionary role in history. The bourgeoisie, wherever it has got the upper hand, has put an end to all feudal, patriarchal, idyllic relations. It has pitilessly torn asunder the motley feudal ties that bound man to his natural superiors, and has left remaining no other bond between man and man than naked self-interest, than callous cash payment. It has

drowned the most heavenly ecstacies of religious fervor, of chivalrous enthusiasm, of philistine sentimentalism, in the icy water of egotistical calculation. It has resolved personal worth into exchange value, and in place of the numberless indefeasible chartered freedoms, has set up that single, unconscionable freedom, Free Trade. In one word, for exploitation, veiled by religious and political illusions, it has substituted naked, shameless, direct, brutal exploitation.

The bourgeoisie has stripped of its halo every occupation hitherto honored and looked up to with reverent awe. It has converted the physician, the lawyer, the priest, the poet, the man of science, into its paid wage-laborers.

The bourgeoisie has torn away from the family its sentimental veil, and has reduced the family relation to a mere money relation.

The bourgeoisie has disclosed how it came to pass that the brutal display of vigor in the Middle Ages, which Reactionists so much admire, found its fitting complement in the most slothful indolence. It has been the first to show what man's activity can bring about. It has accomplished wonders far surpassing Egyptian pyramids, Roman aqueducts, and Gothic cathedrals; it has conducted expeditions that put in the shade all former migrations of nations and crusades.

The bourgeoisie cannot exist without constantly revolutionizing the instruments of production, and thereby the relations of production, and with them the whole relations of society. Conservation of the old modes of production in unaltered form was, on the contrary, the first condition of existence for all earlier industrial classes. Constant revolutionizing of production, uninterrupted disturbance of all social conditions, everlasting certainty and agitation distinguish the bourgeois epoch from all earlier ones. All fixed, fast-frozen relations, with their train of ancient and venerable prejudices and opinions, are swept away, all new-formed ones become antiquated before they can ossify. All that is solid melts into air, all that is holy is profaned, and man is at last compelled to face with sober senses his real conditions of life, and his relations with his kind. The need of a constantly expanding market chases the bourgeoisie over the whole surface of the globe. It must nestle everywhere, settle everywhere, establish connections everywhere.

The bourgeoisie has through its exploitation of the world-market given a cosmopolitan character to production and consumption in every country. To the great chagrin of Reactionists, it has drawn from under the feet of industry the national ground on which it stood. All old-established national industries have been destroyed or are daily being destroyed. They are dislodged by new industries, whose introduction becomes a life and death question for all civilized nations, by industries that no longer work up indigenous raw material, but raw material drawn from the remotest zones; industries whose products are consumed, not only at home, but in every quarter of the globe. In place of the old wants, satisfied by the production of the country, we find new wants, requiring for their satisfaction the products of distant lands and climes. In place of the old local and national seclusion and self-sufficiency, we have intercourse in every direction, universal interdependence of nations. And as in material, so also in intellectual production. The intellectual creations of individual nations become common property. National one-sidedness and narrow-mindedness become more and more impossible, and from the numerous national and local literatures there arises a world literature.

The bourgeoisie, by the rapid improvement of all instruments of production, by the immensely facilitated means of communication, draws all, even the most barbarian, nations into civilization. The cheap prices of its commodities are the heavy artillery with which it batters down all Chinese walls, with which it forces the barbarians' intensely obstinate hatred of foreigners to capitulate. It compels all nations, on pain of extinction, to adopt the bourgeois mode of production; it compels them to introduce what it calls civilization into their midst, i.e., to become bourgeois themselves. In a word, it creates a world after its own image.

The bourgeoisie has subjected the country to the rule of the towns. It has created enormous cities, has greatly increased the urban population as compared with the rural, and has thus rescued a considerable part of the population from the idiocy of rural life. Just as it has made the country dependent on the towns, so it has made barbarian and semi-barbarian countries dependent on the civilized ones, nations of peasants on nations of bourgeois, the East on the West.

The bourgeoisie keeps more and more doing away with the scattered state of the population, of the means of production, and of property. It has agglomerated population, centralized means of production, and has concentrated property in a few hands. The necessary consequence of this was political centralization. Independent, or but loosely connected provinces, with separate interests, laws, systems of taxation, and governments, became lumped together in one nation, with one government, one code of laws, one national class-interest, one frontier, and one customs tariff.

The bourgeoisie, during its rule of scarce one hundred years, has created more massive and more colossal productive forces than have all preceding generations together. Subjection of Nature's forces to man, machinery, application of chemistry to industry and agriculture, steam-navigation, railways, electric telegraphs, clearing of whole continents for cultivation, canalization of rivers, whole populations conjured out of the ground. What earlier century had even a presentiment that such productive forces slumbered in the lap of social labor?. . .

Modern bourgeois society with its relations of production, of exchange and of property, a society that has conjured up such gigantic means of production and of exchange, is like the sorcerer, who is no longer able to control the powers of the nether world whom he has called up by his spells. For many a decade past the history of industry and commerce is but the history of the revolt of modern productive forces against modern conditions of production, against the property relations that are the conditions for the existence of the bourgeoisie and of its rule. It is enough to mention the commercial crises that by their periodical return put on its trial, each time more threateningly, the existence of the entire bourgeois society. In these crises a great part not only of the existing products but also of the previously created forces are periodically destroyed. In these crises, there breaks out an epidemic that, in all earlier epochs, would have seemed an absurdity, the epidemic of overproduction. Society suddenly finds itself put back into a state of momentary barbarism, it appears as if a famine, a universal war of devastation had cut off the supply of every means of subsistence, industry and commerce seem to be destroyed; and why? Because there is too much civilization, too much means of subsistence, too much industry, too much commerce. . . .

And how does the bourgeoisie get over these crises? On the one hand by enforced destruction of a mass of productive forces; on the other, by the conquest of new markets, and by the more thorough exploitation of the old ones. That is to say, by paving the way for more extensive and more destructive crises, and by diminishing the means whereby crises are prevented.

The weapons with which the bourgeoisie felled feudalism to the ground are now turned against the bourgeoisie itself.

But not only has the bourgeoisie forged the weapons that bring death to itself, it has also called into existence the men who are to wield those weapons, the modern working-class, the proletarians.

In proportion as the bourgeoisie, i.e., capital, is developed, in the same proportion is the proletariat, the modern working-class, developed a class of laborers, who live only so long as they find work, and who find work only so long as their labor increases capital. These laborers, who must sell themselves piecemeal, are a commodity, like every other article of commerce, and are consequently exposed to all the vicissitudes of the market.

Owing to the extensive use of machinery and to division of labor, the work of the proletarians has lost all individual character, and, consequently, all charm for the workman. He becomes an appendage of the machine, and it is only the most simple, most

monotonous, and most easily acquired knack that is required of him. . . .

Modern industry has converted the little workshop of the patriarchal master into the great factory of the industrial capitalist. Masses of laborers, crowded into the factory, are organized like soldiers. As privates of the industrial army they are placed under the command of a perfect hierarchy of officers and sergeants. Not only are they the slaves of the bourgeois class, and of the bourgeois State, they are daily and hourly enslaved by the machine, by the overlooker, and, above all, by the individual bourgeois manufacturer himself. The more openly this despotism proclaims gain to be its end and aim, the more petty, the more hateful and the more embittering it is. . . .

The lower strata of the middle class, the small tradespeople, shopkeepers, and retired tradesmen generally, the handicraftsman and peasants, all these sink gradually into the proletariat, partly because their diminutive capital does not suffice for the scale on which Modern Industry is carried on, and is swamped in the competition with the large capitalists, partly because their specialized skill is rendered worthless by new methods of production. Thus the proletariat is recruited from all classes of the population.

The proletariat goes through various stages of development. With its birth begins its struggle with the bourgeoisie. At first the contest is carried on by individual laborers, then by the workpeople of a factory, then by the operatives of one trade, in one locality, against the individual bourgeois who directly exploits them. They direct their attacks not against the bourgeois conditions of production, but against the instruments of production themselves; they destroy imported wares that compete with their labor, they smash to pieces machinery, they set factories ablaze, they seek to restore by force the vanished status of the workman of the Middle Ages.

At this stage the laborers still form an incoherent mass scattered over the whole country, and broken up by their mutual competition. If anywhere they unite to form more compact bodies, this is not yet the consequence of their own active union, but of the union of the bourgeoisie, which class, in order to attain its own political ends, is compelled to set the whole proletariat in motion, and is moreover yet, for a time, able to do so. At this stage, therefore, the proletarians do not fight their enemies, but the enemies of their enemies, the remnants of absolute monarchy, the landowners, the non-industrial bourgeois, the petty bourgeoisie. Thus the whole historical movement is concentrated in the hands of the bourgeoisie; every victory so obtained is a victory for the bourgeoisie.

But with the development of industry the proletariat not only increases in number, it becomes concentrated in greater masses, its strength grows, and it feels that strength more. The various interests and conditions of life within the ranks of the proletariat are more and more equalized, in proportion as machinery obliterates all distinctions of labor and nearly everywhere reduces wages to the same low level. The growing competition among the bourgeoisie, and the resulting commercial crises, make the wages of the workers ever more fluctuating. The unceasing improvement of machinery, ever more rapidly developing, makes their livelihood more and more precarious; the collisions between individual workmen and individual bourgeoisie take more and more the character of collisions between two classes. Thereupon the workers begin to form combinations (Trades' Unions) against the bourgeois, they club together in order to keep up the rate of wages; they found permanent associations in order to make provision beforehand for these occasional revolts. Here and there the contest breaks out into riots.

Now and then the workers are victorious, but only for a time. The real fruit of their battles lies not in the immediate result, but in the ever expanding union of the workers. This union is helped on by the improved means of communication that are created by modern industry, and that place the workers of different localities in contact with one another. It was just this contact that was needed to centralize the numerous local struggles, all of the same character, into one national struggle between classes. But every

class struggle is a political struggle. And that union, to attain which the burghers of the Middle Ages, with their miserable highways, required centuries, the modern proletarians, thanks to railways, achieve in a few years.

This organization of the proletarians into a class, and consequently into a political party, is continually being upset again by the competition between the workers themselves. But it ever rises up again, stronger, firmer, mightier. . . .

Further, as we have already seen, entire sections of the ruling classes are, by the advance of industry, precipitated into the proletariat, or are at least threatened in their conditions of existence. These also supply the proletariat with fresh elements of enlightenment and progress.

Finally, in times when the class-struggle nears the decisive hour, the process of dissolution going on within the ruling class, in fact, within the whole range of old society, assumes such a violent, glaring character, that a small section of the ruling class cuts itself adrift, and joins the revolutionary class, the class that holds the future in its hands. Just as, therefore, at an earlier period, a section of the nobility went over to the bourgeoisie, so now a portion of the bourgeoisie goes over to the proletariat, and in particular, a portion of the bourgeois ideologists, who have raised themselves to the level of comprehending theoretically the historical movements as a whole.

Of all the classes that stand face to face with the bourgeoisie today, the proletariat alone is a really revolutionary class. The other classes decay and finally disappear in the face of modern industry; the proletariat is its special and essential product.

The lower middle class, the small manufacturer, the shopkeeper, the artisan, the peasant, all these fight against the bourgeoisie, to save from extinction their existence as fractions of the middle class. They are, therefore, not revolutionary, but conservative. Even more, they are reactionary, for they try to roll back the wheel of history. If by chance they are revolutionary, they are so, only in view of their impending transfer into the proletariat, they thus defend not their present, but their future interests, they desert their own standpoint to place themselves at that of the proletariat. . . .

All previous historical movements were movements of minorities, or in the interest of minorities. The proletarian movement is the self-conscious, independent movement of the immense majority, in the interest of the immense majority. The proletariat, the lowest stratum of our present society, cannot stir, cannot raise itself up, without the whole super-incumbent strata of official society being sprung into the air.

Though not in substance, yet in form, the struggle of the proletariat with the bourgeoisie is at first a national struggle. The proletariat of each country must first of all settle matters with its bourgeoisie.

In depicting the most general phases of the development of the proletariat, we traced the more or less veiled civil war, raging within existing society, up to the point where that war breaks out into open revolution, and where the violent overthrow of the bourgeoisie lays the foundation for the sway of the proletariat.

Hitherto, every form of society has been based, as we have already seen, on the antagonism of oppressing and oppressed classes. But in order to oppress a class, certain conditions must be assured to it under which it can, at least, continue its slavish existence. The serf, in the period of serfdom, raised himself to membership in the commune, just as the petty bourgeois, under the yoke of feudal absolutism, managed to develop into a bourgeois. The modern laborer, on the contrary, instead of rising with the progress of industry, sinks deeper and deeper below the conditions of existence of his own class. He becomes a pauper, and pauperism develops more rapidly than population and wealth. And here it becomes evident that the bourgeoisie is unfit any longer to be the ruling class in society, and to impose its conditions of existence upon society, as an overriding law. It is unfit to rule, because it is incompetent to assure an existence to its slave within his slavery, because it cannot help letting him sink into such a state that it has to feed him. Society can no longer live under this bourgeoisie, in other words, its existence is no longer compatible with society.

The essential condition for the existence, and for the sway, of the bourgeois class is the formation and augmentation of capital; the condition for capital is wage-labor. Wage-labor rests exclusively on competition between the laborers. The advance of industry, whose involuntary promoter is the bourgeoisie, replaces the isolation of the laborers, due to competition, by their involuntary combination, due to association. The development of Modern Industry therefore cuts from under its feet the very foundation on which the bourgeoisie produces and appropriates products. What the bourgeoisie therefore produces, above all, are its own grave-diggers. Its fall and the victory of the proletariat are equal. . . .

The Communist revolution is the most radical rupture with traditional property relations; no wonder its development involves the most radical rupture with the traditional ideas of all of the bourgeoisie. But let us have done with the bourgeois objections to Communism.

We have seen above, that the first step in the revolution by the working class, is to raise the proletariat to the position of ruling class, to win the battle of democracy.

The proletariat will use its political supremacy to wrest, by degrees, all capital from the bourgeoisie, to centralize all instruments of production in the hands of the State, i.e., of the proletariat organized as the ruling class, and to increase the total of productive forces as rapidly as possible.

Of course, in the beginning, this cannot be effected except by means of despotic inroads on the rights of property, and on the conditions of bourgeois production; by means of measures, therefore, which appear economically insufficient and untenable, but which, in the course of the movement, outstrip themselves, necessitate further inroads upon the old social order, and are unavoidable as a means of entirely revolutionizing the mode of production.

These measures will of course be different in different countries.

Nevertheless in the most advanced countries the following will be found pretty generally applicable:

1. Abolition of property in land and application of all rents of land to public purposes.

2. A heavy progressive or graduated income tax.

3. Abolition of all right of inheritance.

4. Confiscation of property of emigrants and rebels.

5. Centralization of credit in the hands of the State, by means of a national bank with State capital and an exclusive monopoly.

6. Centralization of the means of communication and transport in the hands of the State.

7. Extension of factories and instruments of production owned by the State; the bringing into cultivation of waste lands, and the improvement of soil generally in accordance with a common plan.

8. Equal liability of all to labor. Establishment of industrial armies, especially for agriculture.

9. Combination of agriculture with manufacturing industries; gradual abolition of the distinction between town and country, by a more equable distribution of population over the country.

10. Free education for all children in public schools. Abolition of children's factory labor in its present form. Combination of education with industrial production, etc.

When, in the course of development, class distinctions have disappeared, and all production has been concentrated in the hands of a vast association of the whole nation, the public power will lose its political character. Political power, properly so called, is merely the organized power of one class for oppressing another. If the proletariat during its contest with the bourgeoisie is compelled, by the force of circumstances, to organize itself as a class, if, by means of a revolution, it makes itself the ruling class, and, as such, sweeps away by force the old conditions of production, then it will, along with these condi-

tions, have swept away the conditions for the existence of class antagonisms, and of classes generally, and will thereby have abolished its own supremacy as a class.

In place of the old bourgeois society, with its classes and class antagonisms, we shall have an association, in which the free development of each is the condition for the free development of all.

Review

1. What has been the role of the bourgeoisie in history?

2. How does the bourgeoisie handle crises?

3. Describe the development and life of the proletariat.

4. How will communism change the nature of social life?

Application

Interview one person in the working class (a member of a labor union) and another person who is an owner or executive. Develop and use a questionnaire that addresses the following:

a. perception of the existence and types of classes in the United States

b. perception of how class conflict is manifested

c. advantages and disadvantages of being in the different classes

d. opinion about Marx's ideas

e. opinion about the amount of inequality in the United States. Is it too much? Why or why not? If so, how could it be reduced?

Summarize your findings, contrasting the responses given by the two respondents.

Reprinted from: Karl Marx and Friedrich Engels, "The Communist Manifesto." In *The Communist Manifesto*. Copyright © 1933 by New York: Monthly Review Press. Reprinted by permission. ✦

15

Between the Executive Office and the Storeroom

How Much Inequality Is Acceptable?

"The rich get richer and the poor get poorer." "America is the land of opportunity." Which of these maxims is true? Actually, there is some truth in both of them, but neither of them accurately reflects what has happened to the distribution of wealth throughout American history. According to Census Bureau figures on aggregate income, for example, those in the lowest 20 percent received 3.7 percent of the nation's income in 1999 (compared to 4.1 percent in 1970). Those in the top 20 percent, in contrast, got 49.3 percent in 1999 (compared to 43.3 percent in 1970). In other words, the top 20 percent of Americans with earned income now receive nearly half of all income, and the gap between the top and the bottom—after some years of decrease after World War II—increased over the last decades of the twentieth century. In fact, by 1999, the wage gap between CEOs and workers was ten times larger than it was in 1980.

The disparity between the top and bottom income earners is highlighted in these two selections. Beth Shulman discusses the plight of those in low-wage jobs, noting how the low wages themselves are only part of the deprivation these workers endure. Holly Sklar portrays those at the other end of the income scale—the CEOs who receive as much in a day as low-wage workers get in a year or more. Few Americans would advocate equality in income. These two articles, however, raise the issue of how much inequality is acceptable.

The Story of Thirty-Five Million Workers in Low-Wage Jobs

Beth Shulman

If the social contract has eroded for many American workers, it is nonexistent for Americans who work in low-wage jobs. As Tom Kochan noted in his IRRA [Industrial Relations Research Association] presidential address, a social contract is "the expectations and obligations that workers, employers, and their communities and societies have for work and employment relationships." If one worked hard, the expectation of a livable income and basic securities for oneself and one's family was the implicit understanding of this social contract. For thirty-five million workers who get up every morning and evening and go to work in low-wage jobs, however, there is no such promise. One in four Americans works in jobs in which the most basic expectations from work—a decent wage, basic benefits, and respect—go unfulfilled.

These low-wage workers educate and train our children; care for our parents and friends; clean and assist us in our hotel rooms and offices; answer our questions on toll-free calls; prepare our food and serve our families in restaurants; protect us in airports, offices, and government buildings; cash our checks and take our deposits; harvest and process the meat, chicken, and food we eat; sew and clean the clothes we wear; wait on us in department, grocery, and drugstores; and enter information into databases. These low-wage jobs are intimately involved in every aspect of our lives, yet they provide workers with wages that are at or near the poverty line. While recent tight labor markets have helped inch up the wages at the bottom, thirty-five million Americans still earn less than $8.75 an hour.

Inadequate wages, however, are only part of the problem. Workers in low-wage jobs lack the basic security, freedom, control, and flexibility in their lives that most other Americans take for granted. Most workers in low-wage jobs are not provided any health coverage.[1] Those that are, generally cannot afford to purchase it.[2] Not surprisingly, these workers are exposed to more physically damaging working conditions and workplace safety and health hazards than most higher-paying jobs, which puts them at a higher risk for sickness and accidents.[3] Their jobs give little leeway to take a day off for illness and, if they can get off, they rarely get paid.[4]

Little flexibility exists to balance work and family responsibilities. Planning for family responsibilities is more difficult in low-wage jobs, because the schedules are less predictable. Low-wage employers give their workers little time to tend to a sick child or for personal needs or emergencies.[5] Because of this inflexibility, tending to family concerns can become a choice between taking care of your family or keeping your job. Paid vacations and holidays are less available than in higher-paying jobs, meaning less time to spend with one's family. A disproportionate burden of working night shifts falls on workers in low-wage jobs, which makes childcare provisions even more expensive and difficult to obtain.[6]

And there is little security in these jobs. These workers experience more frequent and recurrent periods of unemployment than workers in higher-paying jobs.[7] Yet it is these workers who receive little if any employer-provided severance pay to help them make the transition to another job.[8] Low-wage jobs provide fewer and more variable hours for workers than higher-paying jobs.[9] Many of these workers have part-time or contingent status and earn a lower hourly wage than a full-time worker in the same job.[10]

Unlike many higher-wage jobs, where cooperative models have been introduced in the workplace and employers value workers' input, most workers in low-wage jobs have little voice or autonomy. Their employers frequently discourage workers from voicing their opinions. Many of these low-wage employers lack basic respect toward their workers. Low-wage jobs are the least likely to have labor-union representation, leaving these workers without power to change their situations.[11] Employer-provided training

opportunities are largely unavailable to workers in low-wage jobs, diminishing their job-advancement possibilities.[12] Profit sharing is half as likely to be given to these workers as workers in higher-paying jobs.[13] At the end of their time on the job, these workers will have minimal employer-provided retirement.[14] When such plans are offered, they require worker contributions, which these workers cannot afford.

The final cruelty is that government programs created over the years to protect workers and their families have excluded this most vulnerable segment of the workforce. Laws covering workplace health and safety, discrimination protections, family and medical leave, wage and hour enforcement, unemployment compensation, workmen's compensation, and business-closing notice bypass many of these workers. A majority of workers in low-wage jobs work in small businesses, which fall outside many worker-protection laws. Some employment and labor statutes' eligibility requirements disqualify many low-wage workers on the number of hours required or minimum income levels. In other words, workers who are the most vulnerable to the dictates of employers are left without assistance from the government.

It is this "piling on" of all the deprivations of these jobs together with the meager earnings that make low-wage jobs not just quantitatively different, but qualitatively different from better-paying jobs. The employers' failure to provide the most basic provisions in low-wage jobs is the antithesis of the reciprocal responsibilities envisioned in the notion of a social contract. Workers in low-wage jobs are meeting their side of the bargain. Employers and politicians are failing to live up to theirs.

If work is to work for all Americans, we must establish a new set of ground rules for these millions of responsible Americans who go to work to provide for themselves and their families, yet get little in return. We need an employee bill of rights. We have established standards and rights in the past to ensure that older Americans would not be impoverished or go without health care; to prevent children from working; to keep our environment clean; and to ensure that workers have equal opportunity regardless of their race, religion, national origin, sex, or age. We must do so now for these thirty-five million Americans. We must also restore the right of workers to organize. In prior generations, we have seen low-wage workers move into the middle class through the power of labor unions. Yet, as Tom Kochan pointed out in his address, "Study after study has documented the failure of labor law to provide workers with the means to implement what the international community has (correctly) described as a fundamental human right, the right to join a union." We must ensure that workers have the tools to improve their situations, including the right to choose to have a union. . . .

Notes

1. Barbara Schone and Philip Cooper, Kaiser Commission, Agency for Health Care Policy and Research, part of the Department of Health and Human Services Study, *Health Affairs,* November 10, 1997.

2. Jack Meyer and Sharon Silow-Carroll, "Policy Options to Assure Access to Health Care for People Leaving Welfare for Work," *Economic and Social Research Institute Report,* September 1996.

3. Daniel S. Hamermesh, "Changing Inequality in Markets for Workplace Amenities," National Bureau of Economic Research Working Paper Series, Working Paper 6515, April 1998.

4. "BLS Report on Employee Benefits in Small Private Industry Establishments," Bureau of Labor Statistics, 1996; "BLS Report on Employee Benefits in Medium and Large Private Establishments," Bureau of Labor Statistics, 1995.

5. "BLS Report on Employee Benefits in Small Private Industry Establishments," Bureau of Labor Statistics 1996; "BLS Report on Employee Benefits in Medium and Large Private Establishments," Bureau of Labor Statistics, 1995.

6. Daniel S. Hamermesh, "The Timing of Work over Time," July 1997; Daniel S. Hamermesh, "Changing Inequality in Markets for Workplace Amenities," National Bureau of Economic Research Working Paper Series, Working Paper 6515, April 1998.

7. Joel F. Handier and Lucie White, eds., *Hard Labor* (Armonk, New York: ME Sharpe, Inc., 1999); Edmund S. Phelps, *Rewarding Work: How to Restore Participation and Self Support to Free Enterprise* (Cambridge, Massachusetts: Harvard University Press, 1997).

8. Peter Cappelli, Laurie Bassi, Harry Katz, David Knoke, Paul Osterman, and Michael Useem, *Change at Work* (New York: Oxford University Press, 1997).

9. Dora L. Costa, "The Unequal Work Day: A Long-Term View," National Bureau of Economic Research Working Paper Series 6419, February 1998.

10. Roberta Spalter-Roth and Heidi Hartmann, "Gauging the Consequences for Gender Relations, Pay Equity, and the Public Purse," in Kathleen Barker and Kathleen Christensen, eds., *Contingent Work: American Employment Relations in Transition* (Ithaca, New York: Cornell University Press, 1998).

11. Lawrence Mishel, Jared Bernstein, and John Schmitt, *The State of Working America 1998–1999* (Ithaca, New York: Cornell University Press, 1999).

12. Laurie J. Bassi, Anne L. Gallagher, and Ed Schroer, *The ASTI Training DataBook,* 1996.

13. Douglas L. Kruse, "Profit Sharing and the Demand for Low-Skill Workers," in Richard B. Freeman and Peter Gottschalk, eds., *Generating Jobs: How to Increase Demand for Less-Skilled Workers* (New York: Russell Sage Foundation, 1998).

14. *EBRI Databook on Employee Benefits,* Fourth Edition.

CEO Gravy Train Keeps On Rolling

Holly Sklar

It's getting harder to tell CEO paychecks from lottery payouts. Except that CEOs expect to win big even when the company loses.

When Coca-Cola CEO Douglas Ivester announced his retirement, Bloomberg compensation analyst Graef Crystal observed, "Here is a man who is resigning after a two-year tenure as CEO that produced a return for shareholders of a negative 7.3 percent. For that, he is walking away with stock options, and other goodies worth at least $120 million." Meanwhile, as the AFL-CIO Executive PayWatch reports, Coca-Cola is laying off thousands of workers and facing a lawsuit alleging the company discriminated against Black employees in promotions, pay, and performance evaluations.

Many CEOs make more in a year than their employees will make in a lifetime. In 1999, the average CEO of a major corporation earned $12.4 million, including salary, bonus, and other compensation such as exercised stock options, according to *Business Week's* latest survey of executive pay. That's $34,000 a day including Saturdays and Sundays.

In 1980, CEOs made 42 times the pay of average factory workers. In 1990, they made 85 times as much. By 1999, CEOs made 475 times as much as workers.

CEOs got a raise of 17 percent last year while blue-collar workers got a raise of 3.5 percent and white-collar workers got a raise of 3.4 percent, just a little ahead of inflation.

The top CEOs earned as much as small countries last year. Computer Associates

CEO Charles Wang led the gravy train with $655 million. Next were Tyco International CEO L. Dennis Kozlowski with $170 million, Charles Schwab CEO David Pottruck with $128 million, Cisco CEO John Chambers with $122 million, and America Online CEO Steve Case with $117 million.

Many CEOs have amassed future fortunes in stock options not yet exercised. Yahoo CEO Timothy Koogle leads with $2.3 billion in unexercised stock options, followed by America Online's Steve Case with $1.3 billion and Barry Diller of USA Networks with $1 billion.

CEOs aren't shy about claiming all the credit for company success to justify taking a big chunk of the rewards. Tyco CEO L. Dennis Kozlowski told *Business Week*, "While I gained $139 million [in stock options], I created about $37 billion in wealth for our shareholders." Thousands of Tyco employees in 80 countries didn't have anything to do with creating that wealth apparently. Kozlowski himself designs and services

Table 15.1
Highest-Paid CEOs, 1999
in Thousands of Dollars

	Salary & Bonus	Long-Term Compensation*	Total Pay
1. Charles Wang—Computer Associates Intl.	$4,600	$650,824	$655,424
2. L. Dennis Kozlowski—Tyco International	4,550	165,446	169,996
3. David Pottruck—Charles Schwab	9,000	118,900	127,900
4. John Chambers—Cisco Systems	943	120,757	121,700
5. Stephen Case—America Online	1,575	115,510	117,085
6. Louis Gerstner—IBM	9,166	91,983	102,250
7. Jack Welch—General Electric	13,325	79,813	93,138
8. Sanford Weil—CitiGroup	10,181	80,049	90,230
9. Peter Karmanos Jr.—Compuware	2,200	85,321	87,521
10. Reuben Mark—Colgate-Palmolive	4,200	81,117	85,318
11. William Esrey—Sprint Fon Group	2,456	74,524	76,980
12. Carleton Florina—Hewlett-Packard	654	68,781	69,435
13. Joseph Nacchio—Quest Communications Intl.	1,543	67,560	69,103
14. Charles Schwab—Charles Schwab	9,000	60,096	69,096
15. Melvin Goodes—Warner-Lambert	1,412	60,442	61,853
16. Robert Bennett—Liberty Media	1,000	54,066	55,066
17. Mark Logan—Visx	1,025	53,810	54,835
18. Robert Cecil—Plantronics	1,053	50,813	51,865
19. Michael Eisner—Walt Disney	750	49,907	50,657
20. Kenneth Lay—Enron	5,407	43,845	49,252

*Includes stock options already exercised. Many of the CEOs listed above have millions of dollars in stock options not yet cashed in.
Source: *Business Week*, "Executive Pay," April 17, 2000.

Tyco's fire safety and electronic security systems and must be very busy building the company's global undersea fiber optic communications network.

GE brings good things to life for CEO Jack Welch. He made $93 million last year and has some $436 million in options he still hasn't cashed in on. According to the AFL-CIO's Executive Pay-Watch, Welch has cut GE's domestic work force by nearly 50 percent since 1986 and relentlessly relocated work to low-wage countries like Mexico and China. Welch told CNN in 1998, "Ideally, you'd have every plant you own on a barge, to move with currencies and changes in the economy."

Most CEOs now get a major chunk of their pay in the form of stock options that don't count against company earnings the way salaries do. Take a leading company like Cisco, where CEO John Chambers hauled in $121.7 million and Donald Listwin hauled in $47,505 last year by *Business Week's* calculations. According to the *New York Times,* "Cisco reported $2.1 billion in net income in 1999, but accounting for options would have erased $500 million of that, according to a footnote in the annual report. That would amount to a 24 percent reduction in earnings per share."

In its April executive pay report, the *New York Times* asked, "Do companies get an extra bang from making their chief executives centimillionaires, for instance, rather than mere decimillionaires?" The *Times* cited a study by Columbia Business School professors examining the performance of 600 companies over the last 20 years. It "showed that increasing an executive's stake in a company did not cause stronger earnings or a higher stock price. Instead, it appears to be other factors, like research spending, that cause a company to perform well." A study by Salomon Smith Barney found that most of the heaviest users of stock options in the S&P 500 underperformed the S&P 500 stock index.

According to *Business Week,* Disney CEO Michael Eisner gave shareholders the least

bang for his bucks in the last three years. Over that period he hauled in $636.9 million.

The *Wall Street Journal's* executive pay report spotlighted "Net envy," an extreme cycle of keeping up with the Joneses in which "the spread of stratospheric compensation for Internet leaders is reverberating . . . in brick-and-mortar boardrooms everywhere." When the Joneses are centimillionaires and billionaires the consequences are enormous.

What kind of society has a minimum wage of $5.15 an hour—$10,712 a year—at the bottom of the pay scale and a *de facto* minimum wage in the millions at the top? . . .

Review

1. What kind of workers fall into the category of "low-wage"?

2. What does Shulman mean when she says that low-wage jobs are not just quantitatively but qualitatively different from better-paying jobs?

3. What kinds of benefits do CEOs get in addition to a salary?

4. Is there a relationship between a CEO's salary and the company's earnings?

Application

According to the Census Bureau, the highest income earned by those households in the lowest 20 percent in 1999 was $17,196, while the lowest income earned by households in the top 5 percent was $142,021. Do you believe that this is too much inequality? If so, why? If not, why not? If it was in your power to alter the amount of inequality in income in the United States, what, if anything, would you do?

16
America's Shame

Women and Children in Shelter

Barbara A. Arrighi

The homeless are at the bottom of the U.S. stratification system. While the United States has always had a population of transients, the character of this segment of the poor has changed in several ways in recent decades. The homeless have become more numerous since about 1980, and they have become more visible, no longer confined to the "skid row" areas of the larger cities. The composition of the homeless has also changed. More women and children are now living on the streets; a third or more of the homeless population are families with children.

In this selection, Barbara Arrighi discusses the ways in which homelessness affects the development of children. Homeless children are deprived of the major benefits of social institutions, such as a stable and secure family life and a good education. The children are living examples of the deprivations and emotional trauma endured by those at the bottom of the stratification system.

What are children who live in poverty, in substandard housing, and in unsafe neighborhoods to believe of a society that claims to revere the family and to hold family values superior to all other values? How does temporary housing affect children? Children who live in a transitional state know no structure, no order, no predictability; they know only chaos. For a child who looks to the adults in her life for security, the sight of her mother or father losing control over life's basic needs can damage her development of trust and sense of security. Many factors can influence the impact of such a transitional state, including the length of time in which the family is without a home, the availability of a support system for the family, and the child's age, sex, and temperament. Even so, the child is influenced by the emotional and physical environment of the available temporary housing.

Loss of home is not the only event that affects a child's sense of security. The process of poverty begins with one or a combination of crises, including separation, divorce, or death of a parent or caretaker, the head of household's loss of employment, declining household income, loss of extended-kin support system, and/or increased family conflict. Any of these factors can affect a child profoundly, and in combination they can have long-term consequences for a child's emotional and physical development. Children require a nurturing, supportive, caring, safe, predictable home life in order to thrive and acquire a sense of self-worth, and a lack of a permanent home disrupts that process.

The institutional environment of a shelter can heighten the crisis of an already tenuous familial relationship and compound the trauma experienced by a child without a home. A parent who is feeling powerless and helpless because of the family's situation is emotionally unable to reassure a frightened child, whose feelings mirror those of the parent. Children typically subjected to conflicting behavior expectations from mothers and staff become overwhelmed and confused. Their anxiety is heightened, not alleviated, by shelter life.

When a child remains largely uncomforted and insecure, she is more likely to exhibit any of an array of maladaptive behaviors, including depression, aggressiveness, restlessness, regressive behavior, hyperactivity, and anxiety. The child's sense of self is traumatized. There is some evidence that the emotional assault that is entwined with being without a permanent space negatively affects a child's expectations about his or her future.

Frequent changes in home environment, structure, and neighborhood can affect a child's sense that she belongs to some place and that some place belongs to her—the child's personal space or turf. Although the environment lacks permanence, one factor that generally remains constant for children living in poverty is the ghettoization of their lives. Typically, any area that they call home has been abandoned by the more affluent and is isolated from the economically vibrant portions of the city.

Poor Children and Schools

For children without a home, school could be a "haven in a heartless world." The few hours a day these children spend at school might well be the only time when they enjoy a sense of order or predictability. Even so, feelings of insecurity and inferiority surrounding these children's home lives can harm them in various areas, including formation of friendships, schoolwork, and attendance. Children who have stayed in a shelter spoke of the ridicule they encountered because of their situation. They coped in various ways. Sometimes they feigned illness to avoid going to school and facing the other children. Another tactic was to get off the school bus before their stop at the shelter so the other children would not see them enter their "home." Children described the pain of being stigmatized by classmates, who frequently taunted them because of their temporary residence.

Unfortunately, some teachers' treatment of the children can be as callous as the taunting by their schoolmates. Often teachers view the issues that children without homes, who live in poverty, bring to the classroom as interfering with teaching. Because any negative reaction on the part of classmates and/or teacher heightens the child's sense of alienation, the child might feel the need to become secretive, protective, and deceptive about her or his personal life. The more often the child employs these defense mechanisms, the more isolated she will be.

Thus life can be a catch-22 for a child without a home. The more she attempts to keep her family situation secret, the more distrusted, suspect, and marginalized she becomes. The most effective way to keep the family secret is to play truant; one study found that 43 percent of school-age children who lacked a permanent home did not attend school. For many children, then, especially adolescents, dropping out is the solution.

Education: Not an Equalizer

Frequently the desperate day-to-day life of poor children and their parents clashes with the educational system. Pierre Bordieu's perspective on education explains the disadvantaged position of poor children in the classroom. Children living in poverty experience the world at a primitive level. Their parents exhaust their psychic energy in search of life's basic needs—food, shelter, and clothing. These children and their families live a concrete existence and speak concrete language about problems relating to their survival. However, the culture of education, disseminated through abstract concepts, presupposes that children have transcended the concrete, essentials of life. Teachers assume that children are prepared for conceptualizing, but children living in poverty generally are not. They have not had the luxury of experiencing abstract ways of thinking. The progressive nature of schoolwork is a constant struggle for them. Bordieu's thinking underscores the point that children living in poverty are excluded from the language and culture of education, and further, that the educational system, portrayed as neutral, is laden with the ideas of the elite. Bordieu's perspective would explain the dropout rate of children in poverty and/or without homes as well as the high proportion of working class and poor children in vocational classes. The language of vocational coursework is familiar. Only 29 percent of children who are poor are placed in the college preparatory track, compared with 65 percent of students from high-income families.

Without a conceptual understanding of their world, the probability intensifies that poor children will be left out of the school curriculum and instruction. Equally important, because of their situation, they risk being excluded from most circles of friends. Thus over time they resort to the most effective exclusion, self-exclusion, which severely decreases their chances for upward mobility. Current research on intergenerational mobility provides evidence supporting the assertion that children whose parents belong to today's underclass have a higher than average probability of taking their parents' place as adults.

The McKinney Act of 1987 mandated that children without homes are entitled to receive an education like all other children. In response to the mandate, the state of Kentucky formed Family Resource Centers in schools in which the majority of students are at or below poverty level. The resource centers facilitate children's attendance in school by assisting them with material needs such as clothing, food, and school supplies, and nonmaterial needs such as counseling and tutoring. In addition, Family Resource Center staff members emphasize to parents the importance of parental involvement with a child's education and encourage parents to volunteer in some way at school. Personnel at the resource center attempt to work with school faculty members to encourage parental involvement. In an interview with a former staff member at a northern Kentucky resource center, however, I learned that school faculty members often do not encourage involvement on the part of these parents. Mothers with whom I spoke told of feeling welcome at the resource center, but not in other areas of the school, especially as classroom mothers. Each mother who had attempted to become an assistant in the classroom told of the teacher's lack of encouragement for the parent's participation. One mother told of an experience where she repeatedly volunteered to assist the teacher while the teacher never asked the mother to assist. Further, the mother maintained that the teacher seemed irritated every time the mother volunteered for classroom activities.

Again, from Bordieu's perspective, teachers typically bring middle-class value systems to education. If they are ill equipped to cope with children living in poverty, their judgment of the children's parents is likely to be even less tolerant, less empathic, less accepting. Indeed, it would be anathema for classrooms laden with middle-class ideology and for the teachers in those classrooms to view a mother who receives AFDC as a potential role model for the students.

If children of parents who are poor and without housing are to reach even half (national test scores indicate many are not achieving even half) of their potential in school, educators must go beyond legal mandates. Flexible school systems and empathic teachers are needed for coping with children's socioeconomic and sociocultural diversity.

Unwelcoming School Structures

Unfortunately, the forbidding atmosphere of school buildings in poor neighborhoods can and does reinforce negative messages that poor children receive from the educational system. Antiquated structures, peeling paint, crumbling plaster, and restrooms in constant disrepair tell children they are unimportant. Children learn a lesson that is as lasting as any classroom instruction, if not more so: not to expect much from any situation they enter. For these children, the atmosphere at school is consistent with the atmosphere at home. They grow up believing that this is all there is, this is all they can expect in life, and this is all they deserve.

As middle-class families continue to flee inner-city school systems, the quality of education in those systems has little chance of improving. Because the proportion of households with children in public schools continues to decrease (currently it is about 24 percent), school levies cannot easily muster support. Increasingly, school systems heavily populated by poor Anglos and members of minorities have fewer resources for basic instructional materials. Poor children are the initial losers, but eventually the whole society loses. Taking care of all children early in their lives is a cost-effective investment; certainly it is less costly to society than rehabilitating or incarcerating adults.

The Role of the Community Environment

Research has established a relationship between dilapidated, economically deprived communities and maladaptive childhood development. Yet there is evidence that even a homogeneous, poor neighborhood can provide children with a buffer against some of the stressors of poverty. Because children living in a totally poor environment are not likely to be in contact with children who enjoy greater material comfort, their self-esteem is less likely to become bruised. They are less likely to be judged by appearances.

Athletic competition frequently brings together children who are disparate in income and race or ethnicity. Differences between lower-income neighborhood schools and middle-income suburban schools are discerned easily in the neighborhood setting, the age and condition of the structure, the quality of the gymnasium, and the team uniforms. Thus even seemingly innocuous athletic meetings have the potential to affect the self-concept of students from schools in poor communities.

On the other hand, children who interact exclusively with persons in their poverty-ridden communities run the risk of adopting characteristics of their neighborhood role models. Two of the children interviewed for this study, sisters aged 9 and 11, spoke matter-of-factly about living in an apartment building in which drug dealers also lived. They recalled the fear they felt when they saw a SWAT (Special Weapons and Tactics) team surround their building in order to apprehend the traffickers. They also reported that the police did not bother to verify whether other tenants were present in the building. Normal police procedure should include ensuring the safety of those in the vicinity of a potentially dangerous arrest. One study suggests that 38 percent of youngsters aged 10 to 17 fear that they could be hurt by someone using drugs. Children should not have to fear being injured by police who are in pursuit of those suspected of committing a crime. Are safety procedures routinely ignored in lower-income neighborhoods? Besides the obvious physical risk to children living among drug dealers, there is the danger that deviance will become normalized in their minds. Children living in such conditions become acutely sensitive to deviance and develop a high tolerance. The sisters giggled, for example, when they described the drug dealers as kind, generous men who

gave neighborhood children candy, money, and motorcycle rides. Perhaps it is to their advantage that they did not fully grasp the immediate danger or the long-term consequences of their circumstances. Yet occasional face-to-face encounters with others outside their community, whose lifestyle is very different, might not be the solution. It might simply emphasize the inequities.

Bringing Order to Unordered Lives

Because the lives of children in poverty and those without housing are out of control, they often fight for control in any arena they enter, such as the classroom, the school playground, the football field, or the gymnasium. In a society that reveres the home, children without a home soon learn from their environment—their classmates, television, films, and the print media—that their situation is considered abnormal and undesirable. And as these children progress through adolescence—these children who have never been allowed to be children, and who live in a society where middle- and upper-class children are idolized and overindulged by their parents—some rebel against their parents, some vandalize their own community, and some choose the safest victims for destruction: themselves. Those who survive childhood will take their place at the lower levels of the class structure, believing that they will achieve parity with those in other social classes if they only work harder and longer. The great majority will never do so.

According to Charles Cooley's "looking glass" theory, which maintains that we see ourselves reflected in the eyes of others, children who lack permanent housing are likely to see themselves as undesirable. Depending on the child's age, temperament, and familial relationships, he or she will develop protective coping mechanisms such as extreme introversion (as in withdrawal) or extreme extroversion (as in acting out in various ways such as aggressive behavior).

Staff members at Hope House have experienced a variety of coping strategies on the part of children. They stated that age is a factor in determining behavior. Older children who could comprehend the total picture were embarrassed about the situation and the lack of privacy; they tended to withdraw. Younger children, who could not verbalize their insecurity, tended to cling to their mothers. Still others, who sensed their mothers' loss of power over them in the shelter, became disruptive.

Children and Shelter Life

Despite the best efforts on the part of an excellent shelter like Hope House, staff members acknowledge that the artificial home environment cannot replace the stabilizing, secure effect of permanent housing for children and their parents. If the familiar constantly gives way to the unfamiliar, a child often ceases to form attachments to people and places. This behavior pattern affects performance of adult roles and places the next generation at risk. The two sisters introduced earlier discussed the difficulty of adapting to shelter life, in which they had lived for 3½ months. Within the shelter, the most troublesome features were sharing their room with another family and the resulting lack of privacy. Another issue (less serious but nonetheless irritating) was the abundance of rules in the shelter: rules that contradicted their way of life outside the shelter, rules for minor things such as snacks in the evening or doing homework at a specified time, rules for everything.

One mother told of her preadolescent son's crying spells. He, his mother, and a younger sibling had to share a room with a family with adolescent girls. Although he had little contact with the girls, sharing a room with strangers was experienced as a tremendous loss of control in his life. He had a sense of dread and mortification about the possibilities the situation presented. Changing his clothes became a battle for the mother because he was afraid the girls would walk in on him. He was fearful, too, of having his few possessions taken. One can only imagine the lifelong consequences for this traumatized child.

Outside the shelter, a major concern for children was hiding their shelter life. The sisters described the measures they took to keep their "home" a secret from their classmates. They made certain that none of their schoolmates ever saw them enter or leave the shelter. Ridicule from classmates who knew they were staying in a shelter was one of their most painful experiences. Former shelter guests confirmed the girls' perceptions and observed that their adolescent children were mortified about their temporary residence. Even at that, not all their experiences with the shelter were negative. The girls spoke positively about some of their shelter experiences. Looking surprised by their own admission, they happily reported that their mother could not whip them when they disobeyed, as was her custom. The girls also pointed out that as shelter guests, they were offered recreational opportunities that would not have been available. Some of the amenities included tickets to concerts and ball games donated by local corporations. A favorite activity was going to the local Boys and Girls Club for swimming and other activities.

An agency in the role of the good provider presents a double-edged sword for families in shelter. Parents, by definition, are supposed to be the providers of the good things in life, including recreational events for children. Parents living in poverty cannot indulge their children in costly leisure activities. Therefore, when an agency replaces the parents as provider, mothers expressed mixed emotions. They were happy to see their children enjoying the event, but they also felt saddened about their inability to be the one making their child's life more enjoyable. It threatened their status as a parent. Perhaps one of the hardest things for us to understand about those living in poverty is their seeming lack of gratitude for works of charity and philanthropy. It is difficult to comprehend that dependency breeds hostility, not gratitude. Most people, given the choice, would choose independence over being on the receiving end of charity.

Familial Relationships in Shelters

When asked about the familial relationships that shelter guests reveal to case managers, Ms. Mayerson and the staff responded without hesitation and almost in unison. Recounting frequent observations of blurred boundaries between mothers and children, they said, "Parents do not parent, and children are not children." Childhood appears to be lost for the youngsters they see. The eldest child or the older children frequently serve as caretakers for the parent as well as the younger children. Although daughters are more likely to be caregivers for all others, staff members reported that typically the sons act like adult male partners for their mothers. Mothers rely on their sons as a wife would rely on a husband. Staff members also pointed out that it was not uncommon for mothers to sleep with their preteen sons . . . (males over age 12 may not stay at Hope House).

Although the mother-child relationships observed by workers seemed to be outside normative expectations from a sociological perspective, a mother's reliance on her children can be understood in several ways. First, from a material standpoint, mothers existing at a survival level have a vague notion of the current cultural prescriptions for performing the mother role, but they have little hope of enacting it. These women have no home, no money, no food, few belongings, and no support system that offers them sustained protection.

Second, the women and their children exhibit vestiges of paradigmatic kin relationships of other eras. For example, families living in poverty resemble members of hunting-and-gathering societies but lack the security and community of a kinship group. The children, like the young of hunting-and-gathering societies, who assisted with sustenance as soon as they could take their place in the group, forage with and sometimes substitute for their parents. Contemporary children whose parents cannot provide for them adequately are producers as well as consumers, like the children of the hunters and gatherers.

Further, families in poverty reflect medieval times, when boundaries between childhood and adulthood hardly existed. During that period, children were treated like small adults (but without the privileges), and took on the roles of caretaker and provider at very young ages. Young boys assumed men's responsibilities; if the father died or departed, the son acted as head of the family. Because

housing was scarce and living space inadequate for the poor in the burgeoning cities of that time (just as they are now), family members frequently slept together.

Families living in poverty today cannot be expected to exhibit twentieth-century middle-class Western norms. Earlier models of family and kinship groups might provide more useful explanations of their existence than the current cultural paradigms of motherhood and parenthood. The latter appear almost irrelevant to the material conditions in which these families find themselves.

We must not assume that such behavior is limited to poor persons and those without homes. We do not know the extent to which the familial relationships revealed to workers in shelters are unique to the guest population and to what extent they reflect the larger society. Certainly the research does not support the conclusion that "deviant" familial behavior is the exclusive domain of the poor. The evidence indicates that maladaptive treatment of children, including incest, cuts across all income levels but too often escapes attention unless the family is forced into public scrutiny for some reason. Families are subjected to public examination, for example, when they apply for assistance with income, housing, and/or food. Although behavior bordering on the incestuous is not to be condoned, we cannot assume that incest is class bound or that it is the cause or the consequence of the circumstances surrounding families without homes.

Deviance of any kind is more likely to be uncovered among persons seeking income assistance than among other families, because higher-income families generally can avoid confrontations with an intrusive legal system. The once-private lives of families who seek federal, state, or local assistance are subjected to scrutiny by numerous strangers. Often such families are asked repeatedly to explain their income and budgetary actions, their lifestyle, and their parenting techniques.

Hope House staff members have been trained to understand and accept the uniqueness of each family's situation. While staying alert to behavior that could harm the children, they work with families without passing judgment. They know the realities of shelter guests' lives and remain alert to their self-conscious struggle to achieve the status of the "normative American family."

Societal Response to Those Without Homes

Our society's response to the growing numbers of people without homes has been ill conceived. It is almost too little, too late. Policies supporting temporary shelter as a solution are based on the assumption that individuals' and families' housing problems are temporary and that people need only a brief stay in a shelter to regain economic solvency. Yet systemic factors beyond individuals' control, such as a shortage of full-time jobs, increased part-time and temporary service work, declining wages, a decrease in affordable housing, and cuts in federal and state assistance for families, have contributed to a crisis-based way of life for increasing numbers of people. Because of unfavorable economic conditions, temporary shelters have become more than a one-time respite; they are a recurring reality for more and more lower-income individuals and families. The dismantling of federal welfare programs that is about to begin means that the chronic crisis of living conditions of poor families will reach epidemic proportions. Temporary housing has not been enough. What will happen when federal funding is completely gone?

Review

1. Why is education "not an equalizer" for homeless children?

2. How do homelessness and poverty affect the self-concept of children?

3. Describe the effects on children of living in a shelter.

4. What has been the societal response to homelessness?

Applications

1. Contact city, county, and state offices and obtain information about the latest official statistics on the number of homeless in your community. Get as much demographic information—sex, race, age, number of dependents, etc.— as you can. Contact a local homeless shelter and ask for a demographic breakdown of the people they serve. Are they similar to the official figures? If not, what could account for the discrepancies?

2. Use the library to consult the archives of your local newspaper. Search for stories on homelessness. How often was the issue addressed? When did the majority of the stories appear? What did the stories indicate about the demographics of the homeless, the causes of homelessness, and efforts to deal with it? Summarize your findings in a brief data table and essay.

Reprinted from: *America's Shame: Women and Children in Shelter and the Degradation of Family Roles,* by Barbara A. Arrighi. Westport, Conn: Praeger, 1997. Copyright © 1997 by Barbara A. Arrighi. Reproduced with permission of Greenwood Publishing Group, Inc., Westport, CT. ✦

Part Two

Racial/Ethnic Inequality

The United States has an increasingly diverse population. The proportion of the population that is white and non-Hispanic continues to decline (from 79.9 percent in 1980 to 71.3 percent in 2000). As the number of racial/ethnic Americans increases, their demands for an equitable share in American life grow stronger. Historically, minorities have not had equal access to the American dream. They have endured considerable **prejudice** (a negative attitude toward those in a different racial/ethnic group that justifies discriminatory behavior) and **discrimination** (arbitrary, unfavorable treatment of people in a different racial/ethnic group). Discrimination against racial/ethnic minorities has been maintained through the policies and practices of institutions, a process that sociologists call institutional racism.

In this part, selections 17 and 18 examine the struggles of African Americans, including an example of institutional racism. Selection 19 shows how prejudice enters into the way we interpret aspects of our culture such as motion pictures. ✦

17
The Job Ghetto

Katherine Newman
Chauncy Lennon

Compared with other economically developed countries, the United States' social safety net is loosely woven. Thus, it is easier for Americans to slip through and end up at the bottom of the social scale. With this weak public support system, having a job is vital; it's the individual's foothold in the private economy. Obtaining the first job provides work experiences essential to moving up the ladder of employment. Employment, even at minimum wage, can also provide a sense of purpose, of having a role and responsibility in society.

On the other hand, when a person cannot find a job even when seriously seeking one, he or she develops a sense of despair or hopelessness. Society places high value on work, and there is a widespread belief that anyone who really wants a job can find one. This attitude often leads to a sharp condemnation of the unemployed, who may also be blamed for expecting too high a wage for the unskilled jobs they seek.

In this social context, it is instructive to look at the experience of poor, minority youth seeking entry-level work in the fast-food industry. Unemployment rates among ghetto youth are the highest in the nation—as high as 40 to 50 percent in some areas. (Keep in mind that the unemployment rate refers to those actively seeking but unable to secure jobs—their lack of jobs is not their choice.) Moreover, in place of the higher-paying, unionized factory jobs once available to inner-city workers, fast-food service employment is now the typical starting point for those poor youth who are able to find a job and enter the world of work. In this selection, Newman and Lennon investigate the search for a job in the ghetto. For many of those studied, this first rung on the employment ladder has proved to be elusive.

To fix the welfare mess, conservatives say, we should stop making life on the dole so comfortable, cut benefits, and force overindulged welfare moms to go out and find honest jobs. . . .

But can just any warm body find a job? For the past two years, we have studied the low-wage labor market in Harlem, focusing on minimum-wage jobs in the fast-food industry, which are typical of the employment opportunities many reformers have in mind for welfare recipients. After all, these jobs presumably demand little skill, education, or prior work experience—or so the public believes.

The fast-food industry is growing more rapidly than almost any other service business and now employs more than 2.3 million workers. One in 15 Americans working today found their first job at McDonald's—not including Burger King and the rest. As a gateway to employment, fast-food establishments are gaining on the armed forces, which have long functioned as a national job-training factory. No wonder the average citizen believes these jobs are wide open! Yet, in inner cities, the picture looks different. With manufacturing gone, fast-food jobs have become the object of fierce competition.

Downward Pressures

Between 1992 and 1994, we tracked the work histories of 200 people working in fast-food restaurants in central Harlem, where according to official data about 18 percent of the population are unemployed and about 40 percent live below the poverty line. These numbers are typical of the communities where many long-term recipients of public assistance will have to look for work if their benefits are cut off. Some 29 percent of the households in Harlem receive public assistance.

Although the 200 workers in our study receive only the minimum wage, they are actually the victors in an intense competition to find work in a community with relatively few jobs to offer. At the restaurants where they work, the ratio of applicants to hires is approximately 14 to 1. Among those people who applied but were rejected for fast-food work in early 1993, 73 percent had not found work of any kind a year later, despite considerable effort. Even the youngest job-hunters in our study (16- to 18-year-olds) had applied for four or five positions before they came looking for these fast-food jobs. The oldest applicants (over 25) had applied for an average of seven or eight jobs.

The oversupply of job-seekers causes a creeping credentialism in the ghetto's low-wage service industries. Older workers in their twenties, who are more often high school graduates, now dominate jobs once taken by school dropouts or other young people first starting out. Long-term welfare recipients will have a tough time beating out their competition even for these low-wage jobs. They will be joining an inner-city labor market that is already saturated with better educated and more experienced workers who are preferred by employers.

Winners and Losers

We tracked nearly 100 people who applied for these minimum-wage jobs but were turned down, and compared them to the fortunate ones who got jobs. The comparison is instructive. Even in Harlem, African Americans are at a disadvantage in hiring compared to Latinos and others. Employers, including black employers, favor applicants who are not African American. Blacks are not shut out of the low-wage labor market; indeed, they represent about 70 percent of the new hires in these jobs. But they are rejected at a much higher rate than applicants from other ethnic groups with the same educational qualifications.

Employers also seem to favor job applicants who commute from more distant neighborhoods. The rejection rate for local applicants is higher than the rate for similarly educated individuals who live farther away. This pattern holds even for people of the same race, sex, and age. Other studies in the warehouse and dockyard industries report the same results. These findings suggest that residents of poor neighborhoods such as central Harlem are at a distinct disadvantage in finding minimum-wage jobs near home.

Mothers of young children face particular problems if they can't find jobs close to home. The costs and logistical complexities of commuting (and paying for longer child care hours to accommodate it) are a big burden.

In searching for jobs, "who you know" makes a big difference. Friends and family members who already have jobs help people get work even in the fast-food industry; those isolated from such networks are less likely to get hired. Personal contacts have long been recognized as crucial for getting higher-skilled employment. This research suggests that contacts are important at the bottom of the job ladder, too.

Native-born applicants are at a disadvantage compared to legal immigrants in securing entry-level work. In fact, even though central Harlem residents are nearly all African American, recent immigrants have a higher probability of being hired for Harlem's fast-food jobs than anyone else. Interviews with employers suggest that they believe immigrants are easier to manage in part because they come from countries where $4.25 an hour represents a king's ransom. Whether or not employers are right about the tractability of immigrants, such attitudes make it harder for the native-born to obtain low-wage jobs.

The people who succeed in getting these minimum-wage jobs are not new to the labor market. More than half of the new hires over the age of 18 found their first jobs when they were younger than 15 years of age. Even the people rejected for the minimum-wage positions had some prior job experience. Half of them also began working before they were 15 years old. Welfare recipients with no prior job experience, or no recent job experience, are going to be at a disadvantage in the competition.

'They Expect Too Much'

One explanation often advanced for low employment in poor communities is that the poor have unrealistic expectations. In this view, they are reluctant to seek (or take) jobs that fall below a "reservation wage," which is supposedly far above the minimum. We asked job-seekers who were refused these entry-level jobs what they were hoping for and what wages they would accept. Their desires were modest: $4.59 per hour on average, which is quite close to the minium wage. The younger the job-seeker, the lower was the expectation.

These job-seekers were willing to accept even more modest wages. On average the lowest they would take was $4.17 per hour, which is less than the minimum level legally permitted for adult workers. It is striking that many applicants previously had higher salaries; the average wage for the best job they had ever held was $6.79 per hour. Many of central Harlem's job-hunters are suffering from downward mobility, falling into the minimum-wage market even though they have done better in the past.

Comparing job-seekers to job-holders shows the intensity of employment competition in the inner city, but it doesn't tell us how welfare recipients will fare. What assets do welfare recipients bring to the competition compared to other job-hunters? The news is grim.

Nationally, one-third of the long-term welfare recipients have received high school diplomas. Recently hired fast-food workers in central Harlem have completed high school at a higher rate—54 percent. Almost 40 percent of welfare recipients have not held jobs in the year preceding their enrollment in welfare. Yet even the central Harlem applicants rejected for fast-food jobs have had more job experience. They have held an average of more than three jobs before applying for these positions.

In short, it is simply not the case that anyone who wants a low-wage job can get one. As is true for almost any glutted labor market, there is a queue of applicants, and employers can be fairly choosy. When conservatives point to the success of immigrants as

proof that jobs are available for welfare moms, they are ignoring the realities of the inner city. Ethnic minorities of all kinds are already locked into a fierce struggle for scarce opportunities at the bottom. . . .

Review

1. In the inner cities, what are the qualifications that determine who does and does not get the minimum-wage jobs?

2. Do Newman and Lennon find support for the argument that residents of poor communities do not take minimum-wage jobs because they have unrealistic wage expectations? What, specifically, are their findings?

3. What puts welfare recipients at a disadvantage should they seek minimum-wage jobs?

Application

Locate one or two local businesses (fast-food, etc.) that hire minimum-wage workers. Arrange to interview the managers about their hiring guidelines and experiences with different groups of applicants. You will want to find out how many applications they receive in a given time period; how many positions they fill; what qualifications they expect; and any other relevant data that will enable you to determine the availability of minimum-wage jobs in your community, and who is getting them. How do your findings correspond to those of Newman and Lennon? Keep in mind the socioeconomic status of the residents of your community.

Reprinted from: Katherine Newman and Chauncy Lennon, "The Job Ghetto." From *The American Prospect*, Summer 1995. Copyright © 1995 New Prospect, Inc. Reprinted by permission. ✦

18
Policies of Prejudice

Gregory Squires

While one might expect that prejudice and discrimination go hand in hand, that is not always the case. An important study done in the United States during the 1930s illustrates this point. Richard LaPiere, a social psychologist, accompanied a Chinese couple on a journey across the country and found that fewer than 1 percent of the food and lodging establishments along the way refused the couple service. However, when LaPiere later wrote the same businesses asking whether they would serve Chinese customers, over 90 percent said they would not. Obviously, action was not consistent with attitude in this instance.

In the United States today, we are likely to find the opposite situation. That is, public expressions of prejudice are less likely to occur, but discrimination in some forms persists. It is important to distinguish between de jure and de facto forms of discrimination. De jure discrimination is formally written into law; de facto discrimination is more subtle and informal, based on customs and existing social arrangements. While de jure discrimination against minorities has been largely eliminated in the United States, it continues in other societies, the most notorious instance being the now abolished apartheid policy in South Africa. De facto discrimination has been more difficult to eliminate in this country, because in some instances it derives from the normal workings of institutions (i.e., institutional racism).

While specific governmental remedies have been used to overcome de facto discrimination in education (for example, voluntary or mandatory busing) and in employment (affirmative action), residential segregation has been more difficult to address. In this selec-tion, Squires shows how so-called redlining practices perpetuate discrimination against minorities in the housing market and in their efforts to develop businesses.

Racial discrimination in the home mortgage market has finally been acknowledged by lenders and regulators in recent years after decades of organizing efforts by community groups around the country. But equally harmful redlining practices by property insurers have received far less attention. Yet property insurance is essential for home ownership, business development, or any urban revitalization effort. The vital role of property insurance for the development of the nation's cities was captured in the following statement of a federal advisory report almost thirty years ago:

> Insurance is essential to revitalize our cities. It is a cornerstone of credit. Without insurance, banks and other financial institutions will not and cannot make loans. New housing cannot be constructed, and existing housing cannot be repaired. New businesses cannot be opened, and existing businesses cannot expand or even survive.

Without insurance, buildings are left to deteriorate; services, goods, and jobs diminish. Efforts to rebuild our nation's inner cities cannot move forward. Communities without insurance are communities without hope.[1]

Despite widespread evidence of discrimination by the property insurance industry, public officials have not pursued remedies to insurance redlining as aggressively as federal financial regulatory agencies have begun to address redlining by mortgage lenders. Where many lenders now acknowledge, perhaps grudgingly, their responsibilities under federal law, the insurance industry's basic response continues to be resistance. However, things may be changing.

The Evidence

The insurance industry, like the housing industry generally, has long utilized race as a factor in appraising and underwriting property. In the past, the Federal Housing Administration (FHA) has warned of "inharmonious racial groups" in its underwriting manuals. Lenders have considered "pride of ownership" in mortgage applications, and homeowners have incorporated racially restrictive covenants in home sales contracts. But insurers were no less concerned with race, sometimes indirectly through vague references to such terms as "character," but often explicitly as well.

In a 1958 report called "Report on Negro Areas of Chicago," the National Inspection Company, which provided technical underwriting consulting services to insurers, noted the "encroachment of Negroes" and observed that "The Puerto Ricans, Mexicans, Japanese and 'Hillbillies' have worked into some colored areas, particularly on the fringe of the cheaper or poorer districts and, in some cases, are in the same category with the lower-class Negroes." The report went on to describe a racially mixed neighborhood in Chicago and concluded, "Any liability in the areas described should be carefully scrutinized and in case of Negro dwellings, usually only the better maintained, owner-occupied risks are considered acceptable for profitable underwriting."

In 1977, the Chief Actuary of the New York Department of Insurance stated, "Take Harlem, for example. They don't need any insurance because they don't have anything of value to insure."

That same year, the Michigan Insurance Commissioner stated that "many of the underwriting rules are not rules at all, but are a conglomeration of myths, notions, perceptions, and beliefs. They are often subjective, not based upon scientific, empirical fact." And in 1994 the Texas Insurance Commissioner told the Senate Banking Committee, "We still find insurance companies making underwriting decisions based on all kinds of factors that have nothing to do with a statistically measured or measurable probability of risk."

The overt use of race in underwriting and pricing of insurance has been reduced in recent years, but it has not disappeared. The sales manager of American Family Insurance, a large insurer, told one agent, "I think you write too many blacks," and instructed several other agents in writing to "quit writing all those blacks. . . ." Until a few years ago, American Family produced a document called "Red Flags for Underwriting," which included "population or racial changes" as one of the flags. And in a 1993 underwriting manual, Nationwide stated that an "applicant must be a person of integrity and financial stability who takes pride in his property"—a phrase that can be understood to mean white people.

More systematic evidence also indicates the continuing role of race in property insurance markets. In 1993, the Missouri Department of Insurance found that residents of low-income minority neighborhoods in St. Louis paid 50 percent more than did residents of low-income white areas for comparable policies, even though losses over the previous five years had been higher in the white communities. Back in 1995, an economist with the department also found that the number of agents in a community was directly related to the racial composition of the area even after controlling for loss history. Ironically, loss costs turned out not to be a significant factor in accounting for the distribution of agents in St. Louis.

The National Association of Insurance Commissioners (NAIC) recently obtained loss data from a sample of insurers in forty-seven communities across thirteen states. Again, even after controlling for losses, the number of policies and the price of those policies in a community remained significantly associated with racial composition of the neighborhood. In their 1995 report, the researchers concluded that the results "lend greater support to concerns that the causes are not confined to higher losses in urban areas."

The National Fair Housing Alliance recently completed a series of paired tests of insurance companies in nine cities. The housing group matched "mystery shoppers" in terms of the structure and value of their homes, their incomes and occupations, and other socioeconomic factors. The only difference was the racial composition of their neighborhoods. In 1995 they reported that discrimination occurred in over half the tests. They found, for example, that when testers from white areas called to inquire about the availability of insurance, agents generally attempted to sell them a policy. But when callers from minority areas inquired about the same insurance needs, the same insurers often denied coverage, offered inferior policies and/or higher rates, referred the caller to a FAIR Plan (publicly administered insurance services that generally provide inferior yet more expensive policies than those available in the regular or "voluntary" insurance market), did not return phone calls, failed to meet scheduled appointments, or otherwise discouraged the callers from pursuing a policy with them.

The industry contends it is risk, not race, that governs its underwriting activities. As the National Association of Independent Insurers—a trade association representing 570 companies who write about one-third of all homeowners insurance—stated in 1978:

> The insurance industry refrains from moral pronouncements about its customers. We measure risk as accurately as we can, applying experience and objective criteria refined for more than two centuries. We leave it to others to speak of discrimination and other such moral terms.

This sentiment has been echoed repeatedly over the years. Insurers often state that underwriting is as much an art as it is a science and, therefore, subjectivity is inevitable. Yet the mounting evidence that has accumulated in recent years demonstrates that race, as well as risk, enters into underwriting, marketing, and sales practices. Even the arguably more objective dimensions of underwriting can have a discriminatory impact on minority applicants and communities and may violate the Federal Fair Housing Act even if there is no evidence of any intent to discriminate. For example, many insurers maintain maximum housing age and minimum housing value requirements to qualify for particular insurance products. Common thresholds exclude homes that are over fifty years of age or valued at less than $50,000. Nationwide, almost half of all black households but less than one-quarter of white

households reside in homes valued under $50,000. Similarly about 40 percent of black households but less than 30 percent of white households live in homes that are more than fifty years old.

The Office of the Public Insurance Counsel in Texas reviewed underwriting guidelines used by major insurers and found that 90 percent of the market in that state was served by companies with age and value restrictions. No doubt Texas is not unique. Such practices have a clear adverse racial impact. Unless there is a business necessity for such practices and no less discriminatory alternative is available that would serve the same business purpose, these practices would violate the Fair Housing Act.

The Law

Insurers contend that even if discrimination occurs, a little-known 1945 statute, the McCarran-Ferguson Act, exempts the industry from the Federal Fair Housing Act. McCarran-Ferguson grants the industry limited immunity from federal antitrust laws and provides for state regulation of the industry. The law states, in part, that "No act of Congress shall be construed to invalidate, impair, or supersede any law enacted by any state for the purpose of regulating the business of insurance." Therefore, insurers contend it is state, not federal, law that would apply to them.

But contrary to the industry's assertions, a proper reading of the law clearly shows that the Federal Fair Housing Act does apply to insurance companies. Under the Fair Housing Act it is unlawful to "otherwise make unavailable or deny a dwelling to any person because of race" or other prohibited classifications (42 U.S.C. Section 3604a) or to "discriminate against any person . . . in the provision of services or facilities in connection therewith" (42 U.S.C. Section 3604b). Because insurance is required to qualify for a mortgage loan, and because home ownership depends on access to mortgage financing, enjoyment of the full rights provided by the Fair Housing Act requires nondiscrimination in the provision of property insurance. HUD made this explicit when it enacted regulations implementing the Fair Housing Amendments Act of 1988 defining as prohibited conduct "Refusing to provide . . . property or hazard insurance for dwellings or providing such services or insurance differently because of race, color, religion, sex, handicap, familial status, or national origin" (24 C.F.R. Section 100.70d [4]).

The courts have consistently interpreted the Fair Housing Act as applying to insurance. In several district court cases, application of the Fair Housing Act has been reaffirmed.[2]

In 1984 the Fourth Circuit ruled to the contrary (Mackey v. Nationwide, 724 F. 2d 419 [Fourth Circuit 1984]). Subsequent to this decision, however, HUD issued its rule explicitly applying the Fair Housing Act to insurance. Pointing to this rule, in 1992 the Seventh Circuit concluded in the American Family case that "events have bypassed Mackey" and found the act did apply. In the Nationwide case the Sixth Circuit observed, "we conclude that HUD's interpretation of the act is consistent with goals of the act and a reasonable interpretation of the statute. . . . We hold that the McCarran-Ferguson Act does not preclude HUD's interpretation of the act." Nationwide filed a petition requesting that the U.S. Supreme Court review this decision, but in February the Court declined, as it did in the 1993 American Family case. Thus, for the second time the Court reaffirmed a circuit court opinion that property insurance is covered by the Fair Housing Act.

State laws do address discrimination, but they do not provide the same protection as the Federal Fair Housing Act. Most states do not provide the same coverage, procedural rights, or range of remedies, such as civil penalties and punitive damages. So, it is not coincidental that virtually all the significant legal challenges to insurance discrimination have been brought under the Fair Housing Act by private attorneys or the federal government rather than under state law by state insurance commissioners. Not only do state laws fail to provide the protections offered by the Fair Housing Act, but state regulators have, in general, failed to enforce state values aggressively and have been unenthusiastic about utilizing the tools available to them.

Responses to Redlining

Some aggressive steps have been taken in recent years to combat insurance redlining. Much more could be done, but the current political climate does not lend itself to optimism on this front, at least for the immediate future.

The most significant development was the 1995 settlement reached by the NAACP and the Justice Department in their lawsuit against American Family. As indicated above, American Family had provided agents with explicit instructions to avoid writing insurance for black applicants. The company also took race into consideration in deciding whether or not to inspect homes and provided different types of policies and levels of service to predominantly black and white neighborhoods.

In a $16 million settlement, the insurer agreed to finance various programs to encourage homeownership in Milwaukee's central city, eliminate the use of housing age and value in its underwriting, appoint four new agents in the central city, expand advertising in electronic and print media directed to the African American community, contract with an independent organization to conduct paired-testing of American Family agents, increase its share of the homeowners insurance market in the central city by at least 1,200 policies within five years, as well as to take other steps to expand its services in Milwaukee's black community. This settlement reverberated throughout the industry. The National Association of Insurance Commissioners labeled it the "mother of all affirmative action plans" and chastised the Justice Department for using "litigation scare tactics" that constituted "Big Brother central planning at its worst."

As a result of its testing program, the National Fair Housing Alliance filed discrimination complaints with HUD against three of the nation's largest insurers: State Farm, Allstate, and Nationwide. And HUD has sponsored similar testing programs in several additional cities that will likely result in more complaints or lawsuits over the next few years.

Several voluntary industry initiatives and partnership activities involving insurers, community-based organizations, and state insurance commissioners have been launched in recent years to increase the insurability of urban properties and educate the industry on business opportunities that currently exist in underserved areas. Among the companies involved in such efforts are Travelers, Hartford, State Farm, Allstate, and Nationwide. Participating community organizations include Habitat for Humanity, Neighborhood Housing Services, and the Association of Community Organizations for Reform Now (ACORN).

For example, Travelers and ACORN recently launched a program in several cities where the company will provide discounts on policies that are tied to anti-crime, fire prevention, and other safety programs that ACORN organizes within its communities. In Atlanta, several insurers are working with the Urban League, the Insurance Commissioner, and industry trade associations to identify and appoint more minority agents in order to increase insurance availability in underserved (often minority) neighborhoods. Several companies and trade associations have initiated mentoring programs enabling more minority agents to obtain contracts with major insurers, again for the primary purpose of expanding business in previously underinsured communities.

More aggressive actions could be taken, but only if a more effective political constituency for such actions can be mobilized. One obvious next step would be an insurance disclosure requirement similar to the Home Mortgage Disclosure Act that currently requires lenders to report lending activity publicly by census tract, the disposition of all loan applications (i.e., whether they were approved or denied), and the race, gender, and income of each applicant. Zip code disclosure bills for insurers were rejected in 1994 and there is little prospect for such legislation in the near future.

Along these same lines, a Community Reinvestment Act (CRA) for insurers similar to the current CRA law requiring federally chartered lenders to be responsive to the credit needs of their entire service, has often been proposed, but not seriously considered at the national level. CRA-type provisions were issued in California in 1994 at the urging of then-Democratic state insurance commissioner, John Garamendi. His Republican successor has proposed new rules that would enable insurers to circumvent these requirements.

HUD could, once again, announce its intent to issue detailed regulations that clarify how the Fair Housing Act applies to insurance. The agency was directed to do so in a 1994 Presidential Executive Order. But the Department recently announced that it would not issue such regulations in the near future.

Linkage requirements could also be established whereby municipalities, unions, churches, and other nonprofit organizations would purchase insurance products only from those companies that demonstrate a commitment to urban communities and to racial minorities wherever they live. But the ethos of the era of privatization and the limited public information documenting where insurers do business make this unlikely in the near future as well.

In sum, the 1994 elections dramatically changed the politics of the insurance redlining debate. Unless there is a reversal of those returns, the likelihood of concerted action to limit the prerogatives of the property insurance industry in the near future is minimal. A major barrier to such action is the political and financial clout of the insurance industry. Property insurance companies control more than $704.6 billion in assets. The 3,300 companies that write property insurance, along with affiliated agencies and technical service organizations, employ more than one million people. Several insurance trade associations lobby actively in state capitals across the country and in Washington, D.C. The American Insurance Association, one of several industry groups with headquarters in the nation's capital, employs a staff of 150 people on an annual budget of $20 million. No doubt the industry's visible presence in Washington is a significant factor in the preservation of state regulation.

Property insurance, and the dynamics of insurance redlining and discrimination, constitute critical components of the uneven development of metropolitan areas. Million-man marches, the debate over the genetic base of racial inequality, and the alleged end of racism and the rationality of discrimination may be more newsworthy. But the fact remains that "communities without insurance are communities without hope."

Any set of long-term recommendations for the development of a healthy city, and stable race relations within those environs, must include detailed attention to some of the more mundane building blocks. Insurance, a risky business as much for consumers as for providers, is an essential part of the formulation.

Endnotes

1. President's National Advisory Panel on Insurance in Riot-Affected Areas, Meeting the Insurance Crisis of Our Cities, 1968.
2. Dunn v. Midwestern, 472 F. Supp. 1106 (S.D. Ohio 1979), McDiarmid v. Economy Fire and Casualty Co., 604 F. Supp. 105 (S.D. Ohio 1984), and Strange v. Nationwide, No. 93-6585 (E.D. Pa. 9-22-94) and two circuit court cases (NAACP v. American Family, 978 F. Circuit 1992) certiorari denied, 113 S. Ct. 2335 (1993), and Nationwide v. Cisneros, No. 94-3296 (Sixth Circuit May 1, 1995).

Review

1. What is meant by the practice of redlining?

2. How much redlining is there, and why does it occur?

3. What kind of legal protection is there against redlining?

4. What action has been taken in recent years to combat redlining?

Application

1. Prepare a map of residential patterns of race or ethnicity in your city. Gather the necessary information by interviewing real estate agents or people in the neighborhood, or by examining U.S. census data.

2. Obtain information from an insurance company or from the state insurance commission on rates of home and auto insurance for the various areas of the city.

3. Compare the two sets of information. Do people in areas with high concentrations of racial/ethnic minorities pay higher rates? If so, ask an insurance agent to explain the rates.

19

Cowboys and Indians

Perceptions of Western Films Among American Indians and Anglos

JoEllen Shively

The French philosopher Pascal once observed that what is true on one side of the Pyrenees, a mountain range separating France and Spain, may not be true on the other side. This basic insight—that one's perception is influenced by one's culture and social identity—has been broadened by sociologists to say that all one's social identities shape one's view of reality. If, for example, a U.S. political leader is supported by a majority of voters, sociologists will examine how the leader's appeal differs according to the gender, social class, and race/ethnicity of voters. Or they might study a new fashion according to its effect on such variables as sex and social class.

In this selection, Shively investigates how different groups respond to the same movie—in this case the "classic" western The Searchers. *Shively shows how Indian and Anglo males (Anglos are defined as non-Indian, non-Hispanic white Americans) identified with the movie's characters, what qualities they perceived in a certain heroic character, what values they interpreted from the story, and why they did or did not like the story. In doing so, Shively goes beyond the common assumptions about how perceptions differ on the basis of race and ethnicity.*

For this study, Shively developed an innovative method for exploring his topic and produced intriguing results. Rather than merely examining the content of the movie in a critical light, she selected specific groups with varying expected attitudes, screened the movie

for them, then elicited their responses in focused discussion groups. Consequently, her findings offer a striking contrast to the expected predictions of armchair speculation.

In the major sociological study of Western films, Wright (1977) used his own viewing of the most popular Western movies from 1931 to 1972 to argue that Westerns resemble primitive myths. Wright's main thesis is that the narrative themes of the Western resolve crucial contradictions in modern capitalism and provide viewers with strategies to deal with their economic worlds. The popularity of Westerns, Wright argued, lies in the genre's reflection of the changing economic system, which allows the viewers to use the Western as a guide for living.

While growing up on an Indian reservation in the Midwestern United States, I observed that fellow Indians loved Western movies and paperbacks. Subsequently, I observed this phenomenon on Indian reservations in Oregon and North Dakota, as well as among Indians who lived off the reservations. As scholars have noted (McNickle 1973; Cornell 1987; Snipp 1991), American Indians have always lived in a culturally, economically, and politically marginal subculture and are ambivalent about American values of achievement and acquisition of material wealth. Thus, it seemed unlikely that Indians who like Westerns would need them as conceptual guides for economic action as Wright alleged. The popularity of Westerns among Indians must be explained in other ways.

In an argument similar to Wright's, Swidler (1986) suggested that cultural works are tools used by people to contend with immediate problems. Swidler discussed "culture" in a broad sense as comprising "symbolic vehicles of meaning including beliefs, ritual practices, art forms, ceremonies as well as language, gossip, stories and rituals of daily life" (p. 272). Swidler was concerned with how culture shapes action and with how people "use" culture. Assuming that Western movies are a story or an art form, how do American Indians use this cultural product?

I address several issues that previous studies have made assumptions about but have not addressed clearly. One issue is the general question of how different groups appropriate and find meaning in cultural products. In particular, does Wright's theory about the cultural use of Westerns hold true for American Indians watching a "cowboys vs. Indians" film? Is the mythic structure of a drama—the "good guy/bad guy" opposition in the Western—more salient than the ethnic aspect of the cultural product, or do Indians in the audience identify with Indians on the screen, regardless of who the good guys and bad guys are? Do Indians prefer Westerns that portray sympathetic and positive images of Indians, e.g., *Broken Arrow* and other movies described by Aleiss (1987) and Parish and Pitts (1976)? Do Indians like only Westerns that show a tribal group other than their own as the villains? Fundamentally, how do Indians link their own ethnic identity to the Western, or limit this identity so they can enter the narrative frame of the Western?

Research Design

Matched samples of 20 Indian males and 20 Anglo[1] males living in a town on an Indian reservation on the Western Plains of the United States watched a Western film, *The Searchers*. Ethnically pure groups were assembled by one Anglo informant and one Indian informant who invited five ethnically similar friends to their homes to watch the film. Written questionnaires were administered immediately after the film, followed by focus-group interviews. An Anglo female conducted the focus-group interviews with Anglos; I conducted the focus-group interviews with Indians. (I am Chippewa.) (Transcripts of the focus interviews are available from the author on request.)

Respondents were asked why they liked or did not like *The Searchers* in particular and Western movies in general. Basic demographic questions included racial identification, including "blood quantum" for Indians.

The research site is the second largest town on the reservation and has a population of about 1,200. Equal numbers of Indians and Anglos live in the town.[2] According to the Tribal Headquarters Enrollment Officer (Bighorn, 12 May 1988), of the 600 Indians approximately 40 percent are Sioux, 10 percent are Assiniboine, 10 percent are Indians of mixed Indian origins, and approximately 40 percent of the self-identified Indians are "mixed-blood," i.e., Indian and white ancestry. Because I wanted to avoid the possible ambiguity of asking how mixed-bloods understand Westerns, all Indians in my sample claim to be "full-blood" Sioux, and all Anglos claim to be white.[3] Because the Western genre is primarily about males, only males were included in the sample.[4]

The respondents did not constitute a representative sample, but were assembled in an effort to create roughly matched groups. I attempted to match Indians and Anglos on age, income, years of education, occupation, and employment status, but succeeded in matching mainly on age, education, and occupation, and was less successful on income and employment status.[5] In the analysis, neither employment status nor income appear to affect the dependent variables. Matching Indians and Anglos on education required me to exclude college-educated respondents.[6] All subjects were between the ages of 36 and 64—the average age of Indian respondents was 51, and the average age of Anglo respondents was 52. Most of the respondents were married.[7]

I chose *The Searchers* (1956) as the Western film to show because its major conflict is between cowboys and Indians. According to Wright (1977), *The Searchers* was one of the period's top-grossing films, a sign of mythical resonance. The film stars John Wayne—a critical advantage for a Western according to Indian and Anglo informants. Briefly, *The Searchers* is about Indian-hating Ethan Edwards's (John Wayne) and Martin Polly's (Jeff Hunter) five-year search to find Debbie Edwards, Ethan's niece (Natalie Wood), who has been kidnapped by Comanche Chief Scar (Henry Brandon). In the end, Scar is killed, and Debbie, who was married to Scar, is taken back to the white civilized world.

Findings

I began my research with the assumption that people understand movies based on their own cultural backgrounds. Therefore, the experience of watching Western movies should be different for Indians and Anglos, especially when watching scenes in which Indians are portrayed in distorted, negative ways. My most striking finding, however, is an overall similarity in the ways Indians and Anglos experienced *The Searchers*.

All respondents—Indians and Anglos—indicated that they liked Western movies in general. Furthermore, in the focus interviews, they said they wished more Westerns were being produced in Hollywood. I asked the respondents to rank the three types of films they most liked to watch from a list of 10 (musical, gangster, horror, and so on). All 40 subjects—both Anglo and Indian—ranked Westerns first or second; the Western was far and away the most popular genre. Seventy-five percent ranked Westerns first. Combat movies were a distant second, and science fiction movies were third.

On both the written questionnaires and in the focus interviews, all respondents indicated that they liked *The Searchers* and considered it a typical Western. One Indian and two Anglos reported that they had seen the film before.

In response to the question, "With whom did you identify most in the film?" 60 percent of the Indians and 50 percent of the Anglos identified with John Wayne, while 40 percent of the Indians and 45 percent of the Anglos identified with Jeff Hunter.[8] None of the Indians (or Anglos) identified with the Indian chief, Scar. Indians did not link their own ethnic identity to Scar and his band of Indians, but instead distanced themselves from the Indians in the film. The Indians, like the Anglos, identified with the characters that the narrative structure tells them to identify with—the good guys. In the focus-group interviews, both Indians and Anglos reiterated their fondness for John Wayne. For both audiences, the Indians in the film were either neutral or negative. What stood out was not that there were Indians on the screen, but that the Indians were the "bad

guys." For example, in the focus groups respondents were asked, "Do you ever root for the Indians?" Both Indians and Anglos consistently responded, "Sometimes, when they're the good guys." Their responses suggest that there is no strong ethnic bias governing whom the respondents root for and identify with. Instead, antagonism is directed against the bad guys. The structure of oppositions that defines the heroes in a film seems to guide viewers' identification with the characters in the film and overrides any ethnic empathy.

The Indians' identification with the good guys in the film is similar to Jahoda's (1961, p. 104) observations of African audiences reacting to films set in Africa that portray Africans as "rude, barbaric savages." Jahoda found that the majority of Africans did not identify with the Africans on the screen—only a minority of highly educated Africans identified with the Africans.

Although Indians and Anglos relied on cues in *The Searchers* about whom to identify with, in other ways the fictional frame of the film did not completely capture these viewers. When discussing *The Searchers*, Indians and Anglos rarely used the main characters' story names. Instead they used the actors' names—John Wayne and Jeff Hunter—which suggests a strong "star effect." Although John Wayne plays different characters in different films, these audiences associated his "cowboy" personality with the off-screen John Wayne, not with specific movie characters. On one level, they saw the actor as embodying all his movie roles. For example, when asked, "Why do you think Ethan Edwards hated the Indians in this movie?" the Indians and Anglos responded in similar ways:

Indians

Well, John Wayne might have hated Indians in this movie, but in other movies he doesn't hate them.
(Mechanic, age 51)

Well, they've killed his brother and his brother's wife. He doesn't hate Indians in all his movies.
(Cook, age 56)

Anglos

John Wayne doesn't like the Indians here because they've killed his brother's family. But in other movies, he's on their side. He sticks up for them.
(Foreman, age 56)

Sometimes he fights for the Indians like in *Fort Apache*.
(Bartender, age 48)

Both Indians and Anglos reported that they liked all of John Wayne's movies, whether he played a boxing champion, a pilot, or a cowboy. In all of his films, they see the strong personality characteristics of "the Duke," or "Dude," as some of the respondents referred to him. For both Indians and Anglos on this reservation, being called "cowboy" or one of John Wayne's nicknames, often "Dude" or "Duke," is a token of respect. Indians often see themselves as "cowboys," greeting each other with, "How ya doing, cowboy?" or "Long time no see, cowboy," and refer to their girlfriends or wives as "cowgirls." Fixico (1986) described a similar emulation of the cowboy among reservation Indians in Arizona and South Dakota.

The respondents talked about John Wayne as if he were one of them and they knew him personally—like a good friend. Believing in John Wayne the man is part of the charisma attached to the cowboy role. It is a self-reinforcing cycle: Because John Wayne always plays good guys—characters with whom viewers empathize—it is easy to identify with John Wayne and all he represents. Levy (1990) noted that, "because acting involves actual role playing and because of the 'realistic' nature of motion pictures, audiences sometimes fail to separate between players' roles onscreen and their real lives offscreen. The difference between life on and offscreen seems to blur" (p. 281). For respondents, John Wayne *is* the Cowboy, both in his movies and in real life. This focus on "John Wayne in real life" is similar to Liebes and Katz's (1990) finding that, when retelling episodes of the TV series "Dallas," Americans and Kibbutzniks talk about the "real life" (behind-the-scene) personalities of the actors.

The Real and the Fictional: Patterns of Differences

Although Anglos and Indians responded in similar ways to the structure of oppositions in the narrative, the two groups interpreted and valued characteristics of the cultural product differently once they "entered" the narrative. The narrative was (re)interpreted to fit their own interests. Although both Indians and Anglos saw some aspects of *The Searchers* as real and others as fictional, the two groups differed on what they saw as authentic and what they saw as fictional.

Table 19.1 shows how the two groups responded when asked to rank their three most

Table 19.1
Ranks of Reasons for Liking The Searchers, by Ethnicity

Reason	American Indians				Anglos			
	Ranked 1st	Ranked 2nd	Ranked 3rd	Weighted Sum of Ranks[a]	Ranked 1st	Ranked 2nd	Ranked 3rd	Weighted Sum of Ranks[a]
Action/Fights	2	4	5	19	2	6	4	22
John Wayne	5	3	2	23	2	3	0	12
It had Cowboys and Indians	6	5	3	31	3	2	5	18
Humor	1	5	6	19	0	1	1	3
Romance	0	0	1	1	0	0	1	1
Authentic Portrayal of Old West	0	0	0	0	10	3	3	39
Other	0	0	1	1	0	0	0	0

[a]Ranks are weighted: 1st x 3; 2nd x 2; 3rd x 1.

important reasons for liking the film. The Kendall rank-order correlation coefficient of $\tau = .29$ indicates that Indians' and Anglos' reasons often differed. The two groups agreed on the importance of "action and fights," "it had cowboys and Indians," and "the scenery and landscape" as reasons for liking the film. They also agreed that "romance" was not an important reason for liking the film. But the differences between Indians and Anglos in Table 19.1 are striking: None of the Indians ranked "authentic portrayal of the Old West" as an important reason for liking the movie, while 50 percent of the Anglos ranked it as the most important reason.

The results in Table 19.1 suggest that the distinctive appeal of the Western for Indians has two elements: (1) the cowboy's way of life—the idealized Western lifestyle seems to make this cultural product resonate for Indians; and (2) the setting of the film, the beauty of the landscape (Monument Valley) moves Indian viewers. When asked in the focus groups, "Why did you like this film, and what makes Westerns better (or worse) than other kinds of movies?" Indians reported: "Westerns relate to the way I wish I could live;" "The cowboy is free;" "He's not tied down to an eight-to-five job, day after day;" "He's his own man;" and "He has friends who are like him." What makes Westerns meaningful to Indians is the fantasy of being free and independent like the cowboy and the familiarity of the landscape or setting.

The setting also resonated for Anglos, but Anglos perceived these films as authentic portrayals of their past. In the focus groups, Anglos, but not Indians, talked about Westerns as accurate chronicles of their history. When asked, "Why did you like this film, and what makes Westerns better (or worse) than other kinds of movies?" Anglos said, "My grandparents were immigrants and Westerns show us the hard life they had;" "Westerns are about my heritage and how we settled the frontier and is about all the problems they had;" "Westerns give us an idea about how things were in the old days;" and "Westerns are true to life." What is meaningful to Anglos is not the fantasy of an idealized lifestyle, but that Western films link Anglos to their own history. For them, Western films are like primitive myths: They affirm and justify that their ancestors' actions when "settling this country" were right and good and necessary.[9]

Indians seemed ambivalent about how the Old West was portrayed in *The Searchers*. In the focus groups, I asked Indians if the film was an authentic portrayal of the Old West and they responded:

> As far as the cowboy's life goes, it's real, but you don't get to know the Indians, so it's hard to say it's totally authentic.
> (Bartender, age 42)

> I think it's real in some ways, like when you see the cowboy and how he was.
> (Mechanic, age 51)

> The cowboys are real to me. That's the way they were. But I don't know about the Indians 'cause you never see much of them.
> (Farm worker, age 50)

> Yeah, the movie is more about the good guys than the bad guys. I mean, the bad guys are there, but you don't get to know them very well. Mostly the movie is about the cowboys, the good guys, anyway.
> (Carpenter, age 48)

For Indians, the film was more about cowboys than about Indians. This does not hinder their enjoyment of the film or make it less meaningful, because they did not view the Indians on the screen as real Indians.

Both Indians and Anglos were asked, "Are Indians and cowboys in this film like Indians and cowboys in the past?" and "Are they like Indians and cowboys today?" Anglos replied:

> I think the cowboys and the settlers are pretty much like those in the old days. It's hard to say if the Indians are like Indians in the past.
> (Mechanic, age 39)

> They're not like Indians today.
> (Foreman, age 56)

> Indians don't go around kidnapping white women and children these days.
> (Bartender, age 48)

> Probably they're similar to how some of the Indians were in the past, I mean Indi-

ans really did scalp white men.
(Postal worker, age 49)

Yeah, and they kidnapped white children and white women.

My grandparents used to tell stories about how their parents told them to be careful when they played outside. They had to stay close to their homes, 'cause the Indians used to kidnap children.
(Bus driver, age 49)

Anglos thought the cowboys in the Western were similar to cowboys of the past, and they suggested that Indians in the film were similar to Indians in the past. However, they did not think Indians today are like Indians in the film.

When asked the same questions about whether Indians and cowboys in the film are like Indians and cowboys today and in the past, Indians replied somewhat differently:

The cowboys are like cowboys in the past. Maybe some Indians in the past were like the Indians in the films.
(Bartender, age 58)

They're not like Indians today. I mean, the only time Indians dress up is for pow-wows.
(Cook, age 60)

In this movie and other movies with Indians, you don't get to know them. I mean, they're not really people, like the cowboys are. It's hard to say they're like Indians in the past. For sure they're not like Indians today.
(Bartender, age 42)

The Indians aren't at all like any of the Indians I know.
(Unemployed factory worker, age 44)

Indians today are the cowboys.
(Bartender, age 42)

The phrase "Indians today are the cowboys" means that contemporary Indians are more like cowboys than Anglos are, in the sense that it is Indians who preserve some commitment to an autonomous way of life that is not fully tied to modern industrial society. Indians want to be, and value being, independent and free—separate from society— more than Anglos do.

Because *The Searchers* portrays Indians not as human beings, but as "wild, blood-thirsty animals," Indians might be expected to report that the Indians on the screen are not like Indians they know today or like Indians in the past. How could they identify with the Indians on the screen when Indians are portrayed in such a caricatured fashion? The only connections that Indians made between the Indians on the screen and Indians of the past and present were with the costumes worn by the Indians on the screen.

On some deeper level, however, Indian respondents may have identified with the Indians on the screen. For example, when asked in the focus groups, "What's a bad Western like?" Indians reported that they like all Westerns except for films like *Soldier Blue*. All of the Indian respondents were familiar with this film. *Soldier Blue* is a 1970 film based on the Sand Creek massacre of 1864, when Colonel Chivington of the U.S. Cavalry ambushed and slaughtered a village of peaceful Arapaho and Cheyenne children, women, and men in Colorado. In all of the Indian focus groups, this title was mentioned as one Western they did not like. This suggests that when films are too realistic and evoke unpleasant emotions, they are no longer enjoyable. This finding resembles Radway's (1984, p. 184) findings about "failed" romance novels. A "failed" romance is one that evokes overly intense feelings of anger, fear, and violence. Such novels are discarded by readers because they are not enjoyable. *Soldier Blue*, however, is sympathetic to the Indians, and the narrative leads the viewer to empathize with the Indians. Unlike the Indians, Anglos reported that they like all Westerns and could not think of an example of a bad Western.

Another striking difference revealed in Table 19.1 is that Indians cited "humor" as an important reason for liking the film, while Anglos did not. In the focus groups, Indians talked about several comic scenes in the film. When asked if humor was important in Western films, they all said, "Yeah." They reported that they liked humor and wit in Western movies and valued this trait in their friends. Humor is a source of joy for them—a gift.

Anglos, in contrast, never mentioned John Wayne's humor. Why did Indians and not Anglos respond to the humor? If Anglos perceived the film as an authentic story of their past, they may have concentrated on the serious problems in the film, i.e., getting the white girl back. Perhaps Anglos were so preoccupied with the film as an affirmation of their past that they were unable to focus on the intended humor, or at least other characteristics of the film were more important. On the other hand, Indians, who did not see the film as an authentic story of their own past, may have focused more on the intended humor in the film.

Ideal Heroes

Indians and Anglos also valued individual traits of the cowboy differently. Table 19.2 shows how the two groups responded when asked to rank the three most important qualities that make a good hero in a good Western. A Kendall rank-order correlation coefficient of $\tau = .167$ shows little agreement between Indian and Anglo rankings. Indians ranked "toughness" and "bravery" as the two most important qualities of a good hero in a good Western, whereas Anglos ranked "integrity/honesty" and "intelligence" as most important. Perhaps audiences look for exceptional characteristics in a good hero—qualities they would like to see in themselves. To live free and close to the land like

Indians wish to live, exceptional bravery and toughness are necessary. Because Anglos do not want to live like cowboys, bravery and toughness are not as important. Responses of Indians in Table 19.2 are similar to responses in Table 19.1 and to the oral responses. For example, when the Indians described John Wayne as a reason why they liked *The Searchers*, they concentrated on John Wayne's toughness.

While the two groups differed on the qualities that make a good hero, Indians and Anglos tended to agree on the characteristics of a good Western. When asked what characteristics they liked in a good Western, a Kendall's rank-order correlation coefficient between Indian and Anglo responses was high, $\tau = .78$, i.e., there were no pronounced differences between Indians and Anglos. For both groups, the three most important characteristics of a good Western were: "a happy ending;" "action/fights;" and "authentic portrayal of Old West." Like the ranking of "a happy ending" as the most important ingredient in a good romance novel (Radway 1984, p. 59), Indian and Anglo viewers ranked "a happy ending" as the most desirable characteristic of a good Western.

For Indians, the importance of a "happy ending" in a good Western film also reflects on their evaluation of *Soldier Blue* as a bad Western—*Soldier Blue* does not fulfill the "happy ending" criterion of a good Western. Although Indians like action or fights, they

---

Table 19.2
Ranks of Qualities That Make a Good Western, by Ethnicity

Quality	American Indians				Anglos			
	Ranked 1st	Ranked 2nd	Ranked 3rd	Weighted Sum of Ranks[a]	Ranked 1st	Ranked 2nd	Ranked 3rd	Weighted Sum of Ranks[a]
Bravery	8	4	4	40	3	4	1	18
Integrity/Honesty	2	2	0	10	8	9	5	47
Independence	0	0	2	2	0	0	1	1
Toughness	8	8	4	44	0	0	0	0
Sense of Humor	0	2	8	12	0	1	1	3
Strength	2	0	0	6	0	0	0	0
Loyalty	0	0	0	0	1	0	7	10
Intelligence	0	2	2	6	8	6	5	41
Other	0	0	0	0	0	0	0	0

[a]Ranks are weighted: 1st x 3; 2nd x 2; 3rd x 1.

are discerning about what kinds of action or fights they enjoy.

For both Anglos and Indians, the three least liked characteristics of a good Western were: "hero rides off into the sunset alone;" "Indians as bad guys;" and "romance between hero and woman."[10]

The Politics of Perception

Some Indians do identify with the Indians in the Western and are not affected by the film's signals about whom to identify with. Before taking my research procedures into the field, I pretested them with 15 American Indian college students at a West Coast university (10 males, 5 females). Because Indians in the reservation sample differed in important characteristics from the Indians in the pretests (9 of the Indian students were "mixed-bloods"), systematic comparisons were not possible.

However, Indian students responded differently from Indians in the reservation sample. Ethnicity was a salient issue for the majority of the students. The narrative of *The Searchers* did not "work" for the students and they were unable to fully enter the drama. For example, unlike the reservation Indians, a majority of the Indian students identified with and rooted for Scar and his Indians or Debbie, the kidnapped girl. They thought Debbie should have been allowed to stay with Scar and that the search should not have taken place at all.

Like the reservation Indians, the college-educated Indians did not view *The Searchers* as an authentic portrayal of the "Old West" and were quick to point out stereotypical portrayals of Indians in the film. They reacted against the negative message in the film that "the only good Indian is a dead one." They also pointed out many inaccuracies in the film, such as the use of Navajos and the Navajo language for Comanche, "Comanche" Indians wearing Sioux war bonnets, and Indians sometimes wearing war bonnets while fishing. Neither the Indians nor the Anglos in the reservation sample mentioned any of these inaccuracies.

All students but one reported that they liked Westerns in general, but preferred Westerns whose plots are about "cowboys vs. cowboys" or "Indians vs. Indians," or a "cowboys vs. Indians" plot in which the Indian point of view is shown. Several male students indicated that they and their friends often rent Western videos and named the video stores nearest the university that had the best selection of Westerns.

None of the students particularly liked John Wayne. Like the reservation sample, the students talked about John Wayne in "real life" and referred to what they considered racist statements he made off-screen in various interviews.

I asked each student, "Do Indians back home on the reservation like Westerns?" and "Do they root for the cowboys?" All of them said, "Oh yeah, sure." One Sioux student said his father had most of John Wayne's films on video, and a Chippewa said that his uncle was named after John Wayne. One Navajo said of his reservation town, "Ever since they closed down the movie theater several years ago, every Friday night they show a movie in the cafeteria room at the high school, and most of the time it's a Western. Everybody goes."

The heightened ethnic awareness of the college students interferes with, or overrides, their responses to the Western so that they do not get caught up in the structure of oppositions in the narrative. Because they identify with their ethnic group, they see *The Searchers* through a different lens. Education increases their awareness of anti-Indian bias in the film, producing a "revised eye" that frames these films in ethnic terms. In this context, ethnicity is a construct of a particular culture or subculture.

Conclusion

Although it would seem problematic for Indians to know which characters to identify with in *The Searchers*, it was not a problem for them at all—they identified with the cowboy and his lifestyle. Indians did not focus on the Indians, who are often portrayed on-screen as a faceless, screaming horde. Instead, they saw the cowboys as they want to see themselves—as the good guys.

What appears to make Westerns meaningful to Indians is the fantasy of being free and independent like the cowboy. In addition, the familiarity of the setting is important. Anglos, on the other hand, respond to the Western as a story about their past and their ancestors. The Western narrative becomes an affirmation of their own social experience—the way they are and what their ancestors strove for and imposed on the West are "good." Thus, for Anglos, the Western resembles a primitive myth. But it is not a myth in this sense for Indians—Indians do not view the Western as authentic.

Both Indians and Anglos found a fantasy in the cowboy story in which the important parts of their ways of life triumph and are morally good, validating their own cultural group in the context of a dramatically satisfying story. Perhaps this motive for ethnic group validation is more general and not peculiar to cowboy movies.

The Indian college students, who by attending college have opted for some of the values of white society, find other meanings in *The Searchers*. Because they are immersed in the intellectual world of the university, the symbolic importance of the film for them lies in its false representation of their ancestry and history.

Endnotes

1. "Anglo" refers to non-Indian white Americans and does not include those of Spanish or Mexican descent.

2. Of the approximately 50,000 residents living on the seven federally recognized reservations in this state in 1980, 48.5 percent are Indian and 51.5 percent are Anglo (Confederation of American Indians 1986, pp. 125–34). Under the 1887 General Allotment Act, more than 100 Indian Reservations on the Plains, along the Pacific Coast and in the Great Lakes states, were divided up and allotted to individual Indians. The remaining land was declared "surplus" and opened up to white homesteaders. Under the terms of this Act, Indians were eventually dispossessed of almost 90 million acres (Talbot 1981, pp. 111–12). Today, whites continue to own land and live on these reservations where their land is "checker-boarded" between Indian-owned land. On some of these reservations, non-Indians own as much or more land than the tribe or Indians do, and the proportion white is equal to or higher than the proportion Indian. The research site is on one of these reservations.

3. I have observed that "mixed-blood" Indians acknowledge and respect both their Indian and white ancestries. To avoid speculation about whether the findings might be associated with the self-identified Indians' "Indianness" or "whiteness," I included only full-bloods.

4. My data show that the Western genre is popular among women, but because the major focus of this study is on racial differences and because I had a limited budget, I controlled for gender by looking [at] males only.

5. The median annual household income for the Indians was $9,000; the median annual household income for the Anglos was $13,000. Seven of the 20 Indian men were unemployed at the time of the research compared to 3 of the Anglo men. Of currently employed Indians, 4 were working part-time; 3 of currently employed Anglos were working part-time. There are no significant differences between the Indians in my study and the 1980 Census data on income and unemployment (U.S. Bureau of the Census 1986, Tables 9, 10, 25; U.S. Bureau of the Census 1988, Table 234). Occupations of the Indians included bartender, farm worker, mechanic, factory worker, carpenter, and food-service worker. Occupations of the Anglos included janitor, school bus driver, bartender, store clerk, factory worker, carpenter, mechanic, foreman, and postal worker.

6. Indians and Anglos differed in the proportion who completed high school, but this difference had no effect on the analysis. Among Indian respondents, 25 percent had completed high school and 60 percent had some high school. For Anglo respondents, 80 percent had completed high school and 20 percent had some high school.

7. To obtain matched 20-person samples, 11 groups comprising 30 Indians and 25 Anglos watched the film. Of these, 2 Indians and 3 Anglos had "some college education" and 8 Indians and 2 Anglos were mixed-blood. These respondents' questionnaires were not used and the respondents were not involved in the focus interviews.

8. One Anglo identified with Laurie, Jeff Hunter's girlfriend. It was difficult to tell why.

9. Describing the role of the myth among Trobriand Islanders, Malinowski (1948) wrote: "The *myth* comes into play when rite, ceremony, or a social or moral rule demands justification, warrant of antiquity, reality, and sanctity" (pp. 84–85).

10. I collected some data in the field on female reservation Indians and female Anglos. These data reveal gender differences as well as differences by ethnicity. For example, women identified with the women in the film, while the men did not. Women ranked "romance" as one of the most important reasons for liking the film, whereas the men ranked it as the least important reason. Women ranked "action/fights" as one of the least important reasons for liking the film, while the men ranked it as one of the most important reasons. Like Anglo men, Anglo women saw the film as an authentic portrayal of the past, while the Indian women, like the Indian men, did not. Indian women like Indian men, also distanced themselves from the Indians on the screen.

References

Aleiss, Angela. 1987. "Hollywood Addresses Postwar Assimilation: Indian/White Attitudes in *Broken Arrow.*"*American Indian Culture and Research Journal* 11:67–79.

Bighorn, Spike N. 1988. Personal communication with author. 12 May.

Confederation of American Indians. 1986. *Indian Reservations: A State and Federal Handbook*. Jefferson, NC: McFarland.

Cornell, Stephen. 1987. "American Indians, American Dreams, and the Meaning of Success." *American Indian Culture and Research Journal* 11:59–70.

Fixico, Donald L. 1986. "From Indians to Cowboys: The Country Western Trend." Pp. 8–14 in *American Indian Identity: Today's Changing Perspectives*, edited by C. E. Trafzer. Sacramento, CA: Sierra Oaks Publishing Company.

Jahoda, Gustav. 1961. *White Man: A Study of the Attitudes of Africans to Europeans in Ghana before Independence*. London: Oxford University Press.

Levy, Emanuel. 1990. *And the Winner Is . . . : The History and Politics of the Oscar Awards*. New York: Continuum.

Liebes, Tamar and Elihu Katz. 1990. *The Export of Meaning: Cross Cultural Readings of DALLAS*. New York: Oxford University Press.

McNickle, DArcy. 1973. *Native American Tribalism: Indian Survivals and Renewals*. New York: Oxford University Press.

Malinowski, Bronislaw. 1948. *Magic, Science, and Religion and Other Essays*. Glencoe, IL: The Free Press.

Parish, James R. and Michael R. Pitts. 1976. *The Great Western Pictures*. Metuchen, NJ: The Scarecrow Press, Inc.

Radway, Janice A. 1984. *Reading the Romance: Women, Patriarchy, and Popular Literature*. Chapel Hill, NC: University of North Carolina Press.

Snipp, C. Manhew. 1991. *American Indians: The First of This Land*. New York: Russell Sage Foundation.

Swidler, Ann. 1986. "Culture in Action: Symbols and Strategies." *American Sociological Review* 51:272–279.

Talbot, Steve. 1981. *Roots of Oppression: The American Indian Question*. New York: International Publishers.

U.S. Bureau of the Census. 1986. *1980 Census of Population. American Indians, Eskimos, and Aleuts on Identified Reservations and in the Historical Areas of Oklahoma*. Vols. 1–2. Subject Report prepared by the U.S. Department of Commerce. Washington, DC: U.S. Government Printing Office.

——. 1988. *1980 County and City Data Book*. Prepared by the U.S. Department of Commerce. Washington, DC: U.S. Government Printing Office.

Wright, Will. 1977. *Sixguns and Society: A Structural Analysis of the Western*. Berkeley, CA: University of California Press.

Review

1. What did Shively expect to find using the film *The Searchers*? Why did she choose this particular film?

2. In what ways were the two audiences similar and different in their views about the film's content?

3. Shively found that Native American college students viewed the film differently from the Native Americans on the reservation. How does she interpret these differences?

4. Contrast the differences between the reservation Native Americans' understanding and the Anglos' understanding of the film's image of the West.

Application

Visit a video store and find a film with a racial or ethnic theme involving both "good" and "bad" guys. View the film with friends from that racial or ethnic group, then note who they identify with and why. Compare your findings with Shively's in a short essay.

Reprinted from: JoEllen Shively, "Cowboys and Indians: Perceptions of Western Films among American Indians and Anglos." In "Cowboys and Indians" by JoEllen Shively, *American Sociological Review*, 57/6, December 1992, pp. 725–34. Copyright © 1992 by the American Sociological Association. Reprinted by permission. ✦

Part Three

Gender Inequality

Prejudice and discrimination against women is called **sexism.** Some Americans believe that women no longer suffer from sexism, that women today face no barriers to their aspirations. Sociological studies, however, identify significant gender inequality. Women more than men are the victims of **sexual harassment,**—unwanted sexual advances by someone in a position of superior power. Inequality also continues in the areas of work (income and opportunities for advancement), politics (office holding), religion (clerical positions), and family (amount of time spent on household tasks).

Selection 20 looks at inequality in the high-status profession of medicine. Selection 21 examines violence in families—another aspect of inequality. For while considerable violence occurs by both men and women in families, women are far more likely than men to be the victims of severe violence. ✦

20

How Unhappy Are Women Doctors?

Robert Lowes

For women who want to work or pursue a career outside of the home, there is good news and bad news. The good news is that the proportion of the labor force that is female has grown dramatically in recent decades, and women are found in increasing numbers even in occupations once reserved for men. The bad news is that women who opt for an occupation traditionally considered more appropriate for men continue to encounter problems of resistance, harassment, and discrimination.

Discrimination occurs in both hiring and promotions. In many occupational categories, women are found disproportionately in the lower-echelon positions. For example, far more women than men are teachers, but far more men than women hold the top administrative jobs in education. In the area of medicine, women make up an increasing proportion of admissions to medical schools, yet they are often encouraged to pursue the more traditional "female" specialties of pediatrics, psychiatry, and preventive medicine.

In this selection, Lowes looks at the world of women doctors. He, too, finds good news and bad news. It is considerably less difficult for a woman to be a physician today than it was in the past. Still, women who want to practice medicine face obstacles, pressures, and problems—both in their professional life and their family life—that men typically do not face. There has been much progress, but medicine is still far from being an area of gender equality.

A Look at the Complex World of Female Physicians

St. Louis ob/gyn Kathy Maupin is a classic multitasker. Once the alarm clock goes off, Maupin's making breakfast for her daughter, Rachel, and husband, John, loading the clothes washer, e-mailing other doctors, and reviewing medical charts. After a day at the office, she comes home to juggle again—dinner, another pile of laundry, more charts.

"I have three businesses," says Maupin. "I practice medicine, I run my office, and I run my household."

Physicians of either sex hustle nonstop in this era of bottom-line medicine, but women such as Maupin encounter other sources of stress. Shouldering a disproportionate share of domestic duties is just one of them. Female doctors also contend with family-unfriendly schedules, gender bias, and sexual harassment.

You'd think that all these challenges would add up to deep demoralization, but by and large, women physicians are a robust, healthy group that's sold on medicine, according to Atlanta preventive medicine specialist Erica Frank, who surveyed 4,500 women about their well-being. In a study published in the *Archives of Internal Medicine* last year, she reported that 84 percent were generally satisfied with their careers. Maupin is part of that group. "I love being a physician," she says. "I would never be anything else."

Interestingly enough, the popular press presented Frank's research as bad news by emphasizing another finding: 31 percent of women physicians, when asked whether they would choose to become a doctor again, said maybe not, probably not, or definitely not. But Frank doesn't find these figures alarming, particularly since half of this group consisted of maybes. And at least one other study indicates this degree of career remorse holds true for all doctors.

Actually, the good news of Frank's research goes deeper than the 84 percent satisfaction rate. The most contented female doctors, it turns out, are the ones who have children. "It's a really toxic myth that if you're a doctor, having children tears you apart," says Frank. "The doctors we studied prove otherwise." And despite all the strikes against women physicians, their rate of depression is about the same as it is for all U.S. women, she adds.

Frank's findings come at a time when women physicians can celebrate much progress—if not complete success—in transforming a male-dominated profession into a more inclusive and hospitable one. In the space of 30 years, the percentage of physicians who are women has grown from a tokenish 8 percent to 23 percent. Almost half of first-year medical school students in 1999 were women. It will take decades, but someday one of every two physicians will be female. And with these rising numbers, old inequities are crumbling.

Medical historian Ellen S. More, author of *Restoring the Balance,* a history of American women doctors from 1850 through 1995, believes that the morale of women physicians has vastly improved since 1970. "It's gotten to the point where younger women have forgotten the degree of discrimination that used to exist. But we still can't afford to lower our guard," says More, who teaches at the University of Texas Medical Branch at Galveston.

To a lesser degree, the career satisfaction of women physicians ebbs and flows on industry and societal trends that doctors in general can't control. The shift to managed care has been a downer, for example. Research suggests that the pressure to squeeze more patients into a day is discouraging female doctors to a greater degree than their male counterparts because women practitioners favor longer patient encounters.

To More and others, though, the knottiest issue is how to accommodate the needs of women physicians who are bearing and rearing children. Yet there's good news on that front, too. Men are beginning to realize that harmonizing home and career isn't just a "chick issue." They're grasping what Frank's study suggests: Doctors who live with balance are happier.

Women Are Closing the Gaps in Income and Leadership

Women physicians don't enjoy playing catch-up with male counterparts when it comes to easily observed measures of equality. Take money. "When women doctors talk to me about gender issues," says AMA past president Nancy Dickey, an FP [family practitioner] at College Station, TX, "one of the first things they mention is unequal pay."

However, women physicians are catching up. In 1991, they earned on average 65 percent of what male physicians earned, according to *Medical Economics' Continuing Survey.* By 1998, they were up to the 72 percent mark.

The gap between male and female earnings isn't entirely the product of discrimination. Women tend to gravitate to lower-paying primary care specialties and work seven fewer hours per week than men, according to the AMA. And because they're younger than the men on the whole, they haven't built their practices up as much.

Yet bald-faced economic injustice continues. One female primary care physician on the East Coast recalls when she and another woman shared a full-time job and a $95,000 salary. Then their employer hired a less experienced man in their specialty on a full-time basis for $120,000. "I told them that was sexist," says the doctor, whose protest led to a small raise, but not enough to bring her pay to half of the [man's].

Women are particularly vulnerable to lowball salaries because 56 percent of them are employees, as opposed to practice partners or shareholders. In contrast, only 35 percent of male doctors are employees.

Leadership is another area of tension. Again, women have made gains, rising to some of the top spots in medicine. Nancy Dickey became the first female president of the AMA in 1998. And just last October, *The Journal of the American Medical Association* hired its first female editor, pediatrician Catherine D. DeAngelis.

Dickey and DeAngelis are more than window-dressing. Leadership by women physicians also is broader. In 1980, when women accounted for 12 percent of all doctors, they made up only 5 percent of the membership in the Tampa, FL-based American College of Physician Executives. Today, however, this group is 17 percent female—far closer to the actual proportion of women in medicine.

Not all the statistics are as sunny. While women constituted about 43 percent of medical school enrollment in 1999, only 27 percent of med school faculty and a mere 11 percent of full professors were female. After-hours faculty meetings and lack of on-site day care penalize women with children, according to those who've researched the problem. Plus, instructors who work part time often aren't eligible for tenure.

"Promotion is tied not to skill, but to schedule, and that's not right," says DeWitt, NY, internist Janice Scully, who was an assistant professor at a New York medical school for eight years.

The same obstacles face part-timers in private practice. Traditionally, they haven't been considered partner or stockholder material, much less potential leaders. To doctors from the 80-hour-a-week generation, the words "part time" translated into "not truly committed to medicine." However, for the sake of accommodating women physicians with children, practices are changing the rules. The Camino Medical Group in Sunnyvale, CA, for example, allows doctors working a three-quarters schedule to become shareholders. They even can slow down to a half-time pace, but only for three years; otherwise, they become employees. Several of those part-time shareholders head up satellite offices while others chair group-wide departments, says internist and board chairman Elizabeth Vilardo.

However, there's no denying that for part-timers, leadership is a stretch. "Leadership takes time—attending meetings, networking, educating yourself about the business of medicine," says Edina, MN, ob/gyn Janette H. Strathy, a member of the Park Nicollet Clinic. "That's going to deter some part-timers."

Strathy, who has a 15-year-old son, predicts that the part-time quandary will disappear for women doctors in her generation when they finish raising their children. "We'll have more time to devote to our groups and organized medicine," she says. "They won't know what to do with us!"

More Freedom To Be Feminine

"You don't change society quickly," observes internist Janice Scully. There's no better proof of that for women physicians than the persistence of harassment, which Erica Frank calls a strong predictor of career dissatisfaction. In Frank's Women Physicians' Health Study, 48 percent of those surveyed reported being hassled in a nonsexual manner simply because they were women, although it was more likely to have happened in medical school and residency than in private practice. Scully recalls such an incident: "When I was a new intern, up all night and exhausted, a male attending told me half-seriously during hospital rounds that he wouldn't talk to me because I was a girl. I went to a stairwell and cried."

Thirty-seven percent of those surveyed reported having been sexually harassed. If you're a man who's too embarrassed to ask a female colleague what it's like, you can read stories posted on the Association of Women Surgeons' Web site (womensurgeons.org). In one recent posting, a West fashion model turned cardiothoracic surgeon described her problems with male doctors: "They stare at my chest and don't take me for my surgical skills. Does anybody have any experience being extremely attractive and a medical professional, too?" Another ex-model ruefully replied: "I tried cutting my hair, dressing in scrubs, no makeup—nothing works. I do, however, wear T-shirts under the scrubs so the V-neck is less enticing."

Discussing what wardrobe will reduce male leers points to a subtler, but no less disconcerting problem: the pressure to deemphasize your femininity to fit in with the boys. That pressure still exists, but to a lesser degree than 30 years ago, say women doctors.

"In the past, the need to conform was critical," says Yarmouth, ME, general surgeon Dixie Mills, president of the AWS. "If you stood out as a woman, you got rejected and didn't make it. But now that there are more women in medicine, we can stand out."

Ferndale, WA, family physician Bertha "Berdi" Safford has experienced that freedom, too. "At first, I didn't let my female self come through," says Safford, who earned her MD in 1976. "I was less personal with people, and tended to give more orders. Today, I'm more myself with my patients—I talk with them about my children. And I'm collaborative as opposed to directive. Its easier now because there are so many more women to reinforce each other."

Maternity Leave: Male Doctors Show Their True Colors

If you take away the pay inequities, the glass ceiling, and the unwanted sexual advances, women physicians still have another challenge—societal attitudes toward mothers in the workplace. "There's one thing that young women doctors often don't understand," says Janice Scully. "Once they have children, the differences between men and women really show up. Before that, they get along fine."

In a classic case of an irresistible force meeting an immovable object, women who want to alter their schedules to fulfill parental roles run headlong into unsympathetic male colleagues. When this happens, mothers feel as if they've lost control of their work environment, says Erica Frank.

The great divide usually begins with maternity leave. According to practice management consultant Gray Tuttle Jr. in Lansing, MI, as recently as the 1970s women found that some practices wouldn't even let them use sick time to cover maternity leave. And there was always the pressure to get back to work fast. "I took five weeks off," says ob/gyn Kathy Maupin, whose daughter is 14, "and after three weeks, my two male partners were telling me over the phone, 'We're tired of doing your work.' They were deplorable."

Granted, there's been progress. The 1993 Family and Medical Leave Act (FMLA) guarantees that in companies of 50 or more employees, a new mother can stay home up to 12 weeks and still keep her job. Uncle Sam doesn't guarantee she'll be paid during that time, but some practices voluntarily compensate their women physicians during maternity leave. Park Nicollet Clinic, for example, lets new mothers take off 12 weeks, eight of them with pay under a short-term disability insurance policy—even for normal childbirth and recovery.

But other groups opt for less expensive disability policies that don't pay anything until 90 days or more of disability. In that scenario, new mothers normally must use up any accrued sick leave and vacation time if they want to maintain cash flow. They have the right to apply such paid leave to their 12 guaranteed weeks under FMLA, but the loss of vacation time is a sore point, says practice management consultant Mike Parshall with The Health Care Group in Plymouth Meeting, PA. "Women don't see maternity leave as a vacation," he explains, "so they don't want to forfeit vacation time."

Consultant Sandra McGraw, also at The Health Care Group, says groups should be more generous about granting paid maternity leave for the sake of retaining women physicians. "Look at the big picture," says McGraw. "We're talking about six to eight weeks, and it may happen only two or three times in the woman's career. Men as well as women need time off on special occasions. They get divorced. A kid gets sick. Stuff will happen."

Requests for part-time schedules after maternity leave also spark discord. More groups are conceding part-time hours, but some still demand that the part-timer take full-time call duty. Others give the part-timers a break and prorate call. The same arguments for liberalizing maternity leave also apply to part-time schedules and variations such as job-sharing. "If you don't treat your part-timers well, you'll lose them," says Ellen More.

Sharing the 50-Pound Knapsack Called Child Rearing

The gains that women have made in medicine are all the more remarkable given the extra burdens that society places on them as wives and mothers; in most cases, they're the default homemakers.

"If medicine is a footrace, then women are running it with a 50-pound knapsack on their back," says Janice Scully. "That knapsack is the work of raising children."

Do men know how heavy that knapsack feels? Memphis pediatrician Nancy Mitchell remembers the efforts she made to breastfeed her third child as a part-timer at a large group practice. "On my lunch hours at the office, I would close the door and pump my breasts, eat lunch, and dictate charts at the same time," says Mitchell. "I was doing it all."

However, multitasking has a dark side. "You're always feeling like you're not getting everything done," says Mitchell. For multitaskers, the result is often guilt. Are they shortchanging their families at the expense of their patients—and vice versa? "When I go home at night, I'm thinking about food, homework, and baths, but I'm also worrying about patients," says Mitchell. "I work in a few telephone calls on some of them, and my kids are saying, 'Read me a book, read me a book.'"

"Would I choose medicine again? On some days, medicine is the most satisfying thing I can do, but on other days, I think, 'This would be great if I were a man.' I used to tell younger women doctors that they could do it all, but now I have some doubts. You can have it all, but at a price." She's hanging in, though.

Mitchell's frustration notwithstanding, Erica Frank's study suggests that immersion in family life actually gives women physicians a brighter outlook on their careers. Frank found that those with no children were less happy. Multiple roles, according to Frank, seem to have benefits that mitigate the wear and tear. The more children female doctors had, in fact, the more content they were. "Children bring us joy," says Frank, the mother of a 3-year-old. And perspective, adds Elizabeth Vilardo. "I have a couple of children," she says. "They help you focus on things besides sick patients."

Author Ellen More echoes these thoughts. "Frank's study indicates that women who experience overall satisfaction with life are better able to cope with the frustrations of work," she says.

If the blend of family and career called the "mommy track" is rewarding, why not a "daddy track" for men? Well, it's under construction. Men are expecting more from themselves as husbands and fathers, which should come as a relief to hard-pressed working mothers. A 1997 study by the Families and Work Institute showed that working fathers spent 4.4 hours per workday caring for their children and doing chores, up from not quite 3 hours in 1977. Working women, in contrast, put in 6.1 hours, a half-hour less than they did 20 years earlier. True, women still shoulder about 60 percent of the load, but ob/gyn Kathy Maupin observes that most women would just as soon have it that way. "We feel the need to have the bigger role," says Maupin. "Maybe we're wired differently."

The awakening of men to hearth and home carries over into medicine. Research shows that young male doctors are twice as likely as older counterparts to make career adjustments—reduce their hours, for example—for the sake of family. Elizabeth Vilardo sees evidence of that in her circle. "The newer male doctors make it a priority to spend more time with their kids and lead a balanced life," says Vilardo, whose husband is a stay-at-home engineer. "The world is changing."

Ellen More sounds a similarly hopeful note at the end of her book: Male physicians are taking up the concerns of their female counterparts as their own. "Can women physicians restore the balance in their profession, in their own lives, and perhaps even in the lives of their patients?" asks More. "It seems clear that the answer is Yes, but they cannot, should not—and may no longer have to—do it alone."

Here's How Women Physicians Can Achieve Balance: Clone John Hruby

FP Bertha "Berdi" Safford in Ferndale, WA, is living proof that if a woman physician wants to balance career and home, she should marry someone who thinks like she does.

Safford and her husband, FP John Hruby, have gotten balance down to a science. Since 1979, the two doctors have shared a practice and split domestic duties on a 50-50 basis.

"I'm blessed with a husband who does the same thing I do," says Safford. "As a result, I don't think I've given up as much for medicine as other women have."

Here's how they slice the pie of life. Safford works in the office on Tuesdays and Fridays; Hruby, on Mondays and Wednesdays. They take Thursdays off together and, when they can, head off to the mountains for skiing and hiking. On the days when one spouse is practicing medicine, the other takes charge of domestic duties from dawn to bedtime (those duties are lighter lately since one of the couple's two children has left the nest).

Safford and Hruby count as one full-timer in their four-doctor practice, so they pull the equivalent of a full-time call schedule. They divide the duty so that the doctor-for-the-day is responsible for any call on his or her evening. "By doing this, we draw boundaries around our jobs," says Hruby. "If I stay home all day, I wash the dishes that night instead of seeing a patient in the ER." On Thursdays and weekends, deciding who takes call comes down to "heavy negotiating," he adds.

Part-time medical schedules have allowed Safford and Hruby to devote more time not only to parenthood, but to labors of love in the outside world. Safford is active in the American Academy of Family Physicians, having served as president of her state chapter. She also squeezes in another part-time job on Wednesdays as medical director of a family physician network. Hruby has [sat] on the local school board for 12 years.

Safford and Hruby married before they entered the University of Washington School of Medicine together. They graduated in 1976. "We knew we wanted children, and we agreed that full-time practice wasn't compatible with raising a family," says Safford. "When we started job-sharing after residency training, nobody else was doing this. It puzzled other doctors. They'd ask John, 'Did you go fishing on your day off?' They couldn't imagine that he was changing diapers instead."

"Today, the reaction is different," adds Hruby. "As doctors have gotten overwhelmed by managed care, they've been envious of us. Some have followed in our footsteps. There are six or seven other physician couples in our area who are job-sharing."

Hruby would like to win over more converts, though. "Society has to allow parents to be parents," he says. "We need more flexibility. Kids come first. Our jobs come second."

What a Mom-Friendly Medical Practice Looks Like

When Memphis pediatrician Aimee Christian wanted to attend her 7-year-old daughter's school play at 9am on a recent Tuesday, nobody at her five-doctor practice objected to rescheduling her patients so she could do so. That's because the other doctors in Memphis Pediatrics are mothers, too. And like Christian, they work less than full-time schedules for the sake of parenting.

Christian, one of three founders, says the group didn't set out to be an all-female—much less all-mom—practice when it formed in 1998. "We were friends in residency, and we wanted to be in a small group," says Christian, a mother of four. Nevertheless, the group oozes the kind of flexibility that working mothers yearn for when they need to take a child to the dentist, watch a softball game, or drive a carpool. "When one of us is rounding at the hospital, somebody else will occasionally have her kids over and watch them," says Christian.

Pediatrician Nancy Mitchell, a mother of three who joined Memphis Pediatrics in 1998, says she used to hear condescending comments from male colleagues in her old practice when she asked for time off to attend to her children. "They acted as if I had something to apologize for," says Mitchell. Not so at Memphis Pediatrics. "There's a more relaxed atmosphere," she says. "Everybody covers for everybody else. We all know, for example, that our kids will get sick and need us. It's not a big deal."

Memphis Pediatrics makes it easier on doctors when illness strikes by maintaining a veritable sick bay in the back of the office, away from patients. It's outfitted with a TV, a VCR, sleeping bags, and toys. Doctors can drop off their sick children here and not miss work, although the room is mostly meant for older children who don't require constant supervision. Other local doctors jokingly refer to Memphis Pediatrics as the "mom group," but the moms are having the last laugh as they watch their practice prosper.

"It took us only a year to pay off the bank loan that got us started," says Christian. "We've been very successful."

What Advice Would You Give Brand-New Women Physicians?

Hold on to your goals, hold on to your passion. You can balance family and career. I used to take my son on hospital rounds when there was nobody to watch him. He would wait at the nurse's station or outside the patient's door. Sometimes a patient would ask to see him and he'd step inside and smile. If you expand your vision, you can make it work.

—General surgeon Dixie Mills, Yarmouth, ME

Maintain at least one hobby or sport in your life that has nothing to do with being a wife, mother, or doctor. I have two—downhill skiing and flying a Cessna TR-1 82.

Exercise. Young mothers often put that last on their list of things to do; they think that chasing their kids equals a workout. But at least take 30 minutes a day for a brisk walk. You'll have more energy to deal with stress.

Pay people to do domestic work that you don't want to do—house cleaning, for example. And pay your child care people well. The best thing I ever did was to employ a live-in nanny for seven years. It gave me peace of mind and made me more productive at work.

—Ob/gyn Janette Strathy, Edina, MN

Become a good negotiator. You can command top dollar from employers by selling the advantages of having a woman physician. Your name on the door will bring in new patients.

Before you sign a contract, hash out the terms of maternity leave. You'll be in a better negotiating position than if you bring this up when you're three months pregnant. And if you decide on three months of maternity leave, stick to your handshake and come back to work after three months. Don't change your mind and take off for another three months. You have an obligation not only to your employer and patients, but to the women physicians who follow you. If you don't stand by your agreement, your employers will be skeptical about hiring the next female applicant.

—FP Nancy Dickey, College Station, TX

Review

1. According to Lowes, women doctors are closing the gaps in income and leadership. What evidence does he present?

2. Discuss the situation of women doctors with regard to looking feminine and taking maternity leave.

3. What are the problems women doctors face when they have children?

Applications

1. Do as the author suggests and go to the Association of Women Surgeons' Web site (womensurgeons.org) to find stories of sexual harassment. What kind of measures would you institute to prevent such incidents?

2. The problems women doctors face are similar to those of women in other professions. Make a list of both the gains and the problems that Lowes notes.

Then talk with a woman in another profession about the extent to which she has experienced, or knows of someone who has experienced, similar gains and problems.

Reprinted from: Robert Lowes, "How Unhappy Are Women Doctors?" In *Medical Economics* 13 (July 10, 2000):80–100. Copyright © 2000 by Medical Economics Publishing. Used by permission from *Medical Economics magazine.* ✦

21
How Women Experience Battering
The Process of Victimization

Kathleen J. Ferraro
John M. Johnson

One of the most tragic expressions of women's inequality in American society is their violent victimization by spouses and lovers. A surprising aspect of this abuse is the extraordinary length of time some women stay in such relationships. In certain cases, women have tolerated their mates' beating so long that some observers have concluded they were willing victims. Such a view is naive. As Ferraro and Johnson make clear, this victimization is closely connected to our culture's conception of women and their position in society. Many women feel they have no choice but to stay in an abusive relationship; they are socialized to accept their subordinate role as natural and are often financially and emotionally dependent on a man. Moreover, some women accept physical violence as a burden to be borne to save their marriage, children, or home. Unfortunately, about half of the women in this study returned to their abusive relationships. The same dependencies and patriarchal perceptions that initially prevented their leaving probably contributed to their return.

Why do battered women stay in abusive relationships?

The socialization of women emphasizes the primary value of being a good wife and mother, at the expense of personal achievement in other spheres of life. The patriarchal ordering of society assigns a secondary status to women, and provides men with ultimate authority, both within and outside the family unity. Economic conditions contribute to the dependency of women on men. In sum, the position of women in U.S. society makes it extremely difficult for them to reject the authority of men and develop independent lives free of marital violence (Dobash and Dobash, 1979; Pagelow, 1981).

Material and cultural conditions are the background in which personal interpretations of events are developed. Women who depend on their husbands for practical support also depend on them as sources of self-esteem, emotional support, and continuity. This paper looks at how women make sense of their victimization within the context of these dependencies.

We first describe six techniques of rationalization used by women who are in relationships where battering has occurred. We then turn to catalysts which may serve as forces to reevaluate rationalizations and to initiate serious attempts at escape. Finally, we outline the consequences of leaving or attempting to leave a violent relationship.

The Data

From July, 1978, to September, 1979, we were participant observers at a shelter for battered women located in the southwestern United States. The shelter was located in a suburban city of a major urban center. The shelter served five cities as well as the downtown population, resulting in a service population of 170,000.

During the time of the research, 120 women passed through the shelters; they brought with them 165 children. The women ranged in age from 17 to 68, generally had family incomes below $15,000, and did not work outside the home.

We established personal relationships with each of these women, and kept records of their experiences and verbal accounts. We also tape-recorded informal conversations, staff meetings, and crisis phone conversations with battered women. This daily interaction with shelter residents and staff permitted first-hand observation of feelings and thoughts about the battering experience. Finally, we taped interviews with 10 residents and five battered women who had left their abusers without entering the shelter. All quotes in this paper are taken from our notes and tapes.

The term battered woman is used in this paper to describe women who are battered repeatedly by men with whom they live as lovers. Marriage is not a prerequisite for being a battered woman. Many of the women who entered the shelter we studied were living with, but were not legally married to, the men who abused them.

Rationalizing Violence

Rather than seeking help or escaping, as people typically do when attacked by strangers, battered women often rationalize violence from their husbands, at least initially. Although remaining with a violent man does not indicate that a woman views violence as an acceptable aspect of the relationship, the length of time that a woman stays in the marriage after abuse begins is a rough index of her efforts to accommodate the situation. In a U.S. study of 350 battered women, Pagelow (1981) found the median length of stay after violence began was four years; some left in less than one year, others stayed as long as 42 years.

Battered women have good reasons to rationalize violence. There are few institutional, legal, or cultural supports for women fleeing violent marriages. Eighty percent of Pagelow's (1981) sample indicated previous, failed attempts to leave their husbands. Despite the development of the international shelter movement, changes in police practices, and legislation to protect battered women since 1975, it remains extraordinarily difficult for a battered woman to escape a violent husband determined to maintain his control. At least one woman, Mary Parziale, has been murdered by an abusive husband while residing in a shelter (Beverly, 1978); others have been murdered after leaving shelters to establish new, independent homes (Garcia, 1978). When practical and social constraints are combined with love for and commitment to an abuser, it is obvious that there is a strong incentive—often a practical necessity—to rationalize violence.

Previous research on the rationalizations of deviant offenders has revealed a typology of "techniques of neutralization," which allow offenders to view their actions as normal, acceptable, or at least justifiable (Sykes and Matza, 1957). A similar typology can be constructed for victims. Extending the concepts developed by Sykes and Matza, we assigned the responses of battered women we interviewed to one of six categories of rationalization: (1) the appeal to the salvation ethic; (2) the denial of the victimizer; (3) the denial of injury; (4) the denial of victimization; (5) the denial of options; and (6) the appeal to higher loyalties. The women usually employed at least one of these techniques to make sense of their situations; often they employed two or more, simultaneously or over time.

1) *The appeal to the salvation ethic:* This rationalization is grounded in a woman's desire to be of service to others. Abusing husbands are viewed as deeply troubled, perhaps "sick" individuals, dependent on their wives' nurturance for survival. Battered women place their own safety and happiness below their commitment to "saving my man" from whatever malady they perceive as the source of their husbands' problems (Ferraro, 1979). The appeal to the salvation ethic is a common response to an alcoholic or drug-dependent abuser. The battered partners of substance-abusers frequently describe the charming, charismatic personality of their sober mates, viewing this appealing personality as the "real man" being destroyed by disease. They then assume responsibility for helping their partners to overcome their problems, viewing the batterings they receive as an index of their partners' pathology. Abuse must be endured while helping the man return to his "normal" self. One woman said:

> I thought I was going to be Florence Nightingale. He had so much potential; I could see how good he really was, and I was going to 'save' him. I thought I was the only thing keeping him going, and that if I left he'd lose his job and wind up in jail. I'd make excuses to everybody for

him. I'd call work and lie when he was drunk, saying he was sick. I never criticized him, because he needed my approval.

2) *The denial of the victimizer:* This technique is similar to the salvation ethic, except that victims do not assume responsibility for solving their abusers' problems. Women perceive battering as an event beyond the control of both spouses, and blame it on some external force. The violence is judged situational and temporary, because it is linked to unusual circumstances or a sickness which can be cured. Pressures at work, the loss of a job, or legal problems are all situations which battered women assume as the causes of their partners' violence. Mental illness, alcoholism, and drug addiction are also viewed as external, uncontrollable afflictions by many battered women who accept the medical perspective on such problems. By focusing on factors beyond the control of their abuser, women deny their husbands' intent to do them harm, and thus rationalize violent episodes.

He's sick. He didn't used to be this way, but he can't handle alcohol. It's really like a disease, being an alcoholic. . . . I think too that this is what he saw at home, his father is a very violent man, and alcoholic too, so it's really not his fault, because this is all he has ever known.

3) *The denial of injury:* For some women, the experience of being battered by a spouse is so discordant with their expectations that they simply refuse to acknowledge it. When hospitalization is not required, routines quickly return to normal. Meals are served, jobs and schools are attended, and daily chores completed. Even with lingering pain, bruises, and cuts, the normality of everyday life overrides the strange, confusing memory of the attack. When husbands refuse to discuss or acknowledge the event, in some cases even accusing their wives of insanity, women sometimes come to believe the violence never occurred. The denial of injury does not mean that women feel no pain. They know they are hurt, but define the hurt as tolerable or normal. Just as individuals tolerate a wide range of physical discomfort before seeking

medical help, battered women tolerate a wide range of physical abuse before defining it as an injurious assault. One woman explained her disbelief at her first battering:

I laid in bed and cried all night. I could not believe it had happened, and I didn't want to believe it. We had only been married a year, and I was pregnant and excited about starting a family. Then all of a sudden, this! The next morning he told me he was sorry and it wouldn't happen again, and I gladly kissed and made up. I wanted to forget the whole thing, and wouldn't let myself worry about what it meant for us.

4) *The denial of victimization:* Victims often blame themselves for the violence, thereby neutralizing the responsibility of the spouse. Pagelow (1981) found that 99.4 percent of battered women felt they did not deserve to be beaten, and 51 percent said they had done nothing to provoke an attack. The battered women in our sample did not believe violence against them was justified, but some felt it could have been avoided if they had been more passive and conciliatory. Both Pagelow's and our samples are biased in this area, because they were made up almost entirely of women who had already left their abusers, and thus would have been likely to feel major responsibility for the abuse they received. Retrospective accounts of victimization in our sample, however, did reveal evidence that some women believed their right to leave violent men was restricted by their participation in the conflicts. One subject said:

Well, I couldn't really do anything about it, because I did ask for it. I knew how to get at him, and I'd keep after it and keep after it until he got fed up and knocked me right out. I can't say I like it, but I shouldn't have nagged him like I did.

As Pagelow (1981) noted, there is a difference between provocation and justification. A battered woman's belief that her actions angered her spouse to the point of violence is not synonymous with the belief that violence was therefore *justified*. But belief in provocation may diminish a woman's capacity for retaliation or self-defense, because it blurs her concept of responsibility. A woman's acceptance of responsibility for the violent incident is encouraged by an abuser who continually denigrates her and makes unrealistic demands. Depending on the social supports available, and the personality of the battered woman, the man's accusations of inadequacy may assume the status of truth. Such beliefs of inferiority inhibit the development of a notion of victimization.

5) *The denial of options:* This technique is composed of two elements: practical options and emotional options. Practical options, including alternative housing, source of income, and protection from an abuser, are clearly limited by the patriarchal structure of Western society. However, there are differences in the ways battered women respond to these obstacles, ranging from determined struggle to acquiescence. For a variety of reasons, some battered women do not take full advantage of the practical opportunities which are available to escape, and some return to abusers voluntarily even after establishing an independent lifestyle. Others ignore the most severe constraints in their efforts to escape their relationships. For example, one resident of the shelter we observed walked 30 miles in her bedroom slippers to get to the shelter, and required medical attention for blisters and cuts to her feet. On the other hand, a woman who had a full-time job, had rented an apartment, and had been given by the shelter all the clothes, furniture, and basics necessary to set up housekeeping, returned to her husband two weeks after leaving the shelter. Other women refused to go to job interviews, keep appointments with social workers, or move out of the state for their own protection (Ferraro, 1981b). Such actions are frightening for women who have led relatively isolated or protected lives, but failure to take action leaves few alternatives to violent marriage. The belief of battered women that they will not be able to make it on their own—a belief often fueled by years of abuse and oppression—is a major impediment to acknowledge that one is a victim and taking action.

The denial of *emotional* options imposes still further restrictions. Battered women

may feel that no one else can provide intimacy and companionship. While physical beating is painful and dangerous, the prospect of a lonely, celibate existence is often too frightening to risk. It is not uncommon for battered women to express the belief that their abuser is the only man they could love, thus severely limiting their opportunities to discover new, more supportive relationships. One woman said:

> He's all I've got. My dad's gone, and my mother disowned me when I married him. And he's really special. He understands me, and I understand him. Nobody could take his place.

6) *The appeal to higher loyalties:* This appeal involves enduring battering for the sake of some higher commitment, either religious or traditional. The Christian belief that women should serve their husbands as men serve God is invoked as a rationalization to endure a husband's violence for later rewards in the afterlife. Clergy may support this view by advising women to pray and try harder to please their husbands (Davidson, 1978; McGlinchey, 1981). Other women have a strong commitment to the nuclear family, and find divorce repugnant. They may believe that for their children's sake, any marriage is better than no marriage. One woman divorced her husband of 35 years after her last child left home. More commonly women who have survived violent relationships for that long do not have the desire or strength to divorce and begin a new life. When the appeal to higher loyalties is employed as a strategy to cope with battering, commitment to and involvement with an ideal overshadows the mundane reality of violence.

Catalysts for Change

Rationalization is a way of coping with a situation in which, for either practical or emotional reasons, or both, a battered woman is stuck. For some women, the situation and the beliefs that rationalize it may continue for a lifetime. For others, changes may occur within the relationship, within individuals, or in available resources which serve as catalysts for redefining the violence. When battered women reject prior rationalizations and begin to view themselves as true victims of abuse, the victimization process begins.

There are a variety of catalysts for redefining abuse; we discuss six: (1) a change in the level of violence; (2) a change in resources; (3) a change in the relationship; (4) despair; (5) a change in the visibility of violence; and (6) external definitions of the relationship.

1) *A change in the level of violence:* Although Gelles (1976) reports that the severity of abuse is an important factor in women's decisions to leave violent situations, Pagelow (1981) found no significant correlation between the number of years spent cohabiting with an abuser and the severity of abuse. On the contrary: the longer women lived with an abuser, the more severe the violence they endured, since violence increased in severity over time. What does seem to serve as a catalyst is a sudden change in the relative level of violence. Women who suddenly realize that battering may be fatal may reject rationalizations in order to save their lives. One woman who had been severely beaten by an alcoholic husband for many years explained her decision to leave on the basis of a direct threat to her life:

> It was like a pendulum. He'd swing to the extremes both ways. He'd get drunk and beat me up, then he'd get sober and treat me like a queen. One day he put a gun to my head and pulled the trigger. It wasn't loaded. But that's when I decided I'd had it. I sued for separation of property. I knew what was coming again, so I got out. I didn't want to. I still loved the guy, but I knew I had to for my own sanity.

There are, of course, many cases of homicide in which women did not escape soon enough. In 1979, 7.6 percent of all murders in the United States where the relationship between the victim and the offender was known were murders of wives by husbands (Flanagan et al., 1982). Increases in severity do not guarantee a reinterpretation of the situation, but may play a part in the process.

2) *A change in resources:* Although some women rationalize cohabiting with an abuser by claiming they have no option, others begin reinterpreting violence when the resources necessary for escape become available. The emergence of safe homes or shelters since 1970 has produced a new resource for battered women. While not completely adequate or satisfactory, the mere existence of a place to go alters the situation in which battering is experienced (Johnson, 1981). Public support of shelters is a statement to battered women that abuse need not be tolerated. Conversely, political trends which limit resources available to women, such as cutbacks in government funding to social programs, increase fears that life outside a violent marriage is economically impossible. One 55-year-old woman discussed this catalyst:

> I stayed with him because I didn't want my kids to have the same life I did. My parents were divorced, and I was always so ashamed of that. . . . Yes, they're all on their own now, so there's no reason left to stay.

3) *A change in the relationship:* Walker (1979), in discussing the stages of a battering relationship, notes that violent incidents are usually followed by periods of remorse and solitude. Such phases deepen the emotional bonds, and make rejection of an abuser more difficult. But as battering progresses, periods of remorse may shorten, or disappear, eliminating the basis for maintaining a positive outlook on the marriage. After a number of episodes of violence, a man may realize that this victim will not retaliate or escape, and thus feel no need to express remorse. Extended periods devoid of kindness or love may alter a woman's feelings toward her partner so much so that she eventually begins to define herself as a victim of abuse. One woman said:

> At first, you know, we used to have so much fun together. He has kind've, you know, a magnetic personality; he can be really charming. But it isn't fun anymore. Since the baby came, it's changed completely. He just wants me to stay at home, while he goes out with his friends. He doesn't even talk to me, most of the time. . . . No, I don't really love him anymore, not like I did.

4) *Despair:* Changes in the relationship may result in a loss of hope that "things will get better." When hope is destroyed and replaced by despair, rationalizations of violence may give way to the recognition of vic-

timization. Feelings of hopelessness or despair are the basis for some efforts to assist battered women, such as Al-Anon. The director of an Al-Anon organized shelter explained the concept of "hitting bottom":

> Before the Al-Anon program can really be of benefit, a woman has to hit bottom. When you hit bottom, you realize that all of your own efforts to control the situation have failed; you feel helpless and lost and worthless and completely disenchanted with the world. Women can't really be helped unless they're ready for it and want it. Some women come here when things get bad, but they aren't really ready to be committed to Al-Anon. Things haven't gotten bad enough for them, and they go right back. We see this all the time.

5) *A change in the visibility of violence:* Creating a web of rationalizations to overlook violence is accomplished more easily if no intruders are present to question their validity. Since most violence between couples occurs in private, there are seldom conflicting interpretations of the event from outsiders. Only 7 percent of the respondents in Gelles' (1979) study who discussed spatial location of violence indicated events which took place outside the home, but all reported incidents within the home. Others report similar findings (Pittman and Handy, 1964; Pokorny, 1965; Wolfgang, 1958). If violence does occur in the presence of others, it may trigger a reinterpretation process. Battering in private is degrading, but battering in public is humiliating, for it is a statement of subordination and powerlessness. Having others witness abuse may create intolerable feelings of shame which undermine prior rationalizations.

> He never hit me in public before—it was always at home. But the Saturday I got back [returned to husband from shelter], we went Christmas shopping and he slapped me in the store because of some stupid joke I made. People saw it, I know, I felt so stupid, like, they must all think what a jerk I am, what a sick couple, and I thought, 'God, I must be crazy to let him do this.'

6) *External definitions of the relationship:* A change in visibility is usually accom-plished by the interjection of external definitions of abuse. External definitions vary depending on their source and the situation; they either reinforce or undermine rationalizations. Battered women who request help frequently find others—and especially officials—don't believe their story or are unsympathetic (Pagelow, 1981; Pizzey, 1974). Experimental research by Shotland and Straw (1976) supports these reports. Observers usually fail to respond when a woman is attacked by a man, and justify nonintervention on the grounds that they assumed the victim and offender were married. One young woman discussed how lack of support from her family left her without hope:

> It wouldn't be so bad if my own family gave a damn about me. . . . Yeah, they know I'm here, and they don't care. They didn't care about me when I was a kid, so why should they care now? I got raped and beat as a kid, and now I get beat as an adult. Life is a big joke.

Clearly, such responses from family members contribute to the belief among battered women that there are no alternatives and that they must tolerate the abuse. However, when outsiders respond with unqualified support of the victim and condemnation of violent men, their definitions can be a potent catalyst toward victimization. Friends and relatives who show genuine concern for a woman's well-being may initiate an awareness of danger which contradicts previous rationalizations.

> My mother-in-law knew what was going on, but she wouldn't admit it. . . . I said, 'Mom, what do you think these bruises are?' and she said 'Well, some people just bruise easy. I do it all the time, bumping into things.'. . . And he just denied it, pretended like nothing happened, and if I'd said I wanted to talk about it, he'd say, 'life goes on, you can't just dwell on things. . . .' But this time, my neighbor knew what happened, she saw it, and when he denied it, she said, 'I can't believe it! You know that's not true!'. . . And I was so happy that finally, somebody else saw what was goin' on, and I just told him then that this time I wasn't gonna come home!

Shelters for battered women serve not only as material resources, but as sources of external definitions which contribute to the victimization process. They offer refuge from a violent situation in which a woman may contemplate her circumstances and what she wants to do about them. Within a shelter, women meet counselors and other battered women who are familiar with rationalizations of violence and the reluctance to give up commitment to a spouse. In counseling sessions, and informal conversations with other residents, women hear horror stories from others who have already defined themselves as victims. They are supported for expressing anger and reflecting responsibility for their abuse (Ferraro, 1981a). The goal of many shelters is to overcome feelings of guilt and inadequacy so that women can make choices in their best interests. In this atmosphere, violent incidents are reexamined and redefined as assaults in which the woman was victimized.

How others respond to a battered woman's situation is critical. The closer the relationship of others, the more significant their response is to a woman's perception of the situation. Thus, children can either help or hinder the victim. Pizzey (1974) found adolescent boys at a shelter in Chiswick, England, often assumed the role of the abusing father and themselves abused their mothers, both verbally and physically. On the other hand, children at the shelter we observed often became extremely protective and nurturing toward their mothers. This phenomenon has been thoroughly described elsewhere (Ferraro, 1981). Children who have been abused by [fathers] who also beat their mothers experience high levels of anxiety, and rarely want to be reunited with their fathers. A 13-year-old abused daughter of a shelter resident wrote the following message to her stepfather:

> I am going to be honest and not lie. No, I don't want you to come back. It's not that I am jealous because mom loves you. It is [I] am afraid I won't live to see 18. I did care about you a long time ago, but now I can't care, for the simple reason you['re] always calling us names, even my friends. And another reason is, I am tired of seeing mom hurt. She has been hurt enough in

her life, and I don't want her to be hurt any more.

No systematic research has been conducted on the influence children exert on their battered mothers, but it seems obvious that the willingness of children to leave a violent father would be an important factor in a woman's own decision to leave.

The relevance of these catalysts to a woman's interpretation of violence vary with her own situation and personality. The process of rejecting rationalizations and becoming a victim is ambiguous, confusing, and emotional. We now turn to the feelings involved in victimization.

The Aftermath

The consequences of leaving a violent husband vary widely and depend on such situational variables as the atmosphere of a shelter, the availability of new partners, success at employment, and the response of the spouse. Interestingly, most battered women, like most divorcees, are optimistic about future relationships (Scanzoni, 1972). When the opportunity presented itself, battered women at the shelter we observed were happy to date and establish new relationships. The idea that battered women seek out violent men has been refuted by both Pagelow (1981) and Walker (1979). However, entering a new relationship shortly after escaping a violent one does interfere with a woman's opportunity to develop autonomy and overcome problems created by years of abuse. Involvement in a new relationship is, however, appealing, because it cushions the impact of divorce and the prospect of making it alone.

Some battered women, however, develop a feeling of repugnance to romantic involvements. They may feel that "men are no good," or simply enjoy their freedom too much to consider entering a relationship. Most women in shelters reject feminism as a total philosophy, but adopt many of its tenets. Living in a shelter operated by and for women changes ideas about the role of women and their ability to run their own lives. It also provides an opportunity to develop female friendships, and to overcome the view of other women as "competitors."

The rights of women to defend themselves and to make their own decisions are not easily given up once they are found. So, while women who have extricated themselves from violent relationships may not call themselves feminists, or become politically active, they do gain a commitment to certain feminist goals (Ridington, 1978).

Some formerly battered women do join in political activity to help other victims. Many of the grass-roots shelters now in existence in the United States and Europe were created by formerly battered women (Warrior, 1978), and some shelters make a special effort to recruit such women for their staffs. Entry into the battered women's movement provides an opportunity to develop a new support group, as well as build feelings of self-worth by contributing service to others.

Of course, some women return to violent relationships. There is a tendency for observers to view such decisions as failures, but they are often part of the process of gaining independence. Women may leave and return to violent relationships a number of times before making a final break. As Pagelow (1981, 219) explains it:

> Women who return home are not 'failures' in any sense of the word. If there was only a short history of abuse and their spouses recognize they have a problem and begin to correct it, there is a possibility of no further violence. But these women had the courage to leave the first time; they were exposed to alternatives and new ideas; they found out that other people outside their homes can and do care for their welfare; they learned that they are not ugly 'freaks' with a rare, individual problem. They may return to the men that abused them, but they do not return the same women they were when they left.

Most shelters are too overworked and understaffed to conduct systematic follow-ups for more than a month or two after women leave. Because our research was participatory, we were able to develop personal knowledge about each resident of the shelter, allowing for a more complete understanding of their post-shelter experiences. If success is defined in terms of life satisfaction (positive relationships with others, self confidence, and optimism about the future), only 30 of the 120 women we met during the study period could be said to have successfully dealt with their battering. An additional 30 women did not return to their marriages, to anyone's knowledge, but continued to face severe problems, either financially, interpersonally, or emotionally. The other 60 shelter residents (50 percent of the sample) returned to their marriages. Further, systematic research on the experiences of battered women who permanently leave violent marriages is needed to expand our knowledge of the battering phenomenon.

Conclusion

The process of victimization is not synonymous with experiencing violent attacks from a spouse. Rationalizing the violence inhibits a sense of outrage and efforts to escape abuse. Only after rationalizations are rejected, through the impact of one or more catalysts, does the victimization process begin. When previously rationalized violence is reinterpreted as dangerous, unjustified assault, battered women actively seek alternatives. The success of their efforts to seek help depends on available resources, external supports, reactions of husbands and children, and their own adaptation to the situation. Victimization includes not only cognitive interpretations, but feelings and physiological responses. Creating a satisfying, peaceful environment after being battered involves emotional confusion and ambiguity, as well as enormous practical and economic obstacles. It may take years of struggle and aborted attempts before a battered woman is able to establish a safe and stable lifestyle, for some, this goal is never achieved.

References

Beverly, "Shelter Resident Murdered by Husband," *Aegis*, September/October, 1978, p. 13.

Davidson, Terry, *Conjugal Crime* (New York: Hawthorn, 1978).

Dobash, R. Emerson, and Russell P. Dobash, *Violence Against Wives* (New York: Free Press, 1979).

Ferraro, Kathleen J., "Hard Love: Letting Go of an Abusive Husband," *Frontiers*, 4, 1979, 2:16–18.

——, "Battered Women and the Shelter Movement," unpublished doctoral dissertation, Arizona State University, 1981a.

——, "Processing Battered Women," *Journal of Family Issues*, 2, 1981b, 4:415–438.

Flanagan, Timothy J., David J. Van Alstyne, and Michael R. Gottfredson (eds.), *Sourcebook of Criminal Justice Statistics 1981*, U.S. Department of Justice, Bureau of Justice Statistics (Washington, D.C.: U.S. Government Printing Office, 1982).

Garcia, Dick, "Slain Women 'Lived in Fear,'" *The Times* (Erie, PA), June 14, 1978, B1.

Gelles, Richard J., "Abused Wives: Why Do They Stay?" *Journal of Marriage and the Family*, 38, 1976, 4:659–668.

Johnson, John M., "Program Enterprise and Official Cooptation of the Battered Women's Shelter Movement," *American Behavioral Scientist*, 24, 1981, 6:827–842.

McGlinchey, Anne, "Woman Battering and the Church's Response," in *Sheltering Battered Women*, ed. Albert R. Roberts (New York: Springer, 1981), pp. 133–140.

Pagelow, Mildred Daley, *Woman-Battering* (Beverly Hills: Sage, 1981).

Pittman, D.J., and W. Handy, "Patterns in Criminal Aggravated Assault," *Journal of Criminal Law, Criminology, and Police Science*, 55, 1964, 4:462–470.

Pizzey, Erin, *Scream Quietly or the Neighbors Will Hear* (Baltimore: Penguin, 1974).

Pokorny, Alex D., "Human Violence: A Comparison of Homicide, Aggravated Assault, Suicide, and Attempted Suicide," *Journal of Criminal Law, Criminology, and Police Science*, 56, December, 1965, pp. 488–497.

Ridington, Jillian, "The Transition Process: A Feminist Environment as Reconstitutive Milieu," *Victimology*, 2, 1978, 3–4:563–576.

Scanzoni, John, *Sexual Bargaining* (Englewood Cliffs, NJ: Prentice-Hall, 1972).

Shotland, R. Lance, and Margret K. Straw, "Bystander Response to an Assault: When a Man Attacks a Woman," *Journal of Personality and Social Psychology*, 34, 1976, 5:990–999.

Sykes, Gresham M., and David Matza, "Techniques of Neutralization: A Theory of Delinquency," *American Sociological Review*, 22, 1957, 6:667–670.

Walker, Lenore E., *The Battered Woman* (New York: Harper and Row, 1979).

Warrior, Betsy, *Working on Wife Abuse* (Cambridge, MA: Betsy Warrior, 1978).

Wolfgang, Marvin E., *Patterns in Criminal Homicide* (New York: John Wiley, 1958).

Review

1. How do Ferraro and Johnson define the term "battered women"?

2. Briefly describe each of the six categories of rationalization used by battered women.

3. What are the six catalysts for redefining abuse? Describe each.

4. What consequences do Ferraro and Johnson find for battered women leaving their violent husbands?

Application

Develop a questionnaire for interviewing a staff member of a shelter for battered women. Address the following points in your interview:

a. shelter's definition of battered women

b. objectives and activities of the shelter

c. statistics about residents, e.g., age, ethnicity, marital status, length of time with their men, average duration of abuse prior to leaving, prior attempts at leaving, number of children, etc.

d. use of rationalization or other techniques of neutralization by residents

e. six catalysts present in redefinition of abuse by victims or others

f. consequences for women of leaving their men and percentage of those who return to their men

If possible, interview one or more of the residents or sit in on a group counseling session.

Part Four

Age Inequality

Ageism is the term used for prejudice and discrimination against the elderly. Ageism is manifested in such things as rules that prevent people from working beyond a certain age or the refusal to hire older people; stereotypes about the elderly (such as the idea that older people lose their intellectual and sexual functioning); patronizing of the elderly (such as talking to them as though they were children); and neglect of the needs and desires of the elderly.

Selection 22 illustrates this last point: neglect of needs and desires. What do you do when you are unable to care for an elderly parent? Many older Americans must necessarily be placed in a nursing home. The care they receive, as the author discovered, may fall short of their needs and desires even in a home that is supposedly adequate. ✦

22

But This Is My Mother!

The Plight of Elders in American Nursing Homes

Cynthia Loucks

The American population is getting older. At the beginning of the twentieth century, about 4 percent of the population was sixty-five years or older. By 2000, the proportion had risen to 12.7 percent, and Census Bureau projections put the proportion at 18.5 percent by 2025. One of the fastest growing segments of the population is those aged eighty-five and above.

The aging of the population means an increasing need for care facilities. Nursing homes are the major providers of long-term care for the elderly in this country; a fourth or more of Americans will spend at least some time in a nursing home before they die. In our society, nursing homes have become a major growth industry, and the provision of long-term care is increasingly defined in terms of cost, profit margin, number of beds, and units of service. The emphasis is on economic and bureaucratic considerations rather than on quality of care.

In her account of her mother's last years in an average-rated nursing home, Cynthia Loucks details the kind of substandard care that has been the target of both government and private investigations. Her mother's paralyzing stroke and dementia forced Loucks to move her to a nursing home. Loucks soon realized that she would have to assume responsibility for ensuring that her mother was not neglected or harmed by the overworked and often indifferent staff. This selection from her book tells of some of the situations she encountered.

Whether elders have bed sores is a good indicator of the quality of care that is being provided. Elders who can no longer move themselves must be repositioned regularly so that their body weight is not resting in any one place for too long. A head nurse on my mother's ward told me that nursing home regulations require that immobile residents be turned every two hours while in bed in order to shift their weight distribution and to vary the pressure on their body parts. If necessary, pillows can be used to position residents on their sides. But when there is a shortage of pillows, the efforts of conscientious aides who try to keep up with the necessary regimen are hampered.

In the course of a person's physical disintegration, bed sores become more difficult to prevent. When someone is very near death, subjecting them to the disturbance of repositioning can be unduly inconsiderate. However, until that point, nursing home staff need to follow the guidelines for preventing bed sores. The reality remains that in many facilities, including the one my mother was in, dependent elders are moved as little as once during an eight hour shift. Even then, most of the movements that occur are merely back and forth between bed and chair, which may not provide any relief if the weight of the body remains on the same spot. In addition, many nursing home residents are in effect lying down even when they are in their chairs, since the recliners are cranked back in order to use gravity to keep flaccid bodies from sliding onto the floor.

Other methods of preventing bed sores, such as gentle massage to stimulate circulation, are seldom employed by overworked staff in nursing homes. Although various devices can be used in chairs and beds to relieve sacral pressure—doughnut-shaped pillows, "egg crate" foam cushions and mattresses, gel-filled mattresses and pillows—these items are often in short supply in many nursing homes. A resident's personal cushion also can lie unnoticed in a closet where one staff person may have stored it and the next staff person does not rediscover it.

It distressed me a great deal to know that Mama couldn't turn herself over in bed or shift her weight in her chair without assistance. She easily could be left in an uncomfortable position for hours, unable to do anything about it. According to her last doctor, the one with geriatric training, part of the nature of Mama's condition was that she no longer felt the uncomfortable pressure or nerve stimuli that prompt the rest of us to shift our positions frequently. I hoped he was right and that Mama never felt too uncomfortable.

When immobile residents aren't being repositioned regularly, it often means they aren't being checked on frequently, either. As a result, nursing home residents have been found stuck in some very bizarre and even potentially life-threatening positions. Sometimes I would find Mama in an incredibly uncomfortable-looking posture. She would be so still, just staring, waiting, as though resigned to something she knew she was helpless to alter. On at least two occasions I know of, Mama somehow rolled to the side of her bed and wound up with her head stuck between the bed rails for who knows how long before someone found her. At the time, I was unaware of how terribly dangerous this phenomenon can actually be. I learned later that many nursing home residents have lost their lives from getting trapped in their bed rails and not being discovered in time to be rescued.

Mama also often slipped down in her chair, another typical side effect of paralysis and other conditions that impede the ability to resist gravity. It was part of the conundrum of having to be left fully upright after meals with no wherewithal to maintain the position herself. I feared that hours might go by before anyone noticed she had slumped. She could even slip all the way out of the chair and wind up injured on the floor before anyone might come to reposition her. I vividly remember one instance when I walked into Mama's room and found that she had slid so far out of her slippery vinyl recliner that only her sacrum and the back of her neck were in contact with the chair. Her chin was pressed to her chest and her legs were sticking out straight in front of her, well beyond the support of the chair's leg rest. She was staring straight ahead, her blank expression revealing little of the soul trapped in that poor old vessel.

I often wondered what Mama was thinking at those times, unsure whether she just checked out or maybe even went into some sort of trance induced by her extreme helplessness. I would notice a particularly blank expression on her face on such occasions, as well as sometimes when the aides were cleaning her, another undoubtedly unpleasant event. This common psychological response of distancing oneself in some way when under such circumstances is called dissociation. When something in life is too disagreeable, people employ defense mechanisms in order to handle the stress. What happens to the people who have to do this every day, several times a day, in order to deal with their circumstances? It is a question that needs to be addressed on behalf of all nursing home residents.

Another highly disconcerting and recurring event in Mama's life took place whenever she had to be transferred. In medical settings, to "transfer" someone is to move an immobilized person from one conveyance to another—from bed to geri-chair or wheelchair, from chair to toilet, etc., and back again. This particular aspect of caring for disabled elders is probably the most strenuous for all concerned. Those elders who cannot bear any weight on their feet are the most difficult to transfer. Even with a small person like Mama, who weighed less than one hundred pounds by the time she was admitted to the nursing home, the bulk and stiffness of the person render the process awkward.

Mama often screamed when she was being transferred, a habit that rattled many of her aides. I think she was frightened to be picked up, afraid she would be dropped or otherwise injured, which is not an unrealistic fear for someone in such impotent circumstances. To ease fears about being transferred and to limit the possibility of injury, there is an approved procedure for moving dependent residents. Two aides or nurses lift the resident along four points—the two armpits and the backs of the two knees—so that the person's weight is evenly distributed. In Mama's case, she was often transferred, whether by one aide or two, by lifting her up by her armpits only. Not only was that a very uncomfortable way to be lifted, but it also risked injury to her unsupported lower torso and limbs. Throughout Mama's stay in the nursing home I tried constantly to get the aides to use their other hand to support Mama beneath her knees. Trying to motivate them, I pointed out that Mama surely wouldn't cry out so much if they used this method. But with each subsequent visit I would see that the aides had reverted to their armpit-only transfer. Considering that Mama was probably transferred between bed and chair an average of 6 times per day, 365 days a year, it was quite an ordeal for her to endure.

There are other chronic physical care issues, albeit non-life-threatening, that are frequently left unattended to in nursing homes. For example, Mama's feet were often cold, so I bought her several pairs of socks and focused on trying to get the aides to remember to put them on her when she needed them. I shouldn't have been surprised when I realized they were putting socks on her all the time, even if her feet weren't cold. At times I would find Mama so hot that she was perspiring. It seemed like such a small thing to pay attention to—a person's skin temperature and then dressing her accordingly. Yet, such consideration was almost totally outside the bounds of the care that Mama received.

The paralysis that followed Mama's stroke and the subsequent lack of movement that ensued resulted in the contraction of her left arm and hand. During the first few months after Mama's arrival at the nursing home, a young woman came in from time to time to perform range-of-motion movements with Mama's limbs, a means for both reducing contraction and improving circulation. When the therapy was discontinued, for whatever reason I do not know, I didn't protest. The young woman had seemed so inexperienced, and Mama clearly didn't enjoy having her arms and legs tugged this way and that. I couldn't bring myself to insist on more.

Mama spent a lot of time either in bed or in her chair with her legs outstretched. Before long, her ankles became rotated such that her feet were always turned in toward one another. Knowing she would never walk again, I didn't think it made a difference how her ankles were positioned so long as there were no indications of discomfort. The color and the condition of her skin looked all right. One of the nurses told me that people's ankles naturally rotated inward once they can no longer walk. I believed her and assumed that she had probably seen it happen many times before. But when I later learned how easily this condition could have been prevented by using pillows to hold her ankles in a neutral position, I felt remorse for having left it at that. I was not aware of the stress that this rotated position placed on all of Mama's connecting joints, and probably on the bones themselves, all the way up to her hips. (To see what this is like, lie down on your back when you are in bed tonight, with your legs outstretched, and slowly rotate your ankles inward as far as they will go. Notice the sensations that occur immediately, even as far up as the small of your back. Ouch!)

Mama's skin had gotten as thin as an old shirt that's been worn and washed so many times it has become transparent and easily torn. Yet, the aides would take a terry washcloth, coarse from heavy bleaching, and scrub her as though she had been digging ditches all day. Although stimulating the skin is beneficial, their methods looked excessive. When I suggested that Mama didn't need such vigorous bathing, they humored me and washed her more gently; but I had no doubt that as soon as I wasn't available to monitor them, they returned to doing it their way.

It wasn't long before Mama developed a skin rash. Considered a redhead (though her hair was more a deep auburn), Mama always had sensitive skin, so it was not surprising that it protested the treatment it received in the nursing home. The doctors and nurses discussed prescribing medication for her, both cortisone-based pills and lotions. As usual, the medical approach was to suppress the symptom without attempting to alleviate its cause.

Aides give bed baths by bringing a plastic tub of warm, soapy water to the bed of a resident, who then gets washed down with a washcloth. To my dismay, I discovered that after washing Mama, some of the aides simply dried her off without first rinsing her skin. Others would bring fresh water for rinsing her but would still use the same sudsy washcloth. The source of Mama's rash seemed obvious to me. When I pointed out the detrimental shortcuts, the aides countered that it was difficult to rinse her properly without getting the bed unduly wet. I suggested that they might try rinsing out the washcloth first with clean water and that if they used less soap when they filled up the plastic tub—it was usually frothing with suds—the rinsing might go more easily. They grudgingly agreed to try it, and Mama's rash soon subsided.

I also had to lobby to add moisturizing lotion to Mama's required skin-care regimen. I scrawled Mama's name in big black letters on her lotion dispenser in the hope that it would actually remain in her room. Since care supplies are seldom adequately stocked in nursing homes, staff freely "borrow" from one resident to give to another—the best solution they can find when needing something otherwise unavailable. Thanks partly to the ongoing vigilance of Aunt Margaret and the steady supply the family provided, lotion was always available. How often it was used on Mama, however, was less reliable. I bought facial moisturizer for Mama, too, but I could tell by how much remained in the jar that it was seldom applied by anyone else but me. I enjoyed rubbing the lotion onto her face. It was a chance to express the gentleness and tenderness that I felt for her, to nurture her in some small way.

It was also apparent that duties such as providing oral care were getting checked off on Mama's chart when they were not actually being performed. Her dentures had disappeared within a few weeks of her arrival at the nursing home. A nurse speculated that they were probably thrown out with her soiled laundry. Their loss, of course, did not preclude her need for oral care. One method of providing this care involves using a little sponge that is attached to the end of a stick. When dipped in water, the sponge emits a mouthwash-like substance. The sponge is then used to massage and freshen a person's

mouth and gums without the need for rinsing. But like most medical supplies, these implements are ridiculously expensive and are invariably in short supply at nursing homes.

The physical care of nursing home residents is further complicated by the maladies that are endemic in today's long term care facilities, and Mama certainly wasn't immune to any of these problems. Urinary tract infections, diarrhea, congestion, dehydration, rashes, and bed sores—these ailments never seem to surprise the doctors, who attribute them to residents' advanced ages and poor physical conditions. While elders do tend to have diminished immune systems and increased susceptibility to sickness, especially when they are inactive, this knowledge should be a warning for increased preventive care rather than an excuse for the various skin, digestive, and bacterial problems that occur. These afflictions could be greatly reduced with good, consistent attention to residents' hygiene as well as to their prescribed care regimens. There should be no excuse for failing to avert the preventable.

When nursing home residents are no longer able to control the flow of their urine, they develop rashes from the prolonged exposure of their skin to the urine in their bedding and diapers. In typical fashion, nursing homes respond to the frequency of these rashes by inserting catheters into aged urethras. While reducing the need for frequent cleanup, catheters provide ideal conditions for the proliferation of infection-causing bacteria. Improperly used and monitored, as they often are in nursing homes, they can present other hazards as well. I once found that my mother had been placed in her bed lying on the tubing, which of course blocked the flow.

In addition, many elderly recipients of these contraptions, no longer constrained by subservience to authority, yank them out, causing subsequent irritation to tender tissue. After Mama suffered through several urinary tract infections, I decided that she, too, had had enough. I told the staff that I did not want any more foreign objects inserted anywhere into my mother and vetoed the further use of a catheter on her. While the doctors never seemed to question writing an order for a catheter and following it with the almost inevitable antibiotic prescription a week or two later, the nursing staff, who saw the human result of that cycle in increased bowel difficulties due to the loss of healthy intestinal flora, were more willing to break the cycle and acquiesce to my request, even though they had requested the catheter in the first place. One nurse admitted to me that she knew I was right, although overall, the staff was miffed that I expected them to keep Mama clean and dry enough to avoid further rashes.

Such medical aspects of Mama's care were never ending. I had to function as a conduit of information among the ever-changing nursing home staff, the doctor, and hospital staff whenever Mama was hospitalized for conditions such as internal bleeding episodes. It was especially important to provide the hospital staff with information because they never seemed to be notified of the particulars of Mama's health care. Once I was just in time to prevent a hospital nurse from attempting to feed Mama solid food, an act that would almost certainly have choked her.

I also had to keep trying to get Mama a diet that took into consideration her pre-existing condition of chronic colitis (inflammation of the colon). I needed to be on the lookout for cuts, sores, infections, and problems with her G-tube, so that these problems were attended to promptly, regularly, and effectively. I tried to be sure that she was not given treatments that would precipitate yet another condition requiring treatment. I checked that she was given sufficient fluids to avoid dehydration, which became a problem due to her inability to consume sufficient quantities at meal times and the unavailability of staff to provide the fluids she needed between meals.

It was very frustrating to review Mama's treatment and consider that she was in a reputable nursing home. At best, her care was tolerable, with rare instances of very good. Frequently, it was heedless, insensitive, rough, and even dangerous. Yet, I was determined to keep fighting for Mama, to keep taking yet another grievance to the head nurse, the doctor, the social worker, whom-

ever I thought might be able to help us. There was never any question of giving up, even though overseeing Mama's care in that nursing home was truly the most demanding, frustrating, and disheartening job I have ever had.

It galled me again and again to witness the indifference with which so many of the nursing home staff treated my mother. They seemed unwilling to look at what they were doing and apparently regarded my efforts to intervene as just so much nagging. Even those who responded positively to my suggestions would either soon revert to their usual methods or not be taking care of my mother any more. Between staff rotations and people quitting, Mama never had the same caregivers for long, which deprived her of the comfort and reassurance that familiarity and continuity could have provided.

The unkindness that some of the aides displayed toward Mama—and that they would behave that way right in front of me—was not only distressing but downright baffling. Throughout her stay at the nursing home, when she wasn't too ill or too sleepy to respond, Mama always had an enthusiastically friendly greeting for one and all. To me it was a reflection of the wonderful graciousness that she managed to retain throughout so much of her ordeal.

One day a young male aide came into Mama's room to attend to her. True to form, Mama called out a cheery "Hi!" when the young man approached her bed. Silence. Seconds passed. Undaunted, Mama said "Hi!" again, with no less warmth or cheer. Her voice and what she said were clear and unmistakable. Still silence. Despite my pounding heart and the fury rising in my throat, I remained calm so as not to make a scene in front of Mama. I said to the young man, "She said 'hi' to you." As though coming out of a trance, he finally uttered a dull, flat "Hello." And without another word, he proceeded to perform his duties in an efficient but perfunctory manner. Mama fell silent.

When I later saw the aide in the corridor, I questioned him about his thoughtless behavior. Vaguely apologetic, he informed me that he had a lot on his mind. I was less than sympathetic and complained about the incident to the head nurse. She shared my dismay at the aide's behavior, agreeing that professional caregivers should leave their personal problems at the door when they come to work. It was good to have her agreement, but it didn't change anything.

I winced whenever I watched aides and nurses tend to Mama without speaking to her or speak to her without looking at her. I desperately wanted them to act in a manner that was kind, civil, and respectful. I knew what a difference it would make for Mama if they took a moment to explain what they were going to do and if they made an effort to listen to her, responding as much as possible to what she indicated.

All nursing home residents have psychological, emotional, and social needs regardless of their conditions. They need eye contact and whatever else seems appropriate to foster a feeling of connection and respect for their basic humanity. The lack of such behavior constitutes an assault on the human spirit and is, in many ways, the most painful offense for people to bear. It wounds more deeply than the discomfort and indignity of poor physical care.

Review

1. Why is the presence or absence of bed sores important? How can nursing homes deal with the problem?

2. What is the problem of "transfer" in a nursing home? Discuss the author's mother's problem with transfer.

3. Describe the difficulties the author had with staff members as they cared for her mother.

Applications

1. If you feel comfortable doing so, try what the author suggests: lay on your back in bed and turn your ankles inward as far as they will go. What sensations do you get? Does the experience give you a greater appreciation for the author's concerns about her mother?

2. A number of government reports have severely criticized the care in nursing homes. See if you can find one in your library. Compare the findings with the experience of the author.

Reprinted from: Cynthia Loucks, *But This Is My Mother! The Plight of Our Elders in American Nursing Homes* (Acton, Mass.: Vanderwyk & Burnham, 2000). Copyright by Cynthia Loucks. Used by permission of VanderWyk & Burnham, Acton, MA. ✦

Part Five

International Inequality

Inequality exists not only between groups within a society, but between societies as well. In other words, we have a global stratification system. The gross national product per capita in rich nations is 400 or more times higher than that of the poorest nations. This difference translates into such things as lower life expectancy, higher rates of disease and infant mortality, lower educational levels, and higher rates of poverty in the poor nations. As selection 23 shows, the rich nations must bear some responsibility for the plight of the poor nations, for the rich nations are able to use those in the poor nations for their own benefit. ✦

23
Sweatshop Barbie

Exploitation of Third World Labor

Anton Foek

The industrialized nations owe much of their current prosperity to the use of extremely cheap labor in Third World countries. One perspective on this economic relationship, called **modernization theory,** *holds that the money and models provided by more advanced nations promote the development of industrial economies and democratic governments in the Third World.* **World system theory,** *in contrast, views the relationship as exploitative of Third World countries and detrimental to their economic development. Researchers have found some support for both positions, suggesting that different outcomes may occur for different nations (for reasons that are not yet clear).*

Whatever the eventual outcome for a Third World nation, the situation of the workers is often deplorable. In this selection, Anton Foek depicts one such situation—women and children in Thailand who make Barbie dolls. Why do they stay in jobs that are killing them? Simple survival is one motivation. Another is their role obligations as family members expected to help poorer relatives.

My daughter Zsa Zsa, seven years old, stands in front of the toy store and can't make up her mind which Barbie doll she wants. Barbie is her idol and role model. I urge her to pick out another present for her birthday but, if I insist, I'll spoil her day altogether. So Barbie it is: four or five to keep the peace and save her birthday.

There is no way for me to explain to her that there is something fundamentally wrong with Barbie. For as financially successful as the doll has been, the story of Barbie is appalling.

Barbie dolls are manufactured in factories in China, Thailand, and Indonesia, where working conditions are radically different from what Americans are used to. Factory workers in these Far Eastern countries are underpaid, overworked, and getting sick—even dying. Just arrived in Bangkok, I see banners that say, "We are not salve labour!" (They were intended to say "slave labour," but the message gets through anyway.) The banners are carried by women and children who work in the Dynamics factory just outside of Bangkok. Only a few men have shown up to support them. I ask these protestors what they want and they answer: to be treated like human beings. They regard themselves as modern-day slaves of a system that exploits them.

One woman, Karim, tells me that more than half of these women are sick. They make Mattel's Barbie dolls in an environment that would probably have been banned as dangerous anywhere in the First World. Many of the workers have respiratory infections, their lungs filled with dust from fabrics in the factory. And not only dust: others work with lead and other chemicals and suffer from chronic lead poisoning. They can wear masks, of course, but first they have to buy them. And as they make a mere four to five dollars a day—from which they must also buy their uniforms and scissors—most simply can't afford the protection.

Thanks to John Osolnick, an American working in Bangkok, I obtained access to the Dynamics factory (naturally, no tape or video recorders were allowed inside). I saw hundreds of women and children stuffing, cutting, dressing, and assembling Barbie dolls—as well as the Lion Kings my daughter worships and other Disney properties that dazzle me.

Many of these factory workers suffer from pains in their hands, necks, and shoulders. Others experience nausea and dizziness and suffer from hair and memory loss. They sleep badly. The most common complaints, however, are a shortage of breath and infections in and around the throat. More than 75 percent of the people working here have breathing problems. The air in the factory is so dusty that even the managers don't come in for fear of being contaminated. And of the hundreds of workers I saw, all of them, without exception, have black circles under their eyes.

One woman told me, "It sometimes gets so hot and moist in here that some of us faint." A small number of workers have tried to organize, she said, but there is an overall fear that they will be fired and that "no one will take care of us if we do not work." There is also the fear of physical harm. "Women in Thailand are vulnerable," another worker tells me. "We have to think of our parents in Chiang Mai and our small brothers and sisters who go to school. Who is going to pay for them if we don't?" It is a catch-22 situation: if they don't work, their relatives get nothing, if they do work, they get sick from all the chemicals and dust.

"I am an old woman even before my twentieth birthday," a third woman said to me. "Maybe I should move to Taiwan or Korea." But even if she wanted to, she wouldn't be allowed to emigrate, because she is too young. This job is a nightmare for her and the 4,500 other people who work at the Dynamics factory, and it is almost standard that Asian women and children are exploited this way. It doesn't really matter what industry you work in, as a woman or child you are always on the bottom of the heap—long hours, low wages, and poor health care. I can't help thinking that health organizations in the West should be able to do something more for them.

Pramitwa doesn't exactly know what to say to me when we meet in a Bangkok hospital. At first, she doesn't really understand why I am there. Dr. Orapun has asked her to come down from the outskirts of this hellish city of six million to the inner city, which is filled with exhaust fumes, noise, and poisoned air.

Dr. Orapun knows that Pramitwa has trouble breathing, but the physician thinks it is important that her story be told to the outside world. Otherwise, Pramitwa does not have a voice. Dr. Orapun is a 42-year-old woman who has an energy and power that is the envy of anyone who meets her. Her office

is small but very well known among the underprivileged here. She has been investigating the widespread illnesses and even deaths of workers at several different factories and assembly plants in and around Bangkok. She knows her work will stir controversy; Thai society is closed and prefers to settle disputes its own way.

Pramitwa is a shy, 22-year-old woman. She is accompanied by two friends, who are also suffering from diseases related to their work at the Dynamics plant. Eye contact with these women is difficult to make, and they all suffer from hair loss and have trouble breathing. When I ask one of them, Sunanta, how she is, she diverts her eyes to the ground and asks me in a whisper if I want to buy a souvenir.

Sunanta is a little older than the rest. I can hear her breathing is heavy and irregular. Dr. Orapun says that Sunanta is in terrible shape. Indeed, most of the women and children working in these toy factories are in terrible shape: besides the asthma, hair and memory loss, and constant pain in their hands, necks, and shoulders, they have episodes of vomiting and the women have irregular periods. Moreover, and without exception, they sleep badly, resulting in fatigue.

Sunanta is a bit more outspoken than the rest and bluntly states that the factory is exploiting them. Most of the Dynamics plant's 4,500 workers come from northeastern Thailand, where the poverty is abject and appalling. It is a frequent practice for parents there to sell their daughters—often not more than 11 or 12 years old—into sex slavery or as cheap labor to Thai gangsters or mafiosi from neighboring countries. The parents generate some income from that—a one-time flat fee of a couple of hundred dollars.

Those who aren't sold outright into slavery at an early age often are sent to the bigger cities like Bangkok, where they generate an even more stable income working in factories. They send the money back home to their parents and very often help pay for their little brothers and sisters to go to school.

Sunanta describes how she has to get up every morning at five o'clock to cook a meal and get ready for work. She also takes care of her neighbor's two children and gets them ready for kindergarten. Then, after a shower from a bucket outside the hut, Sunanta gets dressed and waits for the motorcycle that will pick up both her and the woman she shares the hut with and take them to the factory. She does this six days a week.

Dr. Orapun translates her words to me: "I have been working there for over six years now. After one year, I already started to have these problems." Sunanta's eyes still don't make contact with mine, and her voice is so low that the doctor has to ask her to repeat what she's saying.

I understand that working conditions, not just at the Dynamics plant but in all factories throughout Thailand and Southeast Asia, are appalling: long hours, hard work, low pay, no vacations, no sick days, no rights. No union and thus no voice.

"When we get sick, they throw us out," Sunanta tells me. "It isn't even the factory itself. The factory knows the standards set by the U.S. mother companies. But as the workers are hired by someone else for a period of 120 days, it is easy to fire us after 118 days of work. Very often we are hired again the very same day we are fired for another period of 120 days."

She says that complaining is of no use and that she wants to start a movement. She would like to get in contact with women from overseas, from countries where rights are guaranteed and a part of daily life. Eventually, the souvenir she wanted to sell me becomes a present simply for listening to her.

Sunanta gets up to go to the bathroom and, when she comes back, I notice that she has put some lipstick on. Her eyes are hollow, but they are making contact now with mine. I discover a proud woman who has redefined her identity.

Dr. Orapun started investigating sweatshops in 1991 as the director of Thailand's National Institute of Occupational and Environmental Medicine. At that time, she was looking into the deaths of several factory workers at Seagate Technology, the subsidiary of a computer company located in Silicon Valley. Seagate was, at that time, one of the world's largest independent computer hard-disk producers. It had opened two assembly plants in Thailand and was said to be one of the country's largest employers, with some 21,000 workers.

Seagate was profitable for a long time because it had based its operations in a low-wage country. Seagate's chief executive officer, Alan Shugart, even stated in a 1991 interview with *Electronic Business* magazine that his company was not very employee-oriented. And when Seagate's profits finally started to fall in the fluid and ever-changing computer market, the last thing the company wanted was to allow its employees to form a union to demand higher wages and better working conditions.

It was in this atmosphere that Dr. Orapun started her investigation. One day, while she was walking the factory assembly line, she was summoned to the company boardroom. There she was confronted by Stapron Kavitanon, the first secretary of the then-prime minister of Thailand and the director-general of the Thai Board of Investment. That meeting confirmed one of Dr. Orapun's misgivings about the goals of Thailand's foreign investors. "I am still furious," she tells me now, "because it was then I began to understand how these companies work. If they think Thailand is becoming too expensive or the workers too difficult, they simply move to cheaper labor countries like Indonesia or China."

Dr. Orapun recalls what Stapron said to her: "What you are doing is hurting your country. You cannot continue to investigate Seagate or any other foreign investor. You are a threat to the workers of this country."

Dr. Orapun refused to be intimidated and continued her investigations. Within a few weeks, she was removed as head of the National Institute of Occupational and Environmental Medicine. But that didn't stop her. She began analyzing blood samples from more than 2,000 workers at several factories (including the Dynamics plant where the Barbie dolls are made) in order to discover what was causing the worker illnesses and deaths.

At this point in the interview, Sunanta again makes eye contact with me and says that, at the Dynamics plant, at least four of her friends have died. I look at her and her almost bald head and listen to her heavy breathing, and I cannot help thinking that she may be dead soon, too.

"I think of quitting work, because it is very difficult for me," she says, gasping for air. "I have to rest. I am very tired." Her eyes turn away again, tiny tears in the corners and her cheeks gaunt.

Days before this interview, Sunanta was at the rally I witnessed upon my arrival in Bangkok. She believes that if she doesn't help the other workers, her life will have had no meaning. Before she dies she wants to do something to help her friends and colleagues keep alive the dream of a better life.

Dr. Orapun takes Sunanta's hands and holds them. She says that the blood samples she analyzed from the Seagate workers had levels of lead greater than 20 micrograms per 100 milliliters. "The fatalities at Seagate may have been caused by chronic poisoning," she tells me. "The main source of lead in electronics factories is the solder that is used to attach components to the circuit boards."

Seagate maintains that the high levels of lead in their workers are more likely the result of their living in a dangerously polluted part of the city. But Dr. Orapun says that this isn't true, because another study indicates that only 4 percent of the traffic police in Bangkok—many of whom are continually exposed to the air pollution caused by the city's traffic—had more lead in their blood than the workers at Seagate. Only 4 percent. So what's going on here?

In other factories, like the Dynamics plant where Sunanta and Pramitwa work, illness is more likely caused by the inhalation of dust and solvents. Sunanta says that, for her, becoming ill without health insurance would be possibly the most humiliating thing of all, because she would have to go back home. She does not want to face her relatives again and spend her remaining days dependent upon their benevolence. She is afraid that, if she loses her job—even a job that has caused her to get sick in the first place—she may end up losing her integrity, her self-esteem, and even her identity. And so she doesn't want to complain much about being paid six or seven dollars for a 12-hour workday. Indeed, by Bangkok standards, she is considered lucky to have found such a good job.

Sunanta herself has never played with a Barbie doll. The Dynamics workers are not allowed to buy them—not at the regular price and certainly not at a discount. She is astonished when I tell her that there are two Barbie dolls sold somewhere in the world every second, and that Mattel made more than $3.2 billion in 1994. Nor does she know that more than a billion pairs of shoes have been made for Barbie, many of them here in Bangkok, or that Barbie has 35 dogs, 10 horses, scores of cats, a panda, a chimpanzee, lion cubs, a giraffe, and a zebra. Sunanta cannot grasp the luxury of Barbie's world, but she certainly is not jealous. She just wishes that she could breathe more easily and that she wouldn't be so tired and that her hair would grow back again. She tells me how pretty she used to be when she was still living at home and even during the years when she had first come to Bangkok. But after working at the Dynamics plant for only a year, she started to develop problems: first, with her period, then headaches, memory loss, and now hair loss. Her health problems have left her depressed and embarrassed, shy and ashamed.

The local press eventually picked up on Dr. Orapun's research but concluded that she never proved her case. John Osolnick, an American researcher working in Bangkok, says that this is par for the course. He is furious over the way factory workers are being treated in Thailand: "They try to raise their voices, and they're fired without any benefit whatsoever. The companies know that, if they support the workers' demands, the American mother companies can easily move to even lower-wage countries. So the pressure from lobbyists is enormous." In Osolnick's office, the very air seems to be filled with his disappointment, anger, and frustration. He is particularly incensed by the way Dr. Orapun was treated. Six weeks after she filed her report, her medical institute was closed. "One day," he recalls, "a bunch of people arrived at her office only to remove the name board."

Dr. Orapun confirms the story and adds that she was informed by the director of the hospital that she no longer had a job there and should start looking elsewhere. Not surprisingly, both the Seagate and Dynamics plants have been officially cleared of any wrongdoing in the Kingdom of Thailand. Osolnick also informs me that another Dynamics employee, Metha, is hospitalized just outside of Bangkok and suggests that I speak with her myself.

The hospital is neat and clean. As it is a national holiday, the Dynamics plant is closed, so two friends are visiting Metha to cheer her up and tell her the latest gossip. Metha is a militant woman in her early twenties, who also came to Bangkok to improve the quality of her life. But she is afraid to talk to me. "Barbie is powerful," she says. "Three friends have already died. If they kill me, who will ever know I lived?"

Metha tried to start a union at the Dynamics plant. She claims that the company not only fired her but threatened to shut her up forever. Then she developed respiratory problems and was transferred to this hospital. It remains unclear who is going to pay the bill: Metha has no money and no insurance, and the company refuses to recognize her illness as work-related. Her illness has left her worn out, weak, and thin.

Metha says that she began to feel sick early in 1995, after having worked at the Dynamics plant since 1992 sorting parts for Barbie dolls. She reports, "When my head and body started to ache, I'd go to the factory doctor, but he wouldn't take me seriously. He said it would go away with time. But then my periods stopped, too, and I really started to worry. I told the manager at the factory, but he laughed at me. The doctor then withdrew the diagnosis of my sickness after he was called by the factory. That set me thinking about the rights and responsibilities we have."

Like the other Dynamics workers I have met, Metha avoids eye contact and speaks in a monotone. The only time she ever shows emotion is when she begins to cry and wonders aloud when it is all going to end.

I cannot help thinking of Cindy Jackson, an American photographer in London who has had 19 cosmetic-surgery operations to make herself look like Barbie—at a cost of some $165,000. I wonder what Jackson would say if she could see these sick and dying women and know how brutally they have been exploited in order to make dolls for First World children. Pramitwa, Sunanta, and Metha have never heard of Cindy Jackson, but my guess is they are glad not to be in her shoes. For them, it would be unbearable to live a life looking like Barbie.

Review

1. In what sense are the workers in the Barbie factory "modern-day slaves of a system that exploits them"?

2. Why do the workers accept the jobs, and why do they remain in them?

3. What happens when someone tries to improve the conditions of the workers?

Application

Make a personal or telephone interview of several buyers or suppliers for department stores, clothing retailers, or toy stores. Find out the following:

a. What proportion of products are made in Third World countries

b. How the wholesale prices of these products compare to products made in the United States

c. Whether the proportion of products made in Third World countries has increased or decreased over the past decade

d. Whether the respondent knows the wages and working conditions of the Third World workers who make the products

Discuss your findings in light of the information found in this article.

Unit IV

Social Institutions

Social institutions are the pillars of society. An **institution** is a collective solution to a problem of social life. Thus, the institutions of any society provide a framework for carrying out that society's essential functions, and they enhance social stability. The institutions found in all societies include family, government, the economy, education, religion, and health care. Note that sociologists define "institution" differently from its common usage. A mental hospital is not an institution in sociological terms; it is an organization, which is one kind of group. The family, in the sense of all families rather than a particular family, is an institution.

Examining a society in terms of its institutions can be revealing, especially when comparing one society with another. For instance, contrast the American practice of marrying for romantic love with the dowry and bride-price systems of certain societies. Or compare the working conditions of those in Third World countries with those in modern nations such as the United States and Canada (selection 23).

The connections between institutions within a single society are also worthy of exploration. For example, what are the effects of rising unemployment on family problems such as divorce and child abuse? Similarly, we might look at how power is apportioned among a society's institutions and the implications of that distribution. Religious institutions were dominant in medieval Europe, for instance, but political institutions are much more powerful today.

Selections 24–36 in this unit touch on each of the major social institutions. As you read the selections, think about how each institution has affected your life. It should be clear that social institutions are the matrix within which each of us is embedded as we live out our lives. ✦

Part One

The Family

Some kind of family is found in every human society, suggesting that the family fills fundamental functions for both individuals and society as a whole. Those functions include socialization, regulation of sexual relationships (in most societies people are expected to confine sex to marriage), reproduction, and the economic cooperation necessary to sustain life and well-being.

Family life has varied over time in the United States. In colonial America, a man was expected to be financially secure before marriage. Once a couple were married, children tended to come rapidly, creating large families. The family was stable; divorce was stigmatized. Because colonial America was primarily an agrarian society, the family also tended to be a self-contained economic unit, producing a great deal of what it consumed.

In contrast, today the average family is small, divorce is frequent, and the family is no longer a self-contained economic unit. Selections 24 and 25 address some of the challenges faced by the modern family. Selection 26 points out that our notions of what the family was in the past are not always accurate. ✦

24
Home Work Time

Marilyn Snell

A *century ago, women and men were widely regarded as having separate spheres of life. Women were viewed as "naturally" suited to child-rearing and housework. Men, on the other hand, were regarded as competitive and logical—well equipped for the world of work and public affairs. While some people still hold these beliefs, the massive influx of women into the labor force makes it difficult to maintain the illusion that they are unsuited to work outside the home. And what about men? Are they suited to, and willing to engage in, household work? When wives share in producing family income, do husbands balance this out by helping with the "second shift" of household work and child care?*

In the 1980s Arlie Hochschild and Anne Machung addressed the issue and concluded that husbands did little to help with household chores; wives simply added a "second shift" to their workday. In the 1990s, Hochschild used participant observation to continue her study of families in which both husband and wife work outside the home. The following interview summarizes and expands somewhat on the major findings reported in her book, The Time Bind.

In the interview, Hochschild notes a number of social factors that draw people's commitment away from family time and toward work time. One such factor is the possibility of social mobility, the movement within or between social classes. Upward mobility is a strong value in American society, but it is a value that is not always consistent with the most satisfying family life.

I n her latest book, *The Time Bind: When Work Becomes Home and Home Becomes Work* (New York: Metropolitan Books,

1997), UC Berkeley sociologist Arlie Hochschild takes a detective's eye to the problem of what's keeping parents at work so long. What she discovered were men and women apparently happily married to their jobs and not the least inclined to take advantage of family-friendly company policies—programs that would have allowed employees to spend more time at home.

Hochschild, who made waves with *The Second Shift*—her groundbreaking 1989 book on gender roles in two-career marriages—this time spent three summers observing employees of a Fortune 500 company she calls "Amerco" to protect the privacy of those she studied. She chose the Northeastern manufacturer precisely for its reputation as a good place for parents to work: A 1991 survey by the Families and Work Institute named it one of the 10 most family-friendly companies in the US.

After visiting company-sponsored childcare centers, tagging along on errands with stressed-out, upper-management moms, and interviewing employees in all sectors of the company—from "Bill," a high-ranking corporate executive, to "Becky," a factory-line worker—Hochschild discovered myriad ways in which the home is being invaded by the pressures of work, while the workplace is becoming a haven from a hectic, unrewarding home life. Her findings offer eloquent, sad, and sometimes chilling evidence of the "time bind" many employees find themselves in and, more broadly, suggest a disturbing cultural transformation in the way Americans feel about home, family, work, and even time itself.

Q: You argue that people are having trouble arranging their work hours to spend more time with their families. But you also contend that men and women alike are choosing to spend less time at home. What's going on? Where's the bind?

A: The bind is between work and home for both women and men. In The Second Shift, I put forward the argument that women have changed more rapidly than men. Women are spending more and more time at work, but men are not spending much more time taking care of needs at home (the second shift). We're still stuck in this stalled revolution, and we've come to think of that stall as "normal." In *The Time Bind*, I've explored ways in which the first shift (paid work) is staging a quiet takeover of life at home.

When I began my research, I thought we were working more for external reasons—for example, we needed the money. When I took a hard look, that explanation didn't fit the facts: At the company I studied, the richer the employees the less interested they were in time at home. The poorer they were, the more interested.

Another explanation I tried out was that with all the downsizing going on, people are working very hard so that they don't get on the layoff list. But when I asked people, "Are you working your 60-hour week because you're afraid of being laid off?" they said, "No. I'm doing it because I love my work." Disbelieving these responses at first, I looked at two different departments of this company, one which was adding people and another which was subtracting people. In comparing the two, I found that there weren't any differences in the number of people applying for family-friendly work schedules.

I'm not saying that fear of being laid off or the financial need to work long hours aren't real issues for people. It's just that they didn't account for the absence of a cultural resistance to long hours at work. I was looking for that kind of cultural resistance. What I found was a company that offered policies that we say we want—paternity and maternity leave, part-time, job sharing, flex-time—but very few employees who were interested in them.

Q: Were these policies really available? I got the sense that while the policies were on company books, they often didn't exist in practice.

A: Indeed, there were some managers who really wanted to sabotage the policies. It was just an extra headache for them. But there were also managers who took pride in offering flexible work arrangements. When I compared people working for rigid managers to those who were working for flexible managers, I found little difference in the number of people who came forward to ask for shorter hours.

Then I thought that perhaps people just didn't know about these policies. Wrong. In fact some workers said, "I'm really proud to be working for an enlightened company." Or, "I really don't know the policy specifics, but I know how I can find out should I need them in an emergency." But they weren't defining the scarcity of time at home as an emergency.

All of these explanations—that people wouldn't want more time at home because they couldn't afford it, or they wouldn't want more time because they were working scared, or they wouldn't want more time because they didn't dare ask a bad boss, or they wouldn't want more time because they didn't know about the policies—hold a little water and, in some cases, were definitive explanations. But they didn't account for the absence of a cultural resistance to long hours at work.

Q: Have we become a workaholic, anti-family culture?

A: This country has become more workaholic, but I don't think Americans are anti-family. It's not a family values issue. We live in two separate cultural worlds, one encompassing the workplace and one encompassing home and family. Over time, the world of the workplace has been transformed by a new kind of cultural engineering—especially in Fortune 500 companies—where the worker is invited to be empowered, to work closely with a team, to be a part of a quality circle, etc. In this new work culture, there is a great premium on reward. Moreover, if you get into a problem, there is somebody there to help you. For all its aggravations, many people like being at work.

I don't think that this new culture is necessarily bad. Rather, I think we need the same kinds of support at home that we are now getting at work. Today we have more recognition ceremonies at work, and fewer recognition ceremonies, so to speak, at home. We're asked to value the individual at work, and nobody's quite holding that ideology at home. It's tempting, therefore, to emotionally relocate to the workplace.

Of course, there are many kinds of workplaces and many kinds of homes. There is also a complicated set of corporate work-family strategies. Some corporations are going in the high-investment direction I saw at Amerco: "We're going to put a lot of effort into making a good workplace, and we're going to get a lot of work out of these folks." Others are following the strategy of divestment: "We're going to lay workers off; we're going to speed up; we're going to go back to Frederick Taylor's efficiency model." [In the early 1900s, Taylor engineered highly rigorous and mechanistic standards for factory work.]

Q: But isn't the company you studied in fact doing this? It has laid people off, it has encouraged a speedup in the sense that people are working a lot longer at their jobs for the same amount of pay. It's Taylorism with a smiley face.

A: You're right. But now workers buy into it. They internalize the speedup; they think their hurry is due to their work ethic. At Amerco, people began to think it was exciting to be in a workaholic environment. They would say, "We're our own worst enemy"; "It's hard to scrape myself up and get home, there's just so much to do"; and "No one does it to us, we're like that to ourselves."

They simply felt very rewarded by work. Moreover, their best friends were at work. Essentially, the neighborhood has gone to work. Corporate engineers have looked at how women are with each other, borrowing the best tips from female neighborhood culture and then transporting them back into the bosom of capitalism. They've feminized capitalism. You have to marvel at such corporate engineering, and then you have to watch it like a hawk because it's stealing family time away from families.

Q: Are you suggesting the workplace has been feminized but that the effect of this feminization has been far different than what the original women's movement might have hoped for?

A: Yes. Absolutely. A lot of feminists in the 1970s were calling for an equality in the workplace based on a female sensibility, as well as for an equality in which men participated more actively at home. But the corporate world was holding out the carrot of another equality in which women became equal on traditionally male terms. And there have been more rewards for women to throw themselves into work, frankly, than there

have been rewards for men to go in the other direction.

I'm a feminist. And I'm certainly not saying it was a mistake for women to enter the labor force. I believe work outside the home is good for women and it's good for families. All the data we have show that working women are more likely to feel good about themselves and positive about their lives, and to feel that their contributions at home are honored and valued—more so than women who permanently stay home.

However, women have entered the work world on male terms, and because of power arrangements they haven't felt able to push back. The strategy we need to pursue is one of recovering our time to push back on our hours of work. We need to form a new alliance between feminist groups, labor unions, child advocates, progressive corporations, and the federal government insofar as it's willing to pursue a family-friendly agenda.

Q: But if people really like to work and they don't want to go home, why should we care about starting a "time movement" that would give us more time away from work to spend with our families?

A: I hope to open up a conversation about the costs of settling for the wrong terms at work. And I think there are enough people who don't feel good about the conditions under which they're working to begin this conversation. People are ambivalent. They feel confused. I hope to appeal to this ambivalence.

Q: Men who would like to take more responsibility for child rearing seem to be in an untenable position, almost worse than that of women, because in today's corporate culture wanting to spend more time with one's family—to be a family man—is taken as a sign of lack of ambition.

A: Yes. I think that when you allow a market culture to prevail, those new men, those heroes of an alternative culture, suffer. For example, I interviewed a young engineer, the first man to apply for formal paternity leave at Amerco—two weeks, unpaid. His own father had left home early in his childhood, and he felt strongly about becoming a real daddy to his child, from the very start. His wife appreciated his doing this. The women in his office appreciated it. But his male co-workers divided into two groups. Acquaintances pretended they didn't know why he'd been absent, though they did know. Friends kidded him, "So, did you catch up on the soaps?" They could understand his wanting to take a holiday, but they couldn't understand paternity leave. They thought family-friendly policies were for women, not men. Of course, if he'd been living in Sweden he wouldn't have gotten the soaps jokes, since he'd be among the 80 percent of all employed fathers who take two weeks paternity leave there.

Q: What's happening to the kids in this time-deprived family dynamic?

A: The children I saw were doing fine in school and weren't beating up kids on the playground. But children feel starved for time, and adults feel guilty for starving children of time. That's a huge problem, not because your kid won't grow up to be bright and successful, but what if they grow up to be bright and successful and replay the same time-starved life that was taught to them? I talked to one child, who said to her grandmother on the telephone: "Grandma, I don't have time to talk to you." Well, this kid was doing beautifully in school, but is that what really matters? If that's what matters most, aren't we missing an important emotional piece of the picture?

We want to live fully human lives. Not only is that the feminist project, it's the progressive project. What I'm talking about is very radical. The time movement is an extension of the labor movement, only it's fundamentally different because it puts family and private life center stage in a way that the labor movement has not done. Even portions of the feminist movement have not yet dared to do it.

A new time movement needs to be critical of market culture; it also needs to critique the ways in which capitalism has incorporated the useful aspects of neighborhood female culture and given itself a humanitarian face.

The subtraction of effort from community life has been seen as the absence of civic virtue. I see it as the result of increasing the number of hours at work. The marketplace has been absorbing more people's time, and that time is coming not just from families but from communities.

The focus of our public discourse has been on how American companies are competing with Japanese, German, and other foreign companies. What this allows us to ignore is how each of those American companies is really in competition with the families of the workers. That's the real competition. And in that competition the American companies are winning hands down.

Q: Why haven't we been able to hold the line, like other nations, against the invasion of work, into the home?

A: I think we have a rawer version of capitalism and a more fragile community and family base than other nations. We are a more individualistic culture. From the Boston Tea Party on, we've had too little faith in government. We also have a higher rate of mobility from one community to another. These American characteristics didn't wreak havoc until other factors came into play—the decline of labor movements and the globalization of capital. We could get along with rugged individualism, social mobility, and the absence of dedication to community before. But when you add on these two extra factors, the balance is tipped in favor of the marketplace. And the marketplace has won—for the moment.

Review

1. What is the "time bind" for men and women working outside the home?

2. Describe the new work culture discussed by Hochschild.

3. In what sense has the workplace been feminized?

4. What are the consequences of the new work culture for children?

Application

Make a list of all the things that consume time for families—work, school, meals, individual recreation, couple (husband and wife) activities, family leisure activities, household chores, and so forth. Provide a separate list for each member of a family in which husband and wife both work outside the home and the children are in school. Ask them to write down an estimate of the amount of time they spend during an average week on each of the activities.

Compare the lists. Discuss possible reasons for any discrepancies. If other families are similar to the one you interviewed, what are the implications for family life today?

Reprinted from: Marilyn Snell, "Home Work Time." In *Mother Jones*, May/June, 1997, pp. 26–30. Reprinted with permission from *Mother Jones* magazine, Copyright © 1997, Foundation for National Progress. ✦

25
The Transformation of Family Life

Lillian B. Rubin

Life is quite different for people in the various social classes. Obviously, those with lower levels of education, income, and power have fewer resources and fewer options than those with higher levels. Sociologists have noted, in fact, a great many differences—ranging from differences in health and lifestyles to differences in values and attitudes—among people of different social classes. In studying the family, therefore, it is important to know the social class of the families involved. While Hochschild's research focuses on dual-career couples in the middle and upper-middle class, the author of this selection, Lillian Rubin, has spent much of her career studying working-class families.

Like their middle-class counterparts, working-class wives and mothers are likely to work outside the home. How do working-class couples handle the tensions? In this selection, based on her in-depth interviews with working-class men and women, Rubin describes some of their struggles with money, child care, sex, and men's attitudes toward housework. She also points out some racial/ethnic differences among the families she studied.

Note that the men and women in her study often have differing perceptions of what's going on in the home. Rubin doesn't use the term **definition of the situation,** but it is an important concept that applies well to her research. It means that if people define a situation as real, it is real in its consequences. Thus, if a husband defines himself as overworked, he will act like someone overworked whether or not his wife or an outside observer agrees with his definition. And if a wife defines

herself as not getting a fair amount of help from her husband, she will act accordingly regardless of his perceptions or those of an outside observer. People act on the basis of how they define the situation. To understand their behavior, therefore, you need to understand their definitions, their perceptions.

"I know my wife works all day, just like I do," says Gary Braunswig, a twenty-nine-year-old white drill press operator, "but it's not the same. She doesn't have to do it. I mean, she has to because we need the money, but it's different. It's not really her job to have to be working; it's mine." He stops, irritated with himself because he can't find exactly the words he wants, and asks, "Know what I mean? I'm not saying it right; I mean, it's the man who's supposed to support his family, so I've got to be responsible for that, not her. And that makes one damn big difference.

"I mean, women complain all the time about how hard they work with the house and the kids and all. I'm not saying it's not hard, but that's her responsibility, just like the finances are mine."

"But she's now sharing that burden with you, isn't she?" I remark.

"Yeah, and I do my share around the house, only she doesn't see it that way. Maybe if you add it all up, I don't do as much as she does, but then she doesn't bring in as much money as I do. And she doesn't always have to be looking for overtime to make an extra buck. I got no complaints about that, so how come she's always complaining about me? I mean, she helps me out financially, and I help her out with the kids and stuff. What's wrong with that? It seems pretty equal to me."

Cast that way, his formulation seems reasonable: They're each responsible for one part of family life; they each help out with the other. But the abstract formula doesn't square with the lived reality. For him, helping her adds relatively little to the burden of household tasks he must do each day. A recent study by University of Wisconsin researchers, for example, found that in families where both wife and husband work full-time, the women average over twenty-six hours a week in household labor, while the men do about ten. That's because there's nothing in the family system to force him to accountability or responsibility on a daily basis. He may "help her out with the kids and stuff" one day and be too busy or preoccupied the next. But for Gary's wife, Irene, helping him means an extra eight hours every working day. Consequently, she wants something more consistent from him than a helping hand with a particular task when he has the time, desire, or feels guilty enough. "Sure, he helps me out," she says, her words tinged with resentment. "He'll give the kids a bath or help with the dishes. But only when I ask him. He doesn't have to ask me to go to work every day, does he? Why should I have to ask him?" "Why should I have to ask him?"—words that suggest a radically different consciousness from the working-class women I met twenty years ago. Then, they counted their blessings. "He's a steady worker; he doesn't drink; he doesn't hit me," they told me by way of explaining why they had "no right to complain." True, these words were reminders to themselves that life could be worse, that they shouldn't take these things for granted—reminders that didn't wholly work to obscure their discontent with other aspects of the marriage. But they were nevertheless meaningful statements of value that put a brake on the kinds of demands they felt they could make of their men, whether about the unequal division of household tasks or about the emotional content of their lives together.

Now, the same women who reminded themselves to be thankful two decades ago speak openly about their dissatisfaction with the role divisions in the family. Some husbands, especially the younger ones, greet their wives' demands sympathetically. "I try to do as much as I can for Sue, and when I can't, I feel bad about it," says twenty-nine-year-old Don Dominguez, a Latino father of three children, who is a construction worker.

Others are more ambivalent. "I don't know, as long as she's got a job, too, I guess it's right that I should help out in the house. But that doesn't mean I've got to like it," says

twenty-eight-year-old Joe Kempinski, a white warehouse worker with two children.

Some men are hostile, insisting that their wives' complaints are unreasonable, unjust, and oppressive. "I'm damn tired of women griping all the time; it's nothing but nags and complaints," Ralph Danesen, a thirty-six-year-old white factory worker and the father of three children, says indignantly. "It's enough! You'd think they're the only ones who've got it hard. What about me? I'm not living in a bed of roses either." "Christ, what does a guy have to do to keep a wife quiet these days? What does she want? It's not like I don't do anything to help her out, but it's never enough."

In the past there was a clear understanding about the obligations and entitlements each partner took on when they married. He was obliged to work outside the home; she would take care of life inside. He was entitled to her ministrations, she to his financial support. But this neat division of labor with its clear-cut separation of rights and obligations no longer works. Now, women feel obliged to hold up their share of the family economy—a partnership men welcome. In return, women believe they're entitled to their husband's full participation in domestic labor. And here is the rub. For while men enjoy the fruits of their wives' paid work outside the home, they have been slow to accept the reciprocal responsibilities—that is, to become real partners in the work inside the home.

The women, exhausted from doing two days' work in one, angry at the need to assume obligations without corresponding entitlements, push their men in ways unknown before. The men, battered by economic uncertainty and by the escalating demands of their wives, feel embattled and victimized on two fronts—one outside the home, the other inside. Consequently, when their wives seem not to see the family work they do, when they don't acknowledge and credit it, when they fail to appreciate them, the men feel violated and betrayed. "You come home and you want to be appreciated a little. But it doesn't work that way, leastwise not here anymore," complains Gary Braunswig, his angry words at odds with sadness in his eyes. "There's no peace, I guess that's the real problem; there's no peace anywhere anymore."

The women often understand what motivates their husbands' sense of victimization and even speak sympathetically about it at times. But to understand and sympathize is not to condone, especially when they feel equally assaulted on both the home and the economic fronts. "I know I complain a lot, but I really don't ask for that much. I just want him to help out a little more," explains Ralph Danesen's wife, Helen, a thirty-five-year-old office worker. "It isn't like I'm asking him to cook the meals or anything like that. I know he can't do that, and I don't expect him to. But every time I try to talk to him, you know, to ask him if I couldn't get a little more help around here, there's a fight."

One of the ways the men excuse their behavior toward family work is by insisting that their responsibility as breadwinner burdens them in ways that are alien to their wives. "The plant's laying off people left and right; it could be me tomorrow. Then what'll we do? Isn't it enough I got to worry about that? I'm the one who's got all the worries; she doesn't. How come that doesn't count?" demands Bob Duckworth, a twenty-nine-year-old factory worker.

But, in fact, the women don't take second place to their men in worrying about what will happen to the family if the husband loses his job. True, the burden of finding another one that will pay the bills isn't theirs—not a trivial difference. But the other side of this truth is that women are stuck with the reality that the financial welfare of the family is out of their control, that they're helpless to do anything to prevent its economic collapse or to rectify it should it happen. "He thinks I've got it easy because it's not my job to support the family," says Bob's wife, Ruthanne. "But sometimes I think it's worse for me. I worry all the time that he's going to get laid off, just like he does. But I can't do anything about it. And if I try to talk to him about it, you know, like maybe make a plan in case it happens, he won't even listen. How does he think *that* makes me feel? It's my life, too, and I can't even talk to him about it."

Not surprisingly, there are generational differences in what fuels the conflict around the division of labor in these families. For the older couples—those who grew up in a different time, whose marriages started with another set of ground rules—the struggle is not simply around how much men do or about whether they take responsibility for the daily tasks of living without being pushed, prodded, and reminded. That's the overt manifestation of the discord, the trigger that starts the fight. But the noise of the explosion when it comes serves to conceal the more fundamental issue underlying the dissension: legitimacy. What does she have a right to expect? "What do I know about doing stuff around the house?" asks Frank Moreno, a forty-eight-year-old foreman in a warehouse. "I wasn't brought up like that. My pop, he never did one damn thing, and my mother never complained. It was her job; she did it and kept quiet. Besides, I work my ass off every day. Isn't that enough?"

For the younger couples, those under forty, the problem is somewhat different. The men may complain about the expectation that they'll participate more fully in the care and feeding of the family, but talk to them about it quietly and they'll usually admit that it's not really unfair, given that their wives also work outside the home. In these homes, the issue between husband and wife isn't only who does what. That's there, and it's a source of more or less conflict, depending upon what the men actually do and how forceful their wives are in their demands. But in most of these families there's at least a verbal consensus that men *ought* to participate in the tasks of daily life. Which raises the next and perhaps more difficult issue in contest between them: Who feels responsible for getting the tasks done? Who regards them as a duty, and for whom are they an option? On this, tradition rules.

Even in families where husbands now share many of the tasks, their wives still bear full responsibility for the organization of family life. A man may help cook the meal these days, but a woman is most likely to be the one who has planned it. He may take the children to child care, but she virtually always has had to arrange it. It's she also who is accountable for the emotional life of the family, for monitoring the emotional temperature of its members and making the necessary corrections. It's this need to be responsible for it all that often feels as burdensome as the tasks themselves. "It's not just doing all the stuff that needs doing," explains Maria Jankowicz, a white twenty-eight-year-old assembler in an electronics factory. "It's worrying all the time about everything and always having to arrange everything, you know what I mean. It's like I run the whole show. If I don't stay on top of it all, things fall apart because nobody else is going to do it. The kids can't and Nick, well, forget it," she concludes angrily.

If, regardless of age, life stage, or verbal consensus, women usually still carry the greatest share of the household burdens, why is it important to notice that younger men grant legitimacy to their wives' demands and older men generally do not? Because men who believe their wives have a right to expect their participation tend to suffer guilt and discomfort when they don't live up to those expectations. And no one lives comfortably with guilt. "I know I don't always help enough, and I feel bad about it, you know, guilty sometimes," explains Bob Beardsley, a thirty-year-old white machine operator, his eyes registering the discomfort he feels as he speaks.

"Does it change anything when you feel guilty?" I ask.

A small smile flits across his face, and he says, "Sometimes. I try to do a little more, but then I get busy with something and forget that she needs me to help out. My wife says I don't pay attention, that's why I forget. But I don't know. Seems like I've just got my mind on other things."

It's possible, of course, that the men who speak of guilt and rights are only trying to impress me by mouthing the politically correct words. But even if true, they display a sensitivity to the issue that's missing from the men who don't speak those words. For words are more than just words. They embody ideas; they are the symbols that give meaning to our thoughts; they shape our consciousness. New ideas come to us on the wings of words. It's words that bring those ideas to life, that allow us to see possibilities unrecognized before we gave them words. Indeed, without words, there is no conscious thought, no possibility for the kind of self-reflection that lights the path of change.

True, there's often a long way between word and deed. But the man who feels guilty when he disappoints his wife's expectations has a different consciousness than the one who doesn't—a difference that usually makes for at least some small change in his behavior. Although the emergence of this changing male consciousness is visible in all the racial groups in this study, there also are differences among them that are worthy of comment.

Virtually all the men do some work inside the family—tending the children, washing dishes, running the vacuum, going to the market. And they generally also remain responsible for those tasks that have always been traditionally male—mowing the lawn, shoveling the snow, fixing the car, cleaning the garage, doing repairs around the house. Among the white families in this study, 16 percent of the men share the family work relatively equally, almost always those who live in families where they and their wives work different shifts or where the men are unemployed. "What choice do I have?" asks Don Bartlett, a thirty-year-old white handyman who works days while his wife is on the swing shift. "I'm the only one here, so I do what's got to be done."

Asian and Latino men of all ages, however, tend to operate more often on the old male model, even when they work different shifts or are unemployed, a finding that puzzled me at first. Why, I wondered, did I find only two Asian men and one Latino who are real partners in the work of the family? Aren't these men subject to the same social and personal pressures others experience?

The answer is both yes and no. The pressures are there but, depending upon where they live, there's more or less support for resisting them. The Latino and Asian men who live in ethnic neighborhoods—settings where they are embedded in an intergenerational community and where the language and culture of the home country is kept alive by a steady stream of new immigrants—find strong support for clinging to the old ways. Therefore, change comes much more slowly in those families. The men who live outside the ethnic quarter are freer from the mandates and constraints of these often tight-knit communities, therefore are more responsive to the winds of change in the larger society.

These distinctions notwithstanding, it's clear that Asian and Latino men generally participate least in the work of the household and are the least likely to believe they have much responsibility there beyond bringing home a paycheck. "Taking care of the house and kids is my wife's job, that's all," says Joe Gomez flatly.

"A Chinese man mopping a floor? I've never seen it yet," says Amy Lee angrily. Her husband, Dennis, trying to make a joke of the conflict with his wife, says with a smile, "In Chinese families men don't do floors and windows. I help with the dishes sometimes if she needs me to or," he laughs, "if she screams loud enough. The rest, well, it's pretty much her job."

The commonly held stereotype about black men abandoning women and children, however, doesn't square with the families in this study. In fact, black men are the most likely to be real participants in the daily life of the family and are more intimately involved in raising their children than any of the others. True, the men's family work load doesn't always match their wives', and the women are articulate in their complaints about this. Nevertheless, compared to their white, Asian, or Latino counterparts, the black families look like models of egalitarianism.

Nearly three-quarters of the men in the African-American families in this study do a substantial amount of the cooking, cleaning, and child care, sometimes even more than their wives. All explain it by saying one version or another of: "I just figure it's my job, too." Which simply says what is, without explaining how it came to be that way.

To understand that, we have to look at family histories that tell the story of generations of African-American women who could find work and men who could not, and to the family culture that grew from this difficult and painful reality. "My mother worked six days a week cleaning other people's houses, and my father was an ordinary laborer, when he could find work, which wasn't very often," explains thirty-two-year-old Troy Payne, a black waiter and father of two children. "So he was home a lot more than she was, and he'd do what he had to do around the house. The kids all had to do their share, too. It seemed only fair, I guess."

Difficult as the conflict around the division of labor is, it's only one of the many issues that have become flash points in family life since mother went to work. Most important, perhaps, is the question: Who will care for the children? For the lack of decent, affordable facilities for the care of the children creates unbearable problems and tensions for these working-class families.

It's hardly news that child care is an enormous headache and expense for all two-job families. In many professional middle-class families, where the child-care bill can be $1,500–2,000 a month, it competes with the mortgage payment as the biggest single monthly expenditure. Problematic as this may be, however, these families are the lucky ones when compared to working-class families, many of whom don't earn much more than the cost of child care in these upper middle-class families. Even the families in this study at the highest end of the earnings scale, those who earn $42,000 a year, can't dream of such costly arrangements.

For most working-class families, therefore, child care often is patched together in ways that leave parents anxious and children in jeopardy. "Care for the little ones, that's a real big problem," says Beverly Waldov, a thirty-year-old white mother of three children, the youngest two, products of a second marriage, under three years old. "My oldest girl is nine, so she's not such a problem. I hate the idea of her being a latchkey kid, but what can I do? We don't even have the money to put the little ones in one of those good day-care places, so I don't have any choice with her. She's just got to be able to take care of herself after school," she says, her words a contest between anxiety and hope.

"We have a kind of complicated arrangement for the little kids. Two days a week, my mom takes care of them. We pay her, but at least I don't have to worry when they're with her; I know it's fine. But she works the rest of the time, so the other days we take them to this woman's house. It's the best we can afford, but it's not great because she keeps too many kids, and I know they don't get good attention. Especially the little one; she's just a baby, you know." She pauses and looks away, anguished. "She's so clingy when I bring her home; she can't let go of me, like nobody's paid her any mind all day. But it's not like I have a choice. We barely make it now; if I stop working, we'd be in real trouble."

Even such makeshift solutions don't work for many families. Some speak of being unable to afford day care at all. "We couldn't pay our bills if we had to pay for somebody to take care of the kids."

Some say they're unwilling to leave the children in the care of strangers. "I just don't believe someone else should be raising our kids, that's all."

Some have tried a variety of child-care arrangements, only to have them fail in a moment of need. "We tried a whole bunch of things, and maybe they work for a little while," says Faye Ensey, a black twenty-eight-year-old office worker. "But what happens when your kid gets sick? Or when the baby sitter's kids get sick? I lost two jobs in a row because my kids kept getting sick and I couldn't go to work. Or else I couldn't take my little one to the baby sitter because her kids were sick. They finally fired me for absenteeism. I didn't really blame them, but it felt terrible anyway. It's such a hassle, I sometimes think I'd be glad to just stay home. But we can't afford for me not to work, so we had to figure out something else."

For such families, that "something else" is the decision to take jobs on different shifts—a decision made by one-fifth of the families in this study. With one working days and the other on swing or graveyard, one parent is home with the children at all times. "We were getting along okay before Daryl junior was born, because Shona, my daughter, was getting on. You know, she didn't need somebody with her all the time, so we could both work days," explains Daryl Adams, a black

thirty-year-old postal clerk with a ten-year-old daughter and a nine-month-old son. "I used to work the early shift—seven to three—so I'd get home a little bit after she got here. It worked out okay. But then this here big surprise came along." He stops, smiles down fondly at his young son and runs his hand over his nearly bald head.

"Now between the two of us working, we don't make enough money to pay for child care and have anything left over, so this is the only way we can manage. Besides, both of us, Alesha and me, we think it's better for one of us to be here, not just for the baby, for my daughter, too. She's growing up and, you know, I think maybe they need even more watching than when they were younger. She's coming to the time when she could get into all kinds of trouble if we're not here to put the brakes on."

But the cost such arrangements exact on a marriage can be very high. When I asked these husbands and wives when they have time to talk, more often than not I got a look of annoyance at a question that, on its face, seemed stupid to them. "Talk? How can we talk when we hardly see each other?" "Talk? What's that?" "Talk? Ha, that's a joke."

Mostly, conversation is limited to the logistics that take place at shift-changing time when children and chores are handed off from one to the other. With children dancing around underfoot, the incoming parent gets a quick summary of the day's or night's events, a list of reminders about things to be done, perhaps about what's cooking in the pot on the stove. "Sometimes when I'm coming home and it's been a hard day, I think: Wouldn't it be wonderful if I could just sit down with Leon for half an hour and we could have a quiet beer together?" thirty-one-year-old Emma Guerrero, a Latina baker, says wistfully.

But it's not to be. If the arriving spouse gets home early enough, there may be an hour when both are there together. But with the pressures of the workday fresh for one and awaiting the other, and with children clamoring for parental attention, this isn't a promising moment for any serious conversation. "I usually get home about forty-five minutes or so before my wife has to leave for work," says Ralph Jo, a thirty-six-year-old Asian repairman whose children, ages three and five, are the product of a second marriage. "So we try to take a few minutes just to make contact. But it's hard with the kids and all. Most days the whole time gets spent with taking care of business—you know, who did what, what the kids need, what's for supper, what bill collector was hassling her while I was gone—all the damn garbage of living. It makes me nuts."

Most of the time even this brief hour isn't available. Then the ritual changing of the guard takes only a few minutes—a quick peck on the cheek in greeting, a few words, and it's over. "It's like we pass each other. He comes in; I go out; that's it."

Some of the luckier couples work different shifts on the same days, so they're home together on weekends. But even in these families there's so little time for normal family life that there's hardly any room for anyone or anything outside. "There's so much to do when I get home that there's no time for anything but the chores and the kids," says Daryl's wife, Alesha Adams. "I never get to see anybody or do anything else anymore and, even so, I'm always feeling upset and guilty because there's not enough time for them. Daryl leaves a few minutes after I get home, and the rest of the night is like a blur—Shona's homework, getting the kids fed and down for the night, cleaning up, getting everything ready for tomorrow. I don't know; there's always something I'm running around doing. I sometimes feel like—What do you call them?—one of those whirling dervishes, rushing around all the time and never getting everything done.

"Then on the weekends, you sort of want to make things nice for the kids—and for us, too. It's the only time we're here together, like a real family, so we always eat with the kids. And we try to take them someplace nice one of the days, like to the park or something. But sometimes we're too tired, or there's too many other catch-up things you have to do. I don't even get to see my sister anymore. She's been working weekends for the last year or so, and I'm too busy week nights, so there's no time.

"I don't mean to complain; we're lucky in a lot of ways. We've got two great kids, and we're a pretty good team, Daryl and me. But I worry sometimes. When you live on this kind of schedule, communication's not so good."

For those whose days off don't match, the problems of sustaining both the couple relationship and family life are magnified enormously. "The last two years have been hell for us," says thirty-five-year-old Tina Mulvaney, a white mother of two teenagers. "My son got into bad company and had some trouble, so Mike and I decided one of us had to be home. But we can't make it without my check, so I can't quit.

"Mike drives a cab and I work in a hospital, so we figured one of us could transfer to nights. We talked it over and decided it would be best if I was here during the day and he was here at night. He controls the kids, especially my son, better than I do. When he lays down the law, they listen." She interrupts her narrative to reflect on the difficulty of raising children. "You know, when they were little, I used to think about how much easier it would be when they got older. But now I see it's not true; that's when you really have to begin to worry about them. This is when they need someone to be here all the time to make sure they stay out of trouble."

She stops again, this time fighting tears, then takes up where she left off. "So now Mike works days and I work graveyard. I hate it, but it's the only answer; at least this way somebody's here all the time. I get home about 8:30 in the morning. The kids and Mike are gone. It's the best time of the day because it's the only time I have a little quiet here. I clean up the house a little, do the shopping and the laundry and whatever, then I go to sleep for a couple of hours until the kids come home from school.

"Mike gets home at five; we eat; then he takes over for the night, and I go back to sleep for another couple of hours. I try to get up by 9 so we can all have a little time together, but I'm so tired that I don't make it a lot of times. And by 10, he's sleeping because he has to be up by 6 in the morning. So if I don't get up, we hardly see each other at all. Mike's here on weekends, but I'm not. Right now I have Tuesday and Wednesday off. I keep hoping for a Monday–Friday shift, but it's what everybody wants, and I don't have the seniority yet. It's hard, very hard; there's no time to live or anything," she concludes with a listless sigh.

Even in families where wife and husband work the same shift, there's less time for leisure pursuits and social activities than ever before, not just because both parents work full-time but also because people work longer hours now than they did twenty years ago. Two decades ago, weekends saw occasional family outings, Friday-evening bowling, a Saturday trip to the shopping mall, a Sunday with extended family, once in a while an evening out without the children. In summer, when the children weren't in school, a week night might find the family paying a short visit to a friend, a relative, or a neighbor. Now almost everyone I speak with complains that it's hard to find time for even these occasional outings. Instead, most off-work hours are spent trying to catch up with the dozens of family and household tasks that were left undone during the regular work week. When they aren't doing chores, parents guiltily try to do in two days a week what usually takes seven—that is, to establish a sense of family life for themselves and their children.

"Leisure," snorts Peter Pittman, a twenty-eight-year-old African-American father of two, married six years. "With both of us working like we do, there's no time for anything. We got two little kids; I commute better than an hour each way to my job. Then we live here for half rent because I take care of the place for the landlord. So if somebody's got a complaint, I've got to take care of it, you know, fix it myself or get the landlord to get somebody out to do it if I can't. Most things I can do myself, but it takes time. I sometimes wonder what this life's all about, because this sure ain't what I call living. We don't go anyplace; we don't do anything; Christ, we hardly have time to go to the toilet. There's always some damn thing, that's waiting that you've got to do."

Clearly, such complaints aren't unique to the working class. The pressures of time, the impoverishment of social life, the anxieties about child care, the fear that children will live in a world of increasing scarcity, the threat of divorce—all these are part of family life today, regardless of class. Nevertheless, there are important differences between those in the higher reaches of the class structure and the families of the working class. The simple fact that middle-class families have more discretionary income is enough to make a big difference in the quality of their social life. For they generally have enough money to pay for a baby-sitter once in a while so that parents can have some time to themselves; enough, too, for a family vacation, for tickets to a concert, a play, or a movie. At $7.50 a ticket in a New York or San Francisco movie house, a working-class couple will settle for a $3.00 rental that the whole family can watch together.

Finding time and energy for sex is also a problem, one that's obviously an issue for two-job families of any class. But it's harder to resolve in working-class families because they have so few resources with which to buy some time and privacy for themselves. Ask about their sex lives and you'll be met with an angry, "What's that?" or a wistful, "I wish." When it happens, it is, as one woman put it, "on the run"—a situation that's particularly unsatisfactory for most women. For them, the pleasure of sex is related to the whole of the interaction—to a sense of intimacy and connection, to at least a few relaxed, loving moments. When they can't have these, they're likely to avoid sex altogether—a situation the men find equally unsatisfactory.

"Sex?" asks Lisa Scranton, a white twenty-nine-year-old mother of three who feigns a puzzled frown, as if she doesn't quite know the meaning of the word. "Oh yeah, that; I remember now," she says, her lips smiling, her eyes sad. "At the beginning, when we first got together, it was, WOW, real hot, great. But after a while it cools down, doesn't it? Right now, it's down the toilet. I wonder, does it happen to everybody like that?" she asks dejectedly.

"I guess the worst is when you work different shifts like we do and you get to see each other maybe six minutes a day. There's no time for sex. Sometimes we try to steal a few minutes for ourselves but, I don't know, I can't get into it that way. He can. You know how men are; they can do it any time. Give them two minutes, and they can get off. But it takes me time; I mean, I like to feel close, and you can't do that in three minutes. And there's the kids; they're right here all the time. I don't want to do it if it means being interrupted. Then he gets mad, so sometimes I do. But it's a problem, a real problem."

The men aren't content with these quick sexual exchanges either. But for them it's generally better than no sex at all, while for the women it's often the other way around. "You want to talk about sex, huh?" asks Lisa's husband, Chuck, his voice crackling with anger. "Yeah, I don't mind; it's fine, only I got nothing to talk about. Far as I'm concerned, that's one of the things I found out about marriage. You get married, you give up sex. We hardly ever do it anymore, and when we do, it's like she's doing me a favor.

"Christ, I know the way we've got to do things now isn't great," he protests, running a hand through his hair agitatedly. "We don't see each other but a few minutes a day, but I don't see why we can't take five and have a little fun in the sack. Sure, I like it better when we've got more time, too. But for her, if it can't be perfect, she gets all wound and uptight and it's like . . ." He stops, groping for words, then explodes, "It's like screwing a cold fish."

She isn't just a "cold fish," however. The problems they face are deeper than that. For once such conflicts arise, spontaneity takes flight and sex becomes a problem that needs attention rather than a time out for pleasure and renewal. Between times, therefore, he's busy calculating how much time has passed: "It's been over two weeks"; nursing his wounds: "I don't want to have to beg her"; feeling deprived and angry: "I don't know why I got married." When they finally do come together, he's disappointed. How could it be otherwise, given the mix of feelings he brings to the bed with him—the frustration and anger, the humiliation of feeling he has to beg her, the wounded sense of manhood.

Meanwhile, she, too, is preoccupied with sex, not with thoughts of pleasure but with figuring out how much time she has before, as she puts it, "he walks around with his mouth stuck out. I know I'm in real big trouble if we don't do it once a week. So I make sure we do, even if I don't want to." She doesn't say those words to him, of course. But he knows. And it's precisely this, the knowledge that she's servicing him rather than desiring him that's so hard for him to take.

The sexual arena is one of the most common places to find a "his and her" marriage—one marriage, two different sex lives. Each partner has a different story to tell; each is convinced that his or her version is the real one. A husband says mournfully, "I'm lucky if we get to make love once a week." His wife reports with irritation, "It's two, sometimes three times a week." It's impossible to know whose account is closest to the reality. And it's irrelevant. If that's what they were after, they could keep tabs and get it straight. But facts and feelings are often at war in family life. And nowhere does right or wrong, true or false count for less than in their sexual interactions. It isn't that people arbitrarily distort the truth. They simply report their experience, and it's feeling, not fact, that dominates that experience; feeling, not fact, that is their truth.

But it's also true that, especially for women, the difference in frequency of sexual desire can be a response—sometimes conscious, sometimes not—to other conflicts in the marriage. It isn't that men never withhold sex as a weapon in the family wars, only that they're much more likely than women to be able to split sex from emotion, to feel their anger and still experience sexual desire. For a man, too, a sexual connection with his wife can relieve the pressures and tensions of the day, can make him feel whole again, even if they've barely spoken a word to each other.

For a woman it's different. What happens—or, more likely, what doesn't happen—in the kitchen, the living room, and the laundry room profoundly affects what's possible in the bedroom. When she feels distant, unconnected, angry; when her pressured life leaves her feeling fragmented; when she hasn't had a real conversation with her husband for a couple of days, sex is very far from either her mind or her loins. "I run around busy all the time, and he just sits there, so by the time we go to bed, I'm too tired," explains

Linda Bloodworth, a white thirty-one-year-old telephone operator.

"Do you think your lack of sexual response has something to do with your anger at your husband's refusal to participate more fully in the household?" I ask.

Her eyes smoldering, her voice tight, she snaps, "No, I'm just tired, that's all." Then noticing something in my response, she adds, "I know what you're thinking; I saw that look. But really, I don't think it's because I'm angry; I really am tired. I have to admit, though, that I tell him if he helped more, maybe I wouldn't be so tired all the time. And," she adds defiantly, "maybe I wouldn't be."

Some couples, of course, manage their sexual relationship with greater ease. Often that's because they have less conflict in other areas of living. But whether they accommodate well or poorly, for all two-job families, sex requires a level of attention and concern that leaves most people wanting much of the time. "It's a problem, and I tell you, it has to be well planned," explains thirty-four-year-old Dan Stolman, a black construction worker. "But we manage okay; we make dates or try to slip it in when the baby's asleep and my daughter's out with a friend or something. I don't mean things are great in that department. I'm not always satisfied and neither is Lorraine. But what can you do? We try to do the best we can. Sex isn't all there is to a marriage, you know. We get along really well, so that makes up for a lot.

"What I really miss is that we don't ever make love anymore. I mean, we have sex like I said, but we don't have the kind of time you need to make love. We talk about getting away for an overnight by ourselves once in a while. Lorraine's mother would come watch the kids if we asked her; the problem is we don't have any extra cash to spare right now."

Time and money—precious commodities in short supply. These are the twin plagues of family life, the missing ingredients that combine to create families that are both frantic and fragile. Yet there's no mystery about what would alleviate the crisis that now threatens to engulf them: A job that pays a living wage, quality child-care facilities at rates people can pay, health care for all, parental leave, flexible work schedules, decent and affordable housing, a shorter work week so that parents and children have time to spend together, tax breaks for those in need rather than for those in greed, to mention just a few. These are the policies we need to put in place if we're to have any hope of making our families stable and healthy.

What we have, instead, are families in which mother goes to work to relieve financial distress, only to find that time takes its place next to money as a source of strain, tension, and conflict. Time for the children, time for the couple's relationship, time for self, time for social life—none of it easily available for anyone in two-job families, not even for the children, who are hurried along at every step of the way. And money! Never enough, not for the clothes children need, not for the doctor's bill, not for a vacation, not even for the kind of child care that would allow parents to go to work in peace. But large as these problems loom in the lives of working-class families, difficult as they are to manage, they pale beside those they face when unemployment strikes, especially if it's father who loses his job.

Review

1. How would you characterize the attitudes of working-class husbands toward housework?

2. What differences did Rubin find between white men and those from other racial/ethnic groups?

3. Describe the problems of child-care arrangements for working-class families.

4. What is the nature of the sex life of the working-class couples Rubin studied?

Application

Interview a working-class couple (interview the husband and wife separately) or two students from working-class homes. Conduct an in-depth interview about the following topics: division of labor in the home (who does what); perception of time and financial pressures and the reasons for them; perceptions of what an ideal marriage and an ideal family life would look like.

How do your results compare with Rubin's descriptions? How do they compare with your own experiences? What are your own ideals for marriage and family life?

Reprinted from: Lillian B. Rubin, "The Transformation of Family Life." In *Families on the Fault Line,* by Lillian B. Rubin, New York: HarperPerennial, 1994. Copyright © 1994 by Lillian B. Rubin. Reprinted by permission of HarperCollins Publishers, Inc. ✦

26

'We Always Stood on Our Own Two Feet'

Self-Reliance and the American Family

Stephanie Coontz

When Americans look at other societies, we often focus on their "quaint" myths and marvel at their inability to compare the myths to realities. Yet our society also has its myths, and we seem equally incapable of realistically evaluating them. Our primary values, for instance, stress the importance of individual effort in achievements. Individuals and families are expected to "make their own way" and not rely on the government or other non-kin groups for financial support. The most evident expression of these values is in our attitudes toward welfare. Many Americans are very critical of anyone who is able-bodied but dependent on government support, especially for long periods of time. And self-reliance appears frequently in the call of political leaders to "get the government off the backs of the people."

Reflecting these values, Americans have well-developed myths about the past. According to popular myth, for instance, our ancestors survived the rigors of life through their toughness and perseverance. However, in fact, American families historically have been dependent for survival on government and other social institutions. As Stephanie Coontz shows in this selection, government initiatives have not only been helpful to Americans, they have often provided the foundation for growth and prosperity.

"They never asked for handouts," my grandfather used to say whenever he and my grandmother regaled me with stories about pioneer life in Puget Sound after George Washington Bush and Michael T. Simmons defied the British and founded the first American settlement in the area. But the homesteaders didn't turn down handouts either during that hard winter of 1852, when speculators had cornered almost all the already low supply of wheat. Fortunately, Bush refused to sell his grain for the high prices the market offered, reserving most of what he did not use himself to feed his neighbors and stake them to the next spring's planting.

The United States' successful claim to Puget Sound was based on the Bush-Simmons settlement. Ironically, once Bush had helped his community become part of the Oregon territory, he became subject to Oregon's exclusionary law prohibiting African Americans from residing in the Territory. His neighbors spearheaded passage of a special legislative bill in 1854, exempting Bush and his family from the law. Bush's descendants became prominent members of what was to become Washington state, and the story of Bush's generosity in 1852 has passed into local lore.[1]

Neither my grandparents' paternalistic attitudes toward blacks nor their fierce hatred of charity led them to downplay how dependent the early settlers had been on Bush's aid, but the knowledge of that dependence did not modify their insistence that decent families were "beholden to no one."

When I was older, I asked my grandfather about the apparent contradiction. "Well," he said, "that was an exception; and they paid him back by getting that bill passed, didn't they? It's not like all these people nowadays, sitting around waiting for the government to take care of them. The government never gave us anything, and we never counted on help from anybody else, either." Unless, of course, they were family. "Blood's thicker than water, after all," my grandparents used to say.

My grandparents are not the only Americans to allow the myth of self-reliance to ob-

213

scure the reality of their own life histories. Politicians are especially likely to fall prey to the convenient amnesia that permits so much self-righteous posturing about how the "dependent poor" ought to develop the self-reliance and independence that "the rest of us" have shown. Sen. Phil Gramm, for example, co-author of the 1985 Gramm-Rudman-Hollings balanced budget amendment, is well known for his opposition to government handouts. However, his personal history is quite different from his political rhetoric.

Born in Georgia in 1942, to a father who was living on a federal veterans disability pension, Gramm attended a publicly funded university on a grant paid for by the federal War Orphans Act. His graduate work was financed by a National Defense Education Act fellowship, and his first job was at Texas A&M University, a federal land-grant institution. Yet when Gramm finally struck out on his own, the first thing he did was set up a consulting business where he could be, in his own words, "an advocate of fiscal responsibility and free enterprise." From there he moved on to Congress, where he has consistently attempted to slash federal assistance programs for low-income people.[2]

Self-reliance is one of the most cherished American values, although there is some ambiguity about what the smallest self-reliant unit is. For some it is the rugged individualist; for most it is the self-sufficient family of the past, in which female nurturing sustained male independence vis-à-vis the outside world. While some people believe that the gender roles within this traditional family were unfair, and others that they were beneficial, most Americans agree that prior to federal "interference" in the 1930s, the self-reliant family was the standard social unit of our society. Dependencies used to be cared for within the "natural family economy," and even today the healthiest families "stand on their own two feet."[3]

The fact is, however, that depending on support beyond the family has been the rule rather than the exception in American history, despite recurring myths about individual achievement and family enterprise. It is true that public aid has become less local and more impersonal over the past two centuries . . . but Americans have been dependent on collective institutions beyond the family, including government, from the very beginning.

A Tradition of Dependence on Others

The tendency of Americans to overestimate what they have accomplished on their own and deny how much they owe to others has been codified in the myth that the colonists came on an "errand into the wilderness" and built a land of plenty out of nothing. In reality, however, the abundant concentrations of game, plants, and berries that so astonished Eastern colonists were not "natural"; they had been produced by the cooperative husbandry and collective land-use patterns of Native Americans. In the Northwest, the valuable Douglas fir forests and plentiful herds of deer and elk found by early settlers existed only because Native American burning practices had created sustained-yield succession forests that maximized use of these resources without exhausting them.[4]

Even after they confiscated the collective work of others, though, European settlers did not suddenly form a society of independent, self-reliant families. Recent research in social history demonstrates that early American families were dependent on a large network of neighbors, church institutions, courts, government officials, and legislative bodies for their sustenance. It is true that in colonial days, the poor or disabled were generally cared for in families, but not, normally, in their own families. Families who did not have enough money to pay their passage to America or establish their own farms were split up, with their members assigned to be educated, fed, and trained for work in various propertied households. Elderly, ill, or orphaned dependents were taken care of in other people's families, and city officials gave allowances in money or kind to facilitate such care. The home-care system, however, soon buckled under the weight of population growth and increasing economic stratification. By the mid-eighteenth century, governments had begun to experiment with poorhouses and outdoor relief.[5]

It was not a colonial value to avoid being beholden to others, even among the nonpoor. Borrowing and lending among neighbors were woven into the very fabric of life. The presence of outstanding accounts assured the continuing circulation of goods, services, and social interactions through the community: Being under obligation to others and having favors owed was the mark of a successful person. Throughout the colonies, life was more corporate than individualistic or familial. People operated within a tight web of obligation, debt, dependence, "treating," and the calling in of favors.[6]

As America made the transition to a wage-earning society in the 1800s, patterns of personal dependence and local community assistance gave way to more formal procedures for organizing work and taking care of those who were unable to work, either temporarily or permanently. But the rise of a generalized market economy did not lessen dependency, nor did it make the family more able to take care of its own, in any sector of society.

Within the upper classes, family partnerships, arranged marriages, dowries, and family loans no longer met the need for capital, recruitment of trusted workers, and exploration of new markets. The business class developed numerous extrafamilial institutions: mercantile associations; credit-pooling consortia; new legal bodies for raising capital, such as corporations or limited liability partnerships; and chambers of commerce. Middle-class fraternal organizations, evangelical groups, and maternal associations also reached beyond kinship ties and local community boundaries to create a vast network of mutual aid organizations. The first half of the nineteenth century is usually called not the age of the family but the age of association.[7]

For the working class throughout the nineteenth century, dependence was "a structural," almost inevitable, part of life. Among workers as well, accordingly, blood was not always thicker than neighborhood, class, ethnicity, or religion. Black, immigrant, and native-born white workers could not survive without sharing and assistance beyond family networks.[8]

Working-class and ethnic subcommunities evolved around mutual aid in finding jobs, surviving tough times, and pooling money for recreation. Immigrants founded lodges to provide material aid and foster cooperation. Laborers formed funeral aid societies and death or sick benefit associations; they held balls and picnics to raise money for injured workers, widows, or orphans, and took collections at the mills or plant gates nearly every payday. Recipients showed the same lack of embarrassment about accepting such help as did colonial families. Reformer Margaret Byington, observing working-class life at the end of the nineteenth century, noted that a gift of money to a fellow worker who was ill or simply down on his luck was "accepted . . . very simply, almost as a matter of course." Among the iron and steelworkers of Pittsburgh, "Innumerable acts of benevolence passed between the residents of the rows and tenements . . . rarely remarked upon except for their absence." Some workers' cultures revolved around religious institutions, some around cooperative societies or militant unionism—but all extended beyond the family. Indeed, historian Michael Katz has found that in parts of early-twentieth-century Philadelphia, "Neighbors seemed more reliable and willing to help one another than did kin."[9]

Among Catholic populations, godparenting was one way of institutionalizing such obligations beyond the family. In traditional Mexican and Mexican-American communities, for example, rites of baptism cut across divisions between rich and poor, Native American, mestizo, and Spanish. Godparents became *comadres* or *compadres* with the biological parents, providing discipline and love as needed. They were morally obliged to give financial assistance in times of need or to take on full parental responsibilities if the biological parents should die. Irish and Italian districts had similar customs. Some Native American groups had special "blood brother" rituals; the notion of "going for sisters" has long and still thriving roots in black communities.[10]

Yet even ties of expanded kinship, class, neighborhood, and ethnicity were never enough to get many families by. Poor Americans, for example, have always needed support from the public purse, even if that support has often been inadequate. Indeed, notes one welfare historian, the history of dependence and assistance in America is marked by "the early and pervasive role of the state. There has never been a golden age of volunteerism."[11]

By the end of the nineteenth century, neither poorhouses, outdoor relief, nor private charity could cope with the dislocations of industrial business cycles. As late as 1929, after nearly a decade of prosperity, the Brookings Institute found that the "natural family economy" was not working for most Americans: Three-fifths of American families earned $2,000 or less a year and were unable to save anything to help them weather spells of unemployment or illness. The Great Depression, of course, left many more families unable to make it on their own.[12]

Even aside from times of depression, the inability of families to survive without public assistance has never been confined to the poor. Middle-class and affluent Americans have been every bit as dependent on public support. In fact, comparatively affluent families have received considerably more public subsidy than those in modest circumstances, while the costs of such subsidies have often been borne by those who derived the least benefit from them.

To illustrate the pervasiveness of dependence in American family history, I will examine in greater detail the two main family types that are usually held up as models of traditional American independence: the frontier family, archetype of American self-reliance, and the 1950s suburban family, whose strong moral values and work ethic are thought to have enabled so many to lift themselves up by their bootstraps. In fact, these two family types probably tie for the honor of being the most heavily subsidized in American history, as well as for the privilege of having had more of their advantages paid for by minorities and the lower classes.

Self-Reliance and the American West

Our image of the self-reliant pioneer family has been bequeathed to us by the *Little House on the Prairie* books and television series, which almost every American has read or seen. What is less well known is that these stories, based on the memoirs of Laura Ingalls Wilder, were extensively revised by her daughter as an ideological attack on government programs. When Wilder's daughter, Rose Wilder Lane, failed to establish a secure income as a freelance writer in the 1930s, she returned to her family home in the Ozarks. Here, historian Linda Kerber reports, "Lane announced that she would no longer write so that she would not have to pay taxes to a New Deal government." However, "she *rewrote* the rough drafts of her mother's memoirs . . . turning them into the *Little House* books in which the isolated family is pitted against the elements and makes it—or doesn't—with no help from the community."[13]

In reality, prairie farmers and other pioneer families owed their existence to massive federal land grants, government-funded military mobilizations that dispossessed hundreds of Native American societies and confiscated half of Mexico, and state-sponsored economic investment in the new lands. Even "volunteers" expected federal pay: Much of the West's historic "antigovernment" sentiment originated in discontent when settlers did not get such pay or were refused government aid for unauthorized raids on Native American territory. It would be hard to find a Western family today or at any time in the past whose land rights, transportation options, economic existence, and even access to water were not dependent on federal funds. "Territorial experience got Westerners in the habit of federal subsidies," remarks Western historian Patricia Nelson Limerick, "and the habit persisted long after other elements of the Old West had vanished."[14]

It has been an expensive habit, in more ways than one. The federal government spent $15 million on the Louisiana Purchase in 1803 and then engaged in three years of costly fighting against the British in order to gain more of Florida. In the 1830s, state governments funded outright or financially guaranteed three-fourths of the $200 million it cost to build canals linking the Atlantic seaboard trading centers with new settlements around the Great Lakes and the Ohio and Mississippi rivers. The government got a bargain in the 1830s when it forced the Cherokees to "sell" their land for $9 million and then deducted $6 million from that for the cost of removing them along "The Trail of Tears," where almost a quarter of the 15,000 Native Americans died. Acquiring northern Mexico was even more expensive: The war of annexation cost $97 million; then, as victor, the United States was able to "buy" Texas, California, southern Arizona, and New Mexico from Mexico for only an additional $25 million.

The land acquired by government military action or purchase, both funded from the public purse, was then sold—at a considerable loss—to private individuals. The Preemption Act of 1841 allowed settlers to buy land at $125 an acre, far below the actual acquisition cost; in 1854, the Graduation Act permitted lands that had been on the market for some time to be sold for even less. The Homestead Act of 1862 provided that a settler could buy 160 acres for $10 if the homesteader lived on the land for five years and made certain improvements. The federal government also gave each state 30,000 acres to help finance colleges that could improve agricultural education and techniques. These land-grant colleges made vital contributions to Western economic expansion.

Even after this generous, government-funded head start, pioneer families did not normally become self-sufficient. The stereotypical solitary Western family, isolated from its neighbors and constantly on the move, did exist, but it was also generally a failure. Economic success in nineteenth-century America, on the frontier as well as in the urban centers, was more frequently linked to persistence and involvement in a community than to family self-reliance or the restless "pioneering spirit."[15]

As historian John Mack Farragher describes frontier life in Sugar Creek, Illinois, between 1820 and 1850, for example, "self-sufficiency" was not a family quality but "a community experience. . . . Sharing work with neighbors at cabin raisings, log rollings, hayings, husking, butchering, harvesting or threshing were all traditionally communal affairs." The prairie was considered common land for grazing, and a " 'borrowing system' allowed scarce tools, labor and products to circulate to the benefit of all." As one contemporary explained to prospective settlers: "Your wheel-barrows, your shovels, your utensils of all sorts, belong not to yourself, but to the public who do not think it necessary even to *ask* a loan, but take it for granted." This community, it must be stressed, was not necessarily egalitarian: One traveler characterized Illinois as "heaven for men and horses, but a very different place for women and oxen." But "mutuality" and "suppression of self-centered behavior," not rugged individualism or even the carving out of a familial "oasis," were what created successful settlements as America moved West, while the bottom line of westward expansion was federal funding of exploration, development, transportation, and communication systems.[16]

In the early twentieth century, a new form of public assistance became crucial to Westerners' existence: construction of dams and other federally subsidized irrigation projects. During the Depression, government electrification projects brought pumps, refrigeration, and household technology to millions of families who had formerly had to hand pump and carry their water and who had lacked the capacity to preserve or export their farm produce. Small farmers depended on the government to slow down foreclosures and protect them from the boom and bust of overproduction, soil exhaustion, and cutthroat competition.[17]

Without public subsidies, the maintenance of independent family farms would have been impossible. Yet even with all this help from government and neighbors, small family enterprises did not turn out to be the major developers of the West. Their dependence on government subsidization, it turned out, produced a political constituency and ideological cover for policies that channeled much greater benefits to wealthy individuals and corporations. Of the billion acres of western land distributed by the end of the century, for example, only 147 million acres became homesteads, and even many of these ended up in speculators' hands. Sociologists Scott and Sally McNall estimate that "probably only one acre in nine went to the small pioneers." One hundred and eighty-three million acres of the public domain were given to railroad companies, generally in alternating square-mile sections to a depth of ten miles on either side of the line. These federal giveaways, not family enterprise, were what built most major western logging companies. Environmental historian John Opie and rural geographer Imhoff Vogeler argue that for 200 years, federal policy has promoted the myth of the independent family farm at the same time it has encouraged waste or misuse of land and water and subsidized huge, though not necessarily efficient, agribusinesses. Yet trying to solve such inequity by simply cutting federal subsidies, as in the 1990 Farm Bill, flies in the face of 200 years of experience: The existence of family farms and diversified agriculture has always depended on public subsidy.[18]

Self-Reliance and the Suburban Family

Another oft-cited example of familial self-reliance is the improvement in living standards experienced by many Americans during the 1950s. The surge in homeownership at that time, most people believe, occurred because families scraped together down payments, paid their mortgages promptly, raised their children to respect private property, and always "stood on their own two feet." An entire generation of working people thereby attained middle-class status, graduating from urban tenements to suburban homeownership, just as Lucille Ball and Desi Arnaz did in their television series.

The 1950s suburban family, however, was far more dependent on government handouts than any so-called "underclass" in recent U.S. history. Historian William Chafe estimates that "most" of the upward mobility

at this time was subsidized in one form or another by government spending. Federal GI benefits, available to 40 percent of the male population between the ages of twenty and twenty-four, permitted a whole generation of men to expand their education and improve their job prospects without foregoing marriage and children. The National Defense Education Act retooled science education, subsidizing both American industry and the education of individual scientists. In addition, the surge in productivity during the 1950s was largely federally financed. More than $50 billion of government-funded wartime inventions and production processes were turned over to private companies after the war, creating whole new fields of employment.[19]

Even more directly, suburban home-ownership depended on an unprecedented enlargement of federal regulation and financing. The first steps were taken in the Great Depression, when the Home Owners Loan Corporation (HOLC) set up low-interest loans to allow people to refinance homes lost through foreclosure. The government began to underwrite the real estate industry by insuring private homeownership lenders, loaning directly to long-term buyers, and subsidizing the extension of electricity to new residential areas. But the real transformation of attitudes and intervention came in the 1950s, with the expansion of the Federal Housing Authority and Veterans' Administration loans.

Before the Second World War, banks often required a 50 percent down payment on homes and normally issued mortgages for only five to ten years. In the postwar period, however, the Federal Housing Authority (FHA), supplemented by the GI Bill, put the federal government in the business of insuring and regulating private loans for single-home construction. FHA policy required down payments of only 5 to 10 percent of the purchase price and guaranteed mortgages of up to thirty years at interest rates of just 2 to 3 percent on the balance. The Veterans Administration asked a mere dollar down from veterans. At the same time, government tax policies were changed to provide substantial incentives for savings and loan institutions to channel their funds almost exclusively into low-interest, long-term mortgages. Consequently, millions of Americans purchased homes with artificially low down payments and interest rates, courtesy of Uncle Sam.[20]

It was not family savings or individual enterprise, but federal housing loans and education payments (along with an unprecedented expansion of debt), that enabled so many 1950s American families to achieve the independence of homeownership. Almost half the housing in suburbia depended on such federal financing. As philosopher Alan Wolfe points out: "Even the money that people borrowed to pay for their houses was not lent to them on market principles; fixed-rate mortgages, for example, absolved an entire generation from inflation for thirty years."[21]

Yet this still understates the extent to which suburbia was a creation of government policy and federal spending. True, it was private real estate agents and construction companies who developed the suburban projects and private families who bought the homes. But it was government-funded research that developed the aluminum clapboards, prefabricated walls and ceilings, and plywood paneling that composed the technological basis of the postwar housing revolution. And few buyers would have been forthcoming for suburban homes without new highways to get them out to the sites, new sewer systems, utilities services, and traffic control programs—all of which were not paid for by the families who used them, but by the general public.

In 1947, the government began a project to build 37,000 miles of new highway. In 1956, the Interstate Highway Act provided for an additional 42,500 miles. Ninety percent of this construction was financed by the government. The prime beneficiaries of this postwar road-building venture, which one textbook calls "the greatest civil engineering project of world history," were suburbanites. Despite arguments that road building served "national interests," urban interstates were primarily "turned into commuter roads serving suburbia."[22]

Such federal patronage might be unobjectionable, even laudable—though hardly a demonstration of self-reliance—if it had been available to all Americans equally. But the other aspect of federal subsidization of suburbia is that it worsened the plight of public transportation, the inner cities, poor families in general, and minority ones in particular.

Federal loan policies systematized and nationalized the pervasive but informal racism that had previously characterized the housing market. FHA redlining practices, for example, took entire urban areas and declared them ineligible for loans. Government policy also shifted resources from urban areas into suburban construction and expansion. At the same time, postwar "urban renewal" and highway construction reduced the housing stock for urban workers. Meanwhile, the federal government's two new mortgage institutions, the Federal National Mortgage Association (Fannie Mae) and the Government National Mortgage Association (Ginnie Mae), made it possible for urban banks to transfer savings out of the cities and into new construction in the South and West—frequently, again, into suburban developments. By the 1970s, for example, savings banks in the Bronx invested just 10 percent of their funds in the borough and only 30 percent elsewhere in the entire state.[23]

In the 1950s and 1960s, while the general public financed roads for suburban commuters, the streetcars and trolleys that served urban and poor families received almost no tax revenues and thus steadily deteriorated, with results we are paying for today. In the nineteenth century, American public transport had been one of the better systems in the world, and one of the most used. In 1890, streetcar ridership in the United States was four times as great as that in Europe on a per capita basis. As late as 1953, a million and a half people traveled by rail each day. But expansion of the highway system undercut this form of public transport as well. Between 1946 and 1980, government aid to highways totaled $103 billion, while railroads received only $6 billion.[24]

We should not overestimate the accessibility of earlier public transport to lower-income families—in the third quarter of the nineteenth century, most people walked to work—nor should we forget the pollution and overcrowding of streets filled with horse-drawn vehicles. Yet the fact remains that government transportation policy systematically fostered improvements in private rather than public conveyances, favoring suburban development over the revitalization of urban life. By the end of the 1950s, Los Angeles epitomized the kind of city such policies produced. Once served by an efficient and widely used mass-transit system, the city was carved up by multilane freeways, overpasses, and viaducts. By the end of the decade, two-thirds of central Los Angeles had been paved over to make room for cars.[25]

. . . Attempts to sustain the myth of family self-reliance in the face of all the historical evidence to the contrary have led policymakers into theoretical convolutions and practical miscalculations that are reminiscent of efforts by medieval philosophers to maintain that the earth, not the sun, was the center of the planetary system. In the sixteenth century, leading European thinkers insisted that the sun and all the planets revolved around the earth, much as Americans insist that our society revolves around family self-reliance. When evidence to the contrary mounted, defenders of the Ptolemaic universe postulated all sorts of elaborate planetary orbits, changes of direction, and even periodic loop-de-loops in order to reconcile observed reality with their cherished theory. Similarly, rather than admit that all families need public support, we have constructed ideological loop-de-loops that explain away each instance of dependence as an "exception," an "abnormality," or even an illusion. . . .

Endnotes

1. For more on Bush's history and that of other black pioneers, see William Loren Katz, *The Black West* (Seattle: Open Hand Publishers, 1987).

2. David Broder, "Phil Gramm's Free Enterprise," *Washington Post*, 16 February 1983; Marian Wright Edelman, *Families in Peril: An Agenda for Social Change* (Cambridge: Harvard University Press, 1987), pp. 27–28.

3. Allan Carlson, "How Uncle Sam Got in the Family's Way," *Wall Street Journal*, 20 April 1988, and "Is Social Security Pro-Family?" *Policy Studies* (Fall 1987): 49.

4. James Axtell, *The European and the Indian: Essays in the Ethnohistory of Colonial North America* (New York: Oxford University Press, 1982), pp. 292–293; William Cronon, *Changes in the Land: Indians, Colonists, and the Ecology of New England* (New York: Hill and Wang, 1983), pp. 37–53; Richard White, *Land Use, Environment, and Social Change: The Shaping of Island County, Washington* (Seattle: University of Washington Press, 1980), pp. 20–26.

5. Lorena Walsh, "Till Death Do Us Part," in *Growing Up in America: Historical Experience*, ed. Harvey Graff (Detroit: Wayne State University Press, 1987); Edmund Morgan, *The Puritan Family: Religion and Domestic Relations in Seventeenth-Century New England* (New York: Harper & Row, 1966); John Demos, *A Little Commonwealth: Family Life in Plymouth Colony* (New York: Oxford University Press, 1970); Lawrence Cremin, *American Education: The Colonial Experience, 1607–1783* (New York: Harper & Row, 1970), pp. 124–37.

6. Laurel Thatcher Ulrich, "Housewife and Gadder: Themes of Self-Sufficiency and Community in Eighteenth-Century New England," in *"To Toil the Livelong Day": America's Women at Work, 1780–1980*, Carol Groneman and Mary Beth Norton (Ithaca, N.Y.: Cornell University Press, 1987); James Henretta, "Families and Farms: Mentalite in Pre-Industrial America," *William and Mary Quarterly* 35 (1978); Rhys Isaac, *The Transformation of Virginia 1740–1790*, (Chapel Hill: University of North Carolina Press, 1982), pp. 11–138.

7. James Henretta, *The Evolution of American Society, 1700–1815* (Lexington, Mass.: Heath, 1973), p. 212; Stuart Blumin, *The Urban Threshold: Growth and Change in a Nineteenth-Century American Community* (Chicago: University of Chicago Press, 1976), p. 46; Paul Johnson, *A Shopkeeper's Millennium: Society and Revivals in Rochester, New York, 1815–1837* (New York: Hill and Wang, 1978).

8. Michael Katz, *Poverty and Policy in American History* (New York: Academic Press, 1983), p. 183.

9. S. J. Kleinberg, *The Shadow of the Mills: Working-Class Families in Pittsburgh, 1870–1907* (Pittsburgh: University of Pittsburgh Press, 1989), pp. 270–75; Herbert Gutman,

Work, Culture, and Society in Industrializing America (New York: Knopf, 1976); John Bodnar, *Natives and Newcomers: Ethnicity in an American Mill Town* (Pittsburgh: University of Pittsburgh Press, 1977); Margaret Byington, *Homestead: The Households of a Mill Town* (Pittsburgh: University of Pittsburgh Press, 1974), p. 16; James Borchert, *Alley Life in Washington: Family, Community, Religion, and Folklife in the City, 1850–1970* (Urbana: University of Illinois Press, 1980); Jacquelyn Dowd Hall et al., *Like a Family: The Making of a Southern Cotton Mill World* (Chapel Hill: University of North Carolina Press, 1987); David Montgomery, *The Fall of the House of Labor* (New York: Cambridge University Press, 1989); David Goldberg, *A Tale of Three Cities: Labor Organization and Protest in Paterson, Passaic, and Lawrence, 1916–1921* (New Brunswick: Rutgers University Press, 1989); Katz, *Poverty and Policy*, p. 49.

10. Richard Griswold Del Castillo, *La Familia: Chicano Families in the Urban Southwest, 1848 to the Present* (Notre Dame: University of Notre Dame Press, 1984), pp. 42–43, 118; Carol Stack, *All Our Kin: Strategies for Survival in a Black Community* (New York: Harper & Row, 1974).

11. Michael B. Katz, *In the Shadow of the Poorhouse: A Social History of Welfare in America* (New York: Basic Books, 1986), pp. 190, 240.

12. Abraham Epstein, *Insecurity: A Challenge to Americans: A Study of Social Insurance in the United States and Abroad* (New York: H. Smith and R. Hass, 1933); Katz, *Poverty and Policy*, pp. 121, 126, 244.

13. Linda Kerber, "Women and Individualism in American History," *The Massachusetts Review* (Winter 1989): 604–5.

14. Patricia Nelson Limerick, *Legacy of Conquest: The Unbroken Past of the American West* (New York: Norton, 1987), p. 82.

15. Stephen Thernstrom, *Poverty and Progress: Social Mobility in a Nineteenth-Century City* (Cambridge: Harvard University Press, 1964); Peter Knights, *The Plain People of Boston: A Study in City Growth* (New York: Oxford University Press, 1971); Lilian Schlissel, Byrd Gibbens, and Elizabeth Hampsten, *Far From Home: Families of the Westward Journey* (New York: Schocken, 1989); John Farragher and Christine Stansell, *Women and Men on the Overland Trail* (New Haven: Yale University Press, 1979).

16. John Mack Farragher, "Open-Country Community: Sugar Creek, Illinois, 1820–1850," in *The Countryside in the Age of Capitalistic Transformation*, ed. Steven Hahmond and Jonathon Prude (Chapel Hill: University of North Carolina Press, 1985), p. 245; John Mack Farragher, *Sugar Creek: Life on the Illinois Prairie* (New Haven: Yale University Press, 1986), pp. 132–33, 114; Michael Cassity, *Defending a Way of Life: An American Community in the Nineteenth Century* (Albany: State University of New York Press, 1989).

17. Steven Mintz and Susan Kellogg, *Domestic Revolutions: A Social History of American Family Life* (New York: Free Press, 1988), pp. 146–47.

18. Limerick, *Legacy of Conquest*, pp. 45–47, 82, 136; Scott and Sally Ann McNall, *Plains Families: Exploring Sociology Through Social History* (New York: St. Martin's, 1983), p. 9; Willard Cochrane, *The Development of American Agriculture: A Historical Analysis* (Minneapolis: University of Minnesota Press, 1979); "Lincoln Policy Shaped Local Forest Landscape," *Seattle Post-Intelligencer*, 20 April 1990; John Opie, *The Law of the Land: Two Hundred Years of American Farmland Policy* (Lincoln: University of Nebraska Press, 1987); Imhoff Vogeler, *The Myth of the Family Farm: Agribusiness Dominance of U.S. Agriculture* (Boulder: Westview Press, 1981).

19. William Chafe, *The Unfinished Journey: America Since World War II* (New York: Oxford University Press, 1986), pp. 113, 143; Susan Hartmann, *The Home Front and Beyond: American Women in the 1940s* (Boston: Twayne Publishers, 1982), p. 165; Michael Parenti, *Democracy for the Few* (New York: St. Martin's, 1988), pp. 82–83.

20. Dwight Lee, "Government Policy and the Distortions in Family Housing," in *The American Family and the State*, ed. Joseph Peden and Fred Glahe (San Francisco: Pacific Research Institute for Public Policy, 1986), p. 312.

21. Kenneth Jackson, *Crabgrass Frontier: The Suburbanization of the United States* (New York: Oxford University Press, 1985), pp. 196–204, 215; Chafe, *Unfinished Journey*, p. 113; Henretta et al., *America's History*, vol. 2, pp. 849–50; Alan Wolfe, *Whose Keeper?: Social Science and Moral Obligation* (Berkeley: University of California Press, 1989), p. 62.

22. James A. Henretta et al., *America's History*, vol. 2 (Chicago: Dorsey Press, 1987), p. 848; Jackson, *Crabgrass Frontier*, pp. 248–50; Neal Pierce, "New Highways Next Big Issue to Divide Nation," *The Olympian*, 28 May 1990, p. 8A.

23. Eric Monkkonen, *America Becomes Urban: The Development of U.S. Cities and Towns, 1780–1980* (Berkeley: University of California Press, 1988), p. 203; George Lipsitz, "Land of a Thousand Dances: Youth, Minorities, and the Rise of Rock and Roll," in *Recasting America: Culture and Politics in the Age of Cold War*, ed. Lary May (Chicago: University of Chicago Press, 1989), p. 269; Jackson, *Crabgrass Frontier*, pp. 190–230; Patricia Burgess Stach, "Building the Suburbs: The Social Structuring of Residential Neighborhoods in Post-War America" (Paper presented at "Ike's America, a conference on the Eisenhower Presidency and American Life in the 1950s," University of Kansas, Lawrence, 4–6 October 1990), pp. 17–18; Michael Danielson, *The Politics of Exclusion* (New York: Columbia University Press, 1976), p. 12; John Bauman, *Public Housing, Race, and Renewal: Urban Planning in Philadelphia 1920–1974*, (Philadelphia: Temple University Press, 1987); Elaine Tyler May, *Homeward Bound: American Families in the Cold War Era* (New York: Basic Books, 1988), pp. 169–70; Charles Hoch and Robert Slayton, *New Homeless and Old: Community and the Skid Row Hotel* (Philadelphia: Temple University Press, 1989); Robert Fairbanks, *Making Better Citizens: Housing Reform and the Community Development Strategy in Cincinnati 1890–1960*, (Urbana: University of Illinois Press, 1988), p. 148 and passim.

24. Jackson, *Crabgrass Frontier*, pp. 169–170; Parenti, *Democracy for the Few*, p. 111.

25. Douglas Miller and Marion Nowak, *The Fifties: The Way We Really Were* (Garden City, N.Y.: Doubleday, 1977), pp. 142–43. Eric Monkkonen's *America Becomes Urban* warns against romanticizing early transportation or blaming too many evils on the car, but the point remains that the dominance of the car, with its attendant problems of pollution and oil dependency, was not a result of free consumer choice alone; it stemmed from government decisions to allow private cars public funding for the "social overhead capital" investments they required, while treating public transport as private investment that must pay for itself.

Review

1. How did the United States government fund the expansion of the American West?

2. What benefits did the federal government provide to American families after World War II that led to the development of suburbs?

3. Considering all the expenditures of government, are the poor or the affluent most likely to be the major beneficiaries? Support your argument by reference to specific government programs and initiatives.

Applications

1. Identify several family members from the post–World War II generation (e.g., parents or grandparents) who would have been family decision-makers during the 1950s. Determine whether they benefited from government programs at the time. Recall the elements of government assistance that benefited some Americans, but not others. If your family did not benefit from the programs, or actually suffered as a result, discuss what factors were responsible for this. If they did benefit, what allowed them to do so?

2. Government programs take many shapes and forms. However, few taxpayers know where their dollars go. Do some library or field research to determine where the government spends its money. How does your community benefit from government expenditures, such as tax deductions for home mortgages, block grants, government facilities, government-supported retirement benefits and welfare programs? Summarize your findings by composing a graph or pie chart that shows the proportion of government support for each of the major categories.

Part Two

Government and Politics

Government is the social institution responsible for protecting the citizenry from foreign enemies and for maintaining law and order within the society. **Politics** are the means people use to attempt to influence or control the government. Through government, **power** (control over the behavior of others) is exercised by those in authority. Through politics, various individuals and groups seek to use the power of government for their own interests.

The selections in this part deal with political activity by two groups historically suffering various kinds of prejudice and discrimination in American life: women and Latinos. Selection 27 examines the role of nonviolence in women's movements. Selection 28 on Latinos analyzes the growing political role of what may soon be the nation's largest racial/ethnic minority. ✦

27

Women's Movements and Nonviolence

Anne N. Costain

In the United States, the government is expected not only to protect the citizenry from foreign threats but to insure equal protection under the law for all groups. That is, no one should be deprived of any rights because of such things as race, religion, gender, age, and sexual orientation.

*The reality, of course, diverges from the theory. American history can be viewed in terms of the ongoing struggle of groups within our society to attain the freedom and opportunities of the majority. People have used various ways to try to secure their rights and redress their grievances. When such common efforts as voting or persuading legislators are unavailable or do not work, people may form or become a part of a **social movement**, an organized effort to promote or resist some kind of change. For example, the enfranchisement of African Americans and women, the right of workers to organize, the right of racial minorities to have equal access to public accommodations, and the right of women to have equal access to any kind of job were all secured because of the pressures brought about by social movements.*

Social movements, then, have always been an important part of the political process in the United States. Their methods have ranged from the mild (e.g., distributing literature and making pleas to officials) to the moderate (e.g., engaging in strikes, threats, and boycotts) to the severe (e.g., resorting to armed attacks and advocating overthrow of the government). In this selection, Anne Costain explores the role of nonviolence in women's rights movements. She argues that the insis-tence on nonviolent methods to achieve their aims helps explain both the appeal and the success of the movements.

The ties between women's rights movements and nonviolence have been deep and enduring. In the United States, they stretch from tactics employed by suffragists and proponents of the Equal Rights Amendment (ERA) through core beliefs espoused by participants in these movements.

The American movement for women's suffrage emerged out of a historic meeting in upstate New York. Five Quaker women, including Lucretia Mott and fellow abolitionist and women's rights advocate, Elizabeth Cady Stanton, gathered in Waterloo, where they agreed to call together a convention in Seneca Falls, New York, to discuss "the social, civil and religious rights of women" (quoted in Flexner 1973, 74). Held in 1848, this convention ended with the issuance of a "Declaration of Sentiments" and a resolution supporting suffrage for women. These actions set the women's movement's agenda for the next seven decades.

The authors of the declaration cataloged the exclusion of women from higher education, professions, and the ministry and asked that women be accorded all the "rights and immunities of citizens" granted by the U.S. Constitution. Since much of the leadership of the new movement was provided by Quaker women, including Susan B. Anthony, who became the best known of all suffrage champions, and Quaker faith and practice hold as central tenets both the rejection of violent conflict and the use of nonviolent means to oppose inequality, it is not surprising that the suffrage movement was advanced using tactics of active resistance. Accordingly, suffragists picketed and chained themselves to the fence of the White House, held hunger strikes, and organized massive marches of supporters and sympathizers (DuBois 1998, 580). American suffragists, particularly those led by Alice Paul, cofounder of the National Woman's Party and also a Quaker, patterned their political crusade on that of the British suffragists and, like them, served time in jail rather than paying fines to the state for their civil disobedience (Cott 1987, 53–62). Modern American women's rights activists have also employed many confrontational but nonviolent tactics, ranging from releasing mice at a bridal fair, holding mass marches in large cities (sometimes dressed in white, acknowledging the legacy of suffrage parades), disrupting congressional hearings, and initiating economic boycotts of states that failed to ratify ERA (Costain 1992, 44–78; Ryan 1992).

This reliance on nonviolent civil disobedience is undergirded by what scholars describe as the single largest difference in women's and men's public opinion: their general attitudes on use of force (Conover and Sapiro 1993; Flammang 1997, 124–31; Shapiro and Mahajan 1986). Women, as a group, consistently and from the start of modern polling, have been far more likely to express negative emotions about violence than men—both when that violence is abstract and when it is a present reality.

More Than a Civil Rights Movement

American women's movements have been represented by most scholars as off-shoots of civil rights struggles (see, e.g., Freeman 1975; Mansbridge 1986; McGlen and O'Connor 1998). In this [chapter] I argue for adjusting that frame to portray women's rights activists as also fundamentally concerned with the advocacy of nonviolence. Although this may, at first, seem to be no more than an academic exercise, since most successful twentieth-century civil rights activists used nonviolence as a primary tactic, I assert that women incorporated calls for peace into their demands for equal rights because the desire to reduce the role of force in society lay at the core of most women's hope for social transformation. I will use evidence from the contemporary women's movement to make this case.

First, however, I will review and acknowledge the civil rights antecedents of the U.S. movements for suffrage and women's rights. Women have long labored to achieve the rights resulting from democratic citizenship—not just the vote, but the opportunity

to petition the government for redress of grievances, to seek employment, to run for public office, and to retain citizenship even when marrying foreign nationals. Ellen DuBois (1978) chided those who saw pursuit of the vote by U.S. women as a narrow and largely symbolic goal. She reminded critics of the full implications of voting. Women granted the vote were given power outside the home and domestic sphere and, once in the public realm, they could raise their voices and express their interests in effective ways.

Likewise, women activists of the 1960s followed the lead of black civil rights advocates. They pointed to promises contained in the great documents of American democracy and demanded that these be fulfilled. Feminists, drawing from the "Declaration of Sentiments" passed at Seneca Falls declared that:

> We hold these truths to be self-evident: that all men and women are created equal; that they are endowed by their Creator with certain inalienable rights: that among these are life, liberty and the pursuit of happiness. . . . (Quoted in Flexner 1973, 75)

They asked for equality with men to serve on juries, to be paid equally for their labor, and to have access to training and financial credit. Participants in this "second" women's movement also revived the great unfinished agenda of the suffrage movement, urging addition of an equal rights amendment to the U.S. Constitution that would guarantee that sex would not be used as a basis for depriving citizens of rights.

As I have written elsewhere, civil rights/equality did not stand unchallenged as the major agenda of the modern women's movement (Costain 1988, 157–67; 1992, 79–99). In many respects, civil rights issues elicited more negative responses from the public and government institutions than did women's competing "special needs" agenda, which emphasized that women constituted a legitimate interest group in politics, much as teachers, members of ethnic groups, or union members did. Acknowledged as a group with articulated and achievable interests, women could more openly press for policies of special benefit to them, such as government support for child care, women's health, domestic violence legislation, and parental leaves. Following defeat of the ERA in 1982, the agenda of the women's movement became far more diverse, retaining civil rights issues while reemphasizing special needs concerns. Yet, just as the eagerness to claim full citizenship is a constant for participants in the movement, I believe that commitment to nonviolence as a value has also been constant. If this is the case, it will complete a historical cycle. One of the arguments put forth by suffragists, which appears to have helped to carry the day for women's vote, was that women held uniquely moral opinions toward politics and, consequently, allowing women to participate in elections would move government away from a politics that was so dependent on self-interest and power (Flexner 1973). Although many advocates oversold this case—as when they argued that if women vote wars will end or political corruption will cease—the argument may have some validity. If, when women mobilize politically, they carry a message of democratic inclusion and of opposition to the use of force to accomplish social or political ends, that is significant for society as a whole.

Data

I first began to awaken to the possibility that nonviolence may be a core idea of American women's movements in a rather tortuous and backhanded way. Several coders, including myself, used the *New York Times Annual Index* to build an events data set on the women's movement extending from 1950 to 1986 (see Costain 1992, app. A). Compiling such data is a method commonly used by social movement scholars to assess the levels of activism on behalf of particular causes across time. Using the headings "Women: General" and "Women: United States," the coders and I found and coded 1777 separate "Women's" events. Patterning our codes on those used by Doug McAdam (1982) for his well-known study of the Civil Rights Movement, one of our events coding

categories was whether the event was violent or nonviolent in character. After coding roughly five years worth of events, my graduate students mounted a rebellion and asked to stop coding for violence. They felt it was a wasted category since so few events could be characterized as violent. I capitulated, but could not help wondering why violence, including destruction of property, was such an infrequent component of women's rights activities.

In an effort to answer this question, I built a second data set on the women's movement using Nexis-Lexis. I was particularly interested in further investigating the relation of the movement to violence. I compiled this next batch of data by filtering every article published between 1980 and 1996 in the *New York Times* and selecting only those that referred specifically to one or more of nine nationally visible "second-wave" feminist groups. This yielded a total of 1772 articles.[1] I chose groups to represent a broad and diverse cross-section of participants in the contemporary women's movement.[2] Unlike with the earlier data set, when coders read only synopses of articles, my students and I downloaded complete texts of the articles and placed them into individual files. During the studied period, the number of articles in the Times mentioning the selected women's groups ranged from a low of 55 in 1996 to a high of 168 in 1984. We used QSR NUD*IST, a content analysis program that allows researchers to look for patterns of language within texts, to identify articles mentioning violence. Specifically, we screened the articles for references to violence, violent, injury, destroy, and injure. Because journalists sometimes use vivid language to characterize more mundane circumstances (e.g., "the presidential candidate vowed not to let his opponent's charges destroy his campaign"), I screened each identified article to determine the context of its references to violence.

To my surprise, 14% (240) of these articles mentioned violence. This was unexpected, first, because so few violent events were mentioned in the articles contained in the earlier data set. There did not seem to be a reason why this later period, when protest activity had diminished, should be characterized by violence. Second, in the eighties and nineties, women activists were widely recognized for transforming themselves into successful actors in the arenas of interest group and electoral politics (Costain 1983, 1992; Gelb and Palley 1987; Schlozman 1990; Spalter-Roth and Schreiber 1995). It seems unlikely that the news media, which frequently does portray social movements as radical and threatening to public order, would have done so in this case. The most likely explanation for the increased reporting of violence in relation to the activities of women's organizations was that a counter-movement consisting of people opposed to the goals and achievements of women activists were increasingly resorting to force to attempt to reverse those gains. This pattern can be seen in the history of most successful movements.

A Place for Nonviolence

As I read through the articles, I began to see what had happened. An active and sometimes violent counter-movement arose among people seeking, primarily, to reverse policies that made abortions legal. Nineteen ninety-four was the high point of this politics of force, with 18 articles discussing bombings of clinics and attacks on abortion providers along with the responses to these acts by second-wave women's groups. Advocates for change often face the threat or reality of violent opposition by defenders of the status quo seeking to raise the costs of pursuing change. However, more was going on than just efforts to reverse earlier movement gains.

Women's groups were hard at work opposing violence in sports, art, pornography, and domestic relations; protesting racism and homophobia; and fighting to strengthen laws against sexual coercion both inside the home and outside it. Sexual harassment surfaced as an important issue in 1991, when law professor Anita Hill revealed charges against Supreme Court nominee Clarence Thomas in televised Senate confirmation hearings. Domestic violence had a similar public airing after the murder of Nicole Brown Simpson—the former wife of sports

celebrity O.J. Simpson—and her male friend, Ron Goldman, in 1995, and Simpson's subsequent arrest, trial, and acquittal for their murders. Although organized women's groups played no more than a supporting role in these high-profile cases, it is not difficult to conclude that the more general discussion of violence against women by representatives of the National Organization for Women and similar groups had effectively prepared the soil so that these politically and socially explosive events could take root in the public consciousness and generate years of public debate and examination.

Reviewing the pattern in which specific issues were linked to the women's movement reveals some interesting shifts over time. First, there has been a sharp increase in the numbers of articles mentioning women and violence in the 1990s. These articles describe actions taken by those wishing to undo gains by women and by women protesting violence in all facets of life. Even as references in the *New York Times* to second-wave women's groups have declined overall, the proportion of articles mentioning both women's groups and violence has increased. Comparing the numbers of articles referring to violence or civil rights with those that mention key "women's issues"—namely, abortion, economy/jobs, and education—shows that civil rights advocacy is the main activity of those in the women's movement but also that opposition to violence in all its forms has become increasingly important to them.

Citizenship and Nonviolence as Identity

Nonviolence and opposition to use of coercive means to achieve goals by women's rights activists may be seen either as a tactical choice or as a framing element of that movement. I believe it is both and, as such, is an important component of their collective identity. A great deal has been written about collective identity and participation in social movements (see, e.g., Friedman and McAdam 1992; Melucci 1995, 1996; Tarrow 1994, 118–20). In simple terms, a collective identity is a public claim to a certain status and to ties, connections, or relationships with others who make the same claim.

Examination of collective identities has become important to social movement scholars as they have come to recognize that the messages advocacy groups share with the public and the actions they can be seen taking are frequently critical in determining which opportunities group members can exploit and which resources and networks of supporters they can access. Any particular cause will not necessarily succeed. Its message, membership, and means must all be appropriate to the desired ends and sociopolitical milieu if a group is to reach its goals. For these reasons, groups that promote democratic citizenship and nonviolence may be attractive outlets for women seeking to give voice to their displeasure with the status quo, because they encourage creation of a desirable collective identity: citizen and peacemaker. The importance of this linkage becomes especially evident when considering who and what existing networks and communities are most likely to form such groups. As I mentioned earlier, a greater number of women than men oppose use of force to achieve political ends. Also, when one considers as a whole women's groups' social critique, which holds society accountable for problems ranging from domestic violence to a criminal justice system that makes convictions for rape and other sexually exploitive crimes hard to obtain, a strong pattern of appeals to women's core concerns emerges. Even the acceptance of calls from feminists such as Catharine MacKinnon (1987) to define violence against women in sufficiently broad terms to encompass pornography and violence in the popular culture, as well as sexual harassment, become easier to understand. Acknowledging that violence reduction is a core feature of the political agenda of women's rights advocates also makes their movement's cross-cultural appeal and its frequent cyclic reappearance easier to understand.

Conclusions

Women's movements, even as they represent democratization and the access of polit-ical spheres to previously excluded groups, contain a broad social critique of violence as well. This reinforces the tactical decision of nearly all women's advocacy groups to employ exclusively nonviolent methods. Use of nonviolent tactics stems from activists' attachment to the core value of opposition to coercive means. This nonviolent identity, along with the civil rights vision of participants in the women's movement, helps to account for both the appeal and the impact that the suffrage and women's rights movement have had on American society and politics.

Notes

1. "First-wave" feminist groups are those formed as part of the movement for women's suffrage, which is generally recognized as the first women's movement in the United States. Examples of first-wave groups active today include the League of Women Voters, the American Association of University Women, and the National Woman's Party. My sample of second-wave groups consisted of the National Organization for Women, National Women's Political Caucus, Women's Equity Action League, Federally Employed Women, Congressional Caucus on Women's Issues, Society to Cut Up Men, Redstockings, Older Women's League, and National Abortion Rights Action League.

2. My sample includes the largest national women's organizations and spans a wide range of feminist interests, issues, and styles. Scholarship on the women's movement identifies each as politically active (Carden 1974; Costain 1980, 1981, 1992; Gelb 1995; Gelb and Palley 1977, 1982, 1987; Katzenstein 1987, 1990, 1995; Schlozman 1990; Spalter-Roth and Schreiber 1995).

References

Carden, Maren Lockwood. 1974. *The New Feminist Movement.* New York: Russell Sage Foundation.

Conover, Pamela Johnston, and Virginia Sapiro. 1993. "Gender, Feminist Consciousness, and War." *American Journal of Political Science* 37 (November): 1079–99.

Costain, Anne N. 1980. "The Struggle for a National Women's Lobby: Organizing a Diffuse Interest." *Western Political Quarterly* 33:476–91.

——. 1981. "Representing Women: The Transition from Social Movement to Interest Group." *Western Political Quarterly* 34:100–15.

——. 1983. "The Women's Lobby: Impact of a Movement on Congress." In *Interest Group Politics*, ed. Allan Cigler and Burdett Loomis. Washington: CQ Press.

——. 1988. "Women's Claims as a Special Interest." In *The Politics of the Gender Gap*, ed. Carol M. Mueller. Newbury Park, CA: Sage.

——. 1992. *Inviting Women's Rebellion: A Political Process Interpretation of the Women's Movement.* Baltimore: Johns Hopkins University Press.

Cott, Nancy F. 1987. *The Grounding of Modern Feminism.* New Haven: Yale University Press.

DuBois, Ellen Carol, 1978. *Feminism and Suffrage: The Emergence of an Independent Women's Movement in America.* 1848–1869. Ithaca: Cornell University Press.

——. 1998. "Suffrage Movement." In *The Reader's Companion to U.S. Women's History*, ed. Wilma Mankiller, Gwendolyn Mink, Marysa Navarro, Barbara Smith, and Gloria Steinem. Boston: Houghton Mifflin.

Flammang, Janet A. 1997. *Women's Political Voice: How Women Are Transforming the Practice and Study of Politics.* Philadelphia: Temple University Press.

Flexner, Eleanor. 1973. *Century of Struggle: The Woman's Rights Movement the United States.* New York: Atheneum.

Freeman, Jo. 1975. *The Politics of Women's Liberation.* New York: David McKay.

Friedman, Deborah, and Doug McAdam. 1992. "Collective Identity and Activism: Networks, Choices, and the Life of a Social Movement" In *Frontiers in Social Movement Theory*, ed. Aldon D. Morris and Carol McClurg Mueller. New Haven: Yale University Press.

Gelb, Joyce. 1995. "Feminist Organization Success and the Polities of Engagement." In *Feminist Organizations: Harvest of the New Women's Movement*, ed. Myra Marx Ferree and Patricia Yancey Martin. Philadelphia: Temple University Press.

Gelb, Joyce, and Marian Lief Palley. 1977. "Women and Interest Group Politics" *America Politics Quarterly* 5:331–52.

Gelb, Joyce, and Marian Lief Palley. 1982. *Women and Public Policies.* Princeton: Princeton University Press.

Gelb, Joyce, and Marian Lief Palley. 1987. *Women and Public Policies.* Rev. ed. Princeton: Princeton University Press.

Katzenstein, Mary Fainsod. 1987. "Comparing the Feminist Movements of the United States and Western Europe: An Overview." In *The Women's Movements of the United States and Western Europe: Consciousness, Political Opportunity and Public Policy*, ed. Mary Fainsod Katzenstein and Carol McClurg Mueller. Philadelphia: Temple University Press.

——. 1990. "Feminism within American Institutions: Unobtrusive Mobilization in the 1980s." *Signs* 16(Fall): 27–54.

——. 1995. "Discursive Politics and Feminist Activism in the Catholic Church." In *Feminist Organization: Harvest of the New Women's Movement*, ed. Myra Marx Ferree and Patricia Yancey Martin. Philadelphia: Temple University Press.

MacKinnon, Catharine. 1987. *Feminism Unmodified. Discourses on Life and Law.* Cambridge, MA: Harvard University.

Mansbridge, Jane. 1986. *Why We Lost the ERA.* Chicago: University of Chicago.

McAdam, Doug. 1982. *Political Process and the Development of Black Insurgency*, 1930–1970. Chicago: University of Chicago.

McGlen, Nancy, and Karen O'Connor. 1998. *Women, Politics, and American Society*, 2nd ed. Upper Saddle River, NJ: Prentice Hall.

Melucci, Alberto. 1995. "The Process of Collective Identity." In *Social Movements and Culture*, ed. Hank Johnston and Bert Klandermans, Minneapolis: University of Minnesota.

——. 1996. *Challenging Codes: Collective Action in the Information Age.* Cambridge: Cambridge University Press.

Ryan, Barbara. 1992. *Feminism and the Women's Movement: Dynamics of Change in Social Movement Ideology and Activism.* New York: Routledge.

Schlozman, Kay Lehman. 1990. "Representing Women in Washington: Sisterhood and Pressure Politics." In *Women, Politics, and Change*, ed. Louise Tilly and Patricia Gurin. New York: Russell Sage Foundation.

Shapiro, Robert Y., and Harpeet Majahan. 1986. "Gender Differences in Policy Preferences: A Summary of Trends from the 1960s to the 1980s." *Public Opinion Quarterly* 50: 42–61.

Spalter-Roth, Roberta, and Ronnee Schreiber. 1995. "Outsider Issues and Insider Tactics: Strategic Tensions in the Women's Policy Network during the 1980s." In *Feminist Organizations: Harvest of the New Women's Movement*, ed. Myra Marx Ferree and Patricia Yancey Martin. New York. Russell Sage Foundation.

Tarrow, Sidney. 1994. *Power in Movement: Social Movements, Collective Action and Politics.* Cambridge: Cambridge University Press.

Review

1. Why does Costain say that women's movements are "more than a civil rights movement"?

2. Explain the reason for an increase in the mention of violence after 1980 in articles reporting women's rights activities.

3. What does Costain mean when she claims that nonviolence is a component of the collective identity of women's movements?

Application

Identify someone who has been involved in a social movement such as the women's movement, the Civil Rights movement, the Gay Rights movement or an environmental movement. Interview that person about the movement and its position on nonviolence. What are the movement's grievances? What is the movement trying to achieve? What is its position on nonviolence? Do some members or factions advocate violence? What does the person you interviewed believe about the relative power of violence and nonviolence? Compare the results of your interview with Costain's materials.

Reprinted from: Anne N. Costain, "Women's Movements and Nonviolence," *PS: Political Science & Politics* 33 (2000):175–180. Reprinted by permission of the American Political Science Association. ✦

28
Latinos and American Politics

Rodney Hero
F. Chris Garcia
John Garcia
Harry Pachon

By 2000, Americans of Hispanic origin (or Latinos) were on the verge of becoming the largest
minority group in the nation. In that year, the
Census Bureau reported 32.8 million Hispanics, representing 11.9 percent of the population. African Americans, the largest minority
group throughout American history, made up
12.8 percent of the population. But from 1990
to 2000, the proportion of African Americans
had risen 0.5 percent, while the proportion of
Hispanics had grown 2.9 percent.

*Numbers are important in the exercise of
political power, particularly if a group tends to
favor one political party over another. When a
minority group functions as a voting bloc, the
group can advance and protect its own interests by electing some of its members to political office, influencing legislation and political
platforms, affecting the outcome of elections,
and bringing pressure to bear on elected officials.*

*African Americans have typically voted
overwhelmingly for the Democratic Party, because most African Americans believe their interests are best represented by that party. As
this selection points out, Latinos (except for
Cuban Americans) also tend to vote Democratic, but that tendency may change as they
become more incorporated into the American
social and economic systems. Latinos are
underrepresented among government officials
in terms of their proportion of the population,
but they have made gains in recent decades.
That, too, may change as Latinos become increasingly politicized. When they become the*

*nation's largest minority group, they will have
the potential to bring considerable influence
to bear on the political process. Much depends
on some of the contingencies the authors note
in this overview of Latino participation, partisanship, and office holding.*

The Latino population in the United States
is growing rapidly, and one possible consequence is increased political participation
and empowerment. Another consequence
may be that Latino communities, voters, and
interests face increasing marginalization
and discrimination. Whatever scenario one
envisions, several realities are clear. Latino
political mobilization is difficult because of
the ambiguous status facing the four in 10
Latinos living in the U.S. who are not, for
whatever reason, U.S. citizens. Moreover,
the Latino population is already large, culturally diverse, and disproportionately poor,
and new migration from Latin America re-
shapes community politics at a rapid pace.
Having to accommodate to these challenges,
it would be understandable if the Latino political community remained, for the near future at least, an underachieving, "sleeping giant." But will this be the case? How might
political science explain the challenges and
prospects for Latino political empowerment? And, what dilemmas or opportunities
might Latino empowerment pose for the nation as a whole?

Will the growing population of Latino
adults develop into a more politically oriented and politically active community? If
so, it will not be easy. Long excluded from
formal politics in the United States, many in
Latino communities face difficulty gaining
access to political institutions, effectively advocating their political interests, learning
the rules of the game and seeking greater political representation and responsiveness.
Latino political participation is influenced
by many factors, including the accumulation and use of individual and group resources, positive or negative participatory
orientations, and the presence or absence of
recruitment efforts by organizations and activists.

Political Participation

Early works on the political participation of Latinos focus almost exclusively on Mexican Americans (Garcia 1981; Tirado 1974). Much of the extent [*sic*] research literature, in fact, has been restricted to specific communities or limited realms of political behaviors (e.g., organizational activities, voting, etc.), but some general conclusions can be drawn (Allsup 1982; Briegal 1985; Garcia 1988, 1997; Garcia and de la Garza 1985; Marquez 1993). As a whole, Latinos have lower overall participation rates than the general population, have generally positive participatory orientations (but actual participation does not follow), have lower rates of organizational memberships and activities, and lower rates of voter registration and turnout. Also, a significant proportion of the Latino community is foreign born, and noncitizens report feelings of distance and disinterest from the political life of the U.S. (Falcon 1988; Garcia 1997; Moreno and Warren 1992).

Indicators comparing political behavior of Latinos and non-Latinos, including data from the Participation in America II study (Verba, Schlozman, and Brady 1995), the Latino National Political Survey (LNPS) (de la Garza et al. 1992), and various Current Population Surveys provide important comparative information about Latino participation. Regarding voting, for example, there is almost a 30 percent gap between Latinos and other groups. The gap decreases when the noncitizens segment is removed from the comparison. Taking socioeconomic factors into account also reduces the voting and registration disparities (Hero 1992; Wolfinger and Rosenstone 1980).

Latino participation remains lower outside the electoral arena, as well. Both for Latinos overall, and for Latino citizens, direct contact with public officials falls short of non-Latinos. On the other hand, twice as many Latinos indicated that they have participated in protest activities. Whereas 52 percent of all whites belong to some organization (political or nonpolitical), 24 percent of Latinos and 27 percent of Latino citizens are members (see Garcia and de la Garza

1985). The category of informal community activity (neighborhood issues, school related matters, etc.) shows that Latino rates are comparable to those of other groups. On the other hand, evidence on the average number of activities involved for each of the groups suggests that the Latino mean is 45 percent less (Verba, Schlozman, and Brady 1995).

Political participation depends significantly on political mobilization, that is, on which persons are targeted for political recruitment. We know that employed status, being part of identifiable social networks, and having higher social and economic resources are major determinants for being mobilized. Only one in seven Latino men and one in 25 Latinas were asked to become politically involved (Verba, Schlozman, and Brady 1995). Other information on political orientations (political engagement, interest, efficacy, and political information) also indicate disparities between Latinos and non-Latinos. Lower levels of participatory orientations, especially political information and interest, are more evident among Latinos (de la Garza et al. 1992).

While the Latino National Political Survey results provide some parallels to the patterns identified in Verba, Schlozman, and Brady (1995), LNPS data show significant internal variation within the Latino community (e.g., Mexican origin, Puerto Ricans, and Cubans). Puerto Ricans have lower organizational involvement (60 percent nonmembers), while Cuban citizens vote at the highest level. Moreover, LNPS results indicate that participation disparities between Latinos and non-Latinos are not as wide as reported elsewhere. In particular, the LNPS' additional battery of items measuring Latinos' involvement in school related matters (PTA, school board meetings, voting, etc.) show Latinos to be quite politically active.

Other factors shaping Latino activation include recent punitive policies directed toward Latinos and minorities (especially Propositions 187 and 209 in California), anti-immigrant movements, a growing young adult population, rising rates of naturalization, and greater socioeconomic mobility. These developments are serving as both catalysts and "wake-up" calls about the consequences of noninvolvement in political affairs.

The exploration of Latino political participation is a dynamic area in which demographic changes, more efficient and resource-rich Latino organizations and effective leaders, greater electoral participation, increased representation, and a greater degree of recognition by political parties, leaders, and organizations strongly suggest a positive trajectory of participation. On the other hand, the Latino emergence remains hampered by a lack of political resources, especially lower socioeconomic status, a youthful population, and a large immigrant population in almost every Latino community. Against this, there is a continued expansion of the Latino political base, especially in strategic, populous states, the slow, but noticeable expansion of middle and entrepreneurial classes, and heightened political awareness among Latinos generally.

Much is still to be explored about Latino political participation, including diversity among the Latino sub-groups, especially since little systematic research has examined Central and South Americans and Dominicans, the role of identity politics, and the mobilization efforts by Latino organizations and their leadership.

Political Parties and Partisanship

Political parties are the "grand coalitions" that bring together various interests into large-scale, semipublic organizations. If for no other reason than the general importance of political parties in the United States, it is essential to understand the relationship Latinos have with political parties.

In addition to the role of political parties as organizations, the sense of identifying with a political party—that is "partisanship"—is also an important variable in American politics. It is well known that identification with a political party serves as a valuable psychological organizing mechanism that assists voters in making sense of the complex political system. For that reason, it is also important for an understanding of Latino political participation to understand Latino partisanship. If they are to

become effective players in the American political system, it is probably a necessary but not sufficient condition that Latinos be involved in political party activities.

With few exceptions, Latinos have not been major participants in national party politics, although there have been some state and local exceptions. Until recently, the major parties generally have either chosen to ignore Latinos or take them for granted. This has been due primarily to the fact that Latinos have historically been a relatively small and geographically concentrated proportion of the nation's population. In general, they lacked a national voice and profile until the advent of the Chicano Movement in the mid-1960s and 1970s. Chicanos' and other Latinos' attempts to exert influence on the governmental system resulted in, among other things, increased attention to and from political parties, especially the Democratic Party. Latino party organizations, such as the "Viva Kennedy" clubs, sprung up during the early 1960s. The period also witnessed the emergence of sharp criticisms of the major political parties and other Anglo-dominated institutions. In a critique similar to today's populists, Chicano leaders criticized the political parties for being unresponsive to Chicanos' needs, and portrayed them as being "two heads of the same monster." A manifestation of this was the effort to establish a third, independent, ethnicity based party, El Partido de la Raza Unida.

Electoral rules pose substantial obstacles for any challengers to the status of the major parties. Procedures such as the winner-take-all system of elections and onerous ballot-qualifying provisions greatly advantage the two major parties. The passing on of partisan loyalties from generation to generation through parental socialization also contributes to the dominance of the major parties. Nevertheless, from the activist 1960s period forward, both the Republicans and Democrats have paid increased attention to Latinos, although the degree has waxed and waned according to circumstances.

Since, for decades, the Democratic Party has been seen as more receptive to the interests and needs of lower socioeconomic and ethnic/racial groups, it has won more support among Latinos than has the Republican Party. The Democrats have taken more supportive positions on ethnocultural issues such as immigrants and immigration, affirmative action, bilingual education, and the protection of the Spanish language. It has also espoused a more activist "service" role for government in many socioeconomic areas, such as protecting labor unions, assuring fair wages and employment, and providing social services. From the New Deal period forward, Democrats (at least nationally) have been the principal proponents of civil rights laws and their enforcement. Thus, Latinos have been a significant component of the Democratic Party coalition at least since the 1930s. (The major exception to this Democratic partisanship is the strong Republicanism of Cuban Americans).

LNPS was the first major national survey that included an exploration of Latino partisanship. Because this survey was nationally representative of the three largest Latino populations, it has provided a baseline for subsequent surveys on the subject. According to LNPS, 71 percent of Puerto Ricans, 67 percent of Mexican Americans (and 53 percent of non-Latino respondents) identified themselves as Democrats or Democratic-leaning. In contrast, 69 percent of Cuban Americans identified with the Republican Party (de la Garza et al. 1992, 127). This survey also showed that almost two-thirds of Latinos perceived that there were important differences between the two major political parties.

Very little analysis has been conducted on the reasons underlying Latinos' preference for the Democratic Party. Much of this scarce research focuses on such economic variables as lower income, more poverty, higher unemployment and lower occupational status—factors that often correlate with Democratic support for an activist government involved in the provision of social services. Studies also suggest the importance of Democrats' support for the protection and promotion of civil rights through affirmative action programs; the preservation of Latino culture through bilingual education, and through opposition to the demotion of the Spanish language; and protection

of the rights of immigrants (de la Garza et al. 1992).

Political ideology, in terms of the familiar liberal and conservative spectrum of U.S. politics, is a major correlate of Latino party identification. However, the degree of impact differs for Mexican Americans, Puerto Ricans, and Cuban Americans. And, perhaps more significantly, it has a considerably lesser effect on the partisan choice of Latinos than of whites (Uhlaner and Garcia 2000).

Political party affiliation is the foremost correlate of the direction of the vote. That is, the single-best indicator of how a person votes in an election remains the person's partisan identification. It is thus no surprise that in national elections and state elections, Latinos tend to vote heavily Democratic. This is readily evident in the results of presidential elections. Although the partisan direction of Latino voting has not been documented carefully until recently, every indication is that roughly 70 percent of Latinos support the Democratic presidential candidate. Data on Latino voting in congressional elections evidences a similar pattern of Democratic support (see, e.g., de la Garza and DeSipio 1999).

As the Latino population grows, the partisan direction of Latino voting will become even more significant. Recognizing this, both parties [made] extensive overtures to Latino voters in 2000, and the Latino vote has been designated by spokespersons of both parties as one of the key electoral "battle grounds." The national Republican Party, which for decades hardly attempted to court Latinos, dedicated $10 million to target the Latino electorate for the 2000 election.

Over the past several years, various Republican Party spokespersons have claimed that Latinos are "natural Republicans" and that Latinos only need to be educated to this fact. The Republican assertion is that Latinos share the GOP's conservative values on such issues as patriotism and national defense, abortion, school vouchers, crime, gay rights, and other "family values." Democrats have countered, however, with assertions that their party's positions on socioeconomic and sociocultural issues are most likely to win Latinos' support.

Over the past few years, the Republican party has driven many Latinos away from the GOP through its positions on anti-immigrant legislation, proposals favoring official English or English-only laws, opposition to affirmative action and bilingual education, and other seemingly xenophobic policies. While some of this has been manifested at the national level, much has occurred in state political arenas, most noticeably California, where certain GOP public officials have been particularly ardent supporters of anti-affirmative action, anti-bilingual education, and anti-immigrant and anti-immigration policies. The reaction against these Republican positions has been intense and widespread and has further reinforced the traditional Latino Democratic partisanship. In fact, the Republicans' embrace of policies that are extremely objectionable to Latinos (if even on a symbolic level), may have halted a gradual weakening of Democratic party ties, thereby allowing the Democrats to hold a share of Latino voters who might otherwise have moved toward the Republican Party.

In fact, there are indications that Latinos become less Democratic as they become more incorporated into the American political, social, and economic systems (Calmes 2000). As Latinos' personal status increases, they show increased attraction to an independent or Republican position.

Hispanic Elected Officials

Over the past decade there has been a growth in numbers of Hispanic Elected Officials (HEOs). Court rulings and the advent of favorable legislation in the 1960s, resulting from the African-American and Latino civil rights movements, created conditions for the emergence of Latino candidates for public office. These structural changes in the political system, combined with ethnic political mobilization in Latino communities and the efforts of such groups as the Mexican American Legal Defense and Educational Fund, the Southwest Voter Registration and Education Project and the Puerto Rican Legal Defense and Educational Fund, contributed to an increase in the electoral clout and political salience of the Latino community (Moore and Pachon 1985; Pachon 1999).

As a result, Latino candidates in the 1970s, 1980s, and 1990s, both men and women, won elected offices at all levels of government at an unprecedented rate (see Table 28.1a,b). Highly publicized victories— such as those of former San Antonio Mayor Henry Cisneros, Los Angeles County Supervisor Gloria Molina, and Orange County Congresswoman Loretta Sanchez—have been accompanied by many local and regional victories. For example, the number of California Latino state legislators increased in the 1998 election to 24.

Table 28.1a,b
Latino Elected Officials by Level of Government and by Gender, 1999

Table 28.1a
Latino Elected Officials by Level of Government

Federal	
Cabinet Member	1
U.S. Senator	0
U.S. Representative	18
State	
Governor	0
State Executives	8
State Legislators	187
Local	
County Offices	375
Municipal Offices	1345
Judicial/Law	493
School Board	1291
Special Districts	128
Total	**3845**

Table 28.1b
Latino Elected Officials by Gender, Selected States

State	Male	Female	Latina %
Arizona	163	101	38.3
California	499	263	34.5
Florida	57	26	31.3
Colorado	107	44	29.1
New York	57	21	26.9
Texas	1312	412	23.9
New Mexico	463	139	23.1
Illinois	27	7	20.6
New Jersey	42	9	17.6
Total	**2727**	**1022**	**27.3**

The victories of these Latino elected officials represent more than a series of individual achievements. Some scholars have suggested that "the most widely used indicator of a group's position in a political system is the presence of that group in elective offices" (Browning, Marshall, and Tabb 1984). In other words, the number of elected officials from any particular ethnic group may serve as a barometer of that group's standing in the political system. Moreover, there are political benefits in electing ethnic officials, leaders who have the potential to legitimize and defend the group's interests in the policy arena, whether in school boards, city councils, state legislatures, or in Congress. In this capacity, minority elected officials have been linked to increased minority government employment (Eisenger 1982), increased numbers of Latino teachers (Fraga, Meier, and England 1986), and more responsive public policies in terms of minority contracting and minority representation on boards and commissions. Therefore, the presence of HEOs will have continued consequences for the political life of the Latino community.

Enumeration of Hispanic Elected Officials

Since 1984, the National Association of Latino Elected and Appointed Officials (NALEO) Educational Fund has conducted an annual survey of Latino office holders nationwide to enumerate the HEOs. NALEO's Educational Fund publishes this directory annually (NALEO 1985–99). The following is an overview of Latino office holders as indicated in the research.

Geographic Distribution of Hispanic Elected Officials

In 1999 Hispanic elected officials held 3,845 of the publicly elected offices nationwide. Thus, Latino elected officials represent less than 1 percent of the nation's 513,200 elected officials (U.S. Bureau of the Census 1992). Although total numbers are low, the number of Hispanic elected officials in selected states is large. Nine states, representing 82 percent of the Latino population, account for more than 97 percent of HEOs in the United States. Texas, California, and New Mexico account for more than 80 percent of all HEOs.

The predominance of HEOs in the Southwest should not obscure the increase in the number of HEOs in other states. New York (in particular New York City), New Jersey, Florida (especially Dade County/Miami), and Illinois have elected more than 246 Latinos at all levels of government in recent years. Illinois has more Latinos than the southwestern states of Arizona, Colorado, or New Mexico.

Table 28.2
Latino Elected Officials by State, 1999

Arizona	264	Montana	2
California	762	Nebraska	2
Colorado	151	Nevada	3
Connecticut	24	New Jersey	51
Delaware	2	New Mexico	602
D.C.	1	New York	78
Florida	83	Ohio	2
Georgia	1	Oregon	2
Hawaii	1	Pennsylvania	5
Idaho	1	Rhode Island	2
Illinois	34	Tennessee	1
Indiana	7	Texas	1724
Kansas	3	Utah	2
Louisiana	5	Washington	10
Massachusetts	10	Wisconsin	2
Michigan	4	Wyoming	1
Minnesota	3		
Total			3845

Source: Tomas Rivera Policy Institute, 1999. National Directory of Latino Elected Officials.

Patterns of Political Office Holding

Latinos hold legislative positions at all levels of government, except for the U.S. Senate. The distribution of the office holding for HEOs bears consequences for the future. The first rung on the political ladder is often a school board or city council seat; notably, there are now more than 3,800 Latinos in such positions. HEOs in these offices represent a potential recruitment pool of Latinos for statewide and national political offices in the coming years.

Partisanship Among Hispanic Elected Officials

Because NALEO only collects partisanship data in selected states and offices at the municipal levels and school board levels are typically nonpartisan, trends in the partisanship of HEOs are difficult to ascertain. Among the HEOs for whom a partisan affiliation can be determined, 65 percent identify themselves as Democrats, 5 percent as Republicans, and the remainder as Independents (NALEO). Although the preponderance of HEOs are Democrats, it is important to note that there are Republican HEOs in each of the nine states with the highest concentrations of Latino office holders and that both New Mexico and California have more Republican HEOs than does Florida. In Florida, significantly, HEOs reporting a partisan preferences are almost twice as likely to identify as Republicans as they are Democrats (NALEO 1999).

The Potential for Continued Growth in the Ranks of HEOs

There are at least five reasons to project continued growth in the number of HEOs. First, the Latino population is geographically concentrated and rapidly growing in numbers. This means the constituencies for Latino candidates will grow. In most states, HEOs represent majority Latino districts and, according to 1998 Census data, there are 53 congressional districts with over 100,000 Latinos.

Second, litigation to eliminate minority vote dilution through at-large districting in California (*Gomez v. The City of Watsonville* 1988) or ethnic gerrymandering (*Garza v. County of Los Angeles* 1990), have increased the potential for Latino electoral clout. Reapportionment that creates single-member districts with significant Latino populations (40 percent or more) frequently results in the election of Latinos from a jurisdiction for the first time. Third, both political parties are now well aware of the increasing Latino electorate and are increasingly nominating Latinos for elected office. Fourth, Latinos have made political gains even though the majority of the Latino population has not been eligible to participate in electoral politics. Youth and noncitizenship continue to limit Latino electoral participation. Increased naturalization rates and the aging of the Latino U.S. citizen population will increase the ratio of those adults eligible to

vote, however (Pachon 1998). Finally, the adoption of term limits in many states may aid Latino candidates by creating more opportunities to win various open seats.

The period after the 2000 election will offer analysts a unique opportunity to again examine Latino participation, partisanship, and office holding. We should thus have solid evidence to better understand the development of Latino political influence as it manifests itself in representation, and as these are propelled by participation and party activities.

References

Allsup, Carl. 1982. *The American G. 1. Forum: Origins and Evolution.* Austin: Center for Mexican American Studies, University of Texas.

Briegal, Kay. 1985. "The Alianza Hispanoamericana: A Mexican American Fraternal Insurance Society," Ph.D. diss., University of California, Los Angeles.

Browning, Rufus, Dale Rogers Marshall, and David Tabb. 1984. *Protest Is Not Enough: The Struggle of Blacks and Hispanics for Equality in Urban Politics.* Berkeley: University of California Press.

Calmes, Jackie. 2000. "Hispanic Middle Class Gets Full Court Press." *The Wall Street Journal*, March 9, A9.

de la Garza, Rodolfo, Louis DeSipio, F. Chris Garcia, John A. Garcia, and Angelo Falcon. 1992. *Latino Voices: Mexican, Puerto and Cuban Perspectives on American Politics.* Boulder: Westview.

de la Garza, Rodolfo, and Louis DeSipio, eds., 1999. *Awash in the Mainstream: Latinos and the 1996 Elections.* Boulder: Westview.

Eisenger, Peter. 1982. "Black Employment in Municipal Jobs: The Impact of Black Political Power." *American Political Science Review* 76(June): 380–92.

Falcon, Angelo. 1988. "Black and Latino Politics in New York City." In *Latinos in the Political System*, ed. F. Chris Garcia. Notre Dame: University of Notre Dame Press.

Fraga, Luis, Kenneth Meier, and Robert England. 1986. "Hispanic Americans and Educational Policy: Limits to Equal Access." *Journal of Politics* 48:850–76.

Garcia, John A. 1981. "Political Integration of Mexican Immigrants: Explorations into the Naturalization Process." *International Migration Review* 15 (Winter).

Garcia, John A., and Carlos H. Arce. 1988 "Political Orientations and Behaviors of Chicanos: Trying to Make Sense Out of Attitudes and Participation." In *Latinos and the Political System*, ed. F. Chris Garcia. Notre Dame: University of Notre Dame Press.

——. 1997. "Hispanic Political Participation and Demographic Correlates." In *Pursuing Power: Latinos and the Political System*, 2nd ed., ed. F. Chris Garcia. Notre Dame: University of Notre Dame Press.

Garcia John A., and R. de la Garza. 1985. "Mobilizing the Mexican Immigrant: The Role of Organizational Involvement." *Western Political Quarterly* 38(December): 551–64.

Garza v. County of Los Angeles. 1990. 918 F. 2nd 763 (9th Cir.).

Gomez v. City of Watsonville. 1988. 863 F. 2nd 1407 (9th Cir.).

Hero, Rodney. 1992. *Latinos and the Political System: A Two-Tiered Pluralism*. Philadelphia: Temple University Press.

Marquez, Benjamin. 1993. *LULAC: Evolution of a Mexican American Political Organization*. Austin: University of Texas Press.

Moore, Joan, and Harry Pachon. 1985. *Hispanics in the United States*. Englewood Cliffs, NJ: Prentice-Hall.

Moreno, Dario, and Christopher Warren. 1992. "The Conservative Enclave: Cubans and Community Power in Florida." In *From Rhetoric to Reality: Latinos Do the 1988 Elections*, ed. Rodolfo de la Garza and Louis DeSipio. Boulder: Westview.

National Association of Latino Elected Officials. 1985–99. Roster of Hispanic Elected Officials. Washington, DC: NALEO Educational Fund.

Pachon, Harry. 1998. "Latino Politics in the Golden State: Ready for the 21st Century?" In *Racial and Ethnic Politics in California*, ed. Byran O. Jackson and Michael B. Preston. Berkeley: Institute for Governmental Studies, University of California.

——. 1999. "California Latino Politics and the 1996 Elections: From Potential to Reality." In *Awash in the Mainstream*, ed. Rodolfo O. de la Garza and Louis DeSipio. Boulder: Westview.

Tirado, Miguel. 1974. "Mexican American Community Political Organizations: The Key to Chicano Political Power." In *La Causa Politics*, ed. F. Chris Garcia. Notre Dame: University of Notre Dame Press.

Uhlaner, Carole J., and F. Chris Garcia. 2000. "Ideology, Issues and Partisanship among Latinos." Paper presented at the 2000 meeting of the Western Political Science Association, San Jose.

U.S. Bureau of the Census. 1992. "Popularly Elected Officials." Census of Governments. Washington, DC: U.S. Department of Commerce.

Verba, Sidney, Kay Schlozman, and Henry Brady. 1995. *Voice and Equality: Civic Volunteerism in American Politics*. Cambridge, MA: Harvard University Press.

Wolfinger, Raymond, and Stephen Rosenstone. 1980. *Who Votes?* New Haven: Yale University Press.

Review

1. Discuss the extent of political participation of Latinos, comparing it with that of other groups in American society.

2. Explain partisanship among Latinos, including variations by country of origin.

3. Discuss the situation of Hispanic elected officials: How many are there? To which party do they belong? What is their geographic distribution?

Applications

1. How many Latinos are elected officials in the largest city in the state where you live? From the city's record offices or Web site, secure a list of all elected officials. Estimate the number of Latino officials by the number of Hispanic surnames. What proportion of the overall list do they represent? If possible, contact one of the Latino officials and get his or her perspective on the challenges and problems of Latinos in politics in the area.

2. Make a list of four fictional candidates for your local school board. Make the first a highly qualified man (with much educational experience) whose background includes being a member of the African Methodist Episcopal Church. Make the second a highly qualified man with a Hispanic surname whose background includes membership in the "Hispanic Educational Association." Make the third a somewhat qualified woman (she was president of the PTA) with roots in the community, and the

fourth a man with an Anglo-Saxon name who is a prominent businessman.

Ask ten white respondents to look at the list and tell you which one of the four they would vote for based only on the information given. Then ask them to make a second choice. What would you conclude from your results?

Reprinted from: Rodney Hero, F. Chris Garcia, John Garcia, and Harry Pachon, "Latino Participation, Partisanship, and Office Holding." In *PS: Political Science & Politics* 33, pp. 529–34. Copyright © 2000 by the American Political Science Association. Reprinted by permission. ✦

Part Three

The Economy

The **economy** is the institution that regulates the production and distribution of goods and services. Some of those goods and services are necessary for the maintenance of life and some are believed to enhance the quality of life. Today, the two basic forms of economy among the nations of the world are capitalism and socialism: a few nations combine the two in some way.

Capitalism is an economic system with private ownership of the means of production and competitive, for-profit distribution of goods and services. **Socialism** is an economic system with state ownership of the means of production and cooperative distribution of goods and services.

The first two selections in this part examine capitalism from two very different perspectives. The third selection deals with a form of organization that pervades all economies and that characterizes both government and private industry—the bureaucracy. ✦

29
Alienation in Work

Karl Marx

In Marx's view, a central problem of labor in a capitalist society is **alienation,** estrangement from the social environment that includes feelings of isolation, powerlessness, and meaninglessness. He believed that it is human nature for people to fulfill their creative potential through labor. In this respect he differed from other early social scientists such as Adam Smith, the eighteenth century political economist, who held that human beings are lazy by nature and would not be productive without the incentives of profit and property. Marx maintained that people's distaste for work is the result of a capitalistic system that serves to alienate workers from the processes and products of their labor, from other workers, and, ultimately, from themselves.

This selection discusses the nature, causes, and effects of work-related alienation and the dehumanizing power of money in capitalist society. Although Marx first put forth these ideas more than a century and a half ago, they are still relevant and thought provoking today.

We shall begin from a *contemporary* economic fact. The worker becomes poorer the more wealth he produces and the more production increases in power and extent. The worker becomes an ever cheaper commodity the more goods he creates. The *devaluation* of the human world increases in direct relation with the *increase in value* of the world of things. Labour does not only create goods; it also produces itself and the worker as a *commodity*, and indeed in the same proportion as it produces goods.

This fact simply implies that the object produced by labour, its product, now stands opposed to it as an *alien being*, as a *power independent* of the producer. The product of labour is labour which has been embodied in an object and turned into a physical thing; this product is an *objectification* of labour. The performance of work is at the same time its objectification.

These consequences follow the fact that the worker is related to the *product of his labour* as to an alien object. For it is clear on this presupposition that the more the worker expends himself in work the more powerful becomes the world of objects which he creates in place of himself, the poorer he becomes in his inner life, and the less he belongs to himself. It is just the same as in religion. The more of himself man attributes to God the less he has left in himself. The worker puts his life into the object, and his life then belongs no longer to himself but to the object. The greater his activity, therefore, the less he possesses. What is embodied in the product of his labour is no longer his own. The greater this product is, therefore, the more he is diminished. The *alienation* of the worker in his product means not only that his labour becomes an object, assumes an *external* existence, but that it exists independently, *outside himself*, and alien to him, and that it stands opposed to him as an autonomous power. The life which he has given to the object sets itself against him as an alien and hostile force.

Labour certainly produces marvels for the rich but it produces privation for the worker. It produces palaces, but hovels for the worker. It produces beauty, but deformity for the worker. It replaces labour by machinery, but it casts some of the workers back into a barbarous kind of work and turns the others into machines. It produces intelligence, but also stupidity and cretinism for the workers.

So far we have considered the alienation of the worker only from one aspect; namely, *his relationship with the products of his labour*. However, alienation appears not merely in the result but also in the *process of production*, within productive activity itself. How could the worker stand in an alien relationship to the product of his activity if he

241

did not alienate himself in the act of production itself? The product is indeed only the *résumé* of activity, of production. Consequently, if the product of labour is alienation, production itself must be active alienation—the alienation of activity and the activity of alienation. The alienation of the object of labour merely summarizes the alienation in the work activity itself.

What constitutes the alienation of labour? First, that the work is *external* to the worker, that it is not part of his nature; and that, consequently, he does not fulfill himself in his work but denies himself, has a feeling of misery rather than well-being, does not develop freely his mental and physical energies but is physically exhausted and mentally debased. The worker, therefore, feels himself at home only during his leisure time, whereas at work he feels homeless. His work is not voluntary but imposed, *forced labour*. It is not the satisfaction of a need, but only a *means* for satisfying other needs. Its alien character is clearly shown by the fact that as soon as there is no physical or other compulsion it is avoided like the plague. External labour, labour in which man alienates himself, is a labour of self-sacrifice, of mortification. Finally, the external character of work for the worker is shown by the fact that it is not his own work but work for someone else, that in work he does not belong to himself but to another person.

We arrive at the result that man (the worker) feels himself to be freely active only in his animal functions—eating, drinking and procreating, or at most also in his dwelling and in personal adornment—while in his human functions he is reduced to an animal.

For labour, *life activity, productive life*, now appear to man only as *means* for the satisfaction of a need, the need to maintain his physical existence. Productive life is, however, species-life. It is life creating life. In the type of life activity resides the whole character of a species, its species-character; and free, conscious activity is the species-character of human beings. Life itself appears only as a *means of life*.

The animal is one with its life activity. It does not distinguish the activity from itself. It is *its activity*. But man makes his life activity itself an object of his will and consciousness. He has a conscious life activity. It is not a determination with which he is completely identified. Conscious life activity distinguishes man from the life activity of animals. Only for this reason is his activity free activity. Alienated labour reverses the relationship, in that man because he is a self-conscious *being* makes his life activity, his being, only a means for his *existence*.

The practical construction of an *objective world*, the *manipulation* of inorganic nature, is the confirmation of man as a conscious species-being, i.e., a being who treats the species as his own being or himself as a species-being. Of course, animals also produce. They construct nests, dwellings, as in the case of bees, beavers, ants, etc. But they only produce what is strictly necessary for themselves or their young. They produce only in a single direction, while man produces universally. They produce only under the compulsion of direct physical needs, while man produces when he is free from physical need and only truly produces in freedom from such need. Animals produce only themselves, while man reproduces the whole of nature. The products of animal production belong directly to their physical bodies, while man is free in face of his product. Animals construct only in accordance with the standards and needs of the species to which they belong, while man knows how to produce in accordance with the standards of every species and knows how to apply the appropriate standard to the object. Thus man constructs also in accordance with the laws of beauty.

A direct consequence of the alienation of man from the product of his labour, from his life activity and from his species-life, is that man is *alienated* from *other* men. When man confronts himself he also confronts *other* men. What is true of man's relationship to his work, to the product of his work and to himself, is also true of his relationship to other men, to their labour and to the objects of their nature.

Thus in the relationship of alienated labour every man regards other men according to the standards and relationships in which he finds himself placed as a worker.

If the product of labour is alien to me and confronts me as an alien power, to whom does it belong?

The *alien* being to whom labour and the product of labour belong, to whose service labour is devoted, and to whose enjoyment the product of labour goes, can only be *man* himself. If the product of labour does not belong to the worker, but confronts him as an alien power, this can only be because it belongs to a *man other than the worker*. If his activity is a torment to him it must be a source of *enjoyment* and pleasure to another. Not the gods, nor nature, but only man himself can be this alien power over men.

Thus, through alienated labour the worker creates the relation of another man, who does not work and is outside the work process, to this labour. The relation of the worker to work also produces the relation of the capitalist (or whatever one likes to call the lord of labour) to work.

Money

Money, since it has the *property* of purchasing everything, of appropriating objects to itself, is, therefore, the *object par excellence*. The universal character of this *property* corresponds to the omnipotence of money, which is regarded as an omnipotent being . . . money is the *pander* between need and object, between human life and the means of subsistence. But *that which* mediates *my* life mediates also the existence of other men for me. It is for me the *other* person.

That which exists for me through the medium of *money*, that which I can pay for (i.e., which money can buy), that *I am*, the possessor of the money. My own power is as great as the power of money. The properties of money are my own (the possessor's) properties and faculties. What *I am* and *can do* is, therefore, not at all determined by my individuality. I *am* ugly, but I can buy the most beautiful woman for myself. Consequently, I am not *ugly*, for the effect of ugliness, its power to repel, is annulled by money. I am a detestable, dishonourable, unscrupulous and stupid man, but money is honoured and so also is its possessor. Money is the highest good, and so its possessor is good. Besides, money saves me the trouble of being dishonest; therefore, I am presumed honest. I who can have, through the power of money, *everything* for which the human heart longs, do I not possess all human abilities? Does not my money, therefore, transform all my incapacities into their opposites?

If *money* is the bond which binds me to *human* life, and society to me, and which links me with nature and man, is it not the bond of all *bonds*? It is the real means of both *separation* and *union*. The difference between effective demand, supported by money, and ineffective demand, based upon my need, my passion, my desire, etc. is the difference between *being* and *thought*, between the merely inner representation and the representation which exists outside myself as a *real object*.

If I have no money for travel I have no *need*—no real and self-realizing need—for travel. If I have a *vocation* for study but no money for it, then I have *no* vocation, i.e., no *effective*, genuine vocation. Conversely, if I really have *no* vocation for study, but have money and the urge for it, then I have an *effective* vocation. *Money* is the external, universal means and power (not derived from man as man nor from human society as society) to change *representation* into *reality* and *reality* into *mere representation*.

Let us assume *man* to be *man*, and his relation to the world to be a human one. Then love can only be exchanged for love, trust for trust, etc. If you wish to enjoy art you must be an artistically cultivated person; if you wish to influence other people you must be a person who really has a stimulating and encouraging effect upon others. Every one of your relations to man and to nature must be a *specific expression*, corresponding to the object of your will, of your *real individual* life.

Review

1. What is the product of labor, according to Marx?

2. What does he mean by the alienation of the worker from the worker's products?

3. When do human beings feel themselves to be freely active, according to Marx?

4. What is the direct consequence of the alienation of humans from the product of their labor?

5. What property and power does money have, according to Marx?

Application

Interview two or three people who have worked at a variety of jobs. Ask what was the best and worst of these jobs and what aspects of the work made it good or bad. Relate their descriptions to these notions from Marx:

a. low pay (exploitation)

b. monotony versus variety of tasks

c. excessive supervision versus autonomy

d. personal profit versus service to others

e. narrowly defined tasks versus creativity

What other aspects of work were seen as particularly satisfying or burdensome? Summarize your findings and use them in evaluating Marx's discussion of work.

Reprinted from: Karl Marx, "Alienation in Work." Excerpted from *Karl Marx: Early Writings* by T. B. Bottomore. Copyright © 1964 by McGraw-Hill Book Company. Reprinted with permission of McGraw-Hill, Inc. ✦

30

The Protestant Ethic and the Spirit of Capitalism

Max Weber

Weber's thesis about the historical relationship between the rise of capitalism and the Protestant Reformation is one of the most widely discussed works in social science. Weber believed that modern capitalism is distinguished by its rationality, which involves the pursuit of profit through ethically controlled competition.

In the Middle Ages, however, there was no specific moral code that applied to economic activity. Thus, tradesmen, merchants, and financiers were free to use force or fraud for profit. But in the sixteenth century, new economic attitudes began to emerge from various Protestant denominations, most notably the **Calvinists**—Puritans and others who followed the beliefs of the Protestant reformer John Calvin (1509–1564). Presbyterians and Reformed groups are present-day descendents of the early Calvinists.

Puritans believed that, because an individual's calling in life was a duty to God, economic activity must be pursued in strict accordance with ethical rules. They also believed that worldly success was a sign of God's salvation. In recognition of this distinctive Puritan contribution, Weber, in his writings, refers to all ascetic Protestant religions as Puritan.

It should be noted that Weber regarded the relationship between Protestantism and capitalism with irony. In his view, the early Protestants were driven by concern for their fate in the next world to transform this world into its modern form. But the materialism engendered *by this transformation proved so alluring it killed off the very spirituality that fostered it.*

An Overview of Weber's Thesis

The basic dogma of strict Calvinism, the doctrine of predestination, makes it impossible for the church to administer sacraments whose reception can have any significance for eternal salvation. Moreover, the actual behavior of the believer is irrelevant to his fate, which has been determined from eternity through God's inscrutable and immutable will.

The inscrutability of predestination to either salvation or damnation was naturally intolerable to the believer; he searched for the *certitudo saluris*, for an indication that he belonged to the elect. He could find this certainty, on the one hand, in the conviction that he was acting according to the letter of the law and according to reason, repressing all animal drives; on the other, he could find it in visible proofs that God blessed his work. "Good works" of the Catholic variety were meaningless in the face of God's unchangeable decree; however, for the believer and his community, his own ethical conduct and fate in the secular social order became supremely important as an indication of his state of grace. A person was judged elect or condemned as an entity; no confession and absolution could relieve him and change his position before God and, in contrast to Catholicism, no individual "good deed" could compensate for his sins. Therefore, the individual could only be sure of his state of grace if he felt reason to believe that, by adhering to a principle of methodical conduct, he pursued the sole correct path in all his action—that he worked for God's glory. Methodical conduct, the rational form of asceticism, is thus carried from the monastery into the world. The ascetic means are in principle identical: Rejected are all vain glorification of the self and of all other things of the flesh, feudal pride, the spontaneous enjoyment of art and life, "levity," all waste of money and time, eroticism, or any other activity that detracts from the rational work in one's private vocation and within the God-willed social order. The curtailment of all feudal ostentation and of all irrational consumption facilitates capital accumulation and the ever-renewed utilization of property for productive purposes.

Life is focused not on persons but on impersonal rational goals. Charity becomes an impersonal operation of poor relief for the greater glory of God. And since the success of work is the surest symptom that it pleases God, capitalist profit is one of the most important criteria for establishing that God's blessing rests on the enterprise.

It is clear that this style of life is very closely related to the self-justification that is customary for bourgeois acquisition: profit and property appear not as ends in themselves but as indications of personal ability. Here has been attained the union of religious postulate and bourgeois style of life that promotes capitalism. Of course, this was not the purpose of the Puritan ethic, especially not the encouragement of money making; on the contrary, as in all Christian denominations, wealth was regarded as dangerous and full of temptation. However, just as the monasteries time and again brought this temptation on themselves by virtue of the ascetic rational work and conduct of their members, so did now the pious bourgeois who lived and worked ascetically.

The Contrast of Catholicism with Protestant Asceticism

The normal mediaeval Catholic layman lived ethically, so to speak, from hand to mouth. In the first place he conscientiously fulfilled his traditional duties. But beyond that minimum his good works did not necessarily form a connected, or at least not a rationalized, system of life, but rather remained a succession of individual acts. He could use them as occasion demanded, to atone for particular sins, to better his chances for salvation, or, toward the end of his life, as a sort of insurance premium. Of course the Catholic ethic was an ethic of intentions. But the concrete *intentio* of the single act determined its value. And the single

good or bad action was credited to the doer determining his temporal and eternal fate. Quite realistically the Church recognized that man was not an absolutely clearly defined unity to be judged one way or the other, but that his moral life was normally subject to conflicting motives and his action contradictory. Of course, it required as an ideal a change of life in principle. But it weakened just this requirement (for the average) by one of its most important means of power and education, the sacrament of absolution, the function of which was connected with the deepest roots of the peculiarly Catholic religion.

To the Catholic, the absolution of his Church was a compensation for his own imperfection. The priest was a magician who performed the miracle of transubstantiation, and who held the key to eternal life in his hand. One could turn to him in grief and penitence. He dispensed atonement, hope of grace, certainty of forgiveness, and thereby granted release from that tremendous tension to which the Calvinist was doomed by an inexorable fate, admitting of no mitigation. For him such friendly and human comforts did not exist. He could not hope to atone for hours of weakness or of thoughtlessness by increased good will at other times, as the Catholic or even the Lutheran could. The God of Calvinism demanded of his believers not single good works, but a life of good works combined into a unified system. There was no place for the very human Catholic cycle of sin, repentance, atonement, release, followed by renewed sin.

The moral conduct of the average man was thus deprived of its planless and unsystematic character and subjected to a consistent method for conduct as a whole. It is no accident that the name of Methodists stuck to the participants in the last great revival of Puritan ideas in the eighteenth century.

Only by a fundamental change in the whole meaning of life at every moment and in every action could the effects of grace . . . be proved.

The Effects of Protestant Asceticism on Everyday Life

If a demonstration of religious fidelity is still to be made within the institutional structure of the world, then the world, for the very reason that it inevitably remains a natural vessel of sin, becomes a challenge for the demonstration of the ascetic temper and for the strongest possible attacks against the world's sins. The world abides in the lowly state appropriate to its status as a created thing. Therefore, any sensuous surrender to the world's goods may imperil concentration upon and possession of the ultimate good of salvation, and may be a symptom of unholiness of spirit and impossibility of rebirth. Nevertheless, the world as a creation of God, whose power comes to expression in it despite its creatureliness, provides the only medium through which one's unique religious charisma may prove itself by means of rational ethical conduct, so that one may become and remain certain of one's own state of grace.

Hence, as the field provided for this active certification, the order of the world in which the ascetic is situated becomes for him a vocation which he must fulfill rationally. As a consequence, and although the enjoyment of wealth is forbidden to the ascetic, it becomes his vocation to engage in economic activity which is faithful to rationalized ethical requirements and which conforms to strict legality. If success supervenes upon such acquisitive activity, it is regarded as the manifestation of God's blessing upon the labor of the pious man and of God's pleasure with his economic pattern of life.

Certain other manifestations of inner-worldly asceticism must be noted. Any excess of emotional feeling for one's fellow man is prohibited as being a deification of the creaturely, which denies the unique value of the divine gift of grace. Yet it is man's vocation to participate rationally and soberly in the various rational, purposive institutions of the world and in their objective goals as set by God's creation. Similarly, any eroticism that tends to deify the human creature is proscribed. On the other hand, it is a divinely imposed vocation of man "to soberly produce children" (as the Puritans expressed it) within marriage. Then, too, there is a prohibition against the exercise of force by an individual against other human beings for reasons of passion or revenge, and above all for purely personal motives. However, it is divinely enjoined that the rationally ordered state shall suppress and punish sins and rebelliousness. Finally, all personal secular enjoyment of power is forbidden as a deification of the creaturely, though it is held that a rational legal order within society is pleasing to God.

The person who lives as a worldly ascetic is a rationalist, not only in the sense that he rationally systematizes his own personal patterning of life, but also in his rejection of everything that is ethically irrational, esthetic, or dependent upon his own emotional reactions to the world and its institutions. The distinctive goal always remains the alert, methodical control of one's own pattern of life and behavior.

***

Waste of time is the first and in principle the deadliest of sins. The span of human life is infinitely short and precious to make sure of one's own election. Loss of time through sociability, idle talk, luxury, even more sleep than is necessary for health, six to at most eight hours, is worthy of absolute moral condemnation. It does not yet hold that time is money, but the proposition is true in a certain spiritual sense. It is infinitely valuable because every hour lost is lost to labour for the glory of God. Thus inactive contemplation is also valueless, or even directly reprehensible if it is at the expense of one's daily work. For it is less pleasing to God than the active performance of His will in a calling.

***

The sexual asceticism of Puritanism differs only in degree, not in fundamental principle, from that of monasticism; and on account of the Puritan conception of marriage, its practical influence is more far-reaching than that of the latter. For sexual intercourse is permitted, even within marriage, only as the means willed by God for the increase of His glory according to the commandment, "Be fruitful and multiply." Along with a moderate vegetable diet and cold baths, the same prescription is given for all sexual temptations as is used against religious doubts and a sense of moral unworthiness: "Work hard in your calling." But the most important thing was that even beyond that labour came to be considered in itself the end of life, ordained as such by God. St. Paul's "He who will not work shall not eat" holds unconditionally for everyone. Unwillingness to work is symptomatic of the lack of grace.

***

The Puritan aversion to sport was by no means simply one of principle. Sport was accepted if it served a rational purpose, that of recreation necessary for physical efficiency. But as a means for the spontaneous expression of undisciplined impulses, it was under suspicion; and in so far as it became purely a means of enjoyment, or awakened pride, raw instincts or the irrational gambling instinct, it was of course strictly condemned. Impulsive enjoyment of life, which leads away both from work in a calling and from religion, was as such the enemy of rational asceticism.

***

The theatre was obnoxious to the Puritans, and with the strict exclusion of the erotic and of nudity from the realm of toleration, a radical view of either literature or art could not exist. The conceptions of idle talk, of superfluities, and of vain ostentation, all designations of an irrational attitude without objective purpose, thus not ascetic, and especially not serving the glory of God, but of man, were always at hand to serve in deciding in favour of sober utility as against any artistic tendencies. This was especially true in the case of decoration of the person, for instance clothing. That powerful tendency toward uniformity of life, which today so immensely aids the capitalistic interest in the standardization of produtition, had its ideal foundations in the repudiation of all idolatry of the flesh.

***

One of the most notable economic effects of Calvinism was its destruction of the traditional forms of charity. First it eliminated miscellaneous almsgiving . . . and especially any benevolent attitude toward the beggar. For Calvinism held that the unsearchable God possessed good reasons for having distributed the gifts of fortune unequally. It never ceased to stress the notion that a man proved himself exclusively in his vocational work. Consequently, begging was explicitly stigmatized as a violation of the injunction to love one's neighbor, in this case the person from whom the beggar solicits.

What is more, all Puritan preachers proceeded from the assumption that the idleness of a person capable of work was inevitably his own fault. But it was felt necessary to organize charity systematically for those incapable of work, such as orphans and cripples, for the greater glory of God. This notion often resulted in such striking phenomena as dressing institutionalized orphans in uniforms reminiscent of fool's attire and parading them through the streets of Amsterdam to divine services with the greatest possible fanfare. Care for the poor was oriented to the goal of discouraging the slothful. In any case, charity itself became a rationalized "enterprise," and its religious significance was therefore eliminated or even transformed into the opposite significance. This was the situation in consistent ascetic and rationalized religions.

***

The pious Puritan could demonstrate his religious merit through his economic activity because he did nothing ethically reprehensible, he did not resort to any lax interpretations of religious codes or to systems of double moralities, and he did not act in a manner that could be indifferent or even reprehensible in the general realm of ethical validity. On the contrary, the Puritan could demonstrate his religious merit precisely in his economic activity. He acted in business with the best possible conscience, since through his rationalistic and legal behavior in his business activity he was factually objectifying the rational methodology of his total life pattern. He legitimated his ethical pattern in his own eyes, and indeed within the circle of his own community, by the extent to which the absolute—not relativized—unassailability of his economic conduct remained beyond question. No really pious Puritan—and this is the crucial point—could have regarded as pleasing to God any profit derived from usury, exploitation of another's mistake, haggling and sharp dealing, or participation in political or colonial exploitation. Quakers and Baptists believed their religious merit to be certified before all mankind by such practices as their fixed prices and their absolutely reliable business relationships with everyone, unconditionally legal and devoid of cupidity. Precisely such practices promoted the irreligious to trade with them rather than with their own kind, and to entrust their money to the trust companies or limited liability enterprises of the religious sectarians rather than those of their own people—all of which made the religious sectarians wealthy, even as their business practices certified them before their God.

The Ironic Consequences of Protestant Asceticism

One of the fundamental elements of the spirit of modern capitalism, and not only of that but of all modern culture, rational conduct on the basis of the idea of the calling was born—that is what this discussion has sought to demonstrate—from the spirit of Christian asceticism.

The Puritan wanted to work in a calling; we are forced to do so. For when asceticism was carried out of monastic cells into everyday life, and began to dominate worldly morality, it did its part in building the tremendous cosmos of the modern economic order. This order is now bound to the technical and economic conditions of machine production which today determine the lives of all the individuals who are born into this mechanism, not only those directly [concerned] with economic acquisition, with irresistible force.

Perhaps it will so determine them until the last ton of fossilized coal is burnt.

Since asceticism undertook to remodel the world and to work out its ideals in the world, material goods have gained an increasing and finally an inexorable power over the lives of men as at no previous period in history. The idea of duty in one's calling prowls about in our lives like the ghost of dead religious beliefs. Where the fulfillment of the calling cannot directly be related to the highest spiritual and cultural values, or when, on the other hand, it need not be felt simply as economic compulsion, the individual generally abandons the attempt to justify it at all. In the field of its highest development, in the United States, the pursuit of wealth, stripped of its religious and ethical meaning, tends to become associated with purely mundane passions, which often actually give it the character of sport.

No one knows who will live in this cage in the future, or whether at the end of this tremendous development entirely new prophets will arise, or there will be a great rebirth of old ideas and ideals, or, if neither, mechanized petrification, embellished with a sort of convulsive self-importance. For of the last stage of this cultural development, it might well be truly said: "Specialists without spirit, sensualists without heart; this nullity imagines that it has attained a level of civilization never before achieved."

Review

1. In what ways are ascetic means and ascetic principles identical, according to Weber?

2. How does Weber define and describe the Puritan Ethic?

3. What function do the sacraments have for Catholics?

4. According to Weber, how has the rise of Protestantism determined the role of material goods in people's lives?

Application

Interview a Catholic and a member of a very traditional Protestant denomination.

Address the following, relating to each person's attitudes on each:

a. fate and salvation and the existence of an afterlife

b. money, wealth, profit, and property ownership

c. work—a necessary evil, pleasure, or means to salvation

d. atonement for sins

e. asceticism—a rational, disciplined life versus enjoyment of people and worldly pleasures

f. time

g. sex

h. sports participation

i. beggars, the poor, and charity

31
Approaches to the Iron Cage

Reconstructing the Bars of Weber's Metaphor

Jay Klagge

At *the turn of the century, Max Weber's writings stimulated interest in the subject of bureaucracy. Weber viewed a* **bureaucracy** *as the most rational, efficient, and predictable way to carry out administrative tasks. Indeed, if you think carefully about the six characteristics of bureaucracy identified by Weber and noted in this article, you would find it difficult or perhaps even impossible to conceive of an alternative form of organization that would be as efficient.*

In a complex, industrial society, bureaucracies are essential. They grow in number and size and eventually become dominant in all kinds of institutions. In fact, whether the prevailing economic ideology of a nation is capitalist, socialist, or communist, the dominant form of organization is the bureaucracy.

Although he recognized its fundamental rationality, Weber had serious reservations about bureaucracy. He believed that its influence on every aspect of life could erode individual freedom and responsibility and that its structuring of behavior could suppress human feelings and values.

Klagge uses Weber's metaphor of the "iron cage" but argues that the metaphor can apply to three very different kinds of organizations. One incorporates all the negative images, another all the positive images, and the third suggests a new and more humane direction for the modern bureaucracy.

Debate about the merits and demerits of bureaucracy has rung in the halls of American academia since the notion was popularized in the 1940s. The classic battles in public administration have revolved around the major tenets of bureaucracy. *Friedrich v. Finer* in the 1940s, *Simon v. Argyris* in the 1970s, and *Goodsell v. Hummel* in the 1980s are examples of the longevity of this debate. The purpose of this article is to refuel and refine the debate for the 1990s. In this article, Weber's metaphor of the "iron cage" is variously reconstructed and used as the unit of analysis for understanding bureaucracy. The two traditional views of bureaucracy are presented en route to the development of a third view—another contender in the battle over bureaucracy.

People use the term bureaucracy to refer to various phenomena. Max Weber, the German sociologist credited with the original conception, used the term as shorthand for a model of modern organizational structure. In Weber's model, bureaucratic organizations had the following characteristics: functional division of labor; hierarchy of authority vested in legal positions; written procedures, records, and files; thoroughly trained, expert employees; specific standards of work and output; and formal rules and policies equally binding on management and labor (Weber, 1968). Academics often use the word bureaucracy when referring to the organizational manipulation of power and people. They see bureaucrats as dehumanizing villains or dehumanized victims of a system that robs people of their individuality and moral instincts (Hummel, 1987). Most people today use the term bureaucracy in a pejorative sense to refer to inefficiency, incompetence, red tape, or government (Goodsell, 1985). In this article the term bureaucracy is used to refer to the major structures and strictures common to most large organizations. This definition corresponds to Weber's and to those generally found in management literature.

Weber clearly understood the dual potentials of bureaucracy as an organizing structure. His keen insight foresaw the benefits to be reaped from the efficiencies achievable through bureaucracy. The stability, reliability, precision, and discipline brought to the workplace by bureaucracy could yield continually higher levels of productivity and higher standards of living (Weber, 1968). Yet Weber's keen instinct told him that this very structure could also become for mankind an iron cage (Weber, 1958, p. 181). Bureaucracy could become a rigid structure in which human feelings and values could be easily lost. Weber's original use of the metaphor of the iron cage was intended as a judgment on institutional constraints—it presented a negative view of bureaucracy. Weber's view is summarized nicely by the statement that "the fate of our times" has given us an "iron cage of a specialized, vocational humanity compelled to renounce the Faustian universality of humankind and to live within a rationalized and disenchanted world" (Scaff, 1989, p. 5).

This article explores two additional reconstructions of Weber's original metaphor. These reconstructions change the meaning of the metaphor and alter our interpretation of bureaucracy.

Metaphors, Perceptual Filters, and 'Reality' Construction

Before exploring bureaucracy using reconstructions of the iron cage metaphor, it is important to understand the nature of metaphoric communication. Metaphors help us understand one thing in terms of another. If bureaucracy can be understood by the metaphor of the iron cage, the major attributes of an iron cage must be attributable to bureaucracy. Our understanding of an iron cage will immediately highlight for us significant aspects of the nature of bureaucracy. At the same time, however, our understanding of the iron cage will hide from us other aspects of bureaucracy. The phenomenon of metaphors highlighting and hiding the true nature of the referent object or reality occurs with all metaphors (Lakoff & Johnson, 1980). In other words, no metaphor is neutral; each metaphor is interpretive of the reality it attempts to describe.

We can use Weber's original metaphor of the iron cage to understand the nature of bureaucracy as long as we recognize how this understanding of the metaphor will set our perceptual filters and construct the "reality" we see. If we get trapped by Weber's negative view of the iron cage metaphor, we will perceive bureaucracy through limited perceptual filters. A limited and faulty view of bureaucracy and reality will result.

The remainder of this article presents three constructions of the metaphor of the iron cage. The first construction is Weber's original. It sees the iron cage as a prisoner's structure holding human beings captive within the organization. The second is a reconstruction of Weber's metaphor. It sees the iron cage as the prerequisite structure required for work to occur in an organized manner. These first and second views are those commonly held. They compete with one another as diametrically opposing views. The third view is different. It has not been greatly explored in public administration. It reconstructs the iron cage as a playground structure. This reconstruction of the iron cage metaphor receives extended treatment and is offered to scholars and practitioners for further consideration.

The Iron Cage as Prisoner's Structure

The iron cage as a prisoner's structure constitutes the first metaphor. Prisoners are held captive by the structure of an iron cage within which iron bars preclude the prisoner from escaping to freedom. Iron bars constrain the lives of human beings as the iron cage permeates the lives of individuals, curtailing their actions and corrupting their attitudes. A jail cell is the image brought to mind by the metaphor tj2of iron cage as a prisoner's structure. Within the iron cage dwell the inmates—prisoners and captives. Life for these unwilling participants is dead, dull, stultified, and restricted, for neither movement nor activities are free. Constraint is the operative word. In sum, the iron cage serves only to imprison those who inhabit its environs.

When the iron cage of bureaucracy is viewed as a prisoner's structure, the foregoing metaphoric description applies. In this metaphor, the constraints of organizational hierarchy and rules become prison bars. In the modern organization, an iron cage of hierarchy and rules imprisons the entire entity. Inside this iron cage are the individuals who have been sentenced to endure inhospitable and inhumane treatment. Lingering within the prison walls are listless human forms constantly beckoned to do the bidding of functional and operational systems that serve only the needs and demands of the organization. In sum, the iron cage of bureaucracy serves to take the rights of freedom, selfhood, and creativity from those held in its bonds.

It is no wonder that those who view the iron cage as a prisoner's structure tend to attribute negative outcomes to bureaucracy. Figure 31.1 summarizes some of the negative outcomes attributed to bureaucracy. Negative outcomes from the prisoner's structure view of the iron cage of bureaucracy accrue societally, organizationally, interpersonally, and personally. Societally, the iron cage is viewed as being the enemy of democracy and community. For Americans this means the violation of our basic social contract. Organizationally, the iron cage as a prisoner's structure affects managers and workers. Managers become self-serving, self-perpetuating, power-hungry overlords. Workers become unadaptive and uncreative underlings awaiting assignments from the boss. Interpersonally, communication and openness are destroyed. Communication is replaced by jargon and groupspeak. Openness wanes as power substitutes for expertise in the decision-making process. Interpersonally, fear becomes the motivator. An unhealthy fear of failure to please the boss replaces a healthy concern for doing one's best. Personally, the prisoner's structure of the iron cage afflicts individuals by taking away their humanity, meaning, and responsibility. In the words of Gareth Morgan (1986), organizations can become a psychic prison. The freedom of people to choose and act is restrained by the iron cage, and two unique qualities of mankind are diminished—creativity is stamped out and ethical behavior is reduced. In this metaphor, society, organizations, relationships, and individuals are held hostage in the prisoner's structure of the iron cage.,

Figure 31.1
Iron Cage as Prisoner's Structure— Negatives Attributed to Bureaucracy

Societal negatives	Interpersonal negatives
Democracy is lessened	Jargon substitutes for communication
Community is lessened	Power substitutes for expertise
Society is lessened	Fear becomes major motivator
Organizational negatives	**Personal negatives**
Unadaptive	Stifles humanity
Uncreative	Lowers human meaning
Self-serving	Lowers personal responsibility
Centralizes power	Reduces human freedom
Disguises power	Stamps out creativity
Top-down over bottom-up	Reduces ethical behavior

SOURCES: Denhardt (1981), Goodsell (1985), Hummel (1987), Perrow (1986).

The Iron Cage as Prerequisite Structure

The iron cage as prerequisite structure constitutes the second metaphor. Modern edifices require the structure provided by an iron cage in the same way as foundations give support to forms. Forms give structure to functions. In the case of the modern high-rise building, an iron cage of steel girders frames the entire edifice. On this iron cage are hung the "curtain" walls that form the exterior of the building, while woven throughout this iron cage are the mechanical and electrical systems that make the interior of the building habitable. In sum, the iron cage serves to give form and function to those who inhabit its environs.

When the iron cage of bureaucracy is viewed as prerequisite structure, the foregoing metaphoric description applies. In this metaphor, organizations are similar to buildings. Prerequisite structure provides the framework upon which other organizational functions are constructed. In the modern organization, an iron cage of hierarchy and rules frames the entire entity. On this iron cage are hung the curtain walls that form the exterior boundaries of the organization. Woven throughout this iron cage are the functional and operational systems that assist those within the organization to fulfill their roles. In sum, the iron cage of bureaucracy serves to give form and function to the work and lives of the members of the organization.

Those who view the iron cage as prerequisite structure tend to attribute positive outcomes to bureaucracy. Figure 31.2 shows some of the positive outcomes attributed to bureaucracy. Positive outcomes from the prerequisite structure view of the iron cage of bureaucracy accrue societally, organizationally, interpersonally, and personally. Societally, the iron cage is viewed as being the precursor of the good life. In the private sector, goods, products, and services are provided at the lowest cost per unit by the structures of bureaucracy. In the public sector, the public good is served and the public interest protected by the organizing and equalizing structures of the iron cage. Organizationally, the iron cage brings order to systems, processes, and people. Systems are given direction, rationality, and stability by the iron cage; processes are made efficient, productive, and predictable through the controls of bureaucracy; and people are given accountability in the dual terms of responsibility and empowerment by the prerequisite structure of the iron cage. Interpersonally, equity and fairness arise from clear standards and defined expectations. Authority is identified through the establishment of interpersonal boundaries. Personally, the prerequisite structure of the iron cage affords individuals the opportunity to develop their own areas of expertise. Skills-based power, work, merit, and compensation are also made possible by the iron cage as clear responsibilities for the worker make individual and team success possible. Additionally, the prerequisite structure of the iron cage identifies the career ladder for those participating in the bureaucratic organization. Each of the foregoing positive outcomes is the result of the prerequisite structure provided by the iron

cage. Bureaucracy gives form to function in this architectural metaphor.

Figure 31.2
Iron Cage as Prerequisite Structure—Positives Attributed to Bureaucracy

Societal positives	Interpersonal positives
Delivers the good life	Equity and fairness
Good products and services	Clear standards and expectations
Public good is served	Identified authority
Public interest is protected	Established boundaries
Organizational positives	**Personal positives**
Efficiency and productivity	Development of expertise
Direction	Multiple power bases
Rationality and stability	Meaningful work
Control	Merit versus politics
Accountability	Clear responsibilities

SOURCES: Denhardt (1981), Goodsell (1985), Hummel (1987), Perrow (1986).

Prescriptions for the Iron Cage

Views of bureaucracy generally arise from the two preceding metaphors. Therefore, opinions about bureaucracy tend to focus on the negatives shown in Figure 31.1 or the positives in Figure 31.2. Prescriptions on how to deal with bureaucracy, however, vary more widely. For instance, from among the four authors used as sources for Figures 31.1 and 31.2, there are four distinct prescriptions for bureaucracy. In summary form, these prescriptions are as follows:

1. Death to bureaucracy: It does not deserve to live! Our new organizations should be based on work teams, communal values, functional unity, and increased communication (Hummel, 1987).

2. Life from bureaucracy: Take the goods and services we get and protect bureaucracy as a valuable social asset (Goodsell, 1985).

3. Evolve from bureaucracy: Extend bureaucracy's bounded rationality by including external environments and considering other externalities (Perrow, 1986).

4. Transcend bureaucracy: Avoid looking for new structures but look to new intrinsic values of individual autonomy and praxis (Denhardt, 1981).

Each of these prescriptions is based on acceptance of the negatives and positives listed in Figures 31.1 and 31.2. The next section sets forth another metaphor of the iron cage as a playground structure—specifically as the monkey bars or "jungle gym." It is hoped that this metaphor for the iron cage will engender additional prescriptions for public bureaucracies.

The Iron Cage as Playground Structure

The iron cage as a playground structure is a different metaphor. This metaphor sees the bureaucratic structure as a neutral backdrop requiring the action of human beings before outcomes can emerge. If those actions are unethical, stifling, lazy, or inhumane, negative outcomes will result. If, on the other hand, those human actions are ethical, creative, energetic, and humane, positive outcomes will result. Activity will be productive and enjoyable, more like creative play than laborious toil. In this metaphor, playgrounds provide apparatuses to exercise, educate, and entertain children. Apparatuses give structure to play, which makes the work of exercise fun. Play provides entertainment while requiring social contact, both of which further the child's education. In the case of the typical school yard playground, iron bars form a cage known as the monkey bars or jungle gym. On this playground apparatus ride the hopes, fears, aspirations, and imaginations of schoolchildren. Inextricably bound together with the bars of this iron cage are the physical growth, social development, and emotional glee of our youth. In sum, the rigid, cold, sterile iron cage of the monkey bars serves as a neutral framework for action, reflection, imagination, and creativity.

When the iron cage of bureaucratic structure is viewed as playground apparatus, the preceding metaphor applies. In this metaphor, bureaucratic structures of organizations are similar to the monkey bars. These structures, although rigid, cold, and sterile, provide the framework upon which and within which organization members act, reflect, imagine, and create. In this metaphor, work is recognized as the creative playground of adults. Life is given to the lifeless structure through the creativity and energy of those who engage it. Organizational life is played out in daily dramas as members give meaning, life, and ethics to the sterile structure. In sum, the iron cage of bureaucracy, being a neutral structure, calls for the creative, ethical, energetic play of adults that most of us know by the name of "work." The following idiosyncratic vignette seeks to give fuller expression to this metaphor of the iron cage as playground structure.

An Idiosyncratic Vignette

I embarked for work that typical spring morning at my typical time, with my typical cup of coffee, and drove to my typical portal to the freeway madness. Another typical day was about to begin. What possessed me to alter my routine remains unclear. Perhaps the coolness in the morning air elicited my fresh response. Maybe the invigorating scents of spring drew me to a different path. Whatever the cause, I found myself driving down a residential street past an elementary school still unsuspecting the significance of the turn I had taken.

Something hauntingly nostalgic lingers in the sounds from a playground. Children squealing with glee, chains clinking from swings in flight, ropes and feet tapping bare earth in rhythmic patterns, and rumblings and squeakings from merry-go-rounds all call one back to an earlier time; a time of innocence, a time of freedom, a time of growth, a time when all of life seemed to blossom with the burgeoning of spring. Those hauntingly nostalgic sounds reached my ear that morning as I drove past the school playground, riveting my eyes on the stage filled with children working hard at play, and raising the curtains of my mind to scenes from my own school yard days.

"Hey Todd, shoot Billy!" I yelled, "He's comin' up the back of the castle."

"Zip! Zip!" the sounds sprang from Todd's mouth, "Both my arrows gotcha Billy the Black Knight . . . you're dead for sure!" "That's the last of those varmints Todd," I heralded. Todd replied, "Hip hip hooray!" "Hip hip hooray!" "We're kings of the castle again today!" "Right Jayboy?" Yes, we were kings again! Competitive kings of the castle created from the monkey bars, the jungle gym, the iron cage . . . that playground apparatus that had become the primary place of our daily conquests.

Rounding the corner from the school and turning south toward town, I continued reminiscing on the many games we played in that iron cage. Amazingly enough, whether that hard, rigid, immovable set of metal pipes appeared to us as a mountain to be climbed, or a jungle to be explored, or a canyon to be crossed, the same mystical, magical sense of true adventure always beat within our breasts. The apparatus itself, changeless and enduring as it should have been, shared in the adventure by taking on the very forms and characteristics of the geography we explored. The external shell became the mountain's surface. The horizontal bars were the limbs of hanging jungle growth. The open spaces within the set gave canyon crevices their negative forms in space.

As I neared my office, memories still pulsed within my mind of the numerous dramas we had played out as kids in that iron cage. Sometimes as a dungeon with dark, dank walls, the cage held captives. Sometimes as a sparkling clean hospital fully staffed with doctors and nurses, the cage became a place of healing. Sometimes as a well-appointed, high-rise office building, the cage contained all the functions of business conceivable to youths. Yet to our constant wonder, that dull, gray, metal cage was able to transcend its bounds, transforming itself into perfect conformity with our images of use, purpose, meaning, and mission. The lifeless form always seemed to breathe with our visions. The motionless stand moved at our very direction. The neutral structure stretched to meet the vibrancy of the roles we chose to play.

Exactly how I made it to the parking lot, I'll never know. To have safely traversed the entire bustling city while unconsciously cuddled in the warm cocoon of my memories was miraculous. It had truly been an "unusual" commute.

Exiting the elevator on the third floor brought an abrupt return of the "usual." My secretary directly escorted me past the files and into the office. Her words ripped past me at her standard mile-a-minute pace. "The boss wants the new mission statement." "Roger wants our help in meeting a deadline." "Tom needs advice on the latest legislative proposal." "And Dale has a question about his budget allocation." "Who would you like to see first?"

After a brief pause of silence to catch my breath and to still the office air, I spoke. "Okay, Mary, let's see if I have it all straight." "Our boss, King Harry, wants to redefine and redirect his kingdom." "Roger needs help in climbing his mountain of work." "Tom is requesting guidance on his journey through the political jungle." "And Dale wants to span the canyon between needs and resources." Mary stood facing me speechless, a mildly quizzical look on her face. "Does that sound accurate?" I asked. "Yes, I believe so," she replied. "Good!" I said with renewed vigor. "I was just mulling over similar events this morning on my way to work." "I'll go see King Harry."

As I left my office I noticed out of the corner of my eye that Mary stood motionless as if glued to the floor. Stopping and leaning back through the doorway, I tried to clarify the meaning of my mutterings. "Ms. Mary, I'd like to welcome you to the iron cage. It's a place where numerous adults can simultaneously play hard at many different games of work. It's a neutral apparatus that appears hard, cold, and rigidly fixed, but actually takes form and life from the meaning and values we bring to it. It's a remarkably productive contrivance that can become a captor's prison or an instrument of health, healing, and wholeness. It all depends on the depth of character and height of energy we bring to the game." Seeing the confusion continue in Mary's eyes, and remembering that Harry was waiting, I postponed the philosophical chatter for another time. With a closing farewell I took my leave. "Mary, have a nice day, a great day! We'll talk more when I get back."

The Meaning of This Metaphor

Postmodernism sees an emerging work environment of deskilled tasks and decentering activities that will yield boredom and meaninglessness for the workers (Smart, 1992). In this new work order, individual effort and energy will be required to bring life to the sterile structures of bureaucracy. The emergence of this new work order is what gives importance to the playground apparatus metaphor for the iron cage. Whereas many have noted the similarity between work and play (Rood & Meneley, 1991), the important aspect of this metaphor is that the neutral structure of the monkey bars can become whatever the workers make it by the purpose, meaning, values, visions, mission, and energy they bring to the iron cage. Hypotheses that assert that this is truer for individuals who occupy higher level positions in bureaucracies have been found false (Koberg & Hood, 1991). In the postmodern era, the personal energy, reflection, imagination, and creativity required of each worker will be greatly increased. All workers will need to energize themselves and those around them within the neutral structures of bureaucracy if personal, organizational, and societal benefits are to result (Rood & Meneley, 1991). Some researchers have suggested a regimen for identifying and removing obstacles in the way of unlocking the personal action, reflection, imagination, and creativity of each worker in the iron cage. Some of these blocks are strategically founded, some are value based, some are perceptual, and some result from an incomplete or flawed self-image (Richards & Jones, 1989). In each case, however, the remedy is the same—personal energy and imagination are required to turn the neutral iron cage into a positive framework for reflective and meaningful action.

Metaphors Compared

Metaphors are comprehended by reference to our own personal experiences. No metaphor can be fully understood, appreciated, or applied without an adequate experiential base. The richer our experiential base is relative to a given metaphor, the more meaningful, the more powerful, and the stronger that metaphor will be for us (Lakoff & Johnson, 1980). The three metaphors for the iron cage of bureaucracy can be examined in light of their linkage to our experience base.

The iron cage as a prisoner's structure is a stronger, more powerful metaphor. The strength of this metaphor does not arise from our personal experience with prisons. Most of us have not been incarcerated. Experientially, however, we have been physically restricted during some portion of our lives. Grounding, detention, or even classroom rigors provide us with an experience base similar to imprisonment. If we extend this metaphor to include emotional or creative restrictions, even more of us can experientially identify bureaucratic structures with bondages. Rules and regulations can be easily seen through perceptual filters that reveal them as restrictions rather than as guides or safeguards.

Therefore, this metaphor tends to be rather strong, which may explain the ease with which we embrace it and the negative aspects of bureaucracy that flow from it. It is also true, however, that this metaphor has much to tell us about how life in a bureaucracy really is. Often, this metaphor grows out of personal experience in an organization and not from the adoption of an a priori view. This reality also makes the prisoner's structure a strong metaphor for bureaucracy.

The iron cage as prerequisite structure is a weaker, less powerful, metaphor because most people lack an experiential basis for viewing bureaucracy as the iron cage of prerequisite structure. Architects, engineers, and contractors are the exception because their livelihoods are literally built upon solid structures. For the rest of us our experiential base for understanding and applying this metaphor arises solely from the referent reality of living with rigid organizational rules. Therefore, this tends to be a metaphor that is hard to relate to our experience. This fact may explain the general reluctance of people to fully embrace it or to affirm the positive aspects of bureaucracy that flow from it. It is also true that this metaphor is better seen from the outside of the structure than it is from the inside. Because most organization members are inside the structure and not outside like the customers, clients, and citizens who benefit from the organization's outputs, they fail to see the benefits of the prerequisite structure. This phenomenon may also help to explain why the structural metaphor for bureaucracy is less prevalent in the literature than the prison metaphor.

The iron cage as a playground structure should be the strongest metaphor. We all have childhood experiences based on the playground. Strong physical, emotional, psychological, and social experiences populate the memory of our school yard days. Relating the work of our adult life to the play of our childhood is only one of the positive linkages afforded us in this metaphor. A second, and in this regard more important, linkage of this metaphor is its neutrality regarding bureaucracy. Using this metaphor, one need not view bureaucracy as a "savior," as in the case of the structure metaphor, or as a "villain," as in the case of the prison metaphor. In this metaphor, the iron cage is a neutral apparatus upon which either positive or negative acts may occur. What is meant by the term neutral in this instance is that the iron cage is merely an apparatus yielding no inherent positive or negative outcomes. How that apparatus is used, on the other hand, certainly can yield positive or negative outcomes. Softening the rigidity of the iron bars, warming the coldness of the cage, and breathing life into the sterile structure can result in positive outcomes. Our childhood memories on the iron cage ought to be the most powerful, positive, and important referents provided by this metaphor. Although research is scant, it seems that this metaphor should be the most beneficial, because no unproductive time is spent attacking or defending the iron cage itself. Rather, more important things receive attention—things like the actions, reflections, and imaginations of people, as well as the social encounters among them. In pursuit of these more important things, everyone has a rich childhood playground experience base from which to draw. Granted this experience base provides positive and negative memories, friendly and unfriendly encounters, and exciting and boring scenes, but these experiences that require energy, imagination, creativity, and commitment also correspond to life in a public bureaucracy.

A Call to Research and Praxis

If a rich experiential base means that a metaphor will be meaningful to us, then the metaphor of the iron cage as a playground structure is worthy of additional examination (Lakoff & Johnson, 1980). If so, public administration scholars and practitioners interested in bureaucratic organization theory and the functioning of the modern public bureaucracy should give serious consideration to this metaphor. The relationship of work to play is worthy of specific exploration in the public sector. The relationship between the social aspects of life in the iron cage and life on the monkey bars begs research beyond the sketches provided by Robert Fulghum in *All I Need to Know I Learned in Kindergarten*. The relationship of visionary imagination and reality creation warrants probing in the public sector along with the notion of ethical, energetic action.

If, as Lakoff and Johnson suggest, we live by metaphors, then exploration of the reconstructed versions of the iron cage is a wise and potentially rewarding pursuit. If metaphors can create realities, guide future action, and reinforce experiential coherence, then reflective, creative, ethical, energetic, playful action on the iron cage can become a daily experience for those living in this metaphor for bureaucracy—the iron cage as playground structure for the public sector agency.

References

Denhardt, R. B. (1981). In the shadow of organization. Lawrence: University Press of Kansas.

Goodsell, C. T. (1985). The case for bureaucracy: a public administration polemic (2nd ed.). Chatham, NJ: Chatham House Publishers.

Hummel, R. P. (1987). The bureaucratic experience (3rd ed.). New York: St. Martin's.

Koberg, C., & Hood, J. N. (1991). Cultures and creativity within hierarchical organizations. Journal of Business and Psychology, 6(2), 265–271.

Lakoff, G., & Johnson, M. (1980). Metaphors we live by. Chicago: University of Chicago Press.

Morgan, G. (1986). Images of Organization. Beverly Hills, CA: Sage.

Perrow, C. (1986). Complex organizations: A critical essay (3rd ed.). New York: McGraw-Hill.

Richards, T., & Jones, L. (1989). Creativity audit: A diagnostic approach to overcoming blocks. Management Decision, 27(1), 58–63.

Rood, R. P., & Meneley, B. L. (1991). Serious play at work. Personnel Journal, 70, 90–99.

Scaff, L. A. (1989). Fleeing the iron cage: Culture, politics, and modernity in the thought of Max Weber. Los Angeles: University of California Press.

Smart, B. (1992). Modern conditions, postmodern controversies. New York: Routledge, Chapman and Hall.

Weber, M. (1958). The Protestant ethic and the spirit of capitalism (T. Parsons, Trans.). New York: Scribners.

Weber, M. (1968). Economy and society: An outline of interpretive sociology (3 vols.; G. Roth & C. Wittch, Eds., E. Fischoff, Trans.). New York: Bedminister.

Review

1. What characteristics does the "iron cage as prisoner's structure" attribute to bureaucracies?

2. What characteristics does the "iron cage as prerequisite structure" attribute to bureaucracies?

3. What kind of organization is described in the metaphor of the "iron cage as playground structure"?

4. How would you compare and critique the three metaphors?

Applications

1. A negative criticism of bureaucracies is that officials become timid and tend to follow the lines of least resistance, for example, by carrying out directives even when they consider them wrong. Describe such a situation that you or someone you know has witnessed or in which you have taken part. What was the effect on you? On the other persons involved? On the organization's purpose and goals? What could be done to minimize the chances of similar situations in the future?

2. Use Figures 31.1 and 31.2 and develop a similar figure for the third metaphor—the iron cage as playground structure. Ask a number of people who work in various kinds of bureaucracies—educational, industrial, religious, governmental—to read the three descriptions and tell you the extent to which each of them describes the organizations in which they work. If your results were valid for all bureaucracies, what conclusions would you draw? Be sure to note which of the three metaphors most accurately describes the organizations and whether the bureaucracies differ by institutional area.

Part Four

Education

Education is the institution involved in socializing people to function in their society. In the United States, education enables people to be effective citizens, to prepare for upward mobility, and to engage in personal development. The value that Americans place on education is reflected in the fact that the proportion of Americans completing four or more years of high school rose from 41.1 percent to 83.4 percent between 1960 and 1999, and the proportion completing four or more years of college rose from 7.7 percent to 25.2 percent.

The two selections in this part illustrate that education in the United States has many problems. The first selection examines the plight of ghetto schools. The second looks at a common problem in schools today—a culture that fosters cruelty and violence. ✦

32
Savage Inequalities

Jonathan Kozol

In theory, social institutions operate for the well-being of people. The government protects citizens and provides essential services for them. The economy allows people to fulfill their basic needs and aspirations. Education provides people with the skills necessary to function in the economy and with the necessary information and understanding to pursue meaningful lives.

However, the fact that inequality pervades every society suggests that institutions do not benefit everyone equally. We have already presented selections about the unequal division of labor in the family and inequalities in the economy. In this selection, we encounter a graphic picture of inequality in education— inequality that exists among schools in the same district.

Americans value education. We tout it as a necessary resource for social mobility and as essential to the pursuit of a fulfilling life. Indeed, education functions in this way for some people, but not for all. Kozol, the author of this selection, has taught in ghetto schools where students face severe hurdles to an adequate education. Those hurdles include inadequate supplies and few well-trained teachers; a climate of fear engendered by gangs and weapons; a student culture of contempt for learning; and homes that may offer little in the way of preparation and support. In sum, the students are in a situation of ritualized deprivation—a school atmosphere in which the rituals of teaching and learning go on while the students focus more on surviving than on learning.

In order to find Public School 261 in District 10, a visitor is told to look for a mortician's office. The funeral home, which faces Jerome Avenue in the North Bronx, is easy to identify by its green awning. The school is next door, in a former roller-skating rink. No sign identifies the building as a school. A metal awning frame without an awning supports a flagpole, but there is no flag.

In the street in front of the school there is an elevated public transit line. Heavy traffic fills the street. The existence of the school is virtually concealed within this crowded city block.

In a vestibule between the outer and inner glass doors of the school there is a sign with these words: "All children are capable of learning."

Beyond the inner doors a guard is seated. The lobby is long and narrow. The ceiling is low. There are no windows. All the teachers that I see at first are middle-aged white women. The principal, who is also a white woman, tells me that the school's "capacity" is 900 but that there are 1,300 children here. The size of classes for fifth and sixth grade children in New York, she says, is "capped" at 32, but she says that class size in the school goes "up to 34." (I later see classes, however, as large as 37.) Classes for younger children, she goes on, are "capped at 25," but a school can go above this limit if it puts an extra adult in the room. Lack of space, she says, prevents the school from operating a prekindergarten program.

I ask the principal where her children go to school. They are enrolled in private school, she says.

"Lunchtime is a challenge for us," she explains. "Limited space obliges us to do it in three shifts, 450 children at a time."

Textbooks are scarce and children have to share their social studies books. The principal says there is one full-time pupil counselor and another who is here two days a week: a ratio of 930 children to one counselor. The carpets are patched and sometimes taped together to conceal an open space. "I could use some new rugs," she observes.

To make up for the building's lack of windows and the crowded feeling that results, the staff puts plants and fish tanks in the corridors. Some of the plants are flourishing. Two boys, released from class, are in a corridor beside a tank, their noses pressed against the glass. A school of pinkish fish inside the tank are darting back and forth. Farther down the corridor a small Hispanic girl is watering the plants.

Two first grade classes share a single room without a window, divided only by a blackboard. Four kindergartens and a sixth grade class of Spanish-speaking children have been packed into a single room in which, again, there is no window. A second grade bilingual class of 37 children has its own room but again there is no window.

By eleven o'clock, the lunchroom is already packed with appetite and life. The kids line up to get their meals, then eat them in ten minutes. After that, with no place they can go to play, they sit and wait until it's time to line up and go back to class.

On the second floor I visit four classes taking place within another undivided space. The room has a low ceiling. File cabinets and movable blackboards give a small degree of isolation to each class. Again, there are no windows.

The library is a tiny, windowless and claustrophobic room. I count approximately 700 books. Seeing no reference books, I ask a teacher if encyclopedias and other reference books are kept in classrooms.

"We don't have encyclopedias in classrooms," she replies. "That is for the suburbs."

The school, I am told, has 26 computers for its 1,300 children. There is one small gym and children get one period, and sometimes two, each week. Recess, however, is not possible because there is no playground. "Head Start," the principal says, "scarcely exists in District 10. We have no space." The school, I am told, is 90 percent black and Hispanic; the other 10 percent are Asian, white or Middle Eastern.

In a sixth grade social studies class the walls are bare of words or decorations. There seems to be no ventilation system, or, if one exists, it isn't working.

The class discusses the Nile River and the Fertile Crescent.

The teacher, in a droning voice: "How is it useful that these civilizations developed close to rivers?"

A child, in a good loud voice: "What kind of question is that?"

In my notes I find these words: "An uncomfortable feeling—being in a building with no windows. There are metal ducts across the room. Do they give air? I feel asphyxiated . . ."

On the top floor of the school, a sixth grade of 30 children shares a room with 29 bilingual second graders. Because of the high class size there is an assistant with each teacher. This means that 59 children and four grown-ups—63 in all—must share a room that, in a suburban school, would hold no more than 20 children and one teacher. There are, at least, some outside windows in this room—it is the only room with windows in the school—and the room has a high ceiling. It is a relief to see some daylight.

I return to see the kindergarten classes on the ground floor and feel stifled once again by lack of air and the low ceiling. Nearly 120 children and adults are doing what they can to make the best of things: 80 children in four kindergarten classes, 30 children in the sixth grade class, and about eight grown-ups who are aides and teachers. The kindergarten children sitting on the worn rug, which is patched with tape, look up at me and turn their heads to follow me as I walk past them.

As I leave the school, a sixth grade teacher stops to talk. I ask her, "Is there air conditioning in warmer weather?"

Teachers, while inside the building, are reluctant to give answers to this kind of question. Outside, on the sidewalk, she is less constrained: "I had an awful room last year. In the winter it was 56 degrees. In the summer it was up to 90. It was sweltering."

I ask her, "Do the children ever comment on the building?"

"They don't say," she answers, "but they know."

I ask her if they see it as a racial message.

"All these children see TV," she says. "They know what suburban schools are like. Then they look around them at their school. This was a roller-rink, you know. . . . They don't comment on it but you see it in their eyes. They understand."

On the following morning I visit P.S. 79, another elementary school in the same district. "We work under difficult circumstances," says the principal, James Carter, who is black. "The school was built to hold one thousand students. We have 1,550. We are badly overcrowded. We need smaller classes but, to do this, we would need more space. I can't add five teachers. I would have no place to put them."

Some experts, I observe, believe that class size isn't a real issue. He dismisses this abruptly. "It doesn't take a genius to discover that you learn more in a smaller class. I have to bus some 60 kindergarten children elsewhere, since I have no space for them. When they return next year, where do I put them?

"I can't set up a computer lab. I have no room. I had to put a class into the library. I have no librarian. There are two gymnasiums upstairs but they cannot be used for sports. We hold more classes there. It's unfair to measure us against the suburbs. They have 17 to 20 children in a class. Average class size in this school is 30.

"The school is 29 percent black, 70 percent Hispanic. Few of these kids get Head Start. There is no space in the district. Of 200 kindergarten children, 50 maybe get some kind of preschool."

I ask him how much difference preschool makes.

"Those who get it do appreciably better. I can't overestimate its impact but, as I have said, we have no space."

The school tracks children by ability, he says. "There are five to seven levels in each grade. The highest level is equivalent to 'gifted' but it's not a full-scale gifted program. We don't have the funds. We have no science room. The science teachers carry their equipment with them."

We sit and talk within the nurse's room. The window is broken. There are two holes in the ceiling. About a quarter of the ceiling has been patched and covered with a plastic garbage bag.

"Ideal class size for these kids would be 15 to 20. Will these children ever get what white kids in the suburbs take for granted? I don't think so. If you ask me why, I'd have to speak of race and social class. I don't think the powers that be in New York City understand, or want to understand, that if they do not give

these children a sufficient education to lead healthy and productive lives, we will be their victims later on. We'll pay the price someday—in violence, in economic costs. I despair of making this appeal in any terms but these. You cannot issue an appeal to conscience in New York today. The fair-play argument won't be accepted. So you speak of violence and hope that it will scare the city into action."

While we talk, three children who look six or seven years old come to the door and ask to see the nurse, who isn't in the school today. One of the children, a Puerto Rican girl, looks haggard. "I have a pain in my tooth," she says. The principal says, "The nurse is out. Why don't you call your mother?" The child says, "My mother doesn't have a phone." The principal sighs. "Then go back to your class." When she leaves, the principal is angry. "It's amazing to me that these children ever make it with the obstacles they face. Many do care and they do try, but there's a feeling of despair. The parents of these children want the same things for their children that the parents in the suburbs want. Drugs are not the cause of this. They are the symptom. Nonetheless, they're used by people in the suburbs and rich people in Manhattan as another reason to keep children of poor people at a distance."

I ask him, "Will white children and black children ever go to school together in New York?"

"I don't see it," he replies. "I just don't think it's going to happen. It's a dream. I simply do not see white folks in Riverdale agreeing to cross-bus with kids like these. A few, maybe. Very few. I don't think I'll live to see it happen."

I ask him whether race is the decisive factor. Many experts, I observe, believe that wealth is more important in determining these inequalities.

"This," he says—and sweeps his hand around him at the room, the garbage bag, the ceiling—"would not happen to white children."

In a kindergarten class the children sit cross-legged on a carpet in a space between two walls of books. Their 26 faces are turned up to watch their teacher, an elderly black woman. A little boy who sits beside me is involved in trying to tie bows in his shoelaces. The children sing a song: "Lift Every Voice." On the wall are these handwritten words: "Beautiful, also, are the souls of my people."

In a very small room on the fourth floor, 52 people in two classes do their best to teach and learn. Both are first grade classes. One, I am informed, is "low ability." The other is bilingual.

"The room is barely large enough for one class," says the principal.

The room is 25 by 50 feet. There are 26 first graders and two adults on the left, 22 others and two adults on the right. On the wall there is the picture of a small white child, circled by a Valentine, and a Gainsborough painting of a child in a formal dress.

"We are handicapped by scarcity," one of the teachers says. "One fifth of these children may be at grade level by the year's end."

A boy who may be seven years old climbs on my lap without an invitation and removes my glasses. He studies my face and runs his fingers through my hair. "You have nice hair," he says. I ask him where he lives and he replies, "Times Square Hotel," which is a homeless shelter in Manhattan.

I ask him how he gets here.

"With my father. On the train," he says.

"How long does it take?"

"It takes an hour and a half."

I ask him when he leaves his home.

"My mother wakes me up at five o'clock."

"When do you leave?"

"Six-thirty."

I ask him how he gets back to Times Square.

"My father comes to get me after school."

From my notes: "He rides the train three hours every day in order to attend this segregated school. It would be a shorter ride to Riverdale. There are rapid shuttle-vans that make that trip in only 20 minutes. Why not let him go to school right in Manhattan, for that matter?"

At three o'clock the nurse arrives to do her recordkeeping. She tells me she is here three days a week. "The public hospital we use for an emergency is called North Central. It's not a hospital that I will use if I am given any choice. Clinics in the private hospitals are far more likely to be staffed by an experienced physician."

She hesitates a bit as I take out my pen, but then goes on: "I'll give you an example. A little girl I saw last week in school was trembling and shaking and could not control the motions of her arms. I was concerned and called her home. Her mother came right up to school and took her to North Central. The intern concluded that the child was upset by 'family matters'—nothing more—that there was nothing wrong with her. The mother was offended by the diagnosis. She did not appreciate his words or his assumptions. The truth is, there was nothing wrong at home. She brought the child back to school. I thought that she was ill. I told her mother, 'Go to Montefiore.' It's a private hospital, and well respected. She took my advice, thank God. It turned out that the child had a neurological disorder. She is now in treatment.

"This is the kind of thing our children face. Am I saying that the city underserves this population? You can draw your own conclusions."

Out on the street, it takes a full half hour to flag down a cab. Taxi drivers in New York are sometimes disconcertingly direct in what they say. When they are contemptuous of poor black people, their contempt is unadorned. When they're sympathetic and compassionate, their observations often go right to the heart of things. "Oh . . . they neglect these children," says the driver. "They leave them in the streets and slums to live and die." We stop at a light. Outside the window of the taxi, aimless men are standing in a semicircle while another man is working on his car. Old four-story buildings with their windows boarded, cracked or missing are on every side.

I ask the driver where he's from. He says Afghanistan. Turning in his seat, he gestures at the street and shrugs. "If you don't, as an American, begin to give these kids the kind of education that you give the kids of Donald Trump, you're asking for disaster."

Two months later, on a day in May, I visit an elementary school in Riverdale. The dogwoods and magnolias on the lawn in front of P.S. 24 are in full blossom on the day I visit.

There is a well-tended park across the street, another larger park three blocks away. To the left of the school is a playground for small children, with an innovative jungle gym, a slide and several climbing toys. Behind the school there are two playing fields for older kids. The grass around the school is neatly trimmed.

The neighborhood around the school, by no means the richest part of Riverdale, is nonetheless expensive and quite beautiful. Residences in the area—some of which are large, free-standing houses, others condominiums in solid redbrick buildings—sell for prices in the region of $400,000; but some of the larger Tudor houses on the winding and tree-shaded streets close to the school can cost up to $1 million. The excellence of P.S. 24, according to the principal, adds to the value of these homes. Advertisements in the *New York Times* will frequently inform prospective buyers that a house is "in the neighborhood of P.S. 24."

The school serves 825 children in the kindergarten through sixth grade. This is approximately half the student population crowded into P.S. 79, where 1,550 children fill a space intended for 1,000, and a great deal smaller than the 1,300 children packed into the former skating rink; but the principal of P.S. 24, a capable and energetic man named David Rothstein, still regards it as excessive for an elementary school.

The school is integrated in the strict sense that the middle- and upper-middle-class white children here do occupy a building that contains some Asian and Hispanic and black children; but there is little integration in the classrooms since the vast majority of the Hispanic and black children are assigned to "special" classes on the basis of evaluations that have classified them "EMR"—"educable mentally retarded"—or else, in the worst of cases, "TMR"—"trainable mentally retarded."

I ask the principal if any of his students qualify for free-lunch programs. "About 130 do," he says. "Perhaps another 35 receive their lunches at reduced price. Most of these kids are in the special classes. They do not come from this neighborhood."

The very few nonwhite children that one sees in mainstream classes tend to be Japanese or else of other Asian origins. Riverdale, I learn, has been the residence of choice for many years to members of the diplomatic corps.

The school therefore contains effectively two separate schools: one of about 130 children, most of whom are poor, Hispanic, black, assigned to one of the 12 special classes; the other of some 700 mainstream students, almost all of whom are white or Asian.

There is a third track also—this one for the students who are labeled "talented" or "gifted." This is termed a "pullout" program since the children who are so identified remain in mainstream classrooms but are taken out for certain periods each week to be provided with intensive and, in my opinion, excellent instruction in some areas of reasoning and logic often known as "higher-order skills" in the contemporary jargon of the public schools. Children identified as "gifted" are admitted to this program in first grade and, in most cases, will remain there for six years. Even here, however, there are two tracks of the gifted. The regular gifted classes are provided with only one semester of this specialized instruction yearly. Those very few children, on the other hand, who are identified as showing the most promise are assigned, beginning in the third grade, to a program that receives a full-year regimen.

In one such class, containing ten intensely verbal and impressive fourth grade children, nine are white and one is Asian. The "special" class I enter first, by way of contrast, has twelve children of whom only one is white and none is Asian. These racial breakdowns prove to be predictive of the school-wide pattern.

In a classroom for the gifted on the first floor of the school, I ask a child what the class is doing. "Logic and syllogisms," she replies. The room is fitted with a planetarium. The principal says that all the elementary schools in District 10 were given the same planetariums ten years ago but that certain schools, because of overcrowding, have been forced to give them up. At P.S. 261, according to my notes, there was a domelike space that had been built to hold a planetarium, but the planetarium had been removed to free up space for the small library collection. P.S. 24, in contrast, has a spacious library that holds almost 8,000 books. The windows are decorated with attractive, brightly colored curtains and look out on flowering trees. The principal says that it's inadequate, but it appears spectacular to me after the cubicle that holds a meager 700 books within the former skating rink.

The district can't afford librarians, the principal says, but P.S. 24, unlike the poorer schools of District 10, can draw on educated parent volunteers who staff the room in shifts three days a week. A parent organization also raises independent funds to buy materials, including books, and will soon be running a fund-raiser to enhance the library's collection.

In a large and sunny first grade classroom that I enter next, I see 23 children, all of whom are white or Asian. In another first grade, there are 22 white children and two others who are Japanese. There is a computer in each class. Every classroom also has a modern fitted sink.

In a second grade class of 22 children, there are two black children and three Asian children. Again, there is a sink and a computer. A sixth grade social studies class has only one black child. The children have an in-class research area that holds some up-to-date resources. A set of encyclopedias (World Book, 1985) is in a rack beside a window. The children are doing a Spanish language lesson when I enter. Foreign languages begin in sixth grade at the school, but Spanish is offered also to the kindergarten children. As in every room at P.S. 24, the window shades are clean and new, the floor is neatly tiled in gray and green, and there is not a single light bulb missing.

Walking next into a special class, I see twelve children. One is white. Eleven are black. There are no Asian children. The room is half the size of mainstream classrooms. "Because of overcrowding," says the principal, "we have had to split these rooms in half." There is no computer and no sink.

I enter another special class. Of seven children, five are black, one is Hispanic, one is white. A little black boy with a large head sits in the far corner and is gazing at the ceiling. "Placement of these kids," the principal explains, "can usually be traced to neurological damage."

In my notes: "How could so many of these children be brain-damaged?"

Next door to the special class is a woodworking shop. "This shop is only for the special classes," says the principal. The children learn to punch in time cards at the door, he says, in order to prepare them for employment.

The fourth grade gifted class, in which I spend the last part of the day, is humming with excitement. "I start with these children in the first grade," says the teacher. "We pull them out of mainstream classes on the basis of their test results and other factors such as the opinion of their teachers. Out of this group, beginning in third grade, I pull out the ones who show the most potential, and they enter classes such as this one."

The curriculum they follow, she explains, "emphasizes critical thinking, reasoning and logic." The planetarium, for instance, is employed not simply for the study of the universe as it exists. "Children also are designing their own galaxies," the teacher says.

A little girl sitting around a table with her classmates speaks with perfect poise: "My name is Susan. We are in the fourth grade gifted program."

I ask them what they're doing and a child says, "My name is Laurie and we're doing problem-solving."

A rather tall, good-natured boy who is half-standing at the table tells me that his name is David. "One thing that we do," he says, "is logical thinking. Some problems, we find, have more than one good answer. We need to learn not simply to be logical in our own thinking but to show respect for someone else's logic even when an answer may be technically incorrect."

When I ask him to explain this, he goes on, "A person who gives an answer that is not 'correct' may nonetheless have done some interesting thinking that we should examine. 'Wrong' answers may be more useful to examine than correct ones."

I ask the children if reasoning and logic are innate or if they're things that you can learn.

"You know some things to start with when you enter school," Susan says. "But we also learn some things that other children don't."

I ask her to explain this.

"We know certain things that other kids don't know because we're taught them."

She has braces on her teeth. Her long brown hair falls almost to her waist. Her loose white T-shirt has the word TRI-LOGIC on the front. She tells me that Tri-Logic is her father's firm.

Laurie elaborates on the same point: "Some things you know. Some kinds of logic are inside of you to start with. There are other things that someone needs to teach you."

David expands on what the other two have said: "Everyone can think and speak in logical ways unless they have a mental problem. What this program does is bring us to a higher form of logic."

The class is writing a new "Bill of Rights." The children already know the U.S. Bill of Rights and they explain its first four items to me with precision. What they are examining today, they tell me, is the very *concept* of a "right." Then they will create their own compendium of rights according to their own analysis and definition. Along one wall of the classroom, opposite the planetarium, are seven Apple II computers on which children have developed rather subtle color animations that express the themes—of greed and domination, for example—that they also have described in writing.

"This is an upwardly mobile group," the teacher later says. "They have exposure to whatever New York City has available. Their parents may take them to the theater, to museums. . . ."

In my notes: "Six girls, four boys. Nine white, one Chinese. I am glad they have this class. But what about the others? Aren't there ten black children in the school who could enjoy this also?"

The teacher gives me a newspaper written, edited and computer-printed by her sixth grade gifted class. The children, she tells me, are provided with a link to kids in Europe for transmission of news stories.

A science story by one student asks if scientists have ever falsified their research. "Gergor Mendel," the sixth grader writes, "the Austrian monk who founded the science of genetics, published papers on his work with peas that some experts say were statistically too good to be true. Isaac Newton, who formulated the law of gravitation, relied on unseemly mathematical sleight of hand in his calculations. . . . Galileo Galilei, founder of modern scientific method, wrote about experiments that were so difficult to duplicate that colleagues doubted he had done them."

Another item in the paper, also by a sixth grade student, is less esoteric: "The Don Cossacks dance company, from Russia, is visiting the United States. The last time it toured America was 1976. . . . The Don Cossacks will be in New York City for two weeks at the Neil Simon Theater. Don't miss it!"

The tone is breezy—and so confident! That phrase—"Don't miss it!"—speaks a volume about life in Riverdale.

"What makes a good school?" asks the principal when we are talking later on. "The building and teachers are part of it, of course. But it isn't just the building and the teachers. Our kids come from good families and the neighborhood is good. In a three-block area we have a public library, a park, a junior high. . . . Our typical sixth grader reads at eighth grade level." In a quieter voice he says, "I see how hard my colleagues work in schools like P.S. 79. You have children in those neighborhoods who live in virtual hell. They enter school five years behind. What do they get?" Then, as he spreads his hands out on his desk, he says: "I have to ask myself why there should be an elementary school in District 10 with fifteen hundred children. Why should there be an elementary school within a skating rink? Why should the Board of Ed allow this? This is not the way that things should be."

Stark as the inequities in District 10 appear, educators say that they are "mild" in comparison to other situations in the city. Some of the most stunning inequality, according to a report by the Community Service Society, derives from allocations granted by state legislators to school districts where they have political allies. The poorest districts in the city get approximately 90 cents per pupil from these legislative grants, while the richest districts have been given $14 for each pupil.

Newspapers in New York City have reported other instances of the misallocation of resources. "The Board of Education," wrote the *New York Post* during July of 1987, "was hit with bombshell charges yesterday that money earmarked for fighting drug abuse and illiteracy in ghetto schools was funneled instead to schools in wealthy areas."

In receipt of extra legislative funds, according to the Post, affluent districts were funded "at a rate 14 times greater than low-income districts." The paper said the city's poorest areas were underfunded "with stunning consistency."

The report by the Community Service Society cites an official of the New York City Board of Education who remarks that there is "no point" in putting further money "into some poor districts" because, in his belief, "new teachers would not stay there." But the report observes that, in an instance where beginning teacher salaries were raised by nearly half, "that problem largely disappeared"—another interesting reminder of the difference money makes when we are willing to invest it. Nonetheless, says the report, "the perceptions that the poorest districts are beyond help still remains. . . ." Perhaps the worst result of such beliefs, says the report, is the message that resources would be "wasted on poor children." This message "trickles down to districts, schools, and classrooms." Children hear and understand this theme—they are poor investments—and behave accordingly. If society's resources would be wasted on their destinies, perhaps their own determination would be wasted too. "Expectations are a powerful force. . . ," the CSS observes.

Despite the evidence, the CSS report leans over backwards not to fuel the flames of racial indignation. "In the present climate," the report says, "suggestions of racism must be made with caution. However, it is ines-capable that these inequities are being perpetrated on [school] districts which are virtually all black and Hispanic. . . ." While the report says, very carefully, that there is no "evidence" of "deliberate individual discrimination," it nonetheless concludes that "those who allocate resources make decisions over and over again which penalize the poorest districts." Analysis of city policy, the study says, "speaks to systemic bias which constitutes a conspiracy of effect. . . . Whether consciously or not, the system writes off its poorest students."

Review

1. Compare the poor schools described by Kozol with those of your own experience.

2. What are the major deficiencies in the poor schools described by Kozol?

3. Contrast the resources and programs in the poor schools with those in Riverdale.

4. Why are resources not allocated more equitably to various schools in the district?

Applications

1. With your instructor's permission, organize a workshop for your class on inequality in education. Among other things, you can:

   a. show clips from movies that portray education in a poor neighborhood

   b. have teachers or administrators from poor and wealthy schools describe their resources and programs

   c. have students from poor and wealthy schools describe their experiences

   d. have students find and report on information culled from popular or professional writings

2. Visit a school in a poor area and one in a wealthy area. Ask for permission to sit in and observe a class for an hour. Tour both schools and note their facilities. Write up a report of your observations.

33
At School, a Cruel Culture

Darcia Harris Bowman

The school, in theory, is a place of learning. Every student is encouraged to maximize his or her potential and to discover the joy of gaining a wide range of understanding about the world in which we live. Yet as Kozol showed, a ghetto school may be a place where students must put as much effort into surviving as into learning, a place where learning is severely impeded by ritualized deprivation.

What about schools in well-to-do neighborhoods? Do they also have problems? In the 1990s the nation was shocked by a series of shootings at schools, none of which were in ghetto areas. The shootings dramatized the fact that school violence is a serious problem. Recent surveys show that literally millions of high school students have had physical fights at school at least once during a year's time (including 20 percent of males), have had property stolen or damaged at school, and have admitted to carrying a weapon to school during the 30 days prior to the survey (13 percent of males and 4 percent of females).

There is an atmosphere of fear in many of the nation's schools. Students may feel more apprehension about safety than excitement about learning opportunities as they go off to school. The threat of violence comes both from the loner who shows up one day with a gun and the known bullies who can make life miserable for others. Darcia Bowman labels this situation a "cruel culture." She notes that those who resort to shooting their classmates have often been the victims of bullying or scorn. Most bullied students do not go to such lengths, of course. But the experience of being bullied or taunted does detract from students' ability to maximize their learning. In an atmosphere of fear, the school becomes something to endure rather than a place to flourish.

Elizabeth Catherine Bush's parents hoped her life would improve after they removed her from the reach of bullies in the Jersey Shore Area School District in Pennsylvania last year and placed her in a small private school.

But even at Bishop Neumann High School—a 230-student Roman Catholic institution in nearby Williamsport with a mission to educate "in a climate of love and hope"—the teasing continued. When the distraught 14-year-old shot and injured a popular cheerleader in the school cafeteria on March 7, and then threatened to turn the gun on herself, some believed the treatment she had received at the hands of other students was to blame.

"At Jersey Shore, she had stones thrown at her, she was chased. There was a note left in her locker that said, 'Get out of this school, get out of this town, or we'll harm your parents,' said the girl's mother, Catherine A. Bush. "[The bullies] just gravitated to her. I think it's anyone who chooses a different path . . . or believes something different from what other kids think."

Teasing, name-calling, and bullying have long been synonymous with adolescence, but the possible consequences of a school-wide culture of casual cruelty have never been as deadly as they are today.

From Jonesboro, Ark., to Santee, Calif., teenagers allegedly abused by classmates have been fighting back with bullets. In the bloodiest of those vengeful rampages, two teenagers in Jefferson County, Colo., killed 12 of their classmates and a teacher before taking their own lives in April of 1999.

While the incidents have prompted many districts to heighten security and crack down on bullies, some experts argue that not enough attention is being paid to changing the unfeeling or openly hostile way so many students treat one another on a day-to-day basis.

"One of the issues that seems to be surfacing more and more is the need to focus on bullies—anti-bullying rules, zero tolerance, classes on how to deal with bullies," said Nancy Guerra, a professor of psychology at the University of California, Riverside. "My only concern here is that bullies are defined as extreme cases of kids who taunt others, pick on those weaker. [They] are few and far between. What is really happening," she said, "is that there is a more general atmosphere of meanness, where teasing and taunting are the norm among most students, rather than the exception."

Young people seem to agree.

In a nationwide survey of nearly 70,000 students in grades 6–12, only 37 percent of the respondents said students showed respect for one another. Fewer than half considered themselves positive role models for other students. And, while 80 percent of the girls surveyed said it bothered them "when others are insulted or hurt verbally," only 57 percent of the boys expressed a similar attitude.

"The only zero tolerance that happens in schools is the zero tolerance between kids," said Russell J. Quaglia, the director of the National Center for Student Aspirations, located at the University of Maine in Orono. "I think we're worse off now than we were in the 1950s with the race issues. We've got 'people' issues now. It's a lack of sensitivity [among students], but it's also a lack of a sense of responsibility for someone other than themselves."

Angry Young Men

Elizabeth Bush of Bishop Neumann High, who according to her lawyer was ridiculed for her strong religious beliefs and her tendency to befriend other ostracized teenagers, is a rarity among the school shooters who have grabbed headlines in recent years. Overwhelmingly, the attackers have been boys: Andrew Golden and Mitchell Johnson at Westside Middle School in Jonesboro, Ark.; Kip Kinkel at Thurston High School in Springfield, Ore.; and Eric and Dylan Klebold at Columbine High School in Colorado.

The country saw yet another name added to the list of boys angry enough to kill on March 5, [2001], when 14-year-old Charles Andrew "Andy" Williams, allegedly opened fire in a restroom at Santana High School in Santee, Calif.

Mr. Williams reloaded his father's .22-caliber handgun four times during the course of the shooting, according to a police affidavit for a search warrant of the boy's home unsealed last week. Two students were killed, and 13 other students or staff members were wounded.

The 9th grader, who faces being prosecuted as an adult, was described by other students as the target of incessant teasing and physical bullying. According to investigators, he said the people in Santee were different from those he had known when he lived in Frederick County, Md., until moving to California with his father last year. And, although he told police he had friends at Santana High, he also said he was disappointed with the school.

What many of the teenagers seem to have in common is a sense of alienation from peers.

In about two-thirds of school shootings that the U.S. Secret Service reviewed for a study last year, the attackers had felt persecuted, bullied, threatened, attacked, or injured by others. The agency found that a number of the teenagers had suffered sustained, severe bullying and harassment. The experience appeared to play a major role in motivating the ensuing violence.

"I think the biggest problem we have is the amount of alienation and rage in our young people," U.S. Secretary of Education Rod Paige said March 11 on the CBS News program "Face the Nation," after the school shootings in Santee and Williamsport.

"We [have] to figure out ways to make sure that a quality adult is in the life of every child, and we hope that quality adult would be a parent," Mr. Paige said. "But if it's not going to be a parent, then the school has to step in and fill the void."

But many researchers contend that some hallmark features of American schools contribute to the isolation of certain students.

Aaron R. Kipnis, the author of the 1999 book *Angry Young Men: How Parents, Teachers, and Counselors Can Help 'Bad Boys' Become Good Men*, maintains that schools condone bullying, teasing, and cliques by labeling and dividing students according to their academic and athletic gifts.

"That automatic sorting," he argues, "strengthens cliques and leaves, some students—particularly nonathletic boys—out in the cold."

"The fact that schools issue varsity sweaters with letters to the top athletes, and not the top physics students, underscores this idea that physical prowess and athletic achievement is really what's most important," Mr. Kipnis said in an interview. "Anything else is geeky, nerdy, kooky, or uncool."

Once the lines have been drawn, he said, the groups on top will do what it takes to stay there. "One of the ways cliques reinforce themselves is by putting down whoever isn't in with them with teasing, taunting, and—in the case of some of these boys we've seen—physical abuse," he said.

Setting an Example

If administrators and teachers hope to prevent violence from erupting in their schools, researchers say, they must reshape not only the attitudes of their students, but their own as well.

"Sometimes, we focus too much on the kids and not enough on the adults who are creating the culture," said Jean A. Baker, the director of the school psychology program at Michigan State University in East Lansing. "Kids see what we choose to show them. Schools that are very effective in preventing this kind of treatment are actively shaping their culture. Modeling the right behavior is a great way to start."

That work in large part falls to teachers and coaches, the adults with whom students have the most contact at school. But whether those authority figures are sending the right messages remains unclear, experts say.

Fewer than half of the students polled by the National Center for Student Aspirations said their teachers valued their opinions, and just 56 percent said teachers respected their thoughts.

"Things aren't going to change because there's a sign on the door that says, 'We care,'" Mr. Quaglia said. "We really need to teach kids respect and tolerance. So how do teachers model this behavior? I'm not sure

they do, judging from the data, but I know they can."

Some experts suggest suburban and rural schools, where most of the highly publicized shooting incidents of recent years have taken place, should look to schools in urban areas for clues on how to foster safer and more tolerant environments. There, where violence is often an everyday part of life, educators must work hard to promote peace and understanding among students from a variety of racial and ethnic backgrounds.

At T. C. Williams High School in Alexandria, Va., a 2,000-student school in a diverse district outside Washington, students are offered a number of avenues for working out their differences, including peer mediation and counseling. But more importantly, Principal John L. Porter said, the adults try to abide by the same code of conduct they want students to follow.

"You don't get on the PA and say 'Hey, we all gotta love one another,'" Mr. Porter said. "You've got to try to promote and show the reasons and the rationale for the behavior and have students understand that we're all different, and we're all people."

In Pennsylvania, Catherine A. Bush has only good things to say about Bishop Neumann High School's efforts and refuses to place the blame for her daughter's actions on students there. But as Elizabeth Bush awaits an uncertain fate in a nearby juvenile jail, her mother can't help but wonder if the cruelty of other students helped put her there.

"I don't know what can be done about this, but we have to do something," Ms. Bush said. "These are children, and we have to help them."

Review

1. What does the author mean by a "cruel culture" at school, and to what extent do students agree that it exists?

2. Describe the characteristics of and situations faced by young males who are involved in school shootings.

3. What can be done to foster safer and more tolerant environments in schools?

Application

Summarize this article for a small group of friends or acquaintances. Ask them to share their own experiences of bullying, threats, intolerance, or violence in elementary and high school (either as victims, perpetrators, or observers). What do they see as the causes of such behavior? What did the teachers or administrators do to address the problem? What would they do to change the culture of casual cruelty in schools?

Part Five

Religion

Religion is the institution that provides meaning for people through beliefs and practices defined as sacred. In symbolic interactionist terms, religion offers a specific kind of meaning to life—transcendent meaning. That is, religion assures people that they are involved in something that goes beyond personal pleasures and pains and has eternal significance.

The great majority of Americans believe in God and practice some kind of religion. At the same time, the extent to which religion is salient to everyday life varies among Americans. The selection in this part describes a group for whom religion is central and pervasive: the Hutterites. ✦

34
A Forgotten People in Our Midst

Donald W. Huffman

People everywhere tend to fall prey to **ethnocentrism,** the view of one's own culture as being the right and best way of life. Ethnocentric individuals evaluate in terms of their own values and beliefs. The more we learn about human diversity, however, the more we understand how ways different from our own can work quite well for other people.

Different ways of life are found within as well as between societies. A **subculture** is a group within a society that shares much of the culture of the larger society while maintaining certain distinctive cultural patterns of its own. The distinctive patterns may be primarily religious (Hasidic Jews, Hare Krishna), racial/ethnic (immigrants who maintain the language and ways of the mother country), political (radical student organizations), or others. Subcultures may be viewed by members of the larger society as irrational, backward, undesirable, odd, dangerous, or some combination of those characteristics. In this selection, Donald Huffman discusses the way of life of the Hutterites, a religious subculture found in the United States and Canada.

The Hutterites fled to North America from Europe in the 1870s to escape persecution. They live in rural communities and practice Christian communism—working, eating, and worshiping together. Members have no personal possessions. The institution of religion dominates all other institutions and governs every aspect of Hutterite life.

There are three main Hutterite groups, which differ in some ways from each other. The Schmiededleut branch, to which Huffman refers, is the most progressive of the groups. But all of the groups have a rigidly structured, highly religious, isolated way of life that holds little or no appeal to outsiders. Nevertheless, as Huffman points out, it works well for them.

I
Introduction

I remember the day well—having said goodbye to my wife in metropolitan Pennsylvania, I quickly traveled by air to another world. In a brief eight hours I had moved from a modern urban world of possessions and conveniences to a radically different subculture, which one scholar characterized in this way: "Probably no other group in North America is further from mainstream Western values than this one." That group was a Hutterite colony located in the western plains of Minnesota.

But one hour from Hector International Airport in Fargo, North Dakota, I entered a subsociety with a distinctive way of life. From my daily experience of the radio, television, and the newspaper, the automobile, the relatively isolated nuclear family, the once-a-week experience of congregational worship, I was now about to enter a radically different world of insulation and isolation from modern society. It was different in terms of mass media exposure and consumption, a tri-lingual world of Tyrolean, German, and English, a world of work trucks and vans, an everyday experience of extended family relations, a world where religious belief and practice permeate daily existence, from the spoken prayers before and after an afternoon snack and every meal, to a worship service each day from 6:00–6:30 p.m., and a one and a half hour service on Sundays. Truly this was a different social and cultural world, one from whose historical roots and experiences in modern society we can learn a great deal, and one that for years has fascinated me, a professor of sociology keenly interested in cultural diversity and varied religious groups.

It was late in October 1998 that I drove into the Spring Prairie Colony in western

Minnesota with the intention to live with the Hutterites. A sabbatical granted me by my college had given me this rich opportunity. With relative ease I had located a number of rich secondary sources on the Hutterites. Then came the more daunting task, that of gaining entrance into one of the more than 300 colonies located in the Plains states and the western provinces of Canada for the purpose of conducting field research. Given the relative isolation of Hutterite colonies, both social and geographical, this was not an easy task. In the end, however, it was a very rewarding process. . . .

What did I discover, both as a sociologist and person who had been granted this unique opportunity to live with the Hutterites?

II
Historical and Religious Background of the Hutterites

Before I elaborate on some of my major findings, it is initially important to place this sect in historical perspective. For, as I quickly learned, to understand the Hutterite way of life one must first understand their roots.

The Hutterites, often referred to as "a forgotten people," have a rich and long history which is well-documented. From their roots in the Protestant Reformation, this Anabaptist group has persevered for well over four centuries as a radical experiment in communal living, what they themselves term "community of goods." In fact, they are the longest surviving experiment in communal living recorded in modern Western history.

Beginning with their roots in the Anabaptist movement in Switzerland in the 1520s, the Hutterites have moved from Moravia (now Czech Republic) to Hungary, Romania, Russia, the United States, and Canada. Their core beliefs—which can be traced to the New and Old Testaments and their beginnings as a distinct Christian sect in the 1530s—include adult baptism, community goods, and the total separation of church and state. This latter belief is attested in the Hutterites' refusal to bear arms or to participate in existing social and political institutions, either through membership or leadership in such activities. Of signal importance—in keeping with the Apostolic Church, particularly as reported in Acts 2, verses 44–47—is the norm of living in colonies where community of goods, or sharing of all their goods in common, is practiced faithfully in each Hutterite colony. These beliefs and practices are directly linked to their frequent migrations from country to country, with reports that these migrations often occurred under the cloak of darkness and over treacherous mountain passes as they fled for their lives. It is a historical fact that the Hutterites have been threatened and persecuted by civil authorities in both Europe and the United States. Even more startling is the fact that their severest persecutors bore the name Christian. The Catholic Church, The Lutheran Church and Reformed Churches of John Calvin and Ulrich Zwingli frequently charged the Hutterites with heresy. Numerous leaders of the early Hutterite movement, including Jacob Hutter himself, were martyred for their faith. They were tortured on the rack for their beliefs and practices such as adult baptism; they were hanged, beheaded, drowned, and burned at the stake by religious authorities of the day who shared the Christian faith with them.

III
Survival and Prosperity: The Significance of Religion and Family In Colony Life

Given the numerous persecutions and hardships the Hutterites have experienced over the past four centuries, the central question I would like to address as a sociologist is: How have they survived and even prospered in the modern world?

I have no doubts that the Hutterite children are key to our understanding here. The 20 to 30 children and teenagers I observed during my week-long stay were, on the surface, like any in wider American society—lively, rambunctious, curious, eager to learn. But they are being molded in a very distinctive way. As children whose lives are lived nearly every moment in a colony largely cut off from the wider world, they are socialized from the day of their birth to become baptized adult members of the colony by the ages of 19 to 21. From early exposure to their deeply religious parents, to other relatives in the community who provide child care while parents engage in tasks assigned to them, to the colony nursery school for three to five year olds, to the colony school for first through ninth grades—children are thoroughly educated in the Hutterian way of life. Their education includes German language training (essential for studying the Bible and understanding the daily worship service conducted in German) in classes which they attend for two hours each school day from the age of six on. The children are early and continuously taught Hutterite history and hymnody and core communal values such as cooperation, shared work, and respect for all elders. In the Spring Prairie Colony a well-equipped print shop publishes a wide range of Hutterite school materials, including history texts, catechisms, workbooks, flash cards, maps, and songbooks, all of which are used in many colony classrooms. The print shop is run by a Hutterite elder (a former school teacher) and his son, with whom I had the privilege of working during my colony stay.

It was startling to me to discover that a group of 130 people, including 55 adults and 75 children, all of whom had unique personalities and talents, could function so well together as a cohesive community. This raised to consciousness a fascinating question: How could such cooperation and obvious unity of purpose exist on a daily basis, given the wide range of tasks that need to be accomplished in order for the colony to survive? One major factor, no doubt, is the division of labor which a number of early socioeconomic theorists, including Adam Smith, Herbert Spencer and Emile Durkheim found to be a powerful form of social cooperation that simultaneously allowed people to greatly increase their production. The labor of each individual, so coordinated, added to the wealth of all. During my stay in the Hutterite colony I observed such well-defined division of labor

and community cohesiveness where carpenters, plumbers, field workers, dairymen, hog and turkey managers and workers, meat processors, machinists, feed mill operators, housekeepers, beekeepers, printers, cooks, ministers, teachers, and mechanics all worked in complementary fashion to enable the colony to exist and thrive day by day. But for the Hutterites the key cohesive factor, as I discovered, is not division of labor, as important as that is to them. It is, without doubt, religious belief, religious practice (ritual), and community of goods that holds them together. Again Durkheim's sociological theory is relevant here. As argued in his *Elementary Forms of the Religious Life*, religion is another powerful force bringing about social cohesion amongst a tribe or group of people. In his classic definition of religion, Durkheim speaks of it in terms of "beliefs and practices which unite into one single moral community . . . all those who adhere to them" (1965, p. 62). I observed the powerful, binding force of religion in Spring Prairie Colony. For the Hutterites, religion permeates life. From the first spoken prayer before breakfast at 7:00 a.m., to the prayer following breakfast (and each meal), to the daily religious instruction of the children and youth (particularly the focus in the daily 4–6 p.m. German school with a Hutterite elder as teacher), to the experience of congregational worship each evening, and the frequently heard affirmation in both work and leisure that "if the Lord wills, it will be" religion is the life and breath of the Hutterite colony.

Religion is the key means of social control and is obviously effective because there has been no crime in Spring Prairie Colony in the 20 years of its existence. Admittedly, this is not a utopia. The minister, as leader of the colony, made that quite clear to me on a number of occasions during the long, broad ranging discussions we had each evening. "We are human beings with our frailties. But with God's help, through repentance and confession should there be any infraction of colony ordinances, things [that] can be are made right again." As for shunning, a practice Hutterites share with their Amish cousins, this extreme means of social control has had to be exercised only once in the colony's

·20-year history. In this instance, within a week of his isolation (meals and lodging were provided the person separate from the colony dining hall), the young man made confession of his wrongdoing before the congregation and was at once fully re-integrated into colony life.

Religion is so effective amongst the Hutterites, not only because it centers the colony by drawing them together in worship, work and leisure time (as I experienced in the Sunday evening "singing" in which many youth gathered in an apartment for socializing, refreshments, and the singing of spiritual songs), but also because of strong family life which is so evident to the observer.

Large families are prized. The norm in Hutterite colonies today is five to six children per family. Each child is seen as a gift of God. For this reason, the minister spoke passionately about his opposition to abortion, which he considered sacrificing young human lives. The Hutterite family reinforces the importance of cooperation, work, and worship, viewing them as ways to glorify the God who both brought their people into existence and strengthened and maintained them through centuries of dislocation and persecution.

Add to this the daily interaction of children, parents, uncles, aunts, cousins, and grandparents, in a true and rare expression of the classic extended family in today's society—all of whom profess and practice their faith. From this, one can only begin to understand the tremendous reinforcement of communal values and standards which the family brings to the Hutterite experience. From this observational and factual base, it can reliably be concluded that faith, family, the living in true community (in the Apostolic sense of "community of goods"), are the keystones of Hutterian cohesion and strength.

IV
Work: Shared Responsibilities and Shared Benefits

Work is another activity which enables Hutterite society to cohere. Here Durkheim's and Smith's division of labor thesis, referred to earlier, is relevant. Max Weber's Protestant Ethic thesis is also instructive, though in a negative way for the Hutterites. For the Hutterite, work is practiced in a complementary, cooperative way. The Hutterite view and practice of work is radically different from the current, largely secularized "work ethic" of individual and corporate competition, a "get as much as you can as quickly as you can" philosophy characteristic of so much of business practice today.

Compared to the Old Order Amish and Mennonites, this Hutterite colony—as with many others, I was told—was extremely modern in terms of utilized technology. Large tractors, modern combines, earthmovers, trucks and vans, modern welding equipment, offset printers, sophisticated milking and feedmixing systems, computers, freezers, and one large microwave oven(!) were found in Spring Prairie Colony. Of course, if you are farming thirty-two hundred acres, raising wheat, barley, soybeans and sunflowers; and if you are raising ten thousand turkeys for market and two hundred hogs for sale each week; and if you are milking one hundred thirty-five cows twice a day, large and efficient equipment and a ready-source of labor is required, as one can easily imagine. In Spring Prairie Colony this labor, both skilled and unskilled, is available to accomplish all of these tasks on a day-to-day basis. No hired help from the outside is needed, since all 55 adult members engage in the economic activity of the colony, as their strength and age allows. All of the work is under the leadership of the two ministers, the steward (who holds and expends all colony monies), and the farm manager. The first-tier leadership positions are filled by vote of all adult male members. The ministers are first nominated by elders within the colony, and then by elders representing colonies in the Schmiedeleut group. Adult males receiving at least five votes are then placed in the "lot." The one who selects the Bible with a slip of paper in it is the one selected by God to be minister, according to Hutterite belief. This elder will soon be ordained by the community as their minister, a position he will hold for the rest of his life. He can only be removed if he is found to be in serious violation of the Ordnung, the long established Hutterite charter, which specifically states the rules which govern colony life. The steward and farm manager are nominated and voted into office by adult colony members. After a period of probation, they may hold their positions on a permanent basis until either incompetence, infirmity, or death requires a new election.

Regarding the workday itself, it is an interesting mix of hard, steady work interspersed with meals, a brief break of family time after lunch, and refreshments in mid-afternoon. Except for demanding times of planting, harvesting, and the occasional processing of ducks and chickens (during which time members may work from twelve to fourteen hours a day), the day's work usually ceases by 5 or 5:30 p.m. This enables members to get ready for the evening worship service at 6 p.m., which is followed by dinner at 6:45 p.m. I was surprised and impressed by the rhythm of the everyday routine, finding hard work in the fields, the shops, the barns, the school, and the home to be balanced in healthy manner, with ample time for refreshing social times with friends and family. A nice pace, though for some—including myself, as I discovered—a bit too structured and ritualized, particularly with such little involvement with the outside world. With the nearest town being 12 miles away, and the nearest city of Fargo, North Dakota being 25 miles away—and with no readily available means of transportation made accessible to individuals and families except for the conducting of official colony business or for an occasional visit to relatives in another colony (the closest being 85 miles away)—such selected isolation and off-work activity in the colony is certainly understandable.

There are changes occurring in the traditional world of the Hutterite colony. Most notable for Spring Prairie Colony is the change that has recently been mandated by the state of Minnesota in the area of education. It is the requirement that all Hutterite youth must move beyond their eighth or ninth grade education to achieve their general education diploma (GED). To respect Hutterite insulation from the wider society, the state has allowed students to do their studies within the colony, with a once-a-week meeting with state qualified teachers in a nearby town. While most colony members that I spoke with think this is a good thing, noting that their youth will be better educated than they are, there appears to be an underlying concern amongst the leadership that higher levels of education may lead more of their youth to chose the modem world over colony life. As sociologists have long known, this is not an unfounded fear or concern, since it is generally recognized that the more education the individual has, the more likely one is to raise questions about traditional ways of life and to seek work that matches one's developing interests and skills.

Since this requirement of a high school education for Hutterian youth has only been in effect for the last several years, it is no doubt too soon to test the effects of increased educational levels on loyalty to and self-selected membership in a colony, which commitment is expressed in the central ritual of adult baptism between the ages of nineteen and twenty-one. This will surely be a rich field for sociological research in the future.

V
Colony Life: Insuring the Future Through Expansion, Hard Work, and 'God's Help'

I explored a final question with the leader of the colony, the senior minister, John Waldner, who has been this colony's spiritual leader for 15 years. I asked him if he expected that Hutterite colonies—over 300 of which are in existence today—will survive in the future.

His response was a thoughtful and candid one. He is quite sure that some existing colonies will die in the future. For what reasons? Some will see the rise of false prophets in their midst, who will preach, "We don't need to be so strict in maintaining communal life" or "We can be making some money out in the outside world, to supplement what we do in the colony." Other colonies will probably fail for reasons of poor management, for as the minister said: "Not everyone can be a manger, it is a gift."

He continued: "But Donald, you can tell your students that colony life does work. It has worked for more than four hundred years. You've experienced community life with us and know that it can and does work. We're not a utopia; we have our problems. But we do strive for perfection, to live as the Lord wills us to live as revealed in Scriptures, with Acts 2 serving as our guide." Expressing deep contentment, the minister added: "What more could a person want? While we have no money as individuals, we have our families, our colony made up of relatives and friends, good shelter, and good food, everything we need to live a good life in Christ."

In a reflective mood one evening, John Waldner told me: "I have no doubts that there will be Hutterite colonies one hundred years from now, perhaps fewer, perhaps more. Given our valued religious heritage, our living faith and daily practice of communal living, I trust, that with God's help, most of the colonies will survive and many will thrive in the next century."

The minister, in his mid-sixties, has lived in four colonies, having moved successively into new colonies as they were established. New colonies are planned and developed when an existing one reaches a "critical mass," so to speak. John Hostetler, the leading authority on the Hutterites in North America, notes that

> The Hutterites manage their expansion so that on the average each colony consists of from ninety to one hundred persons. When colonies are too small they become clannish and dominated by a single family, and when too large they do not provide enough employment for the members. When a colony reaches from 120 to 130 persons, it will seek second location. The 'mother' colony will form a new 'daughter' colony by the process of "cell division." This planned method of splitting is commonly referred to as branching out (1983, p. 17).

Hostetler later adds an important note to the effect that one of the internal threats to the well-being of a colony—a threat of which

most Hutterite leaders are very aware—is encountered when the colony's "population exceeds the positions available in the labor force." In such cases "polarization between family members may become a problem" (1983, p. 39).

The Hutterites, in their experience of colony life over a period of 470 years, appear to have satisfactorily resolved the tensions between the costs associated with their colony size and the benefits which they derive as a small community operating in the context of the larger society which surrounds them. In contrast to the Shaker communal experience in which, according to Metin, Miceli, and Murray, "the initially single group was divided into two or more independent groups" (called "Families") to address the costs of work incentives and coordination, most Hutterite colonies of the size of 100 to 130 members have been effective as "income sharing groups." They have been able through their unique organization to maintain "face-to-face contact and to establish trust relations" (1997, p. 140), qualities which are essential to their maximum socioeconomic functioning in the colony form.

No doubt the success of the Hutterites in this regard can further be attributed to their unity of belief and religious devotion, their "linking of work with religion" (ibid.), and their provision of meaningful work for all adults in the colony, which is complemented by the well-organized apprenticeship of youth in all phases of colony economic life. Additionally the Hutterites have developed a distinctive "centralized distribution mechanism" (1997, p. 133) represented in the office of the steward, who, in consultation with the council of the elders, seeks to achieve equality and justice in the communal sense of "from each according to his ability and to each according to his need."

With regard to a colony's "branching out" when it reaches maximum size, I was indeed fortunate to learn firsthand of the process and plans of the Spring Prairie Colony. John Waldner fully informed me of the colony's intention to purchase a thirty-four hundred acre farm some thirty miles southwest of the home colony, at a price of $1,100 per acre. The colony will purchase the land, then rent it to the former owner for four to five years, with the intent at the end of that time to create a new colony to accommodate the growth of the existing one. This new colony development occurs about every 20 to 25 years in a number of colonies located in the United States and Canada. This results in the growth of the number of colonies to offset those that may, for reasons cited above, go out of existence.

VI
What Mainstream American Society Can Learn from the Hutterites

In this last section of my article I want to address the following major question which has been in the back of my mind since conceptualizing this research topic. What can be learned from this intentional religious group of the Hutterites which might well have wider American sociocultural application in terms of values; family stability, community cohesion, and social welfare, with particular interest in their treatment of the elderly and the infirm?

First, the Hutterites remind us of the significance of beliefs—both religious and moral/ethical ones—in preserving a way of life, a culture. For the Hutterites, it is clear that religion is the life-giving energy of their existence. Specific beliefs and practices called them into being as a distinctive people in the early sixteenth century, alongside the better known Lutheran and Reformed churches. And religious beliefs continue to structure the way they live, from the moment of their birth, through daily education and worship experiences, through their baptism as adults, to whom one will marry, and even the desired size of their families.

The Hutterites' ethical or prescriptive beliefs—their values, the way they perceive is the right way to live their lives in relation to one another, and the ultimate goals they want to achieve—are again closely woven from the fabric of their religion. Faith in God, community, love, honesty, cooperation, forgiveness, and helpfulness shown in service to one another are values that they seek to live out in their daily existence.

To be sure, the Hutterites exhibit a number of qualities which are in line with broader American culture. It was clear to this observer that they share a number of values with their neighbors and fellow citizens outside their colonies. Such shared values include honesty, helpfulness, family security, friendship, politeness, and responsibility.

But the Hutterites' value system varies from wider American norms in significant ways. The center of their value system, both individually and corporately viewed, is God. The Hutterite norm of community, defined in terms of community of goods and cooperating with and serving fellow members, is clearly an outgrowth of their belief in and valuing of God and his will for their lives as revealed in Acts 2 and other Biblical passages.

In contrast to wider American life, little emphasis is found in the Hutterite colony on competition, on seeking a comfortable, prosperous life as individuals or nuclear family units, on personal freedom, on ambition, or on independence.

Clearly, as this researcher found, there is a sharp contrast between valuing the individual and valuing the community, indicative of a substantive value conflict between mainstream American culture and the Hutterite subculture. Time after time, in the midst of late hours of stimulating conversation with the minister, this point was impressed upon this "outsider" who had been given entrance to the colony to try to understand their way of life.

What can we learn from the Hutterites that is framed by this substantive value conflict? Imagine, if you will, what we as neighborhoods, as work groups, as towns and cities, and as a nation might become if we were to seek more of a balance of these rich value objects. As difficult as it would be to achieve, might this not be a desired goal, a positive aim worthy of investment and of time and energy—to improve the overall quality of our life together as a people, whether we be young or old, black, Hispanic or white, Catholic, Jew or Protestant?

A renewed emphasis on the value of community in the midst of the dominant individualistic ethos of modern American life could lead us in the direction of a new chapter of what has rightly been called "the American experiment."

A second area from which we as "mainstream" Americans can learn from the Hutterites concerns the subject of family stability. Let me initially share some observations regarding family life in a Hutterite colony.

1. The expectation is that everyone (except in rare cases such as illness, for example) will marry, usually shortly after baptism, which occurs between the ages of 19 and 21.

2. The sexual norm for the youth, which appears to be violated only in rare cases, is sex within marriage. Premarital and extramarital sexual relations are strictly forbidden.

3. Once married, each couple is expected, indeed encouraged by the community, to have children since children are so prized, both in terms of their innocent new lives and as future adult members who will perpetuate the colony way of life.

4. The average number of children per family is between five and six.

5. The Hutterites have a ready-made child care system at hand. This includes the primary care of the "housechildren"—ages birth to two years—by the mother, for whom homemaking is the primary profession. At the same time every mother—as is the case with all members—has specific tasks in the wider colony, from cooking, dishwashing, laundry, and the making of almost all of the clothing her family wears, to the occasional colony-wide slaughter and processing of hundreds of chickens and ducks in marathons of two to four days. Beyond the immediate parents, those engaged in child care and nurturance are older brothers and sisters who "watch" the younger children while the adults eat and worship. Aunts and grandparents are also regularly engaged in child care. I observed all of these relatives tending young children

in my brief stay in Spring Prairie Colony. In fact, one of the most delightful experiences I had was to go with a grandfather to baby-sit his grandchildren several evenings after dinner while the mother and grandmother were completing their work of dishwashing in the community kitchen. Every woman engages in dishwashing every eleventh week, according to one community informant. While child-sitting, the grandfather and I read to and played with the children, who were as lively and curious as are my own grandchildren.

I asked one mother who is 35 years of age with seven children, how she could keep up with and care for so many children. Her response was an interesting one and to the point. She said: "I think it would be harder to raise two or three children alone outside the colony than it is raising seven here. We have all our clothing, meals, and child care provided by the colony. What more could we need?"

6. Further contributing to family stability is the fact that relations between husband and wife are viewed as sacred. This relation has some distinctive features, arising out of Hutterite religious beliefs and community traditions: (a) The husband has the final word; he is the authority figure in all married life. This reflects a classic patriarchal pattern. The wife's power is, however, demonstrated and effective in child-rearing. (b) While one observed no public show of affection between husband and wife, there is obvious devotion, respect and care for one another, evident in the observed informal home environment. (c) No divorce is allowed in Hutterite culture. This prohibition is clearly and forcefully stated in the Ordnung, the rules that have governed community life since the sixteenth century. In relation to this, we might well ask the question: How do couples who are unhappy or dissatisfied with one another maintain lifetime monogamy? Clues to the

answer to this question certainly lie in the fact mentioned earlier, that religion permeates and is at the center of every Hutterite's life. The belief that Christ forbade divorce is for them a major deterrent to separation and divorce. In addition, the very nature of colony life, with its daily enforcement of norms and the provision of support to couples or families facing hardship, works in helping couples maintain their marriage vows throughout their lives, literally "until death do us part." Further, the relatively large number of children born to a couple, children who are prized and cherished as gifts from God, helps to hold husband and wife together even if their relationship may not be all that it could be. As part of this no-divorce ethos, mention must be made again of the classic extended family pattern operative in a Hutterite colony. In nearly every family situation there is daily interaction between at least three generations. They visit in each other's homes; they worship together; and they work side by side in the fields, in shop work, cooking and dishwashing, and in the canning of hundreds of large jars of fruits and vegetables. These tasks require nearly every adult member to be engaged intensely in colony life. One gets a sense of being part of one large extended family of 40 to 50 adults every day, so close is the cooperation and accomplishment of the work at hand.

All of these socio-religious factors, the strength of religious norms, the expectation of marriage and the corollary of a large number of children, the provision of family support through a very effective child care system providing relief for parents who might otherwise be stressed by large numbers living in relatively small quarters (basically a living-dining room and all the rest bedrooms), the clear authority structure, the devotion of husband and wife to each other, the stricture of no divorce, and the religious and social resources made available to insure that family ties are maintained, including an effective extended family network of sup-

port—all of these factors assist in the achievement of family stability which I observed and [have] been well documented in respected studies.

This is not to say that the Hutterites are free of problems in their colony and family life. As the head minister told me: "We are human, with human weaknesses and shortcomings. So we must work at it, keeping our colonies and families strong and thriving, day by day. It is an ongoing challenge. But with assurance that God has and will provide for what we need in every way, in terms of personal, social and material need, we trust that our ways will be preserved, if it is his will."

So, what applications to modern American life can be drawn from Hutterite family structure? In what ways can we perhaps be instructed by this social aspect of this distinctive subculture in our midst who have often been called "the forgotten people"?

First, the Hutterites remind us of the importance of extended family ties, of the strength that is derived from regular and meaningful cross-generational relationships. I observed this firsthand and wondered how we as mainstream Americans might recapture more of the richness of at least three generational family ties in the midst of our modern urban, industrial, information age. What new forms of extended family patterns and participation can we create as we move into the twenty-first century?

Secondly, we are reminded by the Hutterites of the importance of putting the needs of dependent children and the welfare of the community ahead of our own personal and often self-centered concerns. Imagine the difference that might make in our relations with our children, our spouses, other relatives, and our neighbors if we were to emulate their behavior in this crucial area of our lives.

Thirdly, the Hutterites clearly demonstrate the significance of religious belief as a unifying factor in family as well as community life. Here Durkheim's thesis in *The Elementary Forms of the Religious Life* is born out to the effect that religion is a constructive and effective unifying force in stabilizing communities. When focusing on families as the key building blocks of community, research has shown that religion often enhances marriages and parent-child relationships, as well as increases concern for one's aged family members.

Religion also assists parents in the moral training of their children; hence it often enables youth to avoid some of the pitfalls that hamper their future development, as well as giving assistance in the form of counseling to marriage partners who are experiencing difficulties.

A third area of Hutterite life and experience which might well have wider American sociocultural application falls in the domain of social welfare, and particularly the treatment of the elderly. . . . The Hutterites, as with other traditional cultures, revere the elderly in their colonies. Always made to feel a part of colony life, no matter how little labor they can contribute or how dependent they are due to illness or infirmity, the elderly clearly have no fear for their future. They know that they will be loved and cared for until the end of their days and that care, in so far as it is humanly possible, will be given them in the familiar surroundings of home and colony life.

One can imagine how the quality of American life and society might be enhanced if we were to regularly express deep respect and genuine care for the elderly in the context of our homes and institutions. With the documented aging of our population, ever larger numbers of the elderly are found in every sphere of the common life—family relations, the economy, politics, and religious life. In many of these areas the wealth of experience and knowledge that the elderly represent in wider American society remains largely untapped, largely because basic and genuine respect for them is lacking. They are often ignored or pushed off to the sidelines by younger family members as "over the hill," often bypassed for jobs that they qualify for if they choose to work in their senior years, and given little serious programmatic attention by most religious organizations. In this respect, it is clear that we can learn much from the Hutterites. Each colony insures that every elderly member is included in meaningful social spheres and activities, taking into account their interests and needs, so that the worth and dignity of their lives is affirmed to the very end.

References

Allard, William A. (1970). "The Hutterites: Plain People of the West." *National Geographic*, July: 99–125.

Bennett, John W. (1967). *Hutterian Brethren: The Agricultural Economy and Social Organization of a Communal People.* Stanford: Stanford University Press.

Durkheim, Emile (1947). *Division of Labor.* New York: Macmillan Co.

——. (1965). *The Elementary Forms of the Religious Life.* New York: Macmillan Co.

Gross, Leonard (1998). *The Golden Years of the Hutterites.* Kitchener, Ontario: Pandora Press.

Holzach, Michael (1993). *The Forgotten People: A Year Among the Hutterites.* Sioux Falls, SD: Ex Machina Publishing Co.

Hostetler, John A. (1974). *Hutterite Society.* Baltimore: Johns Hopkins University Press.

——. (1983). *Hutterite Life.* Scottdale, PA: Herald Press.

Metin, M. Cosgel, Thomas J. Miceli, and John E. Murray (1997). "Organization and Distributional Equality in a Network of Communes: The Shakers," *The American Journal of Economics and Sociology* 56(2): 129–143.

Peters, Victor (1965). *All Things Common: The Hutterian Way of Life.* University of Minnesota Press.

Rideman, Peter (1970 [1545]). *Confession of Faith: Account of Our Religion, Doctrine and Faith.* Rifton, New York: Plough Publishing House.

Smith, Adam (1976a). *An Inquiry into the Nature and Causes of the Wealth of Nations.* Chicago: University of Chicago Press.

——. (1976b). *The Theory of Moral Sentiments.* Oxford: Clarendon Press.

Spencer, Herbert (1976). *The Evolution of Society.* Chicago: University of Chicago Press.

Weber, Max (1958). *The Protestant Ethic and the Spirit of Capitalism.* New York: Charles Scribner's Sons.

Review

1. Discuss the role of religion in a Hutterite community.

2. Describe the family life of the Hutterites.

3. How is work organized among the Hutterites?

4. Briefly explain what the author says mainstream American society can learn from the Hutterites.

Applications

1. Religion is central to Hutterite life. How central is it to mainstream Americans? Find some recent information on the involvement of Americans in religion (from the Internet, a book on religion, a Gallup poll, etc.). How would you compare the role of religion among the Hutterites with its role among the majority of Americans? What, if any, aspects of Hutterite life would you like to incorporate more thoroughly into mainstream American life?

2. Keeping in mind that a subculture is simply a group that shares most of the culture of the larger society while maintaining some distinctive elements of its own, identify as many subcultures as you can that exist in the area where you live. How many people do you know who belong to a subculture? Talk with one of them about how and why they differ from mainstream Americans.

Reprinted from: Donald W. Huffman, "Life in a Hutterite Colony: An Outsider's Experience and Reflections on a Forgotten People in Our Midst." In *American Journal of Economics and Sociology* 59 (Oct 2000), pp. 549–71. Copyright © 2000 by American Journal of Economics and Sociology, Inc. Reprinted by permission. ✦

Part Six

Health Care

Surveys of Americans about the important factors in their life satisfaction show that good health is at, or near, the top of the list. Like people everywhere, Americans place a high value on health. The health care system, therefore, is a matter of great concern. To what extent do people receive adequate care? To what extent can all Americans afford needed health care? Such questions lead to periodic demands for changes in the nation's health care system so that all Americans can receive adequate care.

One such change has been the emergence and growth of health maintenance organizations, a topic dealt with in the first selection in this part. The second selection illustrates another aspect of health care—the relationship between physical and mental health. The two are closely interrelated, with each affecting the other for good or ill, as dramatized by the dying AIDS patients described in selection 36. ✦

35
Unhealthy Partnership

How Managed Care Wrecks Mental Health for Kids

Joshua Sharfstein

Health care is one of the most vexing social policy issues in the United States. Americans are disturbed by the escalating costs and by what some regard as substandard care in the various methods of managed care, including the proliferating health maintenance organizations (HMOs). According to public opinion polls, a majority of Americans believe that the tendency of HMOs to deny some medical procedures to patients is a "very serious" problem. And when asked to give an overall view of the American health care system, a majority agree that although there are some good things about it, fundamental changes are needed. At the least, respondents affirm the need for reform in the health care system, and some assert the need for a national health care plan.

The costs of health care have risen dramatically faster than the cost of living generally. By the end of the 1990s, Americans spent more than $1.1 trillion for health care, an increase of 65 percent from 1990 and more than 4.6 times the amount spent in 1980! Moreover, in the face of escalating costs, the proportion of Americans without health insurance rose during the decade of the 1990s; by the end of the decade, around 16 percent were not covered.

While much attention has been given to problems in physical health care, mental health care is equally troublesome. According to the U.S. Public Health Service, about 28 to 30 percent of the population have a mental or an addictive disorder, and about 9 percent of all American adults have a disorder that involves some significant functional impairment. In addition, approximately 20 percent of children have mental disorders with at least mild functional impairment.

In this selection, Joshua Sharfstein examines the impact of managed care on the mental health of children. He shows that managed care is as problematic for mental as for physical health care: profit gets priority over patient well-being.

Fourteen years old and sullen, he came to the hospital on a Sunday afternoon for evaluation of long-standing abdominal pain. As a first-year pediatric intern, I thought of incredible diagnoses: An intermittent twisting of the bowel? A rare parasite? When the preliminary tests came back negative, I told my patient the good news. He just cried, looked away, and held his stomach.

The next morning, a senior pediatrician remarked that abdominal pain is often the only obvious manifestation of depression in children. Returning to the patient's room, I elicited a story of loneliness, anger at his siblings, and unwillingness to confide in his parents. Then I drew in a slow breath and ventured that some people do not find life to be worth living. Doctor, he replied, at night I stand in the kitchen with a knife to my neck and pray for the courage to kill myself.

The next couple of hours passed quickly. I consulted with the primary care pediatrician and explained the situation to my patient's family. After a quick phone call from the psychiatry service to the insurance company, the patient was approved for treatment in a psychiatric hospital.

While I've changed some identifying details of the story for confidentiality, this part can't be altered: It was the closest I came to saving a life in my first year of training. I imagined that referring troubled children to the mental health care system for timely and effective treatment would continue to be an important part of my job as a pediatrician.

But it was not to be. Over the next three years, I observed from a front-row seat as mental health services for children in Massachusetts deteriorated. During my first night shifts in the emergency department, I often heard psychiatrists argue with managed care reviewers over approval for inpatient stays. Over time the next step—finding an available bed in a psychiatric hospital in New England—became the bigger hurdle. Late one night, I watched a frustrated social worker give up after several hours of calling area hospitals and ask a troubled adolescent's mother whether she could just take him home. The mother reluctantly agreed, but when they woke up the boy, he bolted. A melee ensued; after the child was restrained, another round of dialing began.

Eventually my experiences with suicidal or out-of-control children led me through the looking glass: I wasn't sending patients to the mental health system for care; the mental health system was sending children with acute psychiatric emergencies to me. About once a day, pediatric residents admitted a child to "board" on the pediatric unit of the hospital until a bed in a psychiatric facility became available.

Some boarders waited hours, others days. Nearly all were kept company by a "sitter" or security guard; some patients had to be sedated or physically restrained for their own safety. Psychiatrists would generally come by once a day to assess the boarders' mental status briefly and then continue with the bed search. Early one morning, I described three boarders admitted overnight to the inpatient team of residents. "Not more psych kids," they moaned.

I fantasized that somewhere in Massachusetts, corrupt officials had absconded with money intended for troubled children. But what I discovered is far more shocking: The Massachusetts Behavioral Health Partnership—the state's largest mental health insurance company and the outfit responsible for managing mental health care benefits for tens of thousands of children on Medicaid—has, in fact, met all of its contractual obligations. What's more, the state pays the plan, known as "the Partnership," millions of dollars each year in performance bonuses. Policy experts and state officials have called it a national model. And in June 2000, the largest HMO in the state, the not-for-profit Harvard Pilgrim Health Care, made plans to contract with the Partnership to provide mental health benefits, yielding the for-profit company approximately 70 percent of the market for children's services.

In New Mexico, Medicaid officials recently pulled the plug on a for-profit managed care experiment after audits showed that 83 percent of patients in one plan were inappropriately treated. In Tennessee and Arizona, the latest studies indicate that half of all children with serious mental illness did not receive any services in the previous six months. In these and several other states, thousands of children have suffered as private managed care plans have reaped profits by denying care.

The Massachusetts experience has led some observers to give for-profit managed mental health care a second chance. But how can a mental health plan be highly regarded even as the service system for children crumbles around it? The answer becomes obvious only with the realization that the plan's purpose was never to ensure access to care for children in need. Indeed, its true function has been to maintain the appearance of success. The company has earned every penny of its more than $200-million plus Medicaid contract by contributing to the illusion that the system is reasonably intact, thereby allowing the state to dodge pressure for more difficult but necessary reform.

The Partnership illustrates what's really missing in public policy for children with mental illness: not more crafty language for managed care contracts, but a political commitment to guaranteeing basic access to care.

A Shaky Model

This story began on July 1, 1996, when the Partnership started to manage mental health benefits for nearly 400,000 Massachusetts Medicaid recipients. Although its name suggests a special relationship between the company and the state, this "partnership" was a joint venture of two of the nation's largest for-profit behavioral health care firms, Connecticut-based Value Behavioral Health and FHC of Virginia. It was the second attempt under the Medicaid program in Massachusetts to carve out mental health benefits. From 1992 to 1996, after obtaining the nation's first waiver for managed mental health care, Massachusetts officials watched helplessly as Mental Health Management of America enraged hospitals and providers by bungling their payments.

Across the country, many other state officials learned the same unfortunate lesson. Hiring the managed care companies that had successfully tamed costs under employer-based coverage in the late 1980s and early 1990s was not a recipe for success in the public sector. These companies had conquered the private insurance market in no small part by leaving vulnerable patients on the tab of state governments. But now that they were working for state governments, the plans could deny care only at the cost of leaving patients totally abandoned. When a for-profit contractor nearly destroyed emergency crisis services across the state, furious state legislators in Montana canceled a five-year contract after just the second year. Arkansas lawmakers waited only six weeks to back out. Connecticut sued its for-profit contractor for what the state's attorney general described as a "purposeful and systematic" scheme to deny necessary care and eventually settled for $4 million.

By 1996 Massachusetts officials were eager for the Partnership to prove that for-profit managed mental health care could actually work. A successful carve-out would demonstrate an easy option for other state governments that were straining to serve increasing numbers of troubled children. The setting seemed right for a breakthrough. "The people in Massachusetts have better resources and better external consultation to deal with managed care," says David Fassler, a child psychiatrist at the University of Vermont who is an expert on Medicaid managed care. "They had the experience with [the first contract], so when they did the [Partnership] negotiations, they weren't coming in blind. They have more resources in Massachusetts—treatment resources—than in a lot of other states."

But skeptics saw danger in the state's desire to declare the new venture a success: "If either the state or the Partnership says it's not working, they both look bad," observes Susan Villani, former medical director of the Gaebler Children's Center. (The last public psychiatric hospital for children in Massachusetts, the center closed in 1995.) "So there's a lot of investment [in looking] good."

Massachusetts officials took pride in the state's model contract with the Partnership. Under the terms of the Partnership contract, Massachusetts paid the company a fixed fee per child and then limited to $2 million the amount of profit it could make by underspending the budget for services. The contract also allowed for $4 million in bonuses for meeting administrative targets and performance standards. Harvard Medical School psychiatrist and managed care expert James Sabin and Tufts University ethicist Norman Daniels raved in the journal *Psychiatric Services* that Massachusetts and the Partnership "may have developed a win-win approach" and noted, "A visitor to the offices of the Partnership sees the performance targets posted on virtually every wall."

The company's initial incentives largely centered on the nuts and bolts of administrative efficiency. For example, the plan processed 99.5 percent of claims within 30 days, besting the contract's requirement of 95 percent. And the Partnership submitted 100 percent of certain agreed-upon reports by 5:00 P.M. on the due date. During the first year of the contract, the Partnership earned the maximum of $4 million in bonuses.

In subsequent years, the performance incentives were expanded, mostly to encourage the company to offer training for providers and state officials and funding for patient surveys and other support services. The Partnership continued to excel at hitting the targets, earning $5 million in bonuses out of a possible $6.7 million in fiscal year 1998.

Yet something important was missing. Nothing in the contract held the Partnership accountable for providing basic access to mental health care for all enrolled children. It is true that Medicaid rewarded the Partnership for showing that its network included hospitals "within 60 minutes or 45 miles" of the homes of 85 percent of children enrolled. But such a guarantee provided no consolation to parents when all the beds at these nearby inpatient facilities were filled.

While the Partnership kept processing claims on time—86 percent were filed electronically in fiscal year 1998—the demand for inpatient hospitalization was steadily rising, with emergency departments seeing more and more acute referrals. Several area inpatient psychiatric units for children folded. Most significant, openings for troubled adolescents in residential settings such as halfway houses overseen by the state's Department of Social Services disappeared, leaving dozens of children in state custody stranded inside psychiatric hospitals, ready for discharge but with no place to go. From July 1998 to June 1999, according to records I obtained under the state's freedom-of-information law, these children spent a collective total of 8,194 unnecessary days in locked wards.

Suicidal and violent children who needed treatment in inpatient psychiatric facilities were put on indefinite hold. Some became boarders in pediatric hospitals; others languished for days in community emergency departments; a few waited in jail. Martha Grace, chief justice of the Massachusetts Juvenile Court, told *The Boston Globe* that judges occasionally had to send troubled children into locked detention simply to protect them while they awaited psychiatric hospitalization. "To put a mentally ill child in a delinquent or criminal population is not good for either population," Grace said. "Now they're being punished for being ill."

In the absence of performance standards requiring access to care during mental health crises, the Partnership did not immediately provide funding for such patients. In a study of 10 boarders covered by Medicaid from January to May 1999, I found that after subtracting the cost of salaries for people to watch the children and psychiatric staff to evaluate them on nights and weekends, my hospital received about $60 per day for nursing services, physician fees, food, medications, and other expenses. At the time, the Partnership did not, as a policy, accept financial responsibility for care. Meanwhile, for the children stuck inside psychiatric facilities, ready for discharge but awaiting community placements, the Partnership paid just $140 per day rather than the usual fee of more than $500. At least through the first half of 1999, the company stood to profit from the shortage of inpatient psychiatric beds.

The Partnership's unwillingness to expand available inpatient treatment might have been more understandable if the company had created a network of community providers to prevent at-risk children from reaching a crisis in the first place. But no performance incentives held the Partnership accountable for significant problems involving access to outpatient care—a bad omen for a business that posts its goals on every wall.

Years of pounding from managed care had left many Massachusetts communities lacking in child psychiatrists, day treatment programs, and other resources. Nationally, from 1988 to 1997, employer spending on mental health services fell by 54 percent in constant dollars. The impact of these cuts on children's services—which often lack strict professional standards on length of treatment—was disproportionately high. As private managed care plans reduced their benefits, families increasingly turned to the state government for assistance. But state spending in Massachusetts and elsewhere did not match the need. For example, the number of patients on waiting lists for case managers from the Department of Mental Health stretched past 2,000—leaving a multitude of families unable to obtain key assistance in finding mental health services, coordinating with local school systems, and accessing other state programs.

Under these dire circumstances, the Partnership did not rise to the challenge of expanding services to meet community needs. Clinicians complain that credentialing with the plan can take months. The Partnership also pays lower rates to many therapists than other insurers do, and clinicians report difficulty in obtaining reimbursement for time spent apart from therapy sessions. (Because children's misbehavior often occurs at home or in school and may have consequences for the criminal justice system, therapists must often work for free making contact with parents, teachers, and school and court officials.)

Until very recently, the Partnership did not even track outpatient waiting times across its system. The net result: In many parts of the state, families covered by the Partnership have waited upwards of five months for a first appointment. "In five or six months, a lot of these kids become much more in crisis," says Lisa Lambert, assistant director of the Parent-Professional Advocacy League, which surveys its members on waits for care. "Their behaviors escalate, and [then] they are looking to access acute services." In March 1999, two state agencies asked Christina Crowe of the Judge Baker Children's Center in Boston to examine why parents were reporting such dissatisfaction with mental health services in northeastern Massachusetts. Her report described a decimated system in which "access to adequate and effective treatment is deficient at every level."

These findings, however, had no implications for the Partnership's stellar record of meeting its performance targets. Within another few months, the company stood to earn another $400,000 bonus by holding two optional training workshops on child and adolescent issues for Partnership providers and state employees. Even in July 2000, as the mental health care system's collapse hit the front page of *The Boston Globe*, an internal Partnership memo boasted in boldface: "All FY 2000 Performance Standards on track for success."

No Accountability

Why can't Massachusetts just hold the Partnership responsible for basic access to care? Partnership CEO Richard Sheola says that such a step would be patently unfair. His reasoning: The Partnership has no control over what's really broken with the mental health care system for children.

This claim enables a for-profit company to escape responsibility for children in distress. But it is also true. Massachusetts state agencies, by leaving dozens of children inappropriately stuck in psychiatric hospitals, are largely responsible for the bed crunch that has forced children to languish in pediatric units, community emergency departments, and jails. The most recent data indicate that children in the care of state agencies spent 20,811 unnecessary days in psychiatric hospitals from July 1999 to June 2000—the equivalent of 57 years of wasted time. Similarly, while the Partnership has not particularly improved community mental health services, the state's support of key elements of the outpatient system has been sorely lacking. At last count, 2,497 children were waiting for case managers from the Department of Mental Health.

It's a catch-22. The state cannot fairly hold the Partnership responsible for basic access to care without first doing a better job itself. But that's exactly what the state government wants to avoid. A real commitment to the mental health needs of children would involve guaranteeing community placements and case management services for all troubled children who need them, backing support teams for families with troubled children, and dedicating additional spending for recruitment and training of new mental health providers. Pilot programs such as the Mental Health Services Program for Youth have reduced foster care rates and improved care for even the most vulnerable children by combining resources from the mental health, education, and criminal justice budgets and creating accountable community-based treatment teams.

But such an investment statewide would be costly up front. Led by tax-cut-obsessed Republican Governor Paul Cellucci, Massachusetts politicians are unlikely to target significant new resources to help such a politically unempowered group. Beyond funding, the political obstacles to reforming the mental health care system are daunting. These would include battles to create new residential treatment centers across the state and to break down the walls between several entrenched bureaucracies. Massachusetts is not alone in failing to tackle these problems: Advocates have recently sued New York and Maine on behalf of emotionally disturbed children who do not receive adequate care, and more than a dozen states have recently reported crises in access to children's mental health services.

Massachusetts, however, has uniquely been able to minimize political embarrassment by hiring a managed care plan, holding it responsible for a limited array of "performance standards," and declaring it a success. Even patient advocates on the national level have been somewhat fooled. In testimony to the New Mexico state legislature, an official of the Bazelon Center for Mental Health Law in Washington, D.C., advised that state to consider a carve-out arrangement for mental health services, citing Massachusetts as a model. The center's policy director, Chris Koyanagi, says approvingly, "People have seen that Massachusetts is monitoring [the Partnership] closely with many performance standards."

"If something is happening in a social system over time, it's been designed in," says managed care expert James Sabin, who early on had high hopes for the Partnership. One could conclude, he adds, that the Massachusetts mental health care system "appears to be designed to keep spending level . . . at the cost of not doing anything for kids."

Last February the health plan moved to dispel the image that it was profiting at the expense of stranded children. According to Partnership Vice President Angelo McClain, "to address any perceptions that [it] stood to gain financially every time a child was 'boarded' in a pediatric unit," the Partnership (in consultation with Medicaid) authorized $502 in daily payments to pediatric hospitals. The plan even increased its reimbursement to psychiatric hospitals for children stranded waiting for community placements.

At times of crisis, the Partnership has stepped in to take some of the heat off the state. In April 1999, *The Boston Globe* reported on its front page: "Suicidal and violent youngsters are languishing in hospital emergency rooms for hours and in pediatric beds for days—and are sometimes simply sent home with panic-stricken parents—because Massachusetts psychiatric hospitals have no room for them." The story made clear that a major cause of the problem was the gridlock generated by children in psychi-

atric hospitals waiting for community placements from state agencies. In response, the Partnership agreed to pay psychiatric hospitals to open more inpatient beds for children, tacitly accepting responsibility and taking pressure off the state.

At first glance, these actions may seem surprising. But they make perfect sense given how the Partnership really earns its money: not by directly shortchanging children, but by fostering the illusion that the system works and earning rewards from the state. Despite a few small steps, the basic dynamic at work in Massachusetts has yet to change. The state government remains unwilling to invest in a comprehensive system of outpatient care that includes residential placements for children who need them. This leaves the Partnership officials on the hook for the bed crisis, a responsibility they do not fully accept. It's a situation that virtually guarantees worsening care.

Massachusetts' unusual relationship with the Partnership could never be sustained if plan officials pushed the state into tackling the bigger issues in children's mental health care. In fact, the Partnership came close to doing just that in the summer of 1998, when the company's leaders decided to cut off payment for children who were waiting beyond a certain number of days for community placements in psychiatric hospitals. After all, they correctly reasoned, Massachusetts was paying the plan to manage medically necessary care, and hospitalization for these children was no longer medically necessary (by anyone's definition).

It didn't take long for hospitals to catch wind of the proposal and start to kick and scream. As pressure mounted, Governor Cellucci's administration faced the choice of finding appropriate placements for the children or simply demanding that the Partnership knuckle under and pay for medically unnecessary care. The knuckling under happened quickly.

Even a trusted not-for-profit health system probably wouldn't risk its own contract by aggressively confronting the state over fundamental problems in the mental health system for children. According to Susan Fendell of the Mental Health Legal Advisers

Committee, "One reason [the Partnership] may not be publicly lobbying for more money spent on the public system of residential services is that they want to be players with the administration." The Partnership is now owned by ValueOptions (the company that resulted when FHC bought out Value Behavioral Health); too much controversy would not make the principals happy.

Carving Out Real Care

So what should happen with private managed care for Medicaid mental health services? In round one, companies tried—and failed—to apply private-sector cost-cutting strategies to a complex public system. States are increasingly abandoning these contracts. In round two, the companies cooperated with governments to placate providers with efficient reimbursement and to meet limited performance goals, sidestepping fundamental problems in the system. Children still suffer.

Is round three coming to a state near you? According to Gail Robinson, vice president of the Lewin Group, an international consulting firm with expertise in mental health issues, the next few years will be a "critical time" in terms of the future of for-profit plans in public mental health services. "A number of states are finishing with three- or five-year contracts," she says. "They will need to consider the benefits and the cost [of renewal]." Preferring to contract with public and not-for-profit groups, some states responsible for millions of Medicaid recipients have not yet embraced for-profit managed mental health care. But that may change.

To succeed, state governments will have to do more than tinker with the contract language in their deals with managed care plans. They'll have to treat children's mental health as a continuum that includes insurance for psychiatric services, residential care, school support, social services, and the criminal justice system. They'll have to foot the bill for comprehensive community-based services. And they'll have to demand and monitor basic access to inpatient and outpatient care as well as actual improvement in the lives of troubled children. It's doubtful that for-profit plans can play anything more than a limited role in such a system.

Even the best managed care plan is only as strong as the political commitment to troubled children that supports it. Legislatures must establish measurable goals for the system and hold agencies responsible for meeting them. Through its oversight of the Medicaid program, Congress can do the same. Virtually all state Medicaid plans have federal waivers to allow managed care for mental health services; Congress should pressure the Department of Health and Human Services to require basic data on access to care before approving renewals. The recent denial of a waiver in New Mexico is a good first step.

In light of the public's interest in avoiding school shootings and youth violence, the political prospects of improved services are not dismal. While laws that mandate parity for mental health benefits can be easily circumvented, their passage indicates that legislators are willing to act to improve children's mental health. Rafael Semansky, a policy research analyst at the Bazelon Center, notes one financial incentive that may push the effort along: When a state uses Medicaid funds to intervene in a troubled child's life, the federal government foots about half the bill, but when that child disrupts school or winds up in jail, it's all on the state's dime.

I have yet to assist another patient as I did the depressed 14-year-old during my internship. Instead, I scramble to coordinate outpatient mental health care, school services, and home supports for troubled children in my primary care practice. Sometimes I help to avert a crisis, but often I fail. When I tell any of the current pediatric trainees of my past hope to detect serious mental illness among children and refer them to the mental health system for effective care, they just laugh. . . .

Review

1. Describe some of the problems that have occurred in the various states as they have tried to utilize managed care for mental patients.

2. Explain what Sharfstein means by the "shaky model" of mental health care.

3. Why is there no accountability in the Massachusetts system?

4. What does Sharfstein say is needed in order for states to provide adequate mental health care?

Applications

1. Through the Internet, a library, or contact with a local mental health professional, find out what kind of mental health care is available to children in your state. Look also for suggestions as to how the care can be improved. Compare your findings with those in Sharfstein's article.

2. Sharfstein focuses on problems involving hospitalization. Private therapists also report annoying issues as they try to provide care to patients covered by a managed-care system. Talk to a therapist who has patients in a managed-care system. Ask the therapist to identify advantages and problems of treating such patients.

Reprinted from: Joshua Sharfstein, "Unhealthy Partnership: How Managed Care Wrecks Mental Health for Kids." In *The American Prospect* 12 (January 1–15, 2001): 24–28. Reprinted with permission from *The American Prospect* Volume 12, Number 1: January 1–15, 2001. The American Prospect, 5 Broad Street, Boston, MA 02109. All rights reserved. ✦

36
Preserving a Vital and Valued Self in the Face of AIDS

Kent L. Sandstrom

tested territory. This view is Sandstrom's point of departure for the study of identity among persons with AIDS. Based on his intensive interviews with a small sample of AIDS victims, Sandstrom describes the challenges faced in the final phases of the illness. He captures the thoughts and feelings of men who struggle with the meaning of their lives, their deaths, and what lies beyond death.

In American society, illness is usually perceived in biomedical terms. A virus or bacterium has invaded the body, the physiological function of an organ has failed, or an essential biochemical has ceased to be adequately produced in the body. In virtually all societies, including our own, some illnesses are considered to have a social or cultural aspect as well. For example, a disease such as asthma is believed to be contracted or its condition worsened when the victim is involved in stressful situations. A disease may also be associated with disapproved behavior patterns, such as cirrhosis of the liver which is associated with the heavy consumption of alcohol. Thus, some kinds of diseases may be stigmatizing, and those afflicted are regarded by some segments of a society as morally suspect and potential pollutants.

This is the prevalent attitude toward AIDS among certain groups in contemporary American society. AIDS, or acquired immune deficiency syndrome, is a viral infection that causes the immune system to stop functioning and is usually fatal. Some people view AIDS as a punishment from God for the victim's immoral behavior. The stigma of AIDS seems to derive from three perceptions: (1) it is a contagious, incurable illness; (2) it can be transmitted by sexual contact; and (3) it is associated largely with two groups of victims: gay men and intravenous drug users.

AIDS is not stigmatized in all circles. There are those who, in fact, have great sympathy for victims of the disease and even those who see its ennobling potential. In short, the moral perception of AIDS in American society is con-

During the past decade sociologists have focused increased attention on the lived experience of HIV disease. Much of their research has concentrated on how persons with HIV disease cope with and counteract stigma (Sandstrom 1990; Siegel and Krauss 1991; Weitz 1991), experience and manage uncertainty (Weitz 1989), negotiate sexual relationships (Sandstrom 1996a), utilize doctors and medical resources (Kayal 1993; Weitz 1991), build support networks (Sandstrom 1996b), and, more generally, reconstruct their lives and selves (Adam 1996; Kotarba and Lang 1986; Sandstrom 1990, 1996a, 1998; Weitz 1991). In addressing these themes, sociologists have insightfully revealed many of the central challenges confronted by persons with HIV disease. However, they have not yet delineated the distinctive challenges to self encountered by people with HIV in the twilight of their moral career—that is, when developing serious AIDS-related complications and facing the prospects of profound debilitation and impending death.

This paper attempts to address this gap in the literature by examining the existential challenges that men with AIDS experience during the final phases of their illness career. These challenges include (1) how to come to terms with debilitating symptoms and a diminishing future; (2) how to offset the threats posed by suffering, dependence, and dying; and (3) how to construct and solidify identities that extend beyond death.

In exploring these issues, this paper extends the sociological literature on illness, death, and dying in a couple of important ways. First, it illustrates some of the most prominent identity dilemmas encountered by men grappling with advanced symptoms of a terminal illness. As Kathy Charmaz (1994, p. 269) has noted, identity dilemmas "include the knotty problems and hard decisions" that emerge as seriously ill people "experience trials, tribulations, and transitions that affect who they are and who they can become." In accord with Charmaz's emphases, this paper highlights the trials, tribulations, and transitions that shape the self-images and identity constructions of men with AIDS, particularly as they come to grips with dying and death.

In addition to this, the paper reveals how men with AIDS construct postmortal identities and sustain a sense of symbolic immortality (Lifton 1978) as they enter the final period of their lives. Through focusing on this phenomenon, the paper offers insight into how people with terminal illnesses fashion enduring selves and futures and, in this process, gain a sense of control and transcendence over death as an ultimate limit. This is an important aspect of their unfolding,"moral experience" (Goffman 1961).

Along with contributing to the sociological literature in the above ways, this paper illustrates and extends the theoretical insights of symbolic interactionism. Symbolic interactionism provides an especially illuminating framework for examining how men with AIDS define themselves and their illness, because it accentuates the processual, interactive, and interpretive dimensions of human experience and selfhood. Following Mead (1934) and Blumer (1969), interactionists assume that (1) people act toward things, including things like AIDS, based on the meanings that those things have for them; (2) the meanings of things are not inherent but rather derive from processes of social and self-interaction (Denzin 1983, 1989a; Durig 1996); (3) meanings have a fluid and mutable quality; and (4) people construct lines of action not only in terms of the meanings they give to objects or events around them or to their internal experiences but also in terms of the meanings they give to themselves. In fact, in fashioning ongoing social acts, the "self" is often the most central and meaningful social object that they take into account (Blumer 1969; Stryker 1980).

Guided by these assumptions, a symbolic interactionist analysis of the experience of men with AIDS focuses significant attention on how they construct meanings for self in light of the unfolding implications of their illness. In a related vein, it also emphasizes how these men's images of self are affected by their visions of and expectations for the future, and vice versa. As implied in the writings of many interactionists, people construct images of self not only in terms of the past and present, but also in terms of their anticipation of the future (Charmaz 1991; Corbin and Strauss 1987; Mead 1934; Markus and Nurius 1986; Strauss 1993). Building upon this premise, this paper examines and portrays how the self-images and identity constructions of men with AIDS both influence and become influenced by their visions of the future, particularly as their illness enters its latter stages.

Finally, in adopting a symbolic interactionist perspective, this paper accentuates how men with AIDS, like all human beings, are actors rather than reactors; that is, they are active agents who, because of their ability to use symbols and engage in self-interaction, do not merely react to the physical and social ramifications of their illness. Instead, they have the capacity to creatively act toward their health situation, to negotiate and transform the meanings attributed to it, and, correspondingly, to exercise a measure of control over its consequences for self (Sandstrom 1990).

Methodology

This study draws on interview data from an availability sample of twenty-one men diagnosed with AIDS. These men volunteered to be interviewed after (1) receiving a descriptive flyer and letter of invitation from a case manager at a local HIV clinic; (2) hearing a presentation made by the author to an AIDS related support group; or (3) getting referred by an acquaintance who had already been interviewed or who knew the author through his involvement in community AIDS work.

The men interviewed in this study ranged in age from 20 to 56; six were in their 20s;

eight were in their 30s; six were in their 40s; and one was in his 50s. The vast majority were White; the only two non-Whites were African American. Fifteen of the twenty-one men had become infected with HIV through having sex with other men. Thirteen of these men identified themselves as gay, while the other two described themselves as bisexual. Among the remaining six men, three had contracted HIV through injection drug use, two had contracted it through sex with infected women, and one had contracted it through blood products he received as a hemophiliac.

All of the men in this study had developed AIDS-related opportunistic infections, such as Kaposi's sarcoma (KS), pneumocystis carinii pneumonia (PCP), cytomegalovirus (CMV), toxoplasmosis, neuropathy, tuberculosis, or dementia. Eighteen of the twenty-one men were suffering from advanced and disabling AIDS-related symptoms during the time that they were interviewed. The remaining three men were comparatively healthy, but they had experienced debilitating and potentially fatal AIDS symptoms in the past.

Everyone in the study was interviewed on at least two occasions, because the interview process was lengthy (an average of four hours), and illness or fatigue made it difficult to talk for more than a couple of hours at a time. I interviewed most of the men at their homes; however, two were interviewed in a private university office because their homes were not conducive to a confidential conversation. The interviews were guided by roughly seventy open-ended questions, including eighteen which explored themes regarding advanced illness, dying, and death. . . .

Challenges to Self Encountered in the Twilight of the AIDS Career

In the earlier phases of their illness, men with HIV/AIDS struggle most centrally with issues of stigma and uncertainty (Sandstrom 1990, 1996a; Weitz 1989, 1991). They worry about how, whether, or when to disclose their health status and how to address or counteract the threat of devaluation it poses.

They also worry about the unpredictable aspects of their HIV infection, such as when it will provoke serious symptoms, what specific symptoms will arise, what treatments will be available for these symptoms, and how both the symptoms and treatments will disrupt their everyday lives.

As their illness unfolds and advances to its latter stages, the concerns of men with HIV/AIDS begin to change. Stigma becomes a less salient issue for them as their social contacts become more restricted and they surround themselves with a trusted and supportive network of others. In addition to this, their struggles with uncertainty diminish. In fact, men with AIDS feel as anguished about the certainties that accompany their advancing illness as the uncertainties, particularly certainties such as debilitating symptoms and a rapidly diminishing future.

Coming to Terms With Debilitation and a Shrinking Future

As they grapple with advanced health complications, men with AIDS find it increasingly difficult to manage their illness and preserve an identity apart from it. They discover that they can no longer contain the disease, as they had in the past, by closely monitoring their health practices and reducing their social involvements. Instead, AIDS becomes a defining feature of their lives—it fills their days and compels them to reorder their priorities, activities, and self-conceptions.

In many cases, AIDS triggers or exacerbates symptoms of unyielding fatigue, pain, indigestion, or diarrhea. These symptoms, in turn, evoke feelings of frustration and demoralization in affected men, as highlighted by one of my informants, Peter, when he remarked: "I'm sick and tired of being sick and tired! I really am. I'm sick and tired all the time, you know. That's the hard part about this damn disease—there's such a constancy to it."

As time passes, men with AIDS no longer experience many good days, or periods of restored health, that offer them respite and renewal. Their lives become a litany of bad days—periods marked by continuous sickness and a profound sense of devitalization.

As Neil, who had lived with AIDS for over five years, described: "I just feel kind of dragged out. I have a lot of days like that now . . . I just feel dragged out, tired, and icky. I don't even have those real good days that I used to have in the middle of bad ones. It's just fatigue, fatigue, fatigue all the time!"

In addition to being plagued by debilitating physical symptoms, men with AIDS may suffer from impaired mental functioning, such as disorientation, memory loss, dementia, and a general slowing of cognitive processes (see also Weitz 1989). These manifestations of their illness, of course, also limit their activities and disrupt their images of self and the future.

In light of the bodily changes they experience, men with AIDS often feel as if they have grown old prematurely. They recognize that they must deal with the same types of symptoms, feelings, and challenges as their aging relatives. As Peter observed:

I feel like it [life with AIDS] is similar to being old! My grandmother and I—we are on the same physical level. She's seventy-nine and I'm thirty-nine but it's like we're dealing with the same kind of problems. You know, I could very, very easily be treated as a geriatric patient and it would be proper care. And when my grandmother complains to me, my final line is "Yeah, look at it, I have all the same problems you do and I'm forty years younger. . . ." I really do feel more related to being old in that sense—more than to having AIDS actually. Because all the symptoms just make you old! And you even look old! . . . Looking at me is the same as looking at my grandmother, but she's seventy-eight years old! And she's got these aches and pains and . . . bad days, just like me.

In a related vein, another of my informants, Greg, emphasized the parallels between the issues he encountered in his daily experiences with AIDS and the existential challenges faced by elderly people:

I know part of it [living with AIDS] is very similar to dealing with issues of being older—of pacing yourself and so on. . . . One of my friends with AIDS said the same kind of thing today at lunch, too. He said, "I feel like I'm ninety years old." And

it is like that! I spoke to a church group lately and I read some poems about my life and stuff. And during the question-and-answer period, this one older gentleman engaged me in discussion in just that way. He said, "I can really identify with where you're at because being seventy-two, I'm dealing with illness and death myself—with things going wrong." And I agreed with him—that it [AIDS] was just, you know, it was just like that. It was like growing old early.

Generally speaking, as their health worsens, men with AIDS—like many elderly people—struggle to come to terms with the threats posed by their diminishing capacities and futures. In addressing these threats, they find it difficult to rely upon the strategies they had adopted in previous phases of their illness, such as maintaining a positive outlook and accentuating the empowering ramifications of life with HIV (Kayal 1993; Sandstrom 1990; Weitz 1991). Instead, these men develop and utilize other adaptive strategies which help them to sustain a sense of control, vitality, and self-value in their daily bouts with advanced illness. One of these strategies is to stop thinking much about the future, as Neil revealed:

I don't look into the future very much anymore because even though I know some good things will come along I anticipate that it's going to get harder and worse. I don't know, from what I've been able to see with other people it doesn't get better. Or, it stays the same, which doesn't offer me much to look forward to either.

As they wrestle with severe manifestations of their illness, men with AIDS become absorbed in the present and try to suppress thoughts of their prospective health situation. When asked, "What do you see as you think about your health in the future?" the men I interviewed typically gave a variation of the following response: "I don't really see much. I try not to think about it. I guess I'm probably going to get even more sick and die. . . . So, I just live day to day."

By choosing to "live one day at a time," men with AIDS derive a greater sense of control in the present and find new sources of personal satisfaction and fulfillment. Many start to notice and appreciate the beauty of little things happening around them and vivid feelings arising within them. Most crucially, through anchoring themselves in an *intense present* (Charmaz 1991), these men discover a rejuvenating sense of joy, vitality, and transcendence, as reflected in the following excerpts:

> You know, I just feel blessed for each day, really—for the sun, the trees, everything. I just feel like I have a more intense experience of life. Yeah, there's times for me when it even comes off as feeling high—like a high from drugs or something like that, except it's not from that. It's just from being so immersed in life—there's a high in that for me. . . . When I got really sick and truly realized that I had a limited amount of time left to live, I started to look at things differently. All of a sudden each new day was precious to me—it was a gift that offered special surprises. I started to see and experience each moment as sacred, at least in some respects.

When living in the intense present, men with AIDS experience not only a revitalizing sense of joy and transcendence, but also a heightened sense of urgency—urgency to act, take risks, experience things, build new or stronger relationships, and, in their own words, "make the most of the opportunity each new day presents." In addition to this, these men often feel an urgency to complete unfinished business. Given their health situation, they realize that they have a limited future, and they feel motivated to achieve something meaningful while they still can. For example, when reflecting upon how his ongoing health problems affected the goals he set for self, Greg asserted:

> I have this kind of, like, drive underneath about, you know, accomplishing something I feel like, "Yeah, I should be doing this, I should be doing that." . . . There's still other things, more things I want to accomplish—like, I have a couple of research and writing projects I want to get finished and published. Although I, you know, make sure I do things to build my self-esteem and take care of myself daily, there are still like some big things that I would like to do.

In a similar vein, Lee stressed how his worsening symptoms had prompted him to try to make a significant contribution through pursuing some larger-scale goals. He also emphasized how AIDS compels those affected to come to grips more quickly with what they want out of their lives:

> I want to work on low-income housing, and I want to teach people how to do carpentry and design and energy efficiency. I mean, all those kinds of things where if you do a little bit it makes a big difference. Suddenly I want to be doing that . . . I want to do something more meaningful—the illness has spurred that. When you hear people [with HIV/AIDS] say, you know, "this illness is a blessing"—well, ugh, that drives me nuts! It's a fucking disease, don't tell me that it's a blessing! But I think that's where I can understand what they're saying. It has kicked them in the butt to say, "Maybe I better do something with my life. It's only going to be a limited time. Let me get out of it what I want to get out of it."

Nevertheless, while advancing illness and a heightened sense of finitude give men with AIDS greater incentive to make and pursue plans for their future, this becomes extremely challenging when they suffer from debilitating (and sometimes erratic) symptoms. These symptoms make it virtually impossible for them to formulate and follow through on long-range plans. The plans they do make are usually tentative or short-term in nature and hinge upon how they feel on a given day, as Vic observed when discussing how he plans for the future:

> I kind of wait till the last minute. I'll say, "Well, I don't know if I can handle that or not. We'll see." Like, there's, um, well, someone's doing a campout at the end of May [about four weeks away]. And I think I'm just going to wait till the last minute to decide. I'll see how my energy level is. Maybe I can do that, maybe not. We'll see. So in a sense, in a general sense, my plans for the future are a little more uncertain and . . . a little more immediate.

In an effort to maximize their flexibility in planning, many men with AIDS work out tacit agreements with lovers, friends, or family members which allow them to easily change or cancel any plans that they make. They rely upon these intimate others to understand that plans or outings depend upon their fluctuating health situation.

Along with limiting the abilities of men with AIDS to plan, seriously debilitating symptoms alter their goals for self. As their health deteriorates and they become more disabled, these men have much greater difficulty imagining themselves pursuing new ambitions, roles, or identities. In light of this, they begin to set more immediate and tangible goals. Through attaining these goals, they can sustain a sense of accomplishment and self-worth. Kirby alluded to this when he reported:

> I try to set goals that I can deal with physically. Right now I'm finishing my basement—putting up some Sheetrock. And I just say, "I'll get a couple of pieces of Sheetrock on the wall today." And then I'll sit back and enjoy that—enjoy having some kind of accomplishment.

Overall, the men who suffer from severe AIDS-related complications orient themselves toward attaining smaller-scale goals, such as exercising regularly, going on outings with friends, attending special parties or events, working on household projects, and, more generally, "taking time to do and appreciate little things." By pursuing and attaining these modest goals, they sustain a sense of mastery and control in their daily battles with debilitating symptoms. In doing so, they experience the self-worth that derives from engaging in efficacious action—action that gives one a sense of being "on top of" rather than merely "up to" the challenges that life poses (Brissett 1972).

Confronting the Threats of Suffering, Dependence, and Dying

As their illness advances and their symptoms become more ominous, men with AIDS struggle to come to grips with their prospective mortality. Yet the threat of mortality is not usually the source of their greatest concerns. When reflecting upon the future, they commonly stress the pain, suffering, and debilitation they are likely to endure as they near the end of their lives. In fact, the men I interviewed felt far more afraid of the dying process than of death itself. When describing their anxieties regarding the future, they shared comments such as the following:

> I'm not afraid of death and what happens after death, I'm more afraid of the transition—it's going from here to there, dying, that's the scary part. . . . The fears that I have connected with it [the future] are to physical pain. I mean death hasn't and doesn't particularly scare me. It's the pain leading up to death that scares me. . . . I've been fairly close to death, but it just doesn't bother me. . . . I guess if anything bothers me it's having to go back to the hospital and go through all those procedures—like having a lung biopsy without anesthesia. That's not fun. . . . Stuff like that is what I don't want to go through again—the pain and discomfort.

In addition to fearing the prospect of pain and suffering, men with AIDS feel concerned about the possibility of losing many of their mental capacities, especially those capacities that are integral to their sense of self. As Lenny remarked:

> It worries me that I might lose my full faculties—my mental faculties. That is one of my major worries. Because I pride myself in being intelligent and rational—and being in control. Yeah, so that is a scary thing for me. And, um, I know it could happen. I mean, I've gone from having an excellent memory to only having an okay memory and things like that. That's been hard to deal with.

Of course, those men who have already experienced symptoms of disorientation or dementia feel particularly anxious about further deterioration of their mental abilities.

At the same time that they grapple with these fears, men with AIDS worry about the prospect of losing valued physical capacities, such as their ability to walk or move around easily. They also feel troubled about losing their sexual capabilities and dealing with the changes this will evoke in their intimate relationships and identities. As Neil indicated:

> As I've gotten more sick I've wondered about how much longer I'll be able to be sexual, I mean, over the last few months

my sexual functioning has just gone downhill. It's hard for me to get excited and, uh, to have sex, especially with my chronic fatigue. Sex takes a lot of energy—it wipes me out for a couple of days. And that doesn't feel very satisfying! But I know it's still important for [my lover]. I just worry about what's going to happen when I get even more sick. I mean, it's gonna get to the point where I'm not going to be able to have sex with him. So then what will happen? How will I feel about that? And how will he react?

As they come to terms with the decline taking place in their bodies and minds, men with AIDS feel especially concerned about the challenges they will face when they become more dependent on others. On one level, they worry about how they will preserve a sense of autonomy, masculinity, and self when they suffer from serious debilitation and have to give others more control over their lives. As Ron observed:

I was thinking lately that if I become an invalid and have to be taken care of all the time, uh, I'd rather kill myself. That's part of dealing with getting really sick—dealing with how am I going to be taken care of or take care of myself. I mean, you know, it's like a progression of giving up your independence, which is, uh, an important part of your manhood. I mean, first of all, you deal with the humility about being sick and then the humility of having to depend on other people. . . . And then when you talk about becoming an invalid, it's like a process of giving up control—giving up control of, uh . . . your identity.

On another level, men with AIDS worry about the burdens they will impose upon their caregivers in the last phases of the disease. Some men hope that they can avoid having relatives, particularly older parents, serve as their primary caregivers. For example, when reflecting upon his deteriorating health and future care, Bob asserted:

I don't want to put them [parents] into that maintenance thing. . . . My dad's old and in pretty crummy health, and my mom's seventy-three. So, I mean, I don't want to put them through that, at least from the standpoint of providing basic

medical care assistance, or that kind of thing. . . . You shouldn't burden your relatives with that kind of bed-changing crap, you know.

In an effort to deal with these concerns and gain a greater sense of control over their future, men with AIDS usually make arrangements that specify who will care for them and how they should be cared for if or when they become incapacitated. Some make plans for their lovers, spouses, or close relatives to serve as key caregivers because they are the most likely or willing persons to serve in this role. Other men, however, make arrangements to receive caregiving assistance from a variety of others—friends, partners, parents, siblings, hospice volunteers, visiting nurses, and other medical specialists—so that they will not overly burden any one person. These men hope to delegate the responsibilities of caregiving so that no one will feel overwhelmed by and resentful about the tasks involved. Dennis reflected the sentiments of those adopting this approach when he remarked, "It's a major burden for one person to have to do—to have to go through—being a primary caregiver. So you have to spread the load out a little bit."

Along with planning for their future care, men with AIDS make arrangements which are designed to enhance their control over the process of dying. For instance, Rick planned to end his life when his symptoms progressed to the point where he had no real hope for recovery. He expected to make this choice in the near future because of the dramatic loss of vision and energy he had recently suffered. When reflecting upon the future, he stated:

I am a firm believer in self-deliverance, or in what some people call voluntary death. . . . You know, there's a time when you've just got to say "good-bye," and when that time comes for me, I'll be ready to do it. Other people might try to hang on and hang on, you know, [through] life support and artificial resuscitation. I think that's ridiculous. . . . I don't want to just hang on and depend on someone else to make decisions for me. I want to have some control over the process. So when the time comes and I've become debilitated and my quality of life has diminished, you know, to an extremely low point, then I'll be ready to perform self-deliverance.

More commonly, men with AIDS exercise control over their dying process by arranging to die a natural death rather than relying upon doctors to make decisions about their health care. They do this in a variety of ways, including filling out living wills which prevent physicians from taking extraordinary measures to prolong their lives (Weitz 1991) and assigning durable power of attorney to loved ones who agree to let them "die with dignity" if they become incapacitated and lose the ability to make their own decisions.

Finally, another way that men with AIDS gain a greater measure of control over their dying and future is through making advanced funeral and burial arrangements, and indicating what types of rituals, memorials, or celebrations they want friends and family to observe.

While discovering ways to gain control over their dying and death is important for men with AIDS, they also devote their energies to sustaining a sense of hope for the future. Some do this by making plans to fulfill lifelong dreams such as finishing treasured projects or traveling to places they had always wanted to see. Others remain hopeful through focusing on the dramatic resurgences of health that they (or their friends) have experienced in the past. Still others derive ongoing hope from the possibility that a medical cure will arrive on the scene before their health deteriorates further. In support of this possibility, they point to the major advances that have taken place in HIV-related medical knowledge and treatments during the past decade. As Alan suggested when discussing his hopes for ongoing survival:

Well, they have come up with medicines, more helpful medicines, you know. . . . And as they come up with better combinations, maybe they can treat me in time. Because I'm still physically intact, you know—my hearing is good, my eyesight is good, and, um, you know, some of the worst things that happen to people I haven't experienced yet. So it's kind of like if they could arrest the virus right

now, I could get back into being a normal, healthy person.

In addition to these strategies, men with AIDS often find hope for the future through prayer and spirituality. As a result of their prayers and spiritual beliefs, they feel better able to cope with their suffering and prospective death. Although their spirituality does not always offer immediate benefits, it helps them to feel more hopeful in coming to terms with the future, as Hal revealed:

My spirituality gives me hope. I don't know if it sustains me all the time. There's times when it doesn't feel like it's doing a damn bit of good. But that's okay, it doesn't have to. I don't think that's what spirituality is about. Um, it's just kind of something that helps me in getting through, you know, getting through the days and what lies ahead.

Yet another strategy that men with AIDS use to sustain hope is focusing on the possibility that they will die a relatively painless and serene death. Usually, they recognize this possibility after seeing a friend or lover have such an experience. For instance, Stuart emphasized how a number of his friends with AIDS had "felt a sense of peace and serenity as their lives drew to a close" and "had come to accept and welcome death." In turn, he anticipated that he could have a similar experience as he underwent the last stages of the dying process.

Transcending Death: Building a Post-Mortal Self

As symbolic interactionist theorists have emphasized, individuals coming to terms with terminal illnesses face the task of making sense of their dying and making sense of themselves as dying persons (Lofland 1978; Marshall 1975, 1980). In doing so, they commonly try to give redemptive meaning to their lives and to sustain a sense of personal continuity, often by "accentuating portions of their personal histories for which they wish to be remembered" (Unruh 1983, p. 342). They also strive to gain a measure of control over the final chapters of their lives and over their post-mortal future. This struggle for control becomes integrally related to their struggle for meaning and continuity. By effectively legitimating or making sense of their unfolding biographies and prospective deaths, terminally ill individuals can gain an enhanced sense of control (Marshall 1980). In fact, through giving redemptive meaning to their lives and deaths, and through defining death as a positive transition for self rather than as a cessation of self, they can gain mastery over it as an ultimate limit. In essence, they can transcend death, at least symbolically (Becker 1975).

As they become increasingly cognizant of their prospective deaths, people with terminal illnesses often experience an "epiphany" (Denzin 1989b)—an existential crisis that challenges or disrupts their fundamental meaning structures and self-understandings. In turn, they begin to reshape their sense of self, linking and anchoring it to what comes after death (Charmaz 1991). In many cases this involves them in efforts to construct or experience an immortal self, or what some analysts call the "postself" (Lifton 1967; Schmidt and Leonard 1986). Through building and becoming anchored in a viable postself, dying individuals find a way to sustain a sense of hope and vitality in their daily lives. They also solidify and preserve important identities and assure themselves that their lives have had or will have an enduring meaning and purpose.

As they come to terms with their prospective deaths, men with AIDS, like others dealing with terminal illness, engage in efforts to anchor their sense of self in a post-mortal future. Those struggling with life-threatening symptoms, such as the men in this study, are especially inclined to devote themselves to the construction of a postself. They do this in a number of ways. (See Table 36.1 for a summary.)

In some cases, men with AIDS focus their energies on maintaining close and caring personal relationships in the hope that after dying they will "be remembered as someone who reached out and did little things for other people." They may also dedicate themselves to collecting artifacts or to writing journals that will be passed on to friends, family, or the wider public. They hope that this will allow their experiences or "stories" to live on in the memories of others.

In addition to using these strategies, many of the men I interviewed anchored a postself, or sense of symbolic immortality (Lifton 1978), in the enduring contributions they had made through their work as artists, writers, teachers, carpenters, businesspeople, or medical specialists. Several also stressed the "legacy" they would leave as a result of their efforts as HIV/AIDS educators and volunteers or as leaders of the gay community. For instance, Hal and Lee emphasized the significant impact they had made through combating homophobia and promoting HIV-related education and support programs in the small towns where they had lived. Others, such as Bob, Dave, and Jay, accentuated how they made a lasting difference through speaking publicly about HIV-related issues, as highlighted in the following excerpt:

> I get up in front of crowds of people and say, "Hey I'm a human being and I have feelings just like you. And I hope that you never find yourself in the same position

---

Table 36.1
Strategies Used to Construct Valued Postselves

Strategies	No. of Interviewees Utilizing
Sustaining close personal relationships to be remembered as a caring person	9*
Passing on personal mementos or journals	6
Highlighting enduring vocational accomplishments	12
Stressing significant volunteer accomplishments (especially AIDS-related education and advocacy)	11
Embracing visions of a spiritual afterlife	16
Linking the AIDS self to enduring social and historical dramas	4

*Many of the men I interviewed used more than one of these strategies in building and sustaining a post-self. As a result, the sum total of the numbers listed in the right column of the table is larger than the sample size of twenty-one men.

that I'm in . . ." I talk about all the things that have happened to me—about getting fired from my job and watching my friends die. And I do it in a way that moves them—that gets them to think more deeply about things and, um, that helps them to focus on their common humanness with me—with us, with people with HIV.

As they come to terms with their finitude, men with AIDS not only construct an enduring self in terms of the legacies they will leave behind, they also anchor a sense of continuity in beliefs that they will live on spiritually after dying. In discussing their future and prospective death, my informants shared remarks that illustrated how their religious beliefs, or spiritual outlooks, provided them with a basis for building and sustaining an immortal self. As Curtis remarked:

I think my spirituality is, very tied to that—to giving me a sense of living on. I don't think there would be any religion or spirituality if people didn't die, you know. And personally, yeah, it's important in coming to terms with that, um, with living on and what that means.

Drawing upon religious or spiritual frameworks, the men I interviewed often saw death as a transition to a new realm of being rather than as an ending to their personal existence. Although some accepted traditional Christian views of the afterlife, most espoused alternative views because of the anti-gay, anti-drug, or anti-sex messages conveyed by many variants of Christian theology. Rather than thinking of the afterlife in terms of Heaven and Hell, they typically embraced philosophies that emphasize how one's life force continues on in a never ending spiritual journey.

Overall, belief in an afterlife offers men with AIDS an important basis of hope and continuity regarding their present and future. By drawing upon these beliefs, they can solidify and preserve their sense of "real self" (Turner 1976) and anchor it in a future beyond death. This makes the prospect of death less ominous and frightening. Moreover, rather than viewing death as the ultimate loss of self, they redefine it as an opening to new experiences and, implicitly, to an enhanced or transformed self. This conception of death is reflected in the following remarks shared by Trent:

Death is the very thing that makes it possible to transcend—the means by which we transcend. It just opens up more and more possibilities and opportunities for wholeness and for unity with God or the Godhead, whatever we might identify as that.

Given their sense of being trapped in a devitalizing present, men with AIDS who embrace this view even look forward to death, at least on one level, because of the new life they anticipate having afterward. Although they feel somewhat fearful of the dying process, they also feel, as Dennis noted, "excited to move on to the new adventure and wonderful possibilities offered in the hereafter."

Yet, while belief in an afterlife can foster feelings of hope and anticipation regarding the future, it can also evoke feelings of anxiety and uncertainty. For instance, Matt and Vic, who accepted traditional Christian conceptions of the afterlife, worried about what would happen after they died. As Matt remarked, "I wonder whether I'll be shoveling coal in one place or pushing clouds in the other." In a related vein, those men who believed in reincarnation also wondered whether their future lives would be more or less rewarding than their present ones. As Neil pointed out:

I believe in reincarnation . . . [and] that serves as a source of hope, but it's a source of worry, too (laughs). You know, in the next life I could come back in Bangladesh, in the midst of a typhoon (laughs). I mean, people always like to think that things would be better in the next life, but who knows where you might pop up? It might not be so great there. In fact, if there's any sense of justice, many of us [Americans] might come back in an impoverished state.

As noted above, the men I interviewed rarely embraced or expressed traditional Christian views when it came to their images of the afterlife and of a postmortal self. At times, however, they drew upon variants of Christianity in their efforts to immortalize the self and to give both redemptive meaning and social significance to their experiences as persons living with AIDS. For instance, Jay utilized Catholic imagery in defining people with AIDS as part of a "litany of saints" who, in suffering, embodied Christ. As he explained:

> I believe, like Mother Teresa says, that those who suffer the most—they're like Jesus. The more you suffer, the closer you are to the face of Jesus. She talks about that imagery—how when she reaches to the beggar, the leper, the dying person in the street, that that is Jesus. . . . She says, "That person is Jesus in a distressing disguise." And I believe that people with AIDS, in the quality of suffering they endure, become—like others who suffer—most like Christ.

By defining the experience of people with AIDS (and, implicitly, his own experience) in this way, Jay not only gave it a redemptive and transcendent meaning, he also connected it to an overarching legacy and an unfolding sociohistorical drama. In fact, he suggested that people with AIDS had a prophetic historical role to play. They were being "called or chosen to convey a message to others about what was happening around them." In elaborating, Jay asserted:

> I think that people with AIDS have an amazing role to play in history. There's so many messages that have been conveyed and are yet to be conveyed—about the disease and what it means for the planet and how we live. There's so much we can learn from this, and I think people with AIDS can be like modern-day prophets. That doesn't mean other people can't be prophetic, too. There are many people in other situations who have that ability as well, but I think AIDS is, uh, is prophetic just because of its connection with sexuality and, um, life-giving things. It reflects the whole paradigm of planetary illness and how Mother Earth is hurting—and when any living, breathing organism is hurting, what happens sooner or later is disease results. And AIDS is an example of that.

Most importantly, by connecting the experience of people with AIDS to larger religious themes and social dramas, Jay legitimized

his own illness experience and gained a sense that it had a redeeming, significant, and enduring purpose. . . .

References

Adam, Barry. 1996. *Experiencing HIV*. New York: Columbia University Press.

Becker, Ernest. 1975. *The Denial of Death*. New York: Free Press

Blumer, Herbert. 1969. *Symbolic Interactionism*. Englewood Cliffs, NJ: Prentice-Hall.

Brissett, Dennis. 1972. "Toward a Clarification of Self-Esteem." *Psychiatry* 35:255–63.

Charmaz, Kathy. 1994, "Identity Dilemmas of Chronically Ill Men." *Sociological Quarterly* 35:269–88.

———. 1991. *Good Days, Bad Days: The Self in Chronic Illness and Time*. New Brunswick, NJ: Rutgers University Press.

———. 1990. "'Discovering' Chronic Illness Using Grounded Theory." *Social Science and Medicine* 30:1161–72.

Corbin, Juliet, and Anselm Strauss. 1987. "Accompaniments of Chronic Illness: Changes in Body, Self, Biography and Biographical Time." Pp. 249–82 in *Research in the Sociology of Health Care*, vol. 6 (*The Experience and Management of Chronic Illness*), edited by J. Roth and P. Conrad. Greenwich, CT: JAI Press.

Denzin, Norman. 1989a. *Interpretive Interactionism*. Beverly Hills, CA: Sage.

———. 1989b. *Interpretive Biography*. Beverly Hills, CA: Sage.

———. 1983. "A Note on Emotionality, Self, and Interaction." *American Journal of Sociology* 89:402–8.

Durig, Alexander. 1996. *Autism and the Crisis of Meaning*. Saratoga Springs, NY: SUNY Press.

Glaser, Barney, and Anselm Strauss. 1967. *The Discovery of Grounded Theory*. Chicago: Aldine.

Goffman, Erving. 1963. *Stigma*. Englewood Cliffs, NJ: Prentice-Hall.

———. 1961. *Asylums*. Garden City, NY: Anchor Books.

Kayal, Philip. 1993. *Bearing Witness: Gay Men's Health Crisis and the Politics of AIDS*. Boulder, CO: Westview Press.

Kotarba, Joseph, and Norris Lang. 1986. "Gay Lifestyle Change and AIDS Preventive Health Care." Pp. 127–43 in *The Social Dimensions of AIDS: Method and Theory*, edited by D. Feldman and T. Johnson. New York: Praeger.

Lifton, Robert Jay. 1978. *The Broken Connection.* New York: Basic Books.

——. 1967. *Death in Life: Survivors of Hiroshima.* New York: Random House.

Lofland, Lyn. 1978. *The Craft of Dying: The Modern Face of Death.* Beverly Hills, CA: Sage.

Markus, Hazel, and P. Nurius. 1986. "Possible Selves." *American Psychologist* 41:954–69.

Marshall, Victor. 1980. *Last Chapters: A Sociology of Aging and Dying.* Monterey, CA: Brooks/Cole.

——. 1975. "Age and Awareness of Finitude in Developmental Gerontology." *Omega* 6:113–29.

Mead, George Herbert. 1934. *Mind, Self, and Society.* Chicago: University of Chicago Press.

Sandstrom, Kent. 1998. "Coming to Terms with Bodily Losses and Disruptions Evoked by AIDS." *Illness, Crisis, and Loss* 48:17–31.

——. 1996a. "Redefining Sex and Intimacy: The Sexual Self-Images, Outlooks, and Relationships of Gay Men Living with HIV Disease." *Symbolic Interaction* 19:241–62.

——. 1996b. "Searching for Information, Understanding, and Self-Value: The Utilization of Peer Support Groups by Gay Men Living with HIV/AIDS." *Social Work in Health Care* 23:51–74.

——. 1990. "Confronting Deadly Disease: The Drama of Identity Construction among Gay Men with AIDS." *Journal of Contemporary Ethnography* 19:271–94.

Schmidt, Raymond, and W. Leonard II. 1986. "Immortalizing the Self Through Sport." *American Journal of Sociology* 91:1088–111.

Strauss, Anselm. 1993. *Continuing Permutations of Action.* New York: Aldine de Gruyter.

Stryker, Sheldon. 1980. *Symbolic Interactionism: A Social Structural Version.* Menlo Park, CA: Benjamin Publications.

Turner, Ralph. 1976. "The Real Self: From Institution to Impulse." *American Journal of Sociology* 81:989–1016.

Unruh, David. 1983. "Death and Personal History Strategies of Identity Preservation." *Social Problems* 30:341–51.

Weitz, Rose. 1991. *Life with AIDS.* New Brunswick, NJ: Rutgers University Press.

——. 1989. "Uncertainty and the Lives of Persons with AIDS." *Journal of Health and Social Behavior* 30:270–81.

Review

1. Discuss the challenges to the self faced by those in the advanced stages of AIDS.

2. How do AIDS victims deal with the threats of suffering, dependence, and dying?

3. Describe how the men try to transcend death by building a post-mortal self.

Applications

1. Find an article or a book that discusses the process of dying. What are the challenges that dying people typically face? What are the emotional stages they go through? How are those dying of AIDS similar to and different from those dying of other causes?

2. Invite someone who works at an AIDS hospice to speak to your class about his or her experiences in being with those dying of the disease. How do his or her experiences compare with Sandstrom's findings?

Unit V

Social Processes

Although social institutions contribute to the stability of societies, every society is also characterized by various processes and change. Traditional societies tend to conform to accepted models from the past and to change more slowly. However, modern societies are distinguished by diversity and dynamism. They are a breeding ground for variations of all kinds, from technological innovations to fundamental changes in religious and political values.

One important process is the emergence of **deviance,** or behavior that violates social norms. In its popular usage, "deviance" connotes something negative and undesirable, but sociologists use the term in a neutral sense. Certain types of deviance, such as the murder of innocent victims, are universally condemned. In other cases, what is considered deviant to one group may be normative behavior to another. And what is deviant to one generation may be applauded by later generations. After all, the Founding Fathers engaged in deviance when they rebelled against the established order. Norm violations that are widely defined as serious and unacceptable may provoke reform or other social changes. Selections 37–40 deal with various aspects of deviant behavior.

The second process is **social change,** which involves alterations in social phenomena at various levels of human life, from the individual to the global. Social change includes population processes. Selection 41 illustrates one type of population shift—immigration and the struggles of immigrants to adapt to their new social setting. Social mobility is also a form of change. Selection 42 looks at a relatively recent kind of mobility, a conscious decision to move down in the social stratification system.

The economy and technology are central elements in social change. Selection 43 addresses the recent and widespread use of credit cards in American society, while selection 44 examines the phenomenon of the growing use of cellular telephones. ✦

Part One

Deviance

How much deviance is there in any society? The answer has to be, a great deal. Think of it this way: Everyone violates the mores and folkways at some time. Indeed, everyone does something at some time that violates the law (such as littering, speeding, or taking office or school supplies home for personal use).

Clearly, however, people regard some kinds of deviance as more serious than others. Crime, urban gang activity, illegal drug use and abuse, and putting children at risk are four such serious types of deviance. These are the topics of the selections in this part. ✦

37
Crime and the Media

Jay Livingston

*How much crime is there is the United States? How do you know? Americans are likely to know about the nature and extent of crime from the media. The **mass media** are those forms of communication that provide information to widespread audiences. Radio, television, newspapers, books, and magazines are all part of the mass media.*

How do the media shape your understandings of such things as crime? Are they simply a mirror of the crime that exists in the society? Or do they select and present information in such a way that the image of crime generated in the audience is inaccurate in some way? In this selection, Livingston describes a number of ways in which the media portray crime in ways that are misleading to the public. His article illustrates how misleading information can become part of the conventional wisdom of a society. It also raises the issue of how much of the conventional wisdom is generated or perpetuated by the mass media.

One of the most successful films of recent years was *The Silence of the Lambs*. It brought in healthy box office receipts and picked up most of the major Academy Awards. Like many other movies, it was about killing. The story pitted a novitiate FBI agent against two homicidal maniacs—one known, for the most part unseen, and largely unremembered; the other, the character everyone was talking about, Hannibal Lecter.

The movie epitomizes some themes that recur in the media's presentation of crime: that crime is mostly murder; killers are motivated by twisted psychopathic fantasies; criminals are fiendishly clever and methodical; and crimes are solved by even more clever and methodical law enforcement officers, often using computers and other high-tech methods that lay people only dimly understand. There are, of course, variations. Murderers also may be motivated by insatiable greed, and the crime-solvers may be civilians.

People know that movies such as *The Silence of the Lambs* or *Basic Instinct* are not factual, like the 11 o'clock news. Yet, in the case of crime, news tries hard to imitate art. More than half the crimes that make it to the TV news are murders, while the far more frequent felonies become newsworthy only under special circumstances (the victim is a celebrity, criminals take hostages, police kill the criminal, etc.). Nor are the murders in the news typical of most murders. Instead, they are those that most resemble a good Hollywood script. Add to this the profusion of made-for-TV movies "based on a true story," and it becomes clear that the distinction between the news and prime time does not much matter, for they convey similar images of crime.

Even "serious" news magazines give a somewhat distorted picture. Every couple of years, for example, *Time* magazine runs a cover story on crime. The 1993 version bore the title "America the Violent." Inside, the featured piece, "Danger in the Safety Zone," carried the subhead: "As violence spreads into small towns, many Americans barricade themselves." The feature focused on five crimes: a revenge-motivated shooting of a nurse by a 31-year-old woman in a hospital; the murder of basketball star Michael Jordan's father; a random shooting in a Kenosha, Wis., McDonald's; the murder of a woman by her 15-year-old son as they sat in a theater at a Kansas City mall; and the strangling of an 82-year-old woman in Tomball, Tex. (pop. 6,370).

The rest of the article was devoted to psychological explanations of violence and the atmosphere of fear that pervades America the Violent. The message was clear—nobody is safe. Yet, by and large, these are not the types of violent crimes Americans risk.

The U.S. does have more violent crime than other industrialized societies, with a murder rate anywhere from three to 12 times higher. Other countries rarely have serial killers or those who arm themselves and start firing randomly in restaurants and workplaces.

Murder makes up only about 0.27% of all the felonies tabulated in the FBI's Index of Serious Crime, and only about 1.25% of all violent incidents. Still, 24,000 homicides a year is a lot. However, the killings that swell this statistic are, for the most part, not the sort featured in *Time*, and they certainly are not like the ones committed by Hannibal Lecter or those that call for the attention of a Columbo or a Jessica Fletcher.

Most murders are unplanned, committed with hardly any thought to escaping detection. Typically, these crimes start with a dispute, often over something trivial, between people (usually men) who know each other. Fueled by alcohol, the dispute quickly escalates to murderous intent. Include some bystanders so that neither party can back down honorably, even if he wanted to, add deadly weapons to the scenario, and someone winds up dead. The largest increase in murder in recent years has occurred among teenage boys, attributable to the ease with which they can obtain deadly weapons. An inner-city 15-year-old, feeling he has been "dissed" by another, borrows a handgun and returns to blow away his antagonist. The scenario, however distressingly frequent it has become, does not have the right stuff for the media. Even on the local news in a large city like New York, it may get only a five-second reading, while Amy Fisher and Joey Buttafuoco appear on the news and in prime time at saturation levels.

Solving Crimes—the Private (Eye) Sector

The media, besides giving a distorted picture of crime and even of the crimes it chooses to depict, also furthers myths about who solves crimes and how they do it.

There is a hierarchy of competence in the world of crime-fighting portrayed in American movies and television. At the top is the private detective, tough, clever, canny, and tenacious. Then comes the police detective and finally, if at all, the patrol officer.

The private eye, the "hard-boiled" private detective, is the decidedly American contribution to the mystery genre. From the heroes of Raymond Chandler and Dashiell Hammett to less literary versions like Mickey Spillane's immensely popular Mike Hammer, this type still dominates the mystery section of the bookstore, though women (such as V. I. Warshawski) now have gotten into the act. Movies and TV have appropriated some of these (Sam Spade, Spenser) and created many knock-offs (Magnum).

The obvious message is, if you need to have a crime solved, go to a private detective. That's what private eyes do better than anyone else, especially the police. In fact, a favorite device in the genre is the interfering cop, a perhaps well-meaning police officer who keeps messing up the private eye's attempt to bring the bad guys to justice. Often, the cops wind up suspecting the hero of the crime and either arresting him or creating other obstacles (which he, of course, overcomes).

Real-life private detectives do decidedly less heroic work. Some of it involves snooping for other parties (insurance companies' lawyers) or working for unhappy families—seeking secret lovers or hidden assets, finding divorce evidence, or tracking down runaway children. There is the occasional case where a private investigator manages to dig up information that sets a wrongfully convicted person free and even finds the real criminal, but most cases are either distasteful or utterly mundane.

If there is no private eye around, crime solving falls to the police, but not, of course, the uniformed force seen every day. The officer in uniform, even in non-comedy films, usually comes off little better than the Keystone Kops. The cops who can solve crimes are the detectives—the guys in plain clothes. This convention sustains the moral of the private-eye theme: the more a person is part of a bureaucratic structure like a police department, the less effective he will be—and what greater symbol of bureaucracy than a uniform?

Often, the crime-busting detective resembles the private investigator. There is something about him that bureaucrats in the department find tainted or threatening. He doesn't play by the rules, and may have trouble with women or alcohol. Most important, rather than approaching the job with bureaucratic detachment, he gets personally involved, leading to the cliché scene in which the hero's superior (even if he is not corrupt, linked to the bad guys, or merely envious of the hero's abilities) says, "You've gotten yourself in too deep, and it's ruined your judgment. I'm taking you off the case before you do something stupid." Or, if the hero has cut a few corners in his pursuit of the bad guys, his boss suspends him from the force altogether. ("O.K., Benson, turn in your badge and your weapon.") Like the private eye, the detective not only must catch the bad guys, who are trying either to avoid him or kill him, but he must do it with one hand behind his back (secured there by department hand-cuffs).

Actual police departments often operate on the detective myth. Most are organized along bureaucratic lines, a structure based on the assumption that things can be handled more efficiently by division of labor and specialization. Detectives, in this model, are crime-solving specialists. When a citizen reports a crime, patrol officers in uniform are dispatched to the scene. They gather the relevant information and turn it over to the detectives, who then solve the crime—just like in the movies.

Clearing Cases in Real Life

What's wrong with this picture? To begin with, there's the problem of batting averages. Fictional cops are batting near 1,000. Before the final credits roll, the bad guys either are arrested or dead. In real life, though, most crimes do not result in arrest.

Police departments compute a statistic called the clearance rate—the percentage of reported crimes for which someone has been arrested (regardless of the outcome of the case). Arrest someone for a crime and it (plus any others the suspect may confess to) is "cleared by arrest." Police departments forward this information to the FBI, which compiles figures for the nation.

Of the eight categories on the FBI's Index of Serious Crime, the one with the highest clearance rate is murder, but even that stands at less than 70%. For robbery, the clearance rate is about 25%; for burglary and theft, less than 20%. When the police do solve these crimes, the process rarely resembles the brilliant deduction, dogged pursuit of leads, or high-tech sleuthing that dominate fictional crimesolving. In most cases— and this especially is true for violent crimes like murder and rape—the police make an arrest when a civilian (usually the victim or a witness) tells them who did it. The comparatively high clearance rate for murder has much less to do with the police than it does with the killers. The murders that are solved are the typical ones—fights between acquaintances or family members that spin out of control and end in death. It doesn't take a Kojak or a report from the ballistics lab to solve crimes like these.

When the murderers are strangers, as in robberies that end in murder, or when the killer takes some minimal steps to avoid detection, as in gangland "hits" or murders between rival drug dealers, it is very unlikely that the police will solve the crime. In New York, for instance, where these types of murders are more frequent, the clearance rate is about 50%. It is not that real-life police are incompetent, but these crimes are very difficult to solve. In big cities, the number of cases is so large that homicide detectives usually cannot devote the kind of time required to pursue leads that might lead to an arrest. Even successful detective work is not so much figuring out who committed the crime as it is gathering evidence so that the suspect will be convicted.

With the more frequent non-lethal violent crimes, police almost completely are dependent on information from victims or witnesses. If the victim can tell the authorities who committed the crime and, better yet, where to find him or her, the perpetrator can be arrested. Otherwise, forget it. TV detectives, of course, working with a physical description and modus operandi, usually can arrest the robber before the last commercial.

By contrast, a RAND study found that for "cold" crimes (i.e., those where the police arrive after the thief has had enough time to leave the area), police solve only two or three cases out of 100. Nearly always, it is the information gathered by the patrol officers that solves the crime. Putting detectives on the case usually is of little avail.

Another staple of fictional crime is the cop killer. In nearly every film or TV show, police get shot at. If the cast is large enough, one or two may get hit and die. This is a useful plot device, for in American films, a hero, no matter how beneficial to society his actions may be, must be motivated by purely personal concerns. Ideologues operating only on abstract principles—even the most basic ones of right and wrong—make the audience suspicious. If viewers are to trust the protagonist, he cannot go after bad guys just because he wants to make the city a nicer place to live in or because he thinks crime is wrong. (For some reason, this restriction does not apply to superheroes like Batman and Superman.) Once a cop is seeking vengeance for a fallen buddy, however, anything goes.

In the non-fiction media as well, a gunned-down police officer almost always is front-page news, with the story usually being played up for several days (the hunt for the killer, the funeral, the arrest). Given these images, the statistical reality probably makes little difference. As Stalin said, "The death of a million Russian soldiers, that is a statistic. The death of one Russian soldier, that is a tragedy." For better or worse, most people are moved more by tragedy than by statistics. Does it matter that the number of police murdered in the line of duty in the U.S. in 1992 was about 65? Or that this annual statistic, despite the widespread perception that criminals have been getting more numerous and dangerous, has been declining more or less steadily since its 1973 high of 131 (a number that still is far lower than what most people would guess)?

An equivalent number of police lose their lives in on-the-job accidents, most of them in automobiles. Apparently, the high-speed chase, a staple of fictional crime-fighting, also is tempting to real-life cops. Here, though, statistics seem finally to have had some impact. In recent years, many departments, realizing the dangers to police and civilians relative to the benefits of catching usually minor offenders, have tightened their restrictions on high-speed pursuit, and accidental police deaths have declined accordingly.

This does not mean that police work is not dangerous. It is certainly more hazardous than, say, accounting or magazine editing. Nevertheless, police officers suffer less on-the-job death than miners (the deadliest occupation), firefighters, or even farm workers.

It is an open question as to what effect the media have on society. People who form their ideas based solely on prime time reporting may not understand the police's inability to solve some serious crimes. A burglary victim may be disappointed that the investigators seemingly just are going through the motions, providing paperwork for insurance claims. "They didn't even dust for fingerprints" is a frequent lament.

The media also can give distorted perceptions of risk. For instance, parents, having heard stories about poisoned candy and other Halloween sadism, now routinely inspect all the candy their offspring bring home; some even may forbid their children to go trick-or-treating. In systematic efforts to track down such stories, however, nearly all of them turn out to have been hoaxes. A 1982 investigation of hundreds of candy-tampering claims found only two injuries, neither requiring medical attention.

There probably is no harm in such parental caution, even though the real risk is minuscule. Yet, the same parents may buy their kids skateboards or rollerblades—sources of more serious injury than all acts of deliberate child abuse. With the occasional exception of fatal accidents, these stories cannot compete with the "glamour" of crime in the media.

Review

1. What are some of the themes that recur in the media's presentation of crime?

2. How do the media distort the picture of crime in the United States?

3. What myths about solving crimes do the media perpetuate?

Applications

1. Conduct a content analysis of a major newspaper and television news program in your community. Note all the stories about crime each day for a period of two weeks. Record the number of stories, the kinds of crimes they deal with, and any information about perpetrators or police officials.

   Get information on the amount of crime in the United States from the most recent *Statistical Abstract of the United States*. Some crimes are broken down by region and state; get the statistics for your area if available.

   Summarize your results. How do the reports from the mass media compare with the government statistics? Do you think any discrepancies are due to reporting decisions or to differences between your community and the larger society? Why?

   Were there any differences in the picture of crime you derived from the newspaper and the television program? If so, what were they and how would you explain them?

2. Interview three men and three women about their understanding of crime in the community. Ask them such things as how much crime there is, how it compares with the nation as a whole, what the most prevalent kinds of crime are, whether most crimes are solved and who solves them, which crimes they fear the most, and so on. Then ask them about the sources of their information.

   Contact a local law enforcement agency for information on crime rates in the community. Summarize your results. Do your respondents have an accurate understanding of crime? Where do they get their information? How do the men's responses compare with those of the women?

Reprinted from: Jay Livingston, "Crime and the Media." In "Crime and the Media: Myths and Reality," *USA Today*, May, 1994, pp. 40–42. Reprinted from *USA Today* magazine, May, copyright © 1994 by the Society for the Advancement of Education. Reprinted by permission. ✦

38
Islands in the Street

Urban Gangs as Economic Organizations

Martin Sánchez Jankowski

A *persistent question in the study of deviant behavior is why people who violate legal and moral rules behave so differently from those in the mainstream of society. Some of the research has proceeded from the assumption that those who engage in deviance are different kinds of people in some sense, and the research has attempted to identify the differences.*

An alternate view, however, takes note of the similarities as well as the differences of those who engage in deviant behavior. Virtually everyone, for example, breaks rules at one time or another. Moreover, there are many gradations or degrees of "evil" between the actions of those who are seriously deviant and those who conform. Every society has areas where normal and deviant phenomena overlap.

This overlap is the subject of the following selection. During ten years of research, Jankowski acted as both an observer and a participant in 37 gangs in Boston, New York, and Los Angeles, including Irish, Latin, and African American gangs. (Entry into Asian and Italian American gangs was not possible.) In this selection he focuses on how gangs harness the individualism, self-reliance, and competitiveness of members and mold them into a viable organization. In some respects, this task is not that different from the one faced by such non-deviant groups as athletic teams and industrial corporations.

If there is one theme that dominates most studies of gangs, it is that gangs are collectives of individuals who are social parasites, and that they are parasitic not only because they lack the skills to be productive members of society but, more important, because they lack the values, particularly the work ethic, that would guide them to be productive members of society.[1] However, one of the most striking factors I observed was how much the entrepreneurial spirit, which most Americans believe is the core of their productive culture, was a driving force in the worldview and behavior of gang members.[2] If entrepreneurial spirit denotes the desire to organize and manage business interests toward some end that results in the accumulation of capital, broadly defined, nearly all the gang members that I studied possessed, in varying degrees, five attributes that are either entrepreneurial in character or that reinforce entrepreneurial behavior.

The first of these entrepreneurial attitudes is competitiveness. Most gang members I spoke with expressed a strong sense of self-competence and a drive to compete with others. They believed in themselves as capable of achieving some level of economic success and saw competition as part of human nature and an opportunity to improve one's self-worth. This belief in oneself often took on a dogmatic character, especially for those individuals who had lost in some form of economic competition. The losers always had ready excuses that placed the blame on something other than their own personal inadequacy, thereby artificially reinforcing their feelings of competence in the face of defeat.[3]

Gang members' sense of competitiveness also reflected their general worldview that life operates under Social Darwinist principles. In the economic realm, they believed there is no ethical code that regulates business ventures, and this attitude exempted them from moral constraints on individual economic-oriented action.[4] The views of Danny, Arrow, and Lobo provide three good examples of this Social Darwinist outlook. Danny was a twenty-year-old Irish gang member from Boston:

I don't worry about whether something is fair or not when I'm making a business deal. There is nothing fair or unfair, you just go about your business of trying to make a buck, and if someone feels you took advantage of him, he has only himself to blame. If someone took advantage of me, I wouldn't sit around bellyaching about it, I'd just go and try to get some of my money back. One just has to ask around here [the neighborhood] and you'll find that nobody expects that every time you're going to make a business deal, that it will be fair—you know, that the other guy is not going to be fair, hell, he is trying to make money, not trying to be fair. This is the way those big business assholes operate too! The whole thing [the system] operates this way.

Arrow was an eighteen-year-old African-American gang member from New York:

Hey, man, what do you mean by ethics? Ethics don't pay bills, money pays bills, and I'm hustling to get money. There ain't nobody interested in ethics, morality, and all that shit—the basic line is, did you make money or not? Fuck those guys who lose and then complain, everybody knows that if they won and I or somebody else lost they wouldn't be saying nothing. Hey, it's dog eat dog, and if you ain't up to it, you get eaten, simple as that! And look at corporate businesses, they ain't moral or ethical, they never have been and they ain't about to be either, 'cause they only know that they want money. Since nobody complains about them, nobody will complain about us.

Lobo was a twenty-year-old Chicano gang member from Los Angeles:

I act like they do in the big time, no different. There ain't no corporation that acts with morals and that ethics shit and I ain't about to either. As they say, if it's good for General Motors, it's good enough for me. . . . It boils down to who is smarter, you either take somebody or get taken, and General Motors, General Dynamics, all those big cats know that shit. They take the government's money— that's really mine and yours—for some type of ride. Check this man, they sell a two cent bolt to the government for thirty dollars and don't blink an eye. They get

caught, but they ain't sorry, they're just sorry they got caught. Who talks ethics and morality to them? They keep doing it because that's the rules, so when I do my business, I just do it and if somebody gets hurt, then they get hurt 'cause that's just the way it is.

The second entrepreneurial attribute I observed is the desire and drive to accumulate money and material possessions. Karl Marx, of course, described this desire as the "profit motive" and attributed it primarily to the bourgeoisie.[5] There is a profit-motive element to the entrepreneurial values of gang members, but it differs significantly from Marx's analysis of the desire to accumulate material and capital for their own sake, largely divorced from the desire to improve one's own material condition. Nor is gang members' ambition to accumulate material possessions related to a need for achievement, which the psychologist David McClelland identifies as more central to entrepreneurial behavior in certain individuals than the profit motive per se.[6] Rather, the entrepreneurial activity of gang members is predicated on their more basic understanding of what money can buy.[7] The ambition to accumulate capital and material possessions is related, in its initial stages (which can last for a considerable number of years), to the desire to improve the comfort of everyday living and the quality of leisure time.

This desire, of course, is shared by most people who live in low-income neighborhoods. Some of them resign themselves to the belief that they will never be able to secure their desires. Others attempt to improve their life situation by using various "incremental approaches," such as working in those jobs that are made available to them and saving their money, or attempting to learn higher-level occupational skills. In contrast, the entrepreneurs of low-income neighborhoods, especially those in gangs, attempt to improve their lives by becoming involved in a business venture, or a series of ventures that has the potential to create large changes in their own or their family's socio-economic condition.

The third attribute of entrepreneurial behavior prevalent in gangs is status-seeking.

Mirroring the dominant values of the larger society, most gang members attempt to achieve some form of status with the acquisition of possessions. However, most of them cannot attain a high degree of status by accumulation alone. To merit high status among peers and in the community, gang members must try, although most will be unsuccessful, to accumulate a large number of possessions and be willing to share them. Once gang members have accumulated sufficient material possessions to provide themselves with a relative level of comfort or leisure above the minimal, they begin to seek the increase in status that generosity affords. (For philanthropic purposes, accumulating cash is preferable to accumulating possessions, because the more money one has, the more flexibility one has in giving away possessions.)

The fourth entrepreneurial attribute one finds among gang members is the ability to plan. Gang members spend an impressive amount of time planning activities that will bring them fortune and fame, or, at least, plenty of spending money in the short term. At their grandest, these plans have the character of dreams, but as the accounts of renowned business tycoons show, having big dreams has always been a hallmark of entrepreneurial endeavors.[8] At the other end of the spectrum are short-range plans (also called small scams) that members try to pull on one another, usually to secure a loan. One member will say, "Can I borrow a few bucks until I get paid?" What he is really saying, however, is, "Can I have so-and-so-many dollars, or any amount to that figure, and if you need some money later yourself, and if I have some, I might give it to you." Once a member has been scammed by another in this way, future requests for "loans" usually elicit some type of respectful refusal.[9] Another common small scam begins with one gang member collecting money from several others for the purpose of obtaining drugs, usually cocaine. Later he returns and claims that he gave the money to the drug dealer, who then ran off with it. Everyone suspects that the gang member used all the dope himself or pocketed the money, and they usually greet the tale with a great deal of hostility, but punishment is seldom administered. The vast majority of small scams within the gang (among members) are tolerated because all the members recognize that they are all continually running scams, and scams, therefore, are considered within the realm of acceptable behavior. But nine of the gangs I studied (14 percent) viewed running a scam on another member to be unacceptable, because it destroyed a sense of group commitment, and severe punishment was administered to those found guilty of being involved in the scam.

Gang members also engage in intermediary and long-range planning. A typical intermediary plan might concern modest efforts to steal some type of merchandise from warehouses, homes, or businesses. Because most of the sites they select are equipped with security systems, a more elaborate plan involving more time is needed than is the case for those internal gang scams just described. Long-range planning and organization, sometimes quite elaborate, are, as other studies have reported, at times executed with remarkable precision.[10]

Finally, the fifth entrepreneurial attribute common among gang members is the ability to undertake risks. Generally, young gang members (nine to fifteen years of age) do not understand risk as part of a risk-reward calculus, and for this age group, risk-taking is nearly always pursued for itself, as an element of what Thrasher calls the "sport motive,"[11] the desire to test oneself. As gang members get older, they gradually develop a more sophisticated understanding of risk-taking, realizing that a certain amount of risk is necessary to secure desired goals. Now they attempt to calculate the risk factors involved for nearly every venture, measuring the risk to their physical well-being, money, and freedom. Just like mainstream businessmen, they discover that risk tends to increase proportionally to the level of innovation undertaken to secure a particular financial objective. Most of these older gang members are willing to assume risks commensurate with the subjective "value" of their designated target, but they will not assume risks just for the sake of risk-taking.

The Source of Entrepreneurial Attitudes

Gang members' entrepreneurial attitudes and behavior can be traced to four distinct sources. First, there are those psychological traits associated with the defiant individualist character into which nearly all gang members have been socialized. Two aspects of defiant individualism that directly relate to entrepreneurial attitudes are: (1) the lack of trust that gang members have of people in general, and (2) the more general acceptance of the Social Darwinist position that only the fit survive. Their lack of trust in people leads them to become self-reliant and confident that they can and must do things for themselves. An example is Circus, a seventeen-year-old African-American gang member from New York:

> Dig, I don't know if you can trust people, but there ain't no way that you should trust them. I mean, I trust myself, I defend and depend on myself, then I got nobody but myself to hold me back or fuck me up . . . what's more, I can do things better on my own than with other dudes who ain't as talented as me. You dig?

The belief that only the fit survive, in turn, lays the foundation for the proposition that one should exploit those opportunities that are present themselves, even if in doing so one hurts other people. The ethic of survival at any cost is somewhat tempered by feelings of attachment (in a number of cases) to family, community, or neighborhood, and some other gang members. Nonetheless, despite some exceptions, gang members generally consider most people as competitors. Take Sweet Cakes, a fifteen-year-old African-American gang member in New York:

> Look, everybody gets certain chances in life and you got to take advantage of them. Those who get ahead are just more better than those that don't. If you mess somebody up by taking advantage of your opportunities, that's just the way it is. You can't worry about it because you were the best this time and you know that if you don't stay competitive, you're done forever. . . . no, I wouldn't mess with my com-

munity that way, but the rest of the folks is all fair game.

A second source of entrepreneurial attitudes arises from the tensions between mainstream American consumer culture and the scarcity of resources in low-income neighborhoods. In all social classes, we have seen in the post-war period a gradual but consistent increase in the degree to which young Americans believe money to be a necessary tool for social interaction. After decades of being courted by American businesses, which correctly saw the potential for vast profits in the youth market, children, teenagers, and young adults have come to accept the premise that having cash is necessary to purchase the goods and services that make life worth living. Activities that do not require cash, the consumerist message reads, are not satisfying. As a result, kids of all ages, especially teenagers, feel the need to have at least some pocket money available at all times.[12] This need becomes a sense of urgency for those kids from low-income areas where there is a scarcity of financial resources. The reality for these kids is the need to struggle for the resources that are available and this acts to stimulate creativity. Without creativity, a youth from a low-income or working-class neighborhood would not be able to secure the money that American culture has established as a high priority. It is the need to be creative in order to secure money that has been one of the underlying elements in building the "entrepreneurial spirit" among gang members. The comments of Mano, a fifteen-year-old Puerto Rican gang member in New York, are representative:

> Let me put it like this. There ain't a lot you can do without some green stuff [money] so if you want to have some good times, you got to get it. . . . hell, yes, it's tough out there, that's why you got to be creative in how you go about raising your cash. Those who ain't creative will be paupers, man! Can you digest that? I sure couldn't.

Another credo of American business culture has also stimulated gang members to think like entrepreneurs: the belief that one can improve oneself with one good idea. In talking to gang members, I repeatedly heard the refrain that all one needs is one good idea, and that what separates successful people from failures is that the former are able to cultivate the necessary contacts to operationalize their big idea. In their search for the big idea that will produce the desired wealth, gang members often generate what in effect are a number of small ideas that take on the character of "conning." Understood in this context, "conning behavior," which has often been misunderstood as the effort of weak-minded and/or parasitic hucksters, is an idiosyncratic variant of the general entrepreneurial spirit. Stake, a twenty-year-old African-American man in a New York gang:

> Yeah, man, what you need in life, no matter who you are, is one, not two, not three, but one good idea that you can get working. You do that and you got yourself some easy life, dig it, man. . . . well, yeah, sometimes you be running some deal down on a dude, but sometimes you get ideas and you got to try out to see how good they are. You know like some experiments that people do. And dig, some experiments they be a job on people [take advantage of people], but that's just the way it is. Hell, medical experiments are just researchers doing a job on some poor sucker, and then they tell him it made a difference to society. What do you call that, science, or a con? It's all the same. It's just some people don't want to see it; or they too stupid to see it.

Finally, gang members' entrepreneurial spirit is both stimulated and reinforced by the desire to resist what they perceive to be their parents' resignation to poverty and failure. As small boys, many gang members were keenly disappointed that their parents had not been successful at becoming self-made people who lifted the family out of poverty. Instead, what they observed was their parents' hopeless inability to do anything that would improve the family's material conditions. What stuck in their minds most vividly was their parents' vulnerability: their objective vulnerability in selling their labor on the market and their feelings of being vulnerable. Here are two representative comments.

Dark, an eighteen-year-old member of an Irish gang:

> A few years ago I would be pissed at my old man 'cause he didn't do things like save his money and move from the projects. He just seemed to be unwilling to have a desire to improve himself so that my mother and us kids were better, you know?. . . Later I could see that he didn't have much of a chance, given that he was just a worker. I resented that, not him, but the situation. But you know, after I talked to him, I was more pissed at the way he felt than anything else. He felt like he had no control over the situation; and I said to myself, I'll do everything I can not to let the fuckers make me feel like that. And I hustle all the time trying to develop projects to get money.

Face-Man, a sixteen-year-old Puerto Rican gang member:

> No, my pop didn't have a chance to make it, 'cause if you're a laborer you don't have any power on the job market. What can he offer that's different than seventy thousand other laborers? Get my point? So he couldn't get out of this hole that we live in or help the rest of us too much. . . . He always was feeling nervous about keeping work or getting it. You could always see him worrying about it. This was a lesson to me, and I said I ain't going to lay down and feel vulnerable to these motherfuckers! So I work hard on my various deals.

Winners and Losers in Entrepreneurial Activity

Most members of gangs, then, have a fairly strong entrepreneurial spirit and engage in a variety of economic activities. Of all the entrepreneurial traits discussed, the one most crucial to an individual gang member's economic success or failure is his pattern of risk-taking. The prevailing view among the public is that nearly all gang activity involves a high degree of risk, but in truth gang members are like other economic actors, making choices among low-risk, moderate-risk, and high-risk ventures. Risk can be defined as the level of jeopardy in the potential loss of material assets, personal freedom, or physical well-being. While the economic environment in which gang members act is a dangerous one, some activities are far more or less risky than others. My observations indicate that gang members who were not successful economically were those whose risk-taking profile fell at either extreme of the spectrum. To be sure, some low and high risk-takers had some successes, but their cumulative efforts were unsuccessful. A good example is the story of Jumbo, an eighteen-year-old member of an ethnically mixed New York gang. Jumbo was always trying to come up with and sell his ideas for making a fortune. He would constantly propose new ideas that had the potential to deliver great profits to himself, those that would help him, and the entire gang, if he could persuade the leadership to commit resources and manpower. During the five years that I studied Jumbo and his particular gang, he had been able to secure gang participation only three times: twice during the first year of his involvement and once only recently for a rather small project. Of Jumbo's numerous entrepreneurial projects involving non-gang members, only a small fraction were successful.

Although each of Jumbo's successful efforts had yielded him several thousand dollars, most had involved high risks. Many of the participants were caught by law enforcement authorities, physically injured, or both. On six occasions, Jumbo had been arrested by the police; he had gone to jail twice. He had also been shot three times and beaten severely four times. Take one episode as an example. Jumbo had decided that a great deal of money could be made distributing cocaine. He was able to get the gang's support in the initial stage, which was to carry on some form of negotiation with the branch of the Mafia in charge of wholesale drug supplies for his area. He made contact, and the Mafia was in principle interested in his offer to have the gang act as the local dispensing agent. In listening to Jumbo's sales pitch, I was struck by how organized and professional it was, but I was also struck by the risks that he took in negotiating with the Mafia, which clearly had more bargaining power. Once the agreement in principle had been made, Jumbo raised the ante by asking for a commission that was so high that everybody (both the syndicate's men and his own) laughed, though the members of his own gang did so in a somewhat uneasy manner. Once it became clear that he was serious, the syndicate made a counterproposal that cut his opening figure by seven-eighths. Jumbo balked at the figure and said he would not make the deal.

After the meeting, he told the leadership of the gang, who were quite angry with him, that he wanted to skip the Mafia as a source and open a drug mill (drug factory) himself. The gang leaders admitted that his idea had the potential to earn big profits, but they were not interested because too many risks were involved. At this juncture, Jumbo said he would do it on his own. In the following weeks, he was able to solicit eighteen people to help him, only three of whom were from the gang. They started to make "treated marijuana" (marijuana spiked with other drugs) and some synthetic LSD. The operation lasted about three weeks, until three of the workers were shot at (no one was actually hit) and the place of business was fire-bombed. Jumbo and another participant escaped with second-degree burns. The money and time that Jumbo had invested in this project were considerable and the potential return was great, but the risks proved too high and the project ended in failure. Yet although his losses repeatedly outran his gains by an overwhelming margin, Jumbo persisted in undertaking high-risk projects, judging the prospects of high returns worth the dangers. However, for Jumbo, as well as others, such ventures generally end in bodily injury and/or loss of time and money.

At the other end of the risk-taking spectrum is Toga, a twenty-year-old member of an Irish gang. On one occasion, he had the idea that he could make good money by stealing car radios and selling them. He found a person who would buy the radios from him and then proceeded to look for radios he could steal. After one week he had become proficient enough to have stolen ten radios. As he became more efficient, he was making several hundred dollars a month from this project. Because the word had spread that he had been relatively success-ful, he was able to persuade a number of peo-ple that a larger operation would be ex-tremely profitable, and they agreed to join him. Before the new group was to start, how-ever, Toga said that they needed to get some equipment that would help them break into cars that had sophisticated alarm systems. All of the new members of the group agreed to invest in the new equipment, which cost several hundred dollars. Having secured this new equipment, the larger group went to work, and within a month they had accumu-lated more than one hundred radios. The man Toga had been selling the radios to now declined to buy them, saying that the opera-tion had gotten too big, and that he would not be able to move that many radios fast enough. Toga then asked if he knew of any-one who would buy in quantity, and the buyer agreed to check around and get back to him. Toga described this conversation to his group, telling them not to worry, that they would start making money as soon as he and the new buyer were able to make a deal.

By now the place where the group was storing the radios was so crowded that they had to rent a small space in an adjoining building. This required still more capital. Toga received a message from his first buyer that he had found a buyer who could handle the volume. But when Toga was told that the new buyer was part of the syndicate, he be-came uneasy. He could not decide whether to go ahead and meet with this new buyer or to try to find another one. He told his group that working with the syndicate would pre-sent some risks to all of them and their oper-ations. Maybe they were being set up by the syndicate, he said, and maybe the syndicate would take all their radios or expect them from now on to work for it. While Toga was trying to decide what to do, the number of ra-dios was rapidly increasing—there were now over eight hundred in storage. Toga finally made a date to meet the syndicate's represen-tative, but then decided not to go, believing, as he told me, that there were too many risks. So he contacted his old buyer and asked him whether he knew of someone else. His old buyer told him that he had blown it: there

was no one else who could deal in such vol-ume.

Needless to say, the other members of Toga's group were frustrated and angry. They had endured personal risks and invested money and time, and all they had to show for it was several rooms filled with stolen radios they could not peddle. Toga's reluctance to take a chance resulted in the failure of the enterprise, and he was given a generous amount of time to return some of their money to his confederates. Though Toga generated more ideas, he found it difficult to get other gang members to participate, and the gang as an organization would not do so. Over the eight years that I observed Toga, he continued to exercise a caution that consis-tently resulted in missed opportunities and failures.

In contrast, the successful gang entrepre-neur tends to assume a moderate risk pro-file. He is likely to pursue a strategy where risk is present, but has been reduced to a moderate level through careful planning: se-lection of the type of activity, location, strat-egy for executing the task, protection from being apprehended. Like a mainstream busi-nessman, the successful gang entrepreneur calculates risk factors, the probability of the venture failing, and the odds of misfortune of various sorts. A good example of this type of gang entrepreneur is Grisly, a nineteen-year-old gang member from New York.

Grisly decided that he would steal stereos and televisions from apartments and then resell them. Before he began his venture, he made contact with two people who bought stolen objects and he entered into an agree-ment to sell to both of them. As he said to me: "The smart thing to do is find more than one buyer, in case one of them is picked up by the police, or if one of them can't buy what you have 'cause they just don't have the money or they can't move them. If you do that, you keep moving your stuff." Then he talked to a number of people in the gang to see if they were interested. He offered a percentage of the amount obtained from the buyer. He then had each of them look at buildings that might have easy access. They also checked out what kinds of locks the apartments had and avoided all those with police locks. They discussed various techniques for ascertaining if people were home before they burglarized a place. They also worked out a warning system to minimize the risk of being caught. Eventually, Grisly decided not to become involved in the burglaries himself, but to buy the stolen objects from those who did and then sell them to his contacts. After accumulating a significant amount of money from this, he moved on to more extensive projects. Because Grisly was well organized and attentive to details, his plans were successful, and most of the gang members wanted to be involved in his projects. In Grisly, then, we see the successful gang entrepreneur who selects enterprises that require some risk but takes steps to ensure that he does not lose everything if the business fails. Because he also works to minimize the risks for his associates, he has little difficulty in recruiting accomplices.

Economic Activity: Accumulating

With a few exceptions, nearly all the literature on gangs focuses on their economic delinquency.[13] This is a very misleading picture, however, for although gangs operate principally in illegal markets, they also are involved in legal markets. Of the thirty-seven gangs observed in the present study, twenty-seven generated some percentage of their revenues through legitimate business activity. It is true that gangs do more of their business activity in illegal markets, but none of them wants to be exclusively active in these markets.[14]

In the illegal market, gangs concentrate their economic activities primarily in goods, services, and recreation. In the area of goods, gangs have been heavily involved in accumulating and selling drugs, liquor, and various stolen products such as guns, auto parts, and assorted electronic equipment. These goods are sometimes bought and sold with the gang acting as wholesaler and/or retailer. At other times, the gang actually produces the goods it sells. For example, while most gangs buy drugs or alcohol and retail them, a few gangs manufacture and market homemade drugs and moonshine liquor. Two gangs (one African-American and one Irish) in this study had purchased stills and sold their moonshine to people on the street, most of whom were derelicts, and to high school kids too young to buy liquor legally.[15] Three other gangs (two Puerto Rican and one Dominican) made a moonshine liquor from fermented fruit and sold it almost exclusively to teenagers. Both types of moonshine were very high in alcohol, always above one hundred proof. While sales of this liquor were not of a magnitude to create fortunes, these projects were quite surprisingly capable of generating substantial amounts of revenue.

The biggest money-maker and the one product nearly every gang tries to market is illegal drugs.[16] The position of the gang within the illegal drug market varies among gangs and between cities. In New York, the size of the gang and how long it has been in existence have a great deal to do with whether it will have access to drug suppliers. The older and larger gangs are able to buy drugs from suppliers and act as wholesalers to pushers. They shun acting as pushers (the lowest level of drug sales) themselves because there are greater risks and little, if any, commensurate increase in profit. In addition, because heroin use is forbidden within most gangs, the gang leaders prefer to establish attitudes oriented to the sale rather than the consumption of drugs within the organization. In the past, when the supply was controlled by the Italian Mafia, it was difficult for gangs to gain access to the quantity of drug supplies necessary to make a profit marketing them. In the past ten years, though, the Mafia has given way (in terms of drug supply) to African-American, Puerto Rican, and Mexican syndicates.[17] In addition, with the increased popularity of cocaine in New York, the African-American, Puerto Rican, and Dominican syndicates' connections to Latin American sources of cocaine supply rival, and in many cases surpass, those of Mafia figures.[18] With better access to supplies, gangs in New York have been able to establish a business attitude toward drugs and to capitalize on the opportunities that drugs now afford them.

Some gangs have developed alternative sources of supply. They do so in two ways.

Some, particularly the Chicano gangs, have sought out pharmacies where an employee can be paid off to steal pills for the gang to sell on the street.[19] Other gangs, particularly in New York, but also some in Los Angeles, have established "drug mills" to produce synthetic drugs such as LSD (or more recently crack cocaine) for sale on the street. The more sophisticated drug mills, which are controlled by various organized crime families, manufacture a whole line of drugs for sale, including cut heroin, but gangs are almost never involved in them. Those gangs that have established a production facility for generating drugs, no matter how crude it may be, generate sizable sums of money. Whether a gang is able to establish a sophisticated production and distribution system for drugs depends on the sophistication of the gang organization and the amount of capital available for start-up purposes.

Stolen guns are another popular and profitable product. Gangs sometimes steal guns and then redistribute them, but most often they buy them from wholesale gun peddlers and then resell them. Sometimes the gang will buy up a small number of shotguns and then cut the barrel and stock down to about 13 to 15 inches in length and then sell them as "easily concealable." A prospective buyer can get whatever he wants if he is willing to pay the going price. In the present study, the Irish gangs have been, commercially speaking, the most involved with guns, often moving relatively large shipments, ranging from sawed-off shotguns to fully automatic rifles and pistols of the most sophisticated types.[20] It was reported that these guns were being moved, with the help of Irish social clubs, to the Catholics of Northern Ireland for their struggle with the Protestants there. No matter what the destination, rather large sums of money were paid to the Irish gangs for their efforts in acquiring the weapons or helping move them. Although all the gangs studied were involved in the sale of illegal guns, illegal gun sales constituted a larger proportion of the economic activities of Irish gangs than they did for the others.

Gangs in all three cities were also involved in the selling of car parts. All the parts sold were stolen, some stolen to fill special orders from customers and others stolen and reworked in members' home garages into customized parts for resale. Business was briskest in Los Angeles, where there is a large market, especially among the low-rider clientele, for customized auto parts.[21] The amount of money made from stolen auto parts varies according to the area, whether or not the gang has an agent to whom to sell the parts, and the types of parts sold. On the whole, revenues from stolen auto parts were not nearly as high as those from selling illegal drugs, guns, or liquor, and so less time is devoted by gangs to this activity.

Gangs' business activities also include a number of services, the three most common being protection, demolition (usually arson), and indirect participation in prostitution. Protection is the most common service, both because there is a demand for it in the low-income areas in which gangs operate and because the gangs find it the easiest service to deliver, since it requires little in the way of resources or training. Gangs offer both personal and business protection. Nearly all the gangs had developed a fee schedule according to the type of protection desired. Most, but certainly not all, of the protection services offered by gangs in this study involved extortion. Usually the gang would go into a store and ask the owner if he felt he needed protection from being robbed. Since it was clear what was being suggested, the owner usually said yes and asked how much it would cost him. When dealing with naive owners, those who did not speak English very well or did not know American ghetto customs, or with owners who flatly resisted their services, the gang would take time to educate or persuade them to retain its services. In the case of the immigrants (most of whom were Asian or Near Eastern), the gang members would begin by explaining the situation, but usually such owners did not understand, and so the gang would demonstrate its point by sending members into the store to steal. Another tactic was to pay a dope addict to go in and rob the store. After such an incident occurred, the gang would return and ask the owner if he now needed protection. If he refused, the tactics were repeated, and almost all owners were finally convinced. However, for those owners who understood and resisted from the start, more aggressive tactics were used, such as destruction of their premises or harassment of patrons. More often than not, continued pressure brought the desired result. However, it should be noted that in the vast majority of cases, no coercion was needed, because owners in high-crime areas were, more often than not, happy to receive protection. As one owner said to me: "I would need to hire a protection company anyway, and frankly the gang provides me much more protection than they could ever do."

Gangs also offer their services as enforcers to clients who need punishment administered to a third party. Small-time hustlers or loan sharks, for example, hired some gangs to administer physical coercion to borrowers delinquent in their repayments. More recently one gang offered and apparently was hired by a foreign government to undertake terrorist acts against the government and people of the United States.[22] Although that was an extreme case, nearly all gangs seek enforcement contracts because the fee is usually high, few resources have to be committed, and relatively little in the way of planning (compared to other projects) is needed.

The permanent elimination of or damage to property is another service gangs offer. This more often than not involves arson, and the buildings hit are commonly dilapidated. The gang's clients are either landlords who want to torch the building to get insurance money or residents who are so frustrated by the landlord's unwillingness to provide the most basic services that they ask the gang to retaliate. In both cases there is usually much discussion of the project within the gang. These service jobs require a good deal of discussion and planning because there is the potential to hurt someone living in the building or to create enormous hardship if people have no alternative place to live, and the gang will do almost anything to avoid injuring people in its community. The gangs of New York have the most business along these lines, particularly in the South Bronx, but arson is a service offered in Detroit, Chicago, and Philadelphia as well. As one gang leader from the Bronx said:

> You just don't bomb or torch any building that someone wants down. You got to find out who lives there, if they got another place to go, if they would be for takin' out the building and if they'd be OK with the folks [law enforcement authorities]. Then you got to get organized to get everybody out and sometimes that ain't many people and sometimes it is. If there is lots of people in the building, we'd just pass [refuse] on the job. . . . [N]ow if we can work all these things out, we take the job and we deliver either a skeleton [outer walls are standing, but nothing else] or a cremation [just ashes].

Many potential clients know that a gang will refuse to burn down a building in its neighborhood if some type of harm will come to residents of its community, and so they contract with a gang from another area to do the job. Such incidents always ignite a war not only between the affected gangs but also between the communities. Take the example of the Hornets, a gang from one borough in New York that had contracted to set on fire a building in another borough. Although no one was killed in the fire, a few people were slightly burned, and of course everyone who lived in the building became homeless. At the request of a number of residents, the Vandals, a gang from the affected area, began to investigate and found out who had contracted to torch the building and who had been responsible. Then, at the request of an overwhelming majority of the community, the Vandals retaliated by burning down a building in the culprit gang's community. Hipper, a twenty-year-old member of the Vandals, said:

> We got to protect our community, they depend on us and they want us to do something so this [the burning of an apartment building in the neighborhood] don't happen again. . . . we be torchin' one of their buildings. I hope this don't hurt anybody, but if we don't do this, they be back hurting the people in our community and we definitely don't be letting that happen!

This is an excellent example of the bond that exists between the community and the gang. There is the understanding, then, among the community that the gang is a resource that can be counted on, particularly in situations where some form of force is necessary. Likewise, the gang knows that its legitimacy and existence are tied to being integrated in and responsible to community needs.

Prostitution is one illegal service in which gangs do not, for the most part, become directly involved. Gangs will accept only the job of protecting pimps and their women for a fee (fifteen, or 40 percent, of the gangs in this study had), and in this way they become indirectly associated with the prostitution business. Yet they generally avoid direct involvement because they feel protective of the females in their communities, and their organizations are wary of being accused by neighborhood residents of exposing female members of the community to the dangers associated with prostitution.

The last type of economic activity in which all the gangs in the present study were involved has to do with providing recreation. Some gangs established numbers games in their neighborhoods.

One New York gang had rented what had been a small Chinese food take-out place and was running numbers from the back where the kitchen had once been. (When I first observed the place, I thought it was a Chinese take-out and even proposed we get some quick food from it, which met with much laughter from the members of the gang I was with.) This gang became so successful that it opened up two other numbers establishments.

One had been a pizza place (and was made to look as though it still served pizza slices); the other was a small variety store, which still functioned in that capacity, but also housed the numbers game in the back rooms.

Setting up gambling rooms is another aspect of the recreation business. Eleven of the gangs (or 30 percent) rented small storefronts, bought tables and chairs, and ran poker and/or domino games. The gang would assume the role of the "house," receiving a commission for each game played. Some of the gangs bought slot machines and placed them in their gambling rooms. Five (or 14 percent) of the gangs had as many as fifteen machines available for use.

Finally, ten gangs (27 percent), primarily those with Latino members, rented old buildings and converted them to accommodate cockfights. The gang would charge each cock owner a fee for entering his bird and an entrance fee for each patron. All of these ventures could, at various times, generate significant amounts of capital. The exact amount would depend on how often they were closed by the police and how well the gang managed the competition in its marketplace.

Turning to the legal economic activities undertaken by gangs, I observed that two ran "mom and pop" stores that sold groceries, candy, and soft drinks. Three gangs had taken over abandoned apartment buildings, renovated them, and rented them very cheaply—not simply because the accommodations were rather stark, but also because the gang wanted to help the less fortunate members of its community. The gangs also used these buildings to house members who had nowhere else to live. Undertaken and governed by social as much as economic concerns, these apartment ventures did not generate much income.

Interestingly, the finances of these legal activities were quite tenuous. The gangs that operated small grocery stores experienced periodic failures during which the stores had to be closed until enough money could be acquired (from other sources) to either pay the increased rent, rebuild shelf stock, or make necessary repairs. For those gangs who operated apartment buildings, in every case observed, the absence of a deed to the building or the land forced the gang to relinquish its holdings to either the city or a new landlord who wanted to build some new structure. Though there was a plentiful supply of abandoned buildings, most gangs lost interest in the renovation-and-rental business because such projects always created a crisis in their capital flow, which in turn precipitated internal bickering and conflict.

Other legal economic activities undertaken by the gangs I studied were automobile and motorcycle repair shops, car parts (quasi junk yards), fruit stands, and hair shops (both barber and styling). However, most of these ventures contributed only very modest revenues to the gangs' treasuries. Furthermore, the gang leadership had difficulty keeping most of the legal economic activities functioning because the rank and file were, by and large, not terribly enthusiastic about such activities. Rank-and-file resistance to most of these activities was of three sorts: members did not want to commit regularly scheduled time to any specific ongoing operation; members felt that legal activities involved considerable overhead costs that lowered the profit rate; and members calculated that the time required to realize a large profit was far too long when compared to illegal economic activity. Thus, when such projects were promoted by the gang leadership and undertaken by the rank-and-file, they were done under the rubric of community service aid projects. The comments of Pin, a nineteen-year-old African-American gang member from New York, are representative of this general position on legal economic activity:

> No, I don't go for those deals where we [the gang] run some kind of hotel out of an old building or run some repair shop or something like that. When you do that you can't make no money, or if you do make something it so small and takes so long to get it that it's just a waste of our [the gang's] money. But when the leadership brings it up as a possibility, well, sometimes I vote for it because I figure you got to help the community, many of them [people in the community] say they sort of depend on our help in one way or another, so I always say this is one way to help the community and me and the brothers go along with it. But everybody knows you can't make no money on shit like this.

Economic Activity: Consuming

Nearly all economic activity that gangs undertake is for the purpose of financing consumption, which takes three forms: goods/commodities, recreation, and basic resources (material and psychological). In the first category, drugs and alcohol are the items most often purchased by gangs, and they try to provide quantities that will satisfy their membership. Some gangs, like Chicano gangs, purchase and use heroin, cocaine, marijuana, and various chemical drugs like barbiturates, amphetamines, and angel dust. Other gangs, like those in New York, forbid the use of heroin, but buy pure cocaine and crack cocaine. Alcohol is used by nearly all the gangs, but I found that the Irish used it most, not so much because they have a tradition of drinking as because the supply of drugs was controlled by nonwhites and they did not want to do business with nonwhites. However, most gangs do not dispense drugs or alcohol free of charge to their members. Rather they sell the drugs or alcohol at cost or provide a limited free supply to members at gang-organized parties. For example, some of the gangs had rather sophisticated clubhouses whose bars sold drinks and small sandwiches (warmed in the microwave) at cost. In addition, at their parties they would have a limited amount of cocaine available to "help people get in the party mood." Furthermore, some of the gangs in all three cities purchased equipment for the members' use: pinball machines, table soccer machines, table tennis, pool tables, and slot machines. They also purchased some athletic equipment: baseball gloves, bats, balls, bases, some basketballs, and handballs. One gang went so far as to purchase a motorcycle for recreational use.

Parties and group recreational activities are an important aspect of gang life, just as they are for other social organizations like the Elks and Moose lodges. A good deal of money is spent on items that will be consumed at their parties, picnics, and outings (barbecues); at times some gangs will rent a hall for a party.

Lastly, gangs allocate money or resources on hand to assist those members and their families who are having difficulty procuring food, clothing, and shelter. A gang's emergency fund serves to reassure members that temporary relief will be available if times are bad for themselves or their families.[23]

Endnotes

1. Nearly all studies of gangs incorporate this theme into their analysis. One of the exceptions is Cloward and Ohlin, *Delinquency and Opportunity*, which argues that many delinquents have the same values as other members of American society. However, even Cloward and Ohlin incorporate some of the conventional argument by accepting the premise that gang members' skills to compete with the larger society have been retarded by a lack of opportunity.

2. See Charles Sabel, *Work and Politics* (Cambridge: Cambridge University Press, 1987), pp. 1–30, on the importance of worldviews in affecting the behavior of individuals in industrial organizations and politics.

3. David Matza mentions a comparable tendency among delinquents to deny guilt associated with wrongdoing when he discusses the delinquent's belief that he is nearly always the victim of a "bum rap" (see Matza, *Delinquency and Drift* [New Brunswick, N.J.: Transaction Books], pp. 108–10).

4. I use the term *economic oriented action* the way Weber does: "Action will be said to be 'economical oriented' so far as, according to its subjective meaning, it is concerned with the satisfaction of a desire for 'utilities' (*Nutzleistung*)" (Weber, *Economy and Society*, I:63).

5. See Karl Marx, *The Economic and Philosophical Manuscripts of 1844*, 4th rev. ed., (Moscow: Progress Publishers, 1974), p. 38.

6. See David C. McClelland, *The Achieving Society* (New York: Free Press, 1961), pp. 233–37.

7. See Lee Rainwater, *What Money Buys: Inequality and the Social Meanings of Income* (New York: Basic Books, 1974). Also see Richard P. Coleman and Lee Rainwater, *Social Standing in America: New Dimensions of Class* (New York: Basic Books, 1978), pp. 29–45.

8. See the accounts of successful entrepreneurs from poor families who dreamed of grandeur and became America's most renowned business tycoons in Matthew Josephson, *The Robber Barons: The Great American Capitalists 1861–1901* (New York: Harcourt, Brace & World, 1962), especially [the] chapter entitled "What Young Men Dream," pp. 32–49.

9. Being respectful maintains the social etiquette established in the gang and acts to deter physical confrontations between members. For an example similar to that reported here, see Kaiser, *Vice Lords*, pp. 41–42.

10. See Thrasher, *The Gang*, pp. 198–200.

11. Ibid., p. 86.

12. In comparing the interviews of older men who had been in gangs during the 1930s, 1940s, 1950s, and 1960s with those who are in gangs today, I found a clear and significant difference in the role that money plays in the everyday lives of these individuals from different generations. Simply stated, the interviews indicate that the importance of money for "normal everyday activity" increases from the 1930s generation to that of today.

13. Both the theoretical and empirical literature focus on the gang's criminal activity. For theoretical discussions, see Kornhauser, *Social Sources of Delinquency*, pp. 51–61. For empirical studies, see nearly all of the classic and contemporary work on gangs. A sample of this literature would include Thrasher, *The Gang;* Herman Schwendinger and Julia Schwendinger, *Adolescent Subcultures and Delinquency* (New York: Praeger, 1985); Cloward and Ohlin, *Delinquency and Opportunity;* Cohen, *Delinquent Boys*. Two exceptions are Horowitz, *Honor and the American Dream*, and Vigil, *Barrio Gangs*.

14. There are two factors that have encouraged gangs to be more active in illegal markets. First, gangs, like organized crime syndicates, attempt to become active in many economic activities that are legal. However, because so much of the legal market is controlled by groups that have established themselves in strategic positions (because they entered that market a considerable time in the past), gangs have found it difficult at best to successfully penetrate legal markets. Further, there are financial incentives that have encouraged gangs to operate in the illegal market. These include the fact that costs are relatively low, and while personal risk (in terms of being incarcerated and/or physically hurt) is rather high, high demand along with high risk can produce greater profit margins. Despite the fact that these two factors have encouraged gangs to be more active in the illegal market it is important to emphasize that nearly all the gangs studied attempted to, and many did, conduct business in the legal market as well.

15. The Schwendingers indicate that "youthful tastes regulate the flow of goods and services in the [adolescent] market" and gangs do take advantage of these tastes. See Schwendinger and Schwendinger, *Adolescent Subcultures and Delinquency*, p. 286.

16. See Fagan, "Social Organization of Drug Use and Drug Dealing Among Urban Gangs," pp. 633–67; and Jerome H. Skolnick, *Forum: The Social Structure of Street Drug Dealing* (Sacramento: Bureau of Criminal Statistics/Office of the Attorney General, 1989).

17. See Francis A. J. Ianni, *Black Mafia: Ethnic Succession in Organized Crime* (New York: Simon & Schuster, 1974). Also see Moore, *Homeboys*, pp. 86–92, 114–16.

18. See Peter Lupsha and K. Schlegel, "The Political Economy of Drug Trafficking: The Herrera Organization (Mexico and the United States)" (Paper presented at the Latin American Studies Association, Philadelphia, 1979).

19. This paying off of employees for drug supplies began, according to Joan Moore, in Los Angeles in the 1940s and 1950s (see Moore, *Homeboys*, pp. 78–82).

20. These gangs can procure fully automatic M-16s, Ingrams, and Uzis.

21. Low riders are people, nearly all of whom are of Mexican descent, who drive customized older automobiles (1950s and 1960s models are preferred), one of the characteristics being that the springs for each wheel are cut away so that the car rides very low to the ground. Some of these cars have hydraulic systems that can be inflated at the flip of a switch so that the car can ride low to the ground at one moment and at the normal level the next. For a discussion of the importance of customized automobiles in Los Angeles, especially among Chicano youth, see Schwendinger and Schwendinger, *Adolescent Subcultures and Delinquency*, pp. 234–45.

22. The El Rukn gang in Chicago was recently indicted and convicted of contracting with the Libyan government to carry out terrorist acts within the United States. See *Chicago Tribune*, 3, 4, 6, 7 November 1987.

23. The gangs give many of their members, and sometimes the community as a whole, the same psychological comfort that the political machine provided urban ethnic groups in the late nineteenth and early twentieth centuries. See Raymond Wolfinger, "Why Political Machines Have Not Withered Away and Other Revisionist Thoughts," *Journal of Politics* 34 (May 1972): 365–98.

Review

1. In his research, Jankowski found that nearly all the gang members studied possessed five attributes that were entrepreneurial in character or that reinforce entrepreneurial behavior. What were these attributes?

2. What are four sources of gang members' entrepreneurial attitudes and behavior?

3. What impact do the risk-taking patterns of individual gang members have on their degree of economic success or failure?

4. The gangs discussed in this article concentrated their illegal economic activities primarily in goods, services, and recreation. In what specific types of goods, services, and recreational activities are gangs most commonly involved?

Application

A juvenile gang is an excellent example of a deviant subculture. It has its own way of life and is separated from the mainstream of society. The purpose of this assignment is to examine how popular movies portray this aspect of gangs. Arrange to rent two or three recent movies that depict gang life. For each movie, make notes about the following features of the gang:

a. norms or rules

b. distinct language

c. values and beliefs

d. rituals

e. division of labor

f. nicknames used by members

Summarize your findings about gang culture and compare its features to the culture of the larger society.

Reprinted from: Martin Sánchez Jankowski, "Islands in the Street: Urban Gangs as Economic Organizations." Excerpted from *Islands in the Street: Gangs and American Urban Society* by Martin Sánchez Jankowski (Berkeley: University of California Press, 1991). Copyright © 1991 by The Regents of the University of California. Reprinted by permission. ✦

39

Crack Cocaine Sentencing: A Racist Policy?

The Sentencing Project

"With liberty and justice for all." *Every U.S. citizen has repeated the phrase from the Pledge of Allegiance countless times. An American ideal is that justice is blind—it is for all because it is dispensed independently of people's class, sex, or race/ethnicity. Justice supposedly differs from electoral politics, in which various interest groups contend over whose political views will dominate in the exercise of power. These conflicts are necessarily partisan and are greatly influenced by the weight of resources each person or group brings to the battle.*

Ideally, justice is dispensed under the law without bias. But is it the reality? According to conflict theorists, the answer is no. Conflict theorists argue that power is the underlying dimension of all social relations, including the dispensing of justice. The writing and enforcement of law reflects the interests of those who hold the most power. Hence, crimes committed by the well-to-do—"white-collar" crime, for example—are not likely to be harshly controlled by the legal system. By the same token, the offenses of the powerless are likely to be sharply punished.

The issue of crack cocaine sentencing policy illustrates this line of analysis. Whatever the intent may have been, the bottom line is that African Americans receive harsher treatment in the criminal justice system than do whites and Hispanics, even though all three groups are charged with using an illegal drug.

Overview

Crack cocaine became prevalent in the mid-1980s and received massive media attention due in part to the death of college basketball star Len Bias (subsequently found to have used powder cocaine on the night of his death and not crack). Crack was portrayed as a violence inducing, highly addictive plague of inner cities, and this media spotlight led to the quick passage of two federal sentencing laws concerning crack cocaine in 1986 and 1988. The laws created a 100:1 quantity ratio between the amount of crack and powder cocaine needed to trigger certain mandatory minimum sentences for trafficking, as well as creating a mandatory minimum penalty for simple possession of crack cocaine. The result of these laws is that crack users and dealers receive much harsher penalties than users and dealers of powder cocaine.

The Difference between Crack and Cocaine Powder

Cocaine powder is derived from coca paste, which is in turn derived from the leaves of the coca plant. Crack cocaine is made by taking cocaine powder and cooking it with baking soda and water until it forms a hard substance. These "rocks" can then be broken into pieces and sold in small quantities. Each gram of powder produces approximately .89 grams of crack.

The psychotropic and physiological effects of all types of cocaine are the same, but the intensity and duration of the high differ according to the route of administration. Crack is always smoked and gives a fast, intense high. Powder cocaine is usually snorted, which gives a slower and less intense high. Supporters of the 100:1 quantity ratio say that the intensity of the high created by crack makes crack more addictive than powder and makes its users more violence prone. Experts believe that crack is more likely to be abused because the high is short, which causes users to desire more of the drug, and because it is cheap and widely available. But when powder cocaine is injected it produces a fast, intense high similar to crack.

The United States Sentencing Commission (USSC) was created by Congress in 1984 to develop federal sentencing guidelines that would, among other goals, reduce unwarranted sentencing disparity. In 1995 the Commission concluded that the violence associated with crack is primarily related to the drug trade and not to the effects of the drug itself. Crack is inexpensive and usually sold in small quantities, so it is often sold in open-air markets which are especially prone to violence. Powder is also distributed in this manner, but it is usually sold in larger wholesale quantities behind closed doors in locations which are inherently more secure. Both powder and crack cocaine cause distribution-related violence, but crack is more often sold in volatile settings.

Sentencing Policy

Although the two types of cocaine cause similar physical reactions, the sentences that users and sellers of the drugs face are vastly different. For powder cocaine, a conviction of possession with intent to distribute carries a five year sentence for quantities of 500 grams or more. But for crack, a conviction of possession with intent to distribute carries a five year sentence for only 5 grams. This is a 100:1 quantity ratio. Under this format, a dealer charged with trafficking 400 grams of powder, worth approximately $40,000, could receive a shorter sentence than a user he supplied with crack valued at $500. Crack is also the only drug that carries a mandatory prison sentence for first offense possession. A person convicted in federal court of possession of 5 grams of crack automatically receives a 5 year prison term. A person convicted of possessing 5 grams of powder cocaine will probably receive a probation sentence. The maximum sentence for simple possession of any other drug, including powder cocaine, is 1 year in jail.

In addition to the federal mandatory minimum sentences, 14 states differentiate between crack and powder cocaine. However, none have a quantity ratio as large as the 100:1 disparity in federal law.

Racial Disparity

Approximately ²/₃ of crack users are white or Hispanic, yet the vast majority of persons convicted of possession in federal courts in 1994 were African American, according to the USSC. Defendants convicted of crack possession in 1994 were 84.5 percent black, 10.3 percent white, and 5.2 percent Hispanic. Trafficking offenders were 4.1 percent white, 88.3 percent black, and 7.1 percent Hispanic. Powder cocaine offenders were more racially mixed. Defendants convicted of simple possession of cocaine powder were 58 percent white, 26.7 percent black, and 15 percent Hispanic. The powder trafficking offenders were 32 percent white, 27.4 percent black, and 39.3 percent Hispanic. The result of the combined difference in sentencing laws and racial disparity is that black men and women are serving longer prison sentences than white men and women.

Legislative History

In 1986 and 1988 Congress adopted mandatory sentencing laws on crack in the wake of widespread media attention. These laws were based on the idea that crack is 50 times more addictive than powder cocaine. Congress doubled that number and came up with the 100:1 quantity ratio currently in effect. As part of the 1994 Omnibus Violent Crime Control and Law Enforcement Act, the U.S. Sentencing Commission was directed to study the differing penalties for powder and crack cocaine. In 1995, the commission recommended equalizing the quantity ratio that would trigger the mandatory sentences. They also pointed out that the Federal Sentencing Guidelines provide criteria other than drug type to determine sentence lengths, so that violent, dangerous dealers receive longer sentences. Congress rejected the recommendation, which marked the first time it had done so since the establishment of the Sentencing Commission. The President then followed Congress and signed the rejection into law.

Litigation

The 100:1 quantity ratio in the federal system has been legally challenged as unconstitutional on the grounds that it denies equal protection or due process, because the penalties constitute cruel and unusual punishment, and because the statutes are unconstitutionally vague. All of these challenges have failed in the federal appellate courts. However, in a state case regarding a statute that enhanced crack cocaine penalties at a 10:3 ratio, the Minnesota Supreme Court struck down the enhancement based on the more expansive equal protection guarantees of its state constitution.

In the case *United States v. Armstrong*, four defendants in Los Angeles charged with trafficking crack cocaine filed a motion for discovery or dismissal, alleging that they were victims of selective prosecution by race. This motion was made after the federal public defender's office found that all 24 crack cocaine cases closed in Los Angeles in 1991 involved blacks. The district court and the circuit court upheld the motion, but the federal prosecutor refused to comply. The government then appealed to the Supreme Court, which decided in favor of the government on the grounds that the defendant did not meet the required threshold showing that similarly situated suspects of other races were not prosecuted.

In 1997, the Supreme Court rejected an appeal of a Washington, D.C. case in which an African American man who received a 10 year prison term for distribution of crack contended that the laws were racially biased in their impact. The U.S. Court of Appeals had previously rejected the challenge, stating that Congress has not acted with a discriminatory purpose in setting greater penalties for cocaine base crimes than for powder cocaine offenses.

Conclusion

The 100:1 quantity ratio in cocaine sentencing causes low-level crack offenders to receive arbitrarily severe sentences compared to high level powder cocaine offend-

ers. The quantity distinction has also resulted in a massive sentencing disparity by race, with African Americans receiving longer sentences than the mostly white and Hispanic powder cocaine offenders. The United States Sentencing Commission recommended revision of the 100:1 quantity ratio in 1995, finding the ratio to be unjustified by the small differences in the two forms of cocaine. Congress ignored the recommendation of the Sentencing Commission though, and refused to change the law. The President went along with the Congressional "tough on crime" stance. In April 1997, the USSC again recommended that the disparity between crack and powder cocaine be reduced, to a ratio of 5:1 by weight. It remains to be seen whether Congress or the Administration will accept this more modest recommendation. Since that time, the Supreme Court has declined to find this law unconstitutional. Ultimately, public opinion will be critical to influencing public policy in this often emotional issue.

Review

1. Explain the differences between crack and cocaine powder.

2. What evidence indicates that the sentencing policy is racist?

3. Discuss the legislative and judicial history of the crack cocaine sentencing policy.

Application

How extensive is racism in the criminal justice system? Look through the criminology journals in your school's library to find other examples. Make a list of the various ways in which the races are treated differently in the system. How would you correct such disparities?

Reprinted from: The Sentencing Project, "Crack Cocaine Sentencing Policy: Unjustified and Unreasonable," From The Sentencing Project Website: *www.sentencingproject.org* Copyright © 2001, by The Sentencing Project. Reprinted by permission. ✦

40

The Razor Blade in the Apple

The Social Construction of Urban Legends

Joel Best
Gerald T. Horiuchi

The legends and myths of traditional societies usually relate heroic exploits and high ideals. Although such stories also have a role in modern society, folk tales of a more contemporary nature, sometimes referred to as urban legends, have evolved alongside them. Characteristically, urban legends focus on the hazards of modern life and the threats they present to the innocent or ignorant. Urban legends often have some basis in fact, and their usual protagonist is not a supernatural being or heroic figure, but an ordinary person. The familiar stories of rats found in soft drink bottles and pets exploded in microwave ovens are typical urban legends that began with actual incidents and evolved through countless tellings and retellings. In some cases, the legends may be pure fiction. Recently, for instance, millions of Americans received e-mail messages warning them against downloading any document containing a certain word in the title. The word varied somewhat, but the message was the same—this document contains a virus that will wipe out your hard drive if you download it. The problem of viruses is a real one, but so far as we know there was no basis for the warnings and no such documents were ever sent or received.

In this selection, Best and Horiuchi examine the frightening urban legend of Halloween sadists who give children dangerous, adulterated treats. The authors describe a typical way in which urban legends can arise and spread. Their detailed analysis of the origin and devel-opment of this particular legend is complemented by a thoughtful discussion of its sociological implications.

The 1970s witnessed the discovery of a frightening new deviant—the Halloween sadist, who gave dangerous, adulterated treats to children. Each year, Halloween's approach brought warnings to parents:

> . . . that plump red apple that Junior gets from a kindly old woman down the block . . . may have a razor blade hidden inside (*New York Times*, 1970).

> If this year's Halloween follows form, a few children will return home with something more than an upset tummy: in recent years, several children have died and hundreds have narrowly escaped injury from razor blades, sewing needles and shards of glass purposefully placed into their goodies by adults (*Newsweek*, 1975).

> It's Halloween again and time to remind you that . . . somebody's child will become violently ill or die after eating poisoned candy or an apple containing a razor blade (Van Buren, 1983).

Various authorities responded to the threat: legislatures in California (1971) and New Jersey (1982) passed laws against Halloween sadism; schools trained children to inspect their treats for signs of tampering; and some communities tried to ban trick-or-treating. According to press reports, many parents restricted their children's trick-or-treating, examined their treats, or arranged parties or other indoor celebrations. By 1984, the threat of Halloween sadists was apparently taken for granted. Doubts about the threat's reality rarely appeared in print. Several Oregon third graders wrote letters to a newspaper: "I wish people wouldn't put poison in our Halloween treats" (*Times*, 1984). Adults questioned for an Illinois newspaper's "Sidewalk Interview" column (*DeKalb Daily Chronicle*, 1984) expressed concern: ". . . part of it is checking to make sure you know your neighbors and checking the candy. I think it's terrible that people are doing this and I guess people's morals have to be examined." "Dear Abby" printed a letter describing a North Carolina hospital's program to X-ray treats (Van Buren, 1984); radiologists at a Hanford, California, hospital checked 500 bags of treats (*Fresno Bee*, 1984).

Halloween sadism is thought to involve random, vicious, unprovoked attacks against small children. The attacks seem irrational, and the attackers are routinely described as disturbed or insane. These "child-haters" are theorized to "have had a really deprived childhood" having been "abused as children," they are now "frustrated and filled with resentment against the world in general" (Isaacs and Royeton, 1982:69). Law enforcement officials and the media reaffirm that the threat is real, urging parents to protect their children against sadistic attacks.

Although Halloween sadism is widely regarded as a serious threat, it has received little scholarly attention. In this paper, we examine the phenomenon from a sociological perspective, addressing three issues. First, we try to assess the incidence of Halloween sadism in order to demonstrate that the threat has been greatly exaggerated. Second, we draw upon a concept from folklore studies to argue that the belief in Halloween sadism is best viewed as an "urban legend." Finally, we suggest that urban legends are a product of social strain and of the social organization of the response to that strain.

A Holiday for Sadists?

There are no reliable official statistics on Halloween sadism. Minor incidents, particularly those that do not involve injuries, may never be reported to the police. Cases that are reported may be classified under a wide range of offenses, and there is no centralized effort to compile cases from different jurisdictions. Moreover, the circumstances of the crime—the young victim, the unfamiliar assailant, the difficulty in remembering which treats came from which houses—make it unlikely that offenders will be arrested.

While the true incidence of Halloween sadism cannot be measured, newspaper reports reveal changes in public reaction to the threat. Therefore, we examined the coverage of Halloween sadism in four daily newspapers between 1959 and 1984. For *The New York Times*, we checked all entries under "Halloween" in the paper's annual indexes for information about Halloween sadism. *The New York Times Index* proved to be unusually complete, listing even short items of a sentence or two. The published indexes for two other major regional newspapers, the *Chicago Tribune* and the *Los Angeles Times*, were less thorough, so for each year, we read both papers' issues for the first three days in November. Finally, we examined all Halloween stories in the files of the *Fresno Bee*. Our search found stories about 76 alleged incidents of Halloween sadism, which included at least the community where the incident occurred and the nature of the attack. Table 40.1 shows the number of incidents reported in each year.

Obviously, the 76 incidents identified through this procedure do not form a complete list of cases of Halloween sadism. However, there are several reasons why it is unlikely that many serious incidents—involving deaths or serious injuries—were overlooked. First, the papers' coverage was national. The 76 reported incidents came from 13 states and two Canadian provinces; while each of the four newspapers concentrated on incidents in its own region, all reported cases from other regions. All four included at least one case from the South—the only major region without a newspaper in the sample. Second, the 76 reported cases were generally not serious. Injuries were reported in only 20 cases, and only two of these involved deaths. It seems unlikely that newspapers would choose to print accounts of minor incidents, while ignoring more serious crimes. This impression is bolstered further by the frequent appearance of stories—often from different states—about other Halloween tragedies: children struck by cars and other accidental deaths; people murdered when they opened their doors, expecting trick-or-treaters; racial disturbances; vandalism; and so on. At least two of the newspapers carried reports on each of the two deaths attributed to Halloween sadists. It is therefore unlikely that the list of 76 incidents excludes any fatal instances of Halloween sadism. Table 40.1 reveals two peaks in the pattern of reporting. Thirty-one of the 76 incidents occurred in the three years from 1969 to 1971. This wave of reports encouraged recognition of Halloween sadism as a threat. As a holiday when millions of children venture out at night, Halloween has a long history of tragic accidents. Routinely, newspapers and magazines print lists of safety tips, warning parents against flammable costumes, masks that obscure the wearer's vision, and the like. A systematic review of such lists found no mention of the danger posed by sadists before 1972; but, from that year on, lists of safety tips almost invariably warned parents to inspect their children's treats for signs of tampering. At the same time that these warnings spread, reports of Halloween sadism fell to a few per year until 1982, when there was a dramatic increase. Of course, this reflected the fear caused by the Tylenol murders. A month before Halloween, seven people died after swallowing poisoned Extra-Strength Tylenol capsules. In the weeks that followed, there were hundreds of reports of "copycats" adulterating food, over-the-counter medications, and other household products. As Halloween approached, the media repeatedly warned parents that trick-or-treaters would be in danger. After raising the specter of Halloween sadism, the press naturally covered the incidents that were reported. A year later, however, coverage fell to pre-Tylenol levels.

Examining the reports of the 76 incidents leads to three conclusions. First, the threat of Halloween sadism has been greatly exaggerated. There is simply no basis for *Newsweek's* (1975) claim that "several children have died." The newspapers attributed only two deaths to Halloween sadists, and neither case fit the image of a maniacal killer randomly attacking children. In 1970, five-year-old Kevin Toston died after eating heroin supposedly hidden in his Halloween candy. While this story received considerable publicity, newspapers gave less coverage to the follow-up report that Kevin had found the heroin in his uncle's home, not his treats (*San Francisco Chronicle*, 1970). The second death is more notorious. In 1974, eight-year-old Timothy O'Bryan died after eating Halloween candy contaminated with

Table 40.1
Reported Incidents of Halloween Sadism, 1958–84

Year	Number of Incidents	Year	Number of Incidents
1958	0	1972	1
1959	1	1973	4
1960	0	1974	1
1961	0	1975	2
1962	1	1976	2
1963	1	1977	0
1964	3	1978	0
1965	1	1979	3
1966	5	1980	0
1967	4	1981	0
1968	3	1982	12
1969	7	1983	1
1970	10	1984	0
1971	14		

cyanide. Investigators concluded that his father had contaminated the treat (Grider, 1982). Thus, both boys' deaths were caused by family members, rather than by anonymous sadists. Similarly, while the newspaper reports rarely gave detailed information about the remaining 18 cases in which injuries were reported, most of the victims were not seriously hurt. Several incidents involved minor cuts and puncture wounds; what was apparently the most serious wound required 11 stitches. In short, there were no reports where an anonymous sadist caused death or a life-threatening injury; there is no justification for the claim that Halloween sadism stands as a major threat to U.S. children.[1]

A second conclusion is that many, if not most, reports of Halloween sadism are of questionable authenticity. Children who go trick-or-treating know about Halloween sadism; they have been warned by their parents, teachers, and friends. A child who "discovers" an adulterated treat stands to be rewarded with the concerned attention of parents and, perhaps, police officers and reporters. Such a hoax is consistent with Halloween traditions of trickery, just as the fear of sadists resembles the more traditional dread of ghosts and witches. The 76 reported incidents included two cases that were identified as hoaxes at the time, and it seems likely that other cases involved undiscovered fraud. After all, it is remarkable that three-quarters of the children who reported receiving contaminated treats had no injuries. Efforts to systematically follow up reports of Halloween sadism have concluded that the vast majority were fabrications. After Halloween of 1972, *Editor and Publisher* (1973)—the trade magazine of the newspaper industry—examined several papers' efforts to trace all local reports of Halloween sadism; it concluded that virtually all the reports were hoaxes. Ten years later, in the wake of the Tylenol scare, the confectionary industry tried to reassure potential customers in a "white paper" on Halloween candy tampering in 1982 (National Confectioners Association et al., n.d.). The report noted that "more than 95 percent of the 270 potential Halloween 1982 candy adulterations analyzed by the Food and Drug Administration have shown no tampering, which has led one FDA official to characterize the period as one of 'psychosomatic mass hysteria.'" Further, a confectionary industry survey of police departments in "24 of the nation's largest cities, as well as smaller towns in which highly-publicized incidents were alleged to have occurred, found two reports of injuries—neither requiring medical treatment—from among the hundreds of claims of candy tampering." Thus, not only does a survey of press coverage reveal fewer reports of Halloween sadism than might be expected, but there is good reason to suspect that many of the reports are unfounded.

Third, the press should not be held responsible for the widespread belief that Halloween sadism poses a serious threat. While the news media can manufacture "crime waves" by suddenly focusing on previously ignored offenses, the press has given Halloween sadism relatively little publicity. Many of the 76 reported incidents received minimal coverage, in news stories of only two or three sentences. Often the reports were embedded in larger stories, such as a wire service summary of Halloween news from around the country. Nor did popular magazines highlight Halloween sadism; before 1982, only two short articles focused on the problem.

The absence of authentic cases of serious injuries caused by Halloween sadism undoubtedly explains this limited coverage. While the publication of annual warnings to parents to inspect their children's treats, as well as occasional short items reporting minor incidents, may help keep the fear of Halloween sadism alive, the media do not seem to be the principal channel by which people learn of the danger. Rather, knowledge of Halloween sadism apparently spreads by word of mouth.

Roots of an Urban Legend

The belief in Halloween sadism as a serious threat can be understood using a concept developed by folklorists: Halloween sadism is an *urban legend*. Urban legends are contemporary, orally transmitted tales that "often depict a clash between modern conditions and some aspect of a traditional lifestyle" (Brunvand, 1981:189). Whereas traditional legends often feature supernatural themes, most urban legends "are grounded in human baseness. . . ." (Fine, 1980:227). They describe criminal attacks, contaminated consumer goods, and other risks of modern life. Halloween sadism combines two themes found in several other urban legends: danger to children (e.g., the babysitter who cooks an infant in a microwave oven; the child kidnapped from a department store or an amusement park); and contamination of food (e.g., the mouse in the soft-drink bottle; the Kentucky Fried Rat). These legends, like that of the Halloween sadist, are typically told as true stories. They "gratify our desire to know about and to try to understand bizarre, frightening, and potentially dangerous or embarrassing events that *may* have happened" (Brunvand, 1981:12). Urban legends may even have a factual basis; soft-drink manufacturers have been sued by people claiming to have found mice in their drinks. Whether a legend begins with a real incident or as a fictional tale, it is told and retold, often evolving as it spreads. On occasion, urban legends appear in newspaper stories, reinforcing the tale's credibility (Brunvand, 1981, 1984). The belief in Halloween sadism is maintained through orally transmitted warnings about the dangers contemporary society poses for the traditional custom of trick-or-treating. These warnings, which greatly exaggerate the threat, are an urban legend. That some incidents of Halloween sadism have occurred, and that the media have reported such incidents, does not disqualify the warnings as legends.

Viewing Halloween sadism as an urban legend helps explain why the belief became widespread when it did. News reports of Halloween sadism are not new. But the general perception that Halloween sadism is a serious threat can be dated to the early 1970s. This was the period when the press began reporting more incidents and warning parents to inspect treats, and legislatures began passing laws against Halloween sadism. In general, urban legends are products of social tension or strain. They express fears that the complexities of modern society threaten the traditional social order. Urban life requires contact with strangers who—the legends suggest—may be homicidal maniacs, unscrupulous merchants, voyeurs, or otherwise threatening. By repeating urban legends, people can respond to social strain, expressing their doubts about the modern world.

While it is obviously impossible to establish a causal link between particular social tensions and the spread of a particular urban legend, folklorists typically examine a legend's element for clues about its roots. Some legends feature a transparent message, but others are more difficult to interpret. In the case of Halloween sadism, a plausible argument can be made that the legend's flowering in the early 1970s was tied to the heightened social strains of that period. The late 1960s and early 1970s were years of unparalleled divisiveness in post–World War II America. The media exposed several serious crises to the public, including an increasingly unpopular war, ghetto riots, student demonstrations, and increased drug use. It was a period of intense social strain. Three forms of strain that emerged or grew during these years seem related to the growing fear of Halloween sadism.

Threats to Children

The form of strain that seems most clearly linked to a belief in Halloween sadism was the growing sense that children were no longer safe in the United States. During the 1960s and early 1970s, physicians and social workers promoted child abuse as a major social problem; the popular press responded with dozens of dramatic stories about children who had been cruelly treated by their parents. The rhetoric of this campaign emphasized that all children were potential victims, that child abuse occurred in all sectors of society. But even parents who remained confident that their children would never be abused could worry about losing their children to other threats. Older children adopted radical political views and experimented with illegal drugs. Other parents found their grown children facing a less symbolic threat—death in Vietnam. The social conflicts that marked America during these years must have left many parents wondering if their hopes for the next generation would be fulfilled.

Since the emergence of the belief in Halloween sadism, the generation gap seems to have narrowed, but threats to children remain visible. The movement against child abuse continues to spread, receiving still more publicity. And, during the late 1970s and early 1980s, emerging campaigns against incest, child pornography, child molesting, and abortion may have contributed to a larger sense of children in jeopardy. Perhaps the clearest link between threats to children and the fear of Halloween sadism appeared during the series of murders of Atlanta schoolchildren. In 1980, STOP, an organization of the victims' parents, argued that "the city should organize Halloween night events that will minimize dangers to the children" (*New York Times*, 1980).

Fear of Crime

Other forms of strain involved more general threats. Survey data reveal that the fear of crime grew substantially between the mid-1960s and the early 1970s (Erskine, 1974; Stinchcombe et al., 1980). Although violent crimes often involve offenders and victims who are acquainted, the fear of crime focuses on the threat of an anonymous attacker. The threat of an unpredictable, unprovoked criminal attack parallels the Halloween sadist menace.

Mistrust of Others

Survey data also reveal rising expressions of general mistrust during the early 1970s. The proportion of Americans who agreed that ". . . you can't be too careful in dealing with people" rose from 45.6 percent in 1966, to 50.0 percent in 1971, to 54.3 percent in 1973 (Converse et al., 1980:28). Studies of urban dwellers in the 1970s found high levels of mistrust for strangers (Fischer, 1982). While warnings about the collapse of the neighborhood in the anonymous modern city have proven exaggerated, the belief that people now live in greater isolation remains widespread. The social conflicts of the 1960s and early 1970s may have encouraged doubts about the trustworthiness of other people. Such doubts provided another form of strain during the period when the belief in Halloween sadism spread.

These sources of strain—threats to children, fear of crime, and mistrust of others—provided a context within which the concern about Halloween sadism could flourish. The Halloween sadist emerged as a symbolic expression of this strain: the sadist, like other dangers, attacks children—society's most vulnerable members; the sadist, like the stereotypical criminal, is an anonymous, unprovoked assailant; and the sadist, like other strangers, must be met by doubt, rather than trust. Placed in the context of the late 1960s and early 1970s, the spread of Halloween sadism is easily understood.

If these sources of strain account for the belief's spread, what explains its persistence? The extraordinary social conflicts of the early 1970s have moderated, yet the belief in Halloween sadism remains. Why? First, some of the same sources of strain continue to exist: the media still publicize threats to children (e.g., child abuse), and the fear of crime and strangers remains high. Second, and more important, Halloween sadism is an established urban legend; it can remain as a taken-for-granted, if dormant, part of American culture. The survey of newspaper stories found only five reports of Halloween sadism from 1976 to 1981—less than one per year. However, warnings about sadists continued to appear during these years and, of course, the Tylenol poisonings in 1982 led to both predictions and reports of Halloween sadism.

Third, folklorists have traced the evolution of some legends over centuries. Legends seem most likely to persist when they have a general, underlying message (for instance, warnings about trusting outsiders) which can be tailored to fit new situations. Thus, the dangers of eating commercially prepared food were detailed in nineteenth-century stories about cat meat in baked pies and, more recently, in tales about rats sold at fried-chicken franchises. Like other urban legends about homicidal maniacs, the Halloween sadist legend expresses fears about criminal attacks. Given the general nature of this threat, the legend may persist as long as the custom of trick-or-treating.

Where do urban legends fit within the broader framework of sociological theory? At first glance, the fear of Halloween sadists resembles some of the instances of collective hysteria in the collective behavior literature. The Halloween sadist can stand beside the "phantom anesthetist" of Mattoon (Johnson, 1945), Taipei's "phantom slasher" (Jacobs, 1965), the "June bug epidemic" in a Southern textile plant (Kerckhoff and Back, 1968), and the windshield pitting in Seattle (Medalia and Larsen, 1958) as a focus of exaggerated fears. Studies of collective hysteria usually account for the emergence of hysterical beliefs as a response to social strain: the Mattoon episode occurred during wartime; the workers in the textile plant were putting in heavy overtime, and so on. In response to this strain, there emerged a belief in some threat, "an ambiguous element in the environment with a generalized power to threaten or destroy" (Smelser, 1962:82). This threat is credible, frightening, and difficult to protect oneself against:

> Instead of simply having a feeling that something is awry, the belief in a tangible threat makes it possible to *explain* and *justify* one's sense of discomfort—instead of anxiety, one experiences fear, and it is

then possible to act in some meaningful way with respect to this tangible threat rather than just feeling frustrated and anxious. (Kerckhoff and Back, 1968:160–61—emphasis in original.)

However, some of this model's key features do not fit the emergence of the belief in Halloween sadism and other urban legends. Collective hysteria is bounded in time and space. Hysterical beliefs are short-lived; they typically emerge, spread, and die within the space of a few days or weeks. Further, they are typically confined to a restricted locality—a single region, town, or facility. In contrast, the belief in Halloween sadists appears to have spread more slowly, over a period of years, and to have become an established, taken-for-granted part of the culture. Nor has the belief observed the normal geographic limits of collective hysteria—reports of Halloween sadism have come from throughout the country, suggesting that the belief is nationwide. If the Halloween sadist resembles the threats identified in instances of collective hysteria, the dynamics of the beliefs spread do not fit the hysterical pattern.

Implications: 'Halloween and the Mass Child' Revisited

Holiday celebrations reflect the larger culture. The events celebrated, as well as the customary ways of celebrating, reveal the society's values and structure. And, as society changes, its holidays often take on new meanings, consistent with the altered culture. Where earlier American celebrations were communal, ceremonial, and often religious or patriotic, contemporary observances tend to be individualistic, materialistic, secular occasions, marked largely by unstructured leisure time.

Gregory P. Stone's (1959) "Halloween and the Mass Child" developed this thesis. Stone traced the evolution of Halloween activities in his lifetime, from the elaborate pranks of adolescents in the 1930s, to the playful trick-or-treating of young children in the 1950s. He found the 1950s children did not understand the extortionate premise of "trick or treat"; for them, Halloween was merely an occasion to receive candy. Stone interpreted

this shift as consistent with the changes in American values described in Riesman's (1950) *The Lonely Crowd*:

> . . . Riesman's character type of 'other-direction' may, indeed, be a *prototype* of American character and not some strange mutation in the northeast. Consumption, tolerance, and conformity were recognizable in the Halloween masquerade of a near-southern town. Production, indignation, and autonomy were not. (Stone, 1959:378—emphasis in original.)

Twenty-five years after Stone's analysis, the fear of Halloween sadism has further altered the meaning of Halloween. While Stone saw trick-or-treating as a part of the emerging culture of consumption, folklorists view Halloween as among the least commercialized of modern holidays. But this informality has been labeled dangerous by those who warn against Halloween sadists. Children are urged to refuse homemade treats and accept only coupons or mass-produced candy with intact wrappings, as though commercialism offers protection. Long celebrated through vandalism and extortion, Halloween has been a symbolic expression of disorder. Today, the Halloween sadist has become an annual reminder of the fragility of the social bond—an expression of growing doubts about the safety of children, the trustworthiness of strangers, and the strength of the modem urban community.

Endnote

1. Certainly other elements of everyday life, while not receiving as much attention, are far more hazardous. In 1980–81, according to the U.S. Product Safety Commission (1982), 60 children under age five died in product associated deaths involving nursery equipment and supplies; another 13 deaths involved toys.

References

Brunvand, Jan Harold, *The Vanishing Hitchhiker* (New York: Norton, 1981).

Converse, Philip E., Jean D. Dotson, Wendy J. Hoag, and William H. McGee III, *American Social Attitudes Data Sourcebook* (Cambridge: Harvard University Press, 1980).

DeKalb Daily Chronicle, "Sidewalk Interview," 1984, October 28:10.

Editor and Publisher, "Press Finds Halloween Sadism Rare but Warns of Danger," 1973, 106 (March 3):22.

Erskine, Hazel, "The Polls: Fear of Crime and Violence," *Public Opinion Quarterly*, 1974, 38:131–45.

Fine, Gary Alan, "The Kentucky Fried Rat," *Journal of the Folklore Institute*, 1980, 17:222–43.

Fischer, Claude S., *To Dwell Among Friends* (Chicago: University of Chicago Press, 1982).

Fresno Bee, "No Tricks Found in Fresno Treats," 1984, November 1:B1.

Grider, Sylvia, "The Razor Blades in the Apples Syndrome," unpublished paper, 1982.

Isaacs, Susan, and Robert Royeton, "Witches, Goblins, Ghosts," *Parents Magazine*, 57, 1982, October: 66–9.

Jacobs, Norman, "The Phantom Slasher of Taipei," *Social Problems*, 1965, 12:318–28.

Johnson, Donald M., "The 'Phantom Anesthetist' of Mattoon," *Journal of Abnormal and Social Psychology*, 1945, 40:175–86.

Kerckhoff, Alan C., and Kurt W. Back, *The June Bug* (New York: Appleton-Century-Crofts, 1968).

Medalia, Nahum Z., and Otto N. Larsen, "Diffusion and Belief in a Collective Delusion," *American Sociological Review*, 1985, 23:180–86.

National Confectioners Association, Chocolate Manufacturers Association, and National Candy Wholesalers Association, "Halloween/ 1982: An Overview," unpublished paper, n.d.

New York Times, "Those Treats May Be Tricks," 1970, October 28:56.

——, "Atlanta and Miami Curbing Halloween," 1980, October 31:A14.

Newsweek, "The Goblins Will Getcha. . .," 1975, 86 November 3:28.

Riesman, David, *The Lonely Crowd* (Yale University Press, 1950).

San Francisco Chronicle, "Capsule Caused Halloween Death," 1970, November 10:3.

Smelser, Neil J., *Theory of Collective Behavior* (New Free Press, 1962).

Stinchcombe, Arthur L., Rebecca Adams, Carol A. Heimer, Kim Lane Scheppele, Tom W. Smith, and D. Garth Taylor, *Crime and Punishment* (San Francisco: Jossey-Bass, 1980).

Stone, Gregory P., "Halloween and the Mass Child," *American Quarterly*, 1959, 11:372–79.

Times (Beaverton, OR), "Letters," 1984, October 25:36.

U.S. Consumer Product Safety Commission, *Annual Report* (Washington: U.S. Government Printing Office).

Van Buren, Abigail, "Dear Abby," *Fresno Bee*, 1983, October 31:D2.

——, "Dear Abby," *Fresno Bee*, 1984, September 30:C4.

Review

1. What are the three issues addressed in this article?

2. What three conclusions were formed by the authors after examining newspaper reports of 76 incidents of Halloween sadism?

3. What forms of strain seem most clearly linked to a belief in Halloween sadism?

4. How does the fear of Halloween sadism fit in with instances of collective hysteria described in the collective behavior literature?

Application

At a library or newspaper office, examine the coverage of Halloween sadism in your local newspaper. Read over specific references and articles for mention of alleged incidents of sadism. Prepare a summary of your findings and contrast them with those of Best and Horiuchi.

Reprinted from: Joel Best and Gerald T. Horiuchi "The Razor Blade in the Apple: The Social Construction of Urban Legends." Edited from the version originally appearing in *Social Problems*, Vol. 32, No. 5, June, 1985, pp. 488–499. Copyright © 1985 by the Society for the Study of Social Problems. Reprinted with permission. ✦

Part Two

Social Change

Social change, as conflict theory asserts, is both normal and pervasive. Fueled by such things as technology, population processes, economic shifts, conflict, and new ideas, every society is in a process of ongoing change. The change is more rapid in some societies than in others, but none escapes the change.

Social change always has consequences for individuals. Some kinds of change are welcomed, while others are resisted. Some changes enhance people's well-being, while others threaten well-being. This interaction between change in the larger society and the struggles of individuals to defend and enhance their well-being is a theme that runs through each of the selections in this part. ✦

41

Life in Big Red

Struggles and Accommodations in a Chicago Polyethnic Tenement

Dwight Conquergood

Beyond birth and death rates, immigration is the social process that most affects a nation's demographic profile. Immigration, which has been an important consideration throughout U.S. history, continues to affect society. Every year a large number of people (970,000 in 2000) legally immigrate to the United States, most of them from Latin America and Asia. And although it is difficult to determine accurate figures, a substantial number enter illegally as well.

Many legal immigrants have come either under certain categories of preference (relatives of current citizens, desirable occupations, etc.) or as political refugees. Certain economic and political problems greet these immigrants when they arrive in the United States. For example, they are more likely to resettle in urban areas where deindustrialization deprives them of jobs that might have been a first step toward upward mobility. In addition, their housing might be owned by absentee landlords who care less about the condition of their property than about maximizing their profits. At the same time, poor housing often becomes a focal point for political and business elites who want to "redevelop" the residences of immigrants into something more acceptable to the middle-class indigenous population.

In this selection, Conquergood addresses these problems from the point of view of the residents of an "urban slum": the Albany Park neighborhood in Chicago. In earlier decades, Albany Park had been predominantly Jewish, but by the 1980s its Latino population had grown to one-third and its Asian population to one-fourth. A section known as "Little Beirut" dramatizes the demographic shifts in Albany Park. This area has more tenements and a higher proportion of nonwhites and residents on public assistance than other parts of Albany Park. Outsiders regard Little Beirut as a "war zone" rampant with crime, drugs, and gangs. In the process of conducting this study, Conquergood himself lived in "Big Red," a three-story, red-brick tenement building in Little Beirut.

When Albany Park developed signs of decline in the 1960s, established residents and community institutions formed the North River Commission (NRC) to slow or reverse the process. By the middle of the 1980s, the NRC began to have some success with new commercial and residential developments in the area. Because Little Beirut stood out as the sore thumb of Albany Park, it eventually became a primary target of NRC redevelopment efforts.

> *Everyday life invents itself by poaching in countless ways on the property of others.*
> —Michel De Certeau,
> *The Practice of Everyday Life* (1984)

I moved into Big Red in December 1987 in order to begin research for the Changing Relations Ford Foundation project.[1] At the time I moved in to the A2R apartment, previously occupied by an Assyrian family, I was the second white resident. An elderly Jewish man lived in C2L. The ethnic breakdown for the other 35 units was 11 Hmong, 10 Mexican, 10 Assyrian, 2 Sino-Cambodian, 1 Puerto Rican, and 1 Puerto Rican-Mexican mixed. During the twenty months I lived in Big Red, the ethnic mix was enriched by African Americans, Appalachian whites, more Puerto Ricans, and new immigrant Poles (see Figure 41.1). I lived in Big Red until the end of August 1989, when along with all my A stairwell neighbors I was displaced and that wing of Big Red was boarded up. I rented an apartment just one block north of Big Red and continue to live in Little Beirut and interact with my Big Red networks at the time of this writing.[2]

Initial inquiries about renting an apartment pulled me immediately into interactions with other tenants. Beyond the "Apartment for Rent" sign, there was no formal assistance for prospective tenants: no rental office, telephone number, or agency address. Yet every vestibule and stairwell was unlocked, open, and filled with friendly people.

Figure 41.1

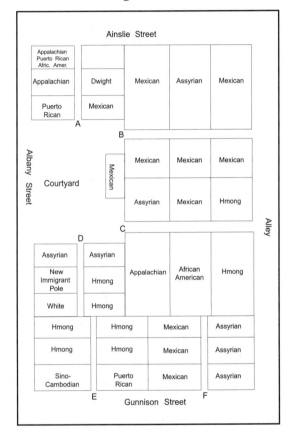

All the business of renting the apartment was conducted informally, through face-to-face interactions with other residents. In twenty months, I never signed or saw a lease. It was a few months before I actually saw the absentee owner. The word-of-mouth way of getting information brought me into contact with a number of neighbors who graciously shared with me what they knew and ventured outside in the bitter chill of Chicago December nights to track down the janitor. Sometimes we would find the janitor, some-

times we would not: he held down another full-time job in order to make ends meet. Sometimes when we found him he would not have the keys.

From one perspective, the rental management of Big Red was highly inefficient and required unnecessary trips, long waits, and delays. On the other hand, the absence of a managing authority made all the residents interdependent. By the time I was ready to move in, I was on friendly terms with several neighbors and had received offers of help with the move, including the loan of a car.

The physical dilapidation of Big Red is even more apparent from the inside than the outside, but it is mitigated by the warmth and friendliness of the people. Indeed, the chronic state of disrepair, breakdowns, and emergencies requires for survival a neighborly interdependence unheard-of in efficiently managed middle-class properties. Crises create community, but this is particularly true when the crisis relates to physical space that people share over time. When the plumbing on the third floor leaks through the second floor ceiling with every toilet flush, the residents of those two floors get to know one another in intimate ways.

It is the human quality of life in Big Red that eludes outsiders. The following NRC memo (1989) captures coldly the physical state of disrepair in Big Red. Even though it notes that "the building is currently fully occupied by low-income families," it discursively evacuates the human element, forgetting that people transform a tenement into a home:

> Due to neglect by the previous owners over the past 15 years, the property has declined into a critical state of deterioration. The building has suffered severely from a lack of any capital improvements. The mechanical systems are only partially operative or not performing at all. Prior attempts at building security have been feeble so that the apartments and common areas are open to abuse by anyone willing to gain access. The major apartment components are functionally obsolete and that, coupled with cosmetic neglect, greatly limits the marketability of the apartments and presents potential health and safety hazards. A few recent

examples include a total lack of hot water, the collapsing of a back porch, rats and roach infestation, and small arson fires in the vestibules.

From the inside, one gets a more detailed experience of the building's deterioration, but that is complemented with a complex understanding of how people maintain human dignity within difficult structures. A casual inspection would reveal scores of housing-ordinance violations but might not capture their meaning in the day-to-day lives of the urban working class and under- and unemployed. The children complain of mice in their beds. Housewives trade stories of "roaches in my refrigerator." They make stoic jokes about this indignity, dubbing them "Eskimo roaches." They say that the roaches move more slowly but can survive in the cold, "just like Eskimos." One day I opened my refrigerator and discovered a mouse scurrying around inside. The refrigerator was decrepit, and the door did not always stay shut. There were jokes about "super-rats" so big that the traps would have to be "anchored." These and other vermin stories about aggressive mice and flying cockroaches resemble "fish stories." Through exaggeration and shared laughter they made the situation more bearable.

To limit the story of Big Red to appalling physical conditions would be misleading. Michel de Certeau in *The Practice of Everyday Life* investigates the creative and manifold "tactics" ordinary people use to resist the "strategies" of the strong—the hegemonic forces of governments, armies, institutions, and landlords. He illuminates the myriad ways vulnerable people "operate" within dominant structures and constraints, what he calls "the art of making do." To illustrate his intellectual project, he uses the metaphor of "dwelling":

> Thus a North African living in Paris or Roubaix [France] insinuates *into* the system imposed on him by the construction of a low-income housing development or of the French language the ways of "dwelling" (in a house or a language) peculiar to his native Kabylia. He superimposes them and, by that combination, creates for himself a space in which he can find *ways of using* the constraining order of the place or of the language. Without leaving the place where he has no choice but to live and which lays down its law for him, he establishes within it a degree of *plurality* and creativity. By an art of being in between, he draws unexpected results from his situation. (de Certeau 1984:30)

Even highly vulnerable people are not simply contained by the structures, both physical and socioeconomic, within which they find themselves. Through imagination and human energy they contest and create "dwelling spaces" inside even forbidding structures.

The tenants of Big Red exploited the marginality, illegalities, and transgressive nature of Big Red in manifold ways. They turned the owner's negligence, which bordered on the criminal, to their advantage. While they suffered, to be sure, from the owner's neglect and lack of building maintenance, they also used his irresponsibility to circumvent typical middle-class restrictions, rules, and "tastes" pertaining to residential life, such as in the use of stairwells, courtyards, and alleys. Hmong women roped off a section of the front courtyard and planted a vegetable garden during the summer of 1988. The rest of the courtyard was an intensively used social space: the center was a playground for a group I will call the Courtyard Kids, while the fence between sidewalk and courtyard served as a volleyball net for teenage girls. The back area bordering on the alley was converted into an unofficial parking lot and open-air garage for working on old cars that were always in need of repair. Some back stairwells were used to sell drugs during the summer of 1989, when dealers set up operations in two Big Red apartments.

The back area also was used for weekend *bracero* alley parties. Whereas the courtyard and front sidewalk of Big Red were informally designated spaces for the evening sociability of women and children, the back alley, at night and on weekends, was a masculine space, so marked by one section of the back wall used as a urinal. This was the time when *braceros* shared the price of a case of beer, with a sensitively enforced code that those who were unemployed or newly arrived would be graciously exempted from any pressure to contribute. For those holding jobs, it was a source of esteem to assume a greater responsibility for financing these parties. This was a time for dramatizing the hardy manliness of their jobs by complaining about sore backs, tight muscles, blisters, and cut hands. Friendship networks of exchange and sharing developed at these alley parties. It was a sign of my acceptance when I first was invited to join these parties and then allowed, after initial protest, to contribute to the cost of a case of beer. Soon afterward, the three neighbors who worked at the Easy Spuds potato-chip factory began offering me free sacks of potatoes that they brought from work. Both the tools and the labor that helped me mount the steel security gate across my back door came from contacts made at the *bracero* parties. The front stairwells and lobbies were prime sites for display of gang graffiti, and during the winter the stairwells were used as spillover rooms for social drinking, talk, and smoking. In some respects, the residents had more autonomy and scope for use of Big Red than would have been possible within a better maintained, middle-class building.

The Art of Making Do: On Kinship, Kindness, and Caring

Tenants stretched scant resources by "doubling up," a common practice enabled by the irregular management of Big Red. In order to save money on rent, two or three families shared a single apartment. The one-bedroom apartment directly above me was home to a Hmong family with three small children, and another newlywed couple with an infant, plus the grandmother. Nine people (five adults and four children) shared this one-bedroom apartment. The one-bedroom basement apartment sheltered two Mexican sisters. One sister slept with her four children (ranging in age from seven to sixteen years old) in the single bedroom, while the other slept with her three small children in the living room. The Assyrian family of twelve lived in a three-bedroom apartment. A Mexican family with six children shared a one-bedroom apartment. These "doubling up" arrangements probably would not be permitted in middle-class-managed buildings.

Perhaps the most vivid example of this practice is the large heteroglot household that lived above me during the summer of 1989. Grace, an Appalachian mother of six children with a Puerto Rican husband, lived with Angel, her Puerto Rican "business" partner, who brought along his girlfriend, his younger brother just released from prison, the brother's girlfriend, and his African-American friend (who before the summer was over went to prison), as well as a single pregnant mother and her best girlfriend—fifteen people in one three-bedroom apartment. The household was anchored by Grace's Public Aid check and Angel's street hustling activities. Two years earlier, Grace had been homeless, living on the streets with her six children; the girls had panhandled and the boys had stolen food and cigarettes from stores. She had a network with street people, and Angel was plugged into the prison culture, so three to five extra people would "crash" at the apartment at any given time. This household was the most multicultural one in Big Red, embracing whites and African Americans who cohabited with several Latinos and one Filipino. The illicit lifestyle of street hustling and drugs brought together these several ethnic groups in strikingly intimate ways. Their unruly household had many problems, but racism and prejudice never surfaced.

The gathering together of extended families and the creation of "fictive kin" (Rapp 1987:232) are primary tactics for "making do" within Big Red. A twelve-year-old Assyrian Courtyard Kid articulated this conventional wisdom: "It's good to have friends and relatives nearby so you can borrow money when you need it." Indeed, the culture of Big Red was characterized by an intimacy of interactions across apartments, expressing in part the kinship networks that laced together these households. When I surveyed the apartments at the end of my first year of residence, I discovered that every household but two (one of those being mine) was tied by kinship to at least one other apartment in Big

Red. The young Mexican family with three small children directly below me in A1R, for example, had strong ties to the B stairwell. The husband's widowed mother lived in B1L, along with his sister, thirty-year-old single brother, and three cousins. His older brother lived across the hall from the mother in B1R, with his five children. Their cousins lived in B3R. Further, the three brothers and half-brothers all worked at the same place: the Easy Spuds potato-chip factory in Evanston. The families all ran back and forth from one another's back porches. Raul in A1R had three children, Salvatore in B1R had five, and two or three children always stayed with the single adults and grandmother in B1L, so there were many cousins to play with, circulate outgrown clothing among, share transportation, and collectively receive parenting from multiple caregivers. The grandmother in B1R had high blood pressure (one of the first things I was told when introduced) and was always surrounded by caring relatives. Maria, the daughter-in-law from A1R, spent so much time with her frail mother-in-law in B1L that it took me some time before I figured out in which apartment Maria actually lived.

The functional importance of this propinquity with immediate relatives became clear when Maria told me about her husband Raul's being laid off from work for seven months. One can get through such a crunch with immediate family close by. This supportive net of family is extended by several friendships with other Latino families in Big Red, as well as more friends and family in or near Albany Park. A more financially successful older brother who is a delivery-truck driver regularly visited from near Hoffman Estates. He had purchased a shiny new Ford truck with a camper cover that was shared with the Big Red kin for shopping trips.

Aurelio (Mexican), who lived across the hall from me in A2L, had a sister with a large family who lived in B2R. Over the summer, two of his younger brothers arrived from Mexico without papers, and they lived with his sister. Aurelio had eight sisters and seven brothers; all but the youngest lived in or near Albany Park. Three brothers and their families lived on Whipple Street around the corner; they and their children visited back and forth all the time. They pooled resources for major family celebrations. For example, Alfredo, Aurelio's baby boy, was baptized with four other cousins; a huge party and feast in the church basement followed for all the extended family and friends. All the working brothers and sisters co-financed the *quinceanera* debutante celebration for Aurelio's niece; Aurelio bought the flowers. Thanksgiving 1989 was celebrated jointly with six turkeys. My first week in Big Red I could not find anyone with the key to get my mailbox unlocked. Gabriel, one of Aurelio's brothers from Whipple, passed by, pulled out a knife from his pocket, and forced it open for me. That incident represented the quality of life in Big Red, the back-and-forth visiting between households and the spontaneous offering of assistance.

Aurelio's family was also tied strongly to the financially strapped family (two sisters rearing their seven children together without husbands) in the basement of B. I think they were cousins, or maybe just good friends, but everyone in A2L looked out for the extended family in the basement because there was no father. The older sister did not speak English.

Alberto, the kid from C2R, practically lived with Aurelio. At first he told me that they were cousins, then later that they really were not blood cousins, but like adopted family because they had lived close together for so long. They had been at Whipple together and then had both moved to Big Red. The same is true for Raul and Hilda, directly below me, and their relatives in B stairwell: they had come from Whipple along with Aurelio. The president of the Whipple block club, a white woman, remembered Aurelio and his relatives; she had had an altercation with them that led to a court hearing and the breaking of all the windows on two sides of her house. She described the entire group negatively as "clannish."

Another example of a kin network in Big Red was the Assyrian family with ten children in D1R. They were on Public Aid with monthly rent of $450. Unable to afford a telephone or transportation, they were among the most needy, even by Big Red standards.

In this case it was the wife who articulated the kinship lines. Her sister and husband lived two floors above them in D3R. The sister drove them to church, which was the hub of their social and economic sustenance (they obtained free meals there and clothes for the kids). The mother lived with the sister on the third floor, but every time I visited the family in D1R, the mother was there helping with caring and cooking for the ten kids, the oldest of whom was sixteen. The wife's brother lived just around the corner on the Gunnison side, in E1R. The brother's apartment was one of the more nicely furnished in Big Red. The D1R family depended on the brother for telephone use. The Assyrian family directly across the hall from them were cousins. The first time I was invited to this family's home for Sunday dinner, the children had picked leaves from trees in River Park; the mother stuffed the leaves with rice and served them with yogurt made from the powdered milk that is distributed once a month at the Albany Park Community Center.

The two ethnic Chinese families from Cambodia were intimately connected. The wife in E1L was the eldest daughter of the family in C1R, and both families helped manage the sewing shop in the basement.

The Hmong are noted for their kinship solidarity. Because they lived on the top floors, by and large, they could leave their doors open. Related families faced one another and shared back and forth, one apartment becoming an extension of the other. The kids ran from one apartment to the other, ate together, and blurred the household boundaries. The Hmong in the United States have not assimilated to the model of the nuclear family. My observations of the Latino and Assyrian families suggest the same, but the extended-family pattern was strongest among the Hmong. The Hmong neighbors directly above me had an apartment the same size as mine, one bedroom. It housed five adults—two brothers, their wives, and a grandmother—as well as the four small children of the older brother (the oldest child is eight) and the baby of the younger brother. They got along handsomely in this one-bedroom apartment. The kids

skipped down to my apartment frequently for cookies. They were extremely happy children, polite and very well-behaved.

This same Hmong family in A3R, the Yangs, demonstrated remarkably the importance of having kinfolk nearby. In December, when their Hmong neighbors across the hall moved to an apartment just across the street because they had suffered for a month with a waterless toilet, the Yangs could not bear to be alone on the top floor of our stairwell. Within two weeks they moved just across the courtyard to the D3L apartment in order to be close to their cousins living one floor below them in D2L. The mother explained that they had moved because she needed kin nearby to help with child care. This was the family's third move within Big Red in order to achieve close communal ties with relatives. Their understanding of "closeness" differed from that of white established residents. First, the Yangs' departing friends from A3L had only moved across the street, still in the 4800 block of Albany, within sight and shouting distance. Further, their cousins in D2L were in the same building, just across the courtyard. The Yangs, however, wanted a degree of intimacy that required side-by-side proximity to relatives or friends.

Even families from different ethnic groups expressed their friendship in "the idiom of kinship"(Stack 1974). The Mexican family in C2R told me that their new downstairs neighbors (Appalachian) in C1R were their "cousins." They claimed knowledge of a family tree that traced the Appalachians' family roots back to Spain, where the connection was made with the Mexicans' forebears. When I pressed the Mexican teenager who told me this, he did not know the specifics. But that did not seem to matter; he was delighted to have "relatives" living directly below him. He informed me that his neighbors—he calls them "hillbillies"—had told his family that they were also related to me, tracing their Irish side to my Scots background.

This interconnectedness with intimate others is highly functional for the people of Big Red. Carol Stack notes: "The poor adopt a variety of tactics in order to survive. They immerse themselves in a domestic circle of kinfolk who will help them. . . . Friends may be incorporated into one's domestic circle" (1974:29). Notwithstanding the unpleasant physical conditions, Big Red was an extraordinarily pleasant and human place to live because of the densely interlaced kin and friendship networks. My neighbors were not self-sufficient; therefore, they did not privilege self-reliance in the same way that the white middle class does. Sometimes they had difficulty making it from one paycheck to the next. They worked at connecting themselves to one another with reciprocal ties of gift-giving and the exchange of goods and services, as well as the less tangible but extremely important mutual offerings of respect and esteem. What Jane Addams observed almost a century ago still applies to Big Red: "I became permanently impressed with the kindness of the poor to each other; the woman who lives upstairs will willingly share her breakfast with the family below because she knows they 'are hard up'; the man who boarded with them last winter will give a month's rent because he knows the father of the family is out of work" (Addams 1910:123–24).

This ethic of care and concern for one another cuts across ethnic groups. The older sister of the Cambodian-Chinese family in C1R cut the hair of Latino neighbors, and the Latino youths in turn "looked out for" her family. I was amazed when the sixteen-year-old Mexican from the basement apartment walked through the courtyard on her way to the high school prom. She was beautifully dressed, with all the accessories. I knew that this household of nine sharing a one-bedroom apartment did not have the resources to finance such an outfit. I learned later that the dress had been borrowed from an aunt, the shoes from a neighbor, the purse from a cousin, and the hair-bow from another neighbor, and that her hair had been styled by the Cambodian neighbor.

This ethos of solidarity was expressed in the common greeting—used by Latino, Hmong, Assyrian—"Where are you going?" "Where have you been?" "I haven't seen you for a while." They expected answers and explanations. They were interested in one another's business. It was from the Mexicans that I learned the Hmong paid $20 a month for their garden plots in the vacant lot down the street. An Assyrian man I had not yet met knocked on my door one day and asked me whether I could help him patent an invention. He explained, "I look through your window and see all the books and thought you must have a book on this."

Taking my cue from neighbors, I started a back-porch "garden" in June 1988. Within the first week of setting out the pots, I had gifts of seeds and cuttings from four of my immediate neighbors.

One of the poignant examples of interethnic sharing deserves a full transcription. Ching, a small eight-year-old Hmong boy from E3R, approached me one day in the courtyard:

> **Ching:** Mr. Dwight, do you know Julio [twenty-year-old Mexican resident of Big Red]?
>
> **DC:** Yes.
>
> **Ching:** [obviously troubled] Is he gang? [In order not to violate street ethics, I deflected Ching's question.]
>
> **DC:** Why are you worried about that, Ching?
>
> **Ching:** [staring at ground, voice sad] Because he's my friend.
>
> **DC:** He's my friend too. How is he your friend, Ching?
>
> **Ching:** Because he's nice to me. He always gives me lots of toys, the toys he used to play with when he was a kid.
>
> **DC:** Why do you think he's in a gang?
>
> **Ching:** Because people say he's gang.

As the example of Ching makes clear, people value the intangibles of friendship and caring as much as the tangibles of money, food, or toys that change hands. That is not to depreciate the real need for material support. Julio's hand-me-down toys are the only ones Ching has. Ching's family moved into Big Red because they had lost their savings on a house they bought. The house had been burglarized twice, and they had lost everything. The father told me that they had moved into Big Red to recoup, to start over again.

The Big Red ethos of familiarity and reciprocity continues, for even though many of us have been displaced from the building, we still live in the area. In early July 1990, two teenagers (Assyrian and Mexican) hailed me as I carried a bag of groceries down one of the streets of Little Beirut. Consistent with local custom, they examined what was in my bag and said, "Thanks, Dwight," as they reached for two yogurts. There was no need to ask for the food. The nature and history of our relationship enabled them to assume this familiarity. Two days later, as they were riding around the neighborhood, they spotted me again and pulled the car over; the Assyrian fellow leaned out the window and offered me some of his food: "Hey Dwight, you want some of this shake?" These two incidents capture the quality of life in the Big Red area. At a micro-level, every day is filled with a host of significant kindnesses and richly nuanced reciprocities. To use a term from the streets, people are "tight" in Little Beirut (meaning tightly connected, not "tight" with their money). These micro-level courtesies provide a buffer against the macro-structures of exclusion and oppression. They enable people to experience dignity and joy in structures like Big Red, refashioning them into "dwelling places."

The fine-grained texture of the daily acknowledgments and courtesies that characterize life in Big Red provides a counterpoint to the blunter treatment the residents sometimes receive when they enter the system controlled by established residents and bureaucracies. Teenagers expelled from school have asked me to accompany their mothers to the principal's office for reinstatement because when the mother went alone, as one student put it, "they did not see her." In a communication system that required a different style of assertiveness, she was invisible. When I accompanied Mexican and Guatemalan mothers to school offices or police stations, all the attention and eye contact would be directed toward me, the white male. One time, after the high school principal had been persuaded to give one of my young neighbors a second chance, the mother gratefully extended her hand to thank him. But the principal reached right past her to shake my hand. Quite literally, he did not see her. A short, dark-complexioned Mexican woman, she had three factors that contributed to her invisibility: race, gender, and class.

Sometimes the erasure is not so subtle. While standing in line at the Perry Drugstore checkout line, one of my Assyrian neighbors gave me an updated report on her finger, which had been bitten by a rat as she slept in Big Red. Although the bandage had been removed, the finger still looked as if it had been slammed in a car door. The cashier, a white woman in her late fifties, treated my neighbors very curtly at the checkout. Before the Assyrian woman was out of earshot, and as the cashier was ringing up my purchases, she began talking to the neighboring cashier, also an older white woman. Here is what the two of them said, in full hearing of the Assyrian woman, her husband, her granddaughter, and me:

Cashier 1: Can you believe it? If my father were alive to see what's happened to the neighborhood!

Cashier 2: I know. Don't get upset.

Cashier 1: I hate getting upset first thing in the morning.

Cashier 2: They're not worth it.

Cashier 1: I know I shouldn't let them upset me.

Cashier 2: They're not worth it. They're trash.

Tactics of Resistance

The residents of Big Red coped with their oppressive circumstances typically through circumventions, survival tactics, and seizing opportunities. They did not have the power and clout to confront the system head-on. They survived via connections, evasions, street-smart maneuvers, making end-runs around authority. De Certeau describes the "tactical" thinking of people everywhere who must find space for themselves within oppressive structures:

The space of a tactic is the space of the other. Thus it must play on and with a terrain imposed on it and organized by the law of a foreign power. . . . It does not, therefore, have the options of planning general strategy and viewing the adversary as a whole within a distinct, visible, and objectifiable space. . . . It must vigilantly make use of the cracks that particular conjunctions open in the surveillance of the proprietary powers. It poaches in them. It creates surprises in them. It can be where it is least expected. It is a guileful ruse. (1984:37)

The Big Red tenants turned the "absenteeism" of the landlord to their advantage to enact spatial practices and temporal rhythms that would not have been tolerated in well-managed buildings. They had their tactics for dealing with the landlord. Mrs. Gutierrez from time to time would unleash a blistering tongue-lashing on him. She always announced to neighbors, days in advance, that she was going to "really shout at him this time." She would gather more complaints from the neighbors, gradually building up steam for one of her anticipated confrontations, and then, at the opportune moment, she would "really let him have it." Though none could match the explosive force of Mrs. Gutierrez, I overheard many women as they stood on back porches and denounced him.

Perhaps the best example of tactical resistance unfolded when the city shut off the water supply to Big Red because the landlord was $26,000 in arrears for payment. This action was taken at the end of June 1988, during a summer in which Chicago broke its previous record for days in which the temperature rose above 100 degrees Fahrenheit. During the three days of the water shutoff, temperatures soared to 105 degrees.

Attempts to work within the system were ineffectual. I contacted NRC, the powerful community organization, but it could do nothing to remedy the immediate crisis. I personally called several agencies and officials in the city, including the Water Department. It is legal, within the City of Chicago, to shut off water supply for a large building as a method of collecting debt payments. The only result my flurry of telephone calls produced was that a city inspector did visit Big

Red during the time we were without water, wrote a report, sympathized with us, then drove away. We never heard from him again. If we had depended on his official intervention, Big Red would still be without water. What all the city bureaucrats told us was that they did not have the authority to turn the water back on until the debt was cleared, or at least a partial payment was deposited. The owner, of course, was unaffected by the city's action. Never easy to reach, insulated in his lakefront condominium, he did not even know that the water had been shut off.

By the third day without water, the situation was intolerable. The gross inconvenience, the outrage of having no water for drink, bathing, or flushing the toilet, intensified by the 105-degree heat, incited radical action. It is hard to say whose idea the final solution was, because I think we came to it collectively. I remember that we were all standing in the courtyard, quite bedraggled and exhausted. Mrs. Yang, the Hmong mother from C3L, kept insisting, "We have to do something!" Spontaneously, we decided to take action into our own hands, dig down to the water main, and turn the water back on ourselves. This action was not only unauthorized, it was illegal.

This plan required several steps of coordinated action across lines of ethnicity, gender, and age. The hue and cry raised during the first day of the water shutoff drew in the white Democratic precinct captain, who lived one block north of Big Red. He became involved in the day-to-day drama of the water crisis as it unfolded. He donated his tools and garage workshop for the Hmong smiths to fashion a custom wrench to turn on the water valve. Mexican, Hmong, and Assyrian residents of Big Red all took turns with the digging. This activity attracted several "sidewalk supervisors," many of whom were homeowners from across the street, others just passersby, including African Americans and whites. The diggers reached the water main only to find the valve sheathed in an eighteen-inch sleeve filled with dirt. A Puerto Rican woman volunteered her vacuum-cleaner hose, and extension cords were plugged into the nearest apartment outlet, which happened to be Assyrian. The Hmong ran back and forth with the white precinct captain to fashion the wrench that would turn the valve. This took several attempts. Once they got it to fit, the next problem to be solved was determining what manipulation turned the water on. A full turn? Half turn? To the right or left? The water company does not make it easy for unauthorized people to take control of their water supply. An elderly Assyrian woman was stationed in the window to check her sink and report the results of each trial turn: "Nothing yet—yes, a trickle, do that again—no, nothing—O.K., that's it."

It was close to midnight by the time the water flowed. Everyone was exhilarated. Several of the men went to the Mexican *bracero* bar down the street on Lawrence to celebrate. No one bought his own beer. Everyone crossed over and spent his money buying someone else's beer, although in the end there was an equal distribution of monies. There was much camaraderie, backslapping, handshaking, and clicking of bottles.

The audience of this drama was enlarged by a front-page story in the *Chicago Tribune*, "In Crisis, Immigrants Learn Who Their True Friends Are." Several follow-up stories and editorials appeared in the Lerner neighborhood newspapers, all supporting the pluck of the Big Red residents and condemning the conditions that allowed a building full of vulnerable people to go for a prolonged time without water during the worst of Chicago's summer heat wave. Spokespersons for the Water Department went on record to say that no legal action would be taken against the Big Red residents who circumvented the law to regain control of their water supply.

This crisis tightened the community. In a crisis, boundaries are suspended or become porous. The sixth month into the project, I had made headway in meeting my Big Red neighbors, but most of the meaningful interaction had been with neighbors sharing my stairwell. By the time the water was turned back on, I had been inside thirty-five of the thirty-seven apartments. The shared hardship of going without water during one of Chicago's most notorious heat waves threw Big Red into a "communitas of crisis," a

heightened sense of "we-feeling" (Turner 1977: 154). It was easy to approach anybody sharing that experience. Residents who had not previously met were greeting one another with warm familiarity by the end of the second day. This crisis transformed my position in the building from semi-outsider to an informal advocate of sorts. It accelerated trust and rapport with neighbors by a great leap.

***

On August 1, 1989, the president of Oakwood Development Company, who was also president of the Albany Park Landlords' Association, took control of Big Red. The absentee owner had failed to make his mortgage payments, and the building was being cited in criminal housing court because of building-code violations and physical deterioration due to his negligence. Notices had gone up warning of another water shutoff because of the owner's failure to pay the water bill. The court appointed Superior Bank as receiver. With NRC urging, the bank appointed Oakwood Development Company as manager of Big Red. Empowered by the state and allied with community organizations, an Oakwood Development crew used sledgehammers to break into the basement of Big Red to take charge of the utility meters and other facilities.

Almost immediately after the takeover, Oakwood and staff interviewed various residents and quickly pinpointed two drug-dealing apartments, the busiest one being the apartment above me that Bao Xiong and her family had formerly occupied. Oakwood used the crisis of drug trafficking as an excuse to evacuate the entire stairwell. With hindsight, I believe the drug dealers, who were real, became the lever Oakwood deployed to start emptying Big Red as quickly as possible.

When Oakwood took control in August, Big Red was fully occupied and still had a vital building culture and ethos of solidarity. Within four months, half of the Big Red households were displaced. One year later, thirty-one of the thirty-seven apartments were vacant. Empty and boarded up, Big

Red looms like a ghost building. The wrenching violence of this intervention was muted in the euphemisms that Oakwood and NRC used to describe their actions: "turning the building around," "turning the neighborhood around."

Oakwood, a multimillion-dollar company that specializes in managing low-income rental properties, works closely with NRC. The NRC director of housing development lives in an Oakwood building. Oakwood and NRC estimate that it will require a $1.5-million loan to purchase and rehabilitate Big Red. NRC Housing Development is working on getting a low-interest loan package through Chicago Equity Fund[3] and Community Investment Incorporation. The NRC Housing Development director explained the plans for Big Red: "We want to make it a community project—bring together Oakwood experience and profitmaking know-how with NRC philosophy and provide quality rehab for poor people. Make it a good solid community, *but integrated with the rest of the community*" (emphasis mine). The partnership of Oakwood's "profit-making know-how with NRC philosophy," united against the market individualism of "slumlords" as much as the transgressive tenants, is a classic example of the complex way investment property mirrors "the internal tensions within the capitalist order" and anchors a coalition between private investment and the public sector in advanced capitalist societies (Harvey 1985:61). The absentee landlord of Big Red was displaced along with the residents: his locks were smashed with Oakwood sledgehammers on the day of takeover. The competitive tensions and profit-making dictates of capitalism are softened, elided, and simultaneously enabled by the moral rhetoric (NRC's "philosophy") of community organizations concerned with the public good. Community organizations like NRC produce strategic definitions of "the public good," "quality of life," and "good solid community" that are advantageous to capital development.

The NRC phrase "but integrated with the rest of the community" codes the middle-class anxiety about Big Red. Big Red transgressed the system by remaining outside it.

With an unresponsive absentee landlord and an array of mostly new-immigrant working-class tenants, Big Red eluded middle-class strategies of containment and control. The plurality, fluidity, and openness that made Big Red accessible and accommodating to new-immigrant and working-class tenants were among the very qualities that the middle class finds forbidding. Situated in the center of Little Beirut, Big Red focused and displayed middle-class fears and ambivalences about difference, density, deterioration, and demographic change.

Endnotes

1. The Northwestern colleagues with whom I worked on the Ford Foundation Changing Relations Project were Paul Fiesema, Jane Mansbridge, and Al Hunter, assisted by graduate students Mary Erdmans, Jeremy Hein, Yvonne Newsome, and Yung-Sun Park. I wish to acknowledge support from the Ford Foundation, which funded the Changing Relations project through the Research Foundation of the State University of New York, Grant 240–1117. The Center for Urban Affairs and Policy Research (CUAPR) at Northwestern University facilitated the work of the Chicago team of the Changing Relations project. I thank the staff of CUAPR for their expertise and cheerful support. I am particularly grateful to my colleague Jane Mansbridge, who carefully read earlier drafts of this chapter and offered many helpful criticisms and suggestions.

2. The conditions and people of Big Red can be seen in segments of two documentaries: *America Becoming*, produced by Dai-Sil Kim-Gibson for the Ford Foundation, and *The Heart Broken in Half*, produced and directed by Taggart Siegel and Dwight Conquergood.

3. Chicago Equity Fund is a not-for-profit loan company for low-income housing funded by a group of Chicago millionaires, who get a special tax break in exchange for the entailment that money go toward housing that will be designated low-income for fifteen years.

References

Addams, Jane. 1960 [1910]. *Twenty Years at Hull-House*. New York: Penguin.

De Certeau, Michel. 1984. *The Practice of Everyday Life*. Translated by Steven Rendall. Berkeley: University of California Press.

Harvey, David. 1985. *Consciousness and the Urban Experience: Studies in the History and Theory of Capitalist Urbanization*. Baltimore: Johns Hopkins University Press.

Rapp, Rayna. 1987. "Urban Kinship in Contemporary America: Families, Classes, and Ideology." In *Cities of the United States: Studies in Urban Anthropology*, edited by Leith Mullings. New York: Columbia University Press.

Stack, Carol B. 1974. *All Our Kin: Strategies for Survival in a Black Community*. New York: Harper and Row.

Turner, Victor. 1977 [1969]. *The Ritual Process: Structure and Anti-Structure*. Ithaca, NY: Cornell University Press.

Review

1. What were the patterns Conquergood found that residents utilized while they were trying to "make do"?

2. How did the crisis of having their water cut off affect the residents of Big Red?

3. What were the factors in the "middle-class anxiety" that led to the demise of Big Red?

Application

Extended familial ties are of major importance to some ethnic groups. Divide your class into sections. Assign each group a different ethnic/immigrant group that came to the United States earlier in the country's history. Using the library to locate historical sources, try to discover the nature of the experience of each ethnic group. Were norms of cooperation and "making do" apparent for these other groups? How important was the extended family in their experiences?

42
Plain Living

Deciding to Move Down

Trudy Bush

Almost every generation in the United States has expected to do better than its predecessor. It has been assumed that in the "land of opportunity" everyone would—and would want to— attain a higher position on the occupational ladder than that of their parents. Thus, not to move up has been a cause for embarrassment for many Americans. Worse yet, those who have experienced downward mobility have often found the experience extremely traumatic. Strained and broken marriages, tension in the family, and personal emotional problems have been associated with people who struggle with downward mobility.

Ironically, during the 1990s, a period of dramatic economic growth and opportunity for upward mobility, some Americans began to question the value of moving up. In particular, they questioned the personal and relational costs of reaching and maintaining the lifestyle to which most people were aspiring. Books, videos, and seminars told Americans how they could simplify their lives. Simplicity Circles emerged—small groups of four to eight people who met regularly to explore ways to simplify their lives. Life simplification does not mean moving down to the poverty level; at the same time, it is a firm rejection of the notion of attaining the highest standard of living you can. Those who participate in the voluntary simplicity movement try to cut back on demands for their time and energy and devote themselves to matters they deem essential— family, friends, personal passions, and so on.

In this selection, Trudy Bush provides some background on the quest for life simplification and relates the stories of a number of Americans who have opted for it. Although some of the people she discusses are motivated to simplify their lives for religious reasons, motiva- tions vary among those who have chosen to simplify. In many cases, the decision is simply a matter of weariness with the "rat race" and a yearning for less tension and a more fulfilling life.

"**T**he Jones' are surrendering!" a TV news reporter proclaims. "The family with whom we've tried to keep up is throwing in the towel!" The camera pans to four desperate looking people standing in front of a large house. "We've had it," the wife says. "We're exhausted. We never see each other. And we have so much debt that we can't keep up anymore. It's just not worth it."

So begins Beyond Affluenza, a recent public television special made in Seattle. The one-hour program and its prequel, Affluenza, document the current expression of an ideal that recurs throughout American history—simplicity. The Puritans and Quakers emigrated here to live out an austere and simple ethic. The founding fathers believed that civic virtue is accompanied by material restraint. In the 1840s, Henry Thoreau sought to live deliberately at Walden Pond, and Ralph Waldo Emerson and Bronson Alcott experimented in simple rural living. That experiment was repeated in the back-to-nature communes of the 1960s and '70s, which were inspired in part by people like Scott and Helen Nearing who had pioneered the simple life of rural homesteading decades earlier.

Many people today are again willing to trade relentless consumption for a more intellectually and spiritually rich life. For most of these people, the pursuit of simplicity means gaining control of their money and their time so that both can be used more intentionally. By downsizing their expectations of material affluence, people are able to discover and invest in what really matters to them, whether that is family, relationships, community involvement, environmental responsibility or a new, more satisfying kind of work.

Who is pursuing the simple life? Among those trying to live more deliberately is a young man who leaves a lucrative position at Microsoft in order to do what he has always wanted—be an actor and help others by volunteering, especially as a Big Brother. A family opts to live on less money after the husband refuses to accept a job transfer that would have him designing weapons and the wife decides she wants to stay at home with their children; to act on these values, the family renovates an old house, relies on bicycles instead of a car, and grows some of its own food. A 50-year-old corporate attorney retires from his practice in order to run an environmental organization; he and his wife recycle and compost so effectively that they fill only one garbage can a month. And a couple who keeps a large home in the suburbs decides to rent out part of it to graduate students from other countries. The rental income frees them to devote fewer hours to paid employment, and they are enriched by their friendship with their tenants.

The idea of living more simply has spawned hundreds of books, videos and seminars. While some of the recent books can be classified with pseudotherapeutic self-help literature, many are both useful and philosophically serious.

What is making this ideal so appealing to people in a time of such conspicuous affluence? The search for a simpler life is usually a response to a crisis like war or economic depression, according to historian David Shi, author of *The Simple Life*. But Shi thinks there is a "psychological malaise" at work in our culture. "We've never before had such high levels of anxiety and depression among affluent people. Though people are materially well off, they're discovering that their lives seem hollow and meaningless. They're searching for meaning and, in many cases, they're also looking for alternatives to the frenetic pace of their lives."

Shi, president of Furman University, points out that during the '90s the work week actually increased for the first time in more than a century. "Even our leisure time has become scheduled, has lost its spontaneity. And among all the hoopla about our prosperity is the disturbing fact that the three most commonly prescribed drugs are an ulcer medication, an antidepressant and a pain reliever. Underneath the surface of success and material splendor, many Americans are struggling to cope."

If the voluntary simplicity movement has a geographical center, it is the Pacific Northwest, particularly Seattle. That's the home of three of the most dedicated practitioners and eloquent advocates of the simple life— Vicki Robin, Cecile Andrews and Janet Luhrs. Seattle is also the home of Earth Ministry, "a Christian, ecumenical, environmental, nonprofit organization" which has just published *Simpler Living, Compassionate Life: A Christian Perspective*, an anthology of essays and a curriculum intended to be used by churches. The people in Seattle are, Shi says, developing an infrastructure that the simplicity movement has seldom had.

On the day I visited Robin at her home near the university, the scene was bustling with people who were carrying around furniture and setting up a picnic table in the garden. "A team is here working on something called the 'ecological footprint,'" Robin explained. The ecological footprint is a concept developed by Mathis Wackernagel of the University of British Columbia to measure humans' impact on the environment. "He worked out a way to translate objects into the number of acres it would take to produce the material for them," Robin said. "This morning the team weighed the futon on which you're sitting to see how many pounds of cotton it contains. They're now working on a bedroom, and they'll do the kitchen next."

By translating everything into acres, Wackernagel (who, with William Rees, published *Our Ecological Footprint: Reducing Human Impact on the Earth* in 1995) has measured the ecological footprints of people in different countries. The average American has a more than ten-square-acre footprint, while the global average is under three. "If you divide all the arable land on the planet by the world's population, you find that we're already overpopulated and overconsuming. We're going into debt globally," Robin says.

The ecological footprint project meshes nicely with Robin's own work—to provide a method for mastering personal finances, as the first step in finding new road maps for living. With the late Joe Dominguez, she coauthored *Your Money or Your Life,* one of the bibles of the voluntary simplicity movement. Still selling briskly, the book (first published in 1992) spent more than a year on *Business Week's* best-seller list. It details nine rigorous steps for gaining financial independence.

Robin, a thoughtful, reserved woman in her 50s, lives frugally, co-owning her house with three other women, driving a well-maintained old car, and buying many of her clothes in thrift stores. She plows the income from her book into the charitable foundation she established with Dominguez. The New Road Map Foundation, staffed by volunteers, provides grants to other nonprofit organizations. "One of my favorites is the Northwest Earth Institute," Robin says. "It was created by a man who had been a partner in a major law firm in Portland, Oregon. He and his wife were concerned about environmental degradation and set out to teach people the basic principles of living in a way that cares for the earth. They and their small staff developed four courses that people take at their workplace during their lunch hours. More than 250 businesses have offered these study groups in ecology and voluntary simplicity."

When I asked her if environmental concerns were the main impetus for her work, she said, "That's a very strong motivator for me—that we're taking God's creation and treating it as though it were ours to use up. But I've always had many layers of passion motivating my decision to live more simply. To me, this movement is spiritual, ecological, social and cultural. Though many of the people I know are deeply engaged in a spiritual quest of one kind or another, it's getting less and less fashionable for Americans to frame their lives around their values and beliefs.

"We need to be more deeply rooted in our values, and more devoted to loving and caring for one another. We need to live in a way that fosters community and that doesn't destroy other cultures. We're losing cultures—that whole web of intelligence that tells us how to survive and live well in a particular environment. It's not just the environmental wall that we'll soon hit; there are many walls.

We're relinquishing species after species, habitat after habitat, social structure after social structure. We have no idea how essential the things we're destroying may be to our own well-being."

These crises give the present interest in simplicity a new urgency, Robin believes. She cites studies that indicate a large cohort of Americans hold values inconsistent with those of the dominant culture, even though many of them are still living as part of that culture. She wonders if the voluntary simplicity movement is like "a change in the geography of the ocean floor that's creating a swell on the surface but won't impact the shore. Or are we seeing such an intense and rapid shift in people's thinking that, like a huge wave hitting the shore, it will really bring about changes?"

Robin wonders if there might be some way to speed up the process, to increase people's awareness of their feelings of discomfort and dissonance so that they become willing to endorse social policies—consumption and energy taxes, for instance—that will change the direction of our culture. Given what we're up against, she asks, "Can we afford to be evolutionary, or do we need to be revolutionary? What form would such a revolution take? And how big is the constituency that would back major changes in our public policies? How much of their lives are people willing to put on the line for their ideals?" She has no answers for these questions, but, she says, "I keep my nose pressed against them."

Cecile Andrews, author of the widely used book *The Circle of Simplicity,* radiates energy and enthusiasm for her ideas and for her region. "People really care about the environment here. The Pacific Northwest is a kind of frontier. Lots of people move here seeking a better life."

As the home of Microsoft, Seattle also is full of people familiar with high-tech industry and the hi-tech lifestyle. But, says Andrews, "People still remember when their lives were more relaxed. Simplicity is kind of a double response—both to the environmental crisis and to the feeling that life has become chaotic and out of control. We're all working so hard that we've almost lost the ability to enjoy ourselves. The high point of people's lives seems to be crossing something off of their to-do list. That's as good as it gets!"

For Andrews, the simple life is the examined life. In its present manifestation, voluntary simplicity is a middle-class movement of well-educated people "who like to think and read, who look thoughtfully at every aspect of their lives and consider the consequences of their decisions." It doesn't necessarily entail a log cabin or pinched frugality. "I hate people to think of simplicity as only frugality," Andrews said. "Rather than frugality, I prefer the term 'morally responsible consumerism.' Paring back is part of simplicity, but an even bigger part is dealing with the inner emptiness that makes people so obsessed with consumerism—the lack of spiritual concerns, of community, of a sense of meaning. Simplicity means being inwardly rich, being joyful, and feeling a sense of connectedness."

Like Robin, Andrews believes that our economy has become so environmentally destructive that we will eventually be forced to change our way of life. But she doesn't see that change coming soon. Though voluntary simplicity is growing, so is consumerism. At this point, the movement is still about individual, not social, change. But eventually the individual movement will affect corporate structures and public policy. Simplicity, she says, is a Trojan horse. "We look so benign that nobody's afraid of us. Then we pop out and change society."

Andrews's favored tool for helping people to examine their lives and to resist consumer culture is the study circle. A former community college administrator, she wants to find a noncompetitive way to bring people together and help them think for themselves. "Simplicity circles are built around people's personal stories," she explained. These small groups usually meet in people's homes once a week for a ten-week period, discussing such topics as how to change consumption habits, build community and transform work.

"During the session on community, we begin by talking about times during our lives when each of us has experienced community. There's no leader—we just go around the circle, and people tell wonderful stories. After we've examined what's happened in our own lives, we go on to critique society. The third step is to brainstorm ways in which we can take action. We plan small, specific things each of us will do that week. If people focus only on what they can do to change the larger society, they begin to feel helpless. But each of us can do something in our own neighborhood, our own community. The following week we report back and compare our experiences. I wanted these study circles to be something people could do without needing training, without relying on experts, without paying any dues. It's something a group can do on its own." Simplicity circles are now meeting throughout the English-speaking world, she said.

Janet Luhrs is a single mother raising an 11-year-old son and a 13-year-old daughter. She said her parents taught her to live below her means and to choose her work according to what she loved to do. Luhrs spent her 20s living frugally so that she could devote herself to writing.

"Then, when I was 30, I thought I was missing out on something, and I went to law school. That's when my life became complicated. I graduated, got my first credit cards and bought expensive, corporate kinds of clothes. We had our first child and decided we would hire a nanny to raise her, while I went out to work as a lawyer. But that lasted only a few weeks, before I asked myself, 'Why am I doing this?' I fired the nanny, stayed home and had another child."

Luhrs's concerns became focused when she took a class on simplicity taught by Andrews. "It was like finding home," she says. Seven years ago she began publishing a quarterly newsletter, *Simple Living: The Journal of Voluntary Simplicity*. "I really started it to teach myself," she explains. "I had known how to live simply as a single woman in my 20s. But I didn't know how to do it, with kids and a mortgage and credit cards."

Four years later, Bantam Doubleday Dell asked her to do a book on simplicity. *The Simple Living Guide: A Sourcebook for Less Stressful, More Joyful Living* (1997) is an encyclopedia of information about everything from the pleasures of simple dating and romance to creative real-estate financing.

Luhrs sees herself as the practical generalist of the simplicity movement, the person who tells people how to do it. All three women think of their work as interrelated and complementary. "Vicki began by focusing more on people's concerns about money, while I was interested in time," Andrews noted. "Janet attracted a lot of people who were fascinated with the ingenuity part—50 ways to have a good time without spending money, or isn't it fun to plant your own garden and cook your own food. My group is probably more the cafe society, who like to talk about the philosophical aspects and the policy implications."

All three bear out Shi's assertion that "the people who have succeeded in maintaining a commitment to simplicity over time are disproportionately people with a powerful spiritual foundation—that is, some sort of transcendent element in their outlook that gives them the fortitude and the tenacity to maintain this mode of living in the face of all of the conflicting tendencies and temptations around us." Robin talks a great deal about God and about the relationship between simpler living and spiritual development. Evy McDonald, who runs the New Road Map Foundation with Robin, has written a "Group Study Guide for Contemporary Christians" to be used with *Your Money or Your Life*. The curriculum has been tested by church groups in a variety of denominations. McDonald is now studying to become a United Methodist pastor. Indeed, Robin and McDonald's work reminds one of the dictum that summarizes John Wesley's economic advice: "Earn all you can, save all you can, give all you can."

Andrews has been a Quaker and is now a Unitarian. She was raised as a Methodist. "My church taught me both to think things through and to be concerned with social justice," she said. "I see simplicity as a core social-issue. People worry about how our way of life, our consumption patterns, are affecting people around the world. They're taking seriously that quote from Gandhi, 'Live simply so that others may simply live.'"

"For years now I've gone back and forth between the Quakers and the Unitarians," Andrews said. "I love the Quaker philosophy, and the silence. But Quakers are quiet people, and I'm not. Unitarians are loud and talkative, like I am. My church voted that morally responsible consumerism should be the main issue Unitarians study and discuss this year. Because they provide both spiritual nurture and community, churches are going to have a central role in the simplicity movement—and the movement may help to revitalize the church."

Luhrs was raised as a Catholic but doesn't belong to a church. "I'm still probably a Catholic at heart," she said. "But I've opened up to a much more eclectic spirituality. I've done a lot of meditation and exploring of different kinds of spiritual traditions. I consider simplicity as a spiritual way of life—if you stop working around the clock or worrying about being in debt or shopping compulsively, then you have time to try to be a better person rather than just an accumulator. Spending time cultivating your virtues rather than your closet is a wonderful way to live."

Robin, Andrews and Luhrs each have projects under way that build on their previous work. Robin is gathering material for a book about how people define and use the freedom that *Your Money or Your Life* is designed to help them find. "Though the book is extremely effective, taking all nine of the steps it advocates is quite challenging because we tend to be uneasy with that degree of freedom. People wonder, 'What will I do with myself if my teacher, my boss, my society aren't telling me what to do? How do I give of myself? What is myself?' We've handed people a solution, but we're also handing them another problem. I've been interviewing people from all kinds of backgrounds and cultures. The variability in the way people define freedom is fascinating. God gave us free will. It's what distinguishes us from other creatures. So not to know how to use our freedom well is misusing our greatest gift."

Andrews is addressing the social-justice implications of simplicity. "I'm trying to figure out how we can talk about this with poor people," she said. "I would never use the word 'simplicity' with people who are struggling to meet their basic needs. Our emphasis on consumption, and the growing gap between the rich and poor, presents a self-esteem issue for poor people and a threat to our democracy. The expense of political campaigns gives the poor less and less of a voice in government and society. A lot of us grew up in families that wouldn't seem at all affluent now. But people felt OK about themselves. Now poor people are learning to judge themselves as losers. They see luxuries on TV and think, 'I should have that, I'd be happy if I had that.' But very few will ever have those luxuries."

"I'm trying out a new idea for how I can talk about values with poor people without coming across as Lady Bountiful. I'm working with a newspaper for the homeless on movie reviews from a poor person's perspective. It's also a way of educating the middle class about the viewpoints of the poor, since middle-class folks buy these newspapers and like to read reviews. And I'm facilitating a writing project for poor people."

Luhrs is working on a book on the effect of simple living on intimate relationships. "I find that the people interested in simplicity live together more consciously, with more awareness," she said. "They really put a lot of time, effort and thought into their relationships. Simple living means a lot of different things for them. Some think of it as a sort of inner simplicity that consists of being more honest about who they are. For some, it's simplifying their outer lives so they're not spending their time fighting about money or worrying about debt. Working together on these lifestyle issues makes people feel closer to each other."

It is significant that these three leaders of the simplicity movement are women, and that women are disproportionately represented throughout the current movement. In holding full time jobs and fighting their way up the corporate ladder while raising children and trying to maintain homes and families, women have perhaps been more conscious of the frenetic demands of life and more inclined to change priorities. (In the past, men like Alcott and Emerson were the public spokesmen for the simplicity ideal, but of course women did much of the work that made simple living possible.)

Though Shi contends that simplicity movements go through cycles and rarely manage to build a long lasting structure, Robin, Andrews and Luhrs think that the movement has become so mainstream that it won't go away. Their own opportunities to speak are increasing, and they see their audiences growing. The call for a simpler and more intentional, sustainable and meaningful way of life continues to find a deep resonance.

Review

1. Is the voluntary simplicity movement a recent phenomenon or does it have historical roots? Explain your answer.

2. Discuss the philosophy of the voluntary simplicity movement.

3. What, according to the advocates, are the implications of simplicity for social justice and intimate relationships?

Applications

1. Interview five students. Ask them about their aspirations for their lives—what kind of work they want to do and what kind of lifestyle they hope to maintain. Also ask them how the lifestyle they hope to achieve compares with that of their parents. Do any of them indicate a desire for simplicity? Or do they aspire to replicate or surpass their parents lifestyle?

2. Do you agree or disagree with the philosophy of the voluntary simplicity movement? Write an essay explaining your position. Point out how your position will affect your life decisions.

Reprinted from: Trudy Bush, "Plain Living: The Search for Simplicity," *Christian Century* 116 (June 30, 1999):676–81. Copyright © 1999 Christian Century Foundation. Reprinted with permission from the June 30, 1999, issue of the *Christian Century*. Subscriptions $42/yr. (36 issues) from P.O. Box 378, Mt. Morris, IL 61054. ✦

43

Credit Cards, Fast-Food Restaurants, and Rationalization

George Ritzer

The founders of sociology—Marx, Weber, and Durkheim—continue to exert significant influence over the discipline. It is a tribute to the clarity of their vision that their writings are still consulted today, a century and more after their work was written. In this sense these early sociologists were superb futurists.

In the following selection, George Ritzer uses Max Weber's concept of rationalization to explain two distinctive developments in modern American society—fast food and charge cards. Weber believed that over the past several centuries Western society has turned away from a reliance on tradition to a preference for "rational" thinking. Rational thinking relies on reasoning and experimentation to find the most efficient and predictable means to accomplish a certain goal. For example, merchants in modern society sell products at fixed prices. In traditional societies, by contrast, prices vary according to the personal relations between buyer and seller and the sometimes interminable "haggling" over price. While the modern system is both more efficient and calculable, it is also more impersonal. Just as Weber lamented this downside of rationalization, so Ritzer points out the common irrationality that often develops out of the process of rationalization.

... [B]oth the credit card and the fast-food restaurant were products of post-World War II changes in American society. Both have, in turn, greatly contributed to an accelerating rate of change in our society. The concern of this chapter . . . is the similarities and differences between these two seemingly mundane but nonetheless enormously important social and economic developments. The main focus is the degree to which the two are part of the general process of the rationalization of society. I will pay special attention to the private troubles and the public issues that accompany the rationalization process in the credit card industry. . . .

Rationalization

. . . [T]he major similarity between fast-food restaurants and credit cards is that both can be seen as part of the process of rationalization. The theory of rationalization is most commonly associated with Max Weber, although, as we have seen, Georg Simmel had a very similar perspective.[1] Weber's theory suggests five basic components of rationalizations:[2]

- *Calculability*. Rationalization involves an emphasis on things that can be calculated, counted, or quantified. There is a tendency to use quantity as a surrogate measure for quality, which leads to a sense that quality is equated with large quantities of things.

- *Efficiency*. Rationalization involves the search for the best possible means to whatever end we have in mind. In a rationalized society, efficiency can become an end in itself.

- *Predictability*. A rationalized world involves as few surprises as possible. Thus, goods and services will be very similar, if not identical, from one time or place to another.

- *Substitution of nonhuman for human technology*. This component is self-explanatory, although it should be noted that often the ultimate objective of such a change is to enhance the amount of control exercised over human beings.

- *Irrationality of rationality*. Rational systems seem inevitably to spawn a series of irrationalities that serve to limit, ultimately compromise, and perhaps even undermine rationality. The major example of such an irrationality is the dehumanization often associated with highly rational systems. Dehumanization causes a series of personal troubles for people, most notably difficulty in finding meaning in their lives. More generally, rationalization leads to what Weber termed the "iron cage" of rationalization. That is, we are increasingly trapped in rationalized structures like bureaucracies and fast-food restaurants from which there is less and less possibility of escape.

Rationalization, then, can be defined as the process by which the five components outlined above come to characterize more sectors of the social world. The process is well underway in the United States and to an increasing degree around the world as well.

The credit card, like the fast-food restaurant, is not only a part of this process of rationalization but is also a significant force in the development and spread of rationalization. Just as McDonald's rationalized the delivery of prepared food, the credit card rationalized (or "McDonaldized") the consumer loan business.[3] Prior to credit cards, the process of obtaining loans was slow, cumbersome, and nonrationalized. But obtaining a modern credit card (which can be thought of as a noncollateralized consumer loan) is now a very efficient process, often requiring little more than filling out a short questionnaire. With credit bureaus and computerization, credit records can be checked and applications approved (or disapproved) very rapidly. Furthermore, the unpredictability of loan approval has been greatly reduced and, in the case of preapproved credit cards, completely eliminated. The decision to offer a preapproved card, or to approve an application for a card, is increasingly left to a non-human technology—the computer. Computerized scoring systems exert control over credit card company employees by, for example, preventing them from approving an application if the score falls below the agreed-on standard. And these scoring systems are, by definition, calculable, relying on quantitative measures rather than qualitative judgments about things like the applicant's "character." Thus, credit card loans, like fast-food hamburgers, are now being served up in a highly rationalized, assembly-line fashion. As a result, a variety of irrationalities of rationality, especially dehumanization, have come to be associated with both.

It is worth noting that the rationalization of credit card loans has played a central role in fostering the rationalization of other types of loans, such as automobile and home equity loans. Automobile loan approvals used to take days, but now a loan can be approved, and one can drive off in a new car, in a matter of hours, if not minutes. Similarly, home equity loans can now be obtained much more quickly and easily than was the case in the past. Such loans rely on many of the same technologies and procedures, such as scoring systems, that are used in decision making involving credit cards.[4] Thus, just as the process of rationalization in society as a whole has been spearheaded by the fast-food industry, it is reverberating across the banking and loan business led by the credit card industry. We can anticipate that over time other types of loans, involving larger and larger sums of money (mortgages and business loans, for example), will be increasingly rationalized. Virtually every facet of banking and finance will be moving in that direction.

We can get a glimpse of the rationalized future of banking at one branch of Huntington Bancshares of Columbus, Ohio. The branch in question is the busiest of the bank's 350 outlets, processing as many home equity loans as 100 typical branches and handling as many new credit cards as 220 of those branches. It is distinguished by the fact that none of its business is done in person—it is all done by telephone. Of the fear of alienating customers because of the dehumanization associated with this type of banking, the chairman of Huntington Bancshares says, "I don't mind offending customers and losing them if it benefits the bank in the long run. . . . I'd rather have fewer customers and make an awful lot of money on them than have a lot of customers and lose our shirt."[5]

Whatever its impact on customers, the branch is certainly efficient. For example, it is able to approve a loan in 10 minutes, even if the request is made by telephone in the middle of the night. Here is the way the system works:

> As soon as a "telephone banker" types the first few identifying details of an application onto the computer, the machine automatically finds the records of the customer's previous activity with Huntington and simultaneously orders an electronic version of the applicant's credit bureau file. The phone banker then contacts by pager one of two seasoned loan officers who roam the maze of office cubicles in the telephone center.

> With printouts of the banking records, credit file and computer-analyzed loan application in hand, a loan officer can generally make a decision in less than a minute. The bank says its credit problems are no greater than for loans from its branches.[6]

Huntington Bancshare's so-called "telephone banker" appears to be the counterpart to the McDonald's counterperson or the worker at the drive-through window. Telephone bankers are clearly far less skilled than their predecessors. They are reduced to glorified computer operators, with the truly important and difficult work (analyses of credit records and loan decisions) being done by the computer and the loan officers. Thus, "McDonaldized" banking brings with it deskilling and the further rationalization of bank work. It is forecast that about 40% of the 100,000 bank branches in the United States are likely to be closed over the next decade. Some of these closures will be due to mergers, but many will be due to the replacement of the less efficient, conventional branches and traditional bankers with new, more efficient branches and telephone bankers. . . .

Now let us turn to a discussion of each of the components of rationalization and the ways in which they apply to the credit card business.

Calculability: The All-Important Credit Report

Calculability is reflected in the fast-food restaurants by, for example, the names they give to their products. These names usually emphasize that the products are large. Examples include the Big Mac, the Whopper, the Whaler, and Biggie fries. The emphasis on things that can be quantified is also reflected in, among other things, products like the Quarter Pounder and publicity on how many billions of hamburgers are sold and how quickly pizzas can be delivered.

The credit card industry also emphasizes things that are quantified, although this more conservative industry generally shies away from the clever names employed in the fast-food industry. (However, one is led to wonder just how long it will be before we see something like the "Whopper Card.") Among the most visible of the quantified aspects of credit cards are their credit limits, interest rates, and annual fees (or lack thereof). Credit cards permit people to maximize the number of things they can buy and optimize the amount of money they spend. By offering instant credit up to a predefined but expandable limit, credit cards allow people not only to spend all their available money but also to go into debt for, in many cases, thousands of dollars. Furthermore, in an effort to increase their level of debt, people often seek to maximize the credit limit on each of their cards and to accumulate as many cards as possible, each with as high a credit limit as possible. In fact, increasingly important status symbols in our society are the number of credit cards one has in one's wallet and the collective credit limit available on those cards. The modern status symbol is thus debt rather than savings. In sum, credit cards emphasize a whole series of things that can be quantified—number of cards, credit limits, amount of debt, number of goods and services that can [be] purchased, and so on.

Calculability involves not only an emphasis on quantity but also a comparative lack of interest in quality. The fast-food industry is concerned with large portions (Big Mac value meals) but not with taste (there is no

"Delicious Mac" for sale at your local Mc-Donald's). Similarly, the emphasis on the quantity of credit card debt allowed tends to lessen people's interest in the quality of the things that they can acquire while running up that debt. With a finite amount of cash on hand or in the bank, consumers tend to be more careful, buying a relatively small number of high-quality goods that promise to have a long and useful life. But consumers who buy things on seemingly ever-expandable credit often have less interest in quality. The accent is on buying large numbers of things, with comparatively little concern that those things might deteriorate swiftly. After all, if things wear out quickly, they can be replaced—perhaps when one's credit card has an even higher credit limit. . . .

Efficiency: The Faster the Better

The second component of rationality—efficiency—is manifest in the fast-food industry, among many other ways, in the drive-through window. For customers the drive-through is a far more efficient way of obtaining a meal than parking one's car, walking to the counter, ordering, paying, and returning to the car. (Walking into the restaurant, of course, is, in turn, a much more efficient method for obtaining a meal than cooking from scratch.) To take one other example, finger foods like Chicken McNuggets are far more efficient to eat than chicken parts like wings, legs, and breasts. Unlike chicken wings, Chicken McNuggets can be tossed into one's mouth as one drives to the next rationally and efficiently organized activity.

Similarly, the credit card is a highly efficient method for obtaining, granting, and expending loans. Applicants need do little more than fill out a brief application, and in the case of preapproved credit cards, even that requirement may be waived. In most cases, the customer is granted a line of credit, which is accessed and expended quickly and easily each time the card is used. Assuming a good credit record, as the credit limit is approached, it will be increased automatically, thereby effortlessly increasing the potential total loan amount.

Furthermore, the credit card tends to greatly enhance the efficiency of virtually all kinds of shopping. Instead of carrying unwieldy amounts of cash, all one needs is a thin piece of plastic. There is no need to plan for purchases by going to the bank to obtain cash, no need to carry burdensome checkbooks and the identification needed to get checks approved. With their credit cards, consumers are no longer even required to know how to count out the needed amount of currency or to make sure the change is correct.

Credit (and debit) cards are also more efficient from the merchant's point of view. The average cash transaction at, for example, a supermarket is still fastest (16 to 30 seconds), but it is closely followed by card payment (20 to 30 seconds); a check transaction lags far behind (45 to 90 seconds). Although it might be a tad slower than cash at the checkout counter, a card transaction is ultimately far more efficient than a cash deal because it requires little from the merchant except the initial electronic transmission of the charge. Handling cash is, as one supermarket electronic banking services executive points out, "labor intensive. From the time it leaves the customer's hands to the time it hits the bank, cash may get handled six to eight different times, both at the store and at the bank level."[7] All these steps are eliminated in a charge (or debit) transaction.

Credit cards and debit cards are unquestionably more efficient than checks as far as the merchant is concerned. Debit cards, which can be thought of as "electronic checks," are more efficient because the amount of the bill is immediately deducted from the customer's account. Eliminated with both credit and debit cards are bounced checks and all the inefficiencies and costs associated with trying to collect on such checks. Furthermore, it is quicker to get a card transaction approved than it is for the customer to write a check and have it approved. Like other businesses, "grocery stores like the cards because they speed up the checkout line."[8] Other EFTS, such as paying bills by computer or telephone, promise even greater efficiencies because customers do not interact on a face-to-face basis with the merchant's staff.

Despite their greater efficiency in comparison to cash, credit and debit cards have rarely been accepted in that center of efficiency, the fast-food restaurant. The executive vice president of Visa describes the problem: "In the fast food arena, we have traditionally had next to no presence for one reason—speed. In a business where fast is beautiful, the card authorization and purchase process has been too slow to make cards attractive." However, some fast-food restaurants have tried to make credit charges more efficient, as the Visa executive explains:

> At the point of sale, the card is passed through a stripe reader and immediately checked against a hot-card file. If a card is good, the amount of the purchase is automatically credited to it. Then the authorization is flashed on a video screen in front of the checker.
>
> The entire process is instantaneous: no phone calls, no imprint and signature procedures. Consumers get more convenience and flexibility. And speedminded merchants get a payment system that's even faster than cash.[9]

The highly rationalized Wal-Mart stores have also installed new technology that makes the process by which card transactions are approved almost instantaneous. According to a spokesperson for the company, "Not too long ago, customers hesitated to use their cards because it took so doggone long to get a transaction processed."[10] Such hesitation is clearly a thing of the past at Wal-Mart and increasingly at many other highly rationalized settings as well.

Predictability: Avoiding Those Painful Lulls

Predictability is manifest in the fast-food restaurant in the fact that the food, the physical structure, and the service are likely to be the same from one time or place to another. Even the demeanor and behavior of the employees is likely to be highly predictable. Predictable behavior is ensured by the fact that franchise owners and managers are social-

ized by institutions like McDonald's Hamburger University. The owners and managers in turn train employees to behave predictably, and they constantly monitor that behavior to be sure it conforms to the norms of the organization. Among other things, the employees often follow scripts that help ensure that they utter the lines expected of them.[11] For example, the Roy Rogers hamburger chain used to have its employees dress like cowboys and cowgirls. Following the corporate script, employees greeted customers with a friendly "Howdy, pardner," and bid them adieu after paying with a hearty "Happy trails."

The credit card has made the process of obtaining a loan quite predictable as well. Consumers have grown accustomed to routine steps (filling out the questionnaire, for example) that lead to the appearance of a new card in the mail. After all, many people have gone through these same steps many times. In the case of preapproved credit cards, the few remaining unpredictabilities have been eliminated, because offer and acceptance arrive in the very same letter.

Credit cards themselves are also highly predictable. Whatever company issues them, they are all likely to be made of the same materials, to feel the same, to be the same shape, to include similar information in similar places, and to do just about the same things. In fact, it is these similarities that prompt the credit card companies to attempt to distinguish their cards by, for example, their distinctive advertisements and array of enhancements. The fast-food restaurants do much the same thing (for example, giving away glasses or selling toys or videotapes of movies at bargain prices) because the hamburgers, fried chicken, french fries, and soft drinks of one are difficult to differentiate from those of competitors. The goal of both the credit card firms and the fast-food restaurants is to manufacture a sense of difference where none, in fact, exists.

Whenever human beings are involved in a transaction, unpredictability increases. Thus both fast-food restaurants and credit card companies seek to minimize interaction between their staff and customers. However, there is far less such human contact in the credit card industry than in the fast-food business. (And there is painfully little genuinely human contact in fast-food restaurants.) The limited contact that does exist in the credit card business is likely to take place over the telephone. It might take the form of unsolicited calls made in an effort to recruit new card users. More likely it involves calls by cardholders to the company to inquire about bills or by employees of the company to cardholders to find out why payments are late. However one comes into contact with employees of the credit card firms, much of the interaction is likely to be scripted. The telephone solicitors are clearly reciting scripts mindlessly. Even those responding to customer inquiries or complaints have been trained to select the appropriate scripts and subscripts depending on the nature of the inquiry or complaint and the direction taken by the conversation. . . .

Nonhuman for Human Technology: No Visitors, No Staff

A variety of nonhuman technologies are found in the fast-food restaurant: soft-drink machines that shut themselves off when the cups are full, french fry machines that buzz when the fries are done and automatically lift the baskets out of the oil—and soon robots rather than real human beings to serve customers. These technologies control employees, deskill jobs by transferring skills from people to machines, and ultimately replace people.

The credit card is itself a kind of nonhuman technology. More important, it has given birth to technologies that intervene between buyer and seller and serve to constrain both. Most notable is the vast computerized system that "decides" whether to authorize a new credit card and whether to authorize a given purchase. Shopkeeper and customer may both want to consummate a deal, but if the computer system says no (because, for example, the consumer's card is over its credit limit), then there is likely to be no sale. Similarly, an employee of a credit card firm may want to approve a sale but be loath, and perhaps forbidden, to do so if the computer

indicates that the sale should be disapproved.

The general trend within rationalized societies is to take decision-making power away from people (customers, shopkeepers, and credit card company employees alike) and give it to nonhuman technologies.

With the advent of smart cards, the card itself will "decide" whether a sale is to be consummated. Embedded in the card's computer chip will be such information as spending limits, so the card itself will be able to reject a purchase that is over the limit. . . .

Irrationality of Rationality: Caught in the Heavy Machinery

The irrationality of rationality takes several forms. At one level, irrationality simply means that what is rational in planning does not work out that way in practice. For example, the drive-through window in the fast-food restaurant is supposed to be a very efficient way of obtaining a meal, but it often ends up being quite inefficient with long lines of cars inching toward the takeout window. Similarly, credit cards are supposed to offer greater efficiency but sometimes are quite inefficient. Take, for example, the Discover Card's program to allow its cardholders access to Sprint's long-distance service. To make a long-distance call with the card, "all you need do is dial Sprint's 11-digit access number. Then 0. Then a 10-digit phone number. Then the 16 digit account number from your Discover Card. Then a four-digit 'Personal Access Code.' "[12] A highly inefficient string of 42 digits must be entered just to make one long-distance telephone call. To take another example, the credit card companies are supposed to function highly predictably. Thus, for example, our bills should be error free. However, billing errors do find their way into monthly statements. For example, there may be charges that we did not make or the amount entered may be incorrect.

The most notable irrationality of rationality in the fast-food industry is the creation of a dehumanized and dehumanizing setting in which to eat or work. Such an inhuman, rationalized world is irrational from the point of view of those who must deal with it. Of course, the credit card world is also highly dehumanized, because people generally interact with nonhuman technologies, with such products as bills or overdue notices, or with people whose actions or decisions are constrained if not determined by nonhuman technologies. Horror stories abound of people caught in the "heavy machinery" of the credit card companies. Pity the poor consumers who get charged for things they did not buy or who are sent a series of computer letters with escalating threats because the computer erroneously considers them to be delinquent in their payments. Then there are the many complaints of people who get turned down for credit because erroneous information has crept into their credit reports. Trying to get satisfaction from the technologies, or from their often robotlike representatives, is perhaps the ultimate in the dehumanization associated with a rationalizing society. . . .

Personal Troubles, Public Issues, and Rationalization

Let us look now more explicitly at the rationalization process as it applies to credit cards from the perspective of the twin themes that inform this [article]—personal troubles and public issues. Rationalization can be seen as a large-scale social process that manifests itself in the credit card industry (among many others) and is, in the process, creating personal troubles for individuals as well as public issues that are of concern to society as a whole.

Although my focus here is the problems that rationalization creates, it certainly carries with it a wide array of benefits.[13] In fact, most of the major components of rationalization may be seen as advantageous. Most of us regard the emphasis on things that can be counted (rather than qualitative judgments), efficient operations, predictable procedures and results, and the advances offered by nonhuman technologies as highly positive characteristics of a rational society.

Still, rationalization creates many personal troubles:

- *Calculability*. Consumerism's emphasis on buying large numbers of easily replaced things leaves us surrounded by poor-quality goods that do not function well and that fall apart quickly. More important, when we can easily acquire, and reacquire, many of the things that we desire, we are left with a cynical and blasé attitude toward the world. In addition, the scoring systems relied on by credit card firms reduce all of us to a single number. Our fundamental character means little, and so society becomes a little more flat, dull, and characterless. Decision making is taken away from human officials and handed to the computers that calculate and assess creditworthiness. Consumers are left feeling that they are controlled by cold, inhuman systems. A perfect example of this control is the fact that, once the credit bureaus have a file on a person, it is impossible for that person to opt out of the system.

- *Efficiency*. The greater efficiency of making purchases with credit cards in comparison to the alternatives, especially cash and checks, exacerbates our society's emphasis on speed. Lost in the process is a concern for the quality of the experience and the quality of the goods and services obtained. Overall, something important but indefinable is lost in a world that sometimes seems to value speed and efficiency above all else.

- *Predictability*. A similar point can be made about the personal troubles associated with predictability. Something very important is lost when all we consume and all the experiences that we have are highly predictable. Life becomes routine, dull, boring. The excitement associated with at least some unpredictability—a surprising discovery or an unexpected experience—is lost. When people had to rely on cash they were likely to experience self-denial at times. But when the cash supply was replenished, there was excitement in finally being able to afford some object or participate in some experience. The tendency to reduce or eliminate periods of self-denial eliminates, in the process, the excitement of obtaining something for which someone has had to wait.

- *Substitution of nonhuman for human technology.* A considerable amount of humanity is lost when people are in the thrall of large-scale computerized systems like those in the credit card industry. Instead of being in control, people are controlled by these systems. This phenomenon is well illustrated by the switch from country-club to descriptive billing in most of the credit card industry. Similarly, the technologies associated with credit cards tend to reduce or eliminate human interaction; tend to eliminate jobs, leaving many people without work and the income and meaning that work accords; and tend to bring with them greater speed and efficiency and thus other kinds of problems.

- *Irrationality of rationality.* Each of the major components of the rationalization of the credit card industry can be seen as causing personal troubles for individuals. Many of those troubles relate to the irrationality of those rational systems, especially their tendency toward dehumanization. In many ways our lives are less human because of the advances in the credit card industry and the rationalization process of which they are part.

What is the public issue associated with rationalization and credit cards? At one level, the aggregation of all these personal troubles can be seen as a public issue. At another level, the policies of the credit card industry that cause these problems can also be viewed as a public issue. However, the broadest public issue is the threat of totalitarianism posed by the credit card industry in concert with the other major elements of the rationalizing society. In his 1980 book, *Charge It*, Terry Galanoy called such a totalitarian system Lifebank, the logical derivative of the credit card society.[14] In the Lifebank system, he speculated, all of a person's assets will be combined into one ac-count, which will be controlled by one or more banks or financial institutions and their computers. All of a person's credit cards will be replaced by a single Lifebank card. Virtually all consumption will be on credit. As the bills come due, they will be automatically deducted from each person's Lifebank account. However, each person will be granted an allowance for day-to-day expenses. There will, as a result, be little cash and little need for it. Checking accounts as we know them will have largely disappeared. Lifebank's computers will make virtually all economic decisions for individuals. Credit ratings will be continually updated. The Lifebank card will be the key to virtually everything, and those without such a card will not only not have any credit in a society that depends on credit but will literally have ceased to exist as far as Lifebank's computers are concerned. In sum:

> We will have lost control. Even the banks will have lost control. The Lifebank-type system will have its own reasoning, its own standards, its own momentum, its own energy, its own life; and operating without conscience, without soul, without social logic, it will also be out of control by all standards we should still live by today.[15]

Although such a system has yet to come into existence, many developments and technological advancements in the credit card industry have made something like Lifebank more possible today, and continued technological advances make it an even greater possibility in the future.

Lifebank does resemble the "iron cage of rationality" that underlay Weber's concern with the rationalization process. Weber feared that the world was moving toward a seamless web of rational systems that would control more and more aspects of our lives. Furthermore, we would be less and less able to escape from the rational society. Eventually, all the escape routes would be closed off (or rationalized). We would be left with little more than the ability to choose among rational systems. . . .

Endnotes

1. For an overview of Weber's theory of rationalization, see Stephen Kalberg. "Max Weber's Types of Rationality: Cornerstones for the Analysis of Rationalization Processes in History." *American Journal of Sociology* 85(1980):1145–1179. See also Bryan S. Turner. "Simmel, Rationalization and the Sociology of Money." *Sociological Review* 34(1986):93–114.

2. For a similar delineation, see Arnold Eisen. "The Meanings and Confusions of Weberian 'Rationality.'" *British Journal of Sociology* 29(1978):57–70.

3. I would like to thank one of my students, Michael Saks, for this point.

4. Kenneth R. Varney. "Automated Credit Scoring Screens Loan Applicants." *Washington Post*, January 15, 1994, pp. E1, E13.

5. Saul Hansell. "Into Banking's Future, Electronically." *New York Times*, March 31,1994, pp. D1, D13.

6. ——. "Into Banking's Future, Electronically." *New York Times*, March 31, 1994, p. D13.

7. "Evaluating the Payments: More Is Better." *Chain Store Executive*, September 1992, p. 28.

8. Michael Quint. "D'Agostino to Accept Debit Cards for Purchases." *New York Times*, May 19, 1990, p. 43.

9. Roger L. Pierce. "Seeking New Opportunities in Tomorrow's Payment-Systems World." *American Banker*, July 5, 1990, p. 11A.

10. Stephanie Strom. "Holiday Shoppers Are Whipping Out the Plastic." *New York Times*, December 18, 1993, p. 45.

11. Robin Leidner. *Fast Food, Fast Talk: Service Work and the Routinization of Everyday Life*. Berkeley: University of California Press, 1993.

12. "Hello, Central, Get Me 180055516960348583 6939416385905045048870348589876." *Consumer Reports*, August 1992, p. 7.

13. For a discussion of the advantages of another key element of the rationalization process, the fast-food restaurant, see George Ritzer,

The McDonaldization of Society. Thousand Oaks, CA: Pine Forge Press, pp. 14–15.

14. Terry Galanoy. *Charge It: Inside the Credit Card Conspiracy*. New York: Putnam, 1980. In fact, Dee Ward Hock, the person responsible for the creation of Visa, actually envisioned an all-purpose card like Lifebank. (See Joseph Nocera. *A Piece of the Action: How the Middle Class Joined the Money Class*. New York: Simon & Schuster, 1994, p. 307.)

15. Terry Galanoy. *Charge It: Inside the Credit Card Conspiracy*. New York: Putnam, 1980, p. 215.

Review

1. What are the five components of rationalization?

2. How do the fast-food and credit card industries fit into the model of rationalization?

3. What are the personal troubles and public issues associated with rationalization?

4. Describe Weber's "iron cage of rationalization."

Application

For as long as possible, every time you call a 1-800 or other customer service number, do not use the automated service. Stay on the line until you must be served by a human. Try this over a period of several weeks. (You rarely get the same agent twice in large companies.) Compare this experience to having computers helping you.

44

The Impact of Mobile Communications

James E. Katz
Philip Aspden

Technological advances hold a particular fascination for Americans. This fascination may be seen in the quickness with which Americans adopt new technologies as if they represent unquestioned life improvements. It is not surprising that an American sociologist, William Ogburn, developed a theory of social change that gave technology a central place. Specifically, Ogburn argued that technological change is the dynamic element in culture with values and beliefs lagging behind. Because all cultures tend to be integrated, the changing technology forces modifications in values and beliefs. For example, the value placed on large families in preindustrial societies gradually changed as industrial technology opened up new opportunities for social mobility and rendered obsolete the need for a large number of workers on the family farm.

*While Ogburn's theory doesn't account for all of the interplay between technology and social factors, it does underscore the fact of that interplay. Social factors can affect the development of technology and new technology always has social consequences. In this selection, Katz and Aspden look at the relationships between social factors and a recent technological development: mobile communications. A few years ago a pager was a **status symbol**, a sign that the owner held an important position such as that of a physician. Is this still true? What about cellular telephones? Are they the tools of the rich and important? These are some of the questions probed in this article.*

Introduction

By 1999 it is expected that there will be more than 120 million cellular phone customers worldwide.[1] In mid-1996, there were already more than 38 million subscribers in the United States alone, or about 14.5% of the entire U.S. population.[2] (This contrasts with about 1% in the mid-1980s.[3]) A cheaper but more limited personal wireless system—the pager—had in 1996 about 8% penetration overall but among older teens it was 17%.[4] Yet this adoption rate is small compared to Singapore, where one out of three adults uses a pager. (There are about 90 million pagers in the Asia-Pacific region.[5]) Paging technology is becoming two way, and predictions are for a five-fold increase in worldwide subscribership by the year 2000.[6]

What has been the impact wrought by this technology in people's personal and business lives? The mass media have presented sundry items ranging from a car-jacked man being rescued from his car trunk to British royalty being eavesdropped. But compared to media attention, the intellectual community has hardly probed the uses and implications of mobile communication.

It appears to us that, from a social analytical viewpoint, wireless personal communication has been overshadowed first by the proliferation of personal computers, then by the Internet. Like its intensively scrutinized, socially transformative cousin, the personal computer, wireless personal communication has experienced a revolution since 1983. And like its socially transformative forebear—the telephone—personal mobile wireless technology has been largely ignored by scholars who claim to study communication modalities and social processes. (For a discussion of the scholarly inattention regarding the telephone, see Reference 7.) . . .

Research Questions

. . . [T]here are numerous questions about mobile communications technology, regarding both how they affect society and human behavior as well as what use reveals about

367

social theory and policy. Our research has focused on some of these. Specifically, we sought to determine:

- The extent ownership is determined by demographic variables. For example, is ownership affluence-driven, gender-based, or ethnically-based?

- The extent ownership reflects functionality needs. For example, are more mobile people more likely to own the technology?

- Whether the technology relieves or generates stress.

Where possible, we also sought to examine how the observed relationship changed over time.

Demographic issues are important given the concern about the commercial uses of mobile communications. There is much riding on whether they are actually a useful tool for economic success. Assuming for the moment that they are, questions of equitable distribution by social class or race assume a great deal of importance. . . .

Another important question is whether wireless communication technologies are fundamentally liberating or enslaving. While the answer is likely to be some combination of both phenomena, it would be helpful to have data which could actually illuminate the question. For instance, while by no means alone, Giddens[8–10] has spoken of the subtle controls over individual movements that technology might give, and Gary Marx,[11, 12] Gandy,[13] and Katz[14, 15] have spoken of the ways in which these technologies can be abused to remove anonymity and freedom.

Method

In an attempt to address our research questions, we have conducted national opinion surveys over a three-year span. The analysis that follows presents data that suggest preliminary answers to our research questions.

Our main source of data is a 2500-person telephone survey (identified as Survey 95). These data were taken from an October 1995 national random telephone sample, surveyed by a commercial firm under contract from Bellcore. The survey sample has a close match on socioeconomic variables compared with the U.S. population as a whole. . . .

Results

Cell-Only and Pager Plus Cell Phone Usage Growing Faster Than Pager-Only Usage

Our approach has been to divide the sample population into four groups—those report owning or using:

1. Neither a pager nor a cellular telephone (the "neither" group).

2. A pager only (the "pager-only" group).

3. A cellular phone only ("the cell-only" group).

4. Both a pager and a cellular phone (the "both" group).

In our 1995 survey, 63% of respondents reported not owning a pager or a cellular phone, 10% reported owning only a pager, and 16% reported owning a cellular phone, while 11% reported owning both a pager and a cellular phone. On the basis of historical data it would appear that over the past few years when there has been significant growth in both cellular and pager usage, pager-only growth has been slow if not static and certainly much slower than growth in cellular-only usage and combined cellular and pager usage. Across our seven surveys spanning nearly three years, 6% to 10% of respondents report being pager-only owners, while cell-only owners grew from 9% to 16% of respondents, and owners of both grew even more rapidly, from 4% to 11% of respondents. . . .

Cell-Only Usage—No Gender Difference; Pager Users More Likely to Be Male

In the 1995 survey 17% of male respondents and 16% of female respondents reported being cell-only users. Our earlier surveys suggest a growing convergence of the male and female ownership rates for cell phones only.

The gender ownership pattern of cell phones only contrasts with ownership of pagers only and both cell phones and pagers, where proportionally more men than women reported owning them. . . . In the 1995 survey 13% of male respondents and 8% of female respondents reported owning only a pager. Most of the earlier surveys also indicated that proportionally more men than women owned only pagers.

Similarly in the 1995 survey for the cell phone plus pager group, 13% of males and 9% of females reported owning both a pager and a cell phone. Again, the earlier surveys indicate that proportionally more men than women owned both pagers and cell phones.

Our surveys show that the gender mix of mobile communications users has changed from 1989 when Rakow and Navarro[16] reported that "more than 90 percent of subscribers were men." Indeed our surveys suggest that the gender gap for cell phone-only usage is on the verge of disappearing.

Declining Age of Cell Phone Users; Pagers Mainly Owned by Young People

In the 1995 survey, respondents who reported only owning a pager were predominantly under 50 years old; moreover, ownership rates were approximately the same for all the five-year age categories below 50. Over 50 years old, ownership rates declined significantly down to 1% for the over 65 category. Earlier surveys had similar patterns. . . .

For those in the 1995 survey who reported owning only a cell phone, the age distribution of ownership was somewhat different from the 1995 pager-only age distribution. . . . Ownership of cell phones was spread fairly evenly over the age range 18 to 64 with ownership rates varying from 15% to 22% per five-year age category. This appears to be a change from the results of our earlier surveys where reported ownership rates tended to be highest in the age range 35–55.

For the group reporting owning both a pager and a cell phone, the 1995 survey results indicate a gradual decline in ownership rates from 16% ownership rate for the youngest age category (18–24) to 9% for the 55–59 category. . . . For the categories 60–64 and 65 and older, the ownership rates are about 3%. The earlier surveys show a slightly different

pattern; the 1993 and 1994 surveys indicate peak ownership rates for ages 35–49.

The results of our surveys provide some proof that cell phones are no longer the preserve of "power elites." Our earlier surveys do indicate highest ownership rates across the age range 35–50; however, the most recent survey shows that the highest ownership rates are spread over the age range 18–64, a much broader age range.

For the pager-only group, our surveys show that over 1993–1995 ownership has continued to be predominantly by younger people, that is people aged less than 45 or 50. There is some suggestion in the results of the 1995 survey that the highest ownership rates are at the younger end of the 18–45 age range.

More Affluent/Better Educated Respondents More Likely to Own Cell Phones

For the cell phone-only group in the 1995 survey, ownership rates increase as household income increases—from 6% for the under $15,000 group to 38% for the $100,000 or more. . . . Similarly for the group which owns both a pager and a cell phone, ownership rates increase as household income increases—from 4% for the under $15,000 group to 26% for the $100,000 or more. The earlier surveys showed a similar pattern of increasing ownership rates as reported household income increases.

For the pager-only group, however, the results for the 1995 survey are somewhat different. Here we see ownership rates independent of household income at around 12% of respondents. This is a change from earlier surveys which show a slight increase in ownership rates as reported household income increases.

We also examined how ownership rates varied with the respondent's highest achieved educational level. . . . In the 1995 survey, ownership rates for the cell phone-only group increase with higher educational levels—from 10% for the group who left school without gaining a high school diploma (or GED) to 28% for the group who gained a Ph.D. The earlier surveys showed a similar pattern.

In the 1995 survey, for the pager-only and the pager plus cell phone groups the relationship between ownership rates and highest education level achieved was less clear and it could be hypothesized that these data indicate no relationship between ownership and highest achieved educational levels. The earlier surveys do suggest a weak trend for both groups toward higher ownership rates for those reporting higher educational levels.

Our survey results suggest that pager-only ownership has become "classless," because ownership rates are independent of income and highest educational level achieved. On the other hand, higher ownership rates of cell phones, either alone or in conjunction with ownership of pagers, continue to be associated with higher income and educational levels. It is possible there are independent income and educational effects, but because income and highest achieved educational levels are highly correlated, it is also possible we are seeing a purely income effect or a purely education effect. Later analysis will probe these issues.

Significant Differences in Ownership Rates Across Ethnic Groups

Analyzing ownership rates by reported ethnic group shows significant differences between ethnic groups in the 1995 survey. Blacks, Hispanics, and Asians (with ownership rates in the range 44%–47%) are more likely than whites (ownership rate 36%) to own mobile communications.

For the pager-only usage, blacks (ownership rate 19%) and Hispanics (ownership rate 17%) have much higher ownership rates than whites (ownership rate 9%) and Asians (ownership rate 5%) have. Asian[s] and whites (ownership rates 23% and 17%, respectively) are more likely to own only cell phones than Hispanics and blacks (ownership rates 12% and 11% respectively). Finally, Asians, blacks, and Hispanics (ownership rates 19%, 17%, and 16%, respectively) are more likely to own both cell phones and pagers than whites (ownership rate 9%).

More Mobile at Work/Socially More Likely to Own Mobile Communications

In the 1995 survey we asked questions about the extent of mobility at work and socially, since a priori highly mobile people should have a disposition to own mobile communications. Respondents were asked the extent they agreed with the statement, "Your job requires you to be frequently away from your place of work." Non-owners of mobile telecommunications systems were less likely to agree with this statement than owners. For the group owning neither a pager nor a cell phone, only 5% strongly agreed and 15% agreed to the statement, whereas for the pager-only group, 13% strongly agreed and 21% agreed, for the cell phone-only group, 10% strongly agreed and 18% agreed, and for the group owning both a pager and a cell phone, 14% strongly agreed and 24% agreed. . . .

Respondents were also asked the extent they agreed with the statement "In your social life you are frequently away from home." Again, non-owners of mobile communications systems were less likely to agree with this statement than owners. . . . For the group owning neither a pager nor a cell phone, 8% strongly agreed and 27% agreed to the statement, whereas for the pager-only group, 12% strongly agreed and 38% agreed; for the cell phone-only group, 12% strongly agreed and 34% agreed, and for the group owning both a pager and a cell phone, 14% strongly agreed and 36% agreed.

We also used the number of children as a proxy measure for daily mobility and examined whether number of children in the household related to reported ownership of mobile communications. In particular, given Rakow and Navarro's work,[16] we might have thought that the need to do parallel social and work activities would result in those individuals whose households contained children would have a greater need for communications, with the result that they would be heavier wireless communication users. For the 1995 survey the results suggest there may be a weak relationship between number of children and ownership of mobile communications. Households with no children were less likely to own mobile communications system[s] than those with children. For households with no children, 33% reported owning either a pager or a cell phone or both. For households with one child, the ownership proportion was 42%, with two children, 44%, and for those with three or more children, 39%.

The results of our surveys regarding mobility support the idea proposed by Davis,[17] that the use of mobile communications provides "a sense of personal control over space and time." In regard to control over space, it would appear that those with greater mobility at work or in their social life are more likely to own mobile communications.

Those Needing to Be in Touch More Likely to Own Mobile Communications

In the 1995 survey we asked respondents the extent they agreed with the statement, "There are often times when you urgently need to get through to another person." Nonowners of mobile telecommunications systems were less likely to agree with this statement than owners. For the group owning neither a pager nor a cell phone, 10% strongly agreed and 36% agreed with the statement, whereas for the pager-only group, 13% strongly agreed and 47% agreed, for the cell phone-only group, 9% strongly agreed and 43% agreed, and for the group owning both a pager and a cell phone, 20% strongly agreed and 45% agreed.

In the only other survey where we asked this question, there was a very similar result. In the late 1993.b survey, for the group owning neither a pager nor a cell phone, 8% strongly agreed and 36% agreed with the statement, whereas for the pager-only group, 13% strongly agreed and 47% agreed, for the cell phone-only group, 13% strongly agreed and 38% agreed, and for the group owning both a pager and a cell phone, 8% strongly agreed and 53% agreed.

Again in the context of controlling time, our results support the idea proposed by Davis,[17] that the use of mobile communications provides "a sense of personal control over space and time." Our surveys indicate that those with a greater need to keep in touch are more likely to own mobile communications.

Stressed Respondents Are More Likely to Own a Pager

We mentioned earlier the ongoing debate about whether mobile communications add to or ease the stress of modern living. To see if we could throw light on this debate we asked, in the 1995 survey, the extent respondents agreed with the statement: "You feel that you have more to do than you can comfortably handle." Those owning a pager reported more agreement with this statement—in the pager-only group 17% agreed very strongly and 37% agreed strongly, and in the pager plus cell phone group 22% agreed very strongly and 26% agreed strongly. For the group without mobile communications and the cell phone-only group, the reported response rates were very similar—17% agreed very strongly and 26%–28% agreed strongly. . . .

In three earlier surveys we also asked this question about the extent respondents have more than they can handle. Taking the four surveys together, the pager-only group reported most agreement with the statement. In each of the surveys, 50% or more respondents either agreed or strongly agreed with the statement.

Earlier we reported that the pager-only group was predominantly under 50 years old. Generally, we have found that younger people are more likely to report that they have more than they can handle, so we investigated whether the fact that the pager-only group was the most likely group to report having too much to handle was just an age effect. For the 1995 survey this proved not to be the case. . . . We divided the sample set into those up to 44 years old and those 45 and over. Anxiety levels for the pager-only group did not decrease with age. For the younger half, 17% strongly agreed and 35% agreed with the statement, while for the older half, 19% strongly agreed and 43% agreed with the statement. For the other ownership groups anxiety levels decreased with age.

Similarly for the early 1993 survey, anxiety levels for the pager-only group did not decrease with age, while anxiety levels for the other three ownership groups did decline with age. For the younger half of the pager-only group, 15% strongly agreed and 38%

agreed with the statement, while for the older half, 11% strongly agreed and 43% agreed with the statement. As in the 1995 survey, the anxiety levels decreased with age for the other groups.

Although our surveys did not explore changes in feeling of overload before and after owning mobile communications, our surveys do indicate that the pager-only group is particularly likely to express feelings of overload. Whether this is a group inherently subject to stress or the ownership of pagers generates stress, we are not able to deduce.

Those Owning Mobile Communications More Likely to Own PCs

In the 1995 survey, those owning a cell phone were more likely to own a PC than those without a pager and a cell phone and those owning only a pager. . . . Sixty-one percent of those only owning a cell phone and 59% of those owning both a pager and a cell phone also owned a PC. The percentage of PC ownership in the other two groups was much less—40% for the group without mobile communications and 43% for the pager-only group.

In our earlier surveys, we observed a somewhat similar pattern with the group without a pager and a cell phone having the lowest PC ownership rates, about 30%. PC ownership rates for the pager-only group were significantly higher than the neither group and were generally in the 40%–55% range. In the 1993 and 1994 surveys, PC ownership rates for the cell phone-only and both groups were significantly higher than the pager-only group. Ownership rates for the cell phone-only group were generally in the 55%–65% range and for the both group in the 60%–80% range. In some cases the ownership rates for the both group were significantly higher than for the cell phone-only group.

There are various plausible explanations for the relationship between mobile communications ownership and PC ownership. A similar relationship exists with the ownership of answering machines.[18] Those owning mobile communications have lifestyles requiring the use of electronic tools such as PCs and answering machines. Alternatively, there are people with a predisposition to want to own new technological devices such as mobile phones, PCs, and answering machines. . . .

Discussion

Our data suggest many interesting relationships upon which theoretical interpretations could be built. Space limitations preclude a full elaboration of these possibilities but, guided by our discussions at the outset of the article, we can highlight a few intriguing possibilities. In particular, we discuss whether wireless communications are "a rich man's toy," assertions that wireless communications are contributing to a stressful or rushed life, and whether wireless communications are a chain of control around the necks of the mobile proletariat.

Digital Divide

Considerable policy attention has been devoted to whether certain ethnic or income groups are going to be at a structural disadvantage as a result of the information revolution. While most attention has been devoted to access to computer resources, issues of universal service have also been the focus of significant work.[19, 20] Our analyses indirectly reflect on this debate and [suggest] some ambivalent conclusions. On the one hand, our model of mobile communications ownership suggests that owners of mobile communications are likely to be from higher income brackets. On the other hand, there appears to be a weak education effect and no gender effect at all. Where one would expect a race effect—whites more likely to own mobile communications—our data suggest otherwise. It is blacks and Hispanic[s] who are more likely to own wireless communications.

The importance of income may be weakening. In general, the ratio of ownership rates of those with reported household incomes above $35,000 to those below $35,000 declines during the period of our surveys for all ownership groups. . . . For the pager-only group, this ratio declines from 2.5 (early 1993 survey), through 1.7 (late 1993 and

1994 surveys) to 1.1 (1995 survey). Thus by 1995, the income effect for pager-only ownership had almost disappeared. For the cell phone-only group, the ratio is 2.3 for the 1995 survey, much less than for the earlier surveys—3.6 for the early 1993 survey, 4.2 for the late 1993 surveys, and 4.2 for the 1994 surveys. For the cell phone plus pager group, the value of the ratio in the 1995 survey (3.0) is the lowest of all the surveys, but the ratios in the other surveys do not display a consistent downward pattern—the ratio is 3.3 for the early 1993 survey, 7.5 for the late 1993 surveys, and 4.4 for the 1994 surveys.

Race/Ethnic Issues

As mentioned earlier, racial/ethnic self-identification was an important predictor variable. In particular, black and Hispanic respondents were much more likely to own either a pager or both a pager and cell phone than were whites. Asians, though, were more likely to have either a cell phone only or both a cell phone and pager than were whites.

For pager-only ownership, we can posit here for discussion an "affordable luxury" hypothesis, which holds that those who do not have status in society will be more likely to buy low-cost items/services that they perceive are associated with high-status individuals. Given this hypothesis, it may be that blacks and Hispanics, if they can afford it, are more likely to buy a pager.

Certainly a competing explanation—that members of these communities might like to be in greater contact or are more out-going and connected than, say, whites, is equally plausible. In fact, given the reports at the outset of our article about Singapore and the popularity of wireless communication in Hong Kong and throughout Asia, the cultural pattern explanation seems also a good fit. For example, this might account for the high cell phone ownership among Asians.

Rather than putting forward definitive answers, we introduce these ideas as possible explanations for our results. By no means do we purport that we have exhausted the range of possible explanations. Instead, we look forward to future studies which can clarify the social role of wireless communication within various cultural settings and identities as well as by demographic categories.

Gender Issues

Mobile communications have been held by many to be a male power tool, yet our models do not suggest any statistical gender effect. Our earlier analyses showed that ownership of mobile communications was related to gender. We speculate that ownership of mobile communications is determined more strongly by social location effects, for example, having a highly mobile job or needing to keep in touch, than by gender. . . .

Rushed Attitudes and Communications Needs

Since "overload" does not have any independent explanatory power in predicting ownership, one might be tempted to say that wireless communication does nothing to relieve such feelings. However, there are competing explanations that cannot be discarded since the data are cross-sectional (as opposed to panel or experimental data). The first possibility is that other variables incorporate its explanatory power. In this case, business and social-related mobility, and "need to keep in touch" attitudes capture whatever statistical power that the feeling of being rushed would have otherwise contributed.

An alternative explanation is that those in our survey who were wireless communication adopters had even higher feelings of overload prior to the technology's adoption. Therefore, the formerly above average feelings of overload have been reduced to those of the average non-adopter. Hence, because we have no prior data, any change in the more overloaded group who adopted the technologyline (non-adopters) level would be masked (see Reference 21). Another plausible explanation is that wireless communication users would have even higher levels of overload were it not for wireless communication. Again, without temporally linked data, we cannot disentangle change over time.

Yet another possibility is that the people who feel overloaded do not perceive that pagers and cell phones can help them reduce overload anxieties. By contrast our model supports the view that those who are highly mobile or need to keep in touch perceive pagers and cell phones as useful to them. While far from definitive, the data do suggest that one prediction about wireless communication's impact, namely that it would add to people's feelings of being rushed and overloaded, does not seem to be borne out. Given that there is no difference between users and non-users of wireless communication regarding their feeling of overload, it seems likely that wireless communication does not add to such feelings. (Of course we cannot definitively rule out the possibility that wireless communication adopters were less rushed than non-wireless communication adopters, prior to their adoption decision.) If this lack of impact were borne out, it would seem to refute some of our arguments made elsewhere[22] as well as those of Gergen[23] and other critics of technological culture.

Age

Usually one of the best predictors of early adoption of technology is age, with younger people being the early adopters. Interestingly, our data suggest that for cell phone usage it is middle-aged people who are the early adopters. This might be because of the cost, but we also believe the nature of one's occupation is probably even more central to the adoption decision. Still our data do not definitively shed light on it, but our background interviews would seem to suggest that occupational category is important in first introducing the user to the technology, and second in creating the environment within which it is adopted.

The one area we do see age making a difference is with pagers. This makes sense, given the relatively low cost of pagers, plus their desirability among youngsters as a prestige symbol.[24]

Conclusion

Our investigation reveals that while no longer "a rich man's toy," cellular telephone ownership is associated with income, although the income affect appears to be declining. Further, in contrast to some of the

more pessimistic speculations about cell phone ownership, including our own, there is as yet little evidence to suggest that cell phone ownership has a pernicious impact on the quality of life. However, as we indicated earlier, we cannot be sure of the antecedent situation in a cross-sectional study, so any claims about impact must be extremely circumscribed.

In general ownership seems guided by what we might call "social location" variables, that is a combination of socioeconomic, demographic, and life-style conditions which influence decisions perhaps more powerfully than individual personality characteristics. People may not personally wish to have wireless communication, but due to conditions of their life—such as job exigencies, work, and personal mobility—they find they need to have wireless communication. Thus while we found no relationship between certain personality measures, such as extroversion or phone liking, perceived "needs" can be an important predictor of service utilization, in this case a perceived need "to keep in touch." This finding is somewhat at odds with an initial analysis of some of the early data reported here, which purported not to find a relationship between needs and telecommunications technology use.[25] Certainly the relationship between needs and gratifications is one that has been explored at length in the mass media literature; that they should be connected in the telecommunications area as well should not come as a surprise. Yet we anticipate that "social location" will eventually become recognized as equal in importance, if not paramount to, the needs-based model.[26]

Interestingly, racial/ethnic self-identification is an important variable. The importance of this variable was somewhat surprising to us. While there are several possible explanations, for example cultural patterns and geographic location of respondents, the importance of this variable also fits with notions we have been working with, which may be characterized as "affordable luxury." This concept means that certain (apparently) high-status items are available for purchase at relatively low cost. Hence groups or individuals who might not have a high status, as defined by the dominant society, might seek to enhance their status in various ways. Certainly the more affordable a luxury is, the easier it would be for people to buy it. Explanations along this path might help us to understand not only wireless communication ownership, but a host of other behaviors as well. Currently we are exploring this area and hope to report on it soon (see Reference 26).

In terms of policy issues, such as information rich–information poor, or the so-called digital divide, some of our findings are troubling. Specifically the income dimension of wireless communication ownership suggests that there is a possibility that those who cannot afford may be shut out of many of society's benefits, with severe personal and political ramifications.[27, 28]

Summing up, we have seen some surprising data shedding light on wireless communication relative to income, age, education, ethnicity/race, household ties, social activity, and job activity mobility and attitudes. These data reflect on important theories of equity, innovation, gender relations, and quality of life issues. While we have only scratched the surface, we believe we have shown that this much-neglected area of wireless communication can have both substantive and theoretical import.

References

1. Staff. *Common Carrier Week*, June 6, 1994.

2. Staff. "Cellular Telecommunications Industry Association, Wireless Growth Sets New Annual Records," Mimeo. September 19, 1996, Washington.

3. Mayer, William G. "The Rise of the New Media," *Public Opinion Quarterly* 58(1),124–146 (1994).

4. Miller, Leslie. "New World to Navigate: New Worries for Adults," *USA Today*, August 27, 1996, D-1.

5. Staff. "Singapore Celebrates 1 Millionth Pager Customer." (0179) AP Wire Services, September 6, 1996.

6. Szaniawski, Kris. "Operations Push Low-Cost Advantage," *Financial Times*, November 27, 1995, 5.

7. Dimmick, John W., Sikand, Jaspreet, and Patterson, Scott J. "The Gratifications of the Household Telephone: Sociability, Instrumentality, and Reassurance," *Communication Research* 21(5), 643–663 (1994).

8. Giddens, Anthony. *The Consequences of Modernity*. Polity Press, Cambridge, in association with Basil Blackwell, Oxford, UK, 1990.

9. ——. *Modernity and Self-Identity*. Stanford University Press, Palo Alto, CA, 1991.

10. Bryant, Christopher G. A., and Jary, David, eds. *Giddens' Theory of Structuration: A Critical Appreciation*. Routledge, London, 1991.

11. Marx, Gary T. "The Surveillance Society: The Threat of 1984-Style Techniques," *The Futurist* 19 (June), 21–26 (1985a).

12. Marx, Gary T. "I'll Be Watching You: Reflections on the New Surveillance," *Dissent* 32 (Winter), 26–34 (1985b).

13. Gandy, Oscar H. *The Panoptic Sort: A Political Economy of Personal Information*. Westview, Boulder, CO, 1993.

14. Katz, James E. "Public Policy Origins of Privacy and the Emerging Issues," *Information Age* 10(3), 47–63 (1988).

15. Katz, James E. "Social Aspects of Telecommunications Security Policy," *IEEE Technology and Society* 9(2), 16–24 (1990).

16. Rakow, Lana F., and Navarro, Vija. "Remote Mothering and the Parallel Shift: Women Meet the Cellular Telephone," *Critical Studies in Mass Communication* 10(2), 144–157 (1993).

17. Davis, Dineh M. "Social Impact of Cellular Telephone Usage in Hawaii," in Pacific Telecommunications Council Fifteenth Annual Conference Proceedings, Session 3.1.1. to 4.4.1. (January 17–20, 1993), Volume 2. James G. Savage and Dan J. Wedemeyer, eds., Pacific Telecommunications Council, Honolulu, HI, 1993, pp. 641–649.

18. Katz, James E., Asp Reich, Warren. "Public Attitudes Toward Voice-Based Electronic Messaging Technologies in the United States," *Behavior & Information Technology* 16(3), 125–144 (1997).

19. Firestone, Charles M. *The Emerging World of Wireless Communications*. The Aspen Institute and Institute for Information Studies, Queenstown, MD, 1996.

20. Anderson, Robert H., Bikson, Tora K., Law, Sally Ann, Mitchell, Bridoer M. *Universal Access to e-mail: Feasibility and Societal Implications*. RAND, Santa Monica, CA, 1995.

21. Campbell, Donald, and Stanley, Julian C. *Experimental and Quasiexperimental Designs for Research*. Rand McNally, Chicago, 1963.

22. Aspden, Philip, and Katz, James. *Mobility and Communications: Analytical Trends and Conceptual Models*. Report for the U.S. Congress, Office of Technology Assessment, OTA N3-16040.0, Washington, D.C. November 1994.

23. Gergen, Kenneth J. *The Saturated Self: Dilemmas of Identity in Contemporary Life*. HarperCollins, New York, 1991.

24. Katz, James, and Wynn, Eleanor. "Teens on the Phone," Technical memorandum number 24350. Bell Communications Research, Morristown, NJ, November 1, 1994.

25. Stienfield, Charles, Dudley, Kathleen, Kraut, Robert, and Katz, James. "Rethinking Household Telecommunications," Paper presented at the International Communications Association Annual Meeting, Miami, FL, 1993.

26. Katz, James, Aspden, Philip, and Fussell, Susan. *Symbolic Aspects of Telecommunications Services: Affordable Luxury and Status Issues*. Bellcore, Morristown, NJ, Mimeo.

27. Aufderheide, Patricia. "Universal Service: Telephone Policy in the Public Interest," *Journal of Communication* 37 (Winter), 81–96 (1987).

28. Sawhney, Harmeet. "Universal Service: Prosaic Motives and Great Ideals," *Journal of Broadcasting & Electronic Media* 38 (Fall), 375–395 (1994).

Review

1. Describe the growth of mobile communications technology.

2. What age and gender differences exist in the use of mobile communications?

3. What racial/ethnic differences exist in the use of mobile communications?

4. How does social class interact with the use of mobile communications?

Applications

1. Perform a content analysis of mobile communication ads to determine to whom and for what purposes they are marketed. Marketing agencies do a good job of determining who uses their products and to whom they should market them. With this in mind, are the findings of Katz and Aspden consistent with what you learned by examining the ads? If not, how would you explain the differences?

2. Interview three men and three women who own cellular telephones. Begin by asking them why they purchased the phones. Then ask them about their schedules—see whether their jobs require them to be frequently away from their place of work and/or their homes. Ask whether they often urgently need to get through to others. Finally, inquire about the effects of the phone on their well-being: in what ways has it added to or diminished the stress in their lives?

   How do your results square with those of Katz and Aspden? Did you find any differences between the answers of the males and those of the females? If so, what were they and how would you explain them?

Reprinted from: James E. Katz and Philip Aspden, "The Impact of Mobile Communications." In "Theories, Data, and Potential Impacts of Mobile Communications: A Longitudinal Analysis of U.S. National Surveys," *Technological Forecasting and Social Change* 57 (1998):133–56. Reprinted by permission from Elsevier Science. ✦